Earth's Landscape

Earth's Landscape

AN ENCYCLOPEDIA OF THE WORLD'S GEOGRAPHIC FEATURES

Volume 2: M–Z

JOYCE A. QUINN AND SUSAN L. WOODWARD

ABC-CLIO

Santa Barbara, California • Denver, Colorado • Oxford, England

Library of Congress Cataloging-in-Publication Data

Quinn, Joyce Ann.
    Earth's landscape : an encyclopedia of the world's geographic features / Joyce A. Quinn and Susan L. Woodward.
        p. cm.
    Includes index.
    ISBN 978-1-61069-445-2 (hardback) — ISBN 978-1-61069-446-9 (ebook)   1. Physical geography—Encyclopedias.   I. Title.
        GB54.5.Q55 2015
        910'.0203—dc23   2014021579

ISBN: 978-1-61069-445-2
EISBN: 978-1-61069-446-9

19 18 17 16 15   1 2 3 4 5

This book is also available on the World Wide Web as an eBook.
Visit www.abc-clio.com for details.

ABC-CLIO, LLC
130 Cremona Drive, P.O. Box 1911
Santa Barbara, California 93116-1911

This book is printed on acid-free paper ∞

Manufactured in the United States of America

Contents

List of Entries by Geographic Location

Continental Features

AFRICA

Algeria (People's Democratic Republic of Algeria)
  Atlas Mountains
  The Sahara
Angola (Republic of Angola)
  Namib Desert
  Zambezi River
Benin (Republic of Benin)
  Niger River
Botswana (Republic of Botswana)
  The Kalahari
  Limpopo River
  Magdakigadi Pans
  Okavango Delta
  Zambezi River
Burkino Faso
  The Sahel
Burundi (Republic of Burundi)
  Lake Tanganyika
  Nile River
Cameroon (Republic of Cameroon)
  African Rainforest
  Lake Chad
  Mount Cameroon
Cape Verde (Republic of Cape Verde)
  Cape Verde Islands
Central African Republic
  African Rainforest
Chad (Republic of Chad)
  Lake Chad
  The Sahara
  The Sahel

Tibesti Mountains
Côte d'Ivoire (Republic of Côte d'Ivoire)
  African Rainforest
Democratic Republic of the Congo
  African Rainforest
  Congo River
  Lake Tanganyika
  Nile River
  Rwenzori Mountains
  Virunga Mountains
Djibouti (Republic of Djibouti)
  Afar Triangle and Danakil Depression
  Red Sea
Egypt (Arab Republic of Egypt)
  Nile River
  Qattara Depression
  Red Sea
  The Sahara
  Sinai Peninsula
  Wadi Al-Hitan (Whale Valley)
Equatorial Guinea (Republic of Equatorial Guinea)
  African Rainforest
Eritrea (State of Eritrea)
  Afar Triangle and Danakil Depression
  Red Sea
Ethiopia (Federal Democratic Republic of Ethiopia)
  Afar Triangle and Danakil Depression
  Ethiopian Highlands
  Lake Turkana
  Nile River
Gabon (Gabonese Republic)
  African Rainforest
Ghana (Republic of Ghana)
  African Rainforest

Turkmenistan
Caspian Sea
Central Asian Deserts—Karakum and Kyzylkum

United Arab Emirates
Arabian Peninsula
Persian Gulf

Uzbekistan (Republic of Uzbekistan)
Aral Sea
Central Asian Deserts—Karakum and Kyzylkum

Vietnam
Ha Long Bay
Mekong River

Yemen (Republic of Yemen)
Arabian Peninsula
Red Sea

AUSTRALIA

Australia
Ediacara Hills
Fraser Island
Gondwana Rainforests
Great Artesian Basin
Great Barrier Reef
Great Dividing Range
Great Victoria Desert
The Kimberley
Lake Eyre Basin and Lake Eyre
Murray-Darling River System
Nullarbor Plain
The Pilbara
Shark Bay
Tasmania
Uluru/Ayers Rock

CENTRAL AMERICA

Belize
Belize Barrier Reef
Central American Isthmus

Costa Rica
Central American Isthmus
Monteverde Cloud Forest Biological Reserve
(Reserva Biológica Bosque Nuboso
Monteverde)
Talamanca Mountains

Volcanic Highlands of Central America

El Salvador
Central American Isthmus
Volcanic Highlands of Central America

Guatemala
Central American Isthmus
Lake Atitlán (Lago de Atitlán)
The Petén
Volcanic Highlands of Central America

Honduras
Central American Isthmus
Miskito Coast
Volcanic Highlands of Central America

Nicaragua
Central American Isthmus
Miskito Coast
Volcanic Highlands of Central America

Panama
Central American Isthmus
Volcanic Highlands of Central America

EUROPE

Albania (Republic of Albania)
Dinaric Alps

Andorra (Principality of Andorra)
Pyrenees Mountains

Austria (Republic of Austria)
Alps
Danube River
Rhine River

Belarus (Republic of Belarus)
Bialowieza Primeval Forest

Bosnia and Herzegovina
Dinaric Alps

Bulgaria (Republic of Bulgaria)
Black Sea and Sea of Azov
Danube River

Croatia (Republic of Croatia)
Dinaric Alps
Plitvice Lakes National Park

Czech Republic
Carpathian Mountains
Elbe River

Denmark (Kingdom of Denmark)
Wadden Sea

Uruguay
  Atlantic Forest (Mata Atlântica)
  The Pampas
  Rio de la Plata
Venezuela
  Amazon Rainforest
  Amazon River
  Andes Mountains
  Angel Falls
  Casiquiare River
  Gran Sabana
  Guácharo Cave (Cueva de Guácharo)
  Lake Maracaibo
  The Llanos
  Mount Roraima
  Orinoco River
  Páramo

Oceanic Features, Including Islands

ARCTIC OCEAN

  Arctic Ocean
  Baffin Island
  Bering Strait and Bering Land Bridge
  Canadian Arctic Archipelago
  Franz Josef Land (Zemlya Frantsa Iosifa)
  Greenland Sea
  Hudson Bay
  Jan Mayen
  Novaya Zemlya Archipelago
  Svalbard Archipelago
  Wrangel Island

ATLANTIC OCEAN

  Ascension Islands
  Atlantic Ocean
  Azores Archipelago
  Baltic Sea
  Bermuda
  Canary Islands
  Cape Verde Islands
  Caribbean Sea
  English Channel
  Faroe Islands
  Fernando de Noronha Archipelago

  Grand Banks
  Greenland
  Gulf of Guinea Islands
  Gulf of Mexico
  Gulf Stream and North Atlantic Current
  Hebrides
  Iceland
  Lost City Hydrothermal Field
  Madeira Archipelago
  Mid-Atlantic Ridge
  Newfoundland
  North Sea
  Orkney Islands
  Saint Helena
  Sargasso Sea
  Shetland Islands
  South Georgia and the South Sandwich Islands
  Strait of Gibraltar
  Surtsey
  Tristan da Cunha and Gough Island
  Wadden Sea

CARIBBEAN SEA

Anguilla
  Lesser Antilles
Antigua and Barbuda
  Lesser Antilles
Aruba
  Lesser Antilles
The Bahamas
  The Bahamas
  Dean's Blue Hole
Barbados
  Lesser Antilles
British Virgin Islands
  Virgin Islands
Cayman Islands
  Greater Antilles
Cuba
  Greater Antilles
  Zapata Swamp (Ciénega de Zapata)
Dominica
  Lesser Antilles

Preface

Nature exists. But the wonders of nature dwell in the minds of sentient beings who are receptive to them.

Bernd Heinrich, *Winter World*, 2003

Our home planet is a fascinating place bearing an enormous variety of natural landscapes and seascapes, each distinguished by one or more distinctive features—landforms, vegetation types, unique plants, characteristic animals—reflecting geomorphic, climatic, evolutionary, and biogeographic processes that have been occurring throughout geologic time. *Earth's Landscape: An Encyclopedia of the World's Geographic Features* offers brief descriptions and explanations of 460 examples of this wonderful diversity from all of the world's continents and oceans. In selecting places to include, the authors tried to cover as full an array of features and landscapes as possible and from as many parts of the world as possible. This was not an easy process and was often hampered by lack of authoritative information. Discovery is an essential part of the study of geography, and we both learned much in preparing the entries. Our hope is that the reader also enjoys learning new things and will be inspired to delve further into places and processes and come away with a greater understanding, appreciation, and wonderment for the natural Earth. This work fills a common gap in physical geography education, the absence of details about specific examples of topics typically covered in the classroom. It also assembles in one place information that usually requires a search through many disparate sources to find. The encyclopedia is aimed at high school and undergraduate students but is accessible to any interested, educated layperson. Each entry about a place is arranged according to the following subheadings, unless one or more is not appropriate to the subject matter or substantiated information is not available on the topic or is not known, in which case it is omitted.

Geographic Overview
Geographic Coordinates
Description
Geologic History
Circulation and Major Currents (in entries for oceans and seas only)
Biota (the plants and animals of the region)
Protected Areas
Environmental Issues
See also
Further Reading

Arrangement and Special Features

The encyclopedia begins with an introduction to the major patterns and processes of physical geography. The entries that follow are arranged alphabetically, but a list of entries by location (continent and country or ocean and its islands) is provided in the beginning of the book, which will be especially useful for those looking for places in a particular country or region. Following the entries, three special features will extend the users' knowledge and interest. Appendix 1 presents information on Earth's dimensions and global comparisons with lists of the top 10 extreme features in several categories, such as highest mountains, lowest points on continents, deepest caves, longest rivers, deepest lakes, and so forth. To encourage critical thinking, Appendix 2 contains a set of opposing viewpoints by knowledgeable writers on six issues related to natural landscapes and their conservation. Each pair of viewpoints is introduced and placed into a larger context. Also for further extending the topics in the book, Appendix 3 is a set of activities and discussion questions for students, which can be addressed in or outside of the classroom.

A generous glossary has definitions for many terms used in the work. The bibliography lists printed matter and Web sites that are good starting points for further research. The comprehensive index is an essential tool for finding sites and topics that may not be the subject of a full entry but are nonetheless discussed.

How to Use This Work

Earth's Landscape presents descriptions of each continent and ocean, as well as many of the major physiographic regions of the landmasses and gulfs, seas, and straits of the oceans. Examples of smaller scale features from mountain ranges to individual volcanoes, from national parks and major wetlands to sites of limited areas such as caves and mountain tops that contain rare or endemic species, unique geologic formations, or globally significant fossils are covered. Oceanic islands and coral reefs appear in the work. The variety of places and types of features are great, sometimes within a given entry, so the reader is cautioned not to rely only on the table of contents, but to use the index to search for items in which he or she may be interested.

Whenever reading about a place, consult a good atlas. Maps are essential to understanding the spatial relationships inherent in geography and understanding why things are where they are. Place names that appear in the encyclopedia generally follow the most common usage, with popular alternatives given in many cases. Names from countries that do not use the Latin or Roman alphabet present special difficulties in transliteration and may appear with other spellings in other works.

Geographic coordinates (latitude and longitude) are provided to help locate places. When a single set of coordinates appears this refers to the center point or global positioning system (GPS) coordinate. Areas are indicated by a range of latitude and longitude that represent the extreme points of the place but do not account for irregularities in shape. In other words, the area in question does not completely fill the box indicated by the coordinates. Most natural regions do not have sharp boundaries, so areal designations are usually approximations.

Indicating the time of geologic events with any degree of consistency is a challenge, because the best estimates of scientists vary according to their area of expertise and change as new knowledge becomes available. The reader should interpret our dates as approximate and consult other authoritative works on particular sites or events for updates, confirmation, or greater precision.

While an attempt was made not to use jargon, some is unavoidable as many terms are specific to a particular science. To assist the reader, a wide-ranging glossary is included and should be consulted. Scientific names of plants and animals were usually avoided unless no common name exists or confusion among common names might make it difficult for the reader to accurately find more on a given species. The latter can happen when common names are shared among different species or when sources give incorrect information, as when, for example, a lichen is called a moss. Only when rare, unusual, or endemic species are mentioned do the Latin names almost always appear.

Acknowledgments

The authors wish to thank the several people who contributed essays, often at short notice, to Appendix 2. Special thanks go to Richard H. Foster, Ph.D., Associate Professor of Geography, Ret., University of Manitoba, for editing and providing useful comments on several of the North American entries. We acknowledge the considerable efforts of Kaitlin Ciarmiello, Senior Acquisitions Editor at ABC-CLIO, in accommodating our ideas into the initial development of the project and in negotiating our contracts. Anne Thompson, Senior Development Editor at ABC-CLIO, graciously answered our many questions and guided the manuscript through to its final draft stage.

Introduction

I. Processes of Landscape Development

The look and characteristics of any landscape are the result of a complex combination of processes. Plate tectonics and mountain building set the stage for subsequent erosion and deposition by various agents, such as water and ice. The combination of weathering and erosion breaks the rocks into smaller pieces and carves the land into a variety of landforms. The resulting sediments, such as sand and mud, may be subsequently transported by water, ice, or wind and deposited elsewhere. Accumulations of sediments may eventually be cemented into rock layers and uplifted to form new mountains, perpetuating the processes. Rock type, elevation, climate, types of weathering, agents of erosion or deposition, plate tectonics, and the passage of geologic time are major variables that determine the final appearance of the landforms and landscape. The following paragraphs provide only a brief introduction to the geological and geomorphological processes pertinent to these volumes. A number of publications, both in print and online, should be consulted for in-depth explanations of processes and results.

Geologic Time

The landscapes we see today are the result of many millions of years of geologic activity. Rocks have been formed at different times, and the geologic time scale (Table 1) represents the sequence in which younger rocks lie above older ones and provides a relative chronology by which we can assign general dates to geologic and evolutionary events. The dates on the scale are not absolute, in part because we still don't know the details of the past. The scientists who study Earth's deep past, mostly geologists and paleontologists, use different criteria—such as indicator rock strata or evidence of mass extinctions in the fossil record—to determine the boundaries between units of geologic time. Nonetheless there is general and universal agreement on the various units and their duration.

The major subdivisions of geologic time are eras, each of which is further partitioned into periods. Periods are broken down in epochs. The first (oldest) unit of time is the Precambrian Supereon, which covers much of Earth's history from its origins roughly 4.55 bya to 545 mya. Very primitive, one-celled life-forms arose as early as 4.0 bya and near the end of the era (570 mya) the oldest known fossils of multicelled organisms appear. The Precambrian ends 545 mya with the Cambrian explosion, a sudden proliferation of complex multicelled organisms thought to have been a response to an increase in oxygen in the atmosphere and seas brought about by early photosynthesizing cyanobacteria. This marks the beginning of the Paleozoic Era (545–251 mya), the time of "ancient life," which included fishes and the first land plants and animals. The last period of this era, the Permian (300–251 mya), saw the final assembly of the ancient continent of Pangaea.

The Mesozoic Era (251–65 mya) followed. This was the time when reptiles, including dinosaurs, dominated the land. The last era, the Cenozoic (65 mya–present) began after a mass extinction in the oceans and on land presumably precipitated by an asteroid strike that left a marker layer of iridium around the world. The Cenozoic Era is separated into two periods, the Tertiary and the Quaternary. The closer we get to today, the more precise the time scale becomes: The Quaternary Period is subdivided into the Pleistocene and Holocene or Recent epochs. The onset of the Quaternary Period (and Pleistocene Epoch) is marked by the first of a series of alternating glacial and interglacial periods at high latitudes and altitudes and the rise of the genus *Homo*, ancestral human beings. The beginning date is set at either 2.6 mya or 1.6–1.8 mya according to the criteria used. The Pleistocene Epoch terminates with the end of the last glacial period 12,000–10,000 years ago. Modern climates and other environmental conditions are established, ushering in the Holocene, the epoch in which we live.

Table I The Geologic Time Scale*

	ERA	PERIOD	EPOCH	MAIN GEOLOGIC and *EVOLUTIONARY* EVENTS
0	**Cenozoic**	Quaternary	Holocene	• *Human disturbances become dominant force in ecological and evolutionary processes*
0.01			Pleistocene	• *Pleistocene megafaunal extinctions*
				• Repeated phases of prolonged glaciations separated by shorter interglacials at high latitudes and elevations
				• *Rise of hominins*
1.6–2.0	Dominance of Angiosperms Age of mammals	Tertiary	Pliocene	• *Great American biotic interchange*
				• Central American isthmus closes
				• Beginning of Cascade volcanism
5.0			Miocene	• Continents in present location
				• *Hominins first appear in Africa*
				• Main uplift of Andes
				• Main uplift of Rocky Mountains
				• Flood basalts on Columbia, Paraná and Deccan plateaus
				• Uplift of Colorado Plateau
				• Uplift of Sierra Nevada
24			Oligocene	• Southern Ocean begins to open
34			Eocene	• Rise of the European Alps and the Himalayas in the Alpine Orogeny
				• Australia collided with Indonesia
55			Palaeocene	• Caribbean and Scotia plates form
65	**Mesozoic** Dominance of conifers, cycads, ferns	Cretaceous		• *Extinction of dinosaurs*
				• Chicxulub asteroid strike
				• *Flowering plants appear*
				• Brazil separates from western Africa
				• Laramide Orogeny begins

			Events
141	Age of Dinosaurs	Jurassic	• Formation of Sierra Nevada • Andes begin to rise • Indian Ocean begins to open • Gondwana begins to break apart • Madagascar separates from Africa • East African Rift System begins to develop • Pacific plate begins to shrink as result of subduction beneath other plates • Atlantic Ocean opened • Tethys Sea begins to close • *Earliest birds*
205		Triassic	• Pangaea begins to break apart: Laurasia separates from Gondwana • *Early mammals*
251	**Paleozoic**	Permian	• *Mass extinction* • Global warming • Pangaea assembled • Closure of Iapetus Ocean • Tethys Sea appears • Final rise of the Appalachian Mountains • Formation of Ural Mountains • *Gymnosperms appear*
298		Carboniferous (Pennsylvanian and Mississippian)	• Glossopteris *seed ferns* • *Early reptiles* • Alleghenian Orogeny • Hercynian (Variscan) Orogeny in Europe
354		Devonian	• Acadian Orogeny in North America • *Amphibians appear*
410		Silurian	• Caledonian Orogeny complete • *Fishes appear*
434		Ordovician	• Caledonian Orogeny begins • Iapetus Ocean begins to close • Taconic Orogeny
490		Cambrian	• Iapetus Ocean appears • Supercontinent Gondwana assembled • Paleo-Tethys Ocean developed • *Hard-shelled fossils first appear in record* • Pannotia splits apart • Cambrian Explosion
545	**Proterozoic**	Ediacaran	• "Snowball Earth" • Supercontinent Pannotia assembled • Rodinia splits apart • Supercontinent Rodinia assembled • *Ediacaran faunas present* • *Multi-celled organisms appear* • First evidence of glaciation
2500	**Archean**		• *Cyanobacteria (stromatolites)* • *Eukaryotes arise* • *Prokaryotes (bacteria) evolve* • Major cratons form
4500– 4600	**Hadean**		• Oldest known land surface (Pilbara region, West Australia) • *No known life* • Earth forms

PRECAMBRIAN

*Numbers are million years ago.

Rock Cycle

Rocks are classified according to their mineral content and method of formation. Over time, they change from one type to another in a process called the rock cycle. Igneous rocks, such as granite and basalt, solidify from molten material. Extrusive igneous rocks form when the molten rock reaches the earth's surface, such as from a volcano. When the molten material solidifies deep within the crust, it is called intrusive igneous rock. The major difference in appearance between extrusive and intrusive rocks is the size of the mineral crystals. Crystal sizes in intrusive rocks are generally large enough to be seen with the naked eye because the molten material cooled slowly and like minerals had time to accumulate. Extrusive igneous rocks are fine-grained, or have small crystals that cannot be seen without magnification, because the molten material cooled quickly. The most common intrusive igneous rocks are forms of granite, with light-colored minerals and large crystals. The extrusive equivalent, which has the same mineral composition but smaller crystals, is rhyolite. The most common extrusive igneous rock is basalt, a dark-colored rock with small crystals. The intrusive equivalent of basalt is gabbro. Between these extremes are many different types of igneous rocks with varying mineral composition and crystal sizes.

Any type of rock exposed long enough to the elements will break down into smaller pieces called sediments. Clastic sediments are small, solid pieces, such as gravel, sand, silt, and clay. Nonclastic sediments are those, such as lime, gypsum, or salt, that are soluble in water. The mineral composition of the sediments may or may not be changed from that of the original rock. Either type of sediment may accumulate in layers, usually according to size, and eventually be compressed and solidified into sedimentary rocks, such as sandstone, shale, or limestone. A major characteristic of sedimentary rocks is their layering, or stratification.

Rock subjected to extreme heat and/or pressure, perhaps from volcanic activity or from being deeply buried, may change its form and mineral composition and become a metamorphic rock. Typical metamorphic rocks include quartzite from sandstone, marble from limestone, and slate from shale. Even metamorphic rocks may be further metamorphosed. Gneiss is a very hard metamorphic rock derived from earlier metamorphic types. If the heat and/or pressure are sufficient, the rocks, whether igneous, sedimentary, or metamorphic, may melt, starting the rock cycle anew.

Different types of rocks react differently to weathering and erosion. Igneous and metamorphic rocks, sometimes referred to collectively as crystalline because of the crystal content, are generally hard or resistant and stand above the general surface as mountains or highlands. Sedimentary rocks are generally soft or less resistant to erosion and are thus more common in lowland landscapes. Of sedimentary rocks, sandstone is most resistant and shale is least resistant, while the resistance of limestone depends on the climate, especially water.

Plate Tectonics

The Earth's crust, overlying the molten core and semimolten mantle, is a relatively thin cover termed either continental crust or oceanic crust according to its mineral composition, which affects rock color, mineral composition, and density. Continental crust is generally 25 mi (32 km) thick, while oceanic crust is 3–5 mi (8 km) thick. Continental crust, also called sial and referred to as acidic due to high silica and aluminum content, can be igneous, sedimentary, or metamorphic. It is usually light both in color and in weight or density. Underlying ocean basins is oceanic crust, also called sima and referred to as basic due to high silica and magnesium content. Igneous in origin, it is dark in color and heavier than sial in weight or density. The difference in density plays a significant role in plate tectonics.

The Earth's crust is not a solid piece covering the entire globe, and the continents and oceans have not always held their present shapes or positions. The crust is broken into sections called plates, usually named for the continent or ocean which comprises its major extent, such as the North American Plate, the African Plate, or the Pacific Plate. The plates, however, are not restricted to their namesake but may include both continental and oceanic crust. The North American Plate, for example, extends from approximately the middle of the Atlantic Ocean west to the San Andreas Fault in western California. The Pacific Plate primarily underlies the Pacific Ocean, but includes the sliver of North America west of the San Andreas Fault. Parts of Earth's major plates—in the Mediterranean region and western Pacific regions, for example—are split into smaller pieces or microplates, further complicating geology and geomorphology.

Earth's crustal plates are not stationary, nor have their sizes and shapes been consistent over geologic time. In places, new oceanic crust emerges as magma rises through fissures and along rifts and in underwater volcanoes, while in other places, oceanic crust is carried deep into the mantle, to emerge as igneous rocks elsewhere. Both continental crust and oceanic crust may be forced together and crumpled upward to form mountain masses, altering the configuration of the surface. Simply stated, Earth's plates are "floating" atop a thick semimolten mass called the mantle. Convection currents in the mantle move the plates around the surface of the globe. A homely analogy is a cold fat layer on top of a pot of soup. Heat from the stove burner causes hot soup to rise to the surface, breaking apart the fat layer, which moves to the edge of the pan with the "current" of soup. The hot soup sinks back to the bottom at the edges of the pan, and the fat layer remaining on the surface may become more broken and crumpled as pieces bump into one another. Unlike the fat layer on the soup, however, the Earth's crustal layer never completely melts.

Types of Plate Margins

Different types of plate margins produce different characteristic landforms. Divergent plate boundaries are created where upwelling in the mantle causes the surface crust to break, allowing magma to extrude onto the surface and create new crust, such as at the Mid-Atlantic Ridge volcanic mountain range in the middle of the Atlantic Ocean. As upwelling continues, mantle currents carry the overlying crust in opposite directions. Upwelling mantle currents may also fracture continental crust and break apart continents, as has happened in the East African Rift Zone. Convergent plate boundaries, defined as active boundaries, occur where mantle currents carry plates toward one another. At a convergent plate margin between an oceanic plate and a continental plate, such as along the western edge of South America, the heavier oceanic crust subducts, or is forced downward beneath the less dense continental plate. A deep trench usually develops along the line of subduction. On the leading edge of the oceanic plate, ahead of the subduction zone and trench, the oceanic crust plunges deep enough to melt. Basic magma of the oceanic crust rises through fractures in the continental rocks of the adjacent plate, often incorporating acidic continental crust and altering the chemical content of the magma. Convergence of the two plates causes the continental plate to crumple, become folded and faulted and uplifted into mountains, which may be accented by stratovolcanoes or intrusive bodies of igneous rock derived from a combination of oceanic and continental crust from below. If two oceanic plates converge, such as the Caribbean and Atlantic plates, one of the oceanic plates will subduct, melt into magma, and create volcanoes along its leading edge ahead of the trench. This can produce a volcanic island arc, such as the Lesser Antilles, that rises above sea level. The best example of convergence of two continental plates is the Himalayan Mountains, between the Eurasian Plate and the Indian Plate. Because of fairly equal densities, neither continental plate subducted and both leading edges crumpled up into the highest mountain range on Earth.

Volcanism, however, may occur without being associated with an active plate margin. The mantle may develop hotspots, isolated areas of upwelling magma not associated with a plate margin but occurring in the center of a plate. The Hawaiian Island chain is a prime example. The hotspot, which remains stationary in the mantle, has melted the oceanic crust and extruded lava onto the ocean floor as the Pacific Plate moved northwestward, resulting in a string of volcanoes built as the plate moves over the upwelling.

The continental margin on the trailing edge of a plate consisting of both oceanic and continental crust, such as on eastern North America and the western Atlantic, is called a passive continental margin. Because it is neither converging nor diverging with another plate, no mountain building occurs and it is usually the site of sediment deposition.

Weathering

Weathering refers to the physical and chemical processes by which rocks are broken down into smaller pieces but not removed from the site. Physical weathering breaks rocks into smaller pieces of the same rock type or composition. A major means of physical weathering is the expansion of ice or plant roots growing in cracks or pores in the rock. Chemical weathering involves the addition of a chemical element, such as water or oxygen, which breaks the rock into smaller pieces that have a different composition than the original. Chemically weathered sediments are usually softer than the parent rock. Although physical and chemical weathering usually work in combination, arid climates usually exhibit more effects of physical weathering while humid climates are more prone to chemical weathering because of the moisture.

Karst landscapes are an exceptional type of chemical weathering. Carbonate-rich rocks such as limestone and dolomite, are susceptible to solution by carbonic acid (H_2CO_3). Over geologic time, rainwater, which is a weak carbonic acid, will dissolve carboniferous rocks both on the surface and underground, forming unique landforms such as cone-shaped hills, sinkholes, and caves.

Erosion, Transportation, and Deposition

Erosion occurs when something such as water, ice, or wind, called an agent of erosion, picks up and transports rocks and weathered material, or sediments, to another site. When for some reason, the sediments can no longer be carried by the agent of erosion, they are deposited. Fluvial processes involve erosion, transportation, and deposition by running water, rivers and streams. Although several factors influence erosion and deposition, in general, rapidly flowing rivers are capable of picking up (eroding) and transporting a lot of sediment. The faster the flow is, the larger the particle size that can be carried. Erosional processes dominate in mountains or hilly regions where stream flow is rapid. As running water decreases its speed, the river first loses its ability to carry the largest particles. Boulders, rocks, and gravel are deposited first, followed by sand, silt, and mud. Fluvial deposition, therefore, is primarily stratified, or layered according to sediment size, which may eventually create layers of different sized sedimentary rocks, such as sandstone, siltstone, and shale. Depositional processes dominate in flat landscapes.

Glacial processes involve movement of ice masses over land surfaces. In circumstances where the climate is either too cold or too snowy for winter snow to melt during the summer, the snow continues to accumulate, eventually turning to ice. When the ice mass becomes thick and heavy enough, it begins to slowly flow (maybe inches [centimeters] each year) due to its own weight. In a mountainous area, the glacier flows downslope, confined to a valley, and is termed a valley glacier or alpine glacier. Moving ice that accumulates on a continent and is not confined to a valley is termed a continental glacier. It spreads in all directions over the landscape like a semisoft chunk of butter on a table top being pushed down from the top. The edges of the continental glacier are not smooth but convoluted into lobes, like fingers spreading out from the center. Both types of glaciers erode as they flow, gouging the valley or scraping the underlying landscape and incorporating the rocks and debris haphazardly into the ice. It is important to emphasize that glacial ice is always moving away from its area of accumulation, acting like a conveyor belt carrying rocks and debris. Movement of the "conveyor belt" never reverses direction. Where the leading edge, or front or snout, of the glacier reaches warmer climates, either due to lower elevation or lower latitude, the rocky and muddy debris inside the ice is deposited as the ice melts. Unlike rivers, however, which sort sediments by size, the glacial ice does not. The debris, called glacial till, is dumped in unsorted, jumbled piles. As long as the rate of accumulation of snow and ice exceeds the rate of ablation (all processes, including melting and sublimation, whereby ice is lost), the glacier's front will continue to move away from its source, both eroding and incorporating the newly deposited till. If the climate changes and the rate of accumulation equals the rate of ablation, the ice front will remain stationary. Till will accumulate in the same location, building moderately high hills called moraines. When the rate of accumulation is less than the rate of ablation, the ice front will retreat, or melt back toward the source, depositing till as it goes. Various factors affect the ways that glacially till is deposited, resulting in several different types of landforms.

Wind processes are most common in sandy deserts or coastal regions, where wind picks up and transports sand, silt, clay, and smaller size sediments. Except within a few feet of ground level where rock may be scoured by windblown sand, wind rarely erodes solid rock. Sand is too heavy for even strong winds to carry very high or for long distances, but dust may be swept thousands of feet into the atmosphere, causing dust storms. In extremely arid climates and over extended geologic time, windblown sand dune accumulations can become thousands of feet deep and solidified; the wind-deposited sandstones of the Colorado Plateau in the United States are an example.

The Pleistocene

The Pleistocene Epoch, which ended approximately 12,000–10,000 years ago, was a period of repeated glaciations with intervening warm periods. Although the Northern Hemisphere bore the bulk of the ice, the impact was global. Huge continental ice sheets extended as far south as 40°N latitude. Extensive ice caps and alpine glaciers covered high mountain areas, such as the Andes in South America, the New Zealand Alps, the European Alps, East African peaks (Mount Kenya, Mount Kilimanjaro, and the Ruwenzori Range), the Himalayas, the Altai, and Tian Shan in Asia. Antarctica was covered by ice. In North America, the Cordilleran Ice Sheet covering the mountainous west merged with the Laurentide Ice Sheet centered on Hudson Bay, which also covered the northern Canadian archipelago. Greenland's ice sheet was even more extensive than it is today. In Europe, the Fennoscandian Ice Sheet extended north to cover the Arctic coast and islands such as Novaya Zemlya, east to cover the Ural Mountains and western Siberia, and south to Great Britain and northern Germany. Isolated icecaps covered northern islands, such as Iceland and Svalbard. Because the ice modified the climate of adjacent areas, a zone of permafrost extended hundreds of miles or kilometers south of the ice front and periglacial features such as patterned ground and pingoes can still be found in areas now far from glaciers.

Ice sheets advanced and retreated (melted back), several times during the Pleistocene. A period of ice advance is called a glacial, while a period of retreat is called an interglacial. Pluvials and interpluvials refer to periods of increased or decreased precipitation, respectively, in non-glaciated areas; they do not usually correlate directly to glacials and interglacials.

An enormous amount of water was tied up in the ice sheets, which were 4,900–9,800 ft (1,500–3,000 m) thick, causing sea level to drop about 300 ft (100 m). During interglacials, coastal areas were inundated by rising oceans. Actual measurements of sea level change are complicated by the fact that the land was depressed by the weight of the overlying ice. When the ice melted, the land rebounded (slowly uplifted).

Many landform features provide evidence of continental glaciation. Because drainage to the north was blocked by ice, lakes, such as Glacial Lake Bonneville in Utah, frequently developed at the southern edges of the ice sheets and temporarily increased in size as the glaciers retreated, with the addition of meltwater. The effects of continental glaciation include not only debris (rocks and sediment) deposited directly by the ice, called glacial till, but also those materials deposited or rearranged by flowing water, wind, or waves. Stratified layers of clay, sand, and gravel typify glacial lakebeds and outwash plains. Fine silt originally carried by ice may be scooped up by wind and deposited elsewhere as loess, such as along the Mississippi River Valley. Waves and currents associated with changing sea levels have reworked glacial deposits along both old and modern shorelines. Regions that are arid today, such as the Basin and Range in the United States and northwestern Mexico or the Central Asian deserts, received more rainfall during the Pleistocene, which allowed an integrated drainage system and lakes to develop. Many of the dry lake beds (playas or salt pans) in now-arid regions owe their existence to pluvial periods of the Pleistocene.

Severe climatic fluctuations associated with glacials and interglacials caused major changes in biogeographic patterns. With each glacial advance, the area beneath the ice was completely depopulated. Plants and animals evolved adaptations, dispersed to new regions of favorable climate, or went extinct. Biomes shifted equatorward and alpine organisms moved downslope. New ecological communities unlike those existing today developed. The late Pleistocene was marked globally by the extinction of the megafauna. In North America, for example, mammoths, mastodons, saber-toothed cats, and ground sloths were lost; while in Australia giant kangaroos and other marsupials vanished. The cause of this mass extinction is still hotly debated, with some scientists pointing to climatic stress, others to habitat change and overhunting by human populations, and many to some combination of climate change and human activity. As the Holocene began 20,000 years ago, plant and animal populations repopulated the formerly ice-covered regions and shifted their distribution areas in response to warming conditions.

Exceptions to this general pattern existed wherever species were able to survive in glacial refugia. "Islands" above the ice, called nunataks, may have retained their biota during a glacial advance, which allowed those taxa to repopulate the ice-covered region more efficiently once the ice retreated. Pockets of favorable environment persisted or formed in nonglaciated areas as well and served as refugia for temperate and subtropical species in the middle latitudes or rainforest species in the drying tropics. Such continental refugia not only preserved plant and animal species but also isolated populations and provided opportunities for new species to arise.

II. Climate

Climate is different from weather. Weather refers to the state of the atmosphere at any one point in time. It is raining, sunny, foggy, windy, hot, or cold. Climate refers to the kind of weather that may be expected at a given time of year. Tropical regions, for example, are expected to be warm all year, while continental mid-latitudes experience a seasonal change of cold and warm temperatures. A combination of several factors—including latitude, Earth's tilt, atmospheric and oceanic circulation, Coriolis effect, and elevation—produce the several climate regions on Earth. (See Table 2.)

Latitude is the major factor that determines receipt of solar radiation, which in turn influences temperature. Temperatures generally decrease with increasing latitude from the equator, culminating in the frozen polar regions. Earth's axis is tilted approximately 23.5° from the vertical and consistently points toward the North Star as our planet makes its annual revolution around the sun. Seasonal receipt of solar radiation in tropical latitudes varies little, resulting in warm temperatures year-round; but because the northern and southern hemispheres alternate between tilting toward the sun or away from the sun, mid-latitudes (roughly 30–60° latitude) have seasonal differences in the receipt of solar energy, giving those regions distinct summers and winters. Although polar regions also experience a seasonal variation in solar energy

Table 2 Major Climate Types[1]

Name	General Location	Description
HUMID TROPICAL CLIMATES		Precipitation sufficient to support tropical forests and savannas; warm all year
Tropical wet or Tropical rainforest	10° N – 10° S Equatorial	Abundant annual precipitation with no dry season
Tropical monsoon	10° N – 20° N & S	Abundant annual precipitation with short (1–3 month) dry season; warm all year
Tropical wet and dry or Tropical savanna	5° – 25° N & S	Abundant to moderate annual precipitation with distinct wet summers and dry winters
DRY CLIMATES		Sparse precipitation supports scrub or grasses
Semiarid or subtropical steppe	15° – 35° N & S	Moderate to sparse annual precipitation; hot summers, mild winters
Subtropical or warm desert	15° – 30° N & S Center or western side of continents	Sparse and sporadic precipitation; hot summers, mild winters
West coast desert	10° – 30° N & S West coast of continents	Sparse and sporadic precipitation; fog may be key source of moisture; mild temperatures all year
Semiarid or midlatitude steppe	35° – 50° N & S Center or western side of continents	Moderate annual precipitation; very hot summers and cold winters.
Arid or midlatitude or cold desert	35° – 50° N & S Center or western side of continents	Sparse and sporadic annual precipitation; very hot summers and cold winters.
HUMID SUBTROPICAL CLIMATES (Temperate climates)		Sufficient precipitation to support forests and woodlands; distinct seasons based on temperature differences; warm to hot summers and mild to cool winters
Humid subtropical	20° – 35° N & S Eastern side of continents	Abundant annual precipitation; hot summers and mild winters
Marine west coast	40° – 60° N & S West coast of continents	Abundant precipitation; mild temperatures all year
Mediterranean	30° – 45° N & S West coast of continents	Moderate to sparse winter precipitation with dry summer season; Warm to hot summers and mild winters
HIGH LATITUDE CLIMATES (Snow climates)		Precipitation sufficient to support forests; extreme seasonal temperature differences.
Humid continental	35° – 60° N & S Center or east side of continents	Moderate precipitation with rainy summers and snowy winters; warm to hot summers and cold winters.
Subarctic	50° – 70° N Large continental areas	Moderate to sparse precipitation with snow; brief mild summers and long, dark, and very cold winters

POLAR CLIMATES		Sparse precipitation, primarily snow; very brief cool summers and no tree growth; long, dark winters
Tundra	North of 55° N South of 50° S	Sparse precipitation, primarily snow, supports low-stature herbaceous growth and dwarf shrubs; very brief cool summers; long, dark winters
Ice cap	Greenland Antarctica	Very sparse precipitation (snow); cold summers; long, dark, extremely cold winters; no month averages above freezing.
HIGHLAND CLIMATES	Mountains	Climate changes rapidly across short map distances as a result of elevational change.

[1] Based on the Koeppen Climate System.

due to the axis's tilt, the total amount of radiation is low, resulting in very cold winters and cool summers. The fact that land absorbs and loses heat more rapidly than water means that continental interiors, especially in the mid-latitudes, experience seasonal temperature extremes; while seasonal temperature differences in coastal locations are modest.

The unequal heating of Earth's surface leads to the circulation of the atmosphere. Heated air at the equator creates an equatorial low pressure zone where air rises, while at each pole cold air forms a polar high pressure cell where air subsides. The result is a giant convection cell. Cold air moves from the poles toward the equator along the surface, and warm air moves aloft from the Equator toward the poles. In its path toward the poles, the warm air aloft sinks back to earth at approximately 30° north and south latitudes, forming a subtropical high pressure cell in each hemisphere. Upon reaching Earth's surface, the subsiding air spreads out in all directions, creating winds moving equatorward, the so-called trade winds, and winds moving into higher latitudes. The trade winds converge at the Intertropical Convergence Zone (ITCZ) near the equator, where they are warmed and rise again, to complete the circulation. The relatively warm winds moving into higher latitudes from the subtropical high pressure meet cold air moving away from the poles. Where these airmasses of different temperature and hence density collide in the mid-latitudes, they create subarctic and subantarctic low pressure belts, where cyclonic storms develop as the warm air rises over the cold air. Winds are deflected by the Coriolis effect, caused by Earth's rotation, to the right in the Northern Hemisphere and to the left in the Southern Hemisphere, a phenomenon which contributes to wind direction.

Interactions among air temperature, water temperature, relative humidity, pressure cells, and wind direction influence precipitation patterns. Warm air has the capacity to hold more water vapor (the source of precipitation) than does cold air, and warm water will more readily evaporate than will cold water. Rising air associated with low pressure expands and cools, increasing relative humidity and facilitating precipitation, while subsiding air associated with high pressure, compresses and warms, decreasing the relative humidity and preventing precipitation. Thus, the combination of warm air, warm water, high relative humidity, and low pressure, such as is common in equatorial regions, often causes frequent and abundant rainfall. Subsidence of air in the subtropics, such as over North Africa or central Australia, combined with minimal water on those continental areas and increasing temperatures produces little precipitation. The zones of subarctic and subantarctic low pressure, where cold air confronts warm air, also produce rising air and the potential for precipitation. This conflict zone between airmasses of different temperatures, called a polar front, is a widely fluctuating belt related to the Jet Stream. Precipitation depends on the location of the Jet Stream and is therefore variable. Distance from water sources often limits precipitation in the centers of large continents. Precipitation in high latitudes or polar regions is sparse due to cold air, cold or frozen water, or land areas from which moisture cannot be evaporated.

Wind direction and ocean currents also play major roles in precipitation patterns. Warm ocean currents increase both the moisture content and temperature of the air, increasing instability, or the potential for that air to rise. Warm winds passing over warm ocean currents, such as those coming from the Gulf of Mexico onto the southeastern United States, evaporate considerable amounts of moisture and carry it inland, where it falls as rain or snow. Cooler, westerly air masses flowing at higher latitudes pass over the warm waters of the North Atlantic Current and bring precipitation to western Europe. Airmasses passing over cold currents, however, are cooled and stabilized, prone to subsidence rather than uplift, which greatly reduces the likelihood of rain. Part of the reason Southern California, for example, receives little rainfall is due to the cold current offshore.

Elevation influences both temperature and precipitation. Temperature generally decreases with increasing elevation, approximately 3.5°F per 1,000 ft (1°C/100 m), explaining why mountains may be snow-covered while adjacent lowlands are warm. Precipitation also generally increases with elevation, although not at a steady rate. Wind direction plays a significant role. The windward side of mountains tends to be wetter because air is forced to rise and cool as it passes over the mountain range (orographic effect). The air subsides and warms on the lee side, which prevents precipitation and creates a dry region called a rain shadow. The Sierra Nevada in California is a prime example, rainy on the western windward side and dry on the eastern lee side, with the rain shadow effect extending eastward well into the continent. Exceedingly high elevations, such as the Tibetan Plateau in Asia and the Altiplano in South America, are dry both because of the rain shadow effect and that fact that moisture in the air is frequently depleted before the air reaches that height.

A major wind pattern is the monsoon system, best developed in Asia. The term "monsoon" refers to a seasonal wind reversal. In winter, the northern part of the large Asian continent becomes very cold, causing high pressure to develop over the interior. Winds circulating from this high pressure flow southeast and south from the continent toward the Pacific and Indian Oceans. Because these winds originate over the cold, dry continent, their moisture content is low and for 1–3 months, they bring no rainfall to southern Asia. In summer, the southern edge of Asia becomes very warm, causing low pressure to develop. In fact, the ITCZ is pulled north from the equator to rest over northern India. For 9–11 months, warm moist air is pulled over southern Asia, often bringing with it the torrential rainfall commonly associated in the popular imagination with monsoons.

Climate Change

Climate has not remained stable through geologic time but has changed as continents shifted latitudinal positions, amassed into supercontinents, and later split apart. Today we are witnessing global climate change with a general warming trend that is affecting not only temperatures, but also storm frequencies, intensity and frequency of tropical cyclones, decreasing snowpack and water availability, coastal flooding and erosion associated with sea-level rise, droughts and decreasing yields of rain-fed agriculture, wildfires, and species extinction.

Causes are still debated. Natural cycles may be partly involved, but human activities, including increased emissions of CO_2 and deforestation, are also part of the problem, globally, regionally, and locally.

III. Major Surface Features

Continents

Continents are the large, continuous land masses consisting of continental crust (or sial) and generally separated by deep ocean basins. Six are conventionally recognized—Africa, Antarctica, Australia, Eurasia (sometimes, as here, divided into Europe and Asia), North America, and South America.

Each continent consists of a core of Precambrian rock, a permanent part of the continent, which is called a craton where it is beneath the surface and a continental shield where it is exposed. After subjection to several episodes of mountain building and erosion throughout geologic time, most continental cores today are eroded to hills, plateaus, or plains. Adjacent to, and perhaps covering, the core are layers of younger sedimentary rocks or more recently uplifted massifs. These younger materials, deposited and eroded through time, alter the shapes of the continents, similar to the way passing waves cover or partially cover a large rock on a beach with sandy layers, continually changing the configuration of the "landmass" above the water line. Sedimentary layers may be a result of coastal deposition or continental deposition from newly eroded mountains. Plate convergence can add to the continental land mass through volcanism or accretion of trench scrapings, terranes, or microplates.

The continental margins, beyond the coastline, are composed of continental shelf, continental slope, and continental rise. The submerged edges of the continents, offshore to depths of approximately 650 ft (200 m) bsl and composed of continental rocks, are the continental shelves. The extension of continental shelves beyond the coastline varies considerably. Continental islands, those composed of continental rather than oceanic crust, rise above sea level on the shelf. The continental slope is where the shelf drops steeply before becoming a more gently sloping surface called the continental rise. Changes in sea level will expose or submerge parts of a continental shelf, altering the configuration of the coastlines and size of continent.

Paleo Continents and Oceans

Continents and supercontinents, separated by ancient oceans, have assembled and disassembled throughout geologic time. Their shifting locations through latitudinal zones have caused climate changes which are often reflected in the rocks and the modern landscape. Assemblage of landmasses, especially Pangaea, affected distribution of land animals by enabling migration.

Approximately 1.3–1.1 bya, in Precambrian time, the supercontinent of Rodinia assembled, with North America (Laurentia) at its core, Australia, East Antarctica, and India forming its western edge, and South America and fragments of proto-Africa close by. Approximately 750 mya, the Panthalassic Ocean (precursor to the Pacific Ocean) opened, splitting Rodinia into two major halves, with the smaller Congo craton between. South America and pieces of Africa drifted eastward to eventually join up with India, Australia, and East Antarctica on the west wide of what was to become the Gondwana supercontinent. Subsequent collision (600–550 mya) of the two halves of Rodinia, along with the Congo craton, initiated mountain building (Pan-African orogeny) and formed a new supercontinent called Pannotia. By the beginning of the Paleozoic Era (545 mya), Pannotia broke into four parts, with the new Iapetus Ocean (proto-Atlantic Ocean) widening between Laurentia (North America), Baltica (Northern Europe), and Angara (Siberia or Asia). The supercontinent of Gondwana, the largest remainder of the short-lived Pannotia continent, contained most of Earth's landmasses clustered around the South Pole. Farther northeast, the Paleo-Tethys Ocean (the proto-Mediterranean Sea) began to develop between Gondwana and Baltica and Angara (the forerunners of Eurasia). By the middle of the Paleozoic Era (ca. 420–370 mya), southeastern Laurentia collided with the microplate Avalonia and western Gondwana, causing the Acadian orogeny and beginning the closure of the southern part of the Iapetus Ocean. Northeastern Laurentia collided with Baltica, beginning the closure of the northern part of the Iapetus Ocean and resulting in the Caledonian orogeny and mountain building in eastern North America, Greenland, and western Europe.

Toward the end of the Paleozoic Era (ca. 251 mya), the Paleozoic oceans between Laurasia (North American and Asia) were completely closed as Gondwana and Laurentia converged to form the supercontinent of Pangaea. Centered on the equator, Pangaea extended from North Pole to South Pole, with a major embayment on the eastern side, the Paleotethys Sea separating Asia from Africa–India–Australia. The Panthalassic Ocean (Panthalassa) surrounded the supercontinent.

Beginning in the early Mesozoic Era (ca. 251 mya), Pangaea broke apart in three main episodes to subsequently form today's continents. The central Atlantic Ocean, along with the Gulf of Mexico, opened in the middle Jurassic (175–145 mya), as North America moved northwest away from Africa and South America. Laurasia (North America and Eurasia) rotated clockwise, pushing Eurasia south toward Africa, which began closure of the Tethys Ocean. Rifting on the east coast of Africa opened the Indian Ocean, which separated India and Madagascar from Africa–Antarctica–Australia. Several events occurred in the late Jurassic to early Cretaceous periods (ca. 150–100 mya). South America began to separate from Africa, opening the South Atlantic Ocean. India and Madagascar rifted away from Antarctica–Australia, and Madagascar separated from India. North America and Eurasia began to separate, opening the North Atlantic Ocean. Shallow seas covered many low-lying continental areas. By the late Cretaceous Period (ca. 65 mya), the oceans had widened. India was moving north toward the southern margin of Asia, with which it began colliding in the early Cenozoic Era (ca. 55–50 mya), and Australia collided with the Indonesian island arc. By 20 mya, the continents had attained their present locations, but the ongoing processes of plate tectonics continue to move them, albeit very slowly.

Oceans

Earth's five oceans cover 71 percent of the planet's surface. They provide innumerable habitats for life, from the intertidal zone along continental shorelines to the deepest oceanic trench.

Ocean currents, which are put into motion by winds, are designated warm if they flow through relatively cooler waters and cool if they flow through relatively warmer waters. Warm current and cool current do not coincide with specific temperatures. The Coriolis effect and prevailing winds drive ocean surface waters in large gyres centered on 30° latitude, clockwise in the Northern Hemisphere and counterclockwise in the Southern Hemisphere. This circulation pattern pushes warm surface waters to the western side of the three largest oceans in tropical and subtropical latitudes and produces warm currents such as the Gulf Stream and its northeastern continuation, the North Atlantic Current, off the eastern side of continents at those latitudes. Water pulled away by winds from the eastern side of these ocean basins allows colder water from depths to upwell toward the surface, contributing to the presence of cool currents on the western side of continents, such as the Humboldt Current off the west coast of South America. The large gyres also bring cold water from the Arctic or Southern oceans into the west coast cold currents. Smaller counterclockwise circulations of wind centered on approximately 60°N latitude in the northern Atlantic and northern Pacific bring warm currents to the more northerly west coasts of North America and Europe, while the eastern coasts are subjected to cool currents. The Arctic Ocean has a small clockwise Beaufort Gyre over its Canada Basin, while the Southern Ocean is dominated by the Antarctic Circumpolar Current, which flows eastward around the frozen continent.

Wave action results in both deposition and erosion. Waves push longshore currents along beaches, moving sediments and building sand spits and bars. In calm areas along soft sediment coastlines, mud flats are deposited. On rocky coasts, sediments in the pounding surf erode the headlands and shape seacliffs, stacks, arches, caves, and wavecut terraces. Lower sea levels during the last glacial period of the Pleistocene Epoch caused rivers entering the sea to seek a new base level, which resulted in valley-deepening. As sea levels rose again, the valleys were flooded and ria coastlines, indented by many bays and estuaries, were produced, perhaps most intricately in northwestern Australia. Glaciers gouged deep valleys, including into the exposed continental shelf, which when inundated by rising sea levels at the end of the Pleistocene, became fjords, such as those found in Norway and in Chile. As continental glaciers covering northern landmasses melted, the land was no longer weighed down by the enormous weight of the ice sheets and began to slowly uplift, or rebound, often resulting in long, straight sandy beaches as marine sediments were exposed. Winds piled loose sand into dunes, and surf and current action continually moved the particles along the shore.

Continental shelves, the submerged parts of the continental masses, are shaped into basins, canyons, and plateaus. Plateaus that rise close to the sea surface become shallow shoals or banks, such as the famous Grand Banks off Newfoundland, Canada. Banks in the high latitudes are often composed of glacial drift, deposited more than 10,000 years ago when sea level was lower. In warm, clear, shallow tropical waters, coral reefs may develop, constructed layer by layer by a thin veneer of living coral polyps and coralline algae over an accumulation of the calcium carbonate skeletons of their predecessors. Reefs take several forms: fringing reefs, patch reefs, barrier reefs, and atolls. They harbor the most diverse marine communities on the planet.

About 65 percent of Earth's ocean waters lie beyond the continental shelf. This is the deep sea overlying the continental slopes and abyssal plain where water depth ranges from 650 ft (200 m) bsl to 36,198 ft (11,033 m) bsl in the Mariana Trench. The oceans are floored by relatively young oceanic crust formed as magma emerges along great rifts at divergent plate boundaries, which pushes aside older volcanic rock. The upwelling magma forces the ocean floor alongside the rift to rise and fracture into tilted blocks, so each ocean is marked by mid-oceanic ridges at the spreading centers. The Mid-Atlantic Oceanic Ridge is a sinuous underwater mountain range, the longest on Earth. Like other mid-oceanic ridges, it is cut by numerous transform faults, themselves the focus of upwelling magma and the sites of features such as seamounts and hydrothermal vents. Submarine volcanoes erupt, often on the flanks of mid-oceanic ridges, where magma breaks through the crust. Where seawater seeps into cracks and is superheated during contact with the magma pool, minerals of the seafloor are dissolved. When the hot water finds a passageway, it rises as a jet of water near 750°F (400°C). Upon reaching the cold bottom waters of an ocean, sulfur compounds (primarily) precipitate out and form the chimneys of white smokers, as found in the Lost City Hydrothermal Field on the Atlantic Mid-Oceanic Ridge. If hydrogen sulfide (H_2S) is emitted, the water is dark and the vent becomes a black smoker.

Seamounts are also abundant along underwater convergent plate boundaries and the tracks of magma hotspots not associated with plate boundaries. Some seamounts once reached above sea level as volcanic islands, but have subsided as they moved away from the upwelling pool of magma and cooled. An estimated 50,000 seamounts occur in the Pacific Ocean and another 50,000 in the world's other oceans.

IV. Geographic Patterns of Life on Earth

A key feature of planet Earth is life, and even the least keen observer can see that life-forms are neither haphazardly nor uniformly distributed. Rather, life assumes distinct geographic patterns that often distinguish one landscape from all others. A major aspect of natural landscapes is plant life, or lack thereof. Types of vegetation, the generalized plant cover of an area, are recognizable by the dominant growth forms (size and shape of plants) and their spatial patterns on the surface and vertically, from ground to top of canopy. The most common vegetation types are forests, woodlands, savannas, grasslands, scrub, and desert. Leaf shape and the timing of leaf replacement (evergreen versus deciduous habit) modify the appearance of similar vegetation types, so that evergreen needleleaf forests, for example, look very unlike deciduous broadleaf forests. Vegetation generally reflects climatic conditions (temperature and precipitation) and so has a broadly latitudinal geographic distribution pattern altered locally and regionally by soils and landforms, especially those producing orographic and rain shadow effects. The same climatic factors also create altitudinal belts (zonation) of vegetation on high mountains.

Similar regional climates give rise to similar structural characteristics of the vegetation and adaptations among animals. The concept of the biome recognizes the relationship between climate and vegetation on global and regional scales and includes the animal life associated with that vegetation. Thus, the tropical rainforest biome occurs around the world in latitudes close to the equator, although different expressions of the biome occur in South and Central America, Africa, and the Indo-Malayan area. Distinct and unique vegetation types such as the caatinga and cerrado of Brazil are considered biomes in that country, because they cover vast territory and are hard to place in the global scheme. A related concept is that of the more inclusive ecoregion, adopted by such international organizations as World Wildlife Fund. An ecoregion focuses on a specific area as identified by its natural features, including climate, surface configuration, drainage systems, plants, and animals.

Each expression of a biome harbors a distinct assemblage of plant and animal species, the product of earth history and evolutionary history. New species arise under a number of conditions, but often some form of barrier—geographic, climatic, genetic—must divide a population before speciation can occur. Isolation and time for changes to evolve are usually prerequisite. The dynamic Earth, through plate tectonics, volcanism, climate change, and sea level changes, has presented opportunities for speciation (and extinction) through geologic time. A changing biota presents still other opportunities for speciation among predators, competitors, pollinators, etc. Species possess varying abilities to disperse from their place of origin; some become widespread while others remain restricted to one area. The result has been geographic patterns in the taxonomic relationships of life across the planet. Different species, genera, families, and even orders may occur on different continents or in different oceans even though similar biomes are present. To address these taxonomic assemblages, botanists, zoologists, and biogeographers recognize six floral kingdoms (Boreal, Paleotropical, Neotropical, Australian, Antarctic, and Cape Province or South African) and six zoogeographic provinces (Palearctic, Nearctic, Neotropical, Ethiopian, Oriental, and Australian). The boundaries of these kingdoms and provinces are functions of barriers to dispersal of organisms, past and present, and do not necessarily coincide with the continents' limits. The Palearctic Zoogeographic Province, for example, extends south of Eurasia into the Sahara, whereas the Ethiopian covers Africa south of the Sahara.

Floral kingdoms and zoogeographic provinces, such as the Cape Province or the Australian province, which have been isolated from other such regions for long periods of geologic time are home to many unique taxa restricted to that geographic area, that is, endemics. The Palearctic and Nearctic provinces, essentially northern Eurasia and North America respectively, have long been connected to other continents and have relatively few endemic families. They, instead, share many families with other regions as well as with each other. Similar patterns hold true for islands. Oceanic islands, never connected to a large landmass, have high rates of endemism. Continental islands, on the other hand, perhaps only recently separated from a nearby landmass by rising sea levels at the end of the Pleistocene Epoch, tend to have many fewer endemic taxa.

Some geographic areas, for reasons not completely understood, have accumulated a great variety of life at all levels: landscape, ecosystem function, community, species, and gene. They are said to possess a high biodiversity, itself a geographic feature. Biodiversity hotspots are those places with high biodiversity, high rates of endemism, and under imminent threat from human activity and global climate change. Currently 34 such hotspots are recognized.

Species that evolved in a particular area or dispersed naturally to that area are considered native. Introduced, nonnative, or alien species are those which were transported to a location, either deliberately or accidentally, by humans. Invasive species, often a major threat on oceanic islands, are those nonnative species which currently are spreading rapidly in a new host territory or have done so in the past and have or may cause ecological and/or economic harm.

Further Reading

Anderson, Bruce, and Alan H. Strahler. 2009. *Visualizing Weather and Climate*. New York: John Wiley & Sons.

Department of Geology. 2014. "GEOL 102 Historical Geology, The History of Earth and Life, Spring Semester 2014." College Park, Maryland: University of Maryland. http://www.geol.umd.edu/~tholtz/G102/102Syl.htm

MacDonald, Glen. 2003. *Biogeography: Introduction to Space, Time and Life*. New York: John Wiley & Sons.

NASA. 2013. *Global Climate Change—Vital Signs of the Planet*. National Aeronautics and Space Administration. Jet Propulsion Laboratory, California Institute of Technology. http://climate.nasa.gov/key_indicators

Scotese, Christopher R. 2002. *Plate Tectonic Maps and Continental Drift Animations*. PALEOMAP Project. http://www.scotese.com/

Strahler, Alan H. 2013. *Introducing Physical Geography*, 6th ed. New York: John Wiley & Sons.

Abbreviations Used

°C	degrees Celsius or Centigrade
°F	degrees Fahrenheit
ac	acre
asl	above sea level
bsl	below sea level
bya	billions of years ago
cm	centimeter
FAO	Food and Agriculture Organization of the United Nations
ft	feet
ft^2	square feet
ft^3	cubic feet
ft^3/sec	cubic feet per second
gal	gallon
GIS	geographic information system
GPS	global positioning system
ha	hectare
in	inches
km	kilometer
km^2	square kilometers
kmph	kilometers per hour
L	liter
M	Magnitude (earthquakes—equivalent to Richter scale)
m	meter
m^2	square meters
m^3	cubic meters
m^3/s	cubic meters per second
MAB	Man and the Biosphere Programme
mi	mile
mi^2	square miles
mph	miles per hour
mya	millions of years ago
NASA	National Aeronautics and Space Administration
NOAA	National Oceanic and Atmospheric Administration
ppm	parts per million
ppt	parts per thousand
UNESCO	United Nations Environmental, Scientific, and Cultural Organization
USGS	United States Geological Survey

M

Mackenzie River

Canada

Geographic Overview. The Mackenzie River, draining 690,000 mi^2 (1,787,000 km^2) in parts of the Northwest Territories, Saskatchewan, Alberta, British Columbia, and the Yukon, covers the largest drainage basin in Canada and is the largest north-flowing river in North America. The system has two large freshwater deltas (the Peace-Athabasca and the Slave) and three major lakes (Athabasca, Great Slave, and Great Bear). From the 1880s to the1940s, the river was a major transportation route from Great Slave Lake to the Beaufort Sea, and barge traffic remains important. Several reaches of the Mackenzie and its tributaries are recognized internationally as important areas for migrating birds.

Geographic Coordinates. Source: 61°12'N, 117° 23'W; Mouth: 68°56'N, 136°10'W

Description. Although the drainage basin includes the catchments of the Athabaska and Peace rivers and Lake Athabasca, the Mackenzie main stem originates at the outflow from Great Slave Lake and flows approximately 1,120 mi (1,800 km) to reach the Beaufort Sea. The Liard River, its major tributary, joins the Mackenzie at Fort Simpson, 185 mi (300 km) downstream from Great Slave Lake. About midway from Great Slave Lake to the Arctic Coast, the Mackenzie is joined by Great Bear River from Great Bear Lake. In its last 150 mi (240 km), the Mackenzie meanders through its delta, where it is joined by the Peel River.

For most of its route, the Mackenzie River has a straight channel, 0.6–1.2 mi (1–2 km) wide, and a low gradient, dropping only 492 ft (150 m). The delta is Canada's largest, 4,700 mi^2 (12,170 km^2), and has the largest concentrations of pingos in the world, approximately 1,500. The river freezes in winter, breaking up late April to May. Runoff is low in winter, peaking in late spring with snowmelt. Mean discharge at the delta is 318,535 ft^3/sec (9,020 m^3/s).

Most of the drainage basin is underlain by glacial drift, and most of the Mackenzie River's route is underlain by permafrost, especially north of 60° north latitude, forming poorly drained wetlands. Permafrost can be 330 ft (100 m) deep in the delta. The tributaries that contribute most of the water are from the mountains in the western part of the drainage basin. The central part of the basin is flat to rolling, part of North America's Great Plains. The east is bounded by the Canadian Shield, with lakes and bogs and few tributaries. Vegetation is boreal forest, grassland, and tundra.

The Liard River, the largest tributary, which contributes a big sediment load and doubles the discharge of the Mackenzie, originates in mountainous southeast Yukon and runs 693 mi (1,115 km) to join the Mackenzie in the Northwest Territories. It flows through glaciated landscapes, from alpine tundra to Great Plains boreal forest, and drops 3,935 ft (1,200 m) from its headwaters to the Mackenzie River. The Liard is known for its wild stretches, such as Rapids of the Drowned and Hell Gate Rapids. A major tributary is the Nahanni River.

The Athabasca River, flowing to the Peace River and then to the Slave River, originates in Jasper National Park, partly in the Columbia Icefield, in western Alberta. The southern-most tributary to the Mackenzie system, it flows approximately 745 mi (1,200 km) northeast across boreal forest and grassland to the

Peace–Athabasca Delta (PAD) and Lake Athabasca. A consistent decrease in gradient changes the river from steep and mountainous in its upper reaches to a broader channel downslope in a flatter landscape. Although the river is unregulated, forestry, agriculture, and mining have contaminated the water.

The Peace River, draining both mountain forests and Great Plains grassland, originates in glacial alpine regions in northeastern British Columbia. Hydroelectric development at W. A. C. Bennett Dam (Williston Reservoir) regulates downstream flow. The river flows 745 mi (1,200 km) from the dam to PAD, for a total length of 1,195 mi (1,923 km). Downstream from the dam, the Upper Peace, 0.3 mi (0.5 km) wide, has incised a straight channel 655 ft (200 m) deep into the plateau. The middle reaches over the Great Plains have irregular entrenched meanders. The lower reaches wind through delta deposits of the PAD, the largest freshwater delta in the world.

The drainage basin of the Slave River, which originates near the confluence of the Peace River and outflow from Lake Athabasca, includes the Peace River, Athabasca River, PAD, and Lake Athabasca. The Slave flows 260 mi (420 km), through glacial drift and alluvial deposits between the Canadian Shield to the east and Great Plains to the west. Upon reaching Great Slave Lake, it meanders through a huge delta for 125 mi (200 km). Strong spring flow from the Peace River can force water upstream to Lake Athabasca, naturally storing it for later release.

The Peel River is the northern-most tributary to the Mackenzie. From its headwaters in the Mackenzie Mountains in northeastern Yukon and northwestern Northwest Territories, it flows 400 mi (644 km) over taiga and tundra to the Mackenzie River delta.

Biota. The main stem of the Mackenzie River and the Laird River are in the Lower Mackenzie freshwater ecoregion. Major fish include Pacific salmon (*Oncorhynchus* spp.), char (*Salvelinus* spp.), whitefish (*Coregonus, Prosopium, Stenodus* spp.), northern pike (*Esox lucius*), minnows (Cyprinidae), and suckers (Catostomidae). Slave River, Athabasca, and Peace River are in the Upper Mackenzie freshwater ecoregion, which is similar to that of the Lower Mackenzie with the exception of anadromous species such as salmon and whitefishes. The Mackenzie River delta is a major calving ground for beluga whales.

Protected Areas. Liard River Hot Springs, a unique swampy microclimate, is a British Columbia provincial park. Nahanni National Park, in the Mackenzie Mountains, is a World Heritage Site where the vertical drop of Virginia Falls is 315 ft (96 m). Large numbers of shorebirds, including geese, swans, and brants, congregate in the Lower Mackenzie River Islands Bird Sanctuary. Wood Buffalo National Park is on the lower reaches of the Peace River. The PAD is a World Heritage Site, critical to migrating birds and home to approximately 5,000 free-roaming bison.

Environmental Issues. In spite of barge traffic and upstream oil production, most of the Mackenzie and its drainage basin is undeveloped and unpolluted. Although there are no dams on the main stem, the drainage basin has eight. The river corridor, however, is a proposed pipeline route to bring natural gas south to the United States. Tar sands in the lower basin of the Athabasca River are the source of the proposed Keystone pipeline from Canada to Gulf Coast oil refineries in the United States.

Further Reading

Burridge, Mary and Nicholas Mandrak. 2013. "104: Upper Mackenzie." World Wildlife Fund and The Nature Conservancy. *Freshwater Ecoregions of the World*. http://www.feow.org/ecoregions/details/upper_mackenzie

Burridge, Mary and Nicholas Mandrak. 2013. "105: Lower Mackenzie." World Wildlife Fund and the Nature Conservancy. *Freshwater Ecoregions of the World*. http://www.feow.org/ecoregions/details/lower_mackenzie

Culp, Joseph M., Terry D. Prowse, and Eric A. Luiker. 2005. "Mackenzie River Basin." In *Rivers of North America*, edited by Arthur C. Benke and Colbert E. Cushing, 804–850. Amsterdam: Elsevier Academic Press.

Parks Canada. 2012. http://www.pc.gc.ca/eng/index.aspx

Madagascar

Indian Ocean

Geographic Overview. Located in the Indian Ocean several hundred miles from Africa's southeastern coast, Madagascar is the world's fourth largest island and a biodiversity hotspot. Millions of years of isolation enabled the evolution of a rich and unique assemblage of plants and animals, many of which are endemic. The unusual biota, especially lemurs, supports a tourism industry that brings millions of dollars into the island's economy.

Geographic Coordinates. 11°57'S–25°36'S; 43°12'E–50°30'E

Description. Madagascar extends approximately 1,000 mi (1,600 km) from north to south, 335 mi (539 km) east to west at its widest point, and covers 226,657 mi² (589,040 km²). The island is asymmetrical, with a 3,950 ft (1,200 m) high mountain ridge, the backbone of the island, close to the east coast. Peaks rise more than 8,530 ft (2,600 m) asl. Five topographic regions are distinct.

The east coast is a strip of lowland with alluvial soils, extending from the Masoala Peninsula in the north to the far southern tip of the island. Except for Antongil Bay, the coastline is straight, with few natural harbors. Canal des Pangalanes, a 375 mi (600 km) stretch of natural lagoons linked by canals, runs from Toamasina south to Farafangana. This canal is a major transportation route and fishing area. The narrow coast, approximately 30 mi (50 km) wide, is backed by ravine-carved steep bluffs at the base of a dissected escarpment extending approximately 1,650 ft (500 m) up to the Central Highlands. At the northern end of the island, the Tsaratanana Massif rises to 9,436 ft (2,876 m) at Maramokotro Peak, the highest point on the island. Further north is the volcanic Montagne d'Ambre. The northern coastline is deeply indented and includes the tourist island of Nosy Be.

The central highlands extend from the Tsaratanana Massif south to the Ivakoany Massif, southwest of Farafagana. The highlands, too irregular to be called a plateau, slope westward from the eastern escarpment. Ranging generally 2,625–5,900 ft (800–1,800 m) asl with local relief of 330–1,650 ft (100–500 m), the highlands include rounded hills, granite outcrops, extinct volcanoes, and peneplains. Most of the alluvial plains and marshes have been converted to terraced rice fields. The region encompasses the Anjafy High Plateaus, volcanic formations of Itasy, and the Ankaratra Massif (which reaches 8,750 ft/2,666 m asl), as well as the Ivakoany Massif.

Isalo Roiniforme Massif is between the central highlands and the west coast. The capital of Madagascar, Antananarivo, is 4,816 ft (1,468 m) asl in the northern part of the highlands. A north–south trending rift valley is prominent east of Antananarivo. Within the rift is Lac Alaotro, the largest lake on the island, at 2,497 ft (761 m) asl and bordered by cliffs, which rise 1,316 ft (701 m) above the lake surface on the west side and 1,601 ft (488 m) on the east side. The rift valley experiences subsidence and earth tremors.

The west coast region consists of sedimentary rock layers and an irregular coastline with several harbors, especially in the northwest. It includes broad alluvial plains between Mahajanga in the north and Toliara in the south. The southwest, bordered on the east by the Ivakoany Massif and on the north by the Isalo Roiniforme Massif, is divided into two regions, the Mahafaly Plateau and the desert region.

The Mananara and Mangoro Rivers, both from the Central Highlands, and the Maningory River from Lake Alaotra flow east to the Indian Ocean. East-flowing rivers are short and steep with several waterfalls. Rivers flowing west to the Mozambique Channel are longer and slower. The Sofia, Mahajamba, Betsiboka, Ikopa, and Mahavary are major rivers flowing to the northwest coast. The Mania and Tsiribihina, Mangoky, and Onilahy flow to the southwest coast. The Mandrare, flowing to the southeast through desert areas, is seasonal.

With the climate controlled by Southeast Trade Winds and currents in the Indian Ocean, Madagascar experiences two seasons: hot and rainy November to April and cool and dry May to October. Variations are caused by elevation and windward or leeward position. The east coast is subequatorial—hot, humid, and subject to tropical cyclones. Annual rainfall may reach 155 in (4,000 mm), and temperatures average 77°F (25°C). The central highlands are cooler due to elevation and drier because the east-facing escarpment promotes rainfall on the coast. Antananarivo receives an annual rainfall of 55 in (1,400 mm). The plateau is 11°–20°F (6°–11°C) cooler than the coasts, with both a seasonal and daily range in temperature. Although frost is rare in Antananarivo, it is common at higher elevations. The northwestern region, slightly protected

The geographic isolation of Madagascar has led to a wide variety of unique plants and animals, illustrated here by Avenue of the Baobabs in Morondava. (Oscar Espinosa Villegas/Dreamstime.com)

from the Southeast Trade Winds, has a 2 month dry season and 71 in (1,800 mm) of rain. Length of the dry season increases southward, and the southwest and south is semidesert, with 12–20 in (300–500 mm) of rain.

Geologic History. Approximately 170 mya, Madagascar was in the middle of the supercontinent Gondwana, between what was to become South America–Africa and India–Australia–Antarctica. When India, with Madagascar attached to its southwest coast and Australia–Antarctica on its east, split from Africa–South America in the middle Jurassic (160 mya), it was first pushed south. In the late Cretaceous (80 mya), seafloor spreading between India–Madagascar and Australia–Antarctica pushed the Indian subcontinent and Madagascar north into the Indian Ocean. Cretaceous age (approximately 85 mya) lava flows and volcanics in eastern Madagascar may have developed as India–Madagascar crossed a hotspot, or they could be related to the Mascarene oceanic plateau or to the rifting at the Mid-Indian Ridge, which separated Madagascar from India.

Madagascar stopped in the Indian Ocean, where it has been isolated for at least 70 million years. In the middle Cenozoic (5–2 mya), east–west extension on Madagascar created the Tsaratanana Massif, the Ankaratra Volcanic Ridge, and the central rift valley.

The bulk of central and eastern Madagascar is composed of metamorphic and igneous rocks. The Precambrian basement rocks in the central highlands date from Gondwana. Basalts and gabbros are common on the east coast and along the rift in the central highlands. The west, south, and northern tip are sedimentary rocks, both continental and marine. Some of the continental sandstone, including glacial conglomerate, is part of the Precambrian Gondwana basement. Marine inundations during the Mesozoic (195–100 mya) deposited limestones and marls in the Ankarana and Bemaraha massifs in western and northern Madagascar. Tertiary (65–7 mya) marine deposits closer to the coast include less eroded marls and chalks.

Biota. More than 90 percent of the island's species, both plants and animals, are endemic. The island's movement through various latitude and climate zones affected extinction or evolution and adaptation of biota. With the initial rift in Gondwana, Madagascar moved as far as south as 40–50°S subjecting the biota to colder temperatures. As it moved back north, the island passed through the arid tropics, causing many extinctions of plants and animals. Habitats and niches, from deserts to rainforests, became available for new species. Some new species, such as the now extinct elephant bird, which evolved from ostrich ancestors, were holdovers from Gondwana. Most Madagascar species, however, descended from species dispersed from nearby Africa much later in geologic time. At least 100 species of lemurs, which are distinct primates endemic to Madagascar but related to African lorises and bushbabies, evolved from an ancestral immigrant. Many typical African animals never arrived. The island has no poisonous snakes, felines, canines,, monkeys, or ungulates.

As the island slowly drifted north, all of Madagascar was subjected to aridity, eliminating all vegetation that was not drought-tolerant. As the island reentered the humid tropics, it developed a new flora. The island has more than 12,000 species of plants, 70–80 percent of which are endemic, including five endemic families. Of eight species of baobab trees (*Adansonia* ssp.) in the world, six are endemic to Madagascar. Although the island was originally covered with natural forests, only 10 percent of the rainforest remains, on steep hills east of the central highlands. Secondary growth consists of travelers palms, raffia, and baobabs. The tropical coast supports crops of bananas, mangoes, coconut, and vanilla, one of the almost 1,000 species of orchids on the island. Natural vegetation in the northwestern part of the island is a monsoon forest, changing to hot and dry deciduous forest as rainfall decreases and length of dry season increases toward the southwest. Most of the central highlands and west coast has been cleared for agriculture and is degraded savanna or fire-adapted grassland. Higher elevations on east-facing windward slopes support small sclerophyllous trees, with mosses and lichens, or Ericaceae thickets. The spiny forest in the southwestern desert, which supports a unique assemblage of highly unusual drought-adapted spiny plants, has the highest degree of endemism of Madagascar's floras. It is also

probably its oldest, the remnants of formerly widespread vegetation squeezed to the southwest corner of the island as the rest of the island became wetter. Many plants are in the Euphorbiaceae and endemic Didiereaceae families; other endemic succulents are also present. Mangrove swamps are found in estuaries in the north and west.

Land mammals dispersed to the island by rafting or swimming after the breakup of Gondwana, and took advantage of the many empty niches to evolve into modern species. Of the approximately 100 native land mammals, nearly all are endemic. Four major groups of mammals—lemurs, carnivores, rodents, and tenrecs—radiated into several species. Insectivores are dominated by the tenrec family (Tenrecidae), small mammals resembling shrews or hedgehogs, with approximately 30 species, most of which are endemic. Ranging in size from 0.1 to 1.4 oz (3–40 g), tenrecs may be terrestrial or arboreal. Primates, in five families (Lemuridae, Indridae, Megaladapidae, and Cheiragaleidae), have a variety of characteristics and live in a variety of habitats. The smallest primate in the world is a mouse lemur (*Microcebus berthae*), weighing 1 oz (30 g). The distinctive and elusive aye-aye (*Daubentonia madagascariensis*) is the only species in its family (Daubentoniidae). Carnivores, including mongoose and the cat-like fossa, number eight species. Native rodents, 22 species, are in the subfamily Nesomyinae. Introduced animals include mice, rats, dogs, cats, Indian civet, pigs, zebu, goat, sheep, and two deer species.

Of the 258 bird species, 44 percent are endemic, with 36 endemic genera and five endemic families. The only amphibians are more than 300 species of frogs, 99 percent of which are endemic. Although the island supports approximately 350 species of reptiles, most of which are endemic, none are dangerous except crocodiles and sea snakes. The 11 families, dominated by geckos, chameleons, and skinks, each have many species. Geckos are most diverse, with 12 genera and 88 species. Chameleon species number approximately 75, 59 of which (approximately half of the world's known chameleons) are found only in Madagascar. The invertebrate population is also varied and distinct, but inadequately described.

Much of the island's more than 3,100 mi (5,000 km) of coastline is outlined by various types of coral reefs. The Grand Recif barrier reef of Toliara off southwestern Madagascar is 11 mi (18 km) long and as much as 2 mi (3 km) wide. The reef system on the rest of the west coast is not continuous. On the east coast, a reef borders the Masoala peninsula. The reefs support many species of global concern, such as dugong, whales, dolphins, sea turtles, sawfish, sharks, coelacanth, and more than 700 species of coral reef fish.

Protected Areas. Although approximately 5 percent of the island has some form of official protection, poverty and government instability limit enforcement of regulations. Madagascar has several national parks, marine national parks, natural reserves, and special reserves, as well as two natural World Heritage Sites, Rainforests of the Atsinanana and Tsingy de Bemaraha Strict Nature Reserve.

Environmental Issues. Madagascar's ecosystems are seriously threatened, primarily due to deforestation and subsequent erosion. Because the majority of mammals are forest dwellers, forest destruction and habitat fragmentation are significant threats. Approximately 80 percent of domestic fuel is derived from charcoal or wood. In 1990, the World Bank funded pine and eucalyptus plantations, in an attempt to stem the destruction of native forests. Madagascar's many cultural groups have different customs and taboos. Some groups actively hunt lemurs for food, while others kill aye ayes because of their unearned reputation for killing chickens and humans.

See also Isalo National Park; Masoala National Park; Menabe Antimena Protected Area; Spiny Forest; Tsingy de Bemaraha National Park; Western Madagascar Wetlands

Further Reading

Garbutt, Nick, Hilary Bradt, and Derek Schuurman. 2008. *Madagascar Wildlife*, 3rd ed. Bradt Travel Guide Madagascar Wildlife. Bradt Travel Guides.

Goodman, Steven M. and Jonathan P. Benstead, editors. 2003. *The Natural History of Madagascar*. Chicago: University of Chicago Press.

Vences, M., K. C. Wollenberg, D. R. Vieites, and D. C. Lees. 2009. "Madagascar as a Model Region of Species Diversification." *Trends in Ecology and Evolution* 24: 456–465.

"Wild Madagascar." 2013. http://www.wildmadagascar.org/

Madeira Archipelago

Atlantic Ocean

Geographic Overview. The Madeira archipelago lies 395 mi (635 km) off the Atlantic coast of Morocco and 250 mi (400 km) north of Tenerife in the Canary Islands. One of the three Macaronesian archipelagos, Madeira hosts the largest relict expanse of the ancient laurel forest that once covered much of southern Europe and North Africa. It is one of Portugal's two autonomous regions (the other being the Azores).

Geographic Coordinates. 32°23'N–33°08'N, 16°17'W–16°65'W

Description. The Madeira archipelago consists of two inhabited islands, the main island of Madeira and the much smaller Porto Santo 23 mi (37 km) to the northeast. In addition, there are three islets off the southeastern shore of Madeira known as the Desertas Islands (Ilheu do Chao, Deserta Grande, and Deserta Pequena) and 10 rocks. Madeira is a massive shield volcano that rises 3.7 mi (6 km) from the ocean floor. Only the top fraction emerges above sea level. Cinder cones and lava flows now cover the eroded shield, which forms an island about 180 mi (290 km) long. More than 90 percent of Madeira stands higher than 1,600 ft (500 m) asl. Most of its coast is bounded by steep sea cliffs. A rugged massif with several peaks over 5,200 ft (1,600 m) high trends east–west through the center of the island. The highest mountain, Pico Ruivo, reaches 6,107 ft (1,862 m) asl. Two steep-walled amphitheaters, products of mass wasting and erosion, open to the south in the central part of the island. The eastern end of the massif is a high plateau with a mean elevation of 5,000 ft (1,550 m), while in the west the island ends in a low, rocky promontory known as Paul de Serra. Porto Santo and the Desertas are lower; elevations do not exceed 1,700 ft (520 m) asl.

Sea cliffs, steep slopes, and deep V-shaped ravines have protected the interior of Madeira and helped keep nearly 90 percent of its native laurel forest (laurisilva) intact. This relict vegetation flourishes at elevations of roughly 1,000–4,000 ft (300–1,300 m) asl and is characterized by a variety of broadleaf evergreen trees and shrubs bearing dark green, laurel-shaped leaves.

This forest type was widespread in southern Europe and North Africa 40–15 mya, but now is restricted to the Azores, Madeira, and Canary islands. At lower elevations the coastal vegetation is dominated by shrubs and herbs with many species endemic to the Macaronesian archipelagos; above this is a belt of evergreen dry forest, now much reduced in area. Above the laurel forest at the highest elevations is an alpine community of herbs and shrubby heaths.

Madeira has a cool mediterranean climate with the characteristic dry summer. In the lowlands, winter months have average highs of 66°F (19°C) and average lows of 55°F (13°C). During the warmest month (August) temperatures range between 78°F (26°C) and 66°F (19°C). Total annual rainfall is 27 in (692 mm), most of it falling between October and March. Less than an inch (25 mm) falls each summer month. Frequent fog and clouds build up at elevations of 2,000–2,600 ft (600–800 m) asl yielding more moisture, up to 63 in (1,600 mm) a year. The low Desertas and Porto Santo are drier than Madeira, averaging less than 16 in (400 mm) of rain a year.

Geologic History. The origin of the Madeira archipelago traces to a magma plume rising in the Mid-Atlantic Ridge about 70 mya. The islands formed about 20 mya over a hotspot then on the African Plate. Porto Santo is the oldest at 14 million years. Madeira is 4.6 million years old and the Desertas about 0.7 million years old. Volcanic activity ceased about 6,000 years ago.

Biota. Madeira maintains a highly diverse biota, mostly in association with the laurisilva. At least 76 plants and more than 500 invertebrates are endemic. The most diverse group is comprised of 250 land snail species, 70 percent of which are endemic. Among the 50 native vertebrates a lizard, two land birds (Madeiran Laurel Pigeon or Trocaz Pigeon and the Madeiran Chaffinch), and one seabird—a petrel, are endemic. Madeira's or Zino's Petrel was believed extinct until rediscovered in the 1960s. Since then a recovery program has resulted in 65–80 breeding pairs nesting on small ledges 5,250 ft (1,600 m) asl and higher in the eastern massif between Pico Ruivo and Pico do Areerio.

After the islands were colonized in 1425, a variety of vertebrates were introduced, including frogs, geckos, fishes, rabbits, rats, mice, goats, pigs, cats, and ferrets.

Protected Areas. About 40 percent of the Madeira Islands are protected. The laurel forest is a UNESCO World Heritage Site and is preserved in Madeira Natural Park. All of the Desertas are natural reserves.

Environmental Issues. Rat and cat control measures are aimed at protecting the rare Madeira's petrel, which nests in burrows in grassy patches. Cattle have been removed from the nesting grounds. Increased tourism could become problematic.

See also Azores Archipelago; Canary Islands

Further Reading

Aguin-Pombo, Dora and Miguel A. A. Pinheiro de Carvalho. 2009. "Madeira Archipelago." In *Encyclopedia of Islands*, edited by Rosemary G. Gillespie and David A. Clague, 582–585. Berkeley: University of California Press.

"Laurisilva of Madeira." n.d. UNESCO. http://whc.unesco.org/en/list/934

"Madeira." n.d. Global Volcanism Program, Smithsonian Institution. http://www.volcano.si.edu/volcano.cfm?vn=382120

"Madeira Nature Park." 2013. Serviço do Parque Natural da Madeira. http://www.pnm.pt/index.php?option=com_content&view=article&id=2&Itemid=17&lang=en

Makgadikgadi Pans

Botswana

Geographic Overview. The Makgadikgadi Pans are one of the largest salt pan complexes in the world. Made up of many discrete salt flats, the largest pan is less than half the size of Bolivia's Salar de Uyuni, which is the largest single salt pan in the world. On the occasions that rainfall floods the pans, they become breeding and feeding grounds for tens of thousands of waterbirds, including flamingos. They also provide important grazing areas for huge herds of zebra and wildebeest that migrate between the Boteti River—an ephemeral link between the pans and the Okavango Delta to the northwest—and the Chobe River east of the salt flats.

Geographic Coordinates. 19°48'S–21°36'S, 25°45'E–26°24'E

Description. A cluster of salt pans left on the former lake bed of Paleolake Makgadikgadi in the Kalahari, the Makgadikgadi Pans are among the largest areas of salt flats in the world. Ntwetwe and Sua (Sowa) pans, separated by a narrow strip of grassland, are the largest. The former measures roughly 65 × 60 mi (106 × 96 km); the latter 70 × 45 mi (112 × 72 km), although the shapes are very irregular. They are surrounded by smaller pans, including Nxai, Kgama-Kgama, and Kudiakam pans, on a broad flat surface at an elevation of 2,920 ft (890 m) asl or slightly higher. During the dry season, the salt-encrusted pans are glistening white. During the rainy season, water may stand a foot (30 cm) deep, and grasses grow on and around the pans. Across the plain or as islands in the pans are isolated granite outcrops (inselbergs) as much as 35 ft (10 m) high.

Precipitation is highly variable from year to year; most falls as downpours associated with thunderstorms during the summer months of October through March. Little or no rain falls between May and August. Average annual rainfall is 18–20 in (450–500 mm), while evapotranspiration in the semiarid Kalahari exceeds 98 in (2,500 mm) annually. Diurnal and seasonal temperature ranges are significant. Summer highs average 95°F (35°C) and can go as high as 111°F (44°C). Winter temperatures can drop below 20°F (–8°C).

Local rains contribute most of the water that collects on the pans, but sporadic inflows of water from ephemeral streams also occur. In exceptionally wet years, the Boteti River, which drains the Okavango Delta, reaches Ntwetwe Pan. In 2010, this happened for the first time since 1981. The ephemeral Nata River, with headwaters in Zimbabwe, empties into Sua Pan, forming a delta in the northeast corner of the pan. Pans may hold water into April and May. The Nata Delta seldom dries out completely and supports reed beds.

Plant life on the pans is limited to cyanobacteria when the flats are inundated in summer. The fringes of the pans are saline environments in which salt-tolerant perennial grasses such as saltgrass (*Sporobolus spicatus*) and spiny grass (*Odyssea paucinervis*) grow. Salt marshes with other halophytic plants, including purslane, a different saltgrass, and sea blite, are scattered at wet spots around the pans' edges. Dry grasslands encircle the pan area. To the north and northwest, these give way to acacia savannas dotted with tall baobabs. Baobabs also grow on some of the islands in the pans. A famous group, painted in 1862 by the British artist Thomas Baines, can still be seen at Kudiakam Pan. To the south, the grasslands grade into mopane woodlands.

When the rainy season brings enough water for shallow lakes to form on the pans, tens of thousands of waterbirds congregate to breed and feed. Sua Pan is the largest breeding area for Greater Flamingo in Africa; the Makgadikgadi Pans also host breeding populations of Lesser Flamingos and Great White Pelicans. The grasslands provide forage for tens of thousands of Burchell zebra, blue wildebeest, and springbok that migrate back and forth between the Boteti River to the northwest and the Chobe River to the east. Few animals occupy the pans during the dry winters. Ostriches are an exception, nesting on the pans beyond the reach of jackals. The herds of grazing animals move to permanent pools in the Boteti River for the winter.

Geologic History. Paleolake Makgadikgadi formed when faults diverted the courses of the Zambezi, Okavango, and Chobe Rivers, which had connected to the Limpopo and Orange Rivers and emptied into the Atlantic Ocean, and sent them into the closed Kalahari basin to create an enormous inland sea. Later tectonic activity formed two basins, one now underlying the Okavango Delta and the other, a bit lower, lying beneath the pans. Stream capture by the lower Zambezi River seems to have drained much of Lake Makgadikgadi, but lower precipitation in the Holocene also contributed to the lake's shrinkage and fragmentation into a number of small bodies of water. Lakes at Ntwetwe and Sua were likely the deepest and the last to dry up. The ancient shoreline is visible as a white calcrete escarpment 100 ft (30 m) or higher near the edges of the basin.

Biota. The pans are on the pathway of a spectacular migration of zebra and wildebeest, and some 90 other mammals make Makgadikgadi home at least seasonally. A total of 35 avian species are reported from the pans, including 104 kinds of waterbirds. Of particular interest and concern are Wattled Cranes, Gray-crowned Cranes, Chestnut-backed Plover, Black-winged Pratincole, and Greater and Lesser

Flamingos. Other vertebrates at the pans and in surrounding grasslands include 18 amphibian species and 71 reptiles, including the endemic Makgadikgadi agama lizard.

Protected Areas. Makgadikgadi and Nxai Pan National Park includes parts or all of several pans, including Kgama-Kgama Pan, Nxai Pan, and Kudiakam Pan with the Baines baobabs. Nata Sanctuary protects the northern part of Sua Pan, including the Nata Delta. However, the main flamingo breeding area remains outside the sanctuary. The area was nominated for inscription as a UNESCO World Heritage Site in 2010 under the name "Makgadikgadi Pans Landscape."

Environmental Issues. Conflicts between wildlife and pastoralists are a recurring fact of life. Trespass and overgrazing by cattle herds is one problem, transmission of diseases another. From the 1950s into the 1980s long veterinary cordon fences were set up south of the Okavango Delta and south of the Makgadikgadi Pans to slow the transmission of pathogens between wildlife and cattle and the spread of such diseases as contagious bovine pleuro-pneumonia, which threatened Botswana's export beef industry. The fences proved ineffective in halting disease, but effective in halting the annual migration of zebra and wildebeest, many of which died as a consequence. Some long stretches of fence have since been removed to allow wildlife to pass through.

A small salt mine on Ntwetwe Pan seems not to pose any ecological problem as long as it stays low-tech. A soda ash extraction facility on Sua Pan has brine wells placed over 190 mi² (500 km²) of the salt flat. The wells themselves are not problematic, but the infrastructure of roads, railroads, and power lines is. The facility lies between the breeding and feeding grounds of flamingos, and young birds especially became tangled in the power lines. The company later buried the lines.

See also The Kalahari; Okavango Delta

Further Reading
Department of Environmental Affairs and Centre for Applied Research, 2010. The Makgadikgadi Framework Management Plan. Government of Botswana, Gaborone. http://www.mewt.gov.bw/uploads/files/DEA/MFMP_report_vol_1_final.pdf

"Makgadikgadi Pans Landscape." n.d. World Heritage Centre, UNESCO. http://whc.unesco.org/en/tentative lists/5559/

Spriggs, Amy. n.d. "Southern Africa: Northern Botswana" (Zambezian Halophytics ecoregion). Terrestrial Ecosystems, World Wildlife Fund. http://worldwildlife.org /ecoregions/at0908

Maldives

Indian Ocean

Geographic Overview. The Maldives are a group of 21 atolls and four reef platforms that extend in a north–south direction southwest of India. They possess globally unique reef structures, and an extremely high diversity of reef animals. The Republic of the Maldives is Asia's smallest nation in terms of both population and land area. With most of the islands less than 3.0 ft (1.0 m) asl, it is also Asia's lowest nation.

Geographic Coordinates. 07°06'N–0°42'S, 72° 33'E–73°46'E

Description. The Maldives consist of a double chain of atolls surrounding an inner sea. At the northern and southern ends, the two lines of atolls converge into single atolls. The network of coral reefs is 540 mi (868 km) long and 5–75 mi (8–120 km) wide. The Maldives lie at the center of the north–south trending submarine Chagos–Laccadive Ridge, some 250 mi (400 km) southwest of India. The group has 16 open atolls with many breaks in the rim. On a map, the open atolls appear to be rings of separate reefs enclosing a central lagoon. These large coral structures range in area from 112 to 1,460 mi² (290–3,790 km²). More than 99 percent of Maldivian reefs are of this type. Within their lagoons are patch reefs and rare ring-shaped reefs known as faros. Islands formed of coral debris emerge along the rims and on some of the patch reefs. The five closed atolls are nearly continuous reef platforms with inner lagoons and are smaller than the open ones. The four oceanic reef platforms have no lagoons and most of their rims are covered by islands. Altogether 2,041 individual reefs and 1,190 reef islands, 200 of which are inhabited, can be identified. Mean elevation of the terrestrial portions of the

Maldives is less than 3 ft (1 m) asl. The highest natural point is but 7 ft 10 in (2.4 m) above the sea.

The nature of the atolls varies along a north–south gradient. Northern atolls are usually open structures with numerous patch reefs and faros in their lagoons. Islands appear on the periphery of the atoll as well as patch reefs within the lagoons. Lagoons are 130–165 ft (40–50 m) deep. Southward more closed reefs occur, lagoons become deeper (230–260 ft or 70–80 m deep), and patch reefs less common. Everywhere, the outer reef drops off rapidly to the seafloor more than 3,200 ft (1,000 m) below.

The impact of the Asian monsoon and the frequency of storms diminish to the south, but rainfall and wave energy increases. Total annual precipitation varies from 100 in (2,540 mm) in the north to 150 in (3,810 mm) in the south.

Geologic History. The Chagos–Laccadive Ridge on which the Maldivian atolls have developed formed 65–40 mya as a product of tectonic plates moving over the Réunion hotspot. The volcanoes formed by that process have since subsided below sea level. The volcanic basement rocks are capped by more than 6,500 ft (2,000 m) of limestone resulting from long periods of coral reef development. The reefs expanded toward the inner sea. During the Quaternary Period, alternating growth and lowering of reefs occurred. When sea levels were higher during the warmer interglacial periods, the reefs grew vertically. With lower sea levels and exposure to rainwater, the reefs dissolved and were lowered. This is a unique form of atoll development unrelated to the model presented by Charles Darwin in which a volcanic island with a fringing reef subsides and leaves a lagoon surrounded by reefs. The origin of the faros has not yet been explained. The islands formed 5,500–4,000 years ago from sands and gravels derived from the reefs themselves. The islands are ever-changing in their morphology in response to changes in wave energy and sea levels.

Biota. Marine life is highly diverse in the coral reefs of the Maldives. Some 250 species of hard and soft corals have been identified as well as many bryozoans and sea slugs and over 1,000 species of fish. Huge numbers of manta rays and whale sharks congregate seasonally, and sea turtles nest on some beaches.

Protected Areas. Some 40 protected areas, including 14 turtle nesting beaches and several spawning grounds for grouper, tuna, and bait fish exist to conserve marine habitats. In 2011, Baa Atoll (05°08'N, 72°57'E) became a World Biosphere Reserve in recognition of its rich coral ecosystem and the long history of sustainable use of the atoll's resources by its human inhabitants. The president has requested inscription of the entire chain of atolls as a Biosphere Reserve.

Environmental Issues. The Maldives have a growing tourism industry and have become one of the world's ultimate luxury destinations. Natural habitats have been reclaimed for urban, airport, and harbor infrastructure to nurture this leading sector of the economy. Waste disposal, depletion and pollution of fresh water, and disturbance of the reef by recreational snorkelers and divers are associated problems. Overharvesting of sharks, sea cucumbers, groupers, giant clams, and lobsters has led to a decline in their numbers. The greatest concern, however, is rising sea level related to warming of the climate. The entire nation is vulnerable to a related increase in land and beach erosion, as well as to simply being underwater.

See also Indian Ocean

Further Reading

Kench, Paul. 2009. "Maldives." In *Encyclopedia of Islands*, edited by Rosemary G. Gillespie and David A. Clague, 586–587. Berkeley: University of California Press.

Moser, Mike and Ilham Atho Mohamed. 2013. "Maldives as a Biosphere Reserve. An Implementation Plan, 2013–2017." 2013. Ministry of Environment and Energy, Republic of the Maldives. http://www.cbd.int/doc/world/mv/mv-biosphere-reserve-en.pdf

UNESCO. 2011. "Baa Atoll." http://www.unesco.org/new/en/natural-sciences/environment/ecological-sciences/biosphere-reserves/asia-and-the-pacific/maldives/baa-atoll/

Mammoth Cave

United States (Kentucky)

Geographic Overview. Mammoth Cave is one of approximately 300 caves in west-central Kentucky. In 1972, a passageway was discovered between Crystal Cave, part of the Flint Ridge Cave group, and

Mammoth Cave, making Mammoth the world's longest cave system.

Geographic Coordinates. 37°11'N, 86°06'W

Description. Mammoth Cave has more than 400 mi (644 km) of explored, interconnected passageways. The cave has at least five known levels, representing sequential elevations of the water table, all of which are connected by occasional vertical shafts. Dripstone formations, such as stalactites and stalagmites, are rare. Flowstone, such as Frozen Niagara at 75 ft (23–m) high and 50 ft (15 m) wide, occurs where water flows over ledges. In the driest part of the cave, long hairlike tendrils of mirabilite and epsomite and gypsum flowers may occur. The surface landscape is hilly and wooded. The limestone surface is dotted with sinkholes, disappearing streams, and springs.

The caves have a long human history. Evidence indicates they were used by the Woodland Group of Native Americans 4,000 years ago. Saltpeter (potassium nitrate), used in fertilizers and gun powder, was extracted from bat guano until the early 1800s. In 1842, a doctor believed that the moist air and constant cave temperature (54°–57°F; 12°–14°C) might cure tuberculosis. An experiment, however, involving patients living in huts inside the cave, failed.

Geologic History. In the Permian, 600 ft (185 m) of fossil-rich limestone was deposited in a shallow, tropical sea. As the Appalachian Mountains rose and eroded, 50 ft (15 m) of sandstone and shale was deposited on top of the limestone. When the area was uplifted to form a plateau, the rock layers were slightly tilted to the northwest, toward the Green River. The large caves occur in the plateau, where the insoluble and impermeable sandstone caprock protects the underlying limestone from completely dissolving. Surface water is funneled to vertical cracks or sinkholes where it is channeled underground. The cave chambers were dissolved by carbonic acid in underground streams at or near the water table. As the land continued to periodically rise, the Green River and its tributaries eroded deeper, and the water table dropped accordingly. The oldest passageways, now dry, are closest to the surface, while the river at the current water table continues to dissolve new cave rooms. Because the cave rock layers are prominently bedded, with few joints cutting across beds, solution predominantly created long passageways. When the broad, lens-shaped passageway was filled with water, solution took place not only on the sides and bottom, but also at the top, resulting in an arched ceiling. The water scalloped the limestone walls, leaving oval depressions in the rock, somewhat like ripple marks, which indicate the speed and direction of flow. Canyon-like passages, tall and narrow, were dissolved through cracks or joints. Vertical shafts occur where streams flow into the cave from sinkholes on the surface.

Biota. More than 200 species use the cave, some of which are limited to the entrance areas. The cave has 42 species of troglobites, organisms adapted to spending their entire life in the cave. As many as 12 species of bats visit the cave, including the endangered Indiana bat (*Myotis sodalis*) and the gray bat (*Myotis grisescens*). Several of the true cave dwellers, including the blindfish (*Amblyopsis spelaea*), a crayfish, a cave shrimp, and a millipede, evolved in the darkness and have no eyes. While those colorless, translucent creatures depend on food brought in by floodwaters, cave crickets, which have retained eyes, travel to the surface to feed.

The surface environment has a variety of terrestrial and aquatic life. Approximately 872 species of flowering plants grow in the park, 21 of which are endangered or threatened. The Big Woods is 300 ac (121 ha) of old growth deciduous forest. The Green River and the Nolin River support 82 species of fish (five of which are endemic), over 51 species of mussels, and approximately 200 species of benthic macroinvertebrates.

Protected Areas. Mammoth Cave National Park covers 52,830 ac (21,380 ha) and is a World Heritage Site and an International Biosphere Reserve.

Environmental Issues. Cave lighting causes growth of algae and moss, which damages formations and provides an unnatural food source for cave dwellers, upsetting the ecosystem. During floods, the rising Green River flows into the cave, an event important to cave life because the water brings in food supplies. The rapid flow of water through the open cave, however, does not allow the water to be filtered and cleaned. Toxic spills, sewage, or any water contaminants threaten the integrity of the cave ecosystem.

See also Appalachian Mountains

Further Reading

Lyons, Joy Medley. 1993. *Mammoth Cave, The Story behind the Scenery*. Las Vegas, NV: KC Publications, Inc.

Palmer, Arthur N. 2004. "Mammoth Cave National Park." In *Geology of National Parks*, 6th ed., edited by Ann G. Harris, Esther Tuttle, and Sherwood D. Tuttle, 191–208. Dubuque, IA: Kendall Hunt.

Uhler, John W. 2007. *Mammoth Cave National Park Information*. http://www.mammoth.cave.national-park.com/

Manú National Park

Peru

Geographic Overview. Manú National Park is a huge preserve in the southwestern corner of the Amazon Basin. Its 6,627 mi^2 (17,163 km^2) span the full range of altitudinal habitats from tropical lowland rainforest through montane rainforest and cloud forest (the Yungas), to a high elevation elfin forest and, above treeline, the puna grasslands. Manú is credited with being the most biologically diverse natural area in the world, although this might be contested by less-studied Madadi National Park in Bolivia (in a similar geographic setting) and Serranía La Macarena National Park in Colombia.

Geographic Coordinates. 11°51'S, 71°43'W

Description. Manú National Park extends down the eastern slopes of the Andes to the Amazon lowlands and encompasses nearly the entire drainage basin of the Manú River and much of the upper basin of the Alto Madre de Dios River. Elevations range from over 13,000 ft (4,000 m) asl at the summit of the Andes to about 500 ft (150 m) in the Amazon region. Most of the area is in the lowlands and consists of broad floodplains separated by low, hilly interfluves. The rainy season here is October–April, at which time the floodplains are inundated. The region remains remote and little studied, so weather records have not been kept for long periods of time. However, a wide range of climate zones occurs between the cold, dry puna of the high Andes and the warm, humid Amazon basin below. Some 47 in (2,100 mm) of rain were recorded during one year at the Cocha Cashu Biological Station in the lowlands, with rainy season months each receiving more than 7.8 in (200 mm) of rain and

dry season months (early May–September) each receiving less than 4 in (100 mm). The cloud forest is enshrouded in fog all year.

Biota. The many habitats of Manú support an estimated 15,000 flowering plants, 140 species of amphibians, 99 species of reptiles, at least 850 species of birds, and about 220 species of mammals. Untold numbers of invertebrate species inhabit the area, including an estimated 500,000 arthropods. The birds amount to more than half of all species found in Peru and about 15 percent of the world's total. Among globally threatened mammals are woolly monkeys, Emperor tamarins, Andean cat, jaguar, small-eared dog, bush dog, and huemal.

Protected Areas. Manú is the core of a still larger UNESCO Biosphere Reserve (total area 7,200 mi^2 or 18,648 km^2), which in addition to the park includes a Reserved Zone for research and tourism and the Manú Cultural Zone, a buffer zone of roughly 350 mi^2 (914 km^2) in which human settlement is permitted, but controlled. The park itself is off limits to all visitors, but about 60 percent of the area is utilized by four native groups who have had little contact with modern civilization: the Machiguena (the largest group), Mascho-Piro, Yamenahua, and Amahuacro. All four are nomadic, depending upon the cultivation of cassava on the floodplains, hunting paca and other animals in the forest, fishing, and collecting turtle eggs from stream banks. They appear to have little, if any, negative impact on Manú's ecosystems.

In recognition of its biological wealth and the traditional hunter-gatherer lifestyles of its human inhabitants, Manú National Park was declared a World Heritage Site by UNESCO in 1987. The declaration also honors research conducted at the Cocha Cashu Biological Station, which has contributed major advances in our understanding of tropical forest ecosystems.

Environmental Issues. Most management concerns for Manú Park are related to land use issues in neighboring areas. Livestock grazing on the puna and colonization of lower slopes by Andean people is one such problem. Others include gas and oil exploration and development north of the park and forest clearing and the encroachment of agriculture along the southeast border.

Further Reading

"Manú National Park." n.d. World Heritage Centre. UNESCO. http://whc.unesco.org/en/list/402

Munn, Charles A. n.d. "The Living Edens: Manu," PBS Online, http://www.pbs.org/edens/manu/conserve.htm

"World Heritage Nomination—IUCN Summary, 402, Manu National Park." 1992. World Heritage Centre, UNESCO. http://whc.unesco.org/archive/advisory_body_evaluation/402bis.pdf

Mariana Islands Archipelago

Pacific Ocean (Micronesia)

Geographic Overview. The Marianas are a volcanic arc of 15 islands at the eastern edge of the Philippine Sea in the western Pacific Ocean. The largest and southernmost is Guam, a U.S. territory. The 14 islands to the north comprise the Commonwealth of the Northern Marianas (CNMI), a separate U.S. territory. Only Guam and three islands in the CNMI (Saipan, Tinian, and Rota) are currently inhabited.

Geographic Coordinates. Approximately 24°N to 12°N, 145°E

Description. The Mariana Islands Archipelago consists of two chains of small islands some 570 mi (920 km) long aligned along the 145°E meridian. The southern group is considerably older than the northern group, which is still volcanically active. The Marianas are remote, about 1,550 mi (2,500 km) north of Papua New Guinea and the same distance east of the Philippine Islands. At their eastern margin is the Mariana Trench, which contains the deepest point on Earth's crust. To the west of the islands is the submarine Mariana Trough, a basin partially filled with young lava flows and sediments of volcanic origin. The Mariana Islands and Trench are on the very active subduction zone where the Pacific Plate is moving beneath the Philippine Plate. The older, southern arc is displaced somewhat east of the northern arc to form an outer arc, and contains six islands: from south to north, Guam, Rota, Aguijan, Tinian, Saipan, and Farallon de Medinilla. The younger islands of the inner arc are: from south to north, Anatahan, Sangan, Guguan, Alamagen, Pagan, Agrihan, Asuncion, the Maug (three islands), and Uracas (Farallon de Pajaros).

The northern islands are mostly conical stratovolcanoes emerging above sea level from the East Mariana Ridge, a submarine structure standing 1.25–2.5 mi (2–4 km) above the seafloor. With increasing age, the steep slopes (>30°) become deeply furrowed with V-shaped valleys. Most have rocky coasts with occasional small sandy beaches. These nine islands continue to be extremely active volcanically. Agrihan is the highest volcano in the Marianas, standing 3,166 ft (965 m) asl, whereas Uracas, the northernmost island, is the most active, its summit crater constantly venting sulfurous fumes. The second most active is Mount Pagan, a peak 1,900 ft (579 m) asl on the northern end of Pagan island; it last erupted in December 2006. Pagan is formed of an unusual northeast–southwest trending group of volcanoes, calderas, and caldera rims that attest to long continuing volcanism. The summit of Anatahan, at the southern end of the inner arc, has an elongate caldera with a pit crater at the eastern end in which sulfurous fumes are emitted and hot springs and mud pots occur. Temperatures of the water and bubbling mud are 153°–210°F (67.4°–98.8°C). The mountain erupted in 2003.

In the old, outer arc, islands tend to be lower, flatter, and capped with limestone. Volcanic activity has long ceased. Saipan rises to a maximum height of 1,550 ft (473 m) asl and has low (<7°) to moderate slope angles. There is a fringing reef along its east coast and a barrier reef enclosing a shallow lagoon along the west. Tinian is a little more than 600 ft (187 m) asl at its highest point and is flat, 99 percent of the island capped by coral and coralline algae limestones. Rota is much like Tinian, low, mostly flat and with a limestone mantle over more than 90 percent of the island.

Guam, 30 mi (48 km) long and 4–12 mi (6–19 km) wide, is the largest island in all of Micronesia. Mount Lamla, its highest point, is 1,332 ft (406 m) asl. About 35 percent of the island, mostly in the south, is exposed volcanic rock; the north is mostly limestone. The coast is lined with sandy beaches, mangroves, or cliffs; and a coral reef with deepwater channels wraps around most of the island.

The Marianas have a tropical maritime climate with warm temperatures all year. Primarily under the influence of the Northeast Trade Winds, seasonal shifts in latitude of global pressure centers produce easterly winds during the rainy season from July to November and prevailing northeast winds July–December. Tropical storms and typhoons are common July–December. Average annual precipitation ranges from 70 in (1,800 mm) to 122 in (3,100 mm).

Most islands have mangroves on their coasts. The high volcanic islands, their peaks often cloud-covered, have interior forests but rarely have distinct life zones developed. Uracas is so volcanically active that very little plant life has been able to establish itself, and its slopes are generally devoid of vegetation.

Geologic History. The Mariana Islands Archipelago is the product of subduction of the Pacific Plate beneath the Philippine Plate 42–8 mya. The northernmost islands emerged as recently as 5 mya and continue to be volcanically active today. Uplift associated with convergence is still raising the island chain; Rota, as an example, has been uplifted about 1,600 ft (500 m) since the end of the Pleistocene.

Biota. The small, remote islands of the Marianas are species-poor. Most native forms seem to have their origins in the Caroline Islands to the south. Of the 325 known native plant species, 25 percent are endemic to the Marianas. As on other oceanic islands, land snails are relatively diverse and 50 percent of the 60 species are endemic to the archipelago. Native vertebrates are limited to small lizards that could have rafted to the islands on floating vegetation and to birds and bats whose ancestors could fly to them. On Guam, most native vertebrates have disappeared due to depredations of the introduced brown tree snake.

A host of plants and animals have been introduced to the islands, some with disastrous consequences. The legume tree tangan-tangan (*Leucaena leucocephala*) has transformed native forests, as have tree-covering vines. Goats, pigs, and the Philippine deer have also negatively impacted vegetation. The most notorious invasive species is on Guam, the brown tree snake (*Boiga irregularis*), accidentally brought to the island by the U.S. military near the end of World War II and responsible for the loss of many of the native birds and reptiles.

Protected Areas. In the Commonwealth of Northern Mariana Islands, the six northern islands (Uracas, the three Maug Islands, Asuncion, and Guguan) are set aside as nature preserves in the constitution of the CNMI. In Guam, the Guam National Wildlife Refuge on the north end of island protects a dwindling population of hawksbill sea turtles and a colony of Mariana fruit bats.

Environmental Issues. Introduced species are the major environmental issue in the Marianas. In addition to trying to control the brown tree snake on Guam and prevent its dispersal to other islands, efforts are underway to manage or extirpate other problematic animals such as water buffalo (carabao), Philippine deer, giant African snail, cane toads, and probably the newest arrival, the noisy coqui tree frog from Puerto Rico.

Further Reading

Rodda, Gordon H. 2009. "Marianas, Biology." In *Encyclopedia of Islands*, edited by Rosemary G. Gillespie and David A. Clague, 593–597. Berkeley: University of California Press.

Trusdell, Frank A. 2009. "Marianas, Geology." In *Encyclopedia of Islands*, edited by Rosemary G. Gillespie and David A. Clague, 598–603. Berkeley: University of California Press.

Mariana Trench

Pacific Ocean

Geographic Overview. The Mariana Trench is the deepest feature of Earth's oceans. The floor of Challenger Deep at the southern end of the trench currently holds the depth record at 36,070 ft (10,994 m) bsl. However, due to the shape of the planet, which is flattened at the poles, places in the Arctic Ocean are actually several miles closer to Earth's center.

Geographic Coordinates. Approximately 12°N–21°N, 142°E–148°E

Description. The Mariana Trench is a long, crescent-shaped oceanic trench to the east of the Mariana Islands in the western Pacific Ocean. It is approximately 1,500 mi (2,550 km) long and 43 mi (69 km) wide. The maximum known depth occurs in a slot canyon near its southern end known as Challenger Deep (11°21'N, 142°12'E); it lies about 36,070 ft (10,994 m) bsl. The extreme conditions at this depth make accurate measurement difficult and estimates are continually being revised as explorers employ ever newer technologies. The dark deep-sea environment of the trench is under water pressures more than 1,000 times greater than sea level atmospheric pressure. At the bottom, pressure reaches over 8 tons/in^2 (15,750 psi or 1,086 bars) compared to sea level pressure of 14.7 lb/in^2 (14.7 psi or 1.013529 bars) and increases water density nearly 5 percent above that of surface waters. Water temperatures near the bottom of the trench have been measured at 34°–39°F (1°–4°C).

Despite the great depth of Challenger Deep, it is not the point closest to Earth's center, just as Mount Everest, Earth's highest peak, is not the point farthest from the center. The equatorial bulge and polar flattening of the planet result in places on the seafloor of the Arctic Ocean being some 8 mi (13 km) closer.

In 1997 a team of researchers from Hawai'i discovered another deep valley in the trench about 124 mi (200 km) east of Challenger Deep at 12°04'N, 144°35'E with a calculated depth of 35,210 ft (10,732 m) bsl. This is currently the third deepest point in the world ocean after Challenger Deep and Horizon Deep in the Tonga Trench (35,702 ft or 10,882 m bsl). Originally the newly found deep was called Hawai'i Mapping Research Group (HMRG) Deep, but this has since been changed to Sirena Deep in celebration of a mermaid in a Guamanian legend.

In 2011, a U.S. Navy hydrographic mission revealed four rocky outcrops at the bottom of Mariana Trench believed to be remnants of old seamounts. Hydrothermal vents and areas where serpentinization of oceanic rock may be occurring have also been discovered. The latter is a process in which water moving up through oceanic crust releases sulfur, methane, and hydrogen.

Geologic History. The Mariana Trench is the product of the subduction of the denser oceanic crust on the western edge of the Pacific Plate beneath the less dense oceanic crust of the Philippine Plate. The oldest rocks at the bottom of the trench date to 180 mya.

Biota. Deep-sea life has been revealed both during manned explorations of the trench and collected by unmanned submersibles. Xenophyophores, giant amoeba up to 4 in (10 cm) in diameter, have been reported at depths of 34,910 ft (10,641 m). Large deep-sea amphipods nearly 7 in (17 cm) long have

been recovered from this and other deep sea trenches. Jellyfish were photographed by *National Geographic*'s dropcam at a depth of 35,630 ft (9,970 m), and a sea cucumber was spotted in photographs taken even deeper. Bacterial mats cover outcrops of rocks in the deepest water. The bacteria may extract energy from the sulfur, methane, and hydrogen seeping through the rock and feed on detritus descending from higher up the water column.

Protected Areas. About 1,000 mi (1,600 km) of the Mariana Trench seafloor are protected in the Trench Unit of the Marianas Trench Marine National Monument, established in 2009. The area is administered by the U.S. Fish and Wildlife Service as part of the U.S. National Wildlife Refuge system.

Environmental Issues. Damage to the pristine environment could come from submersibles exploring the deeps. Special permits are required for exploration within the Marianas Trench Marine National Monument to manage such entry. In the past the trench has been considered for a depository for nuclear wastes or other harmful products of civilization.

See also Mariana Islands Archipelago

Further Reading

"Biology." 2013. Deepsea Challenge, National Geographic. http://deepseachallenge.com/the-science/biology/
"The Mariana Trench." 2013. www.marianatrench.com
"Marianas Trench Marine National Monument." 2012. U.S. Fish and Wildlife Service. http://www.fws.gov/refuge/mariana_trench_marine_national_monument/

Marshall Islands

Pacific Ocean (Micronesia)

Geographic Overview. The Marshall Islands are a group of 29 atolls and five separate, small coral islands arranged in a double archipelago in the central Pacific Ocean. The atolls are the oldest on Earth; Kwajalein, the southernmost atoll, is one of the world's largest. The Marshall Islands are known for the stick charts islanders once used to navigate among the atolls. The maps were constructed of the midribs of coconut palm fronds bent to represent ocean swells and their defraction around islands, which were indicated by shells.

Two atolls in the north, Bikini and Enewetak, were nuclear bomb test sites. In 1990, the islands became the independent Republic of the Marshall Islands (RMI).

Geographic Coordinates. 14°03'N, 160°55'E–04°03'N, 172°9'E

Description. The Marshall Islands consist primarily of two strings of atolls bearing a total of 1,125 low, flat islands and islets that are strewn across 750,000 mi² (1,945,000 km²) of the Pacific Ocean. Wake Island lies to their north, Kiribati to their south. The two chains, one lying east of the other, are known as Retak (sunrise) and Rälik (sunset). The Marshall atolls are much larger than those in the Indian Ocean, and most are elongated rather than circular in shape. The average elevation of dry land on the atolls is 7 ft (2 m) asl. Many islets are mere sand spits; others are vegetated but are submerged during extreme high tides and during storms. More islets occur on the windward side of

---

Bombs and Bathing Suits

Bikini Atoll's lagoon had become a naval ship graveyard after World War II; and from 1946 to 1958, the atoll in the north of the Rälik chain was used for 23 nuclear weapon tests in a U.S. program called Operation Crossroads. In October 1952, the first test of a human-made nuclear fusion explosion occurred on Bikini, and on March 1, 1954 the first operational-scale hydrogen bomb was detonated in what became the largest nuclear weapons test ever made by the U.S. military. The latter test, known as Castle Bravo, contaminated an extensive area of the Marshall Islands with radioactive fallout. Because of its significance to the dawning of the nuclear age, UNESCO has inscribed Bikini Atoll as a cultural World Heritage Site. The two-piece bikini swimsuit was introduced soon after the first test in 1946 and was so-named because of the atoll's newfound fame.

Enewetak Atoll, also in the Rälik chain, was used by the United States for 43 nuclear weapons tests during the same time period. Decontamination began in 1977. Radioactive soil was mixed with Portland cement and buried in an atomic blast crater on Runit Island in the northern part of the atoll, since the island had been deemed uninhabitable for at least 24,000 years. A concrete dome 18 in (46 cm) thick was then constructed over the burial site. Residents were allowed to return to the southern islands of the atoll in 1980.

---

atolls than the leeward side. Each atoll is fringed by coral reefs; most enclose a deep central lagoon, often large enough to have its own circulation pattern. Almost all lagoons are entered by at least one deep channel. The largest atoll is Kwajalein at the southern end of the archipelago. Its 97 islands and islets account for a total land area of 6.3 mi² (16.4 km²). The central lagoon covers 849 mi² (2,174 km²). The smallest atolls are Bikar with 0.2 mi² (0.5 km²) of land and a 14 mi² (37.4 km²) lagoon and Namduk with 1.0 mi² (2.7 km²) of dry land and a lagoon of merely 3.25 mi² (8.4 km²).

The tropical climate is characterized by warm temperatures and high humidity, although these conditions are relieved by the constant trade winds. Temperatures vary little through the year, averaging 80°F (27°C). Nights tend to be 2°–4°F (1°–2°C) warmer than daytime highs due to clouds and heavy rains in the afternoon. The southern atolls receive about 160 in (4,064 mm) of rain a year, but the northern atolls are much drier with average annual precipitation around 20 in (508 mm). During drought years, the northern atolls may get no rain at all.

The coastal zone has single-species stands of a salt-tolerant shrub or small tree, *Pemphis acidula*. Mangroves are common in the intertidal zone; the orange mangrove *Bruguiera gymnorrhiza* is most common. About 60 percent of the dry land of the RMI is covered with coconut palms.

Geologic History. The atoll reefs are more than 50 million years old. They have formed on subsided volcanoes that initially developed over hotspots in French Polynesia 97–67 mya. The atolls began as fringing reefs and kept building near sea level as the mountain cores sank and became seamounts, guyots, and pinnacles. Coral reefs capped their volcanic bases with limestone up to a mile (1.6 km) thick. The atolls may have been just reefs as recently as 4,000–6,000 years ago, when sea level was 3–5 ft (1–1.5 m) higher than today. The islands and islets are very young, coming into being either after sea level dropped 4,000 years ago or when storms piled coral rubble and sand on to the shallow reefs.

Biota. The coral reefs of the Marshall Island atolls have a species-rich fauna closely related to species from the far western Pacific Ocean. Equatorial currents, seabirds, and winds provide a steady flow of plants and invertebrates to these remote islands. Fewer than 750 native plants form the terrestrial flora, each atoll home to fewer than 12 species. Native vertebrates include seven lizards and one blind snake, plus the only native mammal, the Polynesian rat. High biodiversity exists in the reefs, where 362 corals and other cnidarians, 40 species of sponge, 1,665 molluscan species, 728 crustaceans, and 126 echinoderms have been identified. More than 860 reef fishes are known from the Marshall Islands; only seven species are endemic, including the three-banded anemonefish (*Amphiprion trinctus*), popular in the aquarium trade.

Protected Areas. There are no protected areas per se on the islands, but a number of government agencies are involved in protecting and managing the reef resources. RMI is also a signatory to a number of international conservation treaties.

Environmental Issues. Modernization of traditional lifestyles and tourism development create potential problems of pollution and mechanical damage to reefs. Collection and export of live corals and reef fish are potential threats to the integrity of the reef ecosystems. However, climate change, warming seas, and rising sea level are the major threats to these low-lying coral atolls. Average water temperature now is 84°F (29°C), near the upper tolerance level of coral polyps. A further rise of 1.8°F (1.0°C) could cause coral bleaching and dying of the reefs that sustain and protect the islanders. The increasing frequency of storms corresponds with greater wave and storm surge damage to the reef.

Radioactive contamination continues to be a concern, although corals at nuclear test sites seem to have recovered. Invasive species are always a threat on oceanic islands, but not yet a problem here.

See also French Polynesia

Further Reading

Birkeland, Charles, Asher Edward, Yimnang Golbuu, Jay Gutierrez, Noah Idechong, James Maragos, Gustav Paulay, Robert Richmond, Andrew Tafileichig, and Nancy Vander Velde. 2002. "Status of Coral Reefs in the Pacific Freely Associated States: The Republic of the Marshall Islands." In "The State of Coral Reef Ecosystems of the United States and Pacific Freely Associated States: 2002," NOAA, 205–212. http://www.rmiembassyus.org/Environ/status_coralreef.pdf

"Official Website of the Republic of the Marshall Islands." 2005. Embassy of the Republic of the Marshall Islands. http://www.rmiembassyus.org/index.htm

Vander Velde, Nancy. 2009. "Marshall Islands." In *Encyclopedia of Islands*, edited by Rosemary G. Gillespie and David A. Clague, 610–612. Berkeley: University of California Press.

Mascarene Islands

Indian Ocean

Geographic Overview. The Mascarene Islands (Réunion, Mauritius, and Rodrigues) are oceanic islands in the southwestern Indian Ocean. Mauritius, home of the extinct Dodo, is emblematic of human-caused extinction, but the island nation has also pioneered habitat restoration and techniques for saving severely endangered birds. The name for the island group honors the Portuguese navigator Pedro Mascarenhas, who in the early 1500s was the first European to visit the islands. Réunion is an overseas department of France; Mauritius is an independent country of which Rodrigues is a part.

Geographic Coordinates. Réunion: 21°12'S, 55°32'E; Mauritius: 20°20'S, 57°30'E; Rodrigues: 19°42'S, 63°25'E

Description. The three Mascarene Islands extend for 370 mi (600 km) along the submarine Mascarene Plateau east of Madagascar. The plateau, of volcanic origin, rises above the abyssal plain 2.5–3.0 mi (4–5 km) below and lies under 25–500 ft (8–150 m) of seawater. The islands are separated from each other by fracture zones; each formed independently of the others.

Réunion Island is the largest and highest of the three and the closest to Madagascar, being 435 mi (700 km) to its east. Composed of two shield volcanoes, it covers 970 mi² (2,512 km²). Piton des Neiges, which has not erupted for 70,000 years, rises 10,073 ft (3,070 m) asl and is the highest peak in the Indian Ocean. Its slopes are deeply eroded and, high on the mountain deep, bowl-shaped depressions occur. Piton des Neiges forms the northwestern two-thirds of the island. The other peak is one of the most active volcanoes in the world; Piton de la Fournaise, which stands

8,632 ft (2,631 m) asl, has developed on the flank of the inactive volcano, its center 19 mi (30 km) from the summit of Piton de Neiges. The west and southwest coasts of Réunion have a discontinuous fringing reef.

Mauritius Island is 102 mi (164 km) northeast of Réunion. It is both smaller and lower than its neighbor, covering 720 mi² (1,865 km²); its highest mountain, Black River Peak, rises only to 2,716 ft (828 m) asl. Mauritius is formed of young lava flows that surround "islands" of much older volcanic rock. Its central plateau stands 900–2,395 ft (275–730 m) asl. White sandy beaches and lagoons line the shore; a discontinuous fringing reef and a small barrier reef lie several hundred yards (meters) to as much as 3 mi (5 km) offshore.

Rodrigues Island is a small island of gentle hills, the erosional remnant of a volcano that has been extinct for 1.5 million years. Part of the island is a limestone plateau of consolidated coral sand with numerous caves. It lies 357 mi (574 km) east of Mauritius near the Central Indian Ridge and has an area of 40 mi² (104 km²). Mount Limon, its highest peak, is 1,306 ft (398 m) asl. A nearly continuous fringing reef surrounds the island.

The Mascarenes are tropical islands with warm temperatures year-round. In summer (December–April), temperatures in the lowlands average 86°F (30°C); in winter (May–November) about 77°F (25°C). Snow falls on the highest peaks, but does not last long. Affected by the Southeast Trade Winds and elevation, there is considerable variation in total annual precipitation. Leeward slopes may receive as little 20 in (500 mm) of rain a year, while windward slopes on Réunion may receive an astonishing 472 in (12,000 mm).

When the islands were discovered in the early 1500s, all were forested. The only exception was Réunion, where mountain slopes above 6,200 ft (1,900 m) had a subalpine scrub vegetation. Today the native vegetation of Mauritius is largely destroyed and the forests of Rodrigues are gone, but Réunion still has about 25 percent of its natural vegetation. The mountains of Réunion exhibit a pattern of altitudinal zonation wherein between and 650 ft (0–200 m) a dry forest of palms, screw-pine (*Pandanas*), and *Terminalia* dominates. Less than 40 in (1,000 mm) of rain falls in this the former habitat of an extinct giant tortoise.

On the west side of the island, from 650–2,460 ft (200–750 m) is sclerophyllous forest, which receives 40–60 in (1,000–1,500 mm) of rain each year. From 2,460–3,600 ft (750–1,100 m) is the richest plant community, a moist forest with trees up to 100 ft (30 m) tall. At this elevation 80–390 in (2,000–10,000 mm) of precipitation falls annually. Dense cloud forests occur above this zone up to treeline at 6,200 ft (1,900 m) on the eastern slopes and up to 6,560 ft (2000 m) on western slopes. The canopy of the cloud forest, which is rich in epiphytic orchids, ferns, mosses, and lichens, is 20–30 ft (6–10 m) above the ground. Tree ferns emerge higher. Above treeline, frost is a common occurrence in winter, and 80–236 in (2,000–6,000 mm) of precipitation falls. A unique scrub vegetation of heaths and shrubs in the daisy family grows in this habitat. The summits of Réunion's high volcanoes are sparsely vegetated with a grassland rich in endemic grasses and orchids.

Geologic History. The Mascarenes derive from a sequence of volcanic activity associated with the rapid movement of the Indian plate northward over the Réunion hotspot 65–36 mya, followed by the slow migration of the African Plate across the hotspot after the Central Indian Ridge crossed it, moving in a southwest-to-northeast direction from 36 mya to the present time. The Deccan flood basalts in western India are some of the earliest manifestations of these movements that began with the breakup of Gondwana. The Chagos–Laccaldive submarine ridge is another part of the Réunion–Deccan hotspot track. Modern volcanic activity on Réunion, beneath which the hotspot is currently located, is the latest episode. The Mascarene Plateau formed on the African Plate and several volcanic islands emerged in progression; some of the older ones have since subsided below sea level to form coral-capped banks. Several larger banks may have been exposed when sea levels were lowered during the last glacial maximum 18,000–10,000 years ago. Mauritius is the oldest of the Mascarenes, with the oldest dated rocks going back 7.8–6.8 mya. Réunion emerged about 2.1 mya. Réunion is currently above the near stationary mantle hotspot.

Biota. The Mascarenes are one of the world's major biodiversity hotspots. The terrestrial biota is characterized by a high degree of endemism. Of 959 known species of flowering plants, 72 percent are endemic. Nonmarine mollusks number 200 species, 90 percent of which are found only on these islands. Similarly 94 percent of nonmarine reptiles (32 species) and 85 percent of landbirds (60 species) are restricted to the island group. Before human settlement and the introduction of nonnative species, the Mascarenes had the richest reptilian fauna of any oceanic island, with 30 endemic species. More than half of these, including the giant tortoises, have become extinct in the last 400 years. Also extinct are three large flightless birds: the Dodo (*Raphus cucullates*) of Mauritius; the Rodrigues Solitaire, a close relative of the Dodo in the pigeon family; and the Réunion Solitaire, an unrelated species in the ibis family.

The marine biota is poorly studied, but 923 reef fish have been identified. Particularly species-rich are wrasses, damselfish, groupers, and surgeonfishes. Few are endemic; affinities are with the Indo-West Pacific region, as is true for the hard corals and other invertebrates inhabiting the reefs.

Protected Areas. Réunion National Park protects some 400 mi² (1,000 km²) of the mountainous interior of the island. This includes a large buffer zone that permits sustainable use and conserves the cultural heritage of the island. Mauritius established a national park in 1966 to protect its scarce natural habitats. It pioneered habitat restoration in successful efforts to rescue three endangered bird species from certain extinction: the Mauritius Kestrel, the Pink Pigeon, and the Echo Parakeet. Round Island, an islet off its north coast, protects a number of endemic reptiles.

Environmental Issues. Deforestation, which peaked in the 19th century, continued into the 20th century as land was converted to agricultural uses. Habitat fragmentation as well as outright habitat loss for native species increased as a consequence. Invasive species continue to be introduced, part of a long history of introductions of nonnatives that began even before settlement and contributed to the extinct of several native species. Only Réunion is relatively free of the wolf snakes, rats, cats, pigs, monkeys, and mongooses brought to the islands. Eradication of nonnative species is a high priority today.

See also Indian Ocean; Seychelles

Further Reading

Duncan, Robert A. 2009. "Mascarene Islands, Geology." In *Encyclopedia of Islands*, edited by Rosemary G. Gillespie and David A. Clague, 620–622. Berkeley: University of California Press.

Schipper, Jan. 2013. "Islands of Réunion, and Mauritius, East of Madagascar." World Wildlife Fund. http://worldwildlife.org/ecoregions/at0120

Thébaud, Christophe, Ben H. Warren, Dominique Strasberg, and Anthony Cheke. 2009. "Mascarene Islands, Biology." In *Encyclopedia of Islands*, edited by Rosemary G. Gillespie and David A. Clague, 612–619. Berkeley: University of California Press.

Masoala National Park

Madagascar

Geographic Overview. Masoala National Park is a large tract of lowland evergreen rainforest in northeastern Madagascar, with coral reefs and mangrove swamps along the coast. The park houses approximately half of Madagascar's protected lowland rainforest, and has a high rate of endemism and a rich biodiversity. Masoala is the largest protected area in Madagascar and one of island's most important.

Geographic Coordinates. 15°12'S–16°00'S; 49°52'E–50°29'E

Description. Masoala National Park, which covers over half of the peninsula of the same name, is a complex of protected areas. Approximately 900 mi² (2,300 km²) of the park is rainforest or littoral forest; 40 mi² (100 km²) is marine. The rainforest extends to the shoreline of pristine golden beaches and rocky coves. On the west, the Andranofotsy and Mahalevona rivers drain south to Antongil Bay. Several east-flowing rivers, including the Onive River, drain to the Indian Ocean. Most of the park is steep and rugged granite mountains, with some basalt and quartzite. The highest mountains, rising from the coast to more than 4,600 ft (1,400 m) asl in the north, dominate the western side of the peninsula. Near Antalavia in the south, the mountains reach 1,650 ft (500 m) asl. Only the southeastern tip of the peninsula is relatively flat. The large peninsula has a variety of habitats, including rainforest, littoral forest, marshes, and mangroves. Coral reefs, lagoons, and estuaries line the east and southern coasts. The largest section of the park is the mountainous rainforest, followed by three small detached littoral forest reserves and three marine parks. The park is accessible and offers many hiking trails.

In the path of Southeast Trade Winds and tropical cyclones, this part of Madagascar is very wet. The high mountains on the western side of the peninsula receive the most rain, an annual mean of 235 in (6,000 mm), with most falling January to March. The lower elevation eastern side receives 108–120 in (2,750–3,055 mm) a year. Temperatures in December and January average 77–86°F (25–30°C), dropping only to 64–72°F (18–22° C) in July through September.

Biota. Biota in the park and peninsula have been incompletely studied and inventoried. The park supports 50 percent of all of Madagascar's plant species, and more than 50 percent of all of Madagascar's mammal, bird, amphibian, and reptile species. The park includes plants unique to Masoala, as well as those representative of the island's rainforest. The flora includes 150 fern species, more than 100 palm species (one of the most diverse palm populations in the world, with 10 endemic to the peninsula), and 22 begonia species (22 endemic to the peninsula). The park has many chameleons, geckos, frogs, butterflies, and fish, many of which are new to science.

From sea level to 4,600 ft (1,400 m) asl, the peninsula was originally dominated by rainforest, with small patches of montane thicket and cloud forest on the highest points. Approximately 72 percent of the original rainforest remains intact in the rugged mountains, while the littoral forest is patchy. Canopy trees in the humid forest include *Canarium, Diospyros, Symphonia, Tambourissa, Weinmannia, Anthostema,* and *Uapaca* species. Evergreen littoral forest, dominated by *Pandanus* and *Lauraceae* species, lined the sandy shores. Both forests are closed canopy with few emergent trees. Marshes consist of several sedge species, and mangrove swamps are dominated by *Avicennia marina* and *Rhizophora mucronata.*

Four of the 10 lemur species in Masoala, including the elusive aye-aye, are on the International Union for Conservation of Nature's (IUCN) Red List of endangered species. The red-ruffed lemur (*Varecia rubra*) is endemic to the Masoala peninsula. The park also has unique species such as the rare fork-marked lemur (*Phaner furcifer*) and hairy-eared dwarf lemur (*Allocebus trichotis*). The brown-tailed mongoose (*Salanoia concolor*) is a rare carnivore. Of the 102 bird species, 60 percent are endemic, including the locally endemic Madagascar Red Owl (*Tyto soumagnei*). The rare Serpent Eagle (*Eutriorchis astur*) is more commonly seen in Masoala than elsewhere. The numerous reptile species include the Madagascar day gecko (*Phelsuma madagascariensis*), leaf-tailed gecko (*Uroplatus* ssp.), gold dust gecko (*Phelsuma laticauda*), scaled turtle (*Eretmochelys imbricata*), and many chameleons. The tomato frog (*Dyscophus* spp.) is a unique amphibian.

Marine life is typical of the high biodiversity in the Indian Ocean, with 41 coral species. More than 3,000 fish species, both saltwater and freshwater, have been identified. From July to September, Antongil Bay is a breeding ground for humpback whales, and dolphins and dugong are frequently seen.

Protected Areas. Masoala National Park is one of the six properties that comprise Madagascar's Rainforests of the Atsinanana World Heritage Site. Originally declared an Integrated Natural Reserve in 1927, the region was declassified in 1964 to allow logging. World attention and monetary aid led to its national park designation in 1997, in an effort to protect remaining forests.

Environmental Issues. The most serious threats are deforestation, habitat conversion, and habitat fragmentation. Unsustainable collection of wood products, hunting, and fishing are also problems. Littoral forests are replaced by fruit trees, mangroves are used for firewood, marshes are converted to rice paddies, and forests are burned to provide pasture for cattle. Red-ruffed lemur and tenrec (*Tenrec ecaudatus*) especially are endangered by excessive hunting. In 2009–2010, loggers illegally harvested rosewood (*Dahlbergia* ssp.) from the park. Invasive species, such as rats (*Rattus* ssp.) and turkey berry (*Solanum torvum*), threaten native species.

See also Madagascar

Further Reading
Kremen, C. 2009. "The Masoala Peninsula." In *The Natural History of Madagascar,* edited by Steven M. Goodman and Jonathan P. Benstead, 1459–1466. Chicago: University of Chicago Press.

Martinez, Barbara T. 2010. *Forest Restoration in Maso-ala National Park, Madagascar: The Contribution of Red-Ruffed Lemur (Verecia rubra) and the Livelihood of Subsistence Farmers at Ambatoladama.* Dissertation, University of Minnesota. http://conservancy.umn.edu/handle/11299/92239

Massif Central

France

Geographic Overview. The Massif Central in south-central France is geologically the oldest and most diverse part of France. It is the largest and most elevated of Europe's Hercynian massifs of crystalline rocks. This rugged region is also the site of deep limestone gorges and recent, but extinct, volcanoes. The volcanic Mont Dore is the highest point on a Hercynian massif on mainland Europe.

Geographic Coordinates. Approximately 44° 30'N–48°00'N, 01°00'E–04°50'E

Description. The Massif Central, approximately 280 mi (450 km) north-to-south and 185 mi (300 km) east-to-west, covers approximately 33,000 mi² (85,500 km²). It is a mountainous plateau with deep valleys, tectonic depressions, and volcanoes. In the east, it is limited by the Rhone–Saone structural trough. The southeast is marked by escarpments, including the south-facing escarpments of the Causses and the Montagne Noire, and the Cevennes, which rises 5,250 ft (1,600 m) above coastal Languedoc. The northern and western boundaries are defined by the 1,000 ft (300 m) elevation level above the Paris and Aquitaine basins. Most of the plateau is 2,000–3,000 ft (600–900 m) asl. Because the plateau dips to the northwest, the high points are on the east and southeast side, as well as on the volcanoes.

Four landscape regions correlate with major rock types. The western area, primarily in Limousin, consists of Hercynian crystalline basement rocks, such as granites and metamorphics, and is characterized by high plateaus cut by deep valleys. The eastern edge, bordering the Rhone–Saone and extending southeast to include the Cevennes, is also Hercynian rocks, marked by deep gorges, narrow ridges, and plateaus, which may be covered locally with volcanoes. The crystalline plateau in the central part, Auvergne, is a landscape of volcanoes, called puys. Puy de Sancy, at 6,187 ft (1,886 m) asl, is the highest peak, followed by Plomb du Cantal at 6,086 ft (1,855 m). The southern region is the Causses, a limestone area broken by north–south faults, with both surface and subsurface karst features, such as disappearing streams and caves. Surface drainage occurs only in major valleys where rivers, such as the Tarn and Ardeche, have carved deep gorges.

The Massif Central is a major divide between the Atlantic Ocean and the Mediterranean Sea. The Seine, Rhone, and Garonne Rivers all have major tributaries from the Massif Central, and the Loire and Dordogne originate there.

Geologic History. Three-quarters of the Massif Central is underlain by Precambrian and Paleozoic Hercynian crystalline rock, including gneiss and schist with granitic intrusions. These mountain roots, with surfaces truncated by erosion, were uplifted in the Mesozoic and surrounded by seas, into which various sedimentary rocks were deposited. The limestone Causses are the remains of a tropical reef dating from this period. During the Alpine Orogeny in the mid-Tertiary, the region was uplifted, fractured, and tilted.

The fault pattern controlled the location of intense volcanic activity, which began in the Miocene (5.3–2.6 mya) and continued through the Pleistocene. Volcanism was at its maximum when Cantal and Mont Dore were formed. Cantal is the oldest and largest, approximately 44 mi (70 km) in diameter and covering 1,050 mi² (2,700 km²). Mont Dore is slightly younger, with several separate centers. Both are major stratovolcanoes, composed of pyroclastics, basalt, and rhyolite, topped by plateau basalts. Necks, plugs, and dikes in the center have been exposed by erosion. Lava from many scattered vents along the fractures created plateau volcanic forms, a cover of basalt with occasional cinder cones and extrusion domes, during the Pliocene and Pleistocene. Plateau basalts and mudflows accumulated to a depth of 3,300 ft (1,000 m). Chain of Puys, approximately 22 mi (35 km) long and 2.5–3.1 mi (4–5 km) wide, from 3,000–40,000 years ago, is the youngest. There are almost 80 individual volcanoes of various types, both explosive and quiet, including steep-sided domes of viscous lava, plugs or spires, maars, and stratovolcanoes with central craters.

The highest parts of the massif, more than 4,600 ft (1,400 m) asl, including the Cantal and Mont Dore volcanoes, were affected by alpine glaciation in the Pleistocene.

Biota. The Massif Central is thickly forested. Agriculture in this rural region is primarily related to raising cattle and sheep or to growing fodder crops.

Further Reading

Ager, Derek V. 1980. "Central Variscides." In *The Geology of Europe*, 214–270. New York: John Wiley & Sons.

Embleton, Clifford and Demek, J. 1984. "Hercynian Europe." In *Geomorphology of Europe*, edited by Clifford Embleton, 165–230. New York: John Wiley & Sons.

Matterhorn

Switzerland

Geographic Overview. The Matterhorn gives its name to the glacial geology term "horn," meaning a steep peak with cirques on at least three sides. The mountain's structural geology illustrates the complexity of various nappes that form the Swiss Alps.

Geographic Coordinates. 45°59'N, 07°40'E

Description. Located in the high Swiss Alps in the Canton of Valais, the Matterhorn is between Zermatt, Switzerland, on the north and Val Tournache in the Aosta Valley, Italy, on the south. At 14,692 ft (4,478 m) asl, it is the second highest peak in the Pennine (or Valais) Alps and the 10th highest peak in Switzerland. Situated on the watershed divide, it separates drainage of the Rhone River to the north from that of the Po River to the south. The name is derived from the German words for meadow and peak. Italians refer to it as *Monte Cervino.*

The pyramid-shaped peak has four ridges separating four steep faces, which are aligned with the cardinal directions. The north face overlooks Zermatt Valley, and the east face overlooks Gornergrat Ridge, both in Switzerland. The south face overlooks the town of Breuil-Cervinia in Italy, and the west face overlooks the mountains of Dent d'Herens on the Swiss–Italian border. The steep faces, which have

little snow and ice, rise abruptly above glaciers. The largest glacier is Zermatt to the west. Furgg Glacier faces east, and Matterhorn Glacier faces north. The east face is 3,300 ft (1,000 m) high, a dangerous ascent marked by rock falls. The north face is 3,950 ft (1,200 m) high, with rockfalls and storms. The south face is 4,430 ft (1,350 m) high, and offers many climbing routes. The west face is the highest, 4,595 ft (1,400 m), with the fewest routes to the summit.

Hornli Ridge, between the east and north faces, is the least technical climb. Zermatt Ridge is between the north and west faces. Lion Ridge, between the south and west faces, is the normal Italian route. Furggen Ridge is between the south and east faces.

The peak of the Matterhorn was first reached in 1865 by climber Edward Whymper, an accomplishment marred by the deaths of four companions who fell on the descent. They pioneered the most common route used today, Hornli Ridge, a climb that usually takes 10 hours round trip. Three days later, three Italians made the second successful ascent, from the Italian side. The particularly arduous north face was first climbed in 1931. More than 500 people have died since 1865, many on the descent. The average is now 12 per year.

Geologic History. The Matterhorn has a complex geology of several overlapping nappes, slices of both oceanic and continental crust, which were thrust northward to form the Alps during the Alpine Orogeny in the Tertiary. A sequence of rifting, subduction, and convergence created the Matterhorn's geology. The upper part of the Matterhorn is a continental crust remnant of an African microplate, the Dent Blanche klippe (an eroded part of a nappe). It is part of the Apulian Plate, which was rifted away from northern Africa when the modern western Mediterranean Sea opened. With the closure of the Tethys Sea in the eastern Mediterranean, oceanic crust was subducted beneath Africa. Slivers of oceanic crust that stuck to the continental edge, however, were subsequently thrust northward during the Alpine Orogeny. The top of the Matterhorn is carved into Paleozoic granitic gneiss and schist. Below is the Tsate nappe, a narrow band of Jurassic and Cretaceous basalt and gabbro, underlain by calcareous schists and shales, derived from oceanic

Although the sheer cirque faces of the Matterhorn give the impression that it is impossible to climb, the peak was first summited in 1865 and continues to attract mountain climbers. (Chaoss/Dreamstime.com)

sediments from the Tethys Sea. The Tsate nappe extends up to an elevation of 11,150 ft (3,400 m) on the mountain. Above that level is the Dent Blanche nappe.

Alpine glaciation eroded steep cirques on four sides of the klippe, creating the four faces of the horn.

Environmental Issues. Because the glaciers are receding, more meltwater seeps into cracks and fissures, where expansion with freezing has caused an increasing frequency of rock falls. In 2003, 50 climbers trapped by a rock fall had to be air lifted to safety. Potentially unstable foundations also pose a safety issue with gondola towers.

See also European Alps; Mediterranean Sea

Further Reading

Marthaler, Michel. 2008. "The African Matterhorn: Yes or No?—A Structural, Geodynamical and Paleogeographical Overview." *Swiss Bulletin für Angewandte Geologie (for Applied Geology)* 13: 11–16. http://www.angewandte-geologie.ch/

McMurdo Dry Valleys and Their Lakes

Antarctica

Geographic Overview. Most of the ice-free areas in Antarctica are found in the McMurdo Dry Valleys, a group of northeast–southwest trending valleys lying between the East Antarctic Ice Sheet and the Ross Sea. These cold, arid valleys, their lakes, and their impoverished flora are being studied as analogs of the Martian surface and habitats that could support life on other planets.

Geographic Coordinates. Approximately 77° 15'S–77°45'S, 160°E–163°E

Description. The McMurdo Dry Valleys are in the central Transantarctic Mountains. Ridges more than 6,500 ft (2,000 m) high separate the valleys. The walls and valley floors of these glacial troughs resemble a cold desert landscape with exposed bedrock, wind-sculpted rocks, desert pavement, salt-encrusted ground, and sand dunes. The three main valleys (from north to south: Victoria, Wright, and Taylor) are each about 50 mi (80 km) long and up to 9 mi (15 km) wide. Perennially ice-capped lakes, small saline ponds, ephemeral streams, and in some cases the rocks themselves support life, primarily bacteria, cyanobacteria, yeasts, algae, and lichens.

The high ridges between the dry valleys deflect easterly winds down-valley. The extreme aridity of these valleys is related to their rain shadow position and downslope winds that warm and reduce humidity as they descend. Annual precipitation is less than 2 in (50 mm) near the coast, even lower inland. Surrounding glaciers are fed by local precipitation and snow blown off the Antarctic Plateau, neither of which is enough to counteract ablation, so the glaciers (such as Taylor Glacier and Upper Wright Glacier) that shaped these valleys are in retreat. Whether originating as katabatic winds off the interior plateau or developing as foehn winds generated locally by pressure differences between highly reflective ice surfaces and heat-absorbing bare valley floors, fierce downslope winds in excess of 100 mph (161 kmph) are commonplace and affect weathering, ablation of glaciers, and landform development. Foehn-like winds often develop suddenly and can quickly raise air temperatures 70 Fahrenheit degrees (40 Celsius degrees) or more—but still not above freezing. Melting of the ice does occur where windblown sand covers it and absorbs solar radiation for 8–12 weeks in summer, especially on north-facing slopes, but most ice loss is due to sublimation under the intense solar radiation of summer.

Three climate zones, with associated landforms, are recognized in the dry valleys: a coastal thaw zone (CTZ), an inland mixed zone (IMZ), and a stable upland zone (SUZ). Southeasterly winds carry moist air masses from the seasonally open Ross Sea reaches into the CTZ, where summer temperatures average 23°F (−5°C) and daily highs reach 28°F (−2°C). The upper layer of the permafrost undergoes expansion and contraction with seasonal temperature changes, and vertical cracks develop that collect snow and liquid water from the thawed top layer of permafrost. As water refreezes, ice wedges form in the cracks and grow over time to create polygon-shaped surface features with raised rims (patterned ground). The polygons attain diameters of 30–65 ft (10–20 m), and ice wedges can become 6.5 ft (2 m) wide. Solid rock surfaces in this zone are affected by salt weathering, which has honeycombed granite boulders (i.e., created tafoni) and smoothed the slopes.

Sand-wedge polygons characterize the IMZ, where winds alternate between down-valley and up-valley directions. It is drier here than in the CTZ and summer temperatures average 19°F (−7°C), with highs reaching 25°F (−4°C). Cracks tend to fill with windblown sand, rather than snow and ice. This zone also has desert pavement and wind-sculpted rocks (ventifacts).

In the SUZ, warming and drying downslope winds dominate; the heads of the valleys are colder than lower elevations. Summer temperatures average 14°F (−10°C), while daily highs only get to 18°F (−8°C). The patterned ground in this zone is a result of sublimation of the underlying permafrost. The finest particles on the surface sink into cracks created below the surface, leaving coarser sands and gravels to form the polygon rims. Fully developed, a polygon may be edged by trenches 6.5–10 ft (2–3 m) deep that surround an interior cone of buried ice. Rock surfaces in this zone are pitted by wind erosion and salt weathering.

Several lakes, covered with thick ice throughout the year, occur in the dry valleys and are fed in summer by ephemeral streams of glacial meltwater. In Taylor Valley, meltwater from the Taylor Glacier first flows into Lake Bonney, a 130 ft (40 m) deep body of water at the western edge of the ice. Blood Falls discharges from halfway up the terminus of Taylor Glacier into this lake. This extraordinary feature is an outflow of iron-rich brine from the ice; upon contact with the air, the iron is oxidized to produce a reddish sludge. Lake Hoare, the freshest lake in the valley, lies in the middle of the valley and has a maximum depth of 111 ft (34 m). Farther down the valley is large, shallow Lake Fryzell, its deepest point about 62 ft (19 m) below the surface. In this lake, relatively fresh water floats atop brackish water. Algal, bacterial, and microbial mats flourish here.

In Wright Valley, the Onyx River—the longest stream in the McMurdo Dry Valleys—flows into

Lake Vanda, reputedly one of the clearest lakes in the world. (The Onyx River is approximately 18.5 mi [30 km] long and flows only 6–10 weeks each year.) Lake Vanda has surprisingly warm water below its cap of ice and supports microbial mats and even some plankters. The uppermost layer averages almost 45°F (7°C); at depths below 158 ft (48 m), the temperature increases to 77°F (25°C). Maximum depth is 223 ft (68 m). The deepest water is a calcium chloride brine lacking oxygen. Higher up the valley, at 530 ft (162 m) asl, is hypersaline Don Juan Pond, which never freezes over. This water body measures 328 ft × 984 ft × 4 in deep (100 m × 300 m × 10 cm). Fed by groundwater but losing water via evaporation, the concentration of calcium chloride in its waters (> 600 ppt) is near the saturation point. It has been estimated that the temperature would have to be lowered to –61°F (–51.8°C) for the water to freeze.

Victoria Valley is the site of a large hypersaline lake, Lake Vida, once believed to be frozen solid. Later a large pool of sodium chloride brine was discovered beneath 65 ft (19.8 m) of ice. Although it has been cut off from the atmosphere for 3,000 years and lacks oxygen, the pool hosts a community of bacteria. The National Aerospace and Space Administration (NASA) sees the lake's extreme habitat as comparable to what may be found in the subsurface waters of Saturn's moon Enceladus and Jupiter's moon Europa.

Protected Areas. The entire Antarctic region is protected and managed by the international Antarctic Treaty System.

Environmental Issues. Contamination by scientists working in the valleys is always a potential threat.

See also Antarctica

Further Reading

Doran, Peter T., W. Berry Lyons, and Diane M. McKnight. 2005. "Introduction." In *Life in Antarctic Deserts and other Cold Dry Environments: Astrobiological Analogs*, edited by Peter T. Doran, W. Berry Lyons, and Diane M. McKnight, 1–8. New York: Cambridge University Press.

"Environment." 2013. McMurdo Dry Valleys. http://www.mcmurdodryvalleys.aq/environment

"Explanation Offered for Antarctica's 'Blood Falls.'" 2003. Science News. http://www.sciencedaily.com/releases/2003/11/031105064856.htm

Mikuki, Jill, W. Berry Lyons, Ian Hawes, Brian D. Lanoil, and Peter T. Doran. 2005. "Saline Lakes and Ponds in the McMurdo Dry Valleys: Ecological Analogs to Martian Paleolake Environments." In *Life in Antarctic Deserts and other Cold Dry Environments: Astrobiological Analogs*, edited by Peter T. Doran, W. Berry Lyons, and Diane McKnight, 160–194. New York: Cambridge University Press.

"Scientists Find Ancient Microbes in Antarctic Lake." 2012. Jet Propulsion Laboratory, California Institute of Technology. http://www.jpl.nasa.gov/news/news.php?release=2012–382

Mediterranean Sea

Geographic Overview. The Mediterranean Sea, linking three continents, has played a major role in Western civilization for thousands of years. Its shores touch several countries in Europe, western Asia, and northern Africa. The sea has a rich biodiversity and several unique and endangered habitats. It supports 30 percent of international maritime freight traffic, and the region is a major tourist destination.

Geographic Coordinates. Approximately 30°–45°N, 05°E–35°E

Description. The Mediterranean is a body of saltwater enclosed by continents but open to the ocean via the Strait of Gibraltar, which is less than 1,050 ft (320 m) deep. Although Gibraltar is the only natural outlet to the ocean, the Dardanelles and the Bosporus Straits, 655 ft (200 m) and 165 ft (50 m) deep respectively, lead to the land-locked Black Sea. The excavated Suez Canal has afforded access to the Red Sea since 1869. The Mediterranean is fed by many rivers, including the Po from Italy, the Rhone from France, the Ebro from Spain, and the Nile from Egypt.

The Mediterranean Sea stretches 2,360 mi (3,800 km) from the Strait of Gibraltar, between Spain and Morocco, east to Syria, and separates Europe from Africa. Its north–south extent varies because of the configuration of adjacent continents. The surface covers approximately 1,146,420 mi² (2,969,000 km²), and the sea holds approximately 1,428,682 mi³ (3,700,000 km³) of water. Total coastline is approximately 28,600 mi (46,000 km), 40 percent of which is around islands. The sea has a mean depth of 4,920 ft (1,500 m), with a maximum depth of more than

16,400 ft (5,000 m). Some shorelines have steep relief from the sea floor to adjacent continental mountains. The sea has several large islands, such as Corsica, Sardinia, Sicily, the Balearic Islands, Crete, Cypress, and Rhodes, and numerable small islands, all primarily along the European coast.

Within its two main basins, western and eastern, separated at the Strait of Sicily by a 1,300 ft (400 m) deep ridge between Sicily and Tunisia, the Mediterranean seafloor is complex. Steep relief separates several seas or basins, the Balearic and Tyrrhenian in the west and the Ionian, Adriatic, Aegean, and Levantine in the east. The western basin is characterized by deep water, often more than 8,200 ft (2,500 m) deep, even close to shore. The Balearic Basin is the area west of Corsica and Sardinia, southeast of the Balearic Islands, and north of Algeria. The Alboran Basin, between Spain and Morocco, is a western subdivision of the Balearic Basin. The Balearic Basin is a flat abyssal plain, approximately 9,850 ft (3,000 m) deep that was downfaulted. Its deep sediment layers cover thin oceanic crust. The Tyrrhenian Basin, located between Sardinia, Sicily, and Italy, is a smaller abyssal plain, approximately 11,500 ft (3,500 m) deep, and underlain by thin oceanic crust covered by sediments. Its surface is interrupted by elongated north–south trending seamounts. The Eastern Basin is larger with even deeper sections. The deepest, 16,802 ft (5,121 m), is in the Hellenic Trench in the Ionian Sea south of the Greek Peloponnesus. Continental shelf areas, mainly in the Adriatic and Aegean Seas, with relatively shallow water less than 2,000 ft (610 m) deep, are more extensive than in the western Mediterranean. The Aegean Sea floor, underlain by continental crust (not oceanic), is block faulted with a number of interconnected basins. The southeastern edge of the Levantine Basin, the biggest basin as deep as 16,000 ft (4,900 m), parallels a narrow continental shelf off northern Egypt. North of the deep basins, the eastern seafloor has a complicated topography of mountains and islands. The Mediterranean Ridge forms an arc of underwater mountain chains, from the Peloponnesus south of Crete stretching to Cypress.

Circulation of water is complex. A single outlet to the ocean and the configuration of islands and basins both play a major role in currents, temperature, and salinity. Atlantic water enters through Gibraltar and flows east along northern Africa as the Algerian Current. One branch heads north at Sicily into the Tyrrhenian Sea, continuing west off France and southern Spain to the Balearic Sea. The other branch continues east along the African coast, past the Ionian Basin to the Levantine Basin on the eastern side of the Mediterranean. Because more evaporation occurs on the east side in the Levantine Basin, the salt content increases and the heavier saltwater sinks. It then flows subsurface west to the Strait of Sicily, turns north and follows the Italian, French, and Spanish coasts to exit at Gibraltar. Within the general circulation are more localized gyres, which may be both large and seasonal.

The Mediterranean Sea gives its name to climates having hot, dry summers, and mild, rainy winters with moderate precipitation. The south and southeast shores are deserts. Because of strong winds and aridity, evaporation is high. Although more water evaporates than can be replaced by precipitation and river inflow, Atlantic water through the Strait of Gibraltar keeps the salinity of the Mediterranean Sea similar to that of the Atlantic Ocean.

Geologic History. Details of the geological development of the Mediterranean Sea are not totally understood. The western part of the modern Mediterranean Sea occupies a former suture zone between Eurasia and Gondwana (Africa) that was later rifted apart, while the eastern part may be a remnant of the Mesozoic Tethys Sea. The geologic history spans a time frame from the Mesozoic into the Tertiary. The Tethys Sea was a wedge-shaped embayment, primarily east of what is now Italy, between Laurasia and Gondwana at the edge of Pangaea. When Pangaea broke up in the Mesozoic, Africa and western Europe rifted apart, opening the western part of the Mediterranean and creating oceanic crust. At the same time, the Tethys Sea in the eastern part began to close due to the counterclockwise rotation of Africa and convergence with Eurasia, culminating in the collision that resulted in the Alpine orogeny in the Tertiary. Microplates broken off from Africa in the eastern Mediterranean then pushed into Europe to form the Alps, Apennines, Dinaric Alps, and other mountains ranges in southeastern Europe. The configuration of the various microplates may have prevented total closure of the eastern Tethys

Sea. After the Tethys Sea subducted, the Mediterranean region was cut off from the ocean and became an evaporation basin, creating a salt desert until the Atlantic flowed in through the Strait of Gibraltar.

The origin of the deep basins in the Mediterranean is highly controversial. The largest and deepest basin in the western Mediterranean is the Balearic Basin, bounded by normal faults and downfaulted. A rift, or split, developed in the Alboran microplate, the northwestern part of Africa. Its northern half became part of Europe, the Baetic Cordillera in southern Spain. The southern half forms the Rif in northern Morocco, the Tellian Atlas Mountains in northern Algeria, and the Mountains of Sicily and Calabria in Italy. At times the basin was covered by a shallow, very saline sea or a brackish lake, which resulted in thick layers of evaporite deposits, such as salt. The basin's oceanic crust is covered with sedimentary deposits to a depth of more than 3 mi (5 km), including evaporites. At the end of the Tertiary, the Gilbraltar Strait developed, allowing the Atlantic to flood the Balearic Basin as well as the rest of the Mediterranean. Weight of the water induced faulting and subsidence of as much as 3,300 ft (1,000 m). The Tyrrhenian Basin also originated by rifting in the Tertiary and has the remains of several volcanoes, seamounts, beneath the water surface. Sediments are thicker on the periphery than in the center of the basin. It is possible that all Tethys Sea oceanic crust in this area may not have been subducted by the end of the early Tertiary (Eocene), due to the triangular configuration of the sea between the microplates of Corsica, Italy, and Sicily.

The Eastern Mediterranean is a complex area of several microplates, parts of both Eurasia and Africa, with both subduction and spreading zones. Crustal structure is difficult to discern because of deep overlying sediments, as much as 10 mi (16 km) thick, over 4.3 mi (7 km) thick oceanic crust. The eastern and southern edges of the Mediterranean Sea are stable continental margins, while the northern margin is active. This remnant of the Mesozoic Tethys Sea continues to subduct beneath the many microplates to the north, with a subduction zone curving south of the Peloponnesus, Crete, and Cyprus. The seafloor physiography is dominated by an arc-shaped submarine mountain range, the Mediterranean Ridge, which

consists of a number of parallel chains. Southwest of the Ridge is the Ionian Abyssal Plain. Southeast, between the Ridge and the Nile River delta is the Levantine Basin. Both the Adriatic Sea and the Aegean Sea are flooded portions of the European continent. The Adriatic is a crustal depression associated with the uplifted Apennine Mountains. The Aegean Sea is a marginal sea behind the island arc associated with the subduction zone. In the early Miocene, the area was an emergent part of Europe. It began to subside in the mid- to late Miocene and is now part of the Mediterranean Sea. It became separated from the Black Sea during the Pliocene and Quaternary. The Aegean Sea may continue to subside and become a deep basin like the Tyrrhenian.

Biota. The Mediterranean Sea is oligotrophic, rich in oxygen and poor in nutrients. Although the Mediterranean occupies just 0.82 percent of the world's ocean area and contains 0.32 percent of the world's ocean volume, it supports 7 percent of the world's marine species. Approximately 17,000 species have been identified, and many areas have not been fully explored. Its basin is one of 34 biodiversity hotspots in the world, with a high degree of endemism. The high diversity and distribution within the Mediterranean can be explained by geologic history and the interface of temperate and tropical biomes. The Mesozoic Tethys Sea, which was open to the Indo-Pacific Ocean until the convergence of Africa with Eurasia, contained tropical species. When the Mediterranean was also cut off from the Atlantic Ocean at the end of the Miocene, it became an evaporation basin, with the result that most of the Indo-Pacific biota were unable to survive. The flooding of the Atlantic through the Strait of Gibraltar brought new species into the Mediterranean. Climate fluctuations during the Pleistocene allowed both boreal and subtropical species to colonize the sea. The opening of the Suez Canal allowed tropical species from the Red Sea to colonize the warmer eastern basin, which is too warm for most Atlantic biota to thrive. The western basin is the most species rich, with numbers declining toward the eastern basin. More than 50 percent of marine species are from the Atlantic, 4 percent are relict tropical, and 17 percent are from the Red Sea, with 20–30 percent endemics.

Biological production decreases west to east and north to south, inversely related to temperature and salinity. Biodiversity and density vary with habitat. Coastal wetlands, such as lagoons and estuaries, serving as nurseries, feeding areas, and wintering sites for birds, have high biodiversity. Most of the biota in the Mediterranean, 90 percent of plant species and 75 percent of fish species, is concentrated along the shore in water 0–165 ft (0–50 m) deep, where photosynthesis is concentrated. Phytoplankton numbers are low, but zooplankton are plentiful. Coastal waters support approximately 1,000 species of macrophytes and almost 6,000 species of benthic invertebrate species, such as sponges, bryozoan, molluscs, and echinoderms. Larger animals or vertebrates include more than 600 fish species, three reptile species, 33 nesting bird species, and 22 mammals. Although the deep sea, below photosynthetic levels, is largely unexplored, it has important habitats such as canyons, hydrothermal springs, cold water corals, and seamounts. The open sea, more than 12 nautical miles from shore, has pockets of high productivity, such as gyres and upwellings, and supports predators such as sharks, rays, cetaceans, and marine turtles.

Environmental Issues. As of 2010, nonnative or invasive species, particularly molluscs, fish, benthic plants, and crustaceans, numbered approximately 1,000 and numbers are increasing. More than 500 species are well established, while others are only occasionally seen. Not all are invasive. Nonnative species in the eastern basin are predominantly from the Red Sea via the Suez Canal, while nonnative species in the western basin originate from maritime transportation and fish farming. Nonnative species threaten endemics and may cause the reduction of genetic diversity. Climate warming may result in elimination of boreal species and favoring of introduced tropical species from the Red Sea.

See also Aeolian Islands; Apennine Mountains; Black Sea and Sea of Azov; Dinaric Alps; European Alps; Mount Etna; Peloponnesus; Strait of Gibraltar; Venice Lagoon

Further Reading

Bazairi, H. et al., editors. RAC/SPA, Tunis. 2010. *The Mediterranean Sea Biodiversity: State of the Ecosystems, Pressures, Impacts and Future Priorities.* UNEP-MAP RAC/SPA. www.rac-spa.org/sites/default/files/doc_cop/biodiversity.pdf

Nairm, Alan E. M., William H. Kanes, and Francis G. Stehli, editors. 1977. *The Ocean Basins and Margins, Volume 4A—The Eastern Mediterranean, Volume 4B—The Western Mediterranean.* New York: Plenum Press.

OCA/CNES. 2000. "The Mediterranean Sea." Extract from educational CD-ROM. *The Geonauts Inquire into the Oceans.* www-g.oca.eu/cerga/gmc/kids/cd/pdfus/Med.pdf

Mekong River

China, Myanmar, Laos, Thailand, Cambodia, and Vietnam

Geographic Overview. The Mekong River, one of the largest and most important rivers in Southeast Asia, flows through or forms the boundary for six countries, each of which refers to it by a different name. The river basin provides food, drinking water, irrigation, transportation, and energy to more than 60 million people. Approximately half of the course of the Mekong River is in China, the remaining half in or bordering Myanmar (Burma), Laos, Thailand, Cambodia, and Vietnam. The river played a major role during the Vietnam War.

Geographic Coordinates. Source: 33°43'N, 94°42'E; Mouth: 09°48'N, 106°36'E

Description. The Mekong River originates on the eastern side of the Tibetan Plateau. Draining a 307,000 mi² (795,000 km²) basin, the Mekong flows generally south for approximately 3,000 mi (4,800 km) to the South China Sea. It was formerly part of a larger, integrated system with other Southeast Asia rivers, now submerged beneath the South China Sea due to sea level rise since the close of the Pleistocene. Although in places, the river flows through an abundance of alluvial deposits, the river's course appears to remain structurally controlled.

The Mekong rises in Lasagongma spring on Mount Guozongmucha in the Tanggula Range in Qinghai Province, eastern Tibet, at approximately 16,725 ft (5,100 m) asl. Both its origin and its upper course are between the Chang Jiang to the northeast and the Salween River to the southwest. The Mekong flows more than 620 mi (1,000 km) south and southeast through China, confined to valleys more than 3,300 ft (1,000 m) deep between high ridges. The upper course is characterized by a steep gradient and many waterfalls. The Chinese call it Lan Tsan Chiang or Lancang, meaning turbulent river.

Upon leaving China, the Mekong briefly forms the border between Myanmar and Laos before turning eastward toward the center of northern Laos. From the China border to just upstream of Vientiane, the Mekong flows on a variety of rocks, including granitic rocks, folded sedimentary and metamorphic rocks, and locally exposed volcanics. The river flows through a region of narrow parallel ridges, oriented north–south and separated by deep valleys where local relief is 2,000–4,000 ft (600–1,200 m). The river alternately flows in straight narrow valleys before turning to flow in deep river gorges through the ridges. Just upstream from Luangphragang, the river makes a large hairpin bend and turns south. Upon reaching Thailand, the river forms the border between Thailand and Laos. An alluvial section begins near Vientiane, where a low gradient produces a meandering and braided channel 0.6 mi (1 km) wide. A short distance past Vientiane, the river flows northeast, then turns east and winds along the foothills to reach the Annamite Range forming the backbone of Vietnam. The river turns south for most of the rest of its course, paralleling the Annamite chain to its east and again flows in long straight reaches separated by sharp bends. Low flow exposes bedrock islands. South of Savannakhet, Laos, the river, 0.9–1.9 mi (1.5–3.0 km) wide with rocky islands, flows in a steep rock-cut channel of Mesozoic sedimentary rocks. Downstream, the river narrows to less than 0.6 mi (1 km), with hairpin bends, sharp turns, rock exposures, rapids, and whirlpools. Where the river leaves the border of Thailand, it is joined on the right bank by a major tributary, the Mun, from the Khorat Upland in Thailand. Below the Mun, the river flows between steep alluvial banks, either as a straight channel or breaking into two or more channels around rocky islands. Just north of the Cambodian border, the so-called 4,000 Islands area, the Mekong cuts through Mesozoic basalt. In this reach, the river is more than 9 mi (15 km) wide, and the rock-cored islands are covered with alluvium. At the border with Cambodia is a 6 mi (10 km) stretch of rapids and falls, known as

Khone Falls, where the river drops 72 ft (22 m). The pattern of different channels, rock islands, and rapids continues into Cambodia. The river in the lowlands of Cambodia, where the gradient is gentle and depth no more than 16.4 ft (5 m), the 1.9 mi (3 km) wide channel meanders over a thick sandy bed and builds a wide floodplain. Three large tributaries, the Srepok, San, and Kong drain the Annamite range and join the Mekong on its left bank in Cambodia.

At Phnom Penh, Cambodia, Tonle Sap River, from the lake of the same name, joins the Mekong on the right bank. Tonle Sap Lake, the largest lake in Southeast Asia, seasonally varies in size and serves as a natural reservoir. During floods, water from the Mekong flows into the lake; during the dry season, water returns to the Mekong. Also at Phnom Penh, the first distributary, the Bassac, leaves the Mekong main stem but parallels it into the delta in southern Vietnam. The active delta, however, begins at the Vietnam border, where the river has a typically low gradient, several distributary channels, alluvial deposition, and wetlands. The delta covers approximately 75,000 mi^2 (194,250 km^2). The tidal range at the mouth is 10.5 ft (3.2 m), and tidal influence is felt upstream to Phnom Penh. Ho Chi Minh City (Saigon), slightly northeast of the delta, is connected to the river by a barge canal.

The watershed is predominantly rural and agricultural. Although ocean traffic is able to go upstream as far as Phnom Penh, rapids and waterfalls along much of the river's route limit river traffic to local use and short distances. The river is navigable north to Luangphragang, Laos. Many small falls and rapids around Khone Falls are now dammed. Although the river receives May snowmelt from Tibet, the Mekong is primarily rain-fed. The lower half of the Mekong River, influenced by monsoon rains, contributes approximately 75 percent of the total flow, compared with 25 percent from the dry Tibetan Plateau. Approximately 80 percent of its flow comes from monsoon rains in June through November. Mean annual discharge is approximately 16,774 billion ft^3 (475 billion m^3).

The highest rainfall along the Mekong's course is 80–160 in (2,000–4,000 mm) in the north and east of Southeast Asia, tapering to approximately 40 in (1,000 mm) in the western and southern lowlands. The Tibetan plateau receives 26 in (650 mm), and freezing temperatures occur as far south as northern Laos. The remainder of Southeast Asia is tropical and warm to hot.

Biota. Due to a variety of landforms and habitats, the drainage area of the Mekong River is one of the most biologically diverse in the world. Ecosystems include upland plateau, evergreen forests, grasslands, savannas, wetlands, and riparian. The basin houses approximately 20,000 plant species, 1,200 bird species, eight reptiles and amphibians, and 430 mammal species. Species are still being discovered, 1,059 from 1997 to 2007. Most of the forest in the primarily rural watershed has been converted to shifting agriculture in the highlands or to rice paddies in the lowlands. The river basin in Southeast Asia has the legacies of war, such as bomb craters and landmines. Because of napalm and agent orange, most trees are less than 20 years old.

The river and its tributaries support 1,300 species of fish, a major source of protein for Southeast Asians. Tonle Sap is not only the center of the world's most productive inland fishery, but also a biodiversity hotspot. Fish species include carp, herring, threadfin, catfish, murrels, and snakehead. Some fish species, such as giant catfish and giant carp, reach 10 ft (3 m) in length.

Environmental Issues. Although the river has undergone water management projects for centuries, such as those implemented by the Khmer Rouge, it remained largely uncontrolled until the 20th century. Plans for more than 50 giant hydroelectric dams and diversion schemes were sidelined during the Vietnam War and aftermath in the 1960s and 1970s. Interest in managing the river, renewed since the 1980s peace, constitutes the greatest threat to the Mekong River system. China has completed seven of several proposed dam projects in Yunnan Province. As Southeast Asian countries modernize, demand for hydroelectric power will increase. Development in Southeast Asia is overseen by the Mekong River Commission (Cambodia, Thailand, Laos, and Vietnam).

Other issues include deforestation, sand mining for construction, overfishing, pollution, and climate change.

Protected Areas. The major protected areas are in China. Three Parallel Rivers of Yunnan Protected Areas (where the Salween, Mekong, and Chiang Jiang are close but run parallel) and Tonle Sap are Biosphere Reserves. Sanjiangyuan National Nature Reserve protects the headwaters of the Huang He, Chiang Jiang, and Mekong Rivers.

Further Reading

Douglas, Ian. 2005. "The Mekong River Basin." In *The Physical Geography of Southeast Asia*, edited by Avijit Gupta, 193–218. Oxford: Oxford University Press.

Great River Partnership. 2013. *Mekong River Basin*. http://www.greatriverspartnership.org/en-us/asiapacific/mekong/pages/default.aspx

Gupta, Avijit. 2005. "Rivers of Southeast Asia." In *The Physical Geography of Southeast Asia*, edited by Avijit Gupta, 65–79. Oxford: Oxford University Press.

Menabe Antimena Protected Area

Madagascar

Geographic Overview. Menabe Antimena Protected Area, formerly known as Central Menabe, is one of the larger blocks of western Madagascar dry forest, an ecosystem more fragile than rainforest because it takes more time to regenerate due to dry conditions. In addition to housing the giant jumping rat, it is a center of local endemism and diversity.

Geographic Coordinates. Approximately 20°S–21°S; 44°E–45°E

Description. The dry forest of Menabe Antimena, a small remnant of what once covered much of western Madagascar, is an area that has seen extensive research. In addition to dry forest, the Menabe Antimena Protected Area, between the Tomitsy River in the south and the Tsirbihina River in the north, includes humid zones, wetlands, and coastal mangroves. The forested Kirindy Private Reserve, 60–130 ft (18–40 m) asl, is 31 mi (50 km) northeast of Morondava and 12 mi (20 km) inland from the coast. Kirindy Mitea National Park is 56 mi (90 km) south of Morondava. It protects a wide variety of ecosystems—tropical dry deciduous forest, littoral spiny forest, coastal mangroves, grassy dunes, beaches, seven small islands, and coral reefs.

The tropical dry climate has two distinct seasons. December through March is rainy and hot, with temperatures as high as 104°F (40°C). Heavy rains may render several areas inaccessible. Rain, however, is variable; any one area may receive more than one-third of its annual total, 30 in (775 mm), in a 10 day downpour. From the end of March through January, temperatures average 59°–77°F (15°–25°C), and little to no rain falls. During the dry season, the forest is leafless, and many reptiles and small mammals hibernate.

Biota. The rich biodiversity of Menabe Antimena has a mixture of southern and western biotas and several locally endemic species of high conservation importance. Plant adaptations to water stress include small leaves, spines, and thick stems or branches. The forest is stratified into canopy, intermediate, and undergrowth layers, with no herbaceous layer. In general, the forest canopy trees are deciduous, flowering before leaves emerge. The most distinctive plants on very dry soils are species of *Commiphora*, *Dalbergia*, and *Delonix*, along with several others. Dry forest trees reach 40–50 ft (12–15 m) tall. Soils along rivers and wetlands that are occasionally flooded are dominated by *Albizia* species, *Colubrina decipiens*, *Dalbergia geveana*, and others, with trees as tall as 82 ft (25 m). An undergrowth of bamboo and *Pandanus* is common on periodically flooded sites. Geophytes, such as *Amorphophallus*, *Dioscorea*, and *Tacca*, along with lianas are locally abundant.

The region is the only home for the giant jumping rat (*Hypogeomys antimena*) and is the last stronghold for several vertebrate taxa native to the western deciduous forest. Endemic birds include the Madagascar Teal (*Anas bernieri*) and Humblot's Heron (*Ardea humbloti*). The side-necked turtle, also called big-headed turtle (*Erymnochelys madagascariensis*), is endemic.

The forest canopy at Kirindy Private Reserve is dominated by tall baobabs, such as *Adansonia rubrostipa* and *Adansonia za*, 46 ft (14 m) tall, and several local endemics. Of the seven lemur species, the most common are common brown lemur (*Eulemur fulvus*) and Verreaux's sifaka (*Propithicus verreauxi*). Nocturnal lemurs include Coquerel's giant mouse (*Mirza coquereli*), pygmy mouse (*Microcebus myoxinus*), gray mouse (*Microcebus murinus*), western

fat-tailed dwarf (*Cheirogaleus medius*), and red-tailed sportive (*Lepilemur ruficaudatus*). The world's smallest primate, Berthe's mouse lemur (*Microcebus berthae*) at 1.1 oz (31 g), first described in 1994, is found only in Kirindy Private Reserve, which is also the best place to see the carnivorous fossas. Several species of bats, tenrecs, mongooses, and rodents are other mammals found in Kirindy. Bird species number 40, reptiles 50, and amphibians 15.

Kirindy Mitea National Park protects three baobab species and seven mangrove species. The park boasts the greatest density of primates in the world. Verreaux's sifaka, ring-tailed lemur (*Lemur catta*), red-tailed sportive lemur, and pale fork-marked lemur (*Phaner pallescens*) are among its 11 species of mammals.

Protected Areas. International and local conservation efforts beginning in 2000 resulted in protected status in 2006 for the region known as Menabe Antimena, named after the giant jumping rat. Kirindy Private Reserve, Centre de Formation Professionelle Forestiere (CFPF), is a private forest covering 40 mi² (100 km²). The CFPF maintains a forestry concession for research. The 280 mi² (722 km²) of Kirindy Mitea National Park, which was established in 1997 and opened to the public in 2006, sees few visitors.

Environmental Issues. The forest has undergone a long period of exploitation, and much has been converted to secondary and/or fallow forest and savanna. Villagers are dependent on the forest for timber

---

Avenue of the Baobabs

The Avenue of the Baobabs, where 20–25 giant trees line a short stretch of dirt road and others emerge from adjacent fields east of Morondava, is the iconic symbol of Madagascar. Once part of a dense dry tropical forest, these smooth-barked trees now stand alone because the forest was used for wood products and the land converted to agriculture. These Grandidieri's baobab (*Adansonia grandidieri*), as old as 800 years, reach 100 ft (30 m) tall with circumferences more than 66 ft (20 m). The Avenue is one of Madagascar's most visited sites and is classified as a National Monument.

products, agricultural land, medicine, food, and fuel. Several development projects in Kirindy Mitea National Park and CFPF involve providing alternatives to slash and burn agriculture, promoting sustainable methods of forest exploitation, or establishing infrastructure for ecotourism. Feral dogs and cats pose a danger to the giant jumping rat.

See also Madagascar; Western Madagascar Wetlands

Further Reading

Durrel Conservation Programme. 2013. "Central Menabe." http://www.durrell.org/library/conservation_report/contentbb84.html?s=3&c=34

Sorg, J.-P., J. U. Ganzhorn, and P. M. Kappeler. 2003. "Forestry and Research in the Kirindy Forest/Centre de Formation Professionnelle Forestiere." In *The Natural History of Madagascar*, edited by Steven M. Goodman and Jonathan P. Benstead, 1512–1519. Chicago: University of Chicago Press.

Trevelyan, Rosie and TBA Staff. 2007. *Primates and Other Mammals of Kirindy*. Tropical Biology Association Field Guides. Cambridge and Nairobi. http://www.tropical-biology.org/resources/site_guides.htm

Mesopotamia, Tigris River, and Euphrates River

Iraq, Turkey, and Syria

Geographic Overview. Mesopotamia, meaning "land between the rivers," is often called the cradle of civilization because it was the homeland for several ancient kingdoms, including Sumeria, Babylonia, and Assyria, and has many historical and archaeological sites. The Tigris and Euphrates are among the world's most famous rivers, and their marshes are the largest wetland in the Middle East. The Euphrates River was considered the eastern limit of Roman rule, and the region has biblical importance. The area has been an agricultural region in the desert Middle East for thousands of years. The region continues to be a focal point in world affairs.

Geographic Coordinates. Mesopotamia: 29° 50'N–35°30'N, 42°00'E–48°34'E; Euphrates River; Source–38°48'N, 38°45'E; Mouth–31°01'N, 47°25'E; Tigris River: Source–38°29'N, 39°24'E; Mouth–31°01'N, 47°25'E; Shattal-Arab: Source–35°32'N, 42°53'E; Mouth–29°51'N, 48°45'E

Description. The combined drainage basin for the Tigris and Euphrates Rivers, both of which originate in eastern Turkey, is approximately 340,000 mi^2 (880,000 km^2). Both rivers flow generally southeast toward the Persian Gulf. Elevations in their headwaters are approximately 8,200 ft (2,500 m), with a steep gradient. Mean elevation in their lower reaches is 650 ft (200 m), with a very low gradient. After approaching each other near Baghdad, Iraq, the rivers flow parallel in their lower courses but are connected by many canals. They merge at Qurnah to form the Shatt al Arab, which develops a delta and continues to the Persian Gulf.

Two streams in the Taurus Mountains of eastern Turkey merge, at approximately 3,770 ft (1,150 m) asl at Lake Hazar, to become the Tigris River, which then flows 1,150 mi (1,850 km) to meet the Euphrates. As it flows southeast, the Tigris briefly forms the border with Syria and enters Iraq at the triple border with Turkey and Syria. South of Baghdad, the bed of the Tigris River is several feet higher than that of the Euphrates, facilitating gravity-fed irrigation between the rivers.

Two headstreams, the Kara and Murat rivers, originating on the Anatolian Plateau in east-central Turkey, join to create the Euphrates at Keban Dam, approximately 2,000 ft (610 m) asl. The river flows approximately 1,300 mi (2,100 km) southeast to meet the Tigris River. The Euphrates first flows south through Turkey, its upper reaches through steep, narrow gorges. Below Euphrates (Tabqa) Dam in northern Syria and after being joined by its two major tributaries, the Belkh and Khabur, it begins to flow southeast across the Syrian Desert and into Iraq. In its lower course, the gradient is low and the river becomes sluggish, with shifting channels through marshlands and lakes.

Shatt al Arab, which begins just above Basra, Iraq, divides into two arms to flow 120 mi (195 km) southeast to the Persian Gulf. The western arm is a narrow inlet, while the eastern is navigable, passing the port of Khorramshahr, Iran. After the channelized Karun River, which originates in the Zagros Mountains, converges with the eastern arm, the river passes the major oil center of Abadan, Iran, and continues to the gulf. The shifting channels of the Shatt al Arab in the delta region define the broad border between Iraq and Iran, triggering boundary disputes. The delta is a complex of marshes, channels, lakes, and islands.

Agricultural fertility in the lowland between the rivers, Mesopotamia, is renewed by silt deposited when the rivers flood. Ancient kingdoms constructed waterworks for both irrigation and drainage, which allowed the land to be cultivated for thousands of years.

The rivers and their tributaries are controlled for water withdrawal and for production of electricity. Ataturk Dam, completed in 1990, is the largest of a series of several dams along the upper courses of both the Euphrates and Tigris Rivers and their tributaries in Turkey, for both electricity generation and irrigation as part of the Southeastern Anatolia Project. The Euphrates Dam at Tabqa, southeast of Aleppo in Syria, is the main unit of another set of dams for both irrigation and electricity. Iraq built Samara Dam on the Tigris, part of the Wadi Ath Tharthar Scheme to control floods and manage the water supply. The Tharthar is a natural depression between the rivers, now used for storage of floodwater.

The Tigris is navigable by small boats and rafts for most of its length. Tidal currents provide channels deep enough for ocean-going vessels to travel upstream to Basra, 60 mi (95 km) inland, and some steamer traffic is possible up to Baghdad. As improvements are made in road and rail systems, the Tigris becomes less important for transportation.

The subtropical desert of Mesopotamia, with a dry-summer mediterranean influence, is hot and arid. Summer daytime temperatures reach 104°–122°F (40–50°C). Winters are mild, averaging 41°F (5°C), with highs sometimes reaching the 70°s F (20°s C). Winter has a brief rainy season with at most 8 in (200 mm) of precipitation.

Biota. Adjacent desert supports only xeric scrub. The delta marshland is covered by reeds (*Phragmites*), papyrus (*Cyperus*), and rushes (*Typha*). Giant reeds, 20 ft (6 m) tall, are harvested for human and livestock food, fuel, weaving material, and for house and boat construction. Unique wildlife includes the Euphrates soft-shell turtle (*Trionyx euphraticus*), Mesopotamia spiny-tailed lizard (*Saara loricata*), and Mesopotamian gerbil (*Gerbillus mesopotamiae*). Smooth-coated otter (*Lutraperspicillata maxwelli maxwelli*) and Bunn's short-tailed bandicoot rat (*Erythronesokia bunnii*) may be extinct. The delta wetlands are important breeding and wintering grounds for migratory birds and support Iraq Babbler (*Turdoides altirostris*) and almost all of the world's population of Basra Reed Warbler (*Acrocephalus giseldis*).

Fish fauna are dominated (75 percent) by cyprinids, members of the carp family. Marine visitors from the Persian Gulf to the brackish lower reaches of the delta may include bull shark (*Carcharhinus leucas*), Hilsa shad (*Tenualosa ilisha*), and yellowfin seabream (*Acanthopagrus latus*). Shrimp and shad are important commercial food species.

Protected Areas. Shadegan Marshes in southern Iran are a Ramsar Site of International Importance. The Central Marshes of Iraq were declared its first national park in July 2013.

Environmental Issues. Canals today are silting up and soils are becoming increasingly saline, a problem that ancient civilizations may have also dealt with. Increased water withdrawal on the Tigris and Euphrates may increase salinity of the Shatt al Arab, damage the reed marsh ecosystem, and promote saltwater intrusion. Dams and water withdrawal upstream threaten water availability downstream, especially in Iraq. Irreplaceable archaeological sites have been inundated by reservoirs. Considerable marshland was drained under Saddam Hussein's regime. Due to ongoing conflicts, restoration efforts are underway on only a limited scale.

See also Anatolian Plateau; Persian Gulf

Further Reading

Aquastat. 2013. *Euphrates–Tigris River Basin*. Food and Agricultural Organization of the United Nations. http://www.fao.org/nr/water/aquastat/basins/euphrates-tigris/index.stm

Coad, Brian. 2013. "Lower Tigris & Euphrates." *Freshwater Ecoregions of the World*. World Wildlife Fund and the Nature Conservancy. http://www.feow.org/ecoregions/details/lower_tigris_euphrates

Penn, James R. 2001. *Rivers of the World*. Santa Barbara, CA: ABC-CLIO.

Meteor Crater

United States (Arizona)

Geographic Overview. Located on the Colorado Plateau about 35 mi (56 km) east of Flagstaff, Arizona,

Meteor Crater is not the largest of its kind but it was the first proven to be a meteorite impact site and is one of the best preserved on Earth. Meteor Crater is so similar to craters on the moon that the site was used to train *Apollo* astronauts for their lunar mission.

Geographic Coordinates. 35°02'N, 111°01'W

Description. Meteor Crater, also called Barringer Meteorite Crater, is a circular depression in the sandstone and limestone of northern Arizona. The impact of a large meteorite left a crater more than 4,000 ft (1,219 m) in diameter and 2.4 mi (3.9 km) in circumference. Although the crater floor is 700 ft (213 m) below the rim, it is only about 550 ft (168 m) deep because it is partially filled in with broken rock.

Long believed by geologists to be a volcanic crater, the concept of a meteorite impact was not seriously considered, except by a mining engineer, until 1929. Beginning in 1902, Daniel Barringer dug extensive shafts through the crater in search of the iron meteorite he believed lay beneath the surface. He was not successful because the meteorite had been destroyed upon impact. Two minerals, derived from highly crystallized or "shocked" quartz from tremendous pressure, found at Meteor Crater are now the diagnostic for determining meteorite impacts. Upheaval Dome, in Canyonlands National Park, southeastern Utah, was believed for years to be a salt dome. Since 1995, new evidence, such as the absence of salt beneath the surface and less rock deformation with depth, suggested something different. With the discovery of shocked quartz grains, the conclusion is that Upheaval Dome is also a meteorite impact crater.

Geologic History. The meteor, probably a piece of asteroid from the Asteroid Belt, sped toward Earth approximately 50,000 years ago at a speed of 16,000 mph (25,750 kmph). It was about 150 ft (15 m) in

Minerals discovered at Meteor Crater, Arizona, the impact site of a nickel-iron meteorite that fell to Earth 49,000 years ago, have become significant in identifying meteor impacts elsewhere on Earth. (Walter Arce/Dreamstime.com)

diameter, composed of iron and nickel, and weighed thousands of tons. Very little of the mass was destroyed in the few seconds it took to go through Earth's atmosphere. The pressure at impact was more than 20 million lb per in^2 (1.4 million kg per cm^2), which melted or vaporized both meteorite and surface rock under the impact and pulverized the surrounding surface rock. A cloud of molten rock and solid debris, ranging in size from microscopic pieces up to 100 ft (30 m) across, blew into the atmosphere, raining down on the impact zone. The force of the impact not only pushed the sedimentary rock layers up and outward, some of the beds in the crater walls were folded back on themselves like an exploding paper rocket. The surrounding debris layer is "inverted." The top rock layers were ejected and deposited first, covered by successively older rocks from beneath. Inside the crater itself, fractured rock and meteorite material is 600 ft (180 m) deep beneath the current bottom of the depression. The larger pieces of rock fell back to Earth first and are the bottom, followed by successively smaller or finer fragments. Talus and alluvial debris from subsequent erosion now cover the surface.

Protected Areas. Although privately owned, the Department of Interior declared it a National Natural Landmark in 1967.

See also Colorado Plateau; Monturaqui Crater; Vredefort Structure (Vredefort Dome)

Further Reading

Buchner, Elmar and Thomas Kenkmann. 2007. "Upheaval Dome, Utah, USA: Impact Origin Confirmed." *Geological Society of American Bulletin* 36: 227–230.
"Meteor Crater." n.d. http://www.meteorcrater.com/
Morgan, Matt. 1996. "The Controversy over Utah's Upheaval Dome." The Meteorite Exchange. http://www.meteorite.com/impact/upheaval.htm

Meteora

Greece

Geographic Overview. Meteora is an area of sandstone rock monoliths that is the second largest center of Eastern Orthodox Monasticism in Greece. The series of monasteries built directly on top of sandstone monoliths and spires, with no additional foundations, blend with the environment. The name *Meteora* can be translated several ways, including "middle of the sky," "suspended in air," and "in the heavens above."

Geographic Coordinates. 39°45'N, 21°37'E

Description. Located in Central Greece on the western edge of the Plain of Thessaly, Meteora is 217 mi (350 km) northwest of Athens. It is on the eastern edge of the Pindus Mountains and on the southern edge of the Andikhasia Mountains near the Pineios River. Its sheer cliffs and spires tower as high as 1,310 ft (400 m) above the town of Kalambaka. The region covers 927 ac (375 ha). The climate is typical mediterranean, with moderately rainy winters and hot, dry summers. The mountains to the east and north have cold winters with snow. Although summers are driest, storms are possible at higher elevations.

Meteora has a long history of alternating periods of use and decay. The first Christian hermits, or ascetics, who took refuge there approximately 1,000 years ago, lived alone in caves and fissures, isolated for religious privacy and safe from political upheaval through the centuries. The first church was built at the beginning of the 12th century, and the first monastery was organized in the 14th century. Several monasteries, 24 total, were built between 1350 and 1500, when the Turks of the Ottoman Empire were conquering and replacing the Byzantine civilization. Monks operated schools in the monasteries to preserve both Christian Orthodoxy and the Greek language. By the early 18th century, the region was in decline and used by the Ottomans as prisons. Revival began in 1920, with the building of roads and bridges and steps cut into the rock to allow pilgrims easier access. Original entry into the monasteries, for both people and goods, was by long ladders, pulled up when not in use, and nets operated by hand-cranked pulleys. The monasteries suffered damage during various conflicts, from Turkish dominance to World War II. Current renovations began in 1960.

Meteora is now primarily a tourist attraction, but the monasteries, six of which remain sparsely inhabited (four by monks, two by nuns), also preserve religious relics, art work, and documents.

Geologic History. In the early to middle Tertiary (60–30 mya), the region from Albania south to

Trikkala, Greece, was a basin, called both the Thessaly Basin and the Meso-Hellenic Basin, between the Pindos Mountains to the west and the Pelagonian zone to the east. This inland sea was the deposition zone for sediments eroded from adjacent mountains. Mud and coarse sands and gravels were deposited, probably in the form of a delta, in the vicinity of the current town of Kalambaka. The sandstones and conglomerates of the Meteora cliffs are the remnants of those deltaic deposits. In the middle Tertiary (30–25 mya), the Pineios River carved Tempe gorge in eastern Greece, allowing the water in the basin to drain into the Aegean Sea. Subsequent tectonic action first downfolded the sedimentary fill into a broad syncline before uplifting the sedimentary rocks to form a plateau. Erosion along faults and fractures incurred during the uplift separated the rock unit into monoliths. The area remains subject to frequent, but not intensive, earthquakes.

Biota. Meteora is in the Balkan Highlands biogeographic province, with forested hills and riparian habitats of oriental plane trees. Endemic species include a bluebell (*Campanula kalambakensis*) and two thistles (*Centaura lactifolia* and *C. kalambakensis*). Forests above 2,300 ft (700 m) may have oaks, hophornbeam, and beech.

Mammals include red fox, gray wolf, beech marten, eastern hedgehog, lesser horsehoe bat, and weasel. Of the 163 bird species, 120 nest in the area and 10 are endangered or threatened, including the Black Kite (*Milvus migrans*). Also important are White Stork, Nightingale, and Black Redstart. Rock and cliff species such as swallows, swifts, and martins, are common. Raptors include Little Owl, Common Kestrel, Lanner Falcon, eagles, and vultures, such as Lammergeier, Griffon, and Egyptian.

Protected Areas. Meteora is a World Heritage Site.

Further Reading

Ferriere, Jacky et al. 2004. "Geologic Evolution and Geodynamic Controls of the Tertiary Intramontane Piggyback Meso-Hellenic basin, Greece." http://www.google.com/url?sa=t&rct=j&q=&esrc=s&source=web&cd=2&cad=rja&uact=8&ved=0CCYQFjAB&url=http%3A%2F%2Fjournalseek.net%2Fcgi-bin%2Fjournalseek%2Fjournalsearch.cgi%3Ffield%3Dissn%26query%3D0037-9409&ei=TlnhU7TeB4_voATnvIKQBQ&usg=AFQjCNHHBlEmRZ0i25HYRMkDuPOYeSo1sA&sig2=0U-FDKQeST-uAZwLenN6pw&bvm=bv.72389368,d.cGU, 175: 361–381. www.geosciences.univ-rennes1.fr/IMG/pdf/Ferriere_2004-BSGF.pdf

"General Info about Meteora." n.d. www.meteora-greece.com/general-info-about-meteora/

"The Summarized History of the Rocks and the Holy Monasteries of the Meteora." n.d. www.kalampaka.com/en/meteora/history.asp

Mexican Plateau (Mexican Altiplano)

Mexico

Geographic Overview. The Mexican Plateau in north central Mexico is an upland that constitutes one of the major landform units of Middle America.

Geographic Coordinates. Approximately 20°45'N–31°50'N, 100°10'W–108°15'W

Description. The Mexican Plateau is a tilted block that increases in elevation toward the south. At the northern limit at the border with the U.S. states of New Mexico and Texas, elevations are less than 4,000 ft (1,220 m) asl, but the surface rises to more than 8,000 ft (2,400 m) in the south. Two sections are recognized: the arid Mesa del Norte north of 22° N latitude, and the Mesa Central to the south. The edge of the plateau is marked by steep escarpments at its western and eastern margins. From the plateau they appear as slightly raised rims, but from the respective coasts they are major mountain ranges, the Sierra Madre Occidental in the west and the Sierra Madre Oriental in the east. The southern end of the plateau occurs at the east–west trending Trans-Mexican Volcanic Axis.

Much of the Mesa del Norte has a basin and range topography in which low mountain ranges stand 500–2,500 ft (150–760 m) above flat-bottomed desert basins (*bolsones*). Mountains in the west are mostly volcanic, whereas those in the east are formed of limestones and shales. Few permanent streams occur, and interior drainage results in many playas. Alluvial fans and rock pediments line the lower slopes of the mountains. The area encompasses eastern Chihuahua, Coahuila, Durango, San Luis Potosi, and northern Zacatecas and corresponds to the distribution of the Chihuahuan Desert. The land is covered with low, largely evergreen shrubs, the dominants of which are creosote bush, tarbush, and the deciduous whitethorn acacia. Among other conspicuous plants are some with basal whorls of succulent leaves such as agaves, bear grass, sotol, and yuccas. Although the diversity of cacti is quite high, they generally are low-growing and do not stand out on the landscape. Swales of tobosa grass and sacaton occur sporadically, especially on limestone. Higher mountains may be cloaked in pine-oak forests.

All or part of many Mexican states are located on the Mesa Central, including Aguascalientes, Guanajuato, Hidalgo, Jalisco, México, Michoacán, Querétaro, and southern Zacatecas. The Mesa Central is an area of geologically recent volcanism, and the surface is one of eroded stumps of old volcanoes with flat basins in between. Low cinder cones and lava flows are prevalent, as are crater lakes. Ashfall and lava flows blocked streams during the wetter periods of the Pleistocene Epoch and created lakes, most of which have now vanished. Some were artificially drained, as was the case with the five interconnected lakes on which the Aztec built their capital, Tenochtitlán, now the site of Mexico City. Lake Pátzcuaro in the state of Michoacán and Lake Chapala in Jalisco and Michoacán are among the surviving lakes. The imprint of the former lakes on the land is distinct, however, as they left behind level and fertile lacustrine deposits. Today's basins vary in size from a few square miles to valleys 30 mi × 40 mi (48 km × 64 km) and are sites of major population centers. The region south of the Sierra Guanajuato contains a series of basins connected by the Rio Lerma-Rio Santiago river system. It includes the valleys of Guadalajara, Puebla, Toluca, Morelia, and the Valley of Mexico. The Lerma River is the largest river in Mexico and empties into Lake Chapala. Rio Santiago, the lake's outlet, cuts through a deep canyon on its way to the Pacific Ocean. The Pánuco–Moctezuma river system drains the eastern third of the Mesa Central, entering the Gulf of Mexico at Tampico. The upper Rio Balsas drains the southeastern part of the plateau along a meandering route through a hot, dry depression into the Pacific Ocean.

The Mesa Central ends at the row of stratovolcanoes forming the Trans-Mexican Volcanic Axis, which forms a southern escarpment above the Balsas Depression. Volcan Colima (14,200 ft or 4,328 m asl) in the west is still active, as is snow-covered Popocatepetl (17,900 ft or 5,456 m asl) near Mexico City. Iztaccihuatl (17,300 ft or 5,230 m asl), next to "Popo" and snowcapped, is dormant. Pico de Orizaba (Citlaltépetl), Mexico's highest mountain (18,491 ft or 5,636 m asl) and the second highest volcanic prominence in the world after Africa's Mount Kilimanjaro, lies at the eastern end of the chain. It has been dormant since the 1800s.

The Mesa Central lies in tropical latitudes, but its high elevations produce a temperate climate. The natural vegetation of the region is a dry shrubland known as Central Mexican matorral. It is similar to the Chihuahuan Desert; and acacias, mimosas, ocotillos, agaves, and *Opuntia* cacti cover large areas. Higher elevations in the mountains may be forested with oaks and pines. Rainfall is generally less than 20 in (500 mm) a year. The region has a particularly rich herpetofauna and high endemism among reptiles and plants. Little of the native vegetation remains unaltered, as the area has long been used for agriculture and the grazing of cattle, sheep, and goats. Illegal collection of cacti for national and international markets has endangered a number of endemic species.

See also Chihuahuan Desert; Sierra Madre Occidental; Sierra Madre Oriental; Trans-Mexican Volcanic Axis (Eje Volcánico Transversal)

Further Reading

"Central Mexican Matorral (NA 1302). n.d. World Wildlife Fund. http://web.archive.org/web/20110605084423/http://www.worldwildlife.org/wildworld/profiles/terrestrial/na/na1302_full.html

West, Robert C. and John P. Augelli. 1989. *Middle America: Its Lands and Peoples.* Englewood Cliffs, NJ: Prentice-Hall.

Mid-Atlantic Ridge

Atlantic Ocean

Geographic Overview. The Mid-Atlantic Ridge, like the rest of the long chain of underwater mountains snaking their way along the floor of the world ocean, has formed where diverging tectonic plates are forced apart by magma rising from the mantle. Volcanic activity in the central rift valley creates new oceanic crust. Volcanic islands occasionally emerge above sea level along the entire length of the ridge system. Where seawater infiltrates cracks in the crest, it becomes superheated and mineral enriched, leading to hydrothermal vent systems that support a unique deep water fauna. When it was first mapped in the 1950s the Mid-Atlantic Ridge gained broad acceptance for Alfred Wegener's Theory of Continental Drift.

Geographic Coordinates. Latitudes: 87°N to 54°S, centered at 28°24'W

Description. The sinuous Mid-Atlantic Ridge (MAR) extends along the Atlantic Ocean seafloor from the Gakkel Ridge northeast of Greenland and some 200 mi (330 km) south of the North Pole to the Bouvet triple junction beneath the subantarctic waters at the edge of the Southern Ocean. It marks the place where seafloor spreading moves the North American plate away from the Eurasian plate in the North Atlantic and moves the South American plate away from the African plate in the South Atlantic. The MAR is categorized as a slow-spreading mid-ocean ridge since it spreads at a rate of about 1.0 in (2.5 cm) per year.

The ridge is a complex system of tilted blocks of ocean floor, volcanoes and seamounts, and rift valleys. Ridge crests rise on average 1.8 mi (3 km) above the abyssal plain to an average depth of 8,200 ft (2,500 m) bsl; the system is 600–900 mi (1,000–1,500 km) wide. A deep rift valley at the center axis of the MAR is 0.6–1.8 mi (1–3 km) deep, comparable in size to the Grand Canyon. This is where active volcanism adds new oceanic crust and pushes aside older crustal material. Rising magma from Earth's mantle bulges the crust upward and fractures the ridge into a series of tilted blocks. Transform faults perpendicular to the axis of the MAR and many lateral offsets have also formed, giving the ridge a corrugated appearance. Lava spilling out of the rift forms hummocky ridges and numerous hummocks 160–650 ft (50–200 m) in diameter and 33–65 ft (10–20 m) high, as well as smooth lava flows. Actual volcanoes are discrete entities and generally form very small, sometimes coalescing seamounts 150–1,800 ft (50–600 m) high. The majority are only 180 ft (60 m) high. The Atlantis Massif, a geologically young part of the ridge centered at 30°N, is unusually wide and high, rising 5,000 ft (1,700 m) above the seafloor.

Where seawater seeps into hot, new oceanic crust, it is heated to temperatures near 750°F (400°C). The superheated water dissolves minerals, primarily sulfides of zinc, copper, and iron, from the mantle. When it finds a conduit, the water streams upward 1,000 ft (300 m) or more into the cold bottom waters of the sea, resembling thick black smoke. Minerals precipitate from these "black smokers" to form towers or chimneys. Such hydrothermal vents are not numerous and are often 100 mi (160 km) or more apart on the slow-spreading MAR. They are short-lived phenomena, becoming extinct as their part of the ridge moves away from the central rift and heat source. Nevertheless, a unique fauna has developed at these and similar sites around the world. Water seeping through chimney walls cools enough to allow specially adapted life forms dependent on chemosynthetic microbes to thrive.

A small number of volcanic islands, emerged parts of the MAR, extend along the ridge. Iceland, straddling the central rift valley is the largest, its close southwestern neighbor, Surtsey, is the youngest. Others, from north to south, are Jan Mayen, the Azores Archipelago, Ascension Island, St. Helena, Tristan da Cunha, Gough Island, and Bouvet Island.

Geologic History. The MAR began to form in the Triassic Period, 220 mya, as magma rising from Earth's asthenosphere began to split apart the supercontinent of Pangaea. A number of rift valleys formed at this time, but many—such as the Fundy Basin—failed to develop into full-fledged ocean basins. The spreading center at the MAR, however, opened the Atlantic Ocean beginning about 150 mya. The formation of new oceanic crust along the axial rift valley is an ongoing process.

Biota. The fauna of deep sea hydrothermal vents includes giant tubeworms, clams, mussels, crabs, vent fish, and octopus.

See also Ascension Island; Azores Archipelago; Iceland; Saint Helena; Surtsey; Tristan de Cunha and Gough Island

Further Reading

MacDonald, Ken. 2010. "What Is the Mid-Oceanic Ridge?" Ocean Explorer, NOAA. http://oceanexplorer. noaa.gov/explorations/05galapagos/background/mid_ocean_ridge/mid_ocean_ridge.html

"The Mid-Atlantic Ridge." n.d. World Heritage Center, UNESCO. http://whc.unesco.org/en/activities/504/

"Submarine Volcanoes at Divergent Plate Boundaries." n.d. http://volcano.oregonstate.edu/book/export/html/140

U.S. Geological Survey and Peter Saundry. 2011. "Mid-Ocean Ridges." In *The Encyclopedia of Earth*, edited by Cutler J. Cleveland. Washington, D.C.: Environmental Information Coalition, National Council for Science and the Environment. http:/www.eoearth.org/article/Mid-Ocean_ridges?topic=50013

Woodward, Susan L. 2009. *Marine Biomes*. Greenwood Guides to Biomes of the World. Westport, CT: Greenwood Press.

Miskito Coast (La Mosquitia)

Honduras and Nicaragua

Geographic Overview. The coastal lowlands of northeastern Honduras and eastern Nicaragua are an ecologically complex region in Central America named for the indigenous peoples, the Miskito Indians, who still make up more than half the human population living there. This is the largest sea turtle feeding ground in the Americas. The Miskito Coast was a British protectorate from 1655 to 1860. In 1894 it passed to Nicaragua, but the International Court of Justice awarded the northern part to Honduras in 1960.

Geographic Coordinates. Approximately 11° 45'N–15°45'N, 83°35'W–84°W

Description. The coast itself is flat with long stretches of sandy beaches, spits, and north–south parallel beach ridges. Behind these is an interconnected system of freshwater and brackish lagoons fed by rivers. The three largest rivers in eastern Nicaragua, however (the Río Coco, Río Grande de Matagalpa, and Prinsapolka River), enter the Caribbean via large deltas. Offshore is a shallow marine shelf supporting seagrass meadows or "turtle banks." Seagrass occurs both in isolated patches some 2–3 mi (3–5 km) in diameter and as broader contiguous areas. The shelf is widest off Cape Gracias a Dios, where it extends 46.5 mi (75 km) beyond the coastline and hosts the Miskito's major Atlantic green sea turtle fishery. Coral reefs and cays, the latter usually fringed with red mangrove or sea grape, dot the offshore region.

On the poor soils of the interior north of the Río Grande in Nicaragua as far as Cabo Camarón,

Honduras, the rolling terrain is covered with grasses and sedges in a savanna containing scattered Caribbean pine (*Pinus caribaea*), stunted sandpaper trees (*Curatella americana*), and nance (*Brysonian crassifolia*). Low-lying areas support papta palms or silver saw palmetto (*Acoelorrhaphe wrightii*). The pine savanna is separated into two sections by the broad gallery forest and palm swamps of the Río Wawa. To its west and south is one of the largest remaining tropical rainforests in Central America. It has the typical three to four layers of foliage and an unbroken canopy of broadleaf evergreen trees.

At these tropical latitudes and with warm, shallow water offshore, the Miskito Coast maintains warm temperatures throughout the year. Rainfall amounts vary with location, being lowest in the north and interior and highest in the southernmost coastal area. Indeed, San Juan del Norte (Greyfield), on the Nicaragua–Costa Rica border, is one of the wettest places in all of Middle America (a world region consisting of Mexico, Central America, and the Caribbean), receiving on average 253 in (6,425 mm) of rain a year. Northward along the coast, Bluefields receives 163 in (4,410 mm) and Puerto Cabezas 130 in (3,300 mm). Interior stations report closer to 110–120 in (2,800–3,050 mm). A distinct dry season occurs at most places from February into May when only 3–4 in (75–100 mm) of rain falls each month. Near constant heavy rains and high winds prevail from June through August.

Biota. Among valuable timber trees in the forest are mahogany (*Swietenia*) and cedar (*Cedrela*). Important game animals that the Miskito people hunt in the forest include Baird's tapir, white-lipped peccary, and white-tailed deer. Threatened species include Scarlet Macaw, Military Macaw, Green Macaw, Great Curassow, Crested Guan, Baird's tapir, manatee, jaguar, ocelot, margay, and jaguarundi.

Protected Areas. Today, Honduras has the main conservation area in Mosquitia in its Río Plátano Biosphere Reserve. The reserve, a 30 mi (50 km) × 93 mi (150 km) strip along Río Plátano, contains a comprehensive sample of Mosquitia's habitats. Three-quarters of the 2,000 mi² (5,250 km²) area lies in mountainous terrain and virgin rainforest in the headwaters region of the river. A gallery forest of rainforest species borders the river as it passes through pine savanna. On the flat coastal plain, the reserve reaches two lagoons on the Caribbean, one freshwater (Laguna de Ibans) and one brackish (Laguna de Brus).

The 200 or more archaeological sites in the reserve include the Mayan Ciudad Blanca (White City) and a place where Christopher Columbus stepped on American soil. With its rich and varied ecological assets and an indigenous population still practicing a subsistence way of life, UNESCO inscribed Río Plátano as a World Heritage Site in 1979.

Environmental Issues. UNESCO placed the Río Plátano Biosphere Reserve on its World Heritage in Danger list in 2011, citing threats from illegal logging, fishing and land occupation; poaching; and the difficulty Honduras has properly managing the site due to increased lawlessness and drug trafficking in the area.

Further Reading

"Mosquitia-Nicaraguan Caribbean Coast mangrove." n.d. *The Encyclopedia of Earth.* http://www.eoearth.org/article /Mosquitia-Nicaraguan_Caribbean_Coast_mangroves? topic=49597

Nietschmann, Bernard Q. 1973. *Between Land and Water: The Subsistence Ecology of the Miskito Indians, Eastern Nicaragua.* New York: Seminar Press.

"Río Plátano Biosphere Reserve." n.d. World Heritage Center, UNESCO. http://whc.unesco.org/en/list/196

Mississippi River System

United States (Alabama, Arkansas, Colorado, Georgia, Illinois, Indiana, Iowa, Kansas, Kentucky, Louisiana, Minnesota, Mississippi, Missouri, Montana, Nebraska, New Mexico, New York, North Dakota, Ohio, Oklahoma, Pennsylvania, South Carolina, South Dakota, Tennessee, Texas, West Virginia, Virginia, Wisconsin, and Wyoming)

Geographic Overview. The Mississippi River drainage system, including both the Missouri and Ohio river systems, drains more than 40 percent of the contiguous United States. Its drainage basin is the largest in North America and the third largest in the world. From its source in Lake Itasca in northern Minnesota, the main stem of the Mississippi flows 2,350 mi (3,782 km) to the Gulf of Mexico. The length from the Missouri River headwaters in Montana to the Gulf of Mexico via the Mississippi is 3,710 mi (5,970 km), making the Mississippi-Missouri River System the fourth longest in the world. For most of its course, the Mississippi main stem forms the borders between several states, from Minnesota and Wisconsin south to Louisiana and Mississippi.

Geographic Coordinates. Source: 47°14'N, 95° 12'W; Mouth: 29°09'N, 89°15'W

Description. The drainage basin of the Mississippi-Missouri-Ohio River System covers approximately 1,250,000 mi^2 (3,240,000 km^2). Of this total, the Missouri River drainage basin covers approximately 530,000 mi^2 (1,370,000 km^2) and the Ohio River approximately 200,000 mi^2 (518,000 km^2). Those two rivers and their basins are each discussed in detail in separate entries.

From its origin in Lake Itasca in Minnesota 1,444 ft (440 m) asl, the Mississippi River flows through deep glacial drift until reaching Minneapolis—St. Paul, where it is joined from the southwest by the Minnesota River. At St. Anthony Falls, now controlled by a lock and dam in Minneapolis, the river drops into the preglacial Mississippi Valley, which was carved by the River Warren's draining of Glacial Lake Agassiz at the close of the Pleistocene Epoch. The Mississippi River follows the preglacial course from Minneapolis to Davenport, Iowa. Shortly downstream from Minneapolis–St. Paul, the St. Croix and Chippewa rivers from northern Wisconsin enter the Mississippi. From Minneapolis downstream to the Driftless Area, the Mississippi Valley is partly filled with outwash sand and gravel, deposited as glacial meltwater flow diminished and created a braided channel. The Wisconsin River is a major tributary coming from the Driftless Area of Wisconsin. Further downstream, other major tributaries include the Wapsipinicon River and Des Moines River from Iowa, and the Rock River and Kaskaskia River from Illinois.

At St. Louis, Missouri, the Missouri River joins the Mississippi from the west, and further downstream at Cairo, Illinois, the Ohio River joins from the east. After its confluence with the Ohio, the Mississippi River enters the Mississippi alluvial plain, called the Mississippi Embayment (also called the Mississippi Delta region), which is underlain by thick deposits

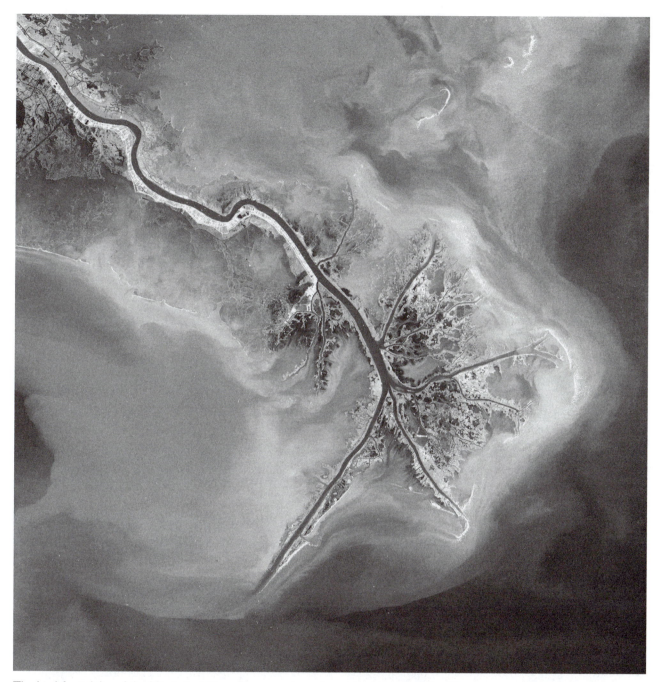

The bird-foot delta of the Mississippi River illustrates how the main channel builds different routes through the vast deltaic deposits. (NASA/Corbis)

of fine alluvium. In east-central Arkansas, both the White River and the Arkansas River enter from the west. The Yazoo River parallels the main stem for several miles in northwestern Mississippi before joining the Mississippi River. Near Shreveport, Louisiana, the Red River and the Ouachita River converge and flow into the Atchafalaya, a drainage basin paralleling the

Mississippi. Near Baton Rouge, the Mississippi River turns southeast to pass through New Orleans and enter the Gulf of Mexico. Over the last 7,000 years, the Mississippi River has taken several paths to the Gulf, depositing sediment in a complex configuration. The irregularity of the Louisiana coastline is a result of several delta lobes. The entire delta covers approximately 4,700 mi^2 (12,180 km^2) and is the seventh largest on Earth. The current river outlet is in the southeast, the Plaquemines—Balize Delta, a bird-foot delta with several narrow channels. The coastline is continually changing as sediments are deposited in the current delta and older areas become eroded or rearranged.

The Upper Mississippi (north of Cairo) is a large floodplain river, meaning that, with some exceptions, the river is allowed to overflow its banks. Although parts are regulated with levees, the Mississippi south of Cairo is a classic meandering river, with sandbars, cutoffs, oxbows, and yazoo streams. From Baton Rouge south to the Gulf, the U.S. Army Corps of Engineers maintains a 12 ft (3.6 m) deep channel for ocean-going ships. The river there is confined by levees and has no floodplain.

In spanning several degrees of latitude and longitude, the Mississippi River and its tributaries flow through several climate zones and vegetation types, from boreal forest in the north through temperate deciduous forest and southern forests to the south. Some tributaries from the west, such as the Minnesota and Red rivers, drain semiarid grasslands. The headwaters and the northern tributaries originate and flow through a region of deep glacial drift with bogs, lakes, and swamps, less than 2,035 ft (620 m) asl with low local relief. The Driftless Area has high relief, with bluffs 330–660 ft (100–200 m) high. Tributaries through Iowa, Illinois, Indiana, and Missouri flow through older or thinner glacial drift, with little relief except along the stream valleys. Below Cairo, the tributaries drain a variety of forest types, although much of the land has been cleared for agriculture and other uses. Some southern tributaries originate in highlands—the White and St. Francis from the Ozark Plateau, the Arkansas from the Rocky Mountains, and the Ouachita from the Ouachita Mountains—and become depositional rivers upon entering the Mississippi alluvial plain.

The Minnesota River, draining glaciated agricultural land that was formerly tallgrass prairie, is the first major tributary below the Mississippi's source. The relatively small river meanders in a wide (0.6–6.2 mi/1–10 km), deep (260 ft/80 m) valley carved by drainage from Glacial Lake Agassiz. Tributaries enter the Minnesota River from hanging valleys, through gorges, waterfalls, or rapids. In spite of several dams, much of the river remains natural. The St. Croix River begins in Upper St. Croix Lake in deep terminal moraine deposits in northern Wisconsin. Forming the Minnesota–Wisconsin border, the St. Croix has a deep channel carved by water that drained Glacial Lake Duluth (forerunner to Lake Superior). Mostly free-flowing and pristine, the lower St. Croix runs through gorges carved into sandstone, dolomite, and basalt. It joins the Mississippi at Lake St. Croix, formed where the Mississippi River deposited sand and silt, naturally damming the St. Croix's flow.

The Wisconsin River, the largest and longest river in Wisconsin, begins in Lac Vieux Desert, a lake in the glaciated landscape of northern Wisconsin at 1,673 ft (510 m) asl. It flows south in a broad valley through glacial drift, forest, and agricultural land, then west through the Driftless Area, entering the Mississippi through limestone and sandstone bluffs. At Wisconsin Dells, on the eastern edge of the Driftless Area, the river flows for 6.8 mi (11 km) between sandstone cliffs as high as 100 ft (30 m). Although heavily dammed for flood control and hydroelectric power, most of the headwaters and the lower 435 mi (133 km) of the Wisconsin River are free-flowing and important for recreation. The Illinois River, the longest in the state of Illinois, begins at the confluence of the Des Plaines and Kankakee Rivers southwest of Chicago and flows over old glacial plains, tallgrass prairie converted to agriculture, southwest to the Mississippi. The Chicago Sanitary and Shipping Canal, which connects the Illinois River to Lake Michigan, was developed in 1900 to protect Chicago's water supply from pollution. It is now a major route for invasive species from the Great Lakes to enter the Mississippi drainage. The Illinois is an aggrading river, with a sandy shoreline, low natural levees, and a broad marshy plain.

The White River, originating in karst landscape in the Boston Mountains, flows through northern Arkansas and is the largest river draining the Ozark Plateau. It artificially joins the Arkansas River in east-central Arkansas via a set of locks and dams designed for navigation between the two rivers. The White is highly regulated except for two free-flowing tributaries, one of which is the Buffalo River. The Yazoo River, the type specimen for a yazoo stream, in north-central and northwestern Mississippi originates in the coastal plain uplands and is a floodplain river. It is highly modified, with dams, channelization, and dredging.

The Atchafalaya River, a former course of the Mississippi River, parallels the lowest stretch of the Mississippi on the west. It receives not only all water from the Red River, but also 19–50 percent of the Mississippi's flow. To protect downstream Baton Rouge and New Orleans from frequent floods, part of the Mississippi's volume is diverted to the Atchafalaya at Old River Control Structure. The U.S. Corps of Engineers maintains an 80–180 ft (24–55 m) deep channel through the Atchafalaya Basin Floodway. Because the levees are not immediately adjacent to the river, a broad region is allowed to flood, in a maze of distribution channels, bayous, lakes, and swamps. The Atchafalaya's bottomland hardwood forest is the largest continuous wetland in the United States.

The Arkansas River and Red River have similarities in that they both drain the Southern Great Plains grassland states of southern Kansas, Oklahoma, and northern Texas. Their upper main stems may be dry at times, and downstream is usually wide, shallow, and sandy. Downstream from its headwaters in the high Rocky Mountains, the Arkansas enters the Great Plains at Pueblo, Colorado, and begins losing water due to dry climate and withdrawal for irrigation. Water is gained from tributaries and rainfall as the river continues east through eastern Kansas and Oklahoma. Control structures and dams allow navigation upstream to Tulsa, Oklahoma. The Canadian River, originating in the southern Rockies and the largest tributary to the Arkansas River, follows a similar pattern. The Red River begins in ephemeral streams in Palo Duro Canyon in the Texas Panhandle, forms the Oklahoma–Texas border, then passes through northern Louisiana and joins the Atchafalaya close to the Mississippi main stem.

Although altered for navigation and floodplain development in lower reaches, most of the headwater and upper reaches of the Mississippi are in natural condition, with fairly natural hydrological patterns. Several locks and dams between St. Paul and the confluence with the Missouri River are designed to maintain sufficient flow for navigation, not for major flood control. Therefore, most the floodplain is still inundated annually according to the natural regime. Levees to protect floodplain agriculture from inundation are more common below the Rock River in Illinois. Although the river maintains a meandering channel below Cairo, Illinois, it is highly regulated for both navigation and flood control. Only 10 percent of the original floodplain is allowed to flood within levees constructed some distance from the channel.

In spite of dams and regulation of flow, the annual pattern of discharge is consistent along the Mississippi's course: highest during spring snowmelt and lowest in winter when northern drainages are frozen. Most of the river's flow comes from the Upper Mississippi basin, Missouri, Ohio, Arkansas, and Red rivers.

Biota. The Upper Mississippi River, north of Cairo, Illinois, has one freshwater ecoregion, the Mississippi, but with differences according to the physiographic province through which a given tributary flows. Common fish species include alligator gar (*Atractosteus spatula*), paddlefish (*Polyodon spathula*), northern pike (*Esox lucius*), and muskellunge (*Esox masquinongy*). The lower river system, south of the confluence with the Ohio River, encompasses all or parts of three freshwater ecoregions—the Mississippi Embayment, the Ozark Highlands, and the Ouachita Highlands. The lower Mississippi is rich in fish species, including lamprey, sturgeon, North American paddlefish, gar, and bowfin. Endemic fish species are few and are limited to tributary drainages.

Protected Areas. The Mississippi River passes through many national park sites and wildlife refuges. A 72-mile stretch of river in Minnesota is protected as Mississippi National River and Recreation Areas. The St. Croix, a tributary from Wisconsin, is one of the original National Wild and Scenic Rivers. The Buffalo River, in Arkansas, is protected along its entire course, either as wilderness or National Scenic Riverway.

Environmental Issues. Major alterations to habitat and biota include engineering for navigation and flood control, chemical contaminants, and nonnative species. Dams and locks designed for navigation have impacted the ecological integrity of the river by limiting or eliminating low-flow habitats and changing sedimentation patterns. Diversion of floodwaters through the Atchafalaya River threatens the current delta by

---

Portage, Wisconsin

In 1876, a navigational canal was completed in Portage, Wisconsin, that connected the Gulf of Mexico with the Great Lakes. Previously, Native Americans and trappers would portage their canoes 1.5–2.0 mi (2.4–3.2 km) between the eastern bend of the Wisconsin River and the Fox River, which flows to Lake Michigan via Green Bay. That route lost its importance and closed in 1951, but remains historically significant.

---

depriving it of sediments. Many wetlands are isolated from the channel by levees or have been reduced by draining. Agricultural runoff is a significant source of pollution, as is municipal and industrial waste and petrochemical contamination. Nonnative species, especially those entering from the Great Lakes such as zebra mussel and grass carp, threaten native species.

See also Driftless Area; Great Lakes; Missouri River System; Ohio River System

Further Reading

Brown, Arthur V. et al. 2005. "Lower Mississippi River and Its Tributaries." In *Rivers of North America*, edited by Arthur C. Benke and Colbert E. Cushing, 231–282. Amsterdam: Elsevier Academic Press.

Delong, Michael D. 2005. "Upper Mississippi River Basin." In *Rivers of North America*, edited by Arthur C. Benke and Colbert E. Cushing, 326–373. Amsterdam: Elsevier Academic Press.

"Mississippi River Trail." 2013. http://www.mississippirivertrail.org/index.html

World Wildlife Fund and The Nature Conservancy. 2013. "Lower Mississippi, Ouachita Highlands, Ozark Highlands, Upper Mississippi." *Freshwater Ecoregions of the World*. http://www.feow.org/

Missouri River System

United States (Montana, Wyoming, Colorado, North Dakota, South Dakota, Nebraska, Kansas, Iowa, Minnesota, and Missouri) and Canada

Geographic Overview. The Missouri River is the longest river in North America. Its drainage basin is second in size only to that of the Mississippi River, of which it is a part. The Missouri drains approximately 17 percent of the country, all or portions of 10 states and two Canadian provinces. After exploration by Lewis and Clark in 1804–1806, the Missouri River became a significant pathway for western movement. Its current importance is primarily water for irrigation and domestic use.

Geographic Coordinates. Source: 45°56'N, 111° 21'W; Mouth: 38°50'N, 90°07'W

Description. Stretching across more than 10 degrees of latitude and more than 25 degrees of longitude, the Missouri River and its tributaries flow through several physiographic provinces and climates and cover a drainage basin of approximately 530,000 mi² (1,370,000 km²). Although the headwaters of the main stem of the Missouri River are believed to be Hell Roaring Creek, Montana, the named Missouri begins at the confluence of the Jefferson, Madison, and Gallatin Rivers near Three Forks, Montana, at an elevation of 4,022 ft (1,226 m) asl. From this point, the river flows 2,341 mi (3,768 km) to the Mississippi River north of St. Louis at an elevation of 400 ft (122 m) asl. Two major northern tributaries are the Milk River, which begins in Glacier National Park, and the Madison River, which begins on the Yellowstone Plateau.

The Missouri River system generally flows from northwest to southeast, following the east slope of the Great Plains across north-central United States. It is joined by the Milk River in northeastern Montana and by the Yellowstone River in northwestern North Dakota before turning abruptly south through central North Dakota and South Dakota. A major tributary in North Dakota is the Little Missouri River from the west. In South Dakota, the Missouri River is joined by the Cheyenne and White rivers and in northeastern Nebraska by the Niobrara River, all from the west. The river jogs to the east in northeastern Nebraska, forming the border between South Dakota and Nebraska, before turning south to form the border between Nebraska and Iowa. The Platte River joins the Missouri south of Omaha. At the junction with the Kansas River in western Missouri, the Missouri River resumes its eastern flow to join the Mississippi River at St Louis.

The limit of continental glaciation defines the present course of the Missouri River. The northeast direction of the upstream Missouri and the Yellowstone Rivers indicates that flow prior to the Pleistocene was to Hudson Bay in Canada. As the ice sheet blocked flow to the north and the Coteau du Missouri escarpment in eastern South Dakota concentrated glacial lobes to the east, the Missouri River was pushed west and forced to flow south through the Dakotas. Because tributaries from the west were not interrupted by glaciers during the Pleistocene, they have well-developed drainage. The small tributaries from the east have had little time to develop since retreat of the ice.

Snowmelt from the Rocky Mountains causes a seasonal input of water, especially in the northern tributaries. Summer thunderstorms in the southern Rockies contribute 50 percent of the water that enters the North and South Platte Rivers. Flow to the South Platte River is also enhanced by diversion of water from the Colorado River Basin drainage, for irrigation east of the Rocky Mountains. Flow in the Missouri River increases slowly across the semiarid plains, then increases rapidly below Omaha due to the wetter climate.

The Missouri River main stem flows largely through the semiarid Great Plains. Headwaters of several major tributaries of the Missouri River, including the Milk, Madison, Yellowstone, and Platte rivers, are in forests and alpine environments on the east slope of the Rocky Mountains. The Cheyenne, White, Niobrara, and Kansas rivers, among others, originate in the semiarid grasslands of the Great Plains. Others, such as Big Sioux and James rivers, originate in the wetter central lowlands, and the Gasconade is a major tributary from the Ozark Plateau.

At 678 mi (1,091 km) long, the Yellowstone River is the longest free-flowing river in conterminous United States. It originates in the Absaroka Range alpine zone at 12,008 ft (3,660 m) asl in northwestern Wyoming, flows into Yellowstone Lake, and through the Grand Canyon of the Yellowstone. Downstream, the river is a braided, alluvial choked channel through the Great Plains. Two major tributaries, the Bighorn and Powder Rivers, drain from the Wyoming Basin. The White River originates on Pine Ridge in northwestern Nebraska and flows unregulated through south-central South Dakota, including Badlands National Park, to Lake Francis Case, a reservoir on the Missouri River. Groundwater sources of the Niobrara River in northern Nebraska contribute a consistent base flow to the Missouri.

Platte River drainage flows through mountains, foothills, and plains, from forests to sagebrush and grasslands. Headwaters of both the North Platte and the South Platte are in the Colorado Rockies more than 10,000 ft (3050 m) asl. The North Platte flows north into Wyoming before curving southeast to Nebraska. The South Platte drains north-central Colorado and flows northeast to the North Platte. Both branches follow braided channels east across the Great Plains to merge in North Platte, Nebraska, at 2,759 ft (841 m) asl. The Platte River then flows east across Nebraska, joining the Missouri just south of Omaha. The Platte and its tributaries are remnants of ancestral rivers that built the Great Plains from Rocky Mountain sediments.

Although water from the Colorado River drainage augments the South Platte, virtually all of its water is diverted for use in the Denver area, and all downstream flow is treated effluent. The Platte is regulated in several places for both power and irrigation. Platte River water is also important for domestic use in Lincoln and Omaha and provides habitat for birds on the Central Flyway, including endangered Whooping Crane.

The Gasconade River, unregulated, flows northeast through the Ozark Plateau to join the Missouri west of St. Louis. In some reaches of the Ozark karst topography, it loses flow to underground drainage, while in others it gains water from springs.

Historically the Missouri River was braided, with shifting sand bars and islands that were an impediment to navigation. Abundant sediment derived from the semiarid landscape gave the river its nickname "Big Muddy." The drainage basin, divided into three zones, has a total of more than 1,300 dams and reservoirs, both large and small, six of which are major dams on the main stem. Sediments are now trapped in reservoirs.

The Upper zone, from Three Forks to the first dam at Fort Lake Peck, Montana, is not channelized and the river flows in a 1.9–3.7 mi (3–6 km) wide valley. Part of that distance, 155 mi (249 km), is the last free-flowing reach of the Missouri, a National Wild and Scenic River. The Middle stretch, also called the Interreservoir Zone, is not channelized but is impounded from Ft. Peck Lake in northeastern Montana to Gavins Pt. Dam, the site of Lewis and Clark Lake on the eastern South Dakota–Nebraska border. The Lower or Channelized zone begins near Sioux City, Iowa, where the banks are stabilized, the river is channelized, and levees emplaced, all of which facilitate navigation. Although regulated by dams, especially in the upper reaches, the lower part is still susceptible to flooding, which can overtop or breach levees.

Biota. The main stem of the Missouri River supports 136 fish species, of which 108 are native. The entire basin has 183 fish species, of which 138 are native. Three freshwater ecosystems, the Upper Missouri, Middle Missouri, and Central Prairie, are distinct but have few endemics. Pallid sturgeon (*Scaphirhynchus albus*), shovelnose sturgeon (*Pseudoscaphirhynchus kaufmanni*), blue sucker (*Cycleptus elongatus*), and sturgeon club (*Macrhybopsis gelida*) are common.

Protected Areas. The route of the Missouri River and its tributaries goes through many protected areas, including Theodore Roosevelt National Park, Upper Missouri River Breaks National Monument, and several wildlife refuges.

See also Colorado River System; Dakota Prairie National Grasslands; Greater Yellowstone Ecosystem; Mississippi River System; Rocky Mountains; Waterton–Glacier International Peace Park

Further Reading

Columbia Environmental Research Center. 2012. *CERC Science Topic: Missouri River.* U.S. Geological Survey. http://www.cerc.usgs.gov/ScienceTopics.aspx?ScienceTopicId=10

Galat, David L. et al. 2005. "Missouri River Basin." In *Rivers of North America*, edited by Arthur C. Benke and Colbert E. Cushing, 426–480. Amsterdam: Elsevier Academic Press.

World Wildlife Fund and the Nature Conservancy. 2013. "Upper Missouri, Middle Missouri." Freshwater Ecoregions of the World. http://www.feow.org/

Mojave Desert

United States (California, Nevada, and Arizona)

Geographic Overview. The landscape of the Mojave Desert in southeastern California, southern Nevada, and extreme northwestern Arizona is characterized by fault-block mountains, alluvial fans, and playas. With the exception of a stand in western Arizona, tall yuccas, called Joshua trees, are endemic to the Mojave Desert.

Geographic Coordinates. Approximately 33°45'N–37°N, 113°30'W–118°20'W

Description. The Mojave Desert covers approximately 25,000 mi^2 (64,750 km^2) of faulted mountains and structural basins with interior drainage, alluvial fans, and salt flats or playas. The general appearance is gravelly slopes and flats covered with widely spaced creosote bushes and, at higher elevations, Joshua trees.

Mojave National Preserve, formerly the East Mojave National Scenic Area, covers approximately 1.6 mil ac (647,500 ha), south of Las Vegas between I-15 on the north and I-40 on the south. One-half of the area is officially designated U.S. Wilderness. Although typical of the Mojave Desert, the preserve's biota is influenced by both the Great Basin and the Sonoran Desert due to its range of elevation, 800 ft (250 m) asl in the western basins to almost 8,000 ft (2,440 m) in the mountains, and variety of habitats. The higher elevations support Great Basin species, such as pinyon pine (*Pinus monophylla*) and juniper (*Juniperus utahensis*) woodlands and sagebrush (*Artemisia* spp.). Several sites within the preserve are representative of Mojave Desert geology. Cinder Cone National Natural Landmark showcases several cinder cones, lava flows, and lava tubes. Hole-in-the-Wall volcanic area is a remnant of the ash beds and lava flows that were deposited during the violent eruptions. The welded rhyolite tuff, which may be several hundred feet thick, is riddled with holes due to weathering. Kelso Dunes is the largest dune field in the Mojave Desert. Northwest winds pick up the sand, primarily from the Mojave River basin, and deposit it at the base of the Granite and Providence Mountains. The dune field is approximately 600 ft (180 m) above the desert floor, and the highest dune stands 300 ft (90 m) above lower, plant-stabilized dunes. The field is known for its "singing sands," sounds made as the grains slide past one another.

Death Valley is the extreme of the Mojave Desert, a fault-block mountain and graben area with elevations ranging from 282 ft (86 m) bsl to 11,049 ft

(3,368 m) asl at the top of Telescope Peak. The valley holds the record for the highest temperature recorded in the western hemisphere, 134°F (56.7°C), and the lowest annual precipitation, 1.84 in (47 mm) in North America. The northern part of Joshua Tree National Park, characterized by granite boulders, supports a large forest of Joshua trees. Lake Mead National Recreation Area includes not only Lake Mead, covering 248 mi² (662 km²) at full capacity, on the Colorado River behind Hoover Dam, but also Lake Mohave, a reservoir 67 mi (108 km) long in the canyon between Hoover Dam and Davis Dam downstream.

The Mojave is considered a warm desert because most of the precipitation falls as rain rather than snow. The majority of the Mojave is high desert, at elevations of 1,850 (550 m) to 3,650 ft (1,100 m) asl. Daytime high temperatures in summer average 90–105°F (32–41°C), while overnight lows in winter have frost. Winters see occasional snowfall. Precipitation, averaging 3.5–9.0 in (90–230 mm) a year, falls primarily in winter due to cyclonic storms from the Pacific Ocean.

Geologic History. The geologic history of the Mojave Desert is similar to that of the greater Basin and Range Physiographic Province of which it is a subsection. The basement rocks are Precambrian schist and gneiss with granite intrusions. During the Paleozoic (550–245 mya), the area was a stable continental margin where deep layers of sediments were deposited, later to become limestone and dolomite. The geology became complicated 250–60 mya, as the western part of North America was uplifted and the rocks folded and faulted. Large granite batholiths were emplaced, which are now exposed as many of the mountains in the Mojave National Preserve and in Joshua Tree National Park. Erosion was the norm until the early Tertiary (30 mya) when the crust was stretched and faulting took place. The faulting caused right lateral displacement, associated with similar movements along the Garlock Fault to the north and the San Andreas Fault further west. Crustal thinning and faulting caused large explosive volcanic eruptions, which blanketed much of the area with volcanic ash and lava flows. Later volcanic activity (7–1 mya) produced cinder cones and basaltic lava flows. The last volcanic episodes occurred approximately 8,000 years ago.

Large alluvial fans and bajadas partially filled valleys as the mountains were eroded and rivers had no outlet in this region of interior drainage. Many playas, centered in the valleys and now encrusted with salt or dried clay sediments, were part of a somewhat integrated drainage system during the wetter Pleistocene, but that drainage still did not reach the sea.

Biota. The Mojave shares many plant and animal species with the Sonoran Desert to the south and the Great Basin Desert to the north and is often considered to be transitional between those two distinct areas. Plants more common in the north and shared with the Great Basin include shadscale and blackbrush shrubs. Plants in common with the Sonoran Desert include bushes, such as creosote bush, all-scale, brittlebush, desert holly, and ocotillo. Other plants in common with the Sonoran Desert are wooly plantain, a forb; several cacti, including prickly pear, cholla, and barrel cactus (*Echinocactus* spp.); and the large leaf succulent, Mojave yucca. Typical vegetation in the Mojave is widely spaced shrubs, yuccas, and winter annuals. Of the 1,750–2,000 species of plants in the Mojave Desert, 25 percent are endemic. Indicator shrubs include spiny menodora (*Menodora spinescens*), bladder-sage (*Salazaria mexicana*), Mojave dalea (*Psorothamnus arborescens*), and scalebroom (*Lepidospartum latisquamum*). Goldenhead (*Acamptopappus shockleyi*), a forb, and Joshua tree (*Yucca brevifolia*), a large leaf succulent, are also indicator species. Joshua trees, many-branched yuccas as tall as 40 ft (12 m), grow at elevations of 3,000–7,000 ft (915–2,135 m) asl, primarily along the boundary with the Great Basin. Cacti are less common than shrubs, and most are small. Although found elsewhere, the distributions of several cactus species, including Mojave prickly pear (*Opuntia erinaceae*), silver cholla (*Opuntia echinocarpa*), beavertail (*Opuntia basilaris*), and many-headed barrel cactus (*Echinocactus polycephalus*), are centered in the Mojave. Of the 250 species of annuals in the Mojave, approximately 80 are endemic. Early spring wildflower displays are sporadic, depending on the amount and timing of precipitation.

Plant assemblages vary with topography and substrate. Creosote bush and white bursage covering 70 percent of the desert is the major plant association at lower elevations. The mid-elevations on the fans and bajadas support a variety of shrubs, including brittlebush, bladder sage, and shadscale, cacti, and Joshua trees. Dry, salty playas may have a sparse cover of saltbush (*Atriplex* spp.) and other halophytes.

More than 300 species of animals make their home in the Mojave. Wildlife, such as coyote, kit fox, bobcat, mountain lion, desert bighorn sheep, and mule deer, is similar to that found in other warm North American Deserts. Large animals require large territories and, except for coyote and mule deer, are rarely seen. Smaller mammals, including white-tailed antelope squirrel, Great Basin pocket mouse, kangaroo rat, and black-tailed jackrabbits are common. The Mojave ground squirrel (*Spermophilus mohaviensis*) is endemic.

All bird and reptile species are found also in other deserts. Birds include Roadrunner, Golden Eagle, Gambel Quail, Mourning Dove, LeConte's Thrasher, Burrowing Owl, Turkey Vulture, and hawks. Lizards and snakes, such as regal horned lizard (*Phrynosoma solare*), Mojave patchnose snake (*Salvadora hexalepis mojavensis*), and Mohave green rattlesnake (*Crotalus scutulatus*), are subspecies of more widely distributed reptiles. Neither the Mojave fringe-toed lizard (*Uma scoparia*) nor the desert night lizard (*Xantusia vigilis*) is endemic, but both are typical. Other common reptiles include desert tortoise, gila monster, chuckwalla, and desert iguana. Kelso Dunes is a distinct community with seven endemic insects.

Protected Areas. The desert physiography and ecosystems are preserved in several publicly owned lands, including Death Valley, Joshua Tree National Park, Lake Mead National Recreation Areas, and Mojave National Preserve.

See also Basin and Range Physiographic Province; Death Valley National Park; San Andreas Fault System

Further Reading

National Park Service. n.d. *Mojave National Preserve, California*. http://www.nps.gov/moja/index.htm

Quinn, Joyce A. 2009. *Desert Biomes*. Greenwood Guides to Biomes of the World. Susan L. Woodward, General Editor. Westport, CT: Greenwood Press.

U.S. Geological Survey. 2009. *Desert Landforms and Surface Processes in the Mojave National Preserve and Vicinity*. USGS Western Region Geology and Geophysics Science Center. http://pubs.usgs.gov/of/2004/1007/intro.html

Mono Lake

United States (California)

Geographic Overview. Mono Lake is a salty lake in the Basin and Range Physiographic Province east of the Sierra Nevada in east-central California. It is surrounded by pumice flats and is adjacent to the volcanic plug domes of Mono Craters. Towers composed of a type of limestone called tufa, which developed from the interaction of calcium with carbonates from the lake, dot both the shoreline and lake itself. Diversion of water that formerly entered the lake to Los Angeles has been a major environmental issue.

Geographic Coordinates. 38°01'N, 119°01'W

Description. Mono Lake, currently 60 mi^2 (155 km^2) with an average depth of 57 ft (17.4 m), is a remnant of a much larger glacial lake in the Great Basin during the Pleistocene. As evidenced by old shorelines in the surrounding area, the older lake covered 338 mi^2 (875 km^2) and was 900 ft (274 m) deep. The glacial lake was large enough to drain via Adobe Valley and into the Owens River. Mono Lake, however, has no outlet, and the salts (chlorides, carbonates, and sulfates) that accumulate as water evaporates make the lake two to three times as salty as the ocean. Evaporation from the surface in this dry climate, which receives less than 5 in (127 mm) annual precipitation, is approximately 45 in (115 cm) per year. The alkaline water (pH of 10) is not suitable for fish and feels soapy or slippery. Mono Lake is surrounded by a dry lake bed, some of it covered with pumice from Mono Craters eruptions. Mono Craters, a series of plug domes south of the lake, developed during the last 40,000 years. Pahoa Island, formed 320 years ago, is a plug dome with a rhyolite core that pushed lake sediments above water level as the dome was forming. Negit Island is a cinder cone which erupted in 1855.

Geologic History. Tufa towers on the south shore, particularly in Mono Lake Tufa State Reserve, are unusual formations. Freshwater springs that are rich in calcium emerge from the ground beneath the lake. When the calcium mixes with the carbonates (the basic ingredient in baking soda) in the lake water, they combine to precipitate calcium carbonate, a form of limestone, around the vent. Water continues to rise from the vent, while a tower of the precipitate is built around it, creating a tube within. Towers may be 30 ft (9 m) or more tall. The tufa towers, which form only underwater, are now exposed by the lower lake level. The towers on the south shore are fewer than 300 years old, while towers higher above the lake were built during higher lake levels in the past.

Biota. Ash deposits related to the Long Valley volcanic eruption in the nearby Sierra Nevada indicate that the lake has held water for at least 700,000 years. Two endemic invertebrate species have evolved—a brine fly (*Ephydra hians*) and a brine shrimp (*Artemia monica*), both of which feed on green algae in the water. Both species are summer phenomena. Only the adult stage of the fly lives above the water, and the water surface and shoreline can be covered with the insects. Both the larval and pupal stages of the fly are spent beneath the surface. Populations of the brine shrimp, 0.5 in (1.27 cm) long, number 8–12 trillion at their peak in summer. They die in fall and overwinter as cysts, or dormant embryos, on the lake bottom. Both species are rich in protein and fat and are an important food source for more than 100 bird species in summer. Mono Lake is important habitat for both nesting and migrant shorebirds. As many as 80,000–100,000 Wilson's Phalaropes (*Phalaropus lobatus*) and Red-necked Phalaropes (*Phalaropus tricolor*) stop at Mono Lake in spring and summer. Eared Grebes (*Podiceps nigricollis*) may number 750,000 to 1.5 million individuals during the August to October migration. As many as 50,000 California Gulls (*Larus californicus*) fly from the Pacific coast to nest at Mono Lake, at the second largest gull rookery in North America.

Environmental Issues. Local farmers initially diverted streams that formerly flowed into Mono Lake for irrigation water, and the volume of the lake decreased. In 1941 the lake environment became severely threatened when Los Angeles began diverting water from the streams and channeling it to southern California, causing the lake level to drop 40 ft (12.2 m). Los Angeles is now required to restore and maintain the lake level to 6,392 ft (1,948 m) asl, a goal estimated to be reached in approximately 20 years.

Further Reading

Alt, David and Donald W. Hyndman. 2000. *Roadside Geology of Northern and Central California*. Missoula, MT: Mountain Press.

"Mono Lake Committee." 2014. http://www.monolake.org

"Mono Lake Tufa State Natural Reserve." 2013. California Department of Parks and Recreation. http://www.parks.ca.gov/?page_id=514

Mont Blanc Massif

France, Italy, and Switzerland

Geographic Overview. Mont Blanc, in the northwestern Alps, is the highest peak in western Europe. It has been the site of many scientific observations related to astronomy, glaciology, meteorology, cartography, botany, physiology, and medicine. Named for its perpetual snow and ice cover (*blanc* means "white" in French), it is a major tourist center for mountain climbers and both winter and summer sports. An extensive cable car system enables visitors to reach high elevations. The mountain is famous for its highly collectible large quartz crystals.

Geographic Coordinates: 45°40'N–46°05'N, 06°45'E–07°04'E

Description. The Mont Blanc Massif, primarily straddling the French–Italian border but also extending into southwestern Switzerland, is bounded by Chamonix Valley in France on the west and the Valley of Courmayeur in Italy on the east. From Martigny, Switzerland, the massif extends southwest to Les Chapieux, France, for approximately 25 mi (40 km) and is at maximum 10 mi (16 km) wide. The summit of the massif is primarily above 11,000 ft (3,350 m) asl, with 17 peaks more than 13,000 ft (3,960 m) asl, including Grandes Jorasses, Aiguille Verte, Mont Mallet, Mont Blanc du Tacul, Mont Maudit, Aiguille du Geant, Mont Dolent, and Aiguille du Midi. The massif also includes the famous aiguilles, needlelike rock spires significant to modern rock climbing.

Several glaciers cover a total of 40–65 mi² (100–170 km²). Bossons and Mont Blanc Glacier is the largest icefield in Europe, and Mer de Glace, one of the most visited glaciers in the world, is second in length in Europe only to the Aletsch in Switzerland.

Mer de Glace was significant to early glacier research and exploration. During the 17th century (Little Ice Age), valley glaciers reached into Chamonix Valley, with subsequent retreats and advances. Ice cores provide records of atmospheric composition for the past 200 years, including the period of intense industrial development. The glaciers are significant sources of water. The Arve River collects water from several glaciers on the west slope of the Mont Blanc Massif, including the Mer de Glace and Argentiere Glacier, and flows through Chamonix to the Rhone River. The Dora Baltea River originates in the eastern massif and flows through Courmayeur to the Po River.

Although the summit of Mont Blanc is accepted to be in France, the border with Italy is disputed. France accepts the border as following a ridge of rocks south of the summit, while Italy prefers to place the border at the line of the watershed, which would put the summit of Mont Blanc in Italy. The official height, 15,771–15,782 ft (4807–4,810 m) asl, varies because it includes the snow cap covering the rock summit. Variation is due to wind sculpting the snow. Local relief is high. Nearby Chamonix and Courmayeur are 3,395 ft (1,904 m) and 4,016 ft (1,224 m) asl, respectively. The first recorded climb was in 1786 by Dr. Michel-Gabriel Paccard and Jacques Balmat, followed by Horace de Saussure, a Swiss geologist, in 1787. More than 20,000 individuals reach the summit each year, via various routes, from both the French and Italian sides.

Mont Blanc Tunnel, completed in 1965, extends for 7.25 mi (11.6 km) beneath Mont Blanc, between France and Italy.

Geologic History. The massif has two main groups of rocks, Hercynian basement core and younger steeply tilting Mesozoic rocks covering the sides. Mont Blanc is a Hercynian massif of ancient gneiss and schist, with granitic intrusions. In the Precambrian and Paleozoic (600–250 mya), the region was part of Africa (Gondwana), separated from Europe by the Tethys Sea. The Mont Blanc Massif area was a continental shelf at the edge of the Tethys and was buried by Jurassic and Cretaceous sediments deposited into that sea. Mont Blanc and the Aiguilles Rouges to the northwest across Chamonix Valley are composed of basement nappes of older, Hercynian rocks. During the Alpine orogeny in the Tertiary, when Africa converged with Europe, these older rocks beneath the Tethys Sea sediments were pushed up into dome-like structures. The sedimentary cover was eroded from the tops of the domes of both mountain masses but remains in the Chamonix Valley between the two. Cracks in the granite, caused by uplift, were filled with gaseous material that solidified to become large quartz crystals. The present landscape was extensively sculpted by glaciers.

Biota. Because the Mont Blanc Massif is surrounded by deep valleys, its biota is geographically isolated. It is at a biogeographic crossroads of western and eastern Alps flora and fauna. Although none are endemic, many plants are rare. Spanning several elevation zones, the massif has many habitats, including deciduous and pine forests, mountain scrub, mountain pastures, lakes, scree, cliffs, and the nival (snow) zone. The most obvious meadow plants are wild orchids, gentians, and edelweiss. The most frequently seen mammals and birds are chamois, ibex, marmot, and Golden Eagle.

See also European Alps

Further Reading

Ehringhaus, Barbara and Jean-Paul Trichet. n.d. "Mont Blanc. A Wonderful Treasure That Is Vulnerable and Unprotected." www.pro-mont-blanc.org/PDF/Mont BlancGB.pdf

Von Raumer, Jürgen F. and François Bussy. 2004. "Mont Blanc and Aiguilles Rouges, Geology of Their Polymetamorphic Basement." *Mémoires de Géologie (Lausanne)* No. 42. doc.rero.ch/record/5019/files/1_ raumer_mba.pdf

Monte Desert

Argentina

Geographic Overview. El Monte is South America's only interior warm desert.

Geographic Coordinates. 24°35'S–44°20'S, 65°20'W–69°50'W

Description. Located in western Argentina, El Monte desert runs from the Quebrada del Toro near Salta south into Chubut Province. The foothills of the

Southern Andes form the western border and create the rain shadow that makes it a dryland. The Monte extends all the way to the Atlantic Ocean at the Golfo San Matias and abuts Patagonia in the south. This is a land of plateaus, basins enclosed by mountains, plains, alluvial fans, and foothills. From its northern limit to about 27°S, the geomorphology is that of high longitudinal valleys paralleling the Andes, some at elevations near 9,000 ft (2,800 m). Between 27°S and 32°S, the terrain consists of isolated basins (*bolsones*) and intermontane valleys in the Andean foothills and the Pampas Mountains. Southward the Monte covers an eastward-sloping sedimentary plain until the Rio Colorado, whereupon it stretches across gravelly plateaus bearing marshy depressions and salars.

The entire region receives on average 8 in (200 mm) of precipitation each year. The wettest areas are in the north, where 13 in (350 mm) of rain may fall, primarily during the summer months. Southern parts of the desert receive precipitation year round since cyclonic storms reach the area in winter. The central Monte between southern La Roija and northern Mendoza provinces is the driest region, with aridity particularly extreme in the Calingasta–Iglesia Valley, which receives about 3 in (80 mm) of precipitation a year. Precipitation everywhere is highly variable from year to year and usually occurs as localized downpours. Due to its position near the Andes Mountains, the region is subject to foehn winds, locally known as *zondas*. These katabatic winds form when polar maritime air masses move onto the ridgeline of the Andes, chiefly during the winter months (May–November) and the dense and heavy cold air slides down the eastern slopes, warming and drying as it descends. Wind speeds can reach 125 mph (200 kmph). Although dessicating the desert below, they produce snow in the mountains. Runoff from spring snowmelt is an important water source for the plants and animals of El Monte.

Due to high elevations in the north and west and maritime influence near the coast, temperatures are cooler than in most warm deserts. Summer maxima commonly reach about 90°F (32°C), while winter temperatures vary between 37° and 70°F (2.8°–21°C). Frosts are rare. The most widespread vegetation type is shrubland (*jarillales*) dominated by creosote bush (*jarilla*) and other members of the Zygophyllaceae family. Two species of creosote bush (*Larrea divarcata* and *Larrea cuneifolia*) are closely related to the one in North American warm deserts. They have small, waxy evergreen leaves and thrive from sea level to 10,000 ft (3,000 m) on plains and plateaus and alluvial fans. The shrub community is 4–6 ft (1.5–2 m) tall. Where their taproots can reach groundwater, mesquites form an open woodland (*algarrobales*) with an understory of herbs and shrubs, including acacias. On the upper slopes of bajadas and on rocky slopes cardons, tall arborescent cacti resembling the saguaro of the Sonoran Desert, grow with an abundance of terrestrial bromeliads in the north and small shrubs in the south. Halophytic communities of saltbush or seepweed and pickleweed grow on clay soils and in salars, respectively.

Biota. The fauna of the Monte has been considered an impoverished version of that of the Gran Chaco. This is true at the species level, but not at higher taxonomic levels; and a number of endemic species enrich the mix. Among vertebrates, birds are most diverse with 235 species. Many are songbirds; the largest are tinamous and the ñandú or rhea. Of the mammals, the rare guanaco is the largest. Small mammals include a number of caviomorph rodents, most typically the mara or Patagonian hare, the gopher-like tuco-tuco, and the plains vizcacha. Xenarthans are another characteristic group and include hairy armadillo, screaming armadillo, dwarf armadillo or *pichi*, and pink fairy armadillo or *pichiciego*. Carnivores include several cats, three foxes, and several mustelids. Reptiles are represented by 63 species, 19 of which are endemic. Iguanid lizards of the genus *Liolaemus* are the most typical group and count ten endemic species among them. Two turtles and a number of snakes, including two poisonous ones, are among other reptiles found here. Amphibians are rare, but include the common toad and a number of frogs.

Protected Areas. The 16 reserves designed to protect landscapes, habitats, or species are all located in the southern and central Monte, although northern parts of the desert are a top priority in conservation.

Environmental Issues. Removal of mesquite for firewood, vineyard posts, and timber in the *algarrobales* and the withdrawal of groundwater for domestic and agriculture use are major concerns. With deforestation, overgrazing of the plains, and erosion, severe desertification and human poverty are expanding.

Further Reading

Quinn, Joyce A. 2009. *Desert Biomes*. Greenwood Guides to Biomes of the World. Westport, CT: Greenwood Press.

Rundel, P. W., P. E. Villagra, M. O. Dillon, S. Roig-Juñent, and G. Debandi. 2007. "Arid and Semi-Arid Ecosystems." In *The Physical Geography of South America*, edited by Thomas T. Veblen, Kenneth R. Young, and Antony R. Orme, 158–183. New York: Oxford University Press.

Monte San Giorgio

Switzerland and Italy

Geographic Overview. Due to the diversity, preservation, rarity, continuous record, and meticulous excavation, Monte San Giorgio, in southern Switzerland, is one of the most important fossil sites in the world. Its rocks have the world's best record of 15 million years of Triassic marine life. Although the mountain is primarily of geological significance, the limestone soils support unique dry meadows and the region is rich in fungi species.

Geographic Coordinates. 45°55'N, 08°57'E

Description. Monte San Giorgio is a wooded mountain, 3,596 ft (1,096 m) asl, on the shore of Lake Lugano in southern Switzerland and adjacent Italy. Its rocks chronicle a sequence of life in a tropical lagoon during the middle Triassic (245–230 mya). Middle Triassic sedimentary rocks lie on top of older Permian andesites and rhyolites exposed on the steep face of the pyramid-shaped mountain. Jurassic limestone is exposed on the lower southern slopes. The gentle slope to the south follows the dip of the strata, and fossil outcrops are exposed near the Italian town of Besano.

The fossil record is diverse—reptiles, fish, bivalves, ammonites, echinoderms, and crustaceans. Most are marine, but reptiles, plants, and insects from the adjacent land are also preserved. Many fossils are complete, with detailed preservation, sometimes illustrating different stages of growth or sex.

The well-managed site has had a long history of research, beginning in 1800. Because of its detailed fossil record, meticulous excavation, and strict systemic research, the site is a point of reference for other fossil sites of Triassic age in the world. The site has yielded more than 20,000 fossil remains, including 30 species of marine and terrestrial reptiles, more than 80 species of fish, and hundreds of invertebrate species, such as ammonites, echinoderms, crustaceans, bivalves, cephalopods, and insects, as well as fossils of terrestrial plants.

The most spectacular fossil fauna are 25 species of reptiles, mostly of marine origin showing different degrees of adaptation to marine life. Paddle-finned eosauropterygians are succeeded by ichthyosaurs with better developed fins. Vertebrate material includes complete articulated skeletons of ichthyosaurs, nothosaurs, placodonts, and the long-necked protorosaur, *Tanystropheus*. Some reptiles were as long as 19.5 ft (6 m). The first complete skeleton of a conodont, an extinct lamprey-like creature known previously only from mouth parts, was excavated in 1983. Cartilaginous fish, such as sharks, are less often preserved, but thousands of boney fish are found. Terrestrial fossils are less numerous. The first complete skeleton found in the northern hemisphere of a *Ticinosuchus*, an archosaur, which were ancestors of dinosaurs and crocodiles, was discovered at Monte San Giorgio. Plant life on the coast included tree ferns and conifers.

Geologic History. Approximately 3,300 ft (1,000 m) of reef limestone, dolomite, and bituminous shales (also called oil shale) were deposited in a shallow lagoon at the western margin of the Tethys Sea, sheltered from the ocean by a barrier reef. The large carbonate structures, the reef and island platforms, were built by calcareous algae, not by corals. Sedimentary deposits, which include conglomerate, sandstone, limestone, dolomite, shale, marl, and gypsum, record successions and transgressions of the sea over the reef. The main fossil-bearing rocks, rich in fishes and reptiles, are also the oldest. The bituminous shales alternating with layers of dolomite and volcanic ash, together called the Besano Formation, are 52.5 ft (16 m) thick. Most of the fossils were covered by stagnant mud on an undisturbed sea floor, where they subsequently became bituminous shales. The five distinct zones in the Besano Formation—in sequence from oldest to youngest, Grenzbitumenzone, Cava Inferiore, Cava Superiore, Cassina Beds, and Kalkschieferzone—provide a chronological record of a critical period of vertebrate species development. The Grenzbitumenzone is richest in fossils, and all zones are still yielding specimens. The four youngest beds are most productive for fossils of insects.

Biota. Plant life on the forested mountain varies with the rock and soil. Acid-loving plants, such as sweet chestnut (*Castanea sativa*), sessile oak (*Quercus petraea*), and ash (*Fraxinus excelsior*) grow on the volcanic north slopes. Broadleaf woodlands with hop-hornbeam (*Ostrya carpinifolia*) grow on moist lime-rich soils, while dry lime-rich soils support pubescent oak (*Quercus pubescens*) and manna ash (*Fraxinus ornus*). Dry meadows on limestone have a high botanic diversity. Total species number more than 100, 38 of which are rare, endemic, or protected. Fungi are especially numerous, 554 species, 130 of which are endemic. The mountain is also rich in animal life, with 109 species of vertebrates, including 27 mammals, 66 birds, 9 reptiles, and 7 amphibians; 37 of the total vertebrates are endangered. The area has a variety of insects, with 63 species of butterflies, 85 of wild bees, 11 of ground beetles, and 47 of crickets and grasshoppers.

Protected Areas. Monte San Giorgio was designated a World Heritage Site in 2003. The Italian side was added in 2010, for a total of 2,098 ac (849 ha), with a 3,432 ac (1,389 ha) buffer zone. Several layers of official protection in both countries further insure the integrity of the site.

See also European Alps

Further Reading

UNESCO. 2013. *Monte San Giorgio*. World Heritage Centre. http://whc.unesco.org/en/list/1090

United Nations Environment Programme-World Conservation M. 2008. "Monte San Giorgio, Switzerland," edited by Mark McGinley. *The Encyclopedia of Earth*. www.eoearth.org/view/article/154678/

Monteverde Cloud Forest Biological Reserve (Reserva Biológica Bosque Nuboso Monteverde)

Costa Rica

Geographic Overview. The Monteverde cloud forest is a misty, soggy high elevation woodland habitat straddling the continental divide of Central America in the Tilarán Mountains. Monteverde is renowned for its high biodiversity and its being the sole home of the now extinct golden toad (*Incilius periglenes*).

Geographic Coordinates. 10°18'N, 84°49'W

Description. The reserve encompasses mountain peaks and ridgelines over 6,000 ft (1, 850 m) asl and descends along both the Pacific slopes and Caribbean slopes to approximately 2,300 ft (700 m). The bright green cloud forest grows in perpetual mist between 4,200 and 5,900 ft (1,300–1,800 m) asl. Moisture in air masses brought in from the Caribbean Sea by the Northeast Trade Winds condenses at an elevation of roughly 4,200 ft (1,300 m) asl, producing a cloud bank over the mountains the base of which marks the lower limit of the cloud forest zone. Saturated air overtops the crestline and descends the Pacific slopes as far as about 4,900 ft (1,500 m), the lower limit of cloud forest on that side of the range. A research station in the cloud forest records 101.5 in (2,579 mm) of rainfall a year. September and October are the wettest months; March and April the driest.

At lower elevations, cloud forest trees attain heights of 100–130 ft (30–40 m), but constant strong winds on exposed mountain tops stunt and deform the trees, creating an elfin woodland 15–30 ft (5–10 m) high. In addition to the cloud forest at the higher elevations, a semideciduous tropical dry forest covers the Pacific slopes and tropical rainforest occurs on the Caribbean side of the mountains.

Biota. Epiphytic plants such as mosses, ferns, orchids and bromeliads cover tree branches in the cloud forest; 800 different kinds of such plants, adapted for extracting moisture and nutrients from the air, can be found here. The reserve may be home to the most diverse orchid flora in the world, with at least 420 species reported. Altogether a total of 3,021 plant species, including 755 kinds of tree and some 200 species of fern, is known from the reserve. The 100 or more mammals represent a mix of Nearctic and Neotropical forms and include six marsupials, three monkeys, two xenarthrans, two peccaries, one tapir, two deer, and a number of squirrels and rabbits. One-fifth of the birds observed in the reserve are North America species wintering in the Tilarán Mountains, but there are also Neotropical species such as the Resplendent Quetzal, Emerald Toucanet, and nearly 30 species of hummingbird.

The high elevation Monteverde Cloud Forest in Costa Rica grows in perpetual mist produced by air masses coming off the Caribbean Sea, overtopping the ridgelines, and descending Pacific slopes. (King Ho Yim/Dreamstime.com)

Monteverde's most famous inhabitant no longer exists. The golden toad, also known as the Monteverde golden toad, was first described in 1966 and so-named for the bright orange color of the male. (The female was a mottled dark brown.) It is known from no other site in the world. In 1987 a scientist reported seeing 1,500 toads in a single pool; the following year only 10 were sighted. The golden toad has not been seen after the single sighting in 1989, and it was declared extinct in 1992. Nineteen other amphibians also went extinct at Monteverde during that time. They are part of a still unexplained disappearance of frogs and toads around the world. Some combination of climate change, infection by chytrid fungus, and habitat loss is likely responsible.

Protected Areas. Monteverde Cloud Forest Biological Preserve was originally set aside for research and for habitat and species protection, but its relatively easy access allowed it to become a pioneer in ecotourism. It is part of a larger conservation area that also includes Santa Elena Cloud Forest and Parque Nacional Arenal. On a rare clear day, from Santa Elena it is possible to see the cone of the Arenal volcano 12.5 mi (20 km) in the distance.

Further Reading

"Monteverde Cloud Forest." n.d. Monte Verde Cloud Forest Biological Reserve. http://www.reservamonteverde.com/cloud-forest.html

"Monteverde Cloud Forest and Santa Elena Cloud Forest Reserves: Facts and History." n.d. MonteverdeCostaRica.info. http://www.monteverdecostarica.info/monteverde_tours/reserves.htm

"Monteverde Cloud Forest Reserve, North Puntarenas." n.d. GoVisitCosta Rica. http://www.govisitcostarica.com/region/city.asp?cID=402

Windeler, Britton. 2005. "The Extinction of the Golden Toad (*Bufo periglenes*)—Symptom of a Worldwide

Crisis." Tropical Ecosystem Field Courses, Miami University, Ohio. http://jrscience.wcp.muohio.edu/fieldcourses05/PapersCostaRicaArticles/TheExtinctionofthe GoldenT.html

Monturaqui Crater

Chile

Geographic Overview. Monturaqui Crater is a small, well-preserved impact crater resulting from an asteroid that struck Earth 780,000–500,000 years ago. It is located about 12.5 mi (20 km) south of Salar de Atacama in northern Chile at an elevation of 9,892 ft (3,015 m) asl. The crater was first discovered in 1962 from aerial photographs and later visited and measured by geologists.

Geographic Coordinates. 23°56'S, 68°17'W

Description. Monturaqui Crater is nearly circular, being slightly elongated in a northwest–southeast direction. It is 1,214 ft (370 m) long, 2,248 ft (350 m) wide, and 112 ft (34 m) deep. The rim rises above the general level of the Altiplano, with the southern rim area 30–50 ft (10–15 m) higher than the northern. The central part of the crater, an area of about 430 ft² (40 m²), is raised about 10 ft (3 m) and capped with a white-to-yellow deposit of lime. The lime is the product of ephemeral lakes that develop after rare summer (December–March) rains.

Impacts of asteroids and meteorites have been a basic process in the building of planets and the modification of planets' landscapes. On Earth they have apparently been significant events in the evolution and extinction of life. Yet, it is rare that impact craters, especially small ones, are not obliterated over time by erosion and deposition. High on the arid Altiplano, Monturaqui Crater has been protected from many geomorphological processes that could have leveled or covered it.

The asteroid struck and penetrated a veneer of volcanic rock and the underlying basement rock of granite. Interactions between the nickel–iron meteorite and the native rocks created impactites, rocks altered by fracturing, shock metamorphism, melting, or fusion caused by the force of and heat generated by an impact. Inside the crater can be found iron shales;

glassy, amorphous impactites; and tiny balls (spherules) formed of previously molten droplets composed of nickel–iron–cobalt–phosphorus.

The shape of the crater and the fact that the steepest slope (35°) is on the southeastern edge lets scientists reconstruct and model the impact itself. An asteroid about 50 ft (15 m) in diameter struck from the northwest at a velocity of 10.5 mi/s (17 kmps) and at an angle of 41°. The force of impact would have hurled debris 7 mi (11.5 km) and dust 14.5 mi (23.6 km) away from the site. Hydrothermal activities generated by the heat of impact in the underlying aquifer lasted some 3,500 years.

When the Mars rover *Spirit* was exploring the surface of that planet in 2004, it found a small, shallow crater with characteristics very similar to Monturaqui. Researchers have named the Martian landscape feature Bonneville Crater.

Further Reading
"Featured Images for March 2009: Impact Craters on Earth and Mars: Monturaqui and Bonneville." 2009. International Association of Geomorphologist Planetary Geomorphology Working Group. http://www.psi.edu/pgwg/images/mar09image.html

Ugalde, Hernan, Millarca Valenzuela, and Bernd Milkereit. 2007. "An Integrated Geophysical and Geological Study of the Monturaqui Impact Crater, Chile." *Meteoritics & Planetary Science* 42(12): 2153–2163. https://journals.uair.arizona.edu/index.php/maps/article/view/15534

Monument Valley

United States (Arizona and Utah)

Geographic Overview. Monument Valley, on the border between Arizona and Utah, is a stark, barren land characterized by red rock mesas, buttes, and sand dunes. It has been the backdrop for many western movies and continues to be home to Navajo sheepherders.

Geographic Coordinates. 36°58'N, 110°06'W

Description. Monument Valley, at approximately 5,500 ft (1,675 m) asl, is a desert landscape of red mesas, buttes, and pinnacles, such as Mitten Buttes and Yebechai Rocks. Spanning the border of Arizona and Utah, it is centered on Monument Valley Navajo

Tribal Park between Kayenta, Arizona, and Mexican Hat, Utah. The rocks here were uplifted into a broad anticline, the Monument Upwarp, most of which was subsequently eroded away. Many of the rock layers are also widespread on other parts of the Colorado Plateau.

The southern part of Monument Valley is part of the Navajo Volcanic Field of dikes and necks, with no trace of the original volcanoes which have eroded away. Approximately 20 diatremes, violent explosive features where volcanic breccia, a combination of igneous and country rock, collected in conduits, are evident. Agathla Peak, 1,225 ft (375 m) above the plain, is the largest. West of Mexican Hat, the San Juan River cuts a 1,000 ft (305 m) gorge of entrenched meanders, often illustrated in textbooks, through deep sedimentary rock layers.

The climate is continental mid-latitude desert, with summer temperatures reaching 90°F (32°C) and winter temperatures below freezing. Because of the high elevation and abundant sunshine, however, winter days usually warm to 40°–50°F (4.5°–10.0°C). Annual precipitation is approximately 7 in (175 mm).

Geologic History. Most of the monuments, or rock formations, are composed of two major Permian formations (270–251 mya). With one exception, all the rock layers were deposited in a continental setting, although a sea existed further west. The following are listed from the bottom up. The Halgaito shale was laid down in a lowland environment of sluggish streams, floodplains, and lakes, followed by an advance of the sea as far east as the eastern monocline of the upwarp. Sand deposited into this sea became the Cedar Mesa sandstone. As the sea retreated westward, it was replaced again by coastal lowlands and tidal flats, where the Organ Rock red shale was deposited in an arid climate. A subsequent sea advance was minor, only reaching the western margin of the upwarp. The region then became a sandy desert, indicated by the massively cross-bedded De Chelly sandstone, which is lithified sand dunes. The De Chelly sandstone is 300–400 ft (90–120 m) thick in Monument Valley, 825 ft (250 m) at Canyon de Chelly to the south, and thins to nonexistent in the north.

During the Laramide Orogeny, the Colorado Plateau was uplifted along with the Rocky Mountains. While rock layers on the Plateau remained essentially horizontal, broad upwarps and basins did develop. The Monument Upwarp, extending roughly from Green River and Moab, Utah, south to Kayenta, Arizona, covers approximately 100 mi (160 km) north to south and 50 mi (80 km) east to west. Rock layers on this asymmetrical oval dome tilt less than 2° on the west, are horizontal across the center, and dip steeply, as much as 50°, on the east side. The south and east side of the upwarp are sharply defined by Comb Ridge, a Wingate and Navajo sandstone hogback, as much as 1,000 ft (305 m) high, a prominent ridge which can be seen stretching from east of Mexican Hat south to Kayenta. Monument Valley occupies the southern part of the upwarp, where most of the horizontal rock layers have been eroded away, leaving remnants as isolated mesas and spires. The Organ Rock shale forms the red lower slopes and ledges while the De Chelly sandstone forms the sheer cliffs. Remnants of Moenkopi shale and Shinarump conglomerate, both from the Triassic, form a caprock on the sandstone. Organ Rock shale and De Chelly sandstone are replaced in the landscape by lower, older rock layers near Mexican Hat, the Cedar Mesa sandstone and the Halgaito shale, which form similar rock formations.

Although wind reshapes sand recycled from the monuments into new sand dunes, most of the erosion is done by water and frost action. As the less-resistant shale layers are eroded away, lack of support causes the sandstone above to break off in vertical slabs, a process which maintains the cliffs but diminishes the width of the mesa or butte.

Biota. Vegetation is sparse, and most of the region is barren rock and sand dunes.

Protected Areas. Monument Valley Tribal Park, straddling the border of Arizona and Utah, covers 91,696 ac (37,108 ha).

See also Colorado Plateau

Further Reading

Baars, D. L. 1973. "Permianland: The Rocks of Monument Valley." In *New Mexico Geological Society Guidebook of Monument Valley*, edited by H. L. James, 68–71. nmgs.nmt.edu/publications/guidebooks/./24/24_p0068_p0071.pdf

Rahm, David A. 1974. *Reading the Rocks. A Guide to the Geologic Secrets of Canyons, Mesas and Buttes of the American Southwest*. San Francisco, CA: Sierra Club.

Mount Cameroon

Cameroon

Geographic Overview. Mount Cameroon is a massive, active stratovolcano on the Gulf of Guinea in Cameroon. It lies on the Cameroon Volcanic Line, a chain of volcanic centers that extends from Pagalu Island in the Gulf, northeastward across the African continent into Chad. Also on this line is Lake Nyos, which ejected a huge bubble of carbon dioxide gas in 1986, suffocating 1,746 people.

Geographic Coordinates. 04°13'N, 09°10'E

Description. Mount Cameroon, the highest peak in West Africa, is an active stratovolcano on the coast of Cameroon, its highest point, Mount Fako, is 13,432 ft (4,095 m) asl. An ultra prominence, the massive volcano is not the classic cone but a broad ridge oriented from southwest to northeast and rising 12,799 ft (3,901) around the surrounding land surface. The base of Mount Cameroon measures 30 mi long and 22 mi wide (50 km × 35 km) and covers an area of 675 mi^2 (1,750 km^2). On its southern flank, near the coast, is Little Mount Cameroon or Etinde, about 5,620 ft (1,713 m) high. More than 100 cinder cones have developed on its slopes and surrounding lowlands parallel to its long axis. The volcano last erupted in 2010.

The volcano built up through a series of eruptions that have given it a step-like edifice with four distinct zones. From sea level to 4,000 ft (1,200 m), is a gently sloping area of montane rainforest now largely cleared for cultivation and settlements. Between 4,000 and 6,500 ft (1200–2,000 m) slopes are considerably steeper and subsistence agriculture is practiced in a disappearing submontane rainforest. Grasslands burned annually by local inhabitants dominate the very steep (>50°) slopes and cliffs of the zone from 6,500–9,000 ft (2,000–2,800 m). From 9,000–13,435 ft (2,800–4,095 m) a subalpine grassland grades into a cover of mosses and lichens above 12,500 ft (3,800 m). The highest peaks are barren moonscapes.

The windward slopes on the southwestern side of Mount Cameroon are one of the wettest places on Earth, receiving more than 400 in (10,160 mm) of rain a year. The northern and eastern sides are in a relative rain shadow and receive less. The summit area is considerably drier, with annual precipitation less than 80 in (2,000 mm). Heavy rains in convectional storms from the Atlantic Ocean occur from June to October; the rest of the year is dry, and dust storms associated with harmattans off the Sahara can greatly reduce visibility. Temperatures are influenced by elevation. Lowlands have daily high temperatures of 90°–95°F (32°–35°C), while the summit experiences nighttime temperatures below freezing and daily highs of about 40°F (4°–5°C).

Mount Cameroon is the only active volcano in the Cameroon Volcanic Line, a chain of more than a dozen volcanic centers that stretches northeast for 995 mi (1,600 km) from the island of Pagalu in the Gulf of Guinea into the African continent as far as the Chad Basin. On one of the extinct volcanoes is the crater lake Lake Nyos (6°26'N, 10°18'E). Magma still lies close beneath the lake and leaks carbon dioxide (CO_2) gas into the groundwater, from which it is transferred to the lake, slowly saturating the bottom waters. The lake does not turnover (as lake waters in temperate regions typically do), so CO_2 builds up until, by an unknown mechanism, the gas is suddenly released. On the night of August 21, 1986, an invisible cloud of CO_2 300 ft (100 m) high burst above the lake and slid downslope, suffocating all living organisms within a 15-mi (25 km) radius of the lake, including 1,746 people. Only two other lakes in the world are known to do this: Lake Monoun, 60 mi (95 km) southeast of Nyos in Cameroon and Lake Kivu, in the Democratic Republic of the Congo.

Geologic History. The Cameroon Volcanic Line occurs along a rift dating to 80 mya and formed when Africa was rotating counterclockwise. The rift failed to split the continent but allowed for magma to rise to the surface through fissures. Some 12 volcanic centers developed in oceanic crust and, unusually, in continental crust as well. Mount Cameroon is the only volcano in the chain that is still active. Lake Nyos fills a 690 ft (208 m) deep maar formed about 500 years ago.

Biota. The flora of the Mount Cameroon region contains some 2,300 species from 800 genera and 210 families. Of these species, 49 are considered endemic and another 50 nearly so. Birds are diverse in the submontane and montane zones, with 210 species reported. Only two are endemic: the Mount Cameroon Francolin and Mount Cameroon Speirops, a songbird. A small, isolated population of forest elephant (*Loxodonta africanus*) survives here.

Protected Areas. The Mount Cameroon National Park was established in 2010 to protect the forest elephants.

Environmental Issues. Forest clearance for agriculture is a major threat to remaining natural habitats. Fuelwood collection and uncontrolled bush burning also diminish and change the natural vegetation. Illegal hunting of mammals is a continuing problem.

See also Gulf of Guinea Islands

Further Reading

Blom, Allard. n.d. Western Africa; Coastal Cameroon and Equatorial Guinea. Tropical and Subtropical Moist Broadleaf Forests. Terrestrial Ecoregions, World Wildlife Fund. http://worldwildlife.org/ecoregions/at0121

"Geography of the Mount Cameroon Region." 2008. Mount Cameroon Inter-communal Ecosystem Board. http://www.mount-cameroon.org/geography.htm

Kayzar, Theresa. n.d. "The Lake Nyos Disaster." http://www.geo.arizona.edu/geo5xx/geos577/projects/kayzar/html/lake_nyos_disaster.html

Mount Erebus

Antarctica

Geographic Overview. Mount Erebus is the southernmost active volcano on Earth. It lies 22 mi (35 km) from the National Science Foundation's McMurdo research station on Ross Island in the Ross Sea, making it a surprisingly accessible site for the study of volcanic activity. Erebus was the Greek god of darkness, the son of Chaos. Erebus and Terror were also the names of the ships of the British explorer James Clark Ross, who discovered the volcano and the island and sea that bear his name in 1841. The tip of the Hut Peninsula on Ross Island is the extreme southern point that can be reached by ships during austral summer, today with the aid of icebreakers. The peninsula is so named, because early 20th-century British Antarctic expeditions led by Captain Robert Falcon Scott and Sir Ernest Shackleton erected huts nearby for their base stations. Both Scott's Hut and Shackleton's Hut are preserved by the Antarctic Heritage Trust, based in New Zealand. Today the peninsula hosts America's McMurdo research station on its western side; New Zealand's research center, Scott Base, is on the eastern side.

Geographic Coordinates. 77°30'S, 167°09'E

Description. Mount Erebus is one of four volcanoes forming Ross Island. Erebus stands 12,448 ft (3,794 m) asl and has been active continuously since 1972. A lava lake in the summit crater is open to the sky, unlike other such lakes that are almost always covered by a rock cap. The other volcanoes—Mount Terror, Mount Terra Nova, and Mount Bird—are dormant or extinct. All are ice-covered. Mount Terror is a shield volcano with numerous satellite cinder cones and lava domes on its flanks. The base of Mount Erebus is also a shield volcano, but the top is a stratocone, which has been leveled several times in the geologic past by the formation of calderas. The summit plateau is 10,500 ft (3,200 m) asl and is the rim of the youngest caldera, which formed during the Late Pleistocene. The contemporary cone built up within this caldera. On its summit is a 360 ft (110 m) deep elliptical crater that measures approximately 1,640 ft × 1,969 ft (500 m × 600 m) in diameter. Within this crater is yet another crater about 820 ft (250 m) wide and 328 ft (100 m) deep. This inner crater contains the lava lake.

Long-lived lakes of molten lava in volcanic craters are extremely rare. Only three or four other volcanoes in the world are known to contain these active features: Mount Kilauea in Hawaii, Erta Ale in Ethiopia, Mount Nyiaragongo in the Democratic Republic of the Congo, and probably Volcán Villarica in Chile. The lava rises from a magma chamber deep beneath the crater, and enormous bubbles of water vapor, carbon dioxide, and carbon monoxide burst forth on a regular basis. These bubbles can be 65–130 ft (20–40 m) across. The lake surface rises and falls by 6.5–10 ft (2–3 m) and emits different gases every 10–18 min.

The world's southernmost active volcano, Mount Erebus, is located on Ross Island in the Ross Sea, Antarctica. (Darryn Schneider/Dreamstime.com)

Occasionally, strong eruptions eject volcanic bombs onto the crater's rim.

Another striking feature of Mount Erebus is the Erebus Glacier, which flows down the southern slopes and moves west into McMurdo Sound, where its tongue floats on the sea during the summer months when the sea ice has melted. This tongue is about 7 mi (11–12 km) long and 30 ft (10 m) high. During the summer, ocean waves eat away at its edges, creating deep ice caves and scalloping the margins of the ice tongue.

Geologic History. Mount Erebus has been active for at least 10,000 years.

Protected Areas. The entire Antarctic region is protected and managed by the international Antarctic Treaty System.

Further Reading

"Erebus." n.d. Global Volcanism Program, Smithsonian Institution. http://www.volcano.si.edu/world/volcano.cfm?vnum=1900-02%3D

"Erebus Glacier." 2011. Earth from Space. http://earthfromspace.photoglobe.info/spc_erebus_glacier.html

Raloff, Janet. 2013. "As Erebus Lives and Breathes." *Science News*. http://www.sciencenews.org/view/feature/id/349079/description/As_Erebus_Lives_and_Breathes

Mount Etna

Italy

Geographic Overview. Mount Etna, the largest active volcano in Europe and the Mediterranean region, is also one of the largest and most active on Earth. Known and observed since Greek and Roman times, it provides a wealth of historic data and research opportunities. It has a diversity of geologic and geomorphologic features and is a natural laboratory for colonization and establishment of plants on new surfaces. It is one of the most visited volcanoes in the world and is a World Heritage Site.

Geographic Coordinates. 37°45'N, 14°58'E

Description. Mount Etna is a large basaltic composite volcano in Northeastern Sicily. Its elliptical base is approximately 24 mi × 29 mi (38 km × 47 km), and the mountain is approximately 10,990 ft (3,350 m) asl. The mountain is a series of stratovolcanoes with summit craters or calderas, including Valle del Bove, 14 mi^2 (37 km^2), with walls as high as 3,300 ft (1,000 m). More than 260 craters on Mount Etna's flanks can produce lava. The most significant summit volcano is Ellittico, formed 14,000–15,000 years ago. The mountain displays a variety of spectacular eruption styles, including summit degassing, explosive eruptions, basaltic lava flows, fire fountaining, steam, and mudflows. Most eruptions are effusive, with a quiet outpouring of lava, but the volcano can also produce pyrotechnic eruptions of tephra. The three summit craters are more frequently explosive while the flank vents produce lava and cinder cones.

Historical records begin in 1500 BC, and approximately 200 eruptions have been documented. One-quarter of Sicily's population lives on Etna's slopes, which are terraced with apple, chestnut, and hazelnut orchards and vineyards. The volcano has directly caused fewer than 100 deaths.

Geologic History. Mount Etna lies above the boundary where the northern edge of the African plate is subducting under the Eurasian plate. Numerous faults in the region, including the Malta–Iblei escarpment, form a structural boundary between the continental crust of Sicily and the oceanic crust of the Ionian Sea floor. The first volcanic activity in the area lasted more than 230 million years, followed by the development of Mount Etna during the last 500,000 years. Eruptive centers shifted during that time, erecting a collage of volcanic cones. Mount Etna sits on an ancient shield base of tholeiites, rocks similar to basalt but richer in silica and iron. The first eruptions took place under water in a shallow bay, eventually building a 9.3 mi (15 km) elongated shield. Approximately 110,000 years ago, fissure flow basalts changed to explosive eruptions, building the first composite cones on the flanks of the shield, the Rocche and Tarderia volcanoes. The Trifoglietto Volcano, in the southeastern part of Valle del Bove, reached a maximum height of approximately 7,875 ft (2,400 m). This marked the end of the eruptive centers in the Valle del Bove and the start of the biggest eruptive center on Etna, the *Ellittico* (meaning "elliptical"), which is now the main

structure. Intense effusive and explosive eruptions created a volcano that may have been 12,000 ft (3,700 m) high, with many flank eruptions. The Ellittico stage ended approximately 15,000 years ago, with explosive eruptions which made a 2.5 mi (4 km) diameter caldera. Subsequent eruptions filled the Ellittico caldera and built the current summit cone, Mongibello, which remains active and periodically remodels the volcano summit.

The most powerful eruption was in 122 BC, when a large volume of pyroclastics (ash and lapilli) damaged the city of Catania on the southeast flank. Fissure flows from an eruption recorded in 1669 reached the sea more than 10 miles away. Eruptions in 1775 melted snow and ice, causing large lahars. An extremely violent eruption in 1852 covered more than 3 mi^2 (7.8 km^2) of the flanks with lava. The longest eruption began in 1979 and lasted for 13 years. Eruptions have occurred almost annually since 2001.

Protected Areas. Etna National Park, 224 mi^2 (581 km^2), was established in 1987.

See also Aeolian Islands; Mediterranean Sea

Further Reading

Seach, John. n.d. "Mt. Etna Volcano—John Seach." Volcano Live. www.volcanolive.com/etna.html

Sistema Rischio Vulcanico. n.d. "Mount Etna Volcano, Sicily." http://srv1.rm.ingv.it/srv/srv/study-sites/mount-etna/mount-etna-volcano-sicily

Mount Everest

Nepal and China

Geographic Overview. Part of the crest of the Himalayan Mountains and on the border of Nepal and Tibet, China, Mount Everest is the highest point on Earth. In spite of extreme conditions, the peak attracts numerous climbers and has been summited by more than 2,700 people. It is called *Chomulungma*, meaning "goddess mother of the world" in Tibetan, and *Sagarmatha*, meaning "ocean mother" in Sanskrit.

Geographic Coordinates. 27°59'N, 86°56'E

Description. Mount Everest was determined to be the highest mountain in 1852 by an Indian surveyor, Radhanath Sikdar. The mountain was known as Peak

XV until 1865 when it was named for Sir George Everest, a British geographer and surveyor in India from 1830 to 1843. Global positioning system (GPS) measurements in 1999 updated the peak's elevation at 29,035 ft (8,850 m). Its pyramid-shaped peak has three fairly flat sides, called faces. The North Face, scored by steep gullies called couloirs, rises 12,000 ft (3,600 m) above the Tibetan Plateau. The Southwest Face rises above Nepal and the South Col. The East Face rises from Tibet. A prominent layer of limestones called the Yellow Band is visible just below the summit. The three ridges separating the faces merge at the summit, which is capped by hard snow overlain by a softer snow. Snow depth, and thus height of the mountain, fluctuates seasonally, but is accepted to be 6.5 ft (2 m) deep.

The mountain is clothed with snow and glaciers—Kangshung Glacier on the east, Rongbuk Glaciers on the north and northwest, Pumori Glacier on the northwest, and Khumbu Glacier on the west and south. Drainage flows to the southwest, north, and east.

July temperatures on the summit may rise to 0°F (−18°C), while January temperatures may plunge to −76°F (−60°C). The mountain is subject to sudden storms and temperature changes. Because its summit penetrates the lower levels of the Jet Stream, sustained winds of more than 100 mph (160 kmph) are frequent.

The first major expeditions were in the 1920s. It is unknown if George Mallory succeeded in reaching the summit in 1924 before he succumbed; his body was found in 1999. The first successful ascent was made in 1953 by New Zealander Edmund Hillary and his Nepalese Sherpa guide, Tenzing Norgay. Since then, many people have completed the climb, and many more have attempted and turned back; 200 have died. A major challenge above 25,000 ft (7,600 m) is hypoxia, which induces physical and mental problems caused by oxygen deprivation. Climbing season is April and May, before summer monsoons bring soft snow and avalanches, and in September, after the monsoons. The most common route is via the Khumbu Icefall and the South Col, but other routes are possible, including from the Tibetan side.

Geologic History. Mount Everest, along with the rest of the Himalayan Mountains, was formed by the closure of the Tethys Sea as it subducted beneath Asia, followed by the collision of the Indian continent with the Asian plate. Part of the Greater Himalayas, Mount Everest began to take its present form during the Pleistocene, beginning 2 mya and continuing to the present. The Himalayas continue to rise and move northward. Three formations derived from the Tethys seafloor comprise the summit of Mount Everest, all divided by low-angle faults, which thrust the formations over one another. From 28,200 ft (8,600 m) to the summit is the Qomolangma, or Jolmo Lungama Formation, consisting of Lower Paleozoic (Ordovician) limestone and recrystallized dolomite and siltstone, white to dark gray in color. The limestone contains fossils of ostracods, trilobites, and crinoids. In the middle, 23,000–28,200 ft (7,000–8,600 m), is the North Col Formation, layers of marble, schist, and phyllite. These layers, also from the Lower Paleozoic but older (Cambrian), are metamorphosed deep sea deposits of sandy limestone, sandstone, and mudstone. The lowest zone, beginning at 23,000 ft (7,000 m), is the Rongbuk Formation of schist, gneiss, and dikes and sills of light-colored granite.

Biota. Lower valleys may be clothed with rhododendrons and birch and pine forests. Higher elevations have alpine vegetation until snowline and glaciers are reached. Lesser pandas and Tibetan bears occupy the forested zone, with rare snow leopards in the alpine. Most of the mountain is unable to support life.

Protected Areas. On the Nepalese side, Sagarmatha National Park is a World Heritage Site.

Environmental Issues. In spite of the expense involved, the mountain is extremely popular with climbers. Trash from climbing expeditions, including oxygen canisters, torn tents, broken equipment, and human waste, litters the mountain. Although expeditions have been mounted to remove debris, bodies remain because they are too heavy to carry down. Deforestation on lower slopes is significant as climbers cut wood to keep themselves warm.

Attributed to world carbon emissions, snowline has retreated upwards more than 500 ft (150 m) and glaciers have melted approximately 13 percent in the last 50 years, threatening the water sources for several Asian rivers.

See also Himalayan Mountains; Tibetan Plateau

Further Reading

GlacierWorks. n.d. "Everest." http://explore.glacierworks .org/en/

Searle, M. P. 2013. *Colliding Continents: A Geological Exploration of the Himalaya, Karakoram, and Tibet.* Oxford: Oxford University Press.

Searle, M. P., R. L. Simpson, R. D. Law, R. R. Parrish, and D. J. Waters. 2003. "The Structural Geometry, Metamorphic and Magmatic Evolution of the Everest Massif, High Himalaya of Nepal—South Tibet." *Journal of the Geological Society, London* 160: 345–366.

Mount Fuji

Japan

Geographic Overview. Mount Fuji, the highest point in Japan, is one of Japan's Three Holy Mountains and the only Japanese volcano composed of basalt. Widely represented in Japanese art as early as the 11th century, the peak has become the sacred icon of the country. More than 300,000 people climb to the crater summit each year.

Geographic Coordinates. 35°22'N, 138°44'E

Description. Mount Fuji, approximately 60 mi (100 km) southwest of Tokyo in south-central Honshu, is a large stratovolcano. Built from multiple eruptions of basaltic lava and pyroclastics, Mount Fuji is contrasted with other Japanese volcanoes, which are andesite. Mount Fuji is one of the few stratovolcanoes in the world composed primarily of basalt, with many lava tubes and tree molds. From a base measuring 32 mi (50 km) in diameter, the picturesque symmetrical cone rises to 12,388 ft (3,776 m) asl. The summit crater is 1,640 ft (500 m) wide and 820 ft (250 m) deep.

The Mount Fuji region is known for an abundance of high-quality water, which is used for both domestic and industrial use. The water is purified as it percolates through porous lava flows, emerging as springs and ponds, such as Wakutama Pond, Shiraito Falls, Kohama Pond, and Kakita River. Summit and flank basalt flows blocked drainages against the Misaka Mountains to the north, creating Fuji Five Lakes, a popular resort.

Temperatures generally decrease 3°F for every 1,000 ft elevation gain (0.6°C/100 m). Except for the months of June through October when the peak is usually snow free, maximum temperatures at the peak are generally below freezing. Temperatures at Mishima, 236 ft (72 m) elevation at the base of the volcano, average 41°F (5°C) in winter and 59–77°F (15–25°C) in summer. Prevailing westerly winds at the peak are strongest in winter, averaging 39 ft/sec (12 m/s).

Climbing Mount Fuji is a very organized, and often crowded, activity. July and August is the official climbing season for both Japanese and foreign visitors. The mountain has 10 stations, the base being Number 1 and the summit Number 10, enabling climbers to mark progress, get refreshments, or rest in a hut before continuing. The mountain has four 5th Stations, offering various routes to the summit. Because it is the easiest to access from Tokyo, the most popular and busiest route is via Kawaguchicho 5th Station. Although steep and rocky, the climb is not technical, but the bare slopes offer no protection from the elements.

Geologic History. Mount Fuji's complex origin is the result of the junction and movement of three tectonic plates. The Pacific Plate is subducting west beneath the Philippine Plate, which is moving north and subducting beneath the Eurasian Plate, of which Japan is a part. Mount Fuji is part of the Fuji Volcanic Zone, a volcanic chain extending north from the Northern Mariana Islands through the Izu Islands and into northern Honshu.

Mount Fuji developed from three major periods of eruption. Komitake, east of Mount Misaka, erupted at least 400,000–300,000 years ago, and some scientists believe 600,000 years ago. Ashitaka volcano, east of Komitake and west of Suruga Bay, erupted during the same time period. Approximately 80,000–20,000 years ago, Kofuji explosively erupted between Komitake and Ashitaka, while those two volcanoes were quiet. Shinfuji, or modern Fuji, began to develop 11,000–8,000 years ago. Huge amounts of basaltic lava and ash incorporated and almost covered Komitake, a remnant cone of which can be seen on Fuji's slope. Early eruptions spread the broad basalt base, while later eruptions were more explosive with less lava. The past 2,000 years has seen more flank eruptions, indicated by more than 100 cones. Mount Fuji last erupted October 26, 1707, blanketing Tokyo with ash and forming a large new crater on the east flank.

Pyroclastic emissions changed to basalt fountaining, and activity ceased January 1, 1708.

Biota. Plant and animal life varies with elevational zone. The alpine belt, 2,300–5,250 ft (700–1,600 m), has a natural deciduous forest of beech, maple, and bamboo, with some plantations of cedar, cypress, and fir. Nikko fir, northern Japanese hemlock, and veitch fir occupy the subalpine belt, 5,250–8,200 ft (1,600–2,500 m). Gold birch, Japanese larch, and veitch fir grow at the treeline transition to the alpine zone, which is bare rock or sparsely covered with mosses and lichens.

The fauna includes 37 mammals, such as the rare Japanese serow (*Capricornis crispus*), an occasional Asiatic black bear, and Japanese squirrels and foxes. Birds are numerous, with approximately 100 breeding species. Owls, warblers, flycatchers, nutcrackers, and thrushes are common. Amphibians are represented by only seven species because of the lack of surface water; reptile species number five. Many insects, especially butterflies, are found in the deciduous forest belt and in the grasslands.

Protected Areas. Several sites on and around Mount Fuji have been declared protected areas, with a variety of names, such as National Natural Treasure or Place of Scenic Beauty. Fuji-Hakone-Izu National Park is included in a World Heritage Site, which incorporates cultural as well as physical features.

Environmental Issues. Because the plate movement that created the volcano has not stopped, the mountain is generally classified as active or dormant. Slightly increased seismic activity in 2000–2001 caused concern. Mount Fuji's water has recently been contaminated, and the water level in Kohama Pond is decreasing to the extent that the lava base is now visible. Climbers and illegal four-wheel drive vehicles and motorcycles mar the landscape and leave litter and trash.

See also Mariana Islands Archipelago

Further Reading

Endo, K. et al. 2003. *Asama and Fuji Volcanoes*, in *IUGG (International Union of Geodesy and Geophysics) 2003 Field Trip Guidebook*, 37–65. Tokyo: Volcanic Society of Japan.

"Fujisan Network." n.d. http://www.fujisan-net.gr.jp/en glish/index.htm

Mount Kenya

Kenya

Geographic Overview. Mount Kenya, an extinct volcano in the eastern branch of the Great Rift Valley of Africa, is the second highest mountain on the African continent. Even though located on the Equator, its jagged peaks still possess several small glaciers. The distinct afroalpine vegetation is well developed on its upper slopes. Mount Kenya is an important catchment area, bringing water to more than two million people.

Geographic Coordinates. 00°09'S, 37°18'E

Description. Mount Kenya is a large, isolated stratovolcano topped by several jagged peaks, the highest of which, Batian, stands 17,057 ft (5,199 m) asl. An ultra prominence, Mount Kenya rises 12,549 ft (3,825 m) above the surrounding landscape. Among other high peaks clustered near the center of the massive mountain are Nelion at 17,021 ft (5,188 m) asl and Point Lenana at 16,355 ft (4,985 m) asl. An ice cap covered the top several times during the Pleistocene Epoch, and the peaks were sculpted by alpine glaciers. U-shaped valleys with steep walls, glacial lakes (tarns), and moraines abound at elevations above 10,800 ft (3,300 m). Ten or more small glaciers still cling to high slopes, but they are rapidly disappearing and expected to be gone in another 25–30 years. Periglacial features found above 13,100 ft (4,000 m), such as patterned ground, blockfields (felsenmeer), and solifluction lobes, are products of continuing freeze–thaw activities associated with permafrost that lies just a few inches (centimeters) below the surface and the nightly freezes experienced at high elevations. The highest peaks and pinnacles (gendarmes) occur at the intersections of rugged, ice- and frost-carved ridgelines. Below 10,800 ft (3,300 m) the mountain was never glaciated and its flanks are generally smooth and dome-like, although many extinct volcanic plugs and craters occur on the northeast side.

Mount Kenya lies on the equator, where seasonal change is dictated by the twice annual passage of the Intertropical Convergence Zone (ITCZ), which draws in moist air masses from the Indian Ocean. Two rainy seasons—a long one from mid-March to June and a short one from October to December—alternate with two dry seasons, one from July to September and the other, the driest time of year, from December to mid-March. Above 14,800 ft (4,500 m), most precipitation occurs as snow, but total amounts are small. The lower southeastern slopes are the wettest, receiving up to 98 in (2,500 mm) of rain annually. Totals diminish with increasing elevation, so that near 12,000 ft (3,650 m) asl only about 35 in (900 mm) falls each year. Currently less snow falls on the summit than is lost by daily melting, so no new ice is being formed.

Temperatures vary with elevation. At 10,000 ft (3,000 m), the mean annual temperature is 45°F (7°C), at 13,750 ft (4,200 m) about 35°F (1.5°C), and at 15,650 ft (4,750 m) near 18°F (−7.5°C). The equatorial position means there is little variation in day length or temperature through the year. However, large diurnal temperature ranges of 22°–32°F (12°–18°C) are encountered. Typically, mornings are sunny, and the highest temperatures of the day occur between 0900 and 1200. Clouds begin to form in the lowlands in the morning as moist air blows in from Lake Victoria and temperatures fall. Upslope winds carry the clouds to the summit in the afternoon, where they shade the remaining glaciers from the most intense sunlight of the day. High air currents are dry, however, and the clouds soon dissipate, leaving clear skies again just before sundown. Radiational cooling at night produces heavy frosts at higher elevations, and nighttime temperatures near the summit can plummet to 23°F (−5°C).

Four clear altitudinal zones form concentric rings around Mount Kenya above the savannas of the surrounding lowlands, which lie at roughly 6,600 ft (2,000 m) asl: montane forests, heathlands, afro-alpine, and nival. A well-defined bamboo zone occurs in the middle of the montane forest. The heathland occurs between 10,500 and 12,500 ft (3,200–3,800 m). Most plants are small-leaved shrubs. The well-developed afroalpine zone, beginning near 13,000 ft (3,500 m) asl, and an analog of the Páramo in the Andes Mountains of South America, is a tussock grassland with giant rosettes—lobelias (*Lobelia* spp.) with towering flower spikes, giant groundsels (*Dendrosenecio* spp.), and tree senecios (*Senecio* spp.), giving an otherworldly look to the high slopes above treeline. Masses of lady's mantle (*Helichrysum* spp.) shrubs cluster around the bases of the giant groundsels. The

nival zone, at elevations above 15,000 ft (4,500 m), is a recently deglaciated landscape of bare rock with lichens and mosses and small, ground-hugging plants tucked into crevices. Exposed ridges, open to frost and wind, support little vegetation other than occasional grass tussocks.

Geologic History. The Mount Kenya stratovolcano was active 3.1–2.6 mya. It may have attained a height of 21,325 ft (6,500 m) or more before becoming extinct and being eroded by ice several times during the Pleistocene. The most extensive ice cap existed about 150,000 years ago, the next to last time the top was covered by ice. The last glacial maximum occurred between 23,000 and 14,500 years ago.

Biota. The afroalpine zone in Africa occurs on several isolated peaks, and each hosts endemic plants adapted to cold and intense sunlight and ultraviolet radiation. On Mount Kenya, the tree-like groundsels include the woody-stemmed *Dendrosenecio keniodendron* and the giant senecio *Senecio brassica*, both unique to the mountain. *Lobelia keniensis*, a low rosette with a 5 ft (1.5 m) flower spike, is also restricted to Mount Kenya, while *Lobelia telekei* is also found on the Aberdares and Mount Elgon. *Lobelia keniensis* responds to the cold nights by closing its leaves around the growth tip to make a safe pocket of air that stays above freezing. The densely haired undersides of the leaves of *S. brassica* similarly insulate tender plant tissue from cold as well as intense solar radiation.

The mammalian fauna of the afroalpine zone consists of few species. Rock hyrax live among the rocks, groove-toothed rats construct burrows at the bases of giant senecios and grass tussocks, and common duiker forage among giant groundsels. The raised mounds of the endemic Mount Kenya mole-rat are conspicuous at elevations up to 13,000 ft (4,000 m) asl. Many plants are pollinated by birds such as the Malachite Sunbird, counterpart of the Andean hummingbirds, since the rarified air prohibits bees, wasps, and mosquitoes.

Protected Areas. Mount Kenya National Park protects Mount Kenya above an elevation of 6,600 ft (2,000 m), from the montane forest zone to the summit peaks. It was set aside to conserve the unique montane and alpine flora and glacial landscapes, as well the water source for millions of Kenyans. A 6-mi (9.8 km) long corridor has been constructed to allow elephants to pass from the Park to the Lewa Wildlife Conservancy and Ngare Ndare Forest Reserve (LWC-NNFR) north of the mountain. The park is otherwise fenced to keep elephants away from neighboring farms. Plans are to construct other wildlife corridors to Samburu National Park and other conservation areas to the south. The Park and LWC-NNR were inscribed as a UNESCO World Heritage Site in 1997.

Environmental Issues. Climate change is a major threat to Mount Kenya ecosystems, as warming will not only melt the last of the glaciers but force habitat zones to shift upward. The proposed corridors to Samburu and other nature preserves are designed to mitigate some of the effects of climate change. The headwaters of two major Kenyan rivers, the Tana and the Ewaso Ng'iro, are on the mountain's slopes. Decreasing precipitation and meltwaters threaten the millions of people who directly depend on these rivers for their water supplies.

See also Mount Kilimanjaro; Páramo; Rwenzori Mountains

Further Reading

"Mount Kenya National Park/Natural Forest." 2013. World Heritage Centre, UNESCO. http://whc.unesco.org/en/list/800

Quinn, Joyce A. 2009. "Afroalpine." In *Arctic and Alpine Biomes*. Greenwood Guides to Biomes of the World. 176–185. Westport, CT: Greenwood Press.

Mount Kilimanjaro

Tanzania

Geographic Overview. Mount Kilimanjaro is the highest mountain in Africa and, as such, is one of the Seven Summits. It can be climbed without special mountaineering gear. Kilimanjaro is also the largest free-standing mountain in the world. UNESCO's World Heritage Center recognizes Kilimanjaro as a "superlative natural phenomenon." The title of Ernest Hemingway's famous 1936 short story, "The Snows of Kilimanjaro," refers to the now disappearing ice cap on this massive dormant stratovolcano located close to the equator.

Geographic Coordinates. 03°05'S, 37°21'E

Description. One of the largest volcanoes on Earth, Kilimanjaro is a cluster of three large stratovolcanoes oriented northwest–southeast some 30 mi (50 km) east of the Great Rift Valley. The highest point, Uhuru Peak, is 19,341 ft (5,895 m) asl. This is an ultra prominence; the impressive mass of the mountain, appearing as a truncated cone, stands 19,308 ft above the surrounding plains, the sole large mountain in the area. The oldest volcano, Shira (13,000 ft or 3,962 m asl), forms the broad shoulder on the west-northwest side of Kilimanjaro; only Shira's western and southern rims remain, so today it appears as a high plateau. East of Shira is Mawenzi, a rugged, sharp-topped peak high on the east-southeast flank of Kilimanjaro. The steep western slopes of its summit area are eroded into crags and pinnacles; on the east, cliffs more than 3,300 ft (1,000 m) high descend toward two gorges, Great Barranca and Lesser Barranca.

The youngest and largest of the volcanoes is the central peak, Kibo. The 1.5 × 2.2 mi (2.4 × 3.6 km) caldera at its summit gives Kilimanjaro its flat-topped profile. Uhuru Peak sits on the southern rim of this caldera. Inside are two concentric craters. Within the nearly 500 ft (150 m) high rim of the inner Reusch Crater is a funnel-shaped deposit of ash called the Ash Pit. The Ash Pit has a diameter of 1,310 ft (400 m) and depth of roughly 500 ft (150 m). The stench of sulfur rises from Reusch Crater, and occasional fumaroles still emit gases from the Ash Pit. More than 250 small parasitic cones occur along a rift northwest and southeast of Kibo. Long ago eruptions from Kibo spewed black obsidian into Shira's caldera and around the base of Mawenzi, forming a high plateau called the Saddle, the largest area of alpine desert (or tundra) in Africa.

Ernest Hemingway's short story, "The Snows of Kilimanjaro," put an ice-covered mountain permanently into the public's imagination, and at one time the ice cap and glaciers on the high slopes (not snow) were part of the landscape. (The classic view of Mount Kilimanjaro is from Kenya's Amboseli National Park a short distance to the north.) In 1912 two icefields covered 4.6 mi² (12 km²) of Kilimanjaro's summit, including both Kibo and Mawenzi. Heat rising from Reusch Crater kept only that area ice-free. By 2007, only 0.7 mi² (1.85 km²) remained, representing a loss of ice mass of nearly 85 percent. Between 2000 and 2007, the icefields and glaciers were not only retreating, but also rapidly thinning. The largest glacier, Furtwänger Glacier, has lost 50 percent of its thickness. A drying climate since the 1960s may be to blame. The remaining ice stands as large, sheer-sided blocks or "cathedrals" with jagged edges reaching upwards or as smaller columns, pillars, and towers.

The long rains of March–May are produced by the Southeast Trade Winds bringing in moisture from the Indian Ocean. From May to October, dry anti-trades arrive and serve to prevent significant precipitation above 10,000 ft (3,000 m). The short rains of November–February are the result of the Northeast Asian Monsoon. Precipitation is again concentrated at elevations below 10,000 ft (3,000 m).

The base of Kilimanjaro is in the East African savanna. Six life zones occur on the mountain's slopes. From 2,600–9,000 ft (800–2800 m) is a moist montane forest composed of gymnosperms such as podocarps and junipers and large broadleaved trees such as rosewood. This zone receives about 90 in (2,300 mm) of rain annually, and much has been converted to agriculture. Unlike the montane zone on other tropical mountains in Africa, there is no bamboo belt on Kilimanjaro. Above the forest, extending to 11,800 ft (3,600 m) is the heather zone, a misty landscape of tree heaths (*Erica arborea*) and tall shrubs such as *Protea kilimandscharica*. Temperatures can drop to freezing at night. About 50 in (1,300 mm) of rain is received each year. From 11,800 to 13,780 ft (3,600 m–4,200 m) is a belt of moorland, a tussock grassland dotted with iconic afroalpine plants such as giant groundsels and lobelias. Total annual precipitation at these elevations is reduced to about 21 in (525 mm). Between 13,000 and 16,000 ft (4,000–5,000 m), on the Saddle, is an alpine desert consisting of three species of tussock grasses and a few everlastings. This is cold, dry zone with intense solar radiation. Less than 8 in (200 mm) of rain and snow falls each year. Finally, from 16,404 to 19,341 ft (5,000–5895 m) the land is barren rock except for occasional lichens.

Geologic History. Shira first erupted along a lateral fault of the Great Rift Valley about 750,000 years ago and continued building for 250,000 years. When it became extinct, it collapsed, forming a caldera.

Mawenzi, the next in age, formed within Shira's caldera. About 460,000 years ago, Kibo rose. The black obsidian covering the Shira caldera and the base of Mawenzi (i.e., forming the Saddle) was produced in one of Kibo's eruptions about 360,000 years ago. The chain of parasitic cones came later, as did Reusch crater. The Ash Pit formed about 200 years ago. The last remaining signs of activity on Kibo are the fumaroles and sulfur fumes emitted by Reusch Crater and the Ash Pit.

The ice in the Northern Icefield has been dated to 11,700 years ago. At maximum glaciations during the Pleistocene Epoch, an ice cap of some 150 mi^2 (400 km^2) covered both Kibo and Mawenzi. Moraines are found as low as 11,800 ft (3,600 m) asl. Permanent ice remains on Kibo, although the Northern and Southern icefields are rapidly losing mass and retreating. In 20–30 years, all ice is expected to be gone.

Biota. The montane forest is species-rich in plants and animals. East African savanna and woodland mammals are well represented by some 140 species, among them seven primates, 25 antelopes, 25 carnivores, and 24 bats. In the heath and moorland zones giant lobelias (*Lobelia deckenii*) sends up flower spikes as much as 30 ft (10 m) tall, and two subspecies of giant senecio or groundsel grow. The endemic *Senecio johnstonii cottonii* is restricted to elevations above 11,800 ft (3,600 m); *S. j. johnstonii* has a greater elevational range, growing between 8,000 and 13,000 ft (2,450–4,000 m) asl.

Protected Areas. Above the 8,850 ft (2,700 m) contour line, the mountain is protected in Mount Kilimanjaro National Park. When it was established in 1973, only areas above treeline were included, but the park was extended in 2005 to include the montane forest zone. The park was inscribed as a UNESCO World Heritage Site in 1987.

Environmental Issues. The area included in Mount Kilimanjaro National Park is threatened by adjacent land-uses and encroachments along its boundaries. Migration routes taken by larger mammals, some of which are endangered species, are vulnerable to blockage as is access to dispersal areas. Poaching, invasive species, fire, and air pollution are additional threats, but the greatest concern is climate change and the loss of summit icefields and glaciers. A drying climate reduces cloud cover and allows more intense solar radiation to increase ablation of the ice. Reduced ice coverage reduces albedo and increases dark surfaces, which absorb heat and further melt the thinning ice. Already several streams flowing from the mountain have dried up.

See also Mount Kenya

Further Reading

"Background Information on Kilimanjaro." *Climb Mount Kilimanjaro: The Trekking Guide to Africa's Highest Mountain.* http://www.climbmountkilimanjaro.com /about-the-mountain/

"Kilimanjaro National Park." n.d. World Heritage Centre, UNESCO. http://whc.unesco.org/en/list/403

Thompson, L. G., H. H. Brecher, E. Mosley-Thompson, D. R. Hardy, and B. G. Mark. 2009. "Glacier Loss on Kilimanjaro Continues Unabated." Proceedings of the National Academy of Sciences of the United States of America. http://www.pnas.org/content/106/47/19770.full

Mount McKinley and Denali National Park and Preserve

United States (Alaska)

Geographic Overview. Denali National Park and Preserve is an example of wild and unspoiled interior Alaska, a wilderness with its natural components of vegetation and wildlife. The area includes Mount McKinley, North America's highest peak, called Denali by native Alaskans. Mount McKinley is part of the 600 mi (965 km) long Alaska Range, a topographic barrier and drainage divide between northern and southern Alaska.

Geographic Coordinates. 63°04'N, 151°00'W

Description. The 7,370 mi² (19,085 km²) of Denali National Park and Preserve are characterized by rugged, glaciated mountain peaks, large valley glaciers, meandering rivers in broad valleys, vast treeless landscapes, an abundance of both large and small wildlife, and migratory and resident birds. Mount McKinley and the other high peaks are part of the granite central massif. The top of Mount McKinley towers approximately 18,000 ft (5485 m) above adjacent lowlands. Recent measurements using new radar mapping technology places the summit of the southern peak, measured at 20,320 ft (6,194 m) in 1952, at 20,237 ft (6,168 m) asl, 83 ft (25 m) shorter than previously thought. The northern peak is 19,470 ft (5,934 km) asl.

Its unaltered landscapes preserve original subarctic ecosystems. Because of both the latitude and elevation, the climate is severe and weather unpredictable. Temperature at 14,500 ft (4,420 m) can be −95°F (−70°C), with wind gusts more than 150 mph (240 kmph). Normal winter temperatures in the park are approximately 0°F (−17.8°C), and summers are 40–80°F (4.5–26.7°C). Snow can occur in any month, and rivers are frozen from late October to late April. More than 50 percent of the mountain mass is covered with permanent snow or ice.

Because most moisture comes from the Gulf of Alaska, the biggest glaciers are on the southeast side of the mountain mass. The five largest are Yentna, Kahiltna, Tokositna, Ruth, and Eldridge, each 20–30 mi (32–48 km) long. Except for Muldrow Glacier, at 35 mi (56 km) long because it follows a fault, most north-facing glaciers are smaller and shorter. The park has discontinuous permafrost and periglacial features, such as solifluction, frost heaving, patterned ground, and ice wedges.

Cretaceous fossils can be found in some sedimentary rocks. Since the first footprint of a theropod, a meat-eating dinosaur, was found in 2005, thousands more have been discovered. Tracks of *Magnoavipes denaliensis*, a 5 ft (1.5 m) tall wading bird, do not match any known fossil. Wood, leaf imprints, and other plant fossils from the Cretaceous also occur.

Geologic History. Several factors contribute to the configuration of Mount McKinley and the Alaska Range. The Denali fault system, North America's largest at 1,300 mi (2,100 km) long, begins south of the Alaskan panhandle, curves northwest into an arc passing just south of Fairbanks, then trends southwest to the Bering Sea. The Alaska Range is in the center of this arc. The Pacific Plate and the North American Plate have been converging since the Paleozoic, causing subduction, deformation of rocks, and uplift. From the Cretaceous through the Tertiary, pieces of oceanic plates and microplates, each terrane with a different assemblage of rocks, were accreted onto North America, complicating the geology of the Alaska Range.

Mount McKinley, the highest peak in North America, rises above Ruth Glacier in Mount McKinley and Denali National Park and Preserve in Alaska. (Danny Lehman/Corbis)

The faults form the boundaries of the many terranes. In the late Mesozoic, the Pacific oceanic plate subducted beneath the North American continental plate, subjecting the various terranes to deformation, metamorphism, and uplift. Volcanoes erupted and many granitic plutons were emplaced. Convergence of the plates at the end of the Tertiary uplifted the McKinley massif. Current movement along the Denali fault system is primarily horizontal or transform, with the southern side moving westward as the Pacific Plate slowly rotates counterclockwise. Confirmed by frequent earthquakes in the region, uplift also continues to occur at approximately 0.04 in (1 mm) per year. During the Pleistocene, an isolated icecap developed on the Alaska Range, and large valley glacier continue to carve the mountains.

Biota. The park has more than 650 species of flowering plants, plus mosses, lichens, fungi, and algae.

Because the Pleistocene ice sheet separated Alaska from the rest of North America, the park's biota has more affinity to that of northeastern Asia. Beringian endemic species are found only in northeastern Asia and in Alaska. Plant associations are taiga and tundra. Taiga, a stunted forest of white spruce and black spruce along with aspen, paper birch alder, and balsam poplar, grows primarily in protected river valleys. Above an elevation of approximately 2,700 ft (825 m), which is the limit of tree growth, are tundra habitats. Moist tundra supports sedge tussocks and cottongrass, and small willow or birch shrubs. Tundra plants, such as moss campion and dwarf rhododendron that grow in dry areas, are tiny and ground-hugging. Above 7,000 ft (2,135 m) asl, even tundra plants become sparse among the rocks.

The park's 39 mammal species are all year-round residents. Large animals include caribou, moose, Dall sheep, grizzly bear, and wolves. Small mammals include fox, weasel, wolverine, lynx, martin, snowshoe hare, hoary marmot, pika, porcupine, beaver, shrew, vole, and lemmings. Of the 169 bird species, 80 percent are migratory, such as wheatears, Arctic terns, and jaegers, which nest on the tundra but spend winters elsewhere, including Africa and Antarctica. Resident birds include ptarmigan, Lapland longspur, grouse, short-eared owls, and many species of shorebirds.

Protected Areas. Established in 1917 as a wildlife refuge, the size, name, and purpose of Denali National Park and Preserve have changed over the years. Three distinct units—Denali Wilderness, Denali National Park additions, and Denali National Preserve—are managed differently. Some are preserved as wilderness, while others allow subsistence use by native Alaskans. The park and reserve was designated a Biosphere Reserve in 1980 because of its pristine subarctic ecosystems.

Further Reading

Brease, Phillip. 2004. "Denali National Park and Preserve." In *Geology of National Parks*, 6th ed., edited by Ann G. Harris, Esther Tuttle, and Sherwood D. Tuttle, 477–501. Dubuque, IA: Kendall Hunt.

National Park Service. n.d. *Denali National Park & Preserve*. www.nps.gov/dena/

National Park Service. n.d. "Denali National Park & Preserve, Alaska." *Geology Fieldnotes*. www.nature.nps.gov/geology/parks/dena/index.cfm

Mount Monadnock

United States (New Hampshire)

Geographic Overview. Mount Monadnock is the highest mountain in southwestern New Hampshire. At 3,165 ft (965 m) asl, its summit stands 1,000 ft (300 m) above all nearby peaks. Mount Monadnock was celebrated in the writings of Ralph Waldo Emerson and Henry David Thoreau and is one of the most popular hiking destinations in the world. The name *Monadnock*, derived from an Abenaki term denoting an isolated peak, has become a generic term in geology for a mountain that is the erosional remnant of a formerly higher surface.

Geographic Coordinates. 42°52'N, 76°06'W

Description. The top 300 ft (90 m) of Mount Monadnock is bare rock, the result of a fire in the early 1800s that destroyed the thin soil cover. An artificial treeline occurs well below what latitude and climate would dictate. The popularity of Mount Monadnock for hiking is due in part to the spectacular panorama from the open crags and exposed ledges at the top, which rises 2,150 ft (655 m) above the surrounding landscape. One can see for 100 mi (160 km) in all directions. On clear days, parts of all six New England states can be seen, including Mount Washington to the north, the Prudential Building in Boston to the east, and the Green Mountains of Vermont and Berkshires of Massachusetts to the west and southwest. The peak is visited by 125,000 hikers a year, making it the third most climbed mountain in the world after Mount Fuji, Japan (200,000 visitors a year), and Tai Shan, China (an estimated 2,000,000 climbers a year), which has been a sacred site for at least 3,000 years.

Composed of schists and quartzites, metamorphic rocks related to those of the White Mountains to the north, the mountain displays small- to medium-scale folds on many of its rock faces; the famous Billings Fold, 450 ft (140 m) west of the summit was featured in an early textbook on structural geology by Marland Billings. "Turkey track" crystals of sillimanite up to 4 in (10 cm) long are another visible product of metamorphism. When William Morris Davis, an American geographer and geomorphologist, developed his theory of the cycle of erosion of landscape development (the geomorphic cycle) in the late 19th and early 20th centuries, he viewed the end product of erosion as a flat plain (peneplain) above which only exceptionally resistant rock remained as isolated mountains. He named these features "monadnocks" after Mount Monadnock.

Geologic History. Mount Monadnock is structurally part of an overturned fold that formed during the Acadian Orogeny some 400 mya.

Biota. Mount Monadnock's base lies in a forest dominated by northern red oak. From 2,000 to 2,500 ft (610–760 m) asl, a northern hardwood forest of oak, red maple, and yellow birch with a ground cover rich in ferns occurs. This transitions into a red spruce-balsam fir forest, which grows to elevations near 2,900 ft (880 m) asl. Above this closed needleleaf forest, short trees of red spruce and paper birch form an open canopy on rocky ridges. Lichens and mosses are abundant. In a narrow band between 2,900 and 3,000 ft (880–915 m) asl, wind and snow have pruned the branches and stunted the growth of small shrubs of the heath family (e.g., sheep laurel, blueberry, mountain cranberry, and rhodora) to create a krummholz in pockets of thin soil among the barren ledges. Above 3,000 ft (915 m), patches of arctic-alpine vegetation grow in cracks and crevices in the bare rock of the burned over area.

Protected Areas. Most of Mount Monadnock is owned by the Society for Protection of New Hampshire Forests, but parts are also owned by the State of New Hampshire and the Town of Jaffery, New Hampshire. It was designated a United States National Landmark in 1987.

See also Appalachian Mountains

Further Reading

Brandon, Craig. "Monadnock: More Than a Mountain." 2008. http://www.monadnockmountain.com/FAQ.htm

Pitcher, Frederick. "Monadnock Trails-Monadnock Mountain." 2011. http://monadnocktrails.com/

Share, Jack. "Written in Stone . . . Seen through My Lens," 2011. http://written-in-stone-seen-through-my-lens.blogspot.com/2011/01/billings-fold.html

Mount Olympus

Greece

Geographic Overview. Mount Olympus was the mythical home of the ancient Greek gods, their palaces hidden from view by frequent misty clouds. It is the highest mountain in Greece and the second highest in the Balkan Peninsula. The complex geology illustrates an unusual sequence of rock units. The Mount Olympus area is one of the most significant botanical sites in Europe and is significant for bird life.

Geographic Coordinates. 40°00'N–40°12'N, 22°27'E–22°43'E

Description. Mount Olympus is located on the border between Thessaly and Macedonia in Greece, on the Aegean coast near the Gulf of Thermai. It is 163 mi (263 km) northwest of Athens, 48 mi (78 km) southwest of Thessaloniki, and 16 mi (24 km) southwest of Katerini. The mountain forms a natural barrier and has been a refuge for Greeks avoiding such enemies as the Turks of the Ottoman Empire and Germans in World War II.

The mountain, not a single peak but a high ridge with a broad summit, rises abruptly from the coast, only 11 mi (18 km) away. The highest point is Mytikas, 9,570 ft (2,917 m) asl. The mountain area is roughly circular, 15.5 mi (25 km) wide, covering more than 193 mi^2 (500 km^2). It is characterized by steep slopes, sharp ridges, deep ravines, and alpine fields. It is frequently called Higher Olympus to avoid confusion with Lower Olympus, at 5,210 ft (1,588 m) asl. Both mountains are separated from Mount Ossa to the south by the Pinios River through the gorge of Tempe.

Few streams are found above 3,300 ft (1,000 m) elevation, and no springs occur above 6,600 ft (2,000 m) because water infiltrates the porous rock. The only lakes, from melting snow, are ephemeral. The upper mountain, above 6,550 ft (2,000 m), has glacial and periglacial features. Thick conglomerate and alluvial deposits cover the lowlands.

The peak's climate resembles that of northern Europe. Annual precipitation is 40–70 in (1,000–1,800 mm), half of which falls as snow, blanketing the mountain from November to May. Summer thunderstorms bring torrential rain and hail. Depending on elevation, winter temperatures average –4° to 14°F (–20° to –10°C), while summer temperatures average 32–65°F (0–20°C). Strong winds, often more than 62 mph (100 kmph), are common.

Geologic History. The geology of Mount Olympus is not well understood. The mountain is primarily late Mesozoic limestone and limestone metamorphosed to schist, with some outcrops of granite and flysch (clastic marine deposits) on the southwestern side. Scientists believe that it is a tectonic window exposing younger limestone that was thrust under the older Pelagonian zone, which stretches from Macedonia southeast to the Cyclades in the Aegean Sea. Pelagonian zone rocks are continental crust of Triassic and Jurassic metamorphosed limestone and Paleozoic gneiss. Cretaceous limestone from western Greece was pushed eastward, under the Pelagonian zone. Erosion through the Pelagonian rocks formed a window, exposing the younger limestone beneath. Mount Olympus has many tectonic units, including carbonates, schist, and pre-Alpine orogeny crystalline and granitic masses, volcanic sediments, and ophiolites (oceanic crust). The convergence of Africa with Europe during the Alpine Orogeny caused complex thrusting and imbrication of these different units.

Biota. Mount Olympus has more than 1,700 species of plants, 25 of which are rare endemics. Four elevation zones are distinguished. From 820 to 1,640 ft (250–500 m), typical mediterranean sclerophyllous maquis is dominated by shrubby oaks, *Arbutus*, junipers, and *Pistacia*. Beech and oak woodlands, 1,640–5,000 ft (500–1,400 m) asl, are predominantly black pine, beech, and oaks. Riparian vegetation in the ravines consists of plane trees, willow, and alder. The rare Bosnian pine (*Pinus heldreichii*) gradually replaces black pine to form pure stands up to 6,550 ft (2,000 m) asl. The forest limit marking the beginning of the alpine zone is at 8,200 ft (2,500 m), where a variety of alpine ecosystems support rare endemic plants. The treeless alpine has 150 species, one-half of which are found only on the Balkan Peninsula.

The mountain supports more than 32 mammal species, the most common being chamois, deer, wolf, wild pig, fox, ferret, and wild cat. Of the 108 bird species, birds of prey are significant, including large populations of species scarce elsewhere in Europe. Many nesting sites are inaccessible, ensuring the birds' safety from both human and natural predators. Mount Olympus is famous for a large number of butterfly species.

Protected Areas. Designated in 1938, Mount Olympus was the first Greek National Park. The park covers 92 mi^2 (238 km^2). The large network of trails was developed primarily by loggers and sheep herders. Several refuges provide services ranging from lodging and meals to basic beds. The area was declared a Biosphere Reserve in 1981 for its beauty and ecological and mythological importance. In 2003, the area below Mount Olympus was incorporated into the European network NATURA 2000 for protection of the natural environment. Mount Olympus is being considered as a World Heritage Site.

Further Reading

Management Agency of Olympus National Park. 2008. *Olympus National Park*. http://www.olympusfd.gr/us/Default.asp

Reischmann, T., D. K. Kostopoulos, S. Los, B. Anders, A. Avgerinas, and S. A. Sklavounos. 2001. "Late Palaeozoic Magmatism in the Basement Rocks Southwest of Mt. Olympus, Central Pelagonian Zone, Greece: Remnants of a Permo-Carboniferous Magmatic Arc." *Bulletin of the Geological Society of Greece* 34: 985–993. http://www.academia.edu/216340/Late_Palaeozoic_magmatism_in_the_basement_rocks_southwest_of_Mt._Olympos_central_Pelagonian_Zone_Greece_Remnants_of_a_Permo-Carboniferous_magmatic_arc

UNESCO. 2014. "The Broader Region of Mount Olympus." http://whc.unesco.org/en/tentativelists/5862/

Mount Pelée (Montagne Pelée)

Martinique

Geographic Overview. Mount Pelée has been the most active volcano in the Lesser Antilles. It is best known for its deadly eruption in 1902, which killed 28,000 people. This was globally the deadliest volcanic eruption of the 20th century and third deadliest in historic time after Tambora in Indonesia in 1815, which killed 92,000 people and Krakatau, also in Indonesia, in 1883, which killed 36,000. After continuous eruptions and lava dome building, Pelée had a spectacular spine extrusion in 1905. The volcano is currently dormant.

Geographic Coordinates. 14°49'N, 61°10'W

Description. Mount Pelée is a stratovolcano rising 4,583 ft (1,397 m) above the Caribbean Sea on the northern end of the island of Martinique. It has had more than 20 major eruptions in the last 5,000 years.

Eruptions at Mount Pelée are explosive and associated with pyroclastic flows and followed by the growth of lava domes in the central vent. Today lava domes produced during the 1902 and 1929 eruptions fill the Etang Sec crater. The latter determines the current morphology of the mountain.

Geologic History. The edifice of the Mount Macouba lava dome formed 100,000 years ago and then collapsed, forming a caldera, the rim of which can still be seen. The southwestern part of the edifice collapsed 25,000 years ago. A new dome rose, called by geologists paleo-Pelée, and then collapsed some 9,000 years ago, leaving a horseshoe-shaped caldera. The current Etang Sec crater at the summit formed on the rim of the paleo-Pelée caldera about 3,000 years ago. In 1902, the mountain had not had a major eruption since 1851–1852. Fumaroles at the summit were reported in 1889, indicating the volcano was still active. In February 1902, the distinctive odor of sulfur was detected in low-lying areas around the volcano, and in April a high column of black smoke rose over 1,600 ft (488 m) into the air from the Etang Sec crater. From late April into early May, rumblings were heard and ashfalls began to coat nearby villages with black dust. On May 5, one side of the Etang Sec crater collapsed, generating a mudflow that reached the sea and killed 25 people. In the early morning hours of May 8, the devastating eruption and pyroclastic flows that completely destroyed the city of Saint-Pierre and all but two of its inhabitants occurred. Violent eruptions, pyroclastic flows, nuées ardentes, and avalanches continued for months. A second deadly eruption on August 30 partially destroyed settlements on the south and east sides of the volcano, killing another 1,000 people. The 1902 lava dome had attained a height of 1,148 ft (350 m) by early July and continued to grow in October into the famous lava spire that towered 1,000 ft (305 m) above the floor of the crater. The solid shaft was 350–500 ft (107–152 m) wide. It proved unstable, however, and crumbled into a pile of rubble in March 1903.

The extremely high temperatures of pyroclastic flows and nuées ardentes accounted for most of the deaths. One survivor of the destruction of Saint-Pierre was a young shoemaker, Léon Compere-Léandre, who had been sitting at his doorstep across the valley from the peak at the edge of the flow. He had raced inside and hidden under a table, but was still badly burned. The other, more famous, survivor was Louis-Auguste Cyparis, who was incarcerated in a nearly windowless dungeon beneath the city jail. He, too, was burned and it took four days for rescuers to find him, but he became a celebrity of sorts and later toured with the Barnum and Bailey Circus.

The mountain erupted again in 1929 and produced a 150 ft (45 m) high spine. Activity continued until 1932, when the last major eruption of Mount Pelée occurred. It has been quiescent since.

Environmental Issues. Volcano-generated earthquakes rattle Martinique a few times a year. The mountain is monitored for signs of activity by the Observatoire Volcanologique de la Montagne Pelée, 5 mi (8 km) away from the volcano.

See also Lesser Antilles

Further Reading

San Diego State University. n.d. "Mount Pelée Eruption (1902)." How Volcanoes Work. http://www.geology.sdsu.edu/how_volcanoes_work/Pelee.html

Smithsonian Institution, Museum of Natural History. "Pelée." n.d. Global Volcanism Program, http://www.volcano.si.edu/volcano.cfm?vn=360120

Mount Pinatubo

Philippines

Geographic Overview. The cataclysmic eruption of Mount Pinatubo in 1991 was the second largest volcanic eruption of the 20th century and the largest to affect a densely populated area. The ash cloud spewed into the stratosphere affected weather worldwide, and its ash deposits devastated a large area of Luzon Island in the Philippines. Although accurate prediction and evacuation saved many lives, the aftermath continues to have a profound impact on the economy and safety of the people of Luzon.

Geographic Coordinates. 15°08'N, 120°21'E

Description. The stratovolcano of Mount Pinatubo, located on the northern island of Luzon in the Philippines 60 mi (100 km) northwest of Manila, is a complex of lava domes. In July 1990, Mount Pinatubo awakened from its 500-year dormancy with an M 7.8 earthquake 60 mi (100 km) to the northeast. By mid-March 1991, earthquakes were occurring frequently around the mountain, followed in April by small explosions, which dusted villages with ash and initiated the evacuation of 5,000 people. The quake and eruption activity continued, and in early June a lava dome began to extrude. A nearby U.S. military base was evacuated of 18,000 people. An explosive eruption occurred on June 12, and more people were evacuated. After beginning eruptions at 1:42 P.M. on June 15, the volcano continued to erupt for nine

Lake Pinatubo fills the crater of Mount Pinatubo, a volcano in the Philippines that explosively erupted in 1991. (Wouter Roesems/Dreamstime.com)

hours, culminating in a massive pyroclastic eruption and collapse of the summit to form a new caldera, 1.6 mi (2.5 km) in diameter and dropping the crest of the mountain by approximately 850 ft (259 m), from a pre-eruption height of 5,725 ft (1,745 m) asl down to 4,875 ft (1,486 m). Smaller, weaker eruptions continued through early September 1991. From July through October 1992, a new lava dome developed to plug the caldera.

Huge pyroclastic flows of hot ash, gas, and pumice filled valleys up to a thickness of 660 ft (200 m). The deep pyroclastic flows remained hot, as much as 900°F (500°C) in 1996. Water reaching these hot areas vaporizes and explodes fine ash into the air.

The ash cloud, 21 mi (34 km) high and more than 250 mi (400 km) wide, extended into the stratosphere. Prevailing winds first pushed it west and southwest toward Asia, but by mid-July, the ash had encircled the globe, and within a year covered the entire Earth. Ash fell as far away as Borneo, Singapore, South Vietnam, and the Indian Ocean. The cloud blocked solar radiation entering the atmosphere, causing a worldwide drop in temperature of approximately 1°F (0.5°C). Complex interactions from the ash cloud may have influenced other weather phenomena, causing floods and droughts. Millions of tons of sulfur dioxide were expelled, which mixed with water to create sulfuric acid, which in turn depleted ozone. In 1992–1993, the hole in the Antarctic ozone layer was the largest ever recorded.

A complication was the passing of Tropical Storm Yunya less than 50 mi (75 km) to the northeast, causing more rain and filling the air with water vapor. The ash mixed with the water vapor created very heavy, wet tephra, which was deposited over most of the island. Approximately 772 mi^2 (2,000 km^2) was covered to a depth of 4 in (10 cm), and in one area the thickness was 13 in (33 cm). Most of the deaths were attributed to roofs collapsing under the weight of the wet ash. Lahars, fast-moving mudflows caused by heavy monsoon and typhoon rains incorporating pyroclastic deposits, continue to destroy homes or bury whole villages, causing more destruction than the eruption itself. Many homes and fields remain covered.

Although approximately 800 people were killed and 100,000 left homeless, forecasts by the Philippine Institute of Volcanology and Seismology and by the United States Geological Survey encouraged evacuation that saved at least 5,000 lives. The disaster cost approximately $0.5 billion in property and economic damage. A second eruption in August 1992 resulted in the death of 72 persons.

Geologic History. Mount Pinatubo is part of the Luzon Arc chain of volcanoes on the west coast of Luzon. A subduction zone and the Manila Trench, dipping eastward beneath the island, is the cause of the volcanic activity. The ancient Pinatubo, which developed approximately 1 mya, was an andesite-dacite stratovolcano. Remnants can be seen in the adjacent peaks of the ancient wide caldera. Several flank vents on this ancestral volcano formed lava domes or plugs—Mounts Negron, Cuadrado, Mataba, Bituin, and Tapungho. It ceased eruption thousands of years before modern Pinatuba developed. Over the last 35,000 years, the young volcano has had at least six periods of strong activity, with many pyroclastic flows.

Environmental Issues. Although not currently active, Mount Pinatubo remains a threat. Lahars continue to occur, usually during the southwest monsoon and typhoon seasons, June to October. Lahar-dammed water courses create temporary lakes that eventually overlap and erode the lahar deposits, creating massive floods that often occur in the absence of concurrent rain. With stream channels filled by previous lahars, the mudflows now flow onto adjacent land. The Institute of Volcanology and Seismology has established a sophisticated warning system for lahar danger.

Further Reading

Newhall, Chris, James W. Hendley II, and Peter H. Stauffer. 1997. *The Cataclysmic 1991 Eruption of Mount Pinatubo, Phillippines*. Fact Sheet 113-97. U.S. Geological Survey. http://pubs.usgs.gov/fs/1997/fs113-97/

Newhall, Chris, Peter H. Stauffer, and James W. Hendley II. 1997. *Lahars of Mount Pinatubo, Phillippines*. Fact Sheet 114-97. U.S. Geological Survey. http://pubs.usgs.gov/fs/1997/fs114–97/

Newhall, Chris and R. G. Punongbayan, editors. 1996. *Fire and Mud: Eruptions and Lahars of Mount Pinatubo, Philippines*. Philippine Institute of Volcanology and Seismology (PHILVOLCS)/USGS/. University of Washington Press.

Mount Rainier

United States (Washington)

Geographic Overview. Mount Rainier (called Tahoma by Native Americans), at 14,410 ft. (4,392 m) asl, rises almost 3 vertical mi (4.8 km) above the lowlands to the west. As part of the volcanic zone where the Juan de Fuca Plate is subducting beneath North America, the mountain remains tectonically active. The national park experiences about 20 small earthquakes each year. The mountain is covered with valley glaciers, currently in retreat. Due to floods and lahars, an eruption on the ice-covered mountain would be extremely hazardous to the heavily populated areas near the volcano.

Geographic Coordinates. 46°51'N, 121°46'W

Description. Mount Rainier is a composite volcano in the Cascade Mountain range in eastern Washington, approximately 50 mi (150 km) southeast of Seattle. Its steep mountain landscape includes forests, meadows, alpine environments, and glacial features. Glaciation has deeply carved a craggy mountain. Mount Rainier is the most glaciated mountain in the lower 48 states, with 25 glaciers radiating from the peak and covering a total of 35 mi² (92 km²). Emmons Glacier is the largest. The mountain is the source of six major rivers—Carbon, Cowlitz, Mowich, Nisqually, Puyallup, and White—and has nine watersheds, 382 lakes, and 470 rivers and streams.

Rainier is a popular climbing site, with climbers traversing glaciers to reach the summit. Several routes are possible, each taking two to four days to complete.

With an elevational change of 12,800 ft (3,900 m), Mount Rainier has a variety of environments and altitudinal zonation. In general, the climate is cool and wet, and Mount Rainier's proximity to the west coast moderates extreme temperatures. Depending on elevation, daytime high temperatures in summer may be in the 50–75°F (10–24 °C) range, potentially dropping to freezing at night. Except on the highest slopes, winters are mild, 20–35°F (−7° to 2°C). Mean annual rainfall averages 75 in (1,900 mm) at the lowest elevations to 126 in (3,200 mm) at Paradise at 5,400 ft (1,645 m) asl. Snowfall is high. The minimum snow recorded at Paradise was 26 ft (7.9 m) in winter of 1939–1940, and the maximum was 93.5 ft (28.5 m) in winter of 1971–72.

Geologic History. Similar to most of the other volcanoes in the Cascade Range, Mount Rainier sits on top of the eroded 40-million-year-old volcanoes of the Western Cascades, which consisted of dark andesite, rhyolite, and volcanic ash. Directly beneath Mount Rainier is a large granite mass, the Tatoosh Pluton, magma that solidified in the Tertiary (18–14 mya). These older rocks are believed to be part of the North Cascades microcontinent. Vented through the pluton, modern Mount Rainier began erupting in the Quaternary, approximately 1.0–0.5 mya. The first lava flows filled canyons carved into the pre-existing surface, while subsequent flows built the volcanic cone. Although Mount Rainier is a stratovolcano, most of the rock is a very dark andesite. Some eruptions occurred beneath glaciers, creating floods and lahars. The cone was 1,000 ft (305 m) higher 75,000 years ago before explosions and landslides removed the top. The summit crater currently has two steam vents.

Biota. The park supports more than 950 species, subspecies, or varieties of vascular plants, many nonvascular plants and fungi, 182 bird species, 65 mammal species, 14 amphibian species, 5 reptile species, and 14 species or subspecies of fish. Over half of the landscape is forested. Forests on disturbed areas are fewer than 100 years old, while old-growth stands are 1,000 or more years old. Higher elevations support alpine meadows with short shrubs and herbaceous wildflowers and sedges among scattered clumps of trees. Above treeline is the alpine zone, half of which is sparsely vegetated with low-growing plants, the other half snow and ice.

Protected Areas. Mount Rainier was established as a national park in 1899. Approximately 97 percent of the park's 236,625 acres (95,762 ha) is official U.S. Wilderness.

Environmental Issues. The most recent volcanic eruption occurred in the 1890s, although there were steam explosions in the 1960s and 1970s. Mount Rainier's future is unknown, but it has hazardous potential. More than 3.3 million people live in the Seattle–Tacoma metropolitan area. Even relatively quiet eruptions would melt glaciers and cause major floods and mudflows. Mudflows are possible even in the absence of an eruption. The Osceola Mudflow, 5,600 years ago, was caused by the collapse of part of the peak, releasing enough debris to cover 100 mi² (160 km²). It is also possible that the mountain could have a source of acidic magma such as rhyolite, which could cause a violent explosion similar to that of Mount Saint Helens or to the eruption which destroyed Mount Mazama and created Crater Lake.

Glaciers are retreating and ice volume is decreasing.

See also Cascade Mountains; Crater Lake; Mount Saint Helens

Further Reading

Alt, David D. and Donald W. Hyndman. 1998. *Roadside Geology of Washington*. Missoula, MT: Mountain Press.

National Park Service. n.d. *Mount Rainier National Park, Washington*. http://www.nps.gov/mora/naturescience /naturalfeaturesandecosystems.htm

United States Geological Survey. n.d. *Volcano Hazards Program—Mount Rainier Geology and History*. http://volcanoes.usgs.gov/volcanoes/mount_rainier /mount_rainier_geo_hist_74.html

Mount Roraima

Brazil and Venezuela

Geographic Overview. Among the easternmost tepuis of the Guiana Shield, at the triple border of Brazil, Guyana, and Venezuela, the tableland of Mount Roraima stands above the clouds like the prow of a great ship.

Geographic Coordinates. 05°09'N, 60°46'W

Description. Mount Roraima has the classic character of eastern tepuis with a thick resistant capstone of horizontal beds of Proterozoic sandstone overlying the less resistant igneous rock of the Guiana Shield. The flat summit covers 12 mi² (31 km²)

and is surrounded by steep escarpments more than 1,000 ft (400 m) high. Its general elevation is 8,858 ft (2,700 m) asl, the highest plateau in a cluster of tepuis stretching 500 mi (800 km) from west to east and known as the Pacaraima Mountains. Mount Roraima's highest prominence, located solely in Venezuela, stands 9,219 ft (2,810 m) asl.

Spectacularly high waterfalls drop down vertical cliffs that end in broad talus slopes. On the southern side, however, is a shelf with a gradual incline known as Whiteley's Ledge, which allows adventurers to ascend to the summit with relatively little difficulty. The top of Mount Roraima is a bizarre world of algae-blackened rock sculpted into intricate shapes by chemical weathering in the constantly wet climate. More like the karst landscapes expected in limestone than typical sandstone environments, the summit is a land of rock towers, arches, great sinkholes, and deep ravines. Below the surface, there is a vast network of caves with underground rivers flowing through a maze of pillars and columns.

An area of 2 mi² (5 km²) on the northwest portion of the plateau known as the great labyrinth contains tens of thousands of sharp, tooth-like rock spires. Igneous intrusions that occurred as South America converged with the Nazca Plate have left an intricate web of dikes and sills, some of pure quartz. A narrow passage in the north of the tepui summit, the Valley of Crystals, is strewn with glistening, loose white and pink quartz crystals an inch or two (2–5 cm) long, so many that it looks like a light snow has fallen. All over the summit pools of standing water, yellowed by tannins and other organic acids, and clumps of low vegetation abound.

The summit experiences a cool, wet climate. Temperatures generally range from 40°F into the upper 70's F (6°–25°C), but may hover near freezing at night on the highest parts of Mount Roraima. More than 350 in (9,000 mm) of rain falls annually as a result of orographic uplift.

Biota. Plant life on top of Mount Roraima is part of a pantepui flora and a vegetation type restricted to elevations above 5,000 ft (1,500 m). Isolated tepui communities typically have few genera but many species, a pattern derived from the adaptive radiation of a few pioneer species much like that found among Darwin's finches on the Galápagos Islands. Endemism is high. The flora is dominated by carnivorous plants: pitcher plants, sundews, and bladderworts. There are also a number of terrestrial orchids and bromeliads. The most inhospitable sites on bare rock may be colonized by algae, lichens, mosses, lithophytic ferns, and orchids, as well as some grasses and other herbs. The larger plants cluster in cracks and depressions and the shelter of rocks wherever sediments and nutrients are trapped for a while before being carried away by rainwater. These areas have been described as "rain deserts" with occasional "oases."

Where thin sandy soil has developed, a "tepui heath" of herbs and dwarfed shrubs exists. The often dense heath is composed of hummocks of carnivorous plants, orchids (e.g., *Epidendrum* spp.), and bromeliads, including the carnivorous *Brocchinia* spp. Low *Bonnetia roraimoe* bushes may be scattered among them. On lower slopes are cloud forests where taller specimens of *Bonnetia* are fed by runoff from above.

The fauna consists mainly of arachnids, insects, and millipedes. Most are dark-colored to blend with the rocks. The tiny endemic toad, *Oreophrynella quelchii*, is also black. Small populations of two rodent and seven bird species have been reported. The cave- and crevasse-nesting oilbird (*Steatornis caripensis*) is the most abundant bird on Mount Roraima. The largest mammal is the coatimundi (*Nasua nasua*).

See also Guiana Shield and Its Tepuis

Further Reading
McPherson, Stewart. 2008. *Lost Worlds of the Guiana Highlands*. Poole, Dorset, England: Redfern Natural History Productions.

Mount Saint Helens

United States (Washington)

Geographic Overview. Until 1980, 9,677 ft (2,950 m) Mount Saint Helens, was a very symmetrical cone. The volcano's violent eruption in 1980 changed the local landscape of the mountain and was the most economically destructive volcanic event in the United States. Mount Saint Helens continues to be a working observatory for scientific research into both volcanic activity and recovery of ecosystems after devastating disasters.

Geographic Coordinates. 46°11'N, 122°12'W

Description. Mount Saint Helens is 96 mi (154 km) south of Seattle and 50 mi (80 km) northeast of Portland, Oregon. The mountain lost 1,316 ft (401 m) of height in the 1980 eruption and now stands 8,363 ft (2,549 m) asl, with a large crater on its north side. The current Mount Saint Helens landscape is a mosaic of devastation and recovering ecosystems. Its forests were blown over like matchsticks, and formerly pristine mountain lakes cloaked in mud and ash debris. In the years since the eruption, however, the biological community has begun to regenerate.

On March 27, 1980, a few days after hundreds of small earthquakes that began on March 16, Mount Saint Helens emitted steam and dark ash, a mild eruption that blew a crater out through the mountain's summit icecap. By mid-April, the amount of ash and steam diminished, but earthquakes indicated that a mass of magma was rising within the volcano, warning of an impending eruption. The rising magma created a bulge on the north flank of the cone. In its later days, the bulge grew at 6 ft (1.8 m) per day until it protruded out at least 450 ft (137 m). On the morning of May 18, a landslide, precipitated by an M 5.1 earthquake and the steepened slope of the bulge, released pressure from within, allowing steam in the magma to be released in an explosive eruption. The energy released was equivalent to that of 21,000 Hiroshima-type atomic bombs. The roar was heard in western Montana. While some of the ash blew 15 mi (24 km) high into the atmosphere, much of it was blown laterally northward at 300–500 mph (485–800 kmph) as far as 17 mi (5.2 km), covering 130 mi² (367 km²). The landslide, the largest ever recorded, travelled 14 mi (22.5 km) downslope to the west, burying the North Fork of the Toutle River to an average depth of 150 ft (45.7 m) and a maximum depth of 600 ft (183 m). Heat from the blast melted snow and ice, creating several lahars, or volcanic mudflows of water, ash, rocks, and debris. The largest lahar traveled, at 10–25 mph (16–40 kmph), down the North Fork of the Toutle River and into the Cowlitz River and Columbia River, about 50 mi (80 km) downstream, destroying

27 bridges and almost 200 homes. Approximately 0.6 mi³ (2.5 km²) of rock and debris were blown out of the mountain, leaving a new crater on the north side 1 mi (1.6 km) wide, and lowering the summit by 1,314 ft (400 m) to its current height of 8,363 ft (2,549 m) asl. Volcanic ash continued to blow out during the day. A heavy pyroclastic flow of hot ash, pumice, and gas reached Spirit Lake 5 mi (8 km) away, burying the landscape in ash an average of 100 ft (30 m) deep. The hot steam and ash devastated everything in more than 150 mi² (388 km²), killing about 7,000 big game animals and 57 humans. Approximately 4 billion board feet of mature timber was blown down and scattered like toothpicks.

The huge volume of ash that was blown into the atmosphere was carried eastward, reaching northern Idaho and western Montana by late afternoon and evening. The falling ash covered 1.5 mil mi² (3.9 mil km²), as much as 10 in (25 cm) deep. After the initial explosion, subsequent eruptions were less violent. After six years of lava extrusions, drier, viscous rhyolite plugged the crater, creating a plug dome about 3,500 ft (1,100 m) in diameter and 876 ft (250 m) high. Although the dome of Mount Saint Helens may (or may not) be permanently plugged, other volcanoes in the High Cascades have similar potential for explosive eruptions.

Geologic History. Like other Cascade volcanoes, the mountain rises on top of an older basaltic shield volcano. The andesite that built Mount Saint Helens was derived from partially melted continental crust and was probably part of the North Cascades microcontinent. Mount Saint Helens has been active since the Pleistocene. A series of eruptions occurred from 1800 to 1857, some historically recorded, and radiocarbon dating indicates that similar eruptions occurred in the 15th and 16th centuries. The oldest deposits are 40,000–50,000 years old, but most of the volcanic rocks are less than 3,000 years old.

Protected Areas. The region, 110,000 ac (44,515 ha), was preserved as Mount Saint Helens National Volcanic Monument in 1982 and is administered by the National Forest Service.

See also Cascade Mountains; Crater Lake; Mount Rainier

Further Reading

Alt, David D. and Donald W. Hyndman. 1998. *Roadside Geology of Washington*. Missoula, MT: Mountain Press.

Brantley, Steve and Bobbie Myers. 2005. *Mount St. Helens—From the 1980 Eruption to 2000*. U.S. Geological Survey, Vancouver, WA. http://pubs.usgs.gov/fs/2000/fs 036-00/

Cascades Volcano Observatory. 2008. *Description: Mount St. Helens Volcano, Washington*. United States Geological Survey, Vancouver, Washington. http://vulcan .wr.usgs.gov/Volcanoes/MSSH/description_msh.html

Mount Vesuvius

Italy

Geographic Overview. The Somma–Vesuvius Volcanic Complex, commonly referred to as Mount Vesuvius, is the only active volcano on mainland Europe.

Its most noted eruption, which destroyed the Roman towns of Pompeii and Herculaneum in AD 79, was described by Pliny the Younger, a Roman historian. Geologists designate violent eruptions Plinian in recognition of his first eyewitness account of a volcanic eruption. Because of its unpredictability, history, and large local population, Mount Vesuvius is considered one of the most dangerous volcanoes in the world.

Geographic Coordinates. 40°49'N, 14°26'E

Description. Mount Vesuvius, rising steeply from a plain on the eastern side of the Gulf of Naples, overlooks the city of Naples to the northwest. The cone of Vesuvius, Gran Cono at 4,203 ft (1,281 m) asl, sits within the Somma Caldera, which has a high point of 4,098 ft (1,249 m) asl. Eruptions range from quiet lava flows and lava fountaining to violently explosive events with pyroclastic flows. Plinian-type eruptions are characterized by massive explosions, causing ash

Mount Vesuvius, an eruption of which destroyed Pompeii and Herculaneum in Roman times, continues to pose a threat of volcanic eruption to nearby cities, such as Naples, in Italy. (Pirus01/Dreamstime.com)

fall and major pyroclastic flows, such as those that buried Pompeii. Major lava flows are associated with Strombolian type eruptions, which may also produce small, more localized pyroclastic events. The last active eruption cycle for Mount Vesuvius ended with an eruption in 1944, which sent lava flows down the valley between the two peaks. Small trees and grasses now cover parts of the crater and caldera, including some on the mostly barren 1944 lava flow. Vesuvius is currently quiet, with only minor earthquake activity and fumarole outgassing. Quiet periods, however, have generally lasted 50–100 years.

Before AD 79, Vesuvius had been quiet for centuries, and the surface and the crater were green with vegetation. In that year, hot ash and pumice buried Pompeii 10 ft (3 m) deep, suffocating the inhabitants, before pyroclastic flows engulfed the town. Pyroclastic flows engulfed Herculaneum before that town was buried 65 ft (20 m) deep by a lahar. The eruption may have killed more than 16,000 people.

Geologic History. Mount Vesuvius is one of a series of volcanic vents on the west coast of Italy. It sits on the Campanian Volcanic Arc, a line of volcanoes over the subduction zone between the African and Eurasian plates. The contact zone crosses southern Sicily, then turns north and northwest along the east coast of the Italian peninsula, almost encircles the Po Valley, and turns back south along the Dinaric Coast. The African plate is moving north, but a finger of the plate underlies the Adriatic Sea, which is subducting west under Italy. Due to changes in magma composition and changes to magma–water interaction, the volcano's andesitic rocks and lava cause it to erupt in a variety of ways. The earliest activity was approximately 300,000 years ago, but the current Vesuvius–Somma complex began to form 25,000 years ago. Quiet lava flows over 6,000 years built Mount Somma, which was probably taller than 6,550 ft (2,000 m) asl. Subsequent explosive Plinian eruptions reduced Somma to a caldera. The AD 79 eruption was the last large Plinian event, which also initiated construction of the Vesuvius cone in the caldera.

Gran Cono's crater is approximately 1,640 ft (500 m) in diameter and 985 ft (300 m) deep. Its conduit is clogged with landslide debris, which increases the pressure in underlying magma. Scientists believe that the magma chamber is 7.5 mi (12 km) below the surface, feeding another chamber 2.5 mi (4 km) below the surface. The magma has a significant mantle (mafic) component as well as andesite (felsic) component. Mafic and felsic magma separate in the chamber, which causes a cycle of quiet basalt flows, ending with a Plinian eruption of explosive felsic material. Volatile components in magma, especially water, vaporize and expand when rising in the conduit, explosively ejecting broken rocks, lava bits, and ash. As the rising cloud cools, it collapses on top of and traps the still rising hot material, sending a pyroclastic flow down the mountain slopes.

Protected Areas. Vesuvius National Park, established in 1995, covers approximately 52 mi^2 (135 km^2).

Further Reading

Popham, Chris. 2011. "Vesuvius: The Most Dangerous Volcano in the World?" Open University Geological Society. http://ougs.org/local_geology/article.php?id-114&&branchcode-=swe

Sistema Rischio Vulcanico. n.d. "Vesuvius Volcano, Campania." http://srv1.rm.ingv.it/srv/srv/study-sites/vesuvius/vesuvius-volcano-campania

Mount Washington and the Presidential Range

United States (New Hampshire)

Geographic Overview. Mount Washington, in the Presidential Range of the White Mountains, New Hampshire, boasts having the "world's worst weather." The summit is the highest peak in the northeastern United States. With its highly changeable weather conditions and its top exposed to fierce winds and often shrouded in dense fog, Washington is a potentially dangerous climb at any time of year. Since 1849, more than 140 people have died on its slopes from hypothermia, falls, and other accidents, many in summer.

Geographic Coordinates. 44°16'N, 71°18'W

Description. Although much lower than peaks in the Rocky Mountains or Sierra Nevada, the summit of Mount Washington, 6,288 ft (1,974 m) asl, reaches well above treeline. The peaks of the Presidential Range are connected by a 12-mi (19-km) northeast–southwest trending ridgeline. North of Mount Washington are Mounts Clay (5,531 ft,

1,681 m asl), Jefferson (5,712 ft, 1,741 m asl), Adams (5,774 ft, 1,760 m asl), and Madison (5,367 ft, 1,636 m asl), the alpine zones of which are all contiguous with Washington's and form the greatest expanse of alpine vegetation east of the Mississippi River. South of Washington are Mounts Monroe (5,371 ft, 1,637 m asl), Eisenhower (4,780 ft, 1,457 m asl), Pierce (4,311 ft, 1,314 m asl), Jackson (4,052 ft, 1,235 m asl), and Webster (3,911 ft, 1,192 m asl). The entire range lies between two large U-shaped valleys scoured by the continental ice sheets, Crawford Notch to the west and Pinkham Notch to the east.

Many types of glacial landforms attest to the presence of Pleistocene ice, which had retreated from the lowlands by 13,000 years ago and from higher elevations about 11,500 years ago. Large cirques with precipitous headwalls occur on Mount Washington's north (The Great Gulf) and east sides (Tuckerman and Huntington ravines). The small ponds known as the Lakes of the Clouds on the col between Washington and Monroe are tarns. Mt. Monroe is a huge roche moutonée planed smooth on the northwest side and plucked into steep, rough slopes by ice passing over its southeast side. The famous Glen Boulder, perched on a spur overlooking Pinkham Notch, is a glacial erratic picked up by the ice 7–8 mi (11–13 km) to the north and dropped at its present, seemingly precarious position. The continental ice sheet, more than 1 mi (1.6 km) thick, left striations or grooves on summit rocks and a 1–2 ft (0.3–0.6 m) thick cover of glacial till. Postglacial freeze-and-thaw processes created a felsenmeer of angular rocks above treeline and patterned ground from solifluction on level surfaces, such as Bigelow Lawn above Tuckerman Ravine.

The infamous weather conditions on Washington are the product of the peak's location at the convergence of three major storm tracks, its exposed position well above other mountains, and upslope acceleration of westerly winds and cooling of air masses. The summit receives storms from the west, nor'easters out of the Canadian Maritimes, and storms from the southeast that often begin in the Gulf of Mexico and follow the Atlantic Coast northward. But, as locals say, the mountain makes its own weather, too, due to orographic uplift. A difference of 30°F (16.7°C) often exists between the base of the mountain and the summit; the hiker dressed for a summer day can suddenly experience freezing temperatures, fierce winds, and dense fog when climbing above a cirque's headwall. The top of Mount Washington has a tundra climate, while lower elevations are subarctic in nature. The summit experiences only 44 sunny days and 77 partly sunny days per year. Temperatures average 6°F (–14°C) in January and rise only to an average of 48°F (8.9°C) in July. Temperatures on the summit have never been above 72°F (22°C), and icicles can hang from the summit buildings in July. Winds greater than hurricane force occur 110 days each year and during every month. On April 12, 1934, wind speed reached 231 mph (372 kmph), the highest ever

Mount Washington

Merlin of Mist

Merlin of mist, merlin of gales
Fearsome pinnacle grazing the stars
Guardian of souls from ancient of times,
Promise of Earth's enduring mind.
Whether spied from great distance
Or snug in the krummholz atop
Merlin of mists, Merlin of gales,
Singular beacon grazing the stars.

Native Algonkian people called it Agiocochook, home of the Great Spirit, a sacred place to which entry was forbidden. In 1852 it became one of the first tourist destinations in the United States, promoted as rivaling Europe's Alps. The oldest hiking trail in the United States, the Crawford Bridle Path, led to the Summit House, the first hotel (1852), which was anchored to the top by heavy chains passing over the roof. It later burned down. The Tip-Top House (1853), a competing establishment constructed of granite, remains. The Mt. Washington Coach Road, now the Mt. Washington Auto Road, opened in 1861, and the Cog Railway on the west side began operations in 1869. Weather observations have been made on the top since 1870. The Mount Washington Observatory began operations in 1932. Meteorologists manned the station throughout the year and for many years broadcast the weather report in evening TV reports. The mountain has long been one of New England's most popular hiking destinations despite the number of lives lost on its slopes.

Verse courtesy of Margot A. Fleck

observed at a manned weather station on Earth's surface. In 1996 record wind speeds of 253 mph (407 kmph) were recorded by instruments over Barrow Island, Australia, during Cyclone Olivia, setting a new world record.

Geologic History. The Presidential Range traces its origins to the Acadian Orogeny 400 mya, when the ancient Iapetus Ocean closed and early continents and microcontinents converged to form Pangaea. Marine sediments caught in between were squeezed and metamorphosed by heat and pressure into quartzite, schist, and gneiss. Continued convergence folded and faulted the rocks and uplifted the Appalachian Mountains, of which the Presidential Range is part. The mountains were shaped during the Wisconsin glacial period, when they were covered by continental ice sheets and then sculpted by alpine glaciers.

Biota. Climatic patterns are reflected in the altitudinal zonation of vegetation. At the lowest elevations, a northern hardwood forest of sugar maple, American beech, and yellow birch prevails, joined by red spruce and balsam fir at approximately 2,000 ft (600 m) asl. By 2,700 ft (820 m), where fog is more frequent and precipitation amounts greater, spruce and fir dominate. By 4,000 ft (1,220 m) only fir persists; becoming increasingly stunted and forming impenetrable thickets called "tuckamores." Still higher, black spruce joins the balsam fir among the dwarfed, gnarled, and flagged trees of the krummholz, patches of which continue above treeline to about 5,400 ft (1,645 m). Treeline and the beginning of the alpine zone occur at approximately 4,500 ft (1,370 m). Alpine species are largely dwarfed shrubs of the heath family such as diapensia, Lapland rosebay, Labrador tea, and alpine azalea growing only a few inches above the surface. The Alpine Gardens on Chandler's Ridge on the south side of the Great Gulf are a favorite destination for the hardy wildflower enthusiast from May into August, when these tiny plants sport pink, white, and yellow blooms.

Protected Areas. Mount Washington is owned by a combination of private, state, and national landholders. Along with the rest of the Presidential Range, it is largely in the White Mountain National Forest.

See also Appalachian Mountains

Further Reading

"Geology of the Mt. Washington Area, Presidential Range, New Hampshire." n.d. Program in Atmospheres, Oceans, and Climates, Massachusetts Institute of Technology. http://paoc.mit.edu/synoptic/courses/deaps/GeologyoftheMt.pdf

Slack, Nancy G. and Allison W. Bell. 1995. *Field Guide to the New England Alpine Summits*. Boston: Appalachian Mountain Club.

"Surviving Mount Washington." n.d. Mount Washington Observatory. http://www.mountwashington.org/about/visitor/surviving.php

Mount Whitney

United States (California)

Geographic Overview. Mount Whitney, in the Sierra Nevada in east-central California, is the tallest mountain in the lower 48 states. The peak is named for Josiah Whitney, California State Geologist in 1864. It is visited and climbed by hundreds of people every year.

Geographic Coordinates. 36°35'N, 118°18'W

Description. Although the brass marker on the summit of Mount Whitney reads 14,494 ft (4,418 m), new measurements by the National Geodetic Survey indicate that the height is 14,505 ft (4,421 m). The mountain rises more than 10,000 ft (3,050 m) above the Owens Valley, less than 10 mi (16 km) to the east. Mount Whitney is located on the Sierra Crest, the 17 mi (27 km) string of high peaks, including 7 that are higher than 14,000 ft (4,265 m) asl, forming the eastern side of the Sierra Nevada. The Sierra Crest is separated from the Great Western Divide, a chain of mountains trending north–south through the center of Sequoia National Park, by the Upper Kern Canyon, a north–south faulted valley deepened by a valley glacier.

The peak was first climbed in 1873, and Lone Pine residents financed the first trail from Whitney Portal in 1904. Mount Whitney is currently the most climbed high peak in the Sierra Nevada, and due to high demand is controlled by a permit system. From the Whitney Portal trailhead, 13 mi (21 km) from Lone Pine in the Owens Valley and 8,360 ft (2,548 m) asl, the 10.7 mi (17.1 km) long trail to the summit gains approximately 6,100 ft (1,900 m) elevation.

Although not a technical climb in late summer, it is an extreme 12–18 hour day hike. Many hikers choose to camp, usually at Outpost Camp (10,360 ft/3,158 m) or Trail Camp (12,039 ft/3,669 m). Alternately, the steep eastern face can be climbed by technical routes. From the western side, access trails beginning in Sequoia National Park require several days of hiking and backpacking through mountainous terrain. All trails travel through forested landscapes at lower elevations, changing to alpine and rocky routes above treeline at 10,000–11,000 ft (3,050–3,350 m).

The stone building on the summit, the Smithsonian Institution Shelter, was completed in 1909 to offer protection for hikers. The building, however, is a high point on the peak and has been closed since the late 1980s when lightning struck the building, killing a hiker taking shelter from the storm.

Geologic History. Mount Whitney is granite, part of the Sierra Nevada Batholith, which intruded into overlying rocks during the Cretaceous as the Pacific Plate subducted beneath North America. The faulting that created the mountain range occurred much later, approximately 10–2 mya. The Sierra Crest is the eastern top of the huge fault-block mountain, tilting to the west, that forms the Sierra Nevada. The Owens Valley on the eastern side dropped down as the Sierra was rising. Uplift was probably associated with development of Great Basin fault-block mountains. Erosion exposed the granite core, which was further sculpted by alpine glaciers. A rugged landscape of arêtes, cirques, and U-shaped valleys is visible from the summit. The steep eastern side of the mountain was eroded back from the fault line. The west slope of the peak is an old erosion surface, now dissected by glaciers except for a small, relatively level area but rocky area near the summit.

The glacial ice did not completely fill the valleys, but stopped somewhat short of the rim. The steep slopes or cliffs down from the summit are due to frost action and avalanche chutes, or gullies, above the level of the glacial ice. Evidence that these chutes were carved during the Pleistocene is that they end at the top of the glacial erosion line. The summit rock is a fine-grained type of granite called aplite, usually found in narrow dikes, which weathers slowly and breaks into angular slabs from frost action.

Protected Areas. Mount Whitney sits astride the boundary between Inyo National Forest and John Muir Wilderness Area to the east and Sequoia National Park and Wilderness Area to the west.

See also Sierra Nevada

Further Reading

Inyo National Forest. 2012. *Hiking the Mt. Whitney Trail.* U.S. National Forest Service. https://fs.usda.gov/Inter net/FSE . . . /stelprdb5333235.pdf

Matthes, Francois. 1962. *François Matthes and the Marks of Time: Yosemite and the High Sierra, The Geologic History of Mount Whitney.* Reprinted from *Sierra Club Bulletin,* 1937, 1–18. http://www.yosemite.ca.us/li brary/matthes/mount_whitney.html

Sierra & Kings Canyon National Parks. 2013. "Climbing Mt. Whitney." www.nps.gov/seki/planyourvisit/whit ney.htm

Murray–Darling River System

Australia

Geographic Overview. The Murray–Darling River System in southeastern Australia is the continent's largest drainage system and contains the three longest rivers in Australia. It drains two distinct basins, which together cover more than 386,100 mi^2 (1,000,000 km^2). The two basins serve as major agricultural areas for the country, producing sheep, cattle, hogs, and irrigated crops.

Geographic Coordinates. Source of River Murray: 36°47'S, 148°12'E; Source of Darling River: 28°40'S, 151°37'E; Mouth of main stem (River Murray): 35°33'S, 138°53'E

Description. The Murray–Darling River Basin is large, a saucer-shaped depression some 310 mi (500 km) wide and nearly 2,000 ft (600 m) long located inside the southeastern arc of the Great Dividing Range in southern Queensland, New South Wales, and Victoria. The lower River Murray, the main stem of the system, flows through South Australia, where it discharges into the Southern Ocean at Encounter Bay. The Northern Basin is drained by the Darling River and its tributaries, including the Severn River in Queensland, which is considered its ultimate source.

The Southern Basin is drained by the River Murray; its main tributary, the Murrumbidgee; and numerous smaller tributaries. The Darling River enters the Murray 93 mi (150 km) from Murray Mouth at the town of Wentworth, New South Wales. The Darling River, measured from its source at the head of the Severn to its junction with the Murray, is 1,708 mi (2,749 km) long. The River Murray has a length of 1,566 mi (2,520 km), the Murrumbidgee River 979 mi (1,575 km). The total length of the Murray–Darling River System from the beginning of the Severn to Murray Mouth is 2,282 mi (3,672 km).

The Northern Basin encompasses more than half of the overall drainage basin, but its rivers provide only 18 percent of the flow of lower River Murray. The main tributaries begin in the Great Dividing Range in southern Queensland, on the tablelands of New South Wales, and in the Blue Mountains. Most of the north receives an average 10 in (250 mm) of precipitation annually from summer rainfall. Rainfall is highly variable from year to year, evaporation rates are high, and many streams are intermittent, most years ending in salt flats. Some, like the Talyawalko Anabranch River or the Great Anabranch River, have channels that leave the Darling only to join up again farther downstream when sufficient flow permits. The basin is flat and rivers meander across broad floodplains. Seasonal wetlands, lakes, and salt flats are abundant.

The Southern Basin is semiarid with a mediterranean regime of winter rains and mild temperatures. The Lower Murray basin receives 8–16 in (210–400 mm) of rain annually. This basin is also quite flat, and its drainages also twist and turn across wide sandy floodplains. Dune fields and salt flats such as the Willandra Lakes, long abandoned by ancient drainage systems, occur in a savanna-like landscape that also has numerous swamps and lakes. The main headwaters of the Murray River lie in the Australian Alps. Almost half the flow of the River Murray derives from runoff in the watersheds of the Goulburn, Murrumbidgee, and Upper Murray rivers. River Murray forms most of the border between New South Wales and Victoria. After its confluence with the Darling River, the River Murray turns due south and enters Lake Alexandrina, a broad, shallow freshwater lake 10–12 ft (3–3.5 m) deep. A short channel, Murray Mouth, leads to Encounter Bay in the Southern Ocean, where near the town of Goolwa, South Australia, some 95 mi (150 km) south of Adelaide. The channel crosses the Coorong, a saline lagoon 60 mi (100 km) long, separated from the open sea by a narrow belt of coastal sand dunes.

The Murray–Darling River System undergoes natural cycles of drought and flood. Flooded wetlands become shallow, still bodies of water which are highly productive and biologically diverse. They are significant breeding and feeding grounds for waterfowl and shorebirds.

Geologic History. The Murray–Darling Basin lies on continental bedrock more than 350 million years old. The basin formed as the southeast Australian mountains were uplifted 65–32 mya and was for millions of years filled by an inland sea, which advanced and retreated several times, leaving behind thick deposits of sand. From 2.0–0.5 mya, a freshwater lake, Lake Bunngunnia, existed while the lower River Murray was blocked by the continuing uplift of the Grampians. Lake bed deposits of sands and clays resulted in the flatness of the region. The natural dam was eventually breached and the lake drained. The River Murray found an outlet through the Murray Mouth to the Southern Ocean. Some of today's salt lakes are remnants of the ancient lake. The glacial periods of the Pleistocene epoch saw the addition of layers of riverine sands to form the contemporary surface of the basin and the main aquifers.

Biota. The rivers, billabongs (ox-bow lakes), and wetlands of the Murray–Darling Basin are home to 46 native fishes, including the largest, the 6 ft (1.8 m) long Murray cod (*Maccullochella peelii peelii*), its numbers in steep decline since the 1950s. The Murray–Darling rainbow fish (*Melanotaenia fluviatilis*) and the nationally endangered trout cod (*Maccullochella macquariensis*) are other examples of native fishes adapted to the irregular flood and drought cycles of the river system. The more than 30,000 wetlands in the basin provide habitat for waterfowl and shorebirds; when floods last 4–6 months, they support large waterbird breeding events. The Barmah–Willema river red gum (*Eucalyptus camaldulensis*) forests on either side of the River Murray in Victoria and New South Wales, respectively, are important riparian habitats now stressed by decreasing water flow.

Protected Areas. A number of national parks conserve natural areas in the basin. The Willandra Lakes World Heritage Site was inscribed in 1981 to protect Pleistocene sand formations and lakes and stream systems that dried out 18,500 years ago, as well as an archeological site documenting the presence of humans 60,000–45,000 years ago, during the time giant marsupials became extinct. Among 12 Ramsar Wetlands of International Importance in the basin is the Coorong and Lakes Alexandrina and Albert Region. The Living Murray Initiative of the Australian Government aims to manage and improve six key sites and restore the River Murray.

Environmental Issues. The river system has seen declining flows in recent decades, in part due to a natural drought cycle and in part due to damming that has changed the flood regime. A decrease in the frequency of natural floods has negative impacts on riparian forests, floodplain billabongs, and wetlands. Acid sulfate soils developed naturally in waterlogged soils have been exposed in Lake Alexandrina and elsewhere as water levels drop. Among other problems are toxic blooms of cyanobacteria, salinization of soils related to irrigation, and invasive plants and animals. Especially troublesome are dense waterweed (*Egeria densa*) native to warm, temperate South America; eastern mosquitofish (*Gambusia holbrooki*), introduced from the United States; and the cane toad (*Bufo marinus*), native to Central and South America.

Further Reading

"About the Basin." 2013. Murray–Darling Basin Authority, Australian Government. http://www.mdba.gov.au/about-basin

"Fishes of the Murray-Darling Basin." 2013. Murray–Darling Basin Authority, Australian Government. http://www.mdba.gov.au/media-pubs/publications/fishes-murray-darling-basin

Mylodon Cave (Cueva del Milodón)

Chile

Geographic Overview. *Mylodon* is a genus of now-extinct giant ground sloths that inhabited Patagonia, South America, during the Pleistocene. Although Mylodon Cave is not the only site with sloth remains, it is one of the most famous and was the first found to contain sloth dung.

Geographic Coordinates. 51°30'S, 72°36'W

Description. Mylodon Cave is situated at the base of the Benitez Mountains, western foothills of the Patagonian Andes northwest of Puerto Natales, Chile, on Seno de Último Esperanza (Last Hope Sound). Its entrance measures approximately 400 ft (121 m) wide × 100 ft (29 m) high, and the grotto extends about 660 ft (200 m) back into the mountain.

The cave was discovered by the German explorer Hermann Eberhard (1852–1908) in 1895. Earlier, Charles Darwin, during his voyage on HMS *Beagle*, had sent specimens of a sloth he had found at Bahía Blanca, Argentina, back to England, where they were identified and named in Darwin's honor by the prominent English paleontologist Richard Owen. Eberhard reported finding skin, bones, teeth and the dung of *Mylodon darwini* in the cave. The 3 ft (1 m) long piece of skin with patches of hair still attached appeared so fresh that Eberhard believed it a recent kill and that the animal still roamed Patagonia. Modern radiocarbon dating revealed that the sloth remains were about 13,000 years old.

The first excavation of the site was made by Otto Nordenskjöld, a Swedish geologist, geographer, and Antarctic explorer, in 1896. His work and that of those who came later have uncovered the remains of other members of the Pleistocene megafauna, including two species of small early horse (*Hippidion saldiasi* and *Onohippidium* spp.), a sabertoothed cat (*Smilodon populator*), and the last member of a uniquely South American mammalian order, the litoptern *Macrauchenia patagonica*. All of these animals were extinct in the area by 10,000 years ago. The cave also produced artifacts from the indigenous Selk'nam people, who lived in the cave about 8,000 years ago during the Holocene Climatic Optimum, a time when global temperatures were warmer than today and a raised sea level brought the waters of Seno de Último Esperanza close to the cave entrance.

The sloth of Mylodon Cave was about 10 ft (3 m) tall when on it stood on its hind feet and weighed about 440 lb (200 kg). It had a thick, tough skin embedded with dermal bones (osteoderms) for added protection. Although it had long claws, it was an herbivore, as revealed in the dung balls (*boñegas*) found in this cave; they contained mainly grasses. At least 80 genera of ground sloth are recognized by paleontologists. Ground sloths were members of the order Xenartha and restricted to the Americas, where they inhabited a variety of environments; five genera are known from North America. Their closest surviving relatives are the small tree sloths of the Neotropics.

The canine teeth in the upper jaw of the sabertoothed cat recovered from Mylodon Cave are the longest of any cat and measured almost a foot (30 cm) in length. The animal itself had a shoulder height of 4.5 ft (1.4 m) and weighed 800–1,000 lb (360–470 kg). A well-preserved specimen from this cave has yielded DNA.

The litoptern represents one of several orders of mammal that arose during the time South America was an island continent. Most species went extinct as a consequence of what is known as the Great American Interchange, the northward or southward migration of animals previously confined to either North America or South America that was made possible by the completion of the Central American isthmus. *Macrauchenia* was the only litoptern to survive the invasion of new competitors from North America. This animal is described as llama-like in general appearance (although not related to these South American camels) with a long neck. Its upper lip was elongated to form a short trunk. A hoofed animal, it had three toes on each foot. *Macrauchenia* went extinct about 20,000 years ago.

Protected Areas. Mylodon Cave is the largest of six limestone caves in the area now protected in Cueva del Milodón Natural Monument. It is developed and managed for tourism.

Further Reading

Martin, Paul S. 2005. *Twilight of the Mammoths: Ice Age Extinctions and the Rewilding of America*. Berkeley: University of California Press.

"Milodon Cave (Cueva del Milodón)." 2012. WonderMondo. http://www.wondermondo.com/Countries/SA/Chile/Magallanes/CuevaMilodon.htm

N

Namib Desert

Angola and Namibia

Geographic Overview. The Namib is generally regarded as the oldest desert on the planet. This west coast fog desert has large sand seas with some of the world's largest dunes and endemic plants and arthropods adapted to extreme drought or extracting moisture from the morning fog. Among the most unusual plants is *Welwetschia mirabilis*, an ancient gymnosperm that lives for 1,000–2,000 years and produces only two long strap-like leaves. The Namib–Nuakluft National Park in Namibia is one of Africa's largest conservation areas. Sossusvlei and its surrounding dunes form an iconic landscape of the Namib within the park's borders.

Geographic Coordinates. Approximately 14°S–28°S, 12°E–16°E

Description. The Namib is a hyperarid region in southwest Africa, a narrow coastal fog desert stretching nearly 1,000 mi (1,600 km) from the Carunjamba River in Angola south to the Orange River on the Namibia–South Africa border. Most of it is only 50–90 mi (80–150 km) wide. Elevations range from sea level to about 3,200 ft (1,000 m) asl in the east. The cold waters of the Benguela Current in the South Atlantic flow along its western margin; the eastern edge is marked by Africa's Great Western Escarpment. In the south, it merges with the Succulent Karoo in the Richtersveld Mountains. It is the only true desert in Southern Africa.

Broad gravelly plains are interrupted by inselbergs of granite, quartzite, marble, and schist and large dry watercourses. Several sand seas (ergs) have formed in western parts of the desert. Three major areas are the Curosa–Bahia dos Tigres Sand Sea in southern Angola, the Kunene–Skeleton Coast Sand Sea in northern Namibia, and, the largest, the Namib Sand Sea south of the Kuiseb River in southern Namibia. The red dunes surrounding the clay pan and marshes of Sossusvlei in the Namib Sand Sea are over 650 ft (200 m high), among the highest in the world. Dunes of all types are found in these areas. On the plains, vegetation is sparse and cryptic. Inland inselbergs such as Gross Spitzkoppe and Brandberg—at 8,550 ft (2,606 m) the highest mountain in Namibia—host larger plants including a number of bizarre stem succulents with swollen caudexes such as *Commiphora* spp., *Moringa ovalifolia*, and *Cyphostemma* spp. The flora and fauna tend to be richer than on the plains, many small organisms finding shelter in cracks and crevices. Camel thorn acacias, salt cedar, and other trees line ephemeral streams that serve as oases with their supplies of groundwater. In the dry streambeds east of Swapokmund, however, *Welwetschia mirabilis*, is about the only plant to found. The Orange River and the Kumene River on the Namibia–Angola border are major perennial streams flowing to the Atlantic Ocean and carrying water in their lower reaches most of the time. Other watercourses, such the Swakop, Kuiseb, Omaruru, and Ugab Rivers, have surface flow in their headwaters but only subterranean water in their lower reaches. Still other ephemeral streams, such as the Tsauchob, which empties into Sossusvlei, have been blocked by sand dunes.

Climate is influenced by the position of the South Atlantic subtropical high pressure system and the presence of the cold Benguela Current offshore. The northern and central Namib receive summer

The high red dunes surrounding the clay pans of Sossusvlei are an iconic landscape of the Namib Desert, but much of the region consists of broad gravelly plains interrupted by inselbergs and dry watercourses. (Jaysi/Dreamstime.com)

precipitation from storms arriving from the Indian Ocean; the Southern Namib south of Lüderitz, Namibia, has a winter precipitation pattern with rains associated with cyclonic storms over the Atlantic Ocean the rule. Annual precipitation ranges from an average 0.6 in (15 mm) on the coast to (4 in) 100 mm in the east, but it occurs irregularly and some years no rain falls at all. Fog formed over the Benguela Current is therefore an important source of moisture for plants and animals. Small hills and other obstructions—even upended beetles—intercept the fog and cause droplets to be deposited in rocks and soil and on plants. At Swakopmund, Namibia, fog contributes about 1.4 in (34 mm) of water a year. This moisture is an important weathering agent, resulting in smooth, rounded profiles on west-facing surfaces, and is an important water source for lichens and small succulents.

Fog at the coast keeps temperatures low and nearly constant, with a daily range of 4°–9°F (2°–5°C)

common in the Northern Namib (14°–20°S), also known as the Kaokeveld Desert. Daily temperatures in the Central and Southern Namib average 60°–73°F (15°–23°C), with daily highs hardly exceeding the average. However, easterly winds descending and warming as they pass over the Great Escarpment can bring highs of 90°–100°F (32°–38°C). In winter temperatures may fall to 36°F (2°C), but frost does not occur.

In the morning, onshore winds move the fog inland, where 20–40 mi (30–60 km) from the coast, at elevations of 1,000–2,000 ft (300–600 m) asl, it is at its densest. Winds also carry detritus, a major food source for Namib invertebrates. The fog evaporates later in the day, allowing great daily fluctuations of both temperature and humidity and creating the most extreme habitats of the Namib.

Even without fog, high humidity along the coast permits a species-rich lichen flora. Low mats of dark orange lichens (*Teleoschistes capensis*) cover as much as 60 percent of the surface near the ocean. Lichens prefer fine-grained soils in crevices and the lee side of stones, where they receive protection from sea spray and sand blast. Inland, in the fog belt, scattered halophytic shrubs 2 ft (0.6–0.7 m) tall dominate the sparse vegetation and trap blowing sand into small mounds called nebkas.

Every kind of dune is found in the Namib ergs. In the Namib Sand Sea, highly mobile barchans (crescentic dunes) occur near the coast, their horns pointing northward in the direction of movement. These dunes average 26 ft (8 m) in height, and 500 ft (155 m) across; they move at a rate of 40–48 ft (12.4–14.6 m)/yr. Inland, the core of the sand sea has great linear dunes oriented north–south and running parallel to each other about 1 mi (1.5 km) apart. In general, they stand 330 ft (100 m) above the surface, but the highest, near Sossusvlei, are over 1,000 ft (325 m) tall. Star dunes develop on some of the dune ridgetops. Inland, north and south of Sossusvlei, stabilized U-shaped or parabolic dunes can be found, the convex side pointing upwind and arms downwind. The slip faces of dunes are home to the greatest variety of animals, including silverfish, tenebrioid beetles, lizards, and golden moles. Water percolating through the sand collects at the base of dunes, often supporting trees.

Geologic History. Aridity in the Namib has been persistent for at least 80 million years and likely developed as the Southern Ocean opened and Africa and South America separated during the late Jurassic–early Cretaceous some 130 mya. The current active dunes lie atop the red Tsondab Sandstone Formation, fossilized dunes from the Early to Mid-Tertiary Period. The Benguela Current developed 5–9 mya and with it came persistent aridity and fog. The Namib Sand Sea probably is more recent and a product of the Pliocene and Pleistocene epochs. The source of the sand is debated; it may be from the alluvial deposits of the Orange River or erosional products of the Great Escarpment. The modern dunes form a young, ever-changing landscape in this the oldest desert on Earth.

Biota. The flora of the Namib is typically small and inconspicuous. Window algae grow in the underside of transparent quartz stones, fruticose lichens hug the ground, succulents such as the endemic *Lithops ruschiorum* and *Hoodia gordonii* hide in the rocks.

Welwetschia, the long-lived strap-leaved gymnosperm, is conspicuous but highly localized in occurrence.

The fauna of the Namib is varied, each species having its own strategy for surviving drought and heat. Mammals range in size from elephants to gemsbok to springbok to the golden mole, which swims through the sand in pursuit of spiders, beetles, and lizards. Endemic dassie rats living on inselbergs in the Kaokoveld are Gondwanan relicts able to flatten their bodies to fit into crevices. The dassie rat can shed its bushy tail much as lizards do. Lions and jackals live in the desert and hunt fur seals along the coast. Fringed-toed lizards stay on the dune surface until temperatures reach 158°F (70°C), when they burrow to cooler depths. The sidewinding adder lurks beneath the surface most of the day with only its eyes and tip of tail above ground. Web-footed geckos let the fog condense on their heads and then lick the water droplets off with long tongues. Among insects, endemic beetles also harvest moisture from the fog. The toktokkie intercepts the fog by standing on its head and letting condensation run down into its mouth. Others (genus *Lepidochora*) dig shallow trenches into the windward sides of dunes in the evening and before sunrise return to drink the dew formed on the ridges between them.

Protected Areas. Namib–Naukluft National Park, covering 19,216 mi^2 (49,768 km^2), is the largest conservation area in Africa. It protects the Namib Sand Sea, which in 2013 was inscribed as a UNESCO World Heritage Site. Angola's coastal Iona National Park will be included with Namibia's Skeleton Coast National Park in a planned Iona–Skeleton Coast Transfrontier Conservation Area. The coastal area extending from Walvis Bay, Namibia, south to the Orange River is the so-called Diamond Coast, an area of dunes strewn with diamonds and carefully guarded to prevent any access.

Environmental Issues. In Namibia, damage from offroad vehicles is a major problem on the fragile gypsum and calcrete crusts protecting many desert soils. Overcollection and an illegal trade in some succulents has decimated certain plant populations. Drops in the water table resulting from groundwater withdrawal for domestic use at Walvis Bay and Swakopmund and for industrial use at the Rossing Uranium Mine threaten the water balance over extensive areas. Goats and donkeys that consume acacia seed pods compete with gemsbok and other native antelopes for food. The future of the Diamond Coast is unknown; leases end in 2020.

In Angola, a 30-year civil war left the Kaokoveld without protection and ravaged. Steps are underway to reestablish parks and create new ones.

See also The Karoo

Further Reading

Goudie, Andrew. 2010. "Namib Sand Sea: Large Dunes in an Ancient Desert." In *Geomorphological Landscapes of the World*, edited by Pietor Mignon. New York: Springer.

Seely, Mary. 2004. *The Namib: Natural History of an Ancient Desert*. Windhoek, Namibia: Desert Research Foundation of Namibia.

Spriggs, Amy. n.d. "Desert and Xeric Shrublands—Africa: Namibia." World Wildlife Fund. http://worldwildlife.org/ecoregions/at1315

World Wildlife Fund and C. Michael Hogan. 2013. "Kaokoveld Desert." *The Encyclopedia of Earth*. http://www.eoearth.org/view/article/153993

Nebraska Sandhills

United States (Nebraska)

Geographic Overview. The Nebraska Sandhills, covering approximately 25 percent of the state, is the largest region of stabilized sand dunes in the Western Hemisphere. Due to a high water table, the region includes 1.3 million ac (526,110 ha) of lakes and wetlands. A native mixed-grass prairie, with both tall and short grasses, covers 95 percent of the area, but there are also patches of coniferous and deciduous forest. A major recharge area for the Ogallala Aquifer, the Sandhills hold approximately 1 billion acre-feet of water.

Geographic Coordinates. Within approximately 41°N–43°N, 98°W–103°W

Description. The Nebraska Sandhills cover 19,600 mi^2 (50,000 km^2) primarily between the Niobrara River and the Platte River in north central Nebraska. Dunes are higher and steeper in the west, with the largest 425 ft (130 m) high.

Although the Sandhills are drained by several rivers, especially the Loup and its tributaries, the drainage is not integrated, meaning that streams or lakes sink into and reemerge from the porous sand in an irregular pattern. Water moves freely through the sand, as far as 500 ft (1.5 m) per year. The groundwater in the Sandhills is recharged by local precipitation, ranging from approximately 16 in (400 mm) in the west to 24 in (610 mm) in the east. Because of the porosity, 25–50 percent of all precipitation percolates through the sand down to the water table. The wetlands, which occur where the water table intersects the surface, serve to maintain the level of the water table under adjacent dunes. Changes in the infiltration or drainage in one area may have major consequences throughout the region, causing the water table to drop in some places while other areas may be flooded. Drainage in the early 1900s started a cycle of erosion and water table drawdown. Settlers dug ditches to interconnect the drainage system. Consequently, streams flowed more freely and drained more water from the dunes, lowering the water table. The increased volume of water eroded streambeds deeper, allowing more water to flow out of the Sandhills.

Geologic History. During the late Pleistocene or Holocene (1 mya), a weathered layer of the Ogallala Formation became the source of the sand, which lies directly on top of the Ogallala Aquifer. The fine silt and clay were blown eastward, while the heavier sand remained. The dunes are primarily transverse, meaning they are perpendicular to the northwesterly prevailing winds. Grass cover is necessary to anchor the dunes. Evidence indicates that during several severe droughts within the last 15,000 years, the dunes moved with the wind when plant cover died.

Biota. A reliable water source in the wet valleys supports dense vegetation, which provides food and shelter for wildlife. The mixed-grass prairie of the Sandhills, with a rich biota, is the largest expanse of native grassland remaining in the United States. It supports 720 species of plants and 314 species of vertebrates, including more than 200 bird species, both nesting and migratory. Major grasses include sand bluestem, little bluestem switchgrass, needle-and-thread grass, and sand dropseed. The prairie also includes many forbs.

Under the Central Flyway migration route, the wetlands are important stopping places for water birds, such as sandhill crane, swans, and geese.

Protected Areas. The Nebraska Sandhills were designated a National Natural Landmark in 1984. Arthur Bowring Sandhills Ranch State Historical Park preserves a turn-of-the-century working cattle ranch. Three national wildlife refuges, Valentine, Fort Niobrara, and Crescent Lake, as well as The Nature Conservancy's Niobrara Valley Preserve protect natural ecosystems and wildlife. The goal of the Sandhills Task Force, a partnership with USDA Fish and Wildlife, is to sustain the water supplies, which in turn sustains both cattle ranching and biotic diversity.

Environmental Issues. Beginning in the 1970s, a number of factors, including advances in irrigation technology, prompted farmers to convert more land to cropland, especially in the eastern part of the Sandhills. More water, pumped up from greater depths, resulted in more water exiting the region through increased stream flow. Additionally, the infertile soil of the new cropland requires input of chemical fertilizers, which are then leached into and contaminate the groundwater. Conversion of Sandhills cropland back to grassland, however, is a slow process. Without the stabilizing grasses, dunes are subject to wind erosion. About 50 percent of the time, winds blowing through the Sandhills region are strong enough to move sand. Even after 80 years, some plots have not recovered to preirrigation standards.

See also Ogallala Aquifer

Further Reading

Johnsgard, Paul A. 2012. *Central Sandhills Trail*. Nebraska Birding Trails. http://www.nebraskabirdingtrails.com/trail.asp?trail=1

Loope, David B. and James Swinehart. 2000. "Thinking Like a Dune Field: Geologic History in the Nebraska Sand Hills. Paper 486." *Great Plains Research: A Journal of Natural and Social Sciences*. http://digitalcommons.unl.edu/greatplainsresearch/486

Nebraska Partners for Fish and Wildlife. n.d. *The Sandhills*. U.S. Fish and Wildlife Service. http://www.fws.gov/mountain-prairie/pfw/ne/ne4.htm

Sandhills Task Force. n.d. *The Nebraska Sandhills*. http://www.sandhillstaskforce.org/sandhills_history.htm

Nevado del Ruiz

Colombia

Geographic Overview. Nevado del Ruiz, 80 mi (129 km) from Bogotá in the Cordillera Central of Colombia, is notorious for the deadly lahar that raced down its slopes after an eruption in 1985. The volcano continues to be active; vapor and ash plumes rose from the summit crater as recently as May 2012.

Geographic Coordinates. 4°53'N, 75°19'W

Description. This snowcapped stratovolcano is part of the Ruiz–Tolima massif and one of seven active volcanoes in a 43.5 mi (50 km) chain in the Northern Volcanic Zone of Andean South America. Shield-shaped, with a broad summit covering some 77 mi² (200 km²), it rises to an elevation of 17,457 ft (5,321 m) asl. Five lava domes are clustered on the summit, and the Arenas crater, which is about 0.4 mi (1 km) wide and 790 ft (240 m) deep lies near its northeast edge.

Above 13,000 ft (4,000 m) Ruiz has steep (20°–30°) slopes, recent volcanic deposits, and deep V-shaped valleys. Below this elevation, the slopes are gentler (10°–20°), consist of older materials, and extend all the way to the floodplains of the Magdalena and Cauca rivers. An ice cap tops the mountain, reaching its maximum thickness of 160 ft (50 m) on the summit plateau and in the Nereides Glacier on the southwest side of the peak. All of its glaciers are rapidly retreating. In 1985, before the eruption, they extended down to elevations of 14,800 ft, but by 2003 had receded to 15,700–16,100 ft (4,800–4,900 m). The greatest losses of ice mass have been on the northern and eastern slopes, closest to the Arenas crater, where glaciers are now only about 100 ft (30 m) thick. Glacial meltwater flows west to the Cauca River and east to the Magdalena River. Some 40 towns depend on runoff from the ice for their water supplies.

The 1985 eruption of Ruiz was well documented, as teams of volcanologists were already studying the volcano's activity. Signs of a pending eruption had been noted for at least a year and included increased seismic activity, increased fumarole activity, deposition of sulfur on the summit, explosive eruptions of steam, and ejection of ash. The main eruption began at 3:06 P.M. on November 13 when tephra was spewed 19 mi (30 km) into the air. Ash began to fall in the surrounding areas to the north-northeast, but local officials were not alarmed. Heavy rains began and obscured the next, more violent eruption around 9 P.M., although the blast was felt by researchers. Subsequent pyroclastic flows melted snow and ice on the summit and produced four lahars, mixtures of water, pumice, clays, and other debris that tore down the mountain at about 20 mph (30–35 kmph). The flow moved through 11 valleys on the flanks of Ruiz and into the Chinchiná River valley, where 1,800 people were killed, and even more devastatingly into the Lagunilla River valley, where around 11 P.M. that night the small town of Armero was buried and an estimated 21,000 people (from a population of 25,000) lost their lives. Overall, at least 23,000 people were killed and another 5,000 injured. This is the deadliest lahar known in history and the second deadliest volcanic eruption of the twentieth century after Mount Pelée, Martinique, which killed some 30,000 people in 1902.

Geologic History. Over the last 11,000 years, there have been numerous eruptive phases characterized by slope failures, pyroclastic flows, and lahars that have partially destroyed the summit. The modern summit is the caldera of a much older Ruiz, now actively rebuilding. During the historic period, it is known to have erupted explosively in 1595 and to have again erupted in 1828 and 1829. Lava flows were produced by an earthquake in 1845. Historic eruptions have been of a type known as Plinian, which have powerful gas explosions and which produce huge amounts of pumice and plumes of gas and ash that reach well into the stratosphere. Such a type of explosion is associated with that of Mount Vesuvius in A.D. 79 and described by Pliny the Younger. So much magma can be lost from the chamber beneath the crater during these explosions that the top of the volcano collapses and produces a caldera, as happened famously with Krakatau in 1883.

See also Mount Vesuvius

Further Reading

Camp, Vic. 1985. "Nevado del Ruis." How Volcanoes Work. Department of Geological Sciences, San Diego State University. http://www.geology.sdsu.edu/how_volcanoes_work/Nevado.html

Committee of Natural Disasters, Division of Natural Hazard Mitigation, National Research Council. 1991. "Eruption of Nevado Del Ruiz Volcano Colombia, South America, November 13, 1985." The National Academies Press. http://www.nap.edu/catalog.php?record_id=1784#toc

"Nevado del Ruiz, Index of Monthly Reports." n.d. Global Volcanism Program, Smithsonian Institution. http://www.volcano.si.edu/world/volcano.cfm?vnum=1501-02=&volpage=var

Nevado Ojos del Salado

Argentina and Chile

Geographic Overview. Nevado Ojos del Salado is a massive stratovolcano on the border between Chile and Argentina and the second highest peak in both the Western and Southern Hemispheres. The volcano is generally considered to be historically active, although its last significant eruption occurred around A.D. 700 ± 300 years. Fumaroles, however, continuously emit gases in the crater and an unconfirmed emission of ash and gas was reported in 1993. If these activities meet the definition of "active," for which there is no consensus, then Ojos del Salado is Earth's highest elevation active volcano.

Geographic Coordinates. 27°07'S, 68°31'W

Description. The rocky summit of Ojos del Salado is the rim of a largely buried caldera. It lies in an extremely dry part of the Andes Mountains bordering the Atacama Desert, so snowfall is limited. Only in winter does snow persist on the peak. The summit area is elongated along a northeast-southwest axis and contains an array of volcanic landforms, including a dozen or so small cinder cones, lava domes, craters, Holocene lava flows, and fumaroles. On the eastern side at 20,960 ft (6,930 m) is a small but permanent crater lake about 300 ft (100 m) in diameter and of undetermined depth. This is likely the highest lake anywhere in the world.

The exact elevation of the summit of the volcano remains somewhat uncertain. The first ascent was made in 1937 by a team of Polish mountain climbers led by Jan Alfred Szczepanski and Justyn Wojsznis, but they provided no estimate of its height. They did, however, give the previously unknown mountain its name, which means "the source of the Salt River" (which it is not). In 1955 the second ascent was made by a Chilean survey team, who determined the elevation was 23,294 ft (7,100 m). If correct, this would have meant Ojos del Salado was higher than Aconcagua, but it turned out that not only was the measurement wrong but the team also had scaled the wrong peak. Others came to conquer the high peak, and in 1956 another Chilean group reached the summit; their aneroid barometers read 23,241 feet (7,083 m), still too high. That same year, an American climbing party used an 18-point triangulation method to determine a truer elevation of 22,580±10 ft (6,885 m). This was essentially confirmed in 2007 by handheld global positioning system (GPS) units. The Smithsonian Institution's Global Volcanism Program currently lists the summit elevation as 22,595 ft (6,887 m).

Aconcagua, now acknowledged as the highest peak in the Americas at 22,837 ft (6,960.8 m), is 370 mi (600 km) to the south. Argentina's Monte Pissis (22,287 ft or 6,793 m) is only 112 mi (180 km) to the south. For a while, Argentina claimed that this mountain was higher than Ojos del Salado, but the modern GPS and digital elevation models generated by the Shuttle Radar Topography Mission flown aboard the space shuttle *Endeavor* in 2000 disproved this and confirmed the elevation of Ojos del Salado. Monte Pissis is about 300 ft (100 m) lower, making it the third highest peak in the Americas. About 175 mi (280 km) north of Ojos del Salado is Volcán Llullailloco, which last erupted in 1887. If Ojos del Salado is considered dormant, Llullailloco holds the record as the highest active volcano in the world. It stands 22,110 ft (6,739 m) asl and is the seventh highest peak in the Andes.

Nevado Ojos del Salado is remote, but more easily accessed from the Chilean side via an international (dirt) road leading out of Copiapo. The climb itself is described as a hike, except for the final approach to the summit, which should be attempted only with ropes. Four-wheel drive vehicles can drive far up the slopes. While this is a convenience, it also contributes to a rapid ascent without proper acclimation to the high altitude and hence can endanger the climber.

Geologic History. Nevado Ojos del Salado is one of several large stratovolcanoes at the western edge of the Altiplano in the Central Volcanic Region of the Andes Mountains. All are products of the subduction of the Nazca Plate beneath the South American Plate that caused magma to rise through 43.5 mi (70 km) of continental crust, providing the necessary materials for the construction of these towering cones.

Further Reading

Falk, Burton. n.d. "Ojos del Salado (Chile): In High Places." Sierra Club. http://angeles.sierraclub.org/sps/archives/sps00074.htm

"Nevado Ojos del Salado." n.d. Global Volcanism Program, Smithsonian Institution. http://www.volcano.si.edu/world/volcano.cfm?vnum=1505-13=

"Nevados Ojos del Salado." n.d. Volcanoes of the Central Andes. Oregon State University. http://volcano.oregonstate.edu/oldroot/CVZ/ojossalado/index.html

New Guinea

Melanesia, South Pacific Ocean

Geographic Overview. New Guinea is the world's second largest island. Located north of Australia, the mountainous island hosts a biodiversity rivaling that of the Amazon Basin, yet it is one of the least studied parts of Earth. Divided at roughly 141°E, the western half of the island is in the Papua and West Papua provinces of Indonesia and the eastern half is the independent nation of Papua New Guinea.

Geographic Coordinates. Approximately 01°S –11°S, 131°E–151°E

Description. Earth's second largest island after Greenland, New Guinea extends 1,367 mi (2,200 km) along a northwest–southeast axis and is as much as 465 mi (750 km) wide. It has an area of 303,380 mi^2 (786,000 km^2). Mountains, the Central Range, run the full length of the island and reach a maximum elevation of 16,023 ft (4,884 m) on the ice-covered summit of Puncak Jaya in the western part of the range. Lower mountains and plains form a band north of the Central range, while a broad plain parallels the mountains to the south. Two prominent peninsulas give the island a distinctive shape. At the northwestern end is Bird's Head and Neck Peninsula; the tail end of the island in the southeast is the Papuan Peninsula. Off the southern coast, the continental shelf connects New Guinea with Australia.

Positioned in equatorial and tropical climate zones, New Guinea experiences uniformly warm temperatures year-round modified by elevation. The mean annual temperature in the lowlands is about 80°F (27°C), while at higher elevations it can be as low as 41°–45°F (5°–7°C). A glacier persists on Puncak Jaya. New Guinea is under the influence of the Asian monsoon, with the northwest monsoon dominating weather patterns from December to March and the southeast monsoon from May to October. The Central Range creates a rain shadow along the southeastern coast and on the Papuan Peninsula, where dry monsoon forests and woodland savannas dominate. Elsewhere lowland and montane rainforests prevail to elevations of 9,800 ft (3,000 m) asl. These forests contain relatives of Gondwanan trees found in South America, such as *Araucaria*, *Nothofagus*, and *Podocarpus*. On higher slopes are successive belts of shrublands, shrub grasslands, and subalpine grasslands until 13,780 ft (4,200 m). Above this elevation, an alpine vegetation of rosette and cushion plants occurs.

Geologic History. New Guinea is on the leading edge of the Australian Plate, and the west-central part of the island south of the Central Range is underlain by part of the Australian craton. The Central Range is a fold belt developed at the convergent boundary between the northward moving Australian Plate and the west-northwest moving Pacific Plate. The peninsulas and northern half of New Guinea are composed of numerous accreted terranes representing former microcontinents and volcanic island arcs caught in the convergence zone and added one by one to the Australian craton. New Guinea and Australia were one land mass (the Sahul continent) until the connecting shelf was flooded by rising sea levels at the end of the last ice age and became the Torres Strait.

Biota. New Guinea may be home to nearly eight percent of the world's species. The extremely rich biota derives from both Southeast Asia and Australia, but over 70 percent of species are endemic to the island. The flora is dominated by forms from the Malesian floristic province, a region that encompasses New Guinea, Indonesia, and the Philippines. Still a research frontier, New Guinea is estimated to have 11,000 to more than 30,000 plant species, including at least 3,000 species of orchid, its most diverse plant family.

The fauna is largely Australian in origin and contains a number of fascinating amphibians and reptiles, such as the world's largest tree frog (*Litoria infrafrenata*) as well as some of the smallest frogs (genus *Oreophyrne*) and frogs with long snouts (*Choerophryne* spp.). The world's largest crocodile lives here, as does the longest lizard, the monitor lizard *Varanus salvadorii*, which grows up to 8 ft (2.4 m) long.

Some 580 known species of bird reside in New Guinea, 60 percent of which are found nowhere else. Most famous are the 42 colorful and often spectacularly plumed birds-of-paradise, but there are also 11 bowerbirds, three large flightless cassowaries, the world's largest pigeon (*Goura victoria*), and the world's smallest parrots (*Micropsitta* spp.), 3.5–4 in (8–10 cm) in total body length. Some of the six brightly colored endemic songbirds (passerines) known as pitohuis contain neurotoxins in their skin and feathers.

Only four major types of mammal are native to New Guinea: monotremes (echidnas), marsupials (including tree kangaroos), rodents, and bats.

The insect fauna has been scarcely examined by scientists, but among those described are the world's largest butterfly (Queen Alexandra's birdwing) and largest moth (atlas moth), a stick insect nearly 8 in (20 cm) long, and a beetle that carries camouflaging algae in pits on its back.

Protected Areas. There are numerous national and provincial parks and wildlife management areas in Papua New Guinea. In Papua Province, Indonesia, Lorentz National Park, which includes the high peak of Puncak Jaya, was inscribed as a World Heritage Site by UNESCO in 1999. It extends from the crest of the Central Range south to the sea, from snow to tropical coast with mangroves.

Environmental Issues. Remoteness has long been thought to protect the people, plants, and animals of New Guinea, but threats do occur. Commercial logging is proceeding in old-growth forest, lowland forests are being converted to oil palm plantations, urbanization is increasing, and poaching and the illegal pet trade threaten certain native animals.

Further Reading

Allison, Allen. 2009. "New Guinea, Biology." In *Encyclopedia of Islands*, edited by Rosemary G. Gillespie and David A. Clague, 652–659. Berkeley: University of California Press.

Davies, Hugh L. 2009. "New Guinea, Geology." In *Encyclopedia of Islands*, edited by Rosemary G. Gillespie and David A. Clague, 659–665. Berkeley: University of California Press.

"WHC Nomination Documentation, Lorentz National Park." 1998. Government of the Republic of Indonesia. http://whc.unesco.org/uploads/nominations/955.pdf

New Zealand

South Pacific Ocean

Geographic Overview. New Zealand is an archipelago consisting of two large "mainland" islands—North Island and South Island—and hundreds of smaller islands and islets lying 900 mi (1,500 km) east of Australia between the Tasman Sea and the Pacific Ocean. Most of the islands represent raised parts of a submerged continent, Zealandia. The archipelago harbors unique animals, including the iconic kiwis, the world's largest extant rail; the flightless takahe; and reptilian "living fossils," the tuatara.

Geographic Coordinates. Approximately 34°S–47°S, 166°30'E–178°30'E

Description. The New Zealand archipelago extends northeast–southwest through 13 degrees of latitude at the southwestern edge of the Pacific Ocean. The main islands are Y-shaped North Island, with an area of 43,911 mi^2 (113,729 km^2), and larger, elongate South Island, with an area of 58,384 mi^2 (150,437 km^2). They are separated by the rough waters of Cook Strait, 22 mi (35 km) wide at its narrowest point. Stewart Island, lying south of South Island across Foveaux Strait, is next in size at 650 mi^2 (1,680 km^2). Among the "offshore" islands are the Chatham Islands 497 mi (800 km) east of South Island.

New Zealand is composed almost exclusively of continental crust and hence, geologically, is considered a group of continental islands. Most islands are parts of a now submerged landmass known as Zealandia, which was once part of Gondwana. Local tectonic activity raised parts of Zealandia above sea level to form the two "mainland" islands and offshore islands such as the Chatham Islands as well as New Caledonia northeast of Australia in the Coral Sea. Former Zealandia is split, however, by the boundary between the Australian and Pacific plates, so that North Island is completely on the Australian Plate and most of South Island lies on the Pacific Plate.

Both mainland islands are mountainous, especially South Island, as a result of uplift associated with a convergent plate boundary. Off the east coast of North Island, the oceanic crust of the Pacific Plate is subducting beneath continental crust on the Australian Plate, giving rise to volcanic arcs offshore (e.g., White Island, a still active volcano) and three active stratovolcanoes in central North Island's Taupo Volcanic Zone (TVZ). The highest peak on the island is Mount Ruapehu at 9,176 ft (2,797 m) asl. The explosive eruptions forming six calderas in the TVZ less than 2 million years ago blanketed the surrounding areas in tephra and ignimbrites. Lake Taupo, New Zealand's largest lake, is a crater lake in the caldera of Taupo Volcano, which erupted 26,500 years ago in what has been the largest volcanic eruption (the Oruanui eruption) on Earth in the past 70,000 years. Auckland, New Zealand's largest city, lies on an active volcanic field less than 250,000 years old and containing some 50 cones, maars, and craters. North Island's volcanoes are part of the Pacific "Ring of Fire."

Along the west coast of South Island, convergence has been between continental crust on both plates and no volcanism has occurred. Instead the Southern Alps, which run the full length of the coast, were formed much as the European Alps or the Himalayas were. The peaks average about 9,800 ft (3,000 m) asl. Aoraki (Mount Cook), New Zealand's highest peak, rises to 12,217 ft (3,724 m) asl in the Southern Alps. In the northeast of South Island, convergence resulted in downwarping, perhaps caused by the drag of the subducting Pacific Plate, which has created Marlborough Sounds, a drowned landscape not caused by rising sea level. The southwest coast of South Island, Fiordland, is a spectacular land of fjords, U-shaped valleys, hanging valleys, and mountain cirques. A few small valley glaciers remain high in the alps as remnants of late Pleistocene ice. Eastern slopes are carved into glacial troughs now filled with long, deep, finger

Aoroki (Mount Cook) in the Southern Alps, South Island, with its remnant Pleistocene glaciers, is the highest peak in New Zealand. (Dmitry Pichugin/Dreamstime.com)

lakes. Along the coast 10 or more marine terraces appear as great flights of stairs. The Canterbury Plains on the central-east coast of South Island are the only major lowland. Large braided streams work their way through alluvial gravels and reworked glacial outwash to outlets in the Pacific.

The climate of much of New Zealand is classified as temperate marine with cool summers and year-round precipitation. Since the islands lie in the path of the Prevailing Westerlies, western slopes are wet; eastern areas in the rain shadows of mountains, such as the Canterbury Plains, are nearly semiarid. Annual precipitation of 118–197 in (3,000–5,000 mm) is recorded on the western flanks of the Southern Alps, while east of the range totals are closer to 40 in (1,000 mm).

Prior to human settlement, which began 1,000–600 years ago, most of New Zealand was covered by a mixed temperate rainforest of podocarps, southern beeches, and tree ferns. About 22 percent of nearly pristine forest remains. Most trees and shrubs are evergreen; white flowers, pollinated by flies, are common. Small-leaved shrubs with interlacing branches are found in 20 families and may represent adaptations to browsing moas (see "Biota" section). The largest tree is the endemic araucaria, kauri (*Agathis australis*) found on the northwestern branch of the Y of North Island. Individuals can be 130–165 ft (40–50 m) tall and have trunk diameters over 16 ft (5 m), rivaling North America's giant sequoias. Above treeline, at about 4,300 ft (1,300 m) asl, an alpine grassland of tussock grasses and cushion plants dominates.

Geologic History. The basement rock of the mainland islands of New Zealand are formed from sediments eroded from Gondwana and deposited off its eastern margin in the Panthalassa Ocean from Cambrian through Cretaceous time. Dominant rock types are graywacke—a muddy sandstone derived from granitic and volcanic rocks—and schists (metamorphosed greywacke). These rocks became a strip of new continental crust attached along the eastern edge of Gondwana and stretched along parts of the supercontinent that are now Australia, East Antarctica, and West Antarctica. Zealandia, as the new segment is called, broke away from Gondwana 83 mya, drifting northeastward as the Tasman Sea opened. Seafloor spreading continued for 60 million years, ceasing about 23 mya. The continental crust of Zealandia stretched, thinned, and cooled and as it moved away from the spreading center, gradually but steadily sank until submerged beneath 8,000 ft (2,500 m) of seawater. Submergence may have been total, although New Caledonia, also part of Zealandia, was above sea level 23 mya. Concurrently, the plate boundary between the Australian and Pacific plates cut through Zealandia. Today, it extends from the Tonga Trench north of New Zealand to the Puysegur Trench south of the islands, passing off the east coast of North Island, cutting across northern South Island (Hope Fault) to connect with the Alpine Fault just off the west coast of South Island, exiting the island at the entrance to Milford Sound in Fiordland. Also the Pacific Plate continues to move westward, while the Australian Plate moves northward. Convergence occurs at a rate of 1.5–2.0 in (4–5 cm)/yr. The islands of contemporary New Zealand emerged as a consequence of plate convergence some time after 23 mya, and both the Southern Alps and the volcanic peaks of North Island are products of this tectonic activity.

New Zealand was glaciated several times in the geologic past, most recently in the late Pleistocene, approximately 20,000 years ago. During glacial periods of the Pleistocene, the three main islands (North, South, and Stewart) were connected. Glaciation sculpted the mountains, gouged the piedmont, and left depositional features such as the curving and looping moraines of Fiordland and the eastern lowlands, the Canterbury Plains. Franz Joseph Glacier and Fox Glacier remain as small tongues of ice flowing several miles down the western flanks of the Southern Alps toward the Tasman Sea.

Biota. Although New Zealand is geologically continental in origin, its biota has been assembled in the manner of oceanic islands by long distance dispersal.

Endemism at the species level is high, but the flora and fauna overall are species-poor. Of 2,300 native plant species, 85 percent are endemic to the archipelago.

Other than three bat species, there are no native terrestrial mammals. Their place was taken by birds. Most famous are New Zealand's now extinct moa (Order Dinornthiformes), ratites and the chief herbivores in the forests. The largest was *Diornis giganteus* [12 ft (3.6 m) tall and weighing up to 510 lbs (230 kg)]. All nine species of moa were extinct by A.D. 1400, about 100 years after the islands were colonized by people. Another endemic order, the kiwis (Apterygidae) has five extant species. Kiwis, the symbol of New Zealand, are the world's smallest ratites and lay the largest egg relative to female body weight known among birds. Flightlessness is a characteristic of both orders, as it is in a variety of bird taxa, among them the large endemic rail (the Takahe), an extinct goose (*Cnemiornis* sp.), an extinct duck (*Chenonetta finschi*), a large parrot (the kakapo, *Strigops habaproptilus*), and the extinct Stephen Island Wren. Like the kiwis, many birds are nocturnal and have low reproductive rates. They tend not to have showy plumage or display sexual dimorphism in plumage.

The herpetofauna is small. An endemic family of frogs (Leiopelmatidae) has four living species, each completing the tadpole stage in the egg and receiving parental care as froglets. Reptiles include only geckos and skinks and, on offshore islands along the north coast of North Island and Cook Strait, two endemic species of tuatara (*Sphenodon punctatus* and *Sphenodon guntheri*), medium-size reptiles that are "living fossils"—the last surviving species of a 200-million-year-old lineage (Order Sphenodontia).

Several of New Zealand's species are alpine specialists. Among plants are snow tussock grass, and the cushion plants called "vegetable sheep" (*Haastia* and *Raoulia*). Animals include skinks and geckos, the takahe and the world's only alpine parrot, the kea (*Nestor notabilis*).

Protected Areas. Te Wahipounamu is a World Heritage Site in southwestern South Island that encompasses four national parks in the Southern Alps: Aoraki/Mount Cook, Fiordland, Mt. Aspiring, and Westland. It protects about 2 million hectares of temperate rainforest and the only wild population of takahe. In the center of North Island, four active volcanoes are contained in Tongariro National Park, a mixed natural and cultural World Heritage Site. A dozen other national parks and other reserves exist. A number of small islands are set aside as sanctuaries to preserve New Zealand's rare and endemic species.

Environmental Issues. Introduced species have been a problem since the Maori arrived from Central Polynesia about 1,000 years ago. They brought with them the Pacific rat and a dog, which undoubtedly contributed to the loss of naïve native island species. Later, European Acclimatization Societies introduced European animals (dogs, cats, pigs, mice, rats, red deer [elk], goats, hares and rabbits, hedgehogs, and numerous "garden birds"). Trout, salmon, and 18 other freshwater fishes were introduced to streams and lakes. Stoats and ferrets were brought in in 1882 in an attempt to control rats and mice, but they preyed upon native birds, reptiles, and invertebrates. The Australian brush-tailed possum is also a major pest. Prevention of new introductions and management of exotic plants and animals are major issues today. Eradication of 12 alien mammalian species has been successful on some of the smaller islands. Climate change and habitat change are also concerns; remaining native forests are now protected so deforestation is no longer a major issue.

Further Reading

Campbell, Hamish and Charles Landis. 2009. "New Zealand, Geology." In *Encyclopedia of Islands*, edited by Rosemary G. Gillespie and David A. Clague, 673–680. Berkeley: University of California Press.

"Te Wahipounamu—South West New Zealand." n.d. World Heritage Centre, UNESCO. http://whc.unesco.org/en/list/551

Trewick, Steven A. and Mary Morgan-Richards. 2009. "New Zealand, Biology." In *Encyclopedia of Islands*, edited by Rosemary G. Gillespie and David A. Clague, 665–673. Berkeley: University of California Press.

Newberry National Volcanic Monument

United States (Oregon)

Geographic Overview. Newberry National Volcanic Monument, south of Bend, Oregon, in the Basin and Range Physiographic Province, preserves a shield volcano, topped by a caldera with two lakes. More recent eruptions occurred approximately 1,300 years ago, blanketing the surrounding area with pumice and ash.

Geographic Coordinates. 43°42'N, 121°15'W

Description. The monument covers 55,000 ac (22,258 ha), including the caldera, the upper slopes, and most of the volcanics in the Northwest Rift Zone. Although related to the Cascade Mountains, Newberry lies 50 mi (80 km) to the east and has a different geologic history and configuration. It is a low-profile shield volcano, more than 25 mi (40 km) in diameter. The volcano and its associated lava flows and cinder cones cover approximately 1,200 mi² (3,200 km²). The summit is a caldera containing two lakes, Paulina Lake and East Lake, drained to the west by Paulina Creek. Paulina Peak is 7,986 ft (2,434 m) asl, approximately 4,000 ft (1,220 m) above Bend.

Geologic History. Approximately 400,000 years ago, fluid basalts built a large, broad shield volcano, similar to those that form the base of the Cascade volcanic chain, but for unknown reasons, a stratovolcano never developed. Explosive eruptions, involving pumice, ash, and pyroclastic flows, took place approximately 75,000 years ago, the most recent of at least three similar eruptions. The summit collapsed into a caldera, 4 mi × 5 mi (6.5 km × 8.0 km). The mountain is estimated to have been 500–1,000 ft (150–400 m) higher than Paulina Peak today. The volcano continued to erupt, but deposits are buried under younger flows.

Recent volcanic activity can be dated by the eruption of Mt. Mazama, which created the caldera at Crater Lake 7,700 years ago. Pumice from that eruption was blown east to Newberry Volcano, covering parts of the mountain with deposits as deep as 6 ft (2 m). Subsequent eruptions from Newberry volcano overlie that pumice and are thus less than 7,700 years old. The first eruptions within the caldera were fissure flows of viscous rhyolite, forming a ridge, which now separates the two lakes. Central Pumice Cone, 700 ft (215 m) above East Lake, developed on the ridge, followed by basalt and basaltic andesite from several cinder and spatter cones along the ridge. Approximately 7,000 years ago, the Northwest Rift Zone opened. This fissure system, extending 20 mi (32 km) northwest from the caldera, had numerous vents and lava flows. Eruptions become successively younger toward the north, and Lava Butte, 500 ft (150 m) tall, is the most recent. One of Lava Butte's flows temporarily dammed the Deschutes River. Lava also engulfed and burned trees, leaving hollow molds or casts in the solidified basalt. Lava River Cave is a 1 mi (1.6 km) long lava tube.

The most recent activity occurred approximately 1,300 years ago within the caldera rim. An explosive eruption involved tephra and pyroclastic flows. Pumice was deposited approximately 10 ft (3 m) thick in the caldera, and westerly winds carried some ash as far east as Idaho. This episode was followed by a less explosive ash flow and thick rhyolite lava, which formed a dome at the vent and the volcanic glass of the Big Obsidian Flow. Covering only 1 mi^2 (1.6 km^2), Big Obsidian Flow is the youngest volcanic feature within the caldera.

Hot springs in the lakes reach 135°F (57.2°C). Temperatures exceeding 500°F (260°C) at the bottom of a 3,000 ft (900 m) drill hole indicate that an active magma chamber still exists.

Protected Areas. Newberry National Volcanic Monument was established in 1990 and is administered by the National Forest Service.

See also Basin and Range Physiographic Province; Cascade Mountains; Columbia Plateau; Crater Lake

Further Reading

Alt, David D. and Donald W. Hyndman. 1978. *Roadside Geology of Oregon*. Missoula, MT: Mountain Press.
U.S. Geological Survey. 2012. "Newberry." Volcanic Hazards Program. http://volcanoes.usgs.gov/volcanoes/newberry/

Newfoundland

North Atlantic Ocean

Geographic Overview. The island of Newfoundland exhibits a detailed assemblage of Appalachian rocks illustrating mountain-building episodes. The island's complex geology records the opening of the Iapetus Ocean, its subsequent closing, and the island's continental collision with Eurasia and Gondwana, which resulted in the supercontinent of Pangaea. The island was a testing ground for new plate tectonics theories of mountain building and key to understanding the origin of the Appalachians Mountains. Parts of the island have oceanic crust and upper mantle rocks, which were pushed onto the land. Some oceanic rock layers preserve rare fossils from the Cambrian Period.

Geographic Coordinates. Approximately 46° 36'N–51°37'N, 52°41'W–59°25'W

Description. Extending 350 mi (560 km) north-to-south and 315 mi (510 km) east-to-west and covering 43,008 mi^2 (111,390 km^2), Newfoundland is separated from eastern mainland Canada by the Strait of Belle Isle. The island has a variety of landscapes, including tundra, sharp glacially carved mountain ranges, barren rocks, lush boreal forest, and rugged coastlines. Much of the island is the northern part of the Appalachian Mountain system and it marks the northernmost point of the International Appalachian Trail, a continuation of the United States Appalachian Trail which terminates at Mount Katahdin, Maine.

Gros Morne, in western Newfoundland, is one of few places in the world where the Mohorovicic Discontinuity, the boundary between crustal rocks and the mantle, can be studied directly. Barren Tablelands in Gros Morne National Park are the ultramafic peridotite, part of the mantle lava, with toxic amounts of heavy metals and lacking nutrients for plant life.

At Mistaken Point Ecological Reserve, just 2.2 mi^2 (5.7 km^2) on the southeastern Avalon Peninsula, mudstones and sandstones preserve examples of the earth's oldest multicell life-forms. Imprints of the soft bodies of Ediacara biota, which predate the development of skeletal support, are imprinted in the muddy ocean floor, preserved by rapid burial in volcanic ash. Distinct fossils on other sites on the island illustrate the diversity of the geology.

The fjord coastline was carved by valley glaciers radiating out from a central ice cap during the Wisconsin glacial period. The extensive coastline is an ideal place for spotting icebergs, whales, and seabirds.

The subarctic climate is moderated by the marine influence, and temperatures are not extreme. Winters hover around freezing, while summers average 60°F (16°C). Annual precipitation is 44 in (1,120 mm), three-quarters falling as rain. Fog is common.

Geologic History. The island has three zones, based on distinct rock assemblages and geologic

Shown here at Ten Mile Pond, Gros Morne National Park in Newfoundland, Canada, is significant for its exposure of the boundary between crustal rocks and mantle, the so-called Mohorovicic Discontinuity. (Photawa/Dreamstime.com)

histories. The Western (Humber) Zone, including eroded granite and gneiss of the southern and northern Long Range Mountains, has been part of North America for more than a billion years, since the late Precambrian. The Central (Dunnage and Gander) and Eastern (Avalon) Zones are accreted terranes, added to North America during the closing of the Iapetus Ocean. The Central Zone is part of the Iapetus Ocean floor, and the Eastern Zone originated east of the ocean, as part of Gondwana, or Africa.

A spreading center split Laurentia (ancestral North America) east of the Long Range Mountains as the Iapetus Ocean (precursor to the Atlantic Ocean) opened during the Cambrian (540 mya), leaving the Western Zone of Newfoundland as part of North America. In the early Ordovician (490 mya), plate movement reversed direction and the Iapetus Ocean began to close.

A subduction zone developed to the east between two oceanic plates, where very basic magma, peridotite, dunnite, and gabbro, flowed up from the mantle to create new oceanic crust. This sequence of basic rocks, called ophiolite, is a complete section of the Iapetus Ocean floor. As subduction and convergence continued, slabs of ocean crust and mantle as large as 25 mi × 6 mi (40 km × 10 km) were pushed to the west coast of Newfoundland, where remnants form the Barren Tablelands of Gros Morne. Volcanics and remnants of oceanic crust also form the Central Zone.

As the ocean closed completely, Laurentia and Gondwana (Europe and Africa) converged to build the huge new mountainous continent of Pangaea in place of the Iapetus Ocean. The Appalachian Mountains, extending from southeastern United States north through Newfoundland, were part of this new continent. With mountain uplift, granite intrusions were emplaced in the Central and Eastern Zones. The region was stable until the Mesozoic Era (250–150 mya) and the opening of the Atlantic Ocean. The rift opened east of the old Iapetus break, leaving part of Gondwana, the Eastern Zone, still attached to Newfoundland, as well as to Nova Scotia, parts of New Brunswick, and northeastern United States. The Eastern Zone is sedimentary and volcanic rocks with younger overlying shale and sandstone with fossil biota different from the rest of Newfoundland. The southern half of the mountains marking the collision zone is the Appalachian Mountains from Alabama north to Newfoundland. The northern half of the collision-zone mountains is separated from North America by the Atlantic Ocean and divided among Greenland, the British Isles, and Scandinavia. The matching of rocks and biota across the Atlantic confirmed the theory of plate tectonics.

Biota. Because the island was completely covered by ice during the Pleistocene, plant and animal life is sparse compared to the subarctic climate of the mainland. The 14 native mammals include caribou, black bears, ermine, otters, beaver, and lynx, but many animals, such as squirrels, chipmunks, and mice, were introduced. Gros Morne National Park supports a large population of introduced moose. Many plants are rare and endemic, such as Long's braya (*Braya longii*) and Fernald's braya (*Braya fernaldii*) in the mustard family.

Protected Areas. Gros Morne National Park, 697 mi² (1805 km²), was recognized as a World Heritage Site because of its exposures of oceanic crust and mantle rock. Mistaken Point Ecological Reserve protects sedimentary rocks with some of the earth's oldest fossils.

See also Appalachian Mountains

Further Reading

Bell, Trevor and David Liverman. 2000. *The Newfoundland Story*. Adapted from Stephen Colman-Sadd and Susan A. Scott, 1994, *Newfoundland and Labrador: Traveller's Guide to the Geology*. www.heritage.nf.ca /environment/nfld_story.html

Parks Canada. 2010. "The Story in Stone." Gros Morne National Park of Canada. www.pc.gc.ca/pn-np/nl /grosmorne/natcul/natcul2.aspx

Ngorongoro Crater

Tanzania

Geographic Overview. Ngorongoro Crater is the world's largest inactive caldera with an unbroken rim. It is world famous for its resident and migratory wildlife. The caldera lies within the Ngorongoro Conservation Area, a protected area that also includes the globally significant paleoanthropological sites at Oldupai Gorge and Laetoli, and lies adjacent to Serengeti National Park. The enormous herds of zebra, wildebeest, and antelopes that migrate through the Serengeti visit Ngorongoro Crater in austral summer.

Geographic Coordinates. 03°10'S, 35°35'E

Description. Ngorongoro Crater is a nearly circular caldera approximately 12 mi (19 km) in diameter located on the southern Serengeti Plain in northern Tanzania. The nearly flat crater floor is at an elevation of 5,900 ft (1,800 m) asl. The unbroken rim rises 1,310–2,000 ft (400–610 m) above the floor, which covers an area of about 96 mi² (250 km²). A seasonal salt lake, Lake Magadi, lies in the southwestern quadrant, fed by Munge Stream, which flows intermittently from the northeast rim. Two large swamps, Goorigor and Manduusi, also occur on the crater floor southeast and north of the lake, respectively. The only other source of surface water is Mgotitokitok Spring, southeast of Lake Magadi.

Ngorongoro Crater lies in a tropical wet and dry climate region with two rainy seasons. The short rains occur in November and December and the long rains fall March through May. With prevailing winds coming from the east, the outer eastern slopes of the caldera receive the most precipitation, averaging 30–47 in (800–1,200 mm) a year. The crater floor and western slopes are drier, receiving about 16–24 in (400–600 mm) a year. Consequently, the eastern slopes are covered by dense montane forests, while the western slopes support xeric shrublands dominated by arborescent spine-shield (*Euphorbia nyikae*). The crater floor is largely an open grassland with scattered umbrella acacia (*Acacia torilis*) and myrrh (*Commiphora africana*) trees. Two woodland areas exist. The Lerai Forest contains yellow fever tree (*Acacia xanthophloea*) and quinine tree (*Rauvolfia caffra*), the Laiyana Forest the flat-topped acacia, *Acacia lahai*.

The crater is home to resident herds of zebra, wildebeest, gazelles, and lions as well as migratory herds that are part of the spectacular ungulate migrations between the Seregenti and Maasai Mara in Kenya. These ungulates support the densest populations of mammalian carnivores in the world, namely dark-maned lions and hyenas.

Ngorongoro is part of the greater Serengeti ecosystem and the centerpiece of the Ngorongoro Conservation Area (NCA), which lies just east and adjacent to Serengeti National Park. Two smaller calderas also occur in the area: Olmoti, known for its waterfalls, and Empakaii, encompassing a deep lake. The NCA is also home to two globally significant paleoanthropological sites: *Oldupai Gorge* (formerly known as *Olduvai Gorge*, but officially renamed in 2005 to use the original Maasai word, which refers to a plant, *Sanseveria ehrenbergii*, that grows there) and Laetoli, worked by Mary and Louis Leakey and their teams. Oldupai Gorge is a 295 ft (90 m) deep valley eroded in a former lake bed over tens of thousands of years by intermittent streams. Nearly 9 mi (14 km) long, the gorge is about midway between Seregenti National Park and Ngorongoro Crater, northwest of the crater. Erosion and archaeological research have revealed the fossilized remains of some of humankind's earliest ancestors, including *Homo habilis, Paranthropus boisei,* and *Homo erectus*, dating to 1.9, 1.75, and 1.2 mya, respectively. Some 30 mi (48 km) to the south is Laetoli, site of an 88 ft (27 m) long trail of about 70 footprints discovered by Paul Abell in 1978 and interpreted as belonging to the early hominin *Australopithecus afarensis* and having been imprinted in wet volcanic ash 3.8 mya.

Geologic History. Ngorongoro Crater is associated with rifting that occurred west of the Gregory Rift (eastern branch of the Great Rift Valley) beginning 20 mya. The Ngorongoro Volcano formed along the Eyasi Rift in which Lake Eyasi now lies sometime in the late Miocene (11.6–5.3 mya). When its magma pool subsided about 2.5 mya, the volcano, estimated to have been anywhere from 14,800–19,000 ft (4,500–5,800 m) high, collapsed, creating the caldera, the rim and floor of which persist to this day. Volcanic

ash from Ngorongoro and other volcanic centers in the volcanic field continued to erupt (Ol Doinyo Lengai is still active) and created ash layers used to date fossilized hominin bones and footprints at paleoarchaeological sites in the vicinity. The ash also created fertile soils that still support nutritious grasslands and the great herds of herbivores that live in or visit the crater.

Biota. Ngorongoro Crater is home to resident populations of an estimated 7,000 wildebeest, 4,000 Burchell's Zebra, and 3,000 antelopes, including Thomson's and Grant's gazelles and eland. A population of 60 or so lions, the males distinguished by their dark manes, also resides in the crater year-round. In December, the annual ungulate migration south from the Maasi Mara in Kenya can bring an additional 1.7 million wildebeest, 260,000 zebras, and 470,000 gazelles into the NCA. At Lake Magadi, Lesser and Greater Flamingos feed on algae and brine shrimp, respectively.

The NCA maintains the highest density of mammalian predators in Africa, including lions and other large cats and hyenas. Endangered species include black rhinoceros, wild hunting dog, and golden cat. Since 1960, buffalo have been replacing wildebeest as the dominant herbivore, presumably because lack of periodic fires have allowed coarser, tall grasses to outcompete shorter, less fibrous grasses in the crater. The warthog first colonized the area in the 1980s.

Protected Areas. The NCA covers almost 3,200 mi^2 (8,280 km^2), encompassing the entire caldera as well as surrounding savanna, woodland, craters, and paleoarchaeological sites. The NCA was separated from Serengeti National Park in 1959, after Tanzania had gained its independence from Great Britain, became a MAB-UNESCO Biosphere Reserve in 1971, and was inscribed as a UNESCO World Heritage Site in 1979.

Environmental Issues. Dramatic declines in population sizes of resident ungulates have been occurring. Vegetation change in the absence of burning has been implicated. Disease may also play a role. Black rhino, which numbered over 100 in the 1960s was down to about 30 animals by 2011 as a result of poaching. In the last 50 years buffalo and warthog have colonized, as have invasive plants. The resident lions are known to lack genetic diversity and their numbers, too, are dropping.

A balance among wildlife conservation, livestock grazing by Maasai pastoralists, and tourism is a constant management goal. Lack of enforcement is a problem, as is a proposed increase of access roads to and other tourist-oriented development at Oldupai Gorge and Laetoli, which could block migration routes and deplete water sources.

See also Serengeti Plain and Maasai Mara

Further Reading

Akyoo, Adam and Marc Nkwame. 2007. "Ngorongoro: A Priceless Asset." Ngorongoro Conservation area Authority. http://www.ngorongorocrater.org/craters.html

Oates, Louisa and Paul A. Rees. 2012. "The Historical Ecology of the Large Mammal Populations of Ngorongoro Crater, Tanzania, East Africa." *Mammal Review*. The Mammal Society and Blackwell Publishing. http://www.rhinoresourcecenter.com/pdf_files/133/1334728220.pdf

Stuart, Chris and Tilde Stuart. 1999. "Ngorongoro: Africa's Cradle of Life. Fiery Origins." The Living Edens, PBS. http://www.pbs.org/edens/ngorongoro/fiery.html

Niagara Falls

United States (New York) and Canada

Geographic Overview. Water draining from the Great Lakes drops from Lake Erie over Niagara Falls, shared by both the United States and Canada, eventually entering Lake Ontario. Ships traveling into the Great Lakes now bypass Niagara Falls via the Welland Canal. Niagara Falls has been a major tourist site since the late 1800s.

Geographic Coordinates. 43°05'N, 79°04'W

Description. The 33 mi (58 km) Niagara River is the only outlet from the Upper Great Lakes, dropping 326 ft (99 m) as it flows from Lake Erie north to Lake Ontario. The river drops half that distance at Niagara Falls, a large cascade over a dolomite cliff. The other half is in rapids both above the falls and in the gorge below the falls. The falls separate into Horseshoe Falls (or Canadian Falls) and American Falls where the river skirts around Goat Island. Small Bridal Veil Falls is also on the American side, separated from the larger cascade by small Luna Island. Horseshoe Falls is the larger of the two main cascades. It carries 90 percent of the flow and drops an average of 188 ft (57 m). The plunge pool at its base is 170 ft (52 m) deep. The crest line of Horseshoe Falls spans approximately 2,200 ft (670 m), compared with 850 ft (260 m) at American Falls. The American Falls drop 70–110 ft (21–34 m) and have no plunge pool because the water falls onto a talus pile of broken rocks.

Geologic History. The Niagara River and its falls developed as glacial ice retreated 12,500 years ago. Water from glacial Lake Tonawanda (between Lake Erie and Lake Ontario) drained north into what would become Lake Ontario, falling over the steep cliff of the Lockport dolomite near Lewiston. As the glacial ice was melting, as many as five waterfall outlets formed over the Niagara escarpment into Lake Ontario. Large waterfalls developed because of differential erosion of gently tilting layers of Paleozoic limestone, sandstone, and shale. Rock layers dip slightly to the south, meaning that escarpments of resistant calcareous rocks face northward. The falls are formed as the water runs over the edge of the Lockport dolomite, 80 ft (24.4 m) of hard rock forming the top layer of the Niagara escarpment. The original falls cut into the escarpment at Lockport, close to Lake Ontario. About 200 ft (61 m) of soft shales beneath the dolomite are easily eroded by the force of falling water. As the cap rock is undercut, losing its support from the shale beneath, it eventually gives way and falls into the river. The process was repeated for 12,500 years and the falls moved 7 mi (11.3 km) upstream, toward Lake Erie, as the cap rock eroded. The process continues today, with Horseshoe Falls eroding upstream more quickly than the American Falls because it receives the greater volume of water. Just north of Lake Erie is the Onondaga scarp, a smaller limestone layer that causes rapids near Buffalo.

Downstream from the falls is Niagara Gorge, variable in width and depth. Increased flow made the gorge wider and deeper, while less flow left a narrow and shallow channel. At one point, water is forced through a narrow part of the gorge, creating a vortex of swirling rapids called the Whirlpool, which drops 50 ft (15 m) and extends 1 mi (1.6 km) downstream. At the Whirlpool, the river makes a 90° turn where it intersected an old river valley and took the easier route.

Since 1950, a treaty between the United States and Canada has regulated the diversion of water for municipal, recreation, and industrial purposes and hydroelectric power, while at the same time maintaining the beauty of the falls. During daylight hours in the tourist season, flow is maintained at approximately one-half of the mean discharge of 202,000 ft³/sec (5,720 m³/s). At night or during the off-season, the flow may be reduced. The rate of erosion and back-cutting of the falls has slowed to 1.6–3.3 ft (0.5–1.0 m) per year because of water diversion. It had been moving back a mean of 3–5 ft (1–1.5 m) per year for the last 560 years. At the current rate, it may take 50,000 years to erode back the 20 mi (32 km) to Lake Erie, at which time the falls would cease to exist.

Protected Areas. Niagara Falls is shared by the United States, as a New York State Park, and Canada, as an Ontario Provincial Park. The U.S. side has been a public area, and America's oldest state park, since 1885.

See also Great Lakes

Further Reading

Maletz, Jörg. n.d. "GLY 103 Niagara Falls Field Trip." Department of Geology, University of Buffalo, New York. http://www.glyfac.buffalo.edu/Faculty/jorgm/WebJorg07/gly103trip.htm

Niagara Parks. n.d. *Niagara Falls Geology Facts & Figures.* Ontario, Canada. http://www.niagaraparks.com/media/geology-facts-figures.html

Van Diver, Bradford B. 1997. *Roadside Geology of New York*. Missoula, MT: Mountain Press.

Niger River

Guinea, Mali, Niger, Benin, and Nigeria

Geographic Overview. The Niger River in West Africa is the third longest river on the African continent after the Nile and Congo. In map view, it is distinctive for its great bend, where it turns sharply south-southeast from the northeastward flow of its upper reaches. Just before the bend is a large inner delta of braided streams and lakes, one of three in Africa (the other two being the Okavango Delta and the Sudd on the Nile River). The inner delta provided water in a parched region and

became the center of two Sahelian empires, Mali (ca. A.D. 1230–1600) and Songhai (ca. A.D. 1340–1591). Timbuktu, just downstream from the inner delta, became an important trading center where Saharan salt was exchanged for West African gold, ivory, and slaves, as well as a major Islamic center of learning in the 15th and 16th centuries. Both Nigeria and Niger take their names from the river.

Geographic Coordinates. Source: Approximately 09°N, 09°W; Mouth: Approximately 04°30'N, 06°E

Description. The Niger River begins 2,625 ft (800 m) asl on Foujta Djallon Plateau of Guinea, only 155 mi (250 km) from the Atlantic Ocean, but it flows northeastward into Mali and the Sahara Desert. A large inner delta has formed just upstream from Timbuktu, Mali (16°46'N, 3°00'W), roughly 600 mi (1000 km) from the source. The delta, with its braided streams and several lakes, is almost 250 mi long and 515 ft (157 m) asl; it marks the end of the Upper Niger. Here 1,540 mi² (4,000 km²) of territory are permanently flooded, expanding to 11,580 mi² (30,000 km²) during the annual flood. This is a vital source of water for aquatic and terrestrial life at the edge of the Sahel and Sahara. Just beyond the inner delta, the river makes a great bend and turns south-southeast into Niger. From the inner delta downstream to the vicinity of Niamey, Niger, is the Middle Niger. Beyond that point is the Lower Niger, which flows through Nigeria into the Gulf of Guinea, terminating 2,585 mi (4,160 km) from the source in a 186 mi (300 km) wide coastal delta.

The river begins in uplands of tropical forest and savanna where rainfall averages 60 in (1,500 mm) a year, but drops into dry grasslands with annual precipitation as low as 8 in (200 mm) in the inner delta. Nearly two-thirds of the water volume is lost between Ségou and Timbuktu through seepage and evaporation. Flow is replenished downstream by the entry of its main tributary, the Benue River, at Lokoja in Nigeria. The Benue's headwaters are in the better-watered highlands of northeast Cameroon. The Niger River floods every year beginning in September at the end of the rainy season. Peak flow in the inner delta occurs in November and water levels return to prerainy season levels by May.

The coastal delta is in a zone of tropical monsoon climate and high precipitation where more than 157 in

(4,000 mm) of rain falls, peaking in winter. The upper coastal delta is swamp forest, the lower delta mangrove swamp.

Geologic History. The Upper Niger and Lower Niger were once two separate rivers. It appears that the Upper Niger River's original northward flow was blocked by sand dunes during a former dry period in the Sahara and a large inland lake formed near Azaouad north of Timbuktu. The lake either overflowed and eroded a sill at Tosaye gorge downstream from Timbuktu or was captured by headward erosion of the Lower Niger 3,000–6,000 years ago.

Biota. The Niger River system contains at least 286 native fish taxa from 36 families. Eighteen of the fish families are endemic to Africa; 20 of the species are endemic to the Niger River. Among the latter are three so-called upside-down catfish (family Mochokidae) and a trunkfish, *Mormyrops oudotea*). Nonendemic fish include the Niger Stingray, tiger fish, and other catfish, including the giant sea catfish (*Arius gigas*) and an electric catfish (*Malapterurus minjiriya*). The lower coastal delta has five species of mangrove and shelters a population of the West African manatee, as well as pygmy hippopotamus and spotted necked otter. Five threatened species of sea turtle and the Nile crocodile also live in the mangroves.

Protected Areas. Edumanon Forest Reserve in the coastal delta is a refuge for chimpanzees. The National Park of Niger, located at the confluence of the Niger and Mekrou Rivers, surrounds a W-shaped meander of the Niger River in the Sudan–Sahelian savanna biome and protects native fishes representative of the river system, 70 mammals, and some 350 bird species. It was inscribed as a UNESCO World Heritage Site in 1996. The park is adjacent to national parks in Benin and Burkino Faso. Plans are to encompass all three in a Transborder Park.

Environmental Issues. Several protected areas occur on paper, but have less than adequate enforcement of use restrictions or protection from the pressures imposed by a growing human population. Irrigation along the Niger and the Benue rivers is reducing discharge from both.

Further Reading

Hogan, C. Michael. 2013. "Niger River." *The Encyclopedia of Earth*. http://www.eoearth.org/view/article/226069/

Nile River

Ethiopia, Sudan, Egypt, Uganda, Democratic Republic of the Congo, Kenya, Tanzania, Rwanda, Burundi, and South Sudan

Geographic Overview. The Nile River is the longest river on Earth. The search for its source, one of the great quests of 19th-century European exploration, may have culminated in 1858, when John Hammond Speke discovered Ripon Falls at the northern end of Lake Victoria. However, the headwater farthest from the mouth is a stream leading into Lake Victoria, and this ultimate source has yet to be determined. The Nile River and life in and beside it were greatly altered by the construction of the Aswan High Dam, which was completed in 1970. Today major issues of water distribution from this international river persist.

Geographic Coordinates. Source of White Nile: 02°17'S, 29°20'E; Source of Blue Nile: 12°00'N, 37°13'E: Mouth: 30°10'N, 31°06'E

Description. The Nile River flows north from the Ethiopian Highlands and equatorial East Africa to empty into the Mediterranean Sea 4,258 mi (6,853 km) from its most distant known source. It drains a river basin of nearly 1.2 million mi^2 (3.1 million km^2) or 10 percent of the African continent.

It has long been accepted that the source of the Nile was at Ripon Falls, the only outlet of Lake Victoria, now submerged beneath a reservoir in Uganda. The first stretch of the river beyond Ripon Falls is known as the Victoria Nile. It enters Lake Kyoga before passing over Murchison Falls about 20 mi (32 km) east of Lake Albert. Here three cascades thunder through a 23 ft (7 m) wide gorge, dropping some 140 ft (43 m). The Victoria Nile continues through Lake Albert, after which it becomes the Albert Nile. As the river crosses into South Sudan 445 mi (716 km) downstream, its name changes to Bahr al Jabal and it passes through the Sudd, a vast wetland. Much of the river's water is lost in the Sudd via evapotranspiration. After passing through Lake No, it becomes the White Nile, a major tributary of the main stem Nile. The Sobat River, a major right bank tributary with headwaters on the Ethiopian Highlands, enters the White Nile at Malakal (9°22'N, 31°33'E). The Sobat undergoes great

The Nile, flowing north from the Ethiopian Highlands and equatorial East Africa to empty into the Mediterranean Sea, is thought to be the longest river on Earth. (Imagineimages/Dreamstime.com)

seasonal fluctuations in its discharge and during flood stage carries the sediments that give the White Nile its name. The White Nile contributes the major part of the flow of the Nile during the low water period.

The other principal tributary of the Nile, the Blue Nile, flows out of Lake Tana in the Ethiopian Highlands 870 mi (1,400 km) to its junction with the White Nile at Khartoum, Sudan, where the two form the main stem of the Nile. The Blue Nile plays a major role in the annual flood pulse of the Nile downstream and provides most of the flow during the high water period. Its peak discharge in late August is 50 times greater than dry season flow.

Another large tributary, the Atbara, enters the Nile 200 mi (300 km) north of Khartoum. This river originates on the Ethiopian Highlands 30 mi (50 km) north of Lake Tana. It is the last of the large right bank tributaries and dries up during the dry season. From this point on, the Nile flows through desert landscapes and only dry river beds (wadis) feed ephemeral streams into it. North of the confluence with the Atbara is the

Great Bend of the Nile, where for 185 mi (300 km) the river turns southwest before looping back to the north. The river passes over resistant crystalline rock between Khartoum and Aswan that gives rise to six cataracts. The first and second cataracts (farthest downstream) were significant obstacles to navigation and in ancient history served to separate Nubia from Upper Egypt. Today they are both submerged beneath the waters of Lake Nassar behind the Aswan High Dam in Egypt. Below the dam, the Nile continues its historic course for another 500 mi (800 km), separating the Western Desert from the Eastern Desert of Egypt and flowing past ancient Thebes, around the bend at Qena, north though the Nile valley with its broad, once fertile floodplains, and past Cairo, where it is about 6 mi (10 km) wide. Just beyond Cairo, it divides into two distributaries and forms the fan-shaped Nile delta. The Nile delta extends 100 mi (160 km) from its apex just north of Cairo to the Mediterranean Sea, where it fans out along 150 mi (240 km) of shoreline. Today there are two distributaries, the Rosetta, on the west side of the delta, and the Damietta on the east. Previously there were seven, but these have either silted up or been lost to flood control projects. The coast is fringed with wetlands, two lagoons, and several lakes. Sandy mounds rising 3–40 ft (1–12 m) above the surrounding delta land were early settlement sites.

Lake Victoria is no longer accepted as the source of the Nile; rather, tributaries of the Kagera River, which flows into the lake, are being explored to find the point most distant from the Nile's mouth. Candidates are either sources of the Ruvyironza River in Burundi or the Rukarara River, a headwater stream of the Nyabarongo River in Rwanda.

Climate varies in the Nile River drainage basin from the cool, summer rainfall regime of the Ethiopian Highlands and the tropical wet and dry climate of equatorial East Africa to the semiarid Sahel in South Sudan and warm deserts of Sudan and Egypt. In the desert, the Nile is a riparian oasis. The delta lies in a mediterranean climate region, receiving most of its limited rainfall in the winter.

Geologic History. The Nile River, thought of as one of the oldest rivers on the planet, began as a chain of separate basins that only became interconnected relatively recently in geologic time. Five main episodes in the development of the present course are recognized, beginning with the *Eonile*, a river that formed as a product of the Messinian Salinity Crisis about 6 mya. At that time, Africa had collided with Europe, isolating the Mediterranean Sea from Atlantic Ocean by closing the entrance at Gibraltar. With no inflow of seawater from the Atlantic and high evaporation rates in the basin, the Mediterranean essentially dried up. As sea level dropped (the floor of the Mediterranean reached almost 10,000 ft [3,000 m] bsl), a lowered base level caused rivers entering the sea to undergo renewed cycles of downcutting and headward erosion. The Eonile carved a deep canyon near its mouth, and stream capture in the upper reaches allowed it to expand southward. The Messinian period ended when the barrier at Gibraltar was breached and the Atlantic flooded in and refilled the Mediterranean Basin. This initiated a new episode in the development of the Nile; the canyon at the mouth of the Eonile became a drowned valley or estuary. A new river regime was established and the *Paleonile* River was born.

Limited to southeastern Egypt, it lasted until about 1.8 mya, by which time the drowned valley had become filled with sediments.

The final three episodes occurred during the changing climates linked to Pleistocene glacial and interglacial periods in Europe and North America. A dry period in North Africa caused the river to cease to flow; sand dunes occupied the dry stream bed. This period marks a transition to a new flow regime, that of the *Protonile*. Flow resumed by 1.5 mya, and the river followed its present course through Egypt, but no evidence of volcanic materials washed from the Ethiopian Highlands has been found to indicate a southward extension of the river via the Blue Nile or Atbara systems. The first such materials appear with the *Prenile*, the river as it existed 700,000–200,000 years ago. At that time the Asian monsoon had intensified and moist air was being brought to the Ethiopian Highlands from the Indian Ocean, increasing the likelihood that runoff now could reach the Nile system, although the geologic history of the Blue Nile remains unknown. The Prenile built a wide floodplain and the delta accumulated sediments 3,300 ft (1,000 m) thick, before the regional climate again became arid.

The Sudd section of the White Nile may be the oldest part of the system as it covers two rift valleys related to uplift during the Cretaceous Period, some 100 mya. The connection of the White Nile to the Nile drainage was made much later when a wet period at the end of the Pleistocene turned the Sahara green and North Africa was dotted with lakes. This period, which began about 120,000 years ago, led to the *Neonile*, which is essentially the modern Nile River. A series of closed basins in Sudan and South Sudan had become filled with sediments and increased rainfall caused them to overflow and become interconnected. The Atbara apparently was first among the major basins to reach the Neonile, establishing an outflow 120,000–100,000 years ago. The Blue Nile connected to the main stem Nile during another wet period 80,000–70,000 years ago. The White Nile system did not become connected to the main stem until after the outlet from Lake Victoria was established about 11,200 years ago.

Biota. Endemism is low in the Nile system. Some species native to the river system, such as the Nile perch, have become major problems in other places to which they have been introduced. The delta and riparian habitats, as well as some islands, are important stopovers for birds migrating from Europe, especially cranes, storks, and raptors.

Protected Areas. Few areas are protected. Lake Burullus Protectorate in the delta conserves marine, brackish, and freshwater habitats. Saluga–Ghazal Protectorate just north of Aswan encompasses two granitic islands in the Nile.

Environmental Issues. The floodplains downstream from the Aswan High Dam and the delta are no longer fertilized naturally by an annual flood, and the papyrus swamps that once lined the banks are nearly gone, having changed to communities of cattail, reeds, rushes, and sedges. The floodplains themselves have been almost completely converted to a human-made landscape of irrigated agriculture or urban land uses. Water pollution from chemical fertilizers and pesticides such as DDT is an ever-growing concern. Rising sea levels in the Mediterranean Sea are causing increased shoreline erosion on the delta and increased saltwater intrusion and salinity levels. Conflicts over water rights among not always friendly countries in the Nile Basin are trying to be resolved through international agreement.

See also Lake Victoria

Further Reading

"Introduction to the Nile." n.d. http://www.utdallas.edu /geosciences/remsens/Nile/geology.html

Parsons, Marie. n.d. "The Nile River." http://www.tour egypt.net/egypt-info/magazine-mag05012001-magf4a .htm

World Wildlife Fund. 2012. "Nile Delta Flooded Savanna." *The Encyclopedia of Earth.* http://www.eoearth.org /view/article/51cbee847896bb431f698675/

North America

Geographic Overview. North America, the world's third largest continent, extends through approximately 75° of latitude, from northern Ellesmere Island in Nunavut, Canada, south to the border between Panama and South America. Geographically, the southernmost point is the Azuero Peninsula in Panama.

Central America, however, is a relatively recently developed (in geologic time) land bridge between North and South America. Although the continent stretches across approximately 135° of longitude, the easternmost and westernmost points are problematic because the western side of the continent crosses the 180° meridian (the International Date Line) into the Eastern Hemisphere. In terms of directional continuity, the westernmost point is Cape Wrangell on Attu Island in the Aleutians. The easternmost point is Cape Spear in Newfoundland, Canada. The continent covers approximately 9,500,000 mi^2 (24,600,000 km^2).

Description. Western North America, from Alaska to Central America, is characterized by north-south trending mountain ranges with intervening plateaus. These ranges are a topographic barrier, causing orographic precipitation on the windward (western) side. In the rain shadow of the mountains, the landscape to the east and in the center of the continent is predominantly semiarid plains. The area in eastern Canada, centered on Hudson Bay, is a rolling to hilly region in old crystalline rocks, the core of North America. South central United States and most of the east coast is characterized by flat-lying sedimentary rocks and sediment deposits. Old, eroded mountains mark the eastern side of the continent, from northeastern Canada south to Alabama. The eastern half of North America receives more precipitation than do the central or southwestern regions.

Landform Regions. The exposed portion of the Canadian Shield covers 1.8 million mi^2 (4.8 million km^2). After several episodes of mountain building during the Precambrian, the region is now eroded to a rolling plateau, or peneplain, generally 0–2,000 ft (0–600 m) elevation, but slightly higher in the east. Hudson Bay is a structural sag or basin. Several large lakes, including Great Bear, Great Slave, Winnipeg, and the Great Lakes, formed in the contact zone between the softer rocks of the surrounding sedimentary layers and the harder crystalline rocks of the shield. Lake Superior occupies a downfaulted syncline in the Precambrian rocks. The shield is characterized by bare rock surfaces, mineral wealth, continental glacial deposits, many lakes, and deranged drainage.

The Interior Plains, which cover most of the continent south of the Shield between the Western

Cordillera and the Appalachian Mountains, are a stable platform of horizontal Paleozoic and Mesozoic sedimentary rocks with only slight upwarps and downwarps. The western part, the Great Plains, is covered by Cretaceous and Tertiary sediments eroded from the rising Rockies. Elevations in this region of little relief gradually increase from 300 ft (90 m) in the east to 5,000 ft (1,500 m) at the base of the Rocky Mountains. Coal deposits occur in some of the structural basins, such as southern Illinois, and karst has developed in some of the structural domes, such as the Ozarks. The southern mountains related to the Appalachian chain, such as the Ouachita and Marathon, have relatively minor outcroppings of Paleozoic rock, but remain primarily buried by the sedimentary cover. The northern and eastern region was covered by continental glaciers, which left continental drift deposits and lakes. Much of the Interior Plains is used for agriculture.

Extending from Newfoundland to northern Alabama, the Appalachian Highlands has a combination of rock types and structures, including Precambrian crystalline rock accreted onto North America, batholith intrusions, sedimentary rocks folded and eroded into a ridge and valley landscape, and horizontal sedimentary plateaus. Elevations vary according to rock type and structure and range from sea level in New England and southeastern Canada to more than 6,000 ft (1,800 m) on the higher mountains. The northern half of the Appalachian Highlands was covered by continental ice and has landscapes of both glacial erosion and deposition. Much of the region is used for agriculture, and Paleozoic rocks have yielded oil, natural gas, and coal.

The Western Cordillera is a complex region of many different landform subdivisions, generally divided into an eastern and western mountainous chain with basins or lower plateaus between. The Rocky Mountain system from Central Alaska south to Colorado and Utah has a variety of rock types and structures, including Precambrian crystalline cores pushed up by tectonic forces, tilted fault-block mountains, complex folding and faulting, Cenozoic batholith intrusions, domed structures, volcanics, and intermontane sedimentary basins. The Snake River Plain and Columbia Plateau are surfaced with basaltic lava

Table 1 Geographic Parameters of North America

Area : 9,500,000 mi² (24,600,000 km²)
Latitudinal extent: 75° degrees of latitude, from 83°06'41"N to 7°40'N
Northernmost point: Cape Columbia, Ellesmere Island, Nunavut, Canada: 83°06'41"N, 69°57'13"W
Southernmost point: Azuero Peninsula, Panama: 07°40'N, 80°34'W
Easternmost point: Cape Spear, Newfoundland, Canada: 47°31'25"N, 52°37'10"W
Westernmost point: Cape Wrangell on Attu Island in the Aleutians, 52°55'24"N, 172°26'30"E
Highest Point: Mount McKinley (Denali), Alaska: 20,237 ft (6,168 m) asl
Lowest Point: Death Valley, California: 282 ft (86 m) bsl

flows. The Great Basin has fault-block mountains and structural valleys filled with alluvial fans and playas. The horizontal sedimentary layers of the Colorado Plateau, characterized by deep canyons and bare rock surfaces, were uplifted with little warping. Much of mountainous Alaska is due to the accretion of several terranes from the Pacific Plate. Subduction zones along southern Alaska and northwestern United States continue to feed active volcanoes in the Aleutian Islands and Cascades. Further south in California, the mountain barrier becomes the large fault-block mountain of the Sierra Nevada. The west coast of the United States is characterized by bluffs and bays where the folded and faulted coastal mountains meet the Pacific Ocean. Elevations in the Western Cordillera vary from sea level to more than 20,000 ft (6,100 m). The northern and high mountains throughout the Western Cordillera, including the fjord coastline of western Canada and southern Alaska, were severely carved by alpine glaciation, and ice fields remain on several of the Canadian mountains.

Central America's landscapes derive from a combination of rock types and structure. The western coast is dominated by both dormant and active volcanoes, while the interior has hilly crystalline massifs. The east coast is characterized by limestone, karst, and a long barrier coral reef.

Climate. Because of its large size, mountainous landscape, and exposure to several ocean currents and air masses, the North American continent covers several climate zones, although most are characterized by a large temperature difference between summer and winter. The extreme northern edge is tundra, changing to subarctic throughout most of Canada and Alaska. The subarctic interior of the continent experiences the coldest conditions, well below 0°F (–18°C). Even the frigid Arctic Ocean moderates winter temperatures on the coast. Summer temperatures are 50°–60°F (10°–15°C) in the subarctic and average below 50°F (10°C) in the tundra. Because of cold air masses in both areas, annual precipitation is less than 20 in (500 mm). Much of the subarctic climate region is underlain by permafrost, permanently frozen ground that affects drainage. Both summer and winter temperatures increase to the south. The northeastern quarter of the United States and adjacent Canada has a humid continental climate, winter snow, and summer rain with either warm or hot summers depending on the latitude. The southeastern quarter is humid subtropical, where snow is rare and does not persist throughout winter. Summers are hot, with high humidity. Annual precipitation in these humid climates is 25–45 in (635–1,400 mm), the higher total occurring toward the south and east. The southern tip of Florida experiences a tropical wet and dry climate, as much as 50 in (1,270 mm) of rain in summer but very little in winter, with hot summers and mild winters. Except for mountain regions and the west coast, climates become drier toward the west. The continental interior, in the rain shadow of the Rocky Mountains, is a steppe climate, with 10–20 in (255–510 mm) of annual precipitation. Temperatures vary according to latitude, as does snow versus rain. Mid-latitude deserts and subtropical deserts, both with annual precipitation of 10–15 in (255–380 mm), lie between the Cascades–Sierra Nevada mountain chain and the Rocky Mountains, both with annual precipitation of 10–15 in (255–380 mm). The mid-latitude desert in the north is colder in winter, with snow, while the subtropical desert further south has mild winters with no snow and very hot summers, over 100°F (38°C). The coastal regions from northwestern United States north through Canada to Alaska is a marine west coast climate, characterized by mild temperatures moderated by proximity to the Pacific Ocean. Moist Pacific air masses combined with mountains paralleling the coastline to foster orographic lifting result in abundant rainfall, 60–80 in (1,525–2,030 mm) or more, with rain changing to snow at higher elevations. Most of coastal California has a mediterranean climate, with warm to hot, dry summers and mild winters. Seasonal temperature variation becomes more extreme with distance from the ocean. Rainfall, 15–25 in (380–635 mm), is restricted to winter. Highland climates vary, but generally become cooler and wetter with increasing elevation.

Most of Mexico has an arid to semiarid climate; the drylands include parts of the Sonoran and Chihuahuan Deserts, which extend north into the United States. Somewhat wetter climates prevail in the southern mountainous areas, which transition into tropical wet and dry and tropical wet climates in Central America, where variation is induced by elevation and windward vs. lee side of highlands.

Drainage. North America is drained by several major river systems and has several continental divides that direct water to one of the surrounding bodies of water. The most recognized divide is the one that sits astride the Rocky Mountains in the United States, separating drainage to the Gulf of Mexico and to the Pacific Ocean. Commonly referred to as The Continental Divide, it extends from the Seward Peninsula in northwestern Alaska south into Mexico. In Alaska, it separates drainages to the Arctic Ocean and the Gulf of Alaska. In Canada, it separates drainages that flow west to the Pacific Ocean from those that flow into the Arctic Ocean or into Hudson Bay. A second major continental divide, the Northern, extends a long distance through the plains near the U.S.–Canadian border before trending northeast through northeastern Canada. It separates drainage to Hudson Bay and the Arctic Ocean from all drainages to the Atlantic, the Gulf of Mexico, and the Pacific. The Eastern Divide follows the crest of the Appalachian Mountains, separating short streams flowing directly into the Atlantic Ocean from the larger Ohio River system flowing west to meet the Mississippi River. The St. Lawrence Seaway Divide runs from northern Wisconsin eastward just south of the Great Lakes, directing flow either into the Great Lakes and ultimately to the Gulf of St. Lawrence or south to the Gulf of Mexico or to the Atlantic Ocean. Numerous other divides at smaller scales similarly separate drainages flowing into various water bodies.

The Mississippi River and its major tributaries, the Missouri River and the Ohio River systems, drain a large portion of the middle part of the United States, which is east of the Continental Divide, south of the Northern Divide, and west of the Eastern Divide, emptying into the Gulf of Mexico. The Colorado River and its tributaries drain a major portion of the western Rocky Mountains and parts of the Colorado Plateau in the American Southwest, flowing into the Gulf of California. The Columbia River rises in the Canadian Rocky Mountains, is joined by the Snake River, which begins in the U.S. Rocky Mountains, and flows west to the Pacific Ocean. The St. Lawrence River drains the Great Lakes and flows into the Atlantic Ocean. In Canada, the Mackenzie River and the Saskatchewan River systems both flow from the Rocky Mountains, but the Mackenzie flows north to the Arctic Ocean at the Beaufort Sea, while the Saskatchewan River flows east to enter Hudson Bay. The Yukon River originates in the Canadian Rockies and flows west through Alaska to the Bering Sea. The Great Basin in western United States is a region with interior drainage, and, with few exceptions, no streams flow to any sea.

Geologic History. The majority of North America, including the northern Canadian islands and Greenland, lies on the North American Plate. A narrow strip west of the San Andreas Fault in California is part of the Pacific Plate which was sutured to North America. Central America lies on the Caribbean Plate. The North American Plate extends west from the Mid-Atlantic Ridge spreading center to the west coast of North America, where it is bounded by the Aleutian Trench off southern Alaska and the subduction zone of the small Juan de Fuca plate off northwestern United States. In California, the San Andreas Fault, which merges with the spreading center in the Gulf of California, marks the transform boundary with the Pacific Plate. The southern plate boundary is marked by the Lesser Antilles in the Caribbean at the margins of the Caribbean Plate and Motagua Valley (Guatemala). Subduction of the Cocos plate southwest of Mexico and Central America marks the southwest boundary of the North American Plate.

The present configuration of North America was developed during a long geologic history of sediment accumulation, several episodes of tectonic activity, accretion of terranes, and erosion. Precambrian rocks of the Canadian Shield underlie 70 percent of the continent and form its stable core. Centered on Hudson Bay, this craton extends deep beneath a surface cover of sedimentary rocks far to the south and west into the continent. After rifting opened the Iapetus Ocean (proto-Atlantic), the eastern edge of the continent was where the Appalachians now stand. The western edge of the continent was roughly where the Rocky Mountains are today. During the Paleozoic, several seas advanced, retreated, and readvanced many times over the continental platform, depositing sedimentary rocks. The advancing seas had two results—the plains of the continent's interior and mountain building episodes on its edges, particularly on the east and west. While shallow seas blanketed much of the continent with relatively flat-lying sedimentary rock, both the eastern and western edges developed geosynclines with deep seas and deep sedimentary deposits. Rock type over the continental platform depended on depth of sea and origin of sediments, and deposits generally are thicker with greater distance from the shield. Geosynclinal rocks on the east margin of the continent were deformed many times as the Iapetus Ocean opened and closed more than once during the Paleozoic. Convergence with Eurasia and Gondwana (Africa) caused subduction, produced volcanic island arcs, accretion of many terranes, and several orogenies that built the Appalachian Mountain system. As the mountains rose and eroded, sediments were washed toward the continental interior to become delta deposits rich in coal, such as that found on the Appalachian Plateau. In the south, collision with northern South America produced the Ouachita Mountains in Arkansas and Oklahoma and the Marathon Mountains in Texas. Complete closure of the Iapetus Ocean and collision of Eurasia, Gondwana, and South America with North America at the end of the Paleozoic formed the supercontinent of Pangaea and ended most tectonic activity in eastern North America.

The geosyncline in the west continued to collect sediments during the Mesozoic, eventually rising to become the Western Cordillera, the mountainous region which extends from Alaska south through the Rocky Mountains. From the late Paleozoic to the Cenozoic, this complex area underwent several orogenies, and uplift continues. As Pangaea began to break up in the Mesozoic and rifting opened the Atlantic Ocean and separated North America from Eurasia and Africa, North America began to move westward. Convergence with the Pacific Plate resulted in a variety of mountain building episodes, including accretion of more than 100 terranes, volcanic activity from subduction of oceanic plates, buckling up of geosyncline sedimentary rocks into mountains, emplacement of batholiths, faulting, and basaltic fissure flows. Part of the Pacific Plate spreading center became the San Andreas Fault, attaching a Pacific Plate terrane onto North America. A hotspot beneath Yellowstone area contributed to mountain building and lava flows on the Snake River Plain. The western continental margin remains active as plates continue to converge. The Atlantic and Gulf Coasts form a passive continental margin, where sediments eroded from the continent form a coastal plain gently sloping toward the ocean. During the Pleistocene, the Laurentide Ice Sheet developed over the Canadian Shield, pushing south to cover and alter the landscape of the northeastern half of the United States.

Assembly of the Central American Isthmus began some 140 mya. Major pieces were added when the Caribbean Plate formed at the Galápagos hotspot 80 mya and moved eastward through a gap between North and South America, initiating a complex combination of events. Oceanic crust was subducted, building the volcanic spine of the isthmus along the western edge. Continental blocks in the north were submerged, where they accumulated layers of limestone. Terranes of both continental and oceanic crust were accreted to become Central America. The Caribbean Plate eventually became sutured to the North American Plate at Motagua Valley, Guatemala. North and South America were finally joined by the Central American land bridge only 3 mya.

Biota. Except where natural vegetation has been cleared for agriculture, lumbering, or urbanization, vegetation in North America generally coincides with climate zones. Because summer temperatures average below the limit needed for tree growth, the tundra is a landscape of low-growing grasses, sedges, and lichens. A coniferous forest is the dominant plant life in the subarctic, scrubby and scattered in the north but increasing in size of trees and density to the south. The humid continental climate supports a forest transition of both coniferous evergreens and broadleaf deciduous trees, while deciduous trees dominate in the humid subtropical. A southern pine forest, however, grows on the sandy soils of the Gulf Coastal Plain, and evergreen live oak festooned with the lichen called Spanish moss grow in the warmest and most humid areas. The Everglades in southern Florida are a unique environment of sawgrass prairies annually flooded with water in winter. Various grasses, along with a variety of flowering forbs, grow in the steppe climate of the plains, taller grasses in the eastern wetter areas and shorter species in the drier west. Natural vegetation of the mid-latitude deserts in the Great Basin, the Columbia Plateau, Snake River Plain, and on the Colorado Plateau is sagebrush shrublands mixed with grasses. Scrubby forests of pinyon pine and juniper grow at slightly higher elevations. The subtropical deserts support a rich variety of drought-tolerant plants, including cactus, small trees, grasses, and large leaf succulents such as agaves. A mid-latitude rainforest, with tall old trees, predominantly coniferous, grows in the wettest parts of the marine west coast climates. The natural vegetation of the mediterranean climate is shrubby chaparral, adapted to summer drought. Vegetation in mountainous areas changes with the elevation, usually coniferous forests thinning out to stunted krummholz at timberline before being replaced by low-growing tundra plants.

North America is mostly in the Nearctic zoogeographic region, which covers North America north of tropical southern Mexico and Central America. The development of the Central American land bridge allowed an exchange of animals between North and South America, but the land bridge served as a filter so distinct biotas exist north and south of it. The isthmus itself remains a mixing zone of Nearctic and Neotropical species. The Nearctic vertebrate fauna is less rich than the Neotropical and has fewer taxa exclusive to North America. North America has a mixture of families shared with the Palearctic, the American tropics, and other parts of the world, with only a few endemics. Genera have more affinity with the Palearctic, with many endemics, especially rodents. Freshwater fishes are numerous and distinctive, with most families either exclusive to North America or shared with the Palearctic faunal region. Fish found only in North America include bass (Centrarchidae), trout perches (Percopsidae), and pirate perch (Aphredoderidae). Dominant Nearctic amphibians include salamanders and frog and toad genera *Rana, Bufo*, and *Hyla*. Reptile, bird, and mammal taxa share an affinity with both Palearctic and Tropical America regions, with few important exclusive groups. Snapping turtles (*Chelydra serpentina*), musk turtles (*Sternotherus odoratus*), iguanas (Iguanidae), and coral snakes (*Micrurus* spp.) are also found in South America. Beaded lizards and Gila monsters (*Heloderma* spp.) and legless lizards (Anniellidae) are limited to southwest United States and adjacent Mexico. In general, Palearctic bird taxa are more common in the north and tropical taxa more common in the south, although many southern birds breed in the north. Approximately 49 bird families, including migratory, are found in North America. Some are widely distributed families, while others are native to the Americas, and a few are Holarctic. Some mammals found in North America, such as shrews, canines, bears, cats, deer, rabbits, and squirrels, are found in several zoogeographic regions. Others, such as armadillo, raccoon, peccary, pocket mice, porcupine, and bats, are shared with Central or South America. Moles, pikas, and beavers are also found in the Palearctic. Pronghorn are endemic to the North American deserts and plains.

Regional differences in fauna exist within North America. Most freshwater fish, turtles, and salamanders are east of the Rocky Mountains. More snake taxa occur in the east, while more lizard taxa are found in the west. Some mammal families, including pronghorn, pika, pocket gophers, and pocket mice, are only distributed in western North America.

See also Aleutian Islands; Appalachian Mountains; Cascade Mountains; Central American Isthmus; Colorado Plateau; Colorado River; Columbia Plateau; Columbia River; Great Bear Lake and Great Slave Lake; Everglades National Park and Great Cypress Swamp; Great Lakes; Greater Yellowstone Ecosystem; Hudson Bay; Mackenzie River; Mexican Plateau (Mexican Altiplano); Missouri River System; Ohio River System; San Andreas Fault System; Sierra Madre Occidental; Sierra Madre Oriental; Sierra Nevada; Snake River; Snake River Plain; Yukon River

Further Reading

Henry, Jim. 2007. *Geomorphic Regions of the United States. A Supplement for Undergraduate Geoscience Courses.* Online Textbook. http://capone.mtsu.edu/mabolins/geomorph.htm

Kummel, Bernhard. 1970. *History of the Earth, An Introduction to Historical Geology*, 2nd ed. San Francisco, CA: W. H. Freeman and Company.

United States. 2013. "Continental Divides in North Dakota and North America." *National Atlas of the United States of America*. Adapted from Gonzalez, Mark A., 2003., *Continental Divides in North Dakota and North America: North Dakota Geological Survey Newsletter*, v. 30, no. 1. http://nationalatlas.gov/articles/geology/a_continentalDiv.html#four

Woodward, Susan L. 2003. *Biomes of Earth, Terrestrial, Aquatic, and Human-Dominated*. Westport, CT: Greenwood Press.

North Sea

Atlantic Ocean

Geographic Overview. The North Sea covers the continental shelf of Northwest Europe. It connects to the Atlantic Ocean in the northwest via the Norwegian Sea and in the southeast via the Strait of Dover and English Channel. Its varied coastline contains fjords, sheer cliffs, and pebbly beaches in the north and sandy beaches and broad mudflats in the south. Most of the sea is very shallow since numerous banks rise above the shelf. The North Sea was once one of the world's great fishing grounds. Today the sea is surrounded by highly industrialized nations. Busy shipping lanes cross the sea, and offshore oil production and the generation of wave and wind power are important economic activities.

Geographic Coordinates. Approximately 51°00'N–60°50'N, 03°40'W–08°45'E

Description. The North Sea covers the continental shelf of Northwest Europe between the British Isles and the continent. It stretches about 600 mi (970 km) from the Shetland Islands south to the coasts of the Netherlands and Belgium and 360 mi (580 km) from the United Kingdom east to Denmark. Average depth is 300 ft (90 m), but in the Norwegian Trench, a glacial trough looping around the southern coast of Norway from Oslo to Bergen, water reaches a maximum depth of 2,373 ft (725 m). The floor of the sea has a varied topography largely shaped by glaciers that traversed the seafloor during the Pleistocene Epoch. Devil's Hole is a cluster of trenches gouged to depths of 750 ft (230 m) east of Dundee, Scotland. Dogger Bank is a moraine 200 mi (324 km) long and 75 mi (120 km) wide that rises to within 50–100 ft (15–30 m) of the sea's surface. Along with a number of other banks, it provides prime habitat for a number of commercially important fish species, but also presents hazards to navigation.

The coastline of the North Sea is varied. The coasts of Scotland and Norway are mountainous, indented with deep fjords, and edged with steep cliffs and numerous offshore islands. Pebble beaches dominate the east coasts of Scotland and northern England, while farther south estuaries such as that of the Thames River and broad areas of sand or mudflats line the shore. Along the English Channel in southeastern England, low cliffs and flooded river valleys are characteristic. In the intertidal zone along the coast of continental Europe from the Netherlands into southern Denmark, a region known as the Wadden Sea, is a 310-mi (500 km)-long expanse of mudflats, the longest unbroken stretch of mudflats in the world. To the south is the rocky coast of Brittany. To the north, in Denmark, are long lagoons separated from the sea by sandy beaches.

Major inflows of fresh water coming from the Rhine and Elbe Rivers and brackish water beginning as meltwater in the many fjords of Norway or from the Baltic Sea keep salinity levels relatively low (32–34.5) in the eastern part of the basin. In the Kattegat and Skarregak at the mouth of the Baltic, salinities are even lower: 10–25 and 25–34. Open water to the west has a salinity of 35. Most North Atlantic water flows in from the north; only about 10 percent of the seawater coming into the North Sea arrives via the English Channel. Average water temperature in summer is 63°F (17°C) and in winter 43°F (6°C). Tidal range is 0–26 ft (0–8 m) depending upon location.

Geologic History. A shallow sea has existed between the Fennoscandian or Baltic Shield and the British Isles since the tectonic uplift of the isles some 150 mya. Sea level dropped during the glacial periods of the Pleistocene Epoch, and the North Sea shrank to nearly oblivion during the glacial maxima, when several times glaciers from Scottish and Scandinavian highlands moved over the exposed seafloor, shaping its topography through erosion and deposition. Glacial moraines formed the Dogger and other banks; glacial scour created Devil's Hole and the Norwegian Trench.

Circulation and Major Currents. Circulation of surface waters in the North Sea is complex, but primarily counterclockwise. The main inflow of Atlantic water comes from the Norwegian Sea to the northwest and follows the western slope of the Norwegian Trench. Two other important sources of North Atlantic seawater are currents passing east of the Shetland Islands and between the Shetlands and the Orkney Islands. These northern waters enter the Skagerrak, where, meeting the outflow from the Baltic, they circle to return north along the Norwegian coast. A minor inflow of warmer water moves northeastward through the English Channel and Strait of Dover, hugging the coast of the continent and also entering the Skagerrak before joining the flow north along the coast of Norway.

Biota. The North Sea was one of the world's great fisheries until the 20th century. More than 230 species of fish live in its waters. Among the commercially important species are cod, haddock, whiting, plaice, sole, mackerel, and herring. Commercially important crustaceans include Norway lobster, deep-water prawns, and brown shrimp. The rich fish and invertebrate fauna support colonies of numerous seabirds, including Black-legged Kittiwakes, Atlantic Puffins, Northern Fulmars, Northern Gannets, petrels, guillemots, sea ducks, gulls, and terns. Marine mammals such as harbor porpoise and common seals also find abundant food.

Protected Areas. The Wadden Sea, a globally important stopover site for migrating birds, is a UNESCO World Heritage Site comprising the Dutch Wadden Sea Conservation Area and the German Wadden Sea National Parks of Lower Saxony and Schleswig-Holstein. Numerous Marine Protected Areas are proposed. A number of coastal areas have been set aside in the United Kingdom to protect habitats of breeding seabirds.

Environmental Issues. Overfishing has diminished the stock of cod, haddock, whiting, and plaice. Beam trawlers damage communities on the seabed.

Land-based pollution, oil spills, and the introduction of alien, invasive species are constant threats. The development of wind farms could be detrimental to benthic organisms since the windmills must be anchored to the seafloor.

See also Baltic Sea; English Channel; Rhine River; Wadden Sea

Further Reading

"Geography, Hydrography and Climate." 2000. Chapter 2 in OPSAR Commission 2000. Region II—Greater North Sea, Quality Status Report 2000. OSPAR Commission. http://www.ospar.org/eng/doc/pdfs/r2c2.pdf

Novaya Zemlya Archipelago

Arctic Ocean

Geographic Overview. The two islands of the Novaya Zemlya archipelago are geologically the northern extension of the Ural Mountains. Cape Flissingsky, protruding from the northern tip, is the easternmost point of Europe. The islands lend their name to the Novaya Zemlya Effect, an atmospheric phenomenon in which the postwinter sun is seen days before it actually rises above the horizon. The archipelago is part of Russia's Arkhangelsk Oblast.

Geographic Coordinates. 70°31'N–77°00'N, 51°10'E–70°00'E

Description. Novaya Zemlya ("new land") archipelago consists of two elongated islands a mere 1–1.5 mi (1.6–2.4 km) apart curving in a north–south direction for over 600 mi (1,000 km) poleward of eastern Russia in the Arctic Ocean. Together, Severny in the north and Yuzhny in the south have an area of about 31,382 mi^2 (81,279 km^2). A narrow strait, Matochkin Shar, separates them while forming a link between the Barents Sea to the west and the shallow Kara Sea to the east. Near the northern tip of Severny, Cape Flissingsky (76°57'N, 68°34'E) sticks into the

The Novaya Zemlya islands are geologically the northernmost section of the Ural Mountains. Outlet glaciers from an icecap that covered the archipelago during the Pleistocene are now in retreat. (Sergey33/Dreamstime.com)

Kara Sea from Cape Zhelaniya to become the easternmost point in Europe.

Severny is a mountainous island with its highest elevation (3,658 ft or 1,115 m), Mt. Sedova, located at the southern end. Much of the northern half of the island is permanently covered in ice. Outlet glaciers approaching the Barents Sea are currently in retreat. The rest of the island is a barren polar desert with large parallel glacial striations filled with water (frozen much of the year), products of the ice sheet that scoured the surface during the last ice age. Yuzhny is hilly and vegetated by arctic tundra. Drumlin fields attest to former continental glaciation.

The polar climate prevailing across the archipelago is severe. Fog is frequent and winds strong. Summer temperatures average 36°–44°F (2°–7°C); winter temperatures –3° to –8°F (–16° to –22°C). Average annual precipitation is 12–16 in (305–405 mm), distributed fairly evenly through the year. The east coast remains inaccessible all year due to sea-ice, but the west coast is influenced by the relatively warm waters of the North Atlantic Drift and is commonly ice-free by midsummer as far north as the Matochkin Strait. The Arctic winter brings 24 hours of darkness from December through January.

Temperature inversions in the lower atmosphere can cause an apparent premature return of the sun in January known as the Novaya Zemlya Effect. First reported by Dutch explorers under Willem Barents's command in 1597, a mirage forms in which the sun seems to be visible days before it is actually above the horizon. The sun may appear to be a glowing square or rectangle or take on a multilayered structure low in the sky. Barents's crew first "saw" the sun on January 24 even though it did not really rise in the Arctic sky again until February 8. A similar phenomenon can bring a premature midnight sun as the region regains 24 hours of daylight in summer.

Geologic History. Novaya Zemlya is the northern extension of the Ural Mountains. Both islands were covered by an ice sheet during the glacial periods of the Pleistocene Epoch.

Biota. Arctic mammals inhabiting Novaya Zemlya include lemmings, arctic fox, and polar bears. The polar bears of the Barents Sea region may be a genetically distinct population. Seabirds such as guillemots breed on rocky sea cliffs.

Environmental Issues. Novaya Zemlya was designated a nuclear bomb testing site by the Soviet Union in 1954, and more than 200 subsequent tests contaminated the land and seas with radioactive fallout. The largest device ever detonated—a 50-megaton hydrogen bomb called Tsar Bomba exploded in 1961—has left a dark scar on the landscape with a lake at it center. The islands largely remain a military installation.

Global warming is implicated in the retreat of outlet glaciers on Severny. Some evidence suggests that the Novaya Zemlya Effect happens more frequently with the changing climate.

See also Ural Mountains

Further Reading

Kusch, Kyle. 2011. "Novaya Zemlya: The Extreme of Europe." Google Sightseeing, http://googlesightseeing.com/2011/05/novaya-zemlya-the-extreme-of-europe/

Lehn, Waldemar. 2011. "The Novaya Zemlya Effect." http://www.humboldtcanada.com/presentations_air/lehn.pdf

"Novaya Zemlya Archipelago." n.d. Novaya Zemlya. http://www.novayazemlya.net/

Nullarbor Plain

Australia

Geographic Overview. Nullarbor Plain is a low, flat, crescent-shaped plateau along the coast of the Great Australian Bight in Western Australia and South Australia. Underlain by horizontal beds of limestone, it is one of the flattest bedrock surfaces on Earth. The rock layers end in long, vertical cliffs paralleling a straight coastline. Recognized in Australia as a distinct biogeographic region, the Nullarbor is a treeless expanse of drought-resistant shrubs with little or no surface water. Some of the numerous caves bear fossils of extinct marsupials.

Geographic Coordinates. Approximately 30°S–32°S, 121°45'E–133°40'E

Description. Nullarbor Plain is a low, flat limestone plateau extending for some 685 mi (1,140 km)

along the coast of the Great Australian Bight from eastern Western Australia into western South Australia. In the north, where it abuts the Great Victoria Desert, the Nullarbor has an elevation of 650–1,000 ft (200–300 m) asl. It slopes for about 185 mi (300 km) toward the Bight, where it is 130–400 ft (40–120 m) asl. The edge of the plateau forms a long, vertical escarpment along the coast that is commonly 250 ft (75 m) high. The uniform bedrock has no weak points that could have been eroded in sea caves or other coastal features, but instead has been undercut by wave action over millennia to produce a straight coastline. In a few places below the escarpment, a narrow coastal plain with sand dunes exists.

The Nullarbor is an ancient karst landscape with collapse dolines (sinkholes) and shallow depressions and no surface drainage. Any rain that falls runs into fractures in the limestone. Extensive cave systems have developed, larger ones extending well below the water table and containing clear underground lakes and water-filled passages. Many caves have what are called breathing holes, narrow, vertical shafts through which air blows out or is sucked in. The changing flow of air is believed a consequence of changing atmospheric pressure outside. At other sites, such as Murrawjinie Cave, several hundred yards (meters) from the coast, blowholes spout seawater that enters the system. Some caves contain Aboriginal artifacts and art; several have been found with fossils of long extinct animals, including 23 marsupials ranging from rat size to giant kangaroos standing 10 ft (3 m) tall. These animals appear to have been trapped when they fell into shafts or collapsed dolines. All forms were extinct by 11,500 years ago. Bones of the extinct marsupial lion, *Thylacoleo carnifex*, also occur. In one case the mummified remains included hair, a dried out eyeball, and tongue. Gut contents of this specimen indicated that 4,600 years ago the vegetation of the Nullarbor was similar to that of today.

Most of the Nullarbor receives less than 10 in (250 mm) of rain each year, making it an arid-to-semiarid environment. Daytime temperatures in summer usually reach 77°F (25°C) and occasionally 122°F (50°C), while nighttime temperatures may dip below freezing. Monthly average temperatures in summer are about 63°F (17°C), in winter 45°F (7°C). Such conditions seem to have existed for thousands if not millions of years and, along with tectonic stability, precluded erosion and deposition and landscape change. As a result, all the meteorites and tektites that fell to Earth over the Nullarbor Plain during that time remain essentially undisturbed on the surface and relatively easy to find.

Dominant plant cover is short shrubs, primarily saltbush (*Atriplex* spp.) and bluebush (*Maireana* spp, *Bassia* spp.). These plants are both drought- and salt-tolerant. Around the margins of the Nullarbor, an upper, open canopy of taller shrubs such as the willow-leaved sticky boobialla (*Myoporum platycapum*) or mallee (*Eucalyptus* spp.) may develop.

Geologic History. The Nullarbor Plain was part of the Bight Basin, the downwarped southern edge of the Australia continent that formed as a result of the rifting that separated Australia from Antarctica. At times in the geologic past, the region was a shallow sea. The first limestone was deposited 45–35 mya; later deposits date to 25–15 mya. The seabed was exposed 15 mya by a combination of continental uplift and lower sea levels. This was followed until the present by a general drying of the climate, which prevented significant erosion of the surface except at the coast. A wet phase 5–3 mya led to the formation of most of the Nullarbor caves as the limestone dissolved and stalagmites and stalactites of calcite grew. Dissolution may have halted more than 1 mya, but caverns continue to enlarge as salt (halite) crystals corrode rock walls.

Biota. The Nullarbor Plain hosts 794 plant species, one frog, 86 reptilian, 249 avian, and 56 mammalian species. Two birds are endemic to the scrubland, the Nullarbor Quail and the Nareth Blue Bonnet. Nullarbor caves have crustaceans, arachnids, and beetles specially adapted to life underground; and an endemic subspecies of the Australian Masked Owl roosts in some caves.

Protected Areas. In 2013 much of the area was placed in the Nullarbor Wilderness Protection Area, receiving Australia's highest level of protection. This incorporated existing Nullarbor National Park, Eucla National Park, and other nature reserves.

Environmental Issues. Tourism is increasing and with it potentially more damage to caves and dolines. Feral camels and invasive rabbits reduce the shrub cover, affecting native birds. Feral cats and introduced foxes prey on ground-dwelling and ground-nesting native animals.

Further Reading

Johnston, David. 2009. "Nullabor Plain." *The Geology of Australia*, 2nd ed., 165–166. New York: Cambridge University Press.

"The Nullarbor Plain—World's Largest Karst Landscape." n.d. The Wilderness Society (Australia). http://www.wilderness.org.au/campaigns/outback-australia/nullarbor-plain-limestone-karst

Ob–Irtysh River System

Russia, Kazakhstan, and China

Geographic Overview. The Ob–Irtysh system in north-central Asia is the world's seventh longest river. It occupies the largest watershed in Russia, primarily on the Western Siberian Plain between the Ural Mountains on the west and the Yenisey River on the east. Navigable for approximately one-half of the year, the Ob–Irtysh is a significant transportation route. Its discharge, third largest of Siberian rivers, provides 12 percent of the Arctic Ocean's freshwater input.

Geographic Coordinates. Ob River—Source: 52°25'N, 85°03'E; Mouth: 66°46'N, 69°10'E; Irtysh River—Source: 47°05'N, 89°20'E; Mouth: 61°05'N, 68°49'E

Description. The Ob-Irtysh river system drains approximately 1,150,000 mi² (2,975,000 km²). Both rivers originate in the Altai Mountains in Central Asia. The Irtysh is 2,640 mi (4,248 km) long. The Ob is 2,268 mi (3,650 km) long. From the source of the Irtysh to the Arctic Ocean, the total length is 3,459 mi (5,568 km). Both rivers are characterized by flat topography, low elevation, low gradient, braided channels, and wide floodplains with swamps and lakes. Maximum elevation in the Western Siberian Lowland is 400 ft (120 m), with a slope of less than 2 in per mile (3 cm/km). Both rivers flow generally northwest and north, becoming wider as they cross the Western Siberian Lowland. Each spring, when the northern reaches are still frozen, the rivers flood a 15–50 mi (24–80 km) width across the flat lowlands. Floods may last 2–3 months. Approximately one-half of Russia's marshes and swamps, including the Vasyugan Swamp, which is the largest in the Northern Hemisphere, are in the Ob drainage. The Upper Ob extends from its headwaters to the confluence with the Tom River, north of Novosibirsk. The Middle Ob is from the Tom to the Irtysh River confluence. The Lower Ob extends from the Irtysh to it mouth at the Gulf of Ob.

The Ob begins near the town of Biysk, near the Russian border with Mongolia, from the confluence of two streams, the Biya and Katun, and descends rapidly to the Western Siberian Lowlands. It enters the Novosibirsk Reservoir prior to the city of the same name. At the confluence with the Tom River, the floodplain is 3 mi (5 km) wide, in a 12 mi (19 km) wide valley. Depth in the upper Orb is 6.5–20 ft (2–6 m). From the Tom confluence, the broad Ob flows northwest, crossing swampy forest taiga in a complex braided network with a wide main channel. Its valley is 18–30 mi (29–48 km) wide, with a floodplain 12–18 mi (19–29 km) wide. In low water, depth is 13–26 ft (4–8 m).

The Irtysh River, flowing 2,640 mi (4,250 km) and draining approximately 615,000 mi² (1,593,000 km²), is the major tributary, joining the Ob from the south near Khanty Mansiysk, The Irtysh rises from glaciers on the southwest slopes of the Altai Mountains in northwestern China, close to Mongolia, and flows through Lake Zaysan in Kazakhstan. It continues through the steppes of northeastern Kazakhstan northwest to Omsk in Russia. Because the steppes to the south are arid, the river has no large tributary for 600 mi (1,000 km). Downstream from Omsk, where it enters the forest zone, it is joined on its west bank first by the Ishim River from the steppe and then by its major tributary, the Tobol River draining the southeastern slope of the Urals. The streams on the divide between the Ob and Irtysh flow southward, following a pattern from the wetter Pleistocene, but terminate in closed lakes before reaching the Irtysh.

Below the Irtysh confluence, the Ob again broadens as it continues through the taiga. After Peregrebnoye, the river splits into two channels, the Great Ob and the Small Ob, as far apart as 200 mi (320 km) before rejoining at Shuryshkary, shortly before crossing the Arctic Circle. The river there is 12 mi (19 km) wide and 130 ft (40 m) deep. The Northern Sosva, a major tributary from the east slope of the Ural Mountains, joins on the west. The river turns briefly east to discharge through a large delta into Ob Bay, an estuary more than 500 mi (800 km) long, and 50 mi (80 km) wide. Two main arms form the delta, the Khamanelsk Ob on the left and the larger Nadym Ob on the right. Mean annual flow at the river's mouth is 448,500 ft³/sec (12,700 m³/s), most from local seasonal snowmelt and precipitation.

The majority of the Ob–Irtysh basin has a dry-winter continental climate, with short warm summers, long cold winters, and temperature extremes from 104°F (40°C) in the arid south to –76°F (–60°C) in the Altai Mountains. Annual precipitation is 16 in (400 mm) in the northern tundra, 20–24 in (500–600 mm) in the taiga, and 12–16 in (300–400 mm) in the steppes. Sparse winter snow cover lasts 160–270 days.

Both rivers remain largely free-flowing. Their vast potential for production of hydroelectric power has been harnessed at only three stations, one at Novosibirsk, and two in the mountainous reaches of the Irtysh. Navigation begins at Biysk when the river is ice free. The Middle and Lower Orb pass through the Western Siberian oil and gas fields. The Trans-Siberian Railway intersects the Ob at Novosibirsk, the largest city in Siberia, and the Irtysh at Omsk. Omsk, Novosibirsk, and Barnaul are industrial and agricultural centers.

Biota. Most of the Ob–Irtysh passes through swampy taiga, with grassland steppe to the south and tundra in the north. The river system supports approximately 45 typically Siberian fish species. Arctic cold-loving species, such as various whitefish (*Coregonus* spp.) and char are found in the lower reaches and adjacent sea. Marine species in the lower reaches include rainbow smelt and flounder. Boreal rivers support pike, roach, dace, perch, carp, and sturgeon.

Environmental Issues. Subsistence hunting and fishing by the native people, the Khanty and Nenets, are threatened by oil and gas development. Oil and gas exploration has polluted the river and damaged the fisheries.

Further Reading

Bogutskaya, Nina. 2013. "Ob." *Freshwater Ecoregions of the World*. www.feow.org/ecoregions/details/ob

Penn, James R. 2001. *Rivers of the World*. Santa Barbara, CA: ABC-CLIO.

Ogallala Aquifer

United States (Colorado, Kansas, Nebraska, New Mexico, Oklahoma, South Dakota, Texas, and Wyoming)

Geographic Overview. The Ogallala Aquifer, also called the High Plains Aquifer, underlies most of Nebraska, one-half of Kansas, the panhandles of Oklahoma and Texas, and adjacent parts of South Dakota, Wyoming, Colorado, and New Mexico. At 174,000 mi² (450,000 km²), it is the world's largest known aquifer and holds enough water to fill Lake Huron. It is the most important source of water in the High Plains region, supplying water for agricultural, municipal, and industrial development.

Geographic Coordinates. Approximately 31° 45'N–43°30'N, 96°20'W–105°30'W

Description. Regional economies are reliant on this water source. Irrigated agriculture, which accounts for 94 percent of use, is the base for a complex tier of economic activities. The crops provide feed for livestock and dairy industries, and the feedlots in turn support the meat-packing industries. The aquifer was first tapped in 1911. The Dust Bowl experience in the 1930s, natural drought cycles, and advances in irrigation technology after World War II all rapidly increased its use. Natural recharge is less than the amount withdrawn, and the rate of depletion depends on several factors, such as thickness of saturation layer and pumping speed. Since the development of large-scale irrigation in the 1940s, the water table has dropped more than 100 ft (30 m) in parts of Kansas, New Mexico, Oklahoma, and Texas. In some areas, thickness of the saturated layer has decreased by more than 60 percent.

Except where the Canadian River in Oklahoma has eroded through the formation, the water-bearing areas of the Ogallala are not separated, meaning that water may freely flow from one region to another. Water flows through the aquifer at an average rate of 12 in (300 mm) per day. The saturated thickness, meaning the part of the aquifer that retains water, varies from only a few feet to over 525 ft (160 m), and is thickest in the Northern Plains. In the Texas Panhandle, the saturated thickness is 50–200 ft (15–61 m). Only 10–25 percent of the aquifer volume, however, is pore space that may be filled with water, so measurement of saturated thickness is not a measurement of amount of water. For example, if the aquifer has 17 percent pore space, removal of one acre-foot of water will cause a drop in the water table of about 6 ft (1.8 m). The average depth to the water table is approximately 400 ft (122 m) in the Northern Plains and 100–200 ft (30–61 m) south of the Canadian River. The current volume of water stored in the Ogallala varies with region, but in 2006, the Northern Plains Groundwater Conservation District, north of the Canadian River, estimated it to be over 133 million acre-feet.

Geologic History. When the Laramide Orogeny uplifted the Rocky Mountains in the Tertiary, east-flowing and southeast-flowing rivers deposited sediments that were eroded from the mountains. After sediments (sand, gravel, silt, and clay) filled existing stream valleys to overflowing, a series of braided streams deposited alluvium over the entire landscape. The thickness of the sediment layer varies, but in some places is more than 500 ft (152 m). Deposits were primarily waterborne in the north, changing to mostly windblown in Texas and New Mexico. Most of the sediments are poorly to moderately consolidated, meaning that they are not yet solid sedimentary rocks. In the Texas and Oklahoma panhandles, the Ogallala Formation forms the surface of the Staked Plains region, where hard caliche forms a caprock.

Water in the aquifer originated from melting glaciers in the Rocky Mountains at the close of the Pleistocene. Today, the aquifer is recharged from local rain and snow, particularly from the Nebraska Sandhills region, but in the semiarid climate of the High Plains, recharge averages less than 1 in (25 mm) each year.

Environmental Issues. Known for its high quality water, which needs no treatment or filtration, the aquifer is threatened by contamination. Traces of pesticides and nitrates have been found. The aquifer crosses state and other political boundaries, and is governed by complex water laws. Research on the sustainability of agriculture and rural communities in the High Plains is monitored by the Ogallala Initiative, a consortium of Kansas and Texas universities along with the U.S. Department of Agriculture. Overuse, or drawdown, of the aquifer is a problem.

See also Nebraska Sandhills

Further Reading
Buchanan, Rex C., Robert R. Buddemeier, and B. Brownie Wilson. 2009. *The High Plains Aquifer. Public Information Circular 18.* Kansas Geological Survey. The University of Kansas. http://www.kgs.ku.edu/Publications/pic18/index.html
Kromm, David E. n.d. *Ogallala Aquifer.* http://www.waterencyclopedia.com/Oc-Po/Ogallala-Aquifer.html
North Plains Groundwater Conservation District. n.d. *Ogallala Aquifer.* http://www.npwd.org/new_page_2.htm

Ohio River System

United States (New York, Pennsylvania, Ohio, Maryland, West Virginia, Virginia, North Carolina, Tennessee, Georgia, Alabama, Mississippi, Kentucky, Indiana, and Illinois)

Geographic Overview. By mean discharge, 308,400 ft³/sec (8,733 m³/s), the Ohio River System is the third largest drainage in the United States, contributing more than 40 percent of the Mississippi River's flow. With a drainage basin covering approximately 200,000 mi² (322,000 km²), the river system drains the major part of eight states and smaller portions of six more, from New York in the northeast, south to Georgia and Alabama, and west to Illinois. The generally southwest or west flowing Ohio, as well as its tributaries, is a major transportation route that supports large urban areas and industrial activities. Discharge, especially for the northern tributaries, is highest in spring, due to snowmelt, and lowest in August and September due to evapotranspiration during hot summer months.

Geographic Coordinates. Allegheny River Source: 41°52'N, 77°53'W; Confluence with Monongahela River: 40°27'N, 80°01'W; Mouth: 36°59'N, 89°08'W

Description. From its headwaters in northern Pennsylvania, the river that will become the Ohio River flows southwest to Ohio, where it is joined by the Kanawha River from West Virginia. Downstream, the Scioto River, from the north through Columbus, enters the Ohio River at Portsmouth. Three of the largest tributaries, Great Miami, Kentucky, and Licking, join the Ohio near Cincinnati. The Great Miami River flows through glacial landscapes from the north, while the Licking and Kentucky Rivers drain karst landscapes in Kentucky and enter the Ohio River from the south. Four additional major tributaries, the Green, Wabash, Cumberland, and Tennessee rivers, join the Ohio between Louisville and Paducah, Kentucky. The Green River flows from the south, through karst landscapes associated with Mammoth Cave before joining the Ohio near Evansville, Indiana. The last major tributary from the north, draining glaciated northern Indiana, is the Wabash River, which joins the Ohio at the Illinois–Indiana border. Prior to the confluence of the Ohio with the Mississippi, both the Cumberland and Tennessee Rivers join the Ohio in southeastern Illinois.

Tributaries in the eastern and southern reaches of the Ohio basin originate in the Appalachian Highlands, while northern tributaries originate just south of the Great Lakes region. All tributaries flow through primarily forest and agriculture land, in a variety of geologic landscapes, including mountains of the Blue Ridge and Ridge and Valley, plateaus in the Appalachian Plateaus, Interior Highlands, glacial till plains of northern Indiana and Ohio, and karst in an area from northern Alabama to central Indiana. Natural vegetation includes coniferous forests, deciduous forests, and grasslands.

The named Ohio River begins at the confluence of the Allegheny and Monongahela rivers near Pittsburgh, Pennsylvania, at an elevation of 712 ft (217 m). It flows 979 mi (1,575 km) to reach the Mississippi River at an elevation of 289 ft (88 m). Although glaciers from the Wisconsin period did not alter the main stem of the Ohio, they changed the drainage patterns of the Wabash and other tributaries from the north. Above Cincinnati, glacial debris forms islands, 21 of which constitute Ohio River National Wildlife Refuge. The channel is generally sandy, and the lower reaches have sand bar islands. The middle third of the river has few islands except for a few limestone outcrops, one of which near Louisville forms the Falls of the Ohio, formerly a series of rapids in a 2.5 mi (4 km) stretch causing the river to drop 26 ft (8 m).

The Ohio River System is highly regulated and used. Approximately 20 locks and dams allow navigation along the entire length of the main stem. Frequent dredging maintains a 10 ft (3 m) deep navigation channel, sufficient for large barge traffic. In spite of regulation, the Ohio is still prone to flooding. Dams and reservoirs on tributaries control floodwaters and also provide water during times of drought.

The Tennessee River, the largest tributary by mean discharge, 70,630 ft³/sec (2,000 m³/s), begins at the confluence of the French Broad River and the Holston River east of Knoxville, Tennessee, in the Appalachian Ridge and Valley. The river flows southwest, its route confined by the parallel ridges and valleys, to Chattanooga, before crossing part of the Cumberland Plateau. After briefly entering northern Alabama, the river cuts into the Interior Low Plateaus in western Tennessee and reaches the Ohio River at Paducah, Kentucky, a journey of 652 mi (1,050 km). Some water is diverted to the Tennessee–Tombigbee waterway, which links the Tennessee River to the Black Warrior–Tombigbee River system in Alabama. From Lake Barkley on the Cumberland River, just upstream from Paducah, a shipping canal to Kentucky Lake, on the Tennessee River, allows free exchange of water between the two rivers.

The Tennessee Valley Authority (TVA) was created in 1933 to provide cheap electricity after the Depression. Approximately 50 multipurpose TVA dams now control water in the Tennessee River Basin, and many others are owned and operated by the U.S. Army Corps of Engineers or private companies. The Tennessee River main stem has nine reservoirs for flood control, power production, and navigation. Except for the extreme upper reaches, the river is totally regulated.

The Cumberland River drains 17,925 mi² (46,430 km²) and flows for 695 mi (1,120 km). It originates at the confluence of the Poor, Martin's, and Clover forks in southeastern Kentucky on the Cumberland Plateau. It runs in a curving arc south into Tennessee through Nashville, then turns northwest to reenter Kentucky. It flows through karst landscape near Nashville, and much of the river's course and its tributaries are incised into the Plateau. At Cumberland Falls, south of Lexington in Kentucky, the river drops 65 ft (20 m) over a sandstone ledge. The Cumberland River closely parallels the Tennessee River before both enter the Ohio upstream of Paducah. The river basin has major multipurpose impoundments, and is navigable for barge traffic upstream to Nashville. Little is free-flowing. The Barkley Canal connects the Cumberland with the Tennessee River. Because they were isolated by Cumberland Falls, pockets of biodiversity still exist in the headwaters, notably the Rockcastle River.

The Wabash River is the second largest tributary to the Ohio in terms of watershed area, 32,950 mi² (85,340 km²). The river originates in rolling agricultural land in west-central Ohio. It flows west over rolling to level glacial till of various ages through Indiana, then south, forming the border between Indiana and Illinois, and enters the Ohio River along that southern boundary. Because the Wabash drained Glacial Lake Maumee (forerunner to Lake Erie), its channel is incised along most of its route. It is mostly free flowing along its 480 mi (772 km) length.

Biota. The Ohio River System has two aquatic ecoregions, the Teays–Old Ohio in most of the drainage basin, and the Tennessee–Cumberland in those two rivers. In spite of impoundments and heavy industrial, urban, and agricultural activities, the Ohio main stem maintains a high biodiversity.

Environmental Issues. With seven large urban areas, many industrial facilities, several power plants, petroleum facilities, grain elevators, chemical plants, and steel mills along the river's course, contaminants can be a problem.

See also Mississippi River System

Further Reading

ORSANCO. n.d. "Ohio River Basin." Ohio River Valley Water Sanitation Commission. http://www.orsanco.org/ohio-river-basin

White, David, Karla Johnston, and Michael Miller. 2005. "Ohio River Basin." In *Rivers of North America*, edited by Arthur C. Benke and Colbert E. Cushing, 374–424. Amsterdam: Elsevier Academic Press.

Okavango Delta

Botswana

Geographic Overview. The Okavango Delta is a very large alluvial fan formed where the Okavango River spills into the Kalahari Basin after crossing the Caprivi Strip of Namibia from Angola. Its position and shape confined by faults, the so-called delta distributes river water into a maze of ever-changing channels and permanent and temporary wetlands. In the dry season, its flooded grasslands support vast herds of large mammals and attract thousands of tourists.

Geographic Coordinates. 18°18'S–20°00'S, approximately 21°30'E–23°30'E

Description. The Okavango Delta consists of a panhandle through which the Okavango River flows southeastward and the fan-shaped delta itself, actually a very large alluvial fan. The panhandle, confined by parallel faults and lined by 65 ft (20 m) high ridges, begins at the Namibia–Botswana international border near the border crossing of Mohembo at an elevation of 3,280 ft (1,000 m) asl. The river's headwaters are in the highlands of Angola; and before it reaches the delta, it is a permanent stream with an annual flood. A very low gradient ensues for the 90 mi (150 km) between Mohembo and the beginning of the delta; the river descends only 16 ft (5 m) over this stretch. The delta's fan shape is determined by three major faults running perpendicular to the river and panhandle. In the north, the Gumare fault marks the beginning of the alluvial fan, which then spreads to a width of 155 mi (250 km) and drops in elevation about 130 ft (40 m) through its full 90 mi (150 km) length. The fan ends where two faults—Kunyere in the southwest and Thamalakane in the east—block the flow, backing it up to create a vast wetland.

Okavanga Delta occupies a downfaulted basin in the Kalahari which is filled with 300–885 ft (100–270 m) of fluvial sediments derived from the Kalahari sands. The delta lies in a semiarid region where average annual precipitation is 19 in (480 mm). Most rainfall occurs in the summer months (November–March). Rainfall collected in headwater streams in the Angolan highlands courses down the Okavango River, reaching the panhandle in

February–April. Peak floods reach Maun at the terminus of the delta from June–August, the driest time of the year in Botswana. In the delta, floodwater is distributed into a myriad of small channels and peaty swamps, which absorb it like a sponge and slow the water. Almost all the inflow is lost to evaporation or seepage. About 3 percent flows out through the Thamalakane River, which makes a right angle turn to the southwest and then again to the east along fault lines and empties (at highwater) into the intermittent Boteti River, which occasionally reaches the Makgadikgadi Pans. With exceptional rains, the delta becomes connected to the Chobe (Kwando)–Zambezi River system via the Selinda Spillway, but this is a rare occurrence. Outlets westward to Lake Ngami more frequently carried water in the recent past than today.

The Okavango encompasses a variety of habitats from the crystal clear open water of channels, oxbow lakes, and lagoons to permanent reed and papyrus swamps, to seasonally flooded grasslands, to riparian woodland and dry woodland savanna. Thousands of islands dot the wetland, many having originated as termitaria, as former levees, or from sediments trapped by plants. Chief Island is the largest, measuring 44 mi (70 km) long and 9 mi (15 km) wide and providing important dry land for wildlife during the annual flood. Many islands have white salt deposits, products of annual desiccation, at their centers, which are barren except for salt-tolerant palms. The wetlands and channels through them are ever-changing. Hippopotamus trails can become new channels, dislodged vegetation can block flows, and the flood can change stream courses.

Okavango Delta is vital habitat for some 200,000 large mammals, mostly migratory, that assemble during the dry season when, paradoxically, vast reed beds and floodplain grasslands are inundated with several inches of water. Most of the animals for which East Africa is famous are also found here.

Geologic History. The Okavango lies in the Kalahari Basin on basement rock uplifted and metamorphosed 700–550 mya. Volcanic, fluvial, and aeolian rocks of the Karoo Group were deposited over the basement rocks 300–180 mya. Some of these ancient rocks are exposed in the Khwebe Hills and Tsodilo Hills nearby. The Kalahari basin formed between cratons as Gondwana rifted apart some 65 mya. For the next 63 million years, it filled with river-borne sediments and lake bed deposits as climate oscillated between wetter and drier conditions. About 2 mya, rifting associated with a southwestward extension of the East African Rift system created a sub-basin now beneath the delta and another underlying the Makgadikgadi Pans. Rivers larger than the Okavango, including some of the upper Zambezi drainage, traversed the area; and Paleo-lake Makgadikgadi filled both sub-basins. Later, windblown Kalahari sands accumulated, forming much of the present surface materials. The faults that control the delta are less than 120,000 years old; the delta is thus considered to be about 120,000 years old.

Biota. Some 150 species of mammal, more than 500 kinds of birds, and 90 fishes have been recorded at Okavango. Among threatened and endangered mammals are wild dog, cheetah, lion, black rhinoceros, white rhinoceros, red lechwe, sitatunga, and hippopotamus. In this still largely intact natural landscape, more than 1,000 plant species have been identified.

Protected Areas. The large Moremi Game Reserve in the eastern corner of the delta is the only nationally protected area. It was founded by the local Batawana inhabitants in 1963 to halt encroachment by hunters and pastoralists. The Okavango Delta was inscribed as a UNESCO World Heritage Site in 2014. The whole area is a Ramsar Wetland of International Importance.

Environmental Issues. The Okavango remains largely intact. Climate change and tourist developments could become concerns.

See also Makgadikgadi Pans; Zambezi River

Further Reading

Mendelsohn, John, Cornelius vanderPost, Lars Ramberg, Mike Muarry-Hudson, Piotr Woski, and Keta Moepele. 2010. "Shaping the Delta." In *Okavango Delta: Floods of Life*. Research and Information Service of Namibia and University of Botswana. http://www.ub.bw/download/doc_id/1499/

"Okavango Delta." 2014. World Heritage Centre, UNESCO. http://whc.unesco.org/en/list/1432/

Olympic Peninsula and Olympic Mountains

United States (Washington)

Geographic Overview. The Olympic Peninsula, in northwestern Washington, is a low mountain area with high relief, isolated by surrounding water or lowlands. Some of the world's largest trees are protected in the temperate rainforest. Although the glaciated peaks retain a system of radiating glaciers, the glaciers are rapidly retreating. The park's island-like position has enabled endemic species, such as the Olympic marmot, to evolve.

Geographic Coordinates. 47°15'N–48°23'N, 122° 05'W–124°43'W

Description. Olympic National Park has two separate units, the mountain interior of the peninsula, which includes temperate rainforest, and a narrow coastal strip. The mountains have been extensively glaciated and exhibit typical alpine features, such as glacial troughs and hanging valleys. The valleys contain lush meadows and forests. Mt. Olympus, with several radiating glaciers and glacial valleys, is 7,480 ft (2,432 m) above the Pacific Ocean just 33 mi (53 km) to the west. The 57 mi (92 km) of coastline is steep and rocky, with turbidite sandstone and conglomerate cliffs. Intensive wave action has carved portions of the cliffs into arches and stacks, with sandy beaches in coves. At the base of the cliffs is a wave-cut platform or bench, eroded level where waves wash debris across the bedrock. Benches at different elevations indicate changing sea level.

Even at the high elevations, temperatures on the Olympic Peninsula are mild. The Cascade Mountains to the east protect it from incursions of frigid Arctic

The many environments of Olympic National Park, including the lush Hoh Rainforest, support a variety of wildlife, including a large herd of Roosevelt elk. (Natalia Bratslavsky/Dreamstime.com)

air, and the ocean moderates temperatures. Coastal summers average 60°–70°F (15°–21°C), and winters rarely drop to freezing. Winter temperatures in the mountains rarely go below 0°F (–18° C). Because of warm, wet Pacific airmasses and orographic lifting, the western side of the mountains is the wettest area in continental United States. The coast and Hoh Rainforest receive an average of 8.5–14 ft (2.6–4.3 m) of rain each year. Higher elevations are snowy, with more than 50 ft (18 m) on Mt. Olympus and 30–35 ft (10 m) on Hurricane Ridge each year. The east side of the mountains is a rain shadow, with only 16 in (400 mm) at Sequim. Summers tend to be dry, although the west and the mountains generally remain wet from fog.

Geologic History. The entire peninsula is composed of material derived from the ocean floor. A small section of oceanic crust at the edge of the continent was pillow basalt, formed from underwater lava eruptions. Turbidites, often caused by underwater landslides, are sediments that settle out of very muddy water, eventually becoming layers of sedimentary rocks at the edge of the oceanic crust. As the Pacific Plate subducted beneath North America, it created a trench. Turbidite rock layers were severely folded and faulted as they were scraped or pushed into the trench. With continued convergence, the trench fillings were upthrust through the ocean crust basalt to become the Olympic Mountains. The basalt forms a rim of upturned ridges on the north, east, and south sides of the mountain core, which is a chaotic assemblage of sandstone, mudstone, conglomerate, and shale cut by faults and folds.

During the Pleistocene, mountain glaciers merged with the ice sheets funneling through Puget Sound and the Strait of Juan de Fuca. The mountains are sculpted into cirques, aretes, and U-shaped valleys, many of which are still occupied by glaciers.

Biota. The mild temperatures and abundant precipitation encourage the growth of a temperate rainforest and record-size trees, particularly in the valleys of the west-flowing rivers. Sitka spruce (*Picea stichensis*) and western hemlock (*Tsuga heterophylla*), which may be more than 200 ft (60 m) tall and more than 500 years old, dominate, most often draped in epiphytes. The cool, moist environment supports more than 130 species of mosses, lichens, liverworts, and ferns. Other forest plants include Douglas fir (*Pseudotsuga menziesii*), western redcedar (*Thuja plicata*), and bigleaf maple (*Acer macrophyllum*), with an understory of salmonberry (*Rubus spectabilis*) and huckleberry (*Vaccinium* spp.) shrubs. Insects and fungi play a major role in plant decay. The range of environments supports a variety of wildlife, including a large herd of Roosevelt elk, mountain lions, black bear, and deer, as well as smaller mammals such as squirrels, moles, bats, and river otters. Frogs and salamanders can be found in aquatic environments, and salmon use the rivers.

Environmental Issues. In a 1982 inventory, 266 glaciers and ice fields were counted, covering a total of 18 mi² (46 km²). From 1948 to 1996, the mean January–March temperature at 4,700 ft (1,450 m) increased approximately 6°F (3.3°C), causing more winter precipitation to fall as rain. Without sufficient snow to feed the ice fields, the glaciers are retreating. Blue Glacier retreated approximately 325 ft (100 m) from 1995 to 2006, while its thickness decreased by 40–175 ft (12–53 m). Lillian Glacier disappeared completely by 2010.

Protected Areas. A large proportion of the peninsula is occupied by Olympic National Park and Olympic National Forest. The park is both a World Heritage Site and Biosphere Reserve.

Further Reading

Alt, David D. and Donald W. Hyndman. 1998. *Roadside Geology of Washington*. Missoula, MT: Mountain Press Publishing Company.

Harris, Ann G., Esther Tuttle, and Sherwood D. Tuttle. 2004. "Olympic National Park." In *Geology of National Parks*, 417–436. Dubuque, IA: Kendall Hunt.

National Park Service. 2013. *Olympic National Park*. www.nps.gov/olym/

Orange River (Gariep River)

Lesotho, Namibia, and South Africa

Geographic Overview. The Orange River flows west from the Drakensberg Mountains in the Kingdom of Lesotho to empty into the Atlantic Ocean at Oranjemund, Namibia. In its lower reaches, it forms the international border between South Africa and Namibia. It was named for the Dutch Royal House of Orange-Nassau. In recent years, the Nama name *Gariep* has become preferred as a way to rebuke South Africa's colonial past. In Lesotho, it is known as the Senqu River.

Geographic Coordinates. Source: 29°34'S, 28°32'E. Mouth: 28°33'S, 16°26'E

Description. The Orange River begins on Thaba Putson, a 10,990 ft (3,350 m) high peak in the Drakensberg (Maloti) Mountains in the Kingdom of Lesotho, 120 mi (193 km) west of the Indian Ocean. In Lesotho, the river flows through a deeply incised valley from the international border to Gariep Dam. The main tributary, the Vaal River, enters southwest of Kimberley, South Africa. Downstream from Kimberley, for the remaining 500 mi (800 km) of its course, it is fed only by intermittent streams and occasional outflow from large wadis. The Fish River, for example, only carries water in March and April. The Orange continues along the southern edge of the Kalahari and, at 20°E longitude, becomes the international boundary between Namibia and the Republic of South Africa. It again enters a deeply incised valley just above Augrabies (or Hundred) Falls, where the river drops 400 ft (126 m) over a 16 mi (26 m) stretch. It reaches the Atlantic Ocean at Oranjemund, Namibia, 1,367 mi (2,200 km) from its source. The mouth lies half way between Walvis Bay, Namibia, and Capetown, South Africa. The final 21 mi (33 km) of the river are interrupted by rapids and sand bars.

In the uplands of Lesotho, the river begins in a region where annual precipitation generally totals 28–32 in (700–800 mm) and orographic uplift can produce as much as 78 in (2,000 mm)/yr. Most of this rainfall falls during austral summer. High elevations mean that headwater streams may freeze over in winter. From the high montane grasslands of the Drakensberg, the Orange River descends through the Highveld of South Africa into the semiarid Nama Karoo, through the Richtersveld Mountains and finally across the southern edge of the hyperarid Namib Desert where annual precipitation is less than 4 in (100 mm) and highly unpredictable.

During the wet season, the murky waters of the Orange River carry a heavy suspended sediment load, much derived from Karoo sandstones. Passing through the Kimberley region of South Africa, a proto-Orange River picked up diamonds eroded from kimberlite pipes and carried them to the coast. The transported sands and diamonds were moved northward along the Namibian coast by longshore drift and strong southerly winds, giving rise to both the sand dunes of the Namib Desert and the alluvial diamonds found on a 60-mile (100 km) strip of land in southwestern Namibia known as the Diamond Coast.

Geologic History. In southern Africa, during the mid- to late Cretaceous Period, two river systems developed after the breakup of Gondwana. The Karoo River consisted of what is now the upper Orange–Vaal system and drained into the Atlantic Ocean near the present day mouth of the Lepelle (Olifants) River. The Kalahari River corresponded to the lower Orange River system and drained southern Botswana and Namibia, both much wetter places than today. Uplift of the southern and eastern coastal margins of Africa 100–80 mya tilted the land to the northwest, encouraging drainage of the Karoo River in that direction. The Kalahari River eroded headward and captured the Karoo system, establishing the modern configuration of the Orange River.

Biota. The Orange–Vaal river system has a relatively low diversity of native fishes. Most of the 21 recorded species feed in the lower part of the water column. Among them are the endemic Orange–Vaal largemouth yellowfish (*Labeobarbus kimberleyensis*), smallmouth yellowfish (*Labeobarbus aeneus*), and Orange River mudfish (*Labeo capensis*).

Protected Areas. Several national parks occur along the Orange River: Sehlabatheke National Park at the headwaters in Lesotho; Mokala National Park near Kimberley and Augrabies Falls National Park in South Africa; the Ais-Ais Richterveld Transfrontier Park, which combines South Africa's Richtersveld National Park and Namibia's Ais-Ais Hot Springs and Fish River Canyon parks; and Sperrbegiet (Prohibited Territory) National Park on the Diamond Coast of Namibia. Sehlabatheke will be part of the Maloti–Drakensberg Transfrontier Conservation Area and Peace Park. Reedbeds and mudflats at the mouth of the Orange River are a Ramsar Wetland of International Importance.

Environmental Issues. A major problem ensues from excessive fertilizer runoff from agricultural lands in the Vaal drainage basin. Algal blooms in the middle Orange basin are a product of the poor land management practices.

See also Drakensberg Mountains; Namib Desert

Further Reading

De Wit, M. C. J. 2004. "Post-Gondwana Drainage and the Development of Diamond Placers in Western South Africa." *Economic Geology*. http://econgeol.geoscience world.org/content/94/5/721.abstract

"Diamond Coast." n.d. Namibia's Geological Treasures. Geological Survey of Namibia. Ministry of Mines and Energy. http://www.mme.gov.na/gsn/posters/geological-attractions/diamondcoast.pdf

Hogan, C. Michael. 2013. "Orange River." *The Encyclopedia of Earth*. http://www.eoearth.org/view/article/22 3561/

Orinoco River

Colombia and Venezuela

Geographic Overview. The Orinoco River is South America's third longest river and the fourth largest river in the world in terms of discharge. It features the only coastal delta on the continent and has a unique distributary in its upper reaches, the Casiquiare River, which links it to the Amazon drainage system. Three-fourths of the watershed of the Orinoco lies in Venezuela, the rest lies in Colombia. In its middle reaches, the river forms the boundary between the two countries. Its name comes from the indigenous Warao people and means "a place to paddle."

Geographic Coordinates. Source: 02°19'N, 63°22'W. Mouth: 08°37'N, 62°15'W

Description. The source of the Orinoco is on Cerro Delgado Chalbard in the Parima Mountains on the Guiana Shield near Venezuela's border with the state of Roraima, Brazil. From there it flows northwest and then turns north, beginning a wide arc around the western side of the shield. It continues to hug the shield as it turns east, forced to the edge of its valley by the southeastward slope of the land surface induced by the uplift of Cordillera Mérida and a thick wedge of sediments extending from the base of these mountains. Bedrock outcrops at eight places along its lower course (downstream of its confluence with the Rio Meta) which creates a series of rapids. Most of the major tributaries are on the left bank, flowing from the Andean Cordillera Oriental and Cordillera Mérida. Much of the sediment load carried from the Andes is deposited in inland deltas formed where the streams join the Orinoco. Right bank tributaries, draining the Guiana Shield, are clearwater streams carrying few sediments. The river ends in a large fan-shaped delta that continues to grow seaward at a rate of 130 ft/yr (40 m/yr). The Orinoco enters the Atlantic Ocean 1,330 mi (2,140 km) from its source.

The Orinoco Basin is located between 10°N and the equator. This tropical region is under the influence of the Intertropical Convergence Zone (ITCZ) and receives abundant precipitation during the wet season, which begins in April and lasts into December. On average 40–80 in (1,000–2,000 mm) of rain falls over the drainage basin each year, resulting in an average annual discharge of 1,271,328 ft³/s or 36,000 m³/s. Maximum discharge during the rainy season is more than twice this amount, reaching 2,860,488 ft³/s (81,000 m³/s). Water levels in the river change dramatically between the dry season and wet season; and the narrow floodplain, inland deltas, and coastal delta are inundated for months at a time. The annual flood maintains the Llanos, the tropical savanna that covers much of the basin.

A striking peculiarity in the Orinoco drainage system is the upriver distributary that deflects 12.5–25 percent, depending upon the season, of the water in the upper reaches of the river to the Amazon River system. The Casiquiare River, or Casiquiare Canal as it sometimes called, splits off the Orinoco just downstream from the town of La Esmeralda, and flows southwest to join the Guainía River at the head of the Rio Negro, the largest tributary of the Amazon River. An example of stream piracy in progress, the Casiquiare eventually will likely capture all the flow from the upper drainages of the Orinoco and convert the upper basin into a section of the Amazon Basin.

The upper Orinoco River passes through tropical rainforest; the middle and lower reaches drain the grasslands of the Llanos. The large delta, covering 2,300 mi² (5957 km²) and having a coastal perimeter 224 mi (360 km) long, is a sandy plain that grades

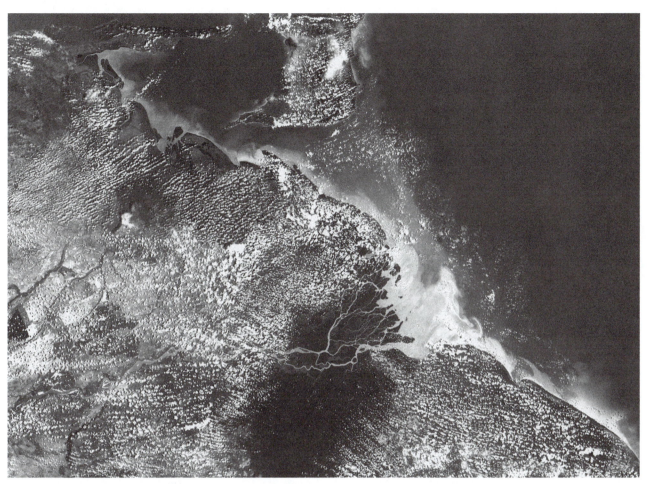

The large fan-shaped delta of the Orinoco River, South America's third-longest river, continues to build seaward at a rapid pace. The island of Trinidad in the Caribbean Sea can be seen to the north in this composite Landsat image. (Planet Observer/Universal Images Group via Getty Images)

into mud and peat near the mouths of its many distributaries. Channels weave in and out of each other creating oxbow lakes, natural levees, and a multitude of low-lying islands. This area is rarely more than 30 ft (9 m) asl and supports a mosaic of seasonally flooded grasslands and swamp forests, palm groves, and mangroves, part of an ecosystem that extends north to Paria Peninsula and south to the Waini River of Guyana.

Geologic History. Prior to the Miocene Epoch, the Orinoco and eastern Amazon rivers were one system and drained north to the Caribbean Sea. The rise of the Vaupés Arch between the Serranía de la Macarena and Andes to the west and the Guiana Shield to the east divided the two basins, and the rise of the

Cordillera Mérida deflected the course of the Orinoco northeast to the Atlantic Ocean.

Biota. The river is home to more than 1,000 species of fish and harbors several critically endangered species, including the Orinoco crocodile, pink river dolphin, giant river otter, and Orinoco Goose.

Protected Area. Delta del Orinoco Biosphere Reserve is the largest protected area.

Environmental Issues. While threats to the river and delta are not severe at this time, oil extraction and exploitation, water pollution from growing metal industries, and flood control measures are of concern. Guri Dam on the Caroni River provides hydroelectric power for steel and aluminum industries in Ciudad Guyana but interrupts seasonal flooding on the lower Orinoco.

See also Casiquiare River

Further Reading

Dunne, Thomas and Leal Anne Kerry Mertes. 2007. "Rivers." In *The Physical Geography of South America*, edited by Thomas T. Veblen, Kenneth R. Young, and Antony R. Orme, 76–90. New York: Oxford University Press.

Schipper, Jan. n.d. "Flooded Grasslands and Savannas: Northern South America: Northeastern Venezuela." World Wildlife Fund. http://worldwildlife.org /ecoregions/nt0906

Winemiller, Kirk O., Hernán López-Fernández, Donald C. Taphorn, Leo G. Nico, and Aniello Barbarino Duque. 2008. "Fish Assemblages of the Casiquiare River, a Corridor and Zoogeographical Filter for Dispersal between the Orinoco and Amazon Basins." *Journal of Biogeography* 35: 1551–1563. http://aquaticecology .tamu.edu/files/2012/07/Winemiller-et-al-JBI-2008.pdf

Orkney Islands

Atlantic Ocean

Geographic Overview. The Orkney Islands, located 6.2 mi (10 km) from the northeast tip of the Scottish mainland, protect several internationally threatened and rare species of both plants and birds. The islands' rocky cliffs provide nesting sites for thousands of seabirds in summer. Many archaeological sites, from the Neolithic period through the Viking era, trace human habitation for the last 6,000 years. The harbor of Scapa Flow played an important part in both world wars.

Geographic Coordinates. 58°41'N–59°24'N, 02°22'W–04°25'W

Description. The Orkney Islands, extending 53 mi (83 km) north to south and 23 mi (37 km) east to west and covering approximately 240,000 ac (100,000 ha), include some 90 islands and skerries. The combined coastlines, which vary from near-vertical cliffs to rocky, sandy, and muddy shores, is 550 mi (880 km) of inlets, coves, and bays. The largest island, called Mainland, is the most populated. Other inhabited islands include Shapinsay, Gairsay, Stronsay, Wyre, Rousay, Egilsay, Eday, Sanday, Westray, Papa Westray, and North Ronaldsay in the northern group and Graemsay, Hoy, South Walls, Bursay, Flotta, and South Ronaldsay in the southern group.

The landscape of the predominantly low-lying islands is gently rolling fields, heather moorland, and lakes. Hoy, with its hills, valleys, and cliffs, is the exception. Old Man of Hoy is part of a cliff complex of sandstone and lava flows, with cliffs 450 ft (137 m) high. Many valleys that produce long, open inlets, locally called voes, indent the shorelines. These river valleys were enlarged by glaciers, but they are not steep-sided like fjords. Sand bars and spits close off many voes, and tombolos connect small islands to the main coasts. The sandstone rock produces fertile soil, which supports hay meadows for beef cattle.

Archaeological sites, including Neolithic tombs and standing stones, Pictish brochs (dwellings from the Iron Age), and Viking settlements dot the islands. Knap of Hower on Papa Westray is the oldest dwelling house in Britain, approximately 5,600 years old. Scara Brae, occupied from 5200 to 2200 BP, is the best preserved Neolithic village in northern Europe. Every part of the dwellings at Scara Brae, including interior furnishings, is made from easily split slabs of sandstone. The chambered tomb at Maes Howe is a large burial mound built out of sandstone. Ring of Brodgar is a major site of standing stones.

Scapa Flow, a protected harbor enclosed by five islands, was used by the British Navy during both world wars for protection against German submarines. The German fleet was scuttled there in 1919 after World War I, but most of the ships were subsequently raised for salvage. Causeways built between islands during World War II provided further security for the harbor as well as road access between islands.

Because the climate is moderated by the North Atlantic Drift, winter and summer temperature differences are small. Winters average 43°F (6°C), and summers average 60°F (15°C). Annual precipitation is 37 in (950 mm), and snow is infrequent except when storms blow from the north. Fog and wind are common.

Geologic History. The Orkney Islands, along with the Shetland Islands, are the northernmost British remnants of the Caledonian Mountains. The surface bedrock of the Orkney Islands is primarily Old Red Sandstone from the Devonian (410–360 mya). Sandstones, mudstones, and other clastic sedimentary rocks were deposited into a large lake at the base of the Caledonian mountains, covering the basement rock of intrusive granites to a depth of almost 5,000 ft (1,500 m). The sandstones are interbedded with occasional lava flows. The islands are crisscrossed by several faults. The erosion of coastal cliffs by wave action into long narrow slots, blowholes, caves, and stacks, followed faults or joints.

Biota. Most plant life is low-growing because of strong winds. Several species of flowering plants, 520 native species and 210 introduced species, grow in diverse habitats, including coastal cliffs, beaches, wetlands, fields, moorland, and salty maritime heath. Two rare plants, Scottish primrose (*Primula scotica*) and oysterplant (*Mertensia maritima*), grow in maritime heath. Gorse and heathers are common moorland plants. Cliffs on western Mainland are topped with grass and heath. Shallow lakes are rich in algae, stoneworts, and pondweeds. Small pockets of machair, which are lime-rich habitats developed on broken shells, support unique plants and meadows.

The largest marine mammals are the grey seal and common seal. Porpoises, whales, and dolphins are also frequent. Otters occupy both lakes and coastal waters. Rabbits, hare, fieldmice, pygmy shrew, and hedgehogs are common. The Orkney vole (*Microtus orcadensis*) is endemic, and mountain hare is found only on Hoy.

Coastline and tidal margins, heath, and lakes provide feeding grounds for thousands of birds that nest on the sea cliffs, including Arctic Skuas, Great Skuas, kittiwakes, guillemots, fulmars, razorbills, and puffins. Other significant birds include divers, knots, turnstones, kestrel, oyster-catcher, ducks, geese, and the rare Corncrake. Waders, such as lapwing and Ringed Plover, frequent meadows or fields. Wetlands are home to rare species, such as Black-tailed Godwits and Northern Pintail, along with more common redshanks, snipe, and curlews. Wintering birds include twite, Reed Bunting, and skylarks. Breeding moorland birds include Hen Harrier, Short-eared Owl, Red Grouse, and merlin.

Protected Areas. Many areas in the Orkney Islands have official protection, including Sites of Special Scientific Interest and Special Protection Areas. Several Neolithic sites comprise the Heart of Neolithic Orkney, a World Heritage Site since 1999.

See also Shetland Islands

Further Reading

McKirdy, Alan. 2010. *Orkney and Shetland, A Landscape Fashioned by Geology.* www.snh.org.uk/pdfs/publications/geology/orkneyshetland.pdf
Orkney College. n.d. "The Orkney Environment." http://www.agronomy.uhi.ac.uk/html/environment.htm

Outer Banks

United States (North Carolina)

Geographic Overview. The Outer Banks is an arc-shaped system of barrier islands off the coast of North Carolina. This region of beaches, dunes, marshes, inlets, and maritime forests supports a variety of sea life and birdlife, and is culturally significant. The shoals off Cape Hatteras, the eastern-most point, are treacherous to navigation. The Wright Brothers took their first historic flight on a barrier island in the Outer Banks.

Geographic Coordinates. 35°22'N, 75°30'W

Description. The Outer Banks extend 140 mi (225 km) from the Virginia border in the north to Cape Lookout in the south. Barrier islands are normally quite close to shore, but the Outer Banks are separated from the mainland by as much as 40 mi (64 km) of the shallow, brackish water of Albemarle–Pamlico Sound. Diamond Shoals, the shifting sand ridges off Cape Hatteras, are referred to as the Graveyard of the Atlantic because of the more than 600 shipwrecks that have occurred there. The lighthouse was built to warn ships of danger. The area has also been nicknamed Torpedo Junction because of the many Allied tankers sunk there by German submarines during World War II. Shipwreck remains can still be uncovered on the beaches.

Wright Brothers National Memorial at Kill Devil Hill, near the town of Kitty Hawk, commemorates the Wright Brothers' first flight.

Geologic History. The layers of poorly consolidated sediment—peat, mud, gravel, and shells—in the Albemarle–Pamlico Sound estuary system, had its origin in the Pleistocene. During glacial periods when sea level was lower, the rivers that flowed to the Atlantic cut deep channels into the coastal alluvial deposits.

The barrier islands of the Outer Banks off North Carolina are marked by navigational aids, such as Bodie Island Lighthouse along Cape Hatteras National Seashore. (Mark Vandyke/Dreamstime.com)

Each readvance of seas during interglacials redistributed sediment. Ocean currents and the configuration of the underlying sediment have determined the shape of the shoreline and barrier bars. While the major rivers, such as the Roanoke, Tar, and Neuse, flowed perpendicular to the coast, their tributaries were parallel to the shore. At the close of the Pleistocene, sea level was 250 ft (75 m) lower, the shore was 40 mi (64 km) to the east, and Pamlico Sound was dry land. The subsequent rise in sea level overtopped the tributary interfluves. At the seaward edge of the flooded interfluve, advancing ocean waves rearranged sediment into the high sand ridge, which is now the Outer Banks island string. Ocean waves, longshore currents, and storms continue to alter shorelines and rearrange islands. The Outer Banks have migrated several miles inland since they were initially formed 3,500–5,000 years ago. In 1870, the lighthouse on Cape Hatteras was built

1,500 ft (455 m) from shore. By 1999, it was 100 ft (30 m) from shore and was moved inland to assure its preservation.

Biota. Ecosystems include beaches, dunes, grasslands, shrub thickets, salt marsh, and maritime forests. Buxton Woods, inland from Cape Hatteras, is 9 mi^2 (23 km^2) of maritime forest, the largest on any barrier island. Live oak, loblolly pine, and laurel oak grow on dune crests, with swamp dogwood, southern bayberry, Carolina willow, and red bay, along with grasses and cattails, in swales. The Gulf Stream veers out into the Atlantic Ocean at Cape Hatteras, making it the northern limit of southern plants, such as Spanish moss, dwarf palmetto, and yaupon.

Under the Atlantic Flyway, the Outer Banks are a Globally Important Bird Area, with more than 360 documented species, including warblers, geese, ducks, swans, terns, willets, black skimmers, and oystercatchers. Ibis, egrets, herons, and Brown Pelicans nest on small islands in Pamlico Sound. The National Park Service maintains a small herd of wild ponies on Oracoke Island, presumed descendants of horses brought by early English colonists. Documented reptile species number 32, including alligators and several turtles, notably the endangered loggerhead sea turtle (*Caretta caretta*).

Protected Areas. Two national park units protect the majority of the Outer Banks. Cape Hatteras National Seashore stretches 72 mi (116 km) from Bodie Island to Ocracoke Inlet. Cape Lookout National Seashore extends from Ocracoke Inlet to Beaufort Inlet, the southern part of the Outer Banks. There are also smaller parks or preserves.

Further Reading

Albermarle-Pamlido Natural Estuary Program. n.d. *Geology of the Albemarle-Pamlico Estuarine System*. North Carolina Department of Environmental and Natural Resources. http://portal.ncdenr.org/web/apnep/geology

National Park Service. 2013. *Cape Hatteras National Seashore*. http://www.nps.gov/caha/index.htm

Ross, John, Bates Littlehales, and Thomas E. Lovejoy. 1995. *The Atlantic Coast and Blue Ridge. The Smithsonian Guides to Natural America*. Washington, D.C.: Smithsonian Books.

P

Pacific Ocean

Geographic Overview. The Pacific is Earth's largest ocean, accounting for about 30 percent of the planet's surface area. Its area is greater than that of all the continents combined and twice the size of the next largest sea, the Atlantic Ocean. The ocean itself is ancient, but the oceanic crust beneath it is relatively young. Subduction at its margins creates the Pacific Ring of Fire and also means that the ocean is shrinking in size—unlike the Atlantic, which is expanding. The Pacific was so-named by Ferdinand Magellan for its seeming calm after his stormy passage through the strait at the tip of South America that now bears his name.

Geographic Coordinates. 65°40'N–60°00'S, approximately 121°E–70°W

Description. The vast Pacific Ocean covers some 63,800,000 mi² (165,250,000 km²) or almost one-third of Earth's surface. At its widest, at 5°N, it is 12,300 mi (19,800 km) across. It not only is the largest ocean on the planet, but it also contains the lowest point on Earth's crust at Challenger Deep, in the Mariana Trench (35,837 ft or 10,924 m bsl). The northern and western margins along the coasts of Alaska and Australia contain numerous large seas and embayments, including the Gulf of Alaska, Bering Sea, Sea of Okhotsk, Sea of Japan (or East Sea), East China Sea, South China Sea, Yellow Sea, Gulf of Thailand, Philippine Sea, Sulu Sea, Celebes Sea, Coral Sea, and Tasman Sea. The eastern margin along the west coasts of the Americas lacks such bodies of water. The southern border occurs at 60°S at the edge of the Southern Ocean. The ocean, which extends some 9,600 mi (15,550 km) south from the Bering Strait to the Southern Ocean, is divided into the North Pacific and South Pacific at the equator.

The Pacific connects with the Arctic Ocean though the narrow Bering Strait and with the Atlantic Ocean via the Strait of Magellan and Drake's Passage. The boundary with the Indian Ocean is drawn from the Malay Peninsula to the north coasts of Borneo and Sulawesi and the Arafura Sea between New Guinea and Australia. The Pacific exchanges water with the cold Southern Ocean at the Antarctic Circumpolar Current, but Antarctic sea-ice does not extend into Pacific waters. Sea-ice is present during winter in the north, however, in both the Bering Sea and the Sea of Okhotsk.

Two-thirds of the ocean is underlain by the Pacific Plate. New oceanic crust forms at the East Pacific Rise (EPR), the world's fastest spreading mid-ocean ridge, pushing out at a rate of 4.5–6.0 in (11–16 cm)/yr. The EPR is a broad ridge with gentle slopes. Together with a few transverse fracture zones emanating from it, the EPR dominates the ocean floor of the eastern Pacific Basin. Much of the remaining one-third of seafloor lies on the Cocos and Nazca plates, which are subducting beneath the South American and Caribbean plates at the eastern edge of the basin. In the western and southwestern Pacific a number of microplates act as buffers between the Pacific Plate and the Australian and Eurasian plates. As a result, oceanic trenches and volcanic islands arcs are prevalent in the western Pacific. Examples are the Aleutian Islands, Marianas Islands, and the Philippines. Most of the plates pass over mantle hotspots where chains of volcanic islands and seamounts are formed; these are most prevalent in the western half of the basin. Examples of such are the Galápagos Islands, Hawaiian Islands, Emperor

Seamounts, Caroline Islands, Marshall Islands, Gilbert Islands, Phoenix Islands, Line Islands, and Samoan Islands.

Except off Australia, the Pacific Ocean is bounded by subduction zones. The presence of subduction zones has created a geologic distinction between the nature of volcanism along margins of the ocean and that occurring beyond in the Pacific Basin. The boundary between these two geologic regions is called the andesite line. It circles the Pacific, tracing the ocean's peripheral deep oceanic trenches. Outside the circle is the Ring of Fire, where rising magma penetrated existing continental crustal material and produced andesitic volcanic rocks. Explosive volcanic eruptions and the cones of large stratovolcanoes are commonplace in this outer region. Inside the circle, basaltic lava rises to the bottom of the ocean along oceanic ridges or at hotspots, unimpeded by existing continental crust and produces the enormous domes of shield volcanoes.

Over such a latitudinal span, salinity can be expected to vary. (Average surface salinity of the world ocean is 35.) It is lowest (near 32) in the high latitudes of the North Pacific, where evaporation rates are lowest. High precipitation offset by high evaporation rates in the wet equatorial climate zone causes salinity to rise to 34. The highest salinity (37) occurs in the eastern South Pacific under the southern subtropical high pressure system, where evaporation rates are high and precipitation low.

Climate patterns also vary across such an expansive body of water that encompasses subpolar, temperate, subtropical, and tropical/equatorial regions. Storms presenting major hazards to western lands in the temperate and tropical Pacific are typhoons, the name given tropical cyclones in the western Pacific. These are most often generated between 180° and 100°E longitude at about 10°N latitude. The western Pacific has the most numerous and intense tropical cyclones in the world, many of which reach full strength in the Philippine Sea and track northwest along the east coast of Asia. Peak season is June–November. Tropical cyclones are also generated in the eastern Pacific off the coast of Mexico and Central America, where they are called hurricanes. The storms are less frequent in the South Pacific, where they are confined to the western part of the basin.

A phenomenon of global significance, the El Niño and Southern Oscillation (ENSO), forms in the tropical Pacific but influences global climate. This has both atmospheric and oceanic ramifications. Normally, high pressure and easterly winds occur over the tropical Pacific in the east and an arid climate prevails along the coast of South America, where the cool Peru-Humboldt Current dominates. In the western tropical Pacific the opposite conditions occur: low pressure and heavy convectional rainfall. During El Niño conditions, the South Pacific High and easterly Trade Winds weaken, allowing warm water and humid air masses to spill eastward. Low pressure and rains come to the eastern South Pacific, while high pressure and arid conditions develop in the west. These changes affect the Asian monsoon and rainfall (or snowfall) amounts around the world.

Geologic History. The history of the Pacific Ocean goes back to the Panthalassa Sea, which surrounded the supercontinent of Pangaea. About 180 mya the Atlantic Ocean began to open with the rifting of Pangaea. By 167 mya, seafloor spreading west of Pangaea began and the earliest oceanic crust of the Pacific Plate was formed, driving the old seafloor westward. Indeed, three major plates developed at the ancestral EPR: the Kula and Farallon plates east of the ridge, and the Pacific Plate to the west. They came together at a triple junction. The Kula Plate moved northward and was subducted beneath the Pacific Northwest region of the United States and Canada. To the south, the Farallon Plate broke in two, becoming the Cocos and Nazcas plates. In the north, the Juan de Fuca Plate is probably the last remnant of the Farallon Plate.

The Pacific Plate continued to expand, pushing older fragments of oceanic crust aside. The EPR was forced eastward until about 30 mya, when it collided with the California coast and contacted the North American plate. Movement of the plates at this contact zone is mostly along the San Andreas Fault, a transform fault that led to the opening of the Gulf of California and continues to see California south of San Francisco as well as the Baja California Peninsula slip northward. The Nazca Plate subducts beneath South America at the Peru-Chile Trench, the world's longest oceanic trench (3,650 mi or 5,900 km). This convergence has raised the Andes and produced the range's spectacular stratovolcanoes. The Cocos Plate subducts beneath the North American and Caribbean Plates at the Middle America Trench. The Pacific Plate continues to slip beneath the North American in the Aleutian Trench at the southern edge of the Bering Sea, the northernmost part of the Ring of Fire.

In the western Pacific, the expanding Pacific Plate encountered the Eurasian and Australian plates and numerous microplates. In the northwestern part of its basin, the Pacific Plate subducts beneath the small Okhotsk Plate at the Kuril Trench, along which the Kuril island arc emerges above sea level. At the Mariana Trench along the eastern margin of the Philippine Sea, the expanding Pacific Plate converges with the tiny Mariana Plate, creating the deepest oceanic trench on Earth. (The Mariana Plate has a divergent boundary with the Philippine Plate to its west. North of the Mariana plate boundary, the Philippine Plate is subducting beneath the Pacific Plate; on its northwestern margin, it subducts beneath the Eurasian Plate in the Ryukyu Trench.) The Pacific Plate also is subducting into the Kermadac-Tonga Trench, which runs between North Island, New Zealand, and the island of Tonga. Here the closing rate between the Pacific and Australian plates is 9 in (24 cm)/yr, the fastest plate movement recorded. Subduction at these and all other convergent plate boundaries more than compensates for new crust formed at the EPR; the Pacific Plate has actually been shrinking in size for the past 165 million years. The oldest Pacific Ocean sea floor, which is also the oldest sea floor on Earth (167 million years old), is found in the westernmost reaches of the basin.

Circulation and Major Currents. With little cold water entering from the Arctic Ocean, the clockwise subtropical gyre of the North Pacific is dominated by warm water. The North Equatorial Current, the world's longest current, transports tropical water some 9,000 mi (14,500 km) westward across the ocean at roughly 5°N, driven by the Northeast Trade Winds. Turning north near the Philippines, it becomes the warm Kuroshio Current, the western boundary current of the North Pacific. Moving north past Taiwan and northeast by Japan, the Kuroshio meets the southward-flowing Oyashio Current near Hokkaido, Japan. The cool Oyashio Current comes from the Bering Sea and forms the western edge of a subpolar gyre. The mixing of waters produces a rich fishing ground. The Kuroshio Current continues past northeast Japan where it merges into the North Pacific Current. At 45°N, it branches into the Aleutian Current, which flows eastward and forks into the north-flowing Alaska Current—which circulates counterclockwise in the Gulf of Alaska, and the south-flowing cool California Current, the eastern boundary current of the subtropical gyre.

The South Equatorial Current flows westward along the equator, propelled by the Southeast Trades. It turns south near New Guinea, becoming the warm East Australian Current, and then east beyond New Zealand to flow eastward just equatorward of the Antarctic Circumpolar Current (ACC). Reaching the west coast of South America, it merges with a branch of the ACC and flows northward as the Peru or Humboldt Current, the eastern boundary current of the South Pacific. These cool waters emanating in part from the Southern Ocean dominate the counterclockwise circulation of the South Pacific.

Regional circulation patterns occur in the marginal seas, which are linked to neighboring seas, if not to the open Pacific itself, by straits and other passages. Some, such as the Sulu Sea, display reversing currents in accord with the Asian monsoon.

Environmental Issues. Natural hazards include volcanic eruptions, earthquakes, tsunamis, and El Niño conditions. Increasingly the effects of global climate change are evidenced in warming surface sea temperatures and rising sea levels, both of which can be devastating to the enormous biodiversity held in coral reefs in the tropical Pacific.

A massive and growing problem is the Great Pacific Garbage Patch in the North Pacific between Hawai'i and California (roughly from 35°–45°N and 135°–155°W). Here, trapped in the middle of the slow-moving North Pacific subtropical gyre, the refuse of civilization collects. The flotsam is mostly plastic—plastic bags, bottles, bottle caps, toys, etc. The upper water column is full of suspended particulates of plastic polymers. Marine life, from jellyfish to albatrosses, consumes the debris, fatally mistaking it for food; the shores of mid-ocean islands become littered with it, threatening the breeding grounds of sea turtles, seabirds, and pinnipeds.

See also Bering Sea; East China Sea; Humboldt Current; Mariana Trench; Sea of Japan (East Sea); South China Sea; Tasman Sea

Further Reading

Cousteau, Fabien. 2006. *Oceans, The Last Wilderness Revealed*. New York: American Museum of Natural History.

Neall, Vincent E. and Steven A. Trewick. 2008. "The Age and Origin of the Pacific Islands: A Geological Overview." *Philosophical Transactions of the Royal Society* 363: 3293–3308. http://rstb.royalsocietypublishing .org/content/363/1508/3293.full#sec-2

Pamirs

Afghanistan, China, Kyrgyzstan, and Tajikistan

Geographic Overview. The Pamirs are high mountains in south-central Asia, more than 20,000 ft (6,100 m) asl, west of and related to the larger Himalayan Mountain complex. The rough translation, high undulating grasslands or roof of the world, describes the treeless expanse of high plateaus, from which high, glaciated peaks rise higher. The Pamirs are the third highest mountain ecosystem in the world.

Geographic Coordinates. Approximately 37° 00'N–39°30'N, 70°15'E–75°00'E

Description. The Pamirs center on a bulge called the Pamir Knot, approximately 310–375 mi (500–600 km) in diameter, from which several mountain ranges, including the Hindu Kush, Karakoram, Kunlun, and Tian Shan, radiate. The core of the Pamirs is in Tajikistan, but they also cross the borders into Afghanistan, China, and Kyrgyzstan. The mountain node is distinctly defined. The Pamirs are bounded in the north by the Gissar-Alay (Trans-Alai) fault, where the Trans-Alai Range drops steeply down to the Alai Valley (Kyzylsu-Surkhob-Vakhsh Rivers) south of the Alai Range in the Tian Shan in Uzbekistan. The eastern boundary is the Sarykol Pamir (Chinese Pamirs), forming the border with China at the western edge of the Tarim Basin. The southern boundary is the Vakhan Valley (Wakhan Corridor) region of Afghanistan, separating the Pamirs from the Hindu Kush. On the west is the Tajik depression.

The Pamirs have very high elevations, 20,000–24,000 ft (6,100–7,300 m) asl. The eastern part is characterized by high plateaus with a mean elevation of 20,000 ft (6,200 m), with rounded peaks rising 3,300–5,900 ft (1,000–1,800 m) higher. The plateaus are separated by wide, flat valleys at 12,000–13,800 ft (3,700–4,200 m). The western Pamirs, with high alpine ridges, glaciers, and deep, narrow gorges, exhibit high relief because they underwent rapid uplift combined with subsidence of the Fergana and Tajik valleys. The highest peak in the Pamirs is Ismail Somoni (Garmo) Peak at 24,590 (7,495 m).

Extensively glaciated, the Pamirs have almost 10,000 glaciers, covering 3,860 mi^2 (10,000 km^2), the single most important source of water for Central Asian plains. Fedchenko Glacier dominates the central Pamirs. Most drainage is north and west to the Panji and Vakhsh Rivers. The Amu Darya begins at the confluence of the Vakhsh and Panji in southwestern Tajikistan.

The Pamirs are rich in minerals, such as gold, silver, molybdenum, and mercury, and in gem stones, including rubies and lazulite.

Climate in the Pamirs is arid continental. The western regions receive 12–24 in (300–600 mm) of annual precipitation, including snow. The eastern Pamirs are very dry, 4 in (100 mm). Because of the dry interior, snowline in the central and eastern Pamirs is high, 17,000 ft (5,200 m). Temperature varies with elevation and location. Extremes in the western Pamirs are generally less drastic. In some parts of the eastern Pamirs, temperatures may drop to –58°F (–50°C), and frost is possible any time of year. The eastern Pamirs have permafrost at elevations above 9,850 ft (3,000 m).

Geologic History. The Pamirs, created by the collision of India and Eurasia, are composed of several distinctive microplates accreted to southern Asia during the late Paleozoic–Mesozoic closure of the Tethys Sea. A number of narrow terranes were pushed north into Asia between the Tajik Basin and the Tarim Basin. As the terranes moved northward, they overthrust and separated the Tajik depression on the west from the Tarim Basin on the east. Sedimentary strata in the Tajik and Tarim Basins were pushed 200 mi (320 km) north, to reappear at the northern edge of the Pamirs. The overthrusting and piling up of terranes continued into the Cenozoic. Active deformation is now dominated by east–west extension along transform faults.

Four accreted terranes are joined by overthrust faults and suture zones. The northern zone is mainly Precambrian to Paleozoic metamorphosed igneous and sedimentary rocks, including basalts, limestones, siltstones, and sandstones, of marine origin from a small ocean that closed by late Carboniferous Period in the Paleozoic. The southern part of this block is andesitic, part of an island arc. The central Pamirs are deformed and metamorphosed Precambrian and Paleozoic basement rocks, a continental fragment accreted in the middle Mesozoic. Fault-bounded schists and gneisses from the Alpine Orogeny in the Tertiary are exposed in cores of anticlines, such as the Central Pamir gneiss domes. The Rushan–Pshart zone has continentally derived sedimentary rocks in the north, grading to a variety of marine limestone and pillow basalts in the south, the remains of a small ocean basin created in the Mesozoic (250–100 mya) by rifting, but which closed by the early Cretaceous (100 mya). The southwestern Pamirs are exposures of metamorphosed Precambrian and Mesozoic rocks, with Miocene granites. The southeast has no exposures of basement rocks. The oldest exposed rocks are late Paleozoic and Mesozoic sedimentary and meta-sedimentaries, including sandstones, limestones, conglomerate, gneiss, marble, and quartzite, believed to be part of the southwestern sedimentary cover that was detached.

Biota. Because of aridity, most of the Pamirs is similar to the treeless Tibetan Plateau or arctic tundra. Vegetation cover is 8–15 percent in these high mountain deserts. The flat expanses in the eastern plateaus, which have little altitudinal zonation, are dominated by *Kobresia* grasses. Drought-tolerant cushion plants are found on rocky slopes. The western Pamirs are wetter, with juniper on valley slopes, giving way to subalpine tall-grass meadows above 10,000 ft (3,000 m) and eventually to low-grass alpine meadows. Watercourses above 6,500 ft (2,000 m) have willows, thornbushes, oleander, and poplar.

High plateaus are breeding grounds for mountain goat and argali. Blue sheep, urial, and ibex are present, and markhor may be seen in the lower ranges. Other mammals include brown bear, marmot, wolf, and a small population of snow leopards. Lammergeier (Bearded Vulture) and Himalayan Griffon frequent the highest peaks. The western mountains support partridges, pheasant, and snow cock. Migratory waterfowl visit lakes in the eastern Pamir.

Protected Areas. Tajik National Park, covering almost the entire Pamir Mountains and including Fedchenko Glacier, is a World Heritage Site.

Environmental Issues. The region is seismically active, with many earthquakes.

See also Aral Sea; Himalayan Mountains; Hindu Kush Mountains; Karakoram Mountains; Kunlun Shan; Tarim Basin and Takla Makan Desert; Tian Shan

Further Reading

Lohr, Tina. 2001. *A Short Story about the Geological History of the Pamir. Department of Tectophysics.* University of Mining and Technology, Freibeg Institute of Geology. www.geo.tu-freiberg.de/hydro/oberseminar /pdf/Tina%20Lohr.pdf

Shahgedanova, Maria et al. 2002. "The Mountains of Central Asia and Kazakhstan." In *The Physical Geography of Northern Eurasia*, edited by Maria Shahgedanova, 375–402. Oxford: Oxford University Press.

The Pampas

Argentina, Brazil, and Uruguay

Geographic Overview. Temperate grasslands rivaling the prairies of North America and the steppes of Eurasia surround the Rio de la Plata on vast, flat to gently rolling plains that cover northeastern Argentina, most of Uruguay, and southeastern Brazil. These are the Pampas, from the Quechan word designating plains. They contain the largest area of fertile soils in South America. Once reaching the Atlantic Ocean in the east, the natural grasslands of the Rio de la Plata area are mostly gone now, converted to agricultural and urban land uses. The Pampas were the home of the legendary gaucho, a folk hero comparable to the cowboy of the American West. His heyday was from the mid-18th to mid-19th centuries, before the pampas were fenced.

Geographic Coordinates. Approximately 28°S–38°S, 50°W–65°W

Description. Seven pampas are commonly delineated. The two in southeastern Brazil and Uruguay are called the Northern Campos and the Southern Campos. The other five all occur in Argentina and are known as pampas. The four eastern pampas, from north to south, are the Mesopotamic Pampa, lying between the Paraná and Uruguay rivers, the Rolling Pampa, the Flooding Pampa, and the Austral Pampa. The Inner Pampa lies to the west of the last three. The subtropical Northern Campos once supported tall-grass prairies and grass steppes on soils derived from basalt. Livestock grazing has now altered these grasslands. The Southern Campos and Rolling Pampa are both hilly with well-defined drainage systems.

The natural vegetation was structurally similar to the North American prairie and consisted of sod-forming grasses such as bahia grass and caminha grass (Southern Campos) and silver beardgrass (Rolling Prairie) 20–40 in (50–100 cm) tall growing with medium height bunchgrasses such as Chilean needlegrass, that stood 20 in (50 cm) high, and short tuft-grasses or *flechillas* 4 in (5 cm) high. Warm-season C4 grasses and cool-season C3 grasses were of equal dominance. In wet areas, the iconic Pampas grass stood 8 ft (2.5 m) tall. Grazing eliminated the tall grasses; and today most of the area is cropland, used primarily for soybean production. The Flooding Pampa has many depressions along the Salado and other rivers that flood each year. Habitats vary from small, low hills that are never submerged to flat areas occasionally flooded to lowlands inundated for several months each year. Repeated inundation followed by evaporation makes some soils saline, capable of supporting only halophytes. The Inner Pampa is semiarid and lacks a well-developed drainage system. Tussock grasses here are less dense than elsewhere. The Austral Pampa occurs on the Tandilia Hills and Sierra de la Ventana. These low ranges rarely exceed 3,000 ft (1,000 m) in elevation. Cool season tussock grasses dominate. Since they maintain dead blades from previous years, the landscape is always yellow. On rocky areas, shrubs are common. High soil fertility has meant that most of this area has been converted to wheat production.

The pampas are located in a subtropical climate region in the north but extend southward into the temperate zone. The tapering shape of the South American continent introduces a maritime moderation of temperatures to much of the region, so the extreme winters of Northern Hemisphere temperate grasslands are not experienced. Mean annual temperatures range from 66°F (19°C) in the north to 57°F (14°C) in the south. Frost is frequent during the winter; first frost occurs in mid-April in the south but is delayed to late May or early June in the north. The growing season is 4–8 months long.

Moist air masses off the South Atlantic Ocean account for most of the precipitation across the Pampas and—together with the lack of topographic barriers—a northeast–southwest gradient in annual totals. The warm air meets cold, polar air masses moving across semiarid Patagonia and produces frontal precipitation. This moisture is augmented in northern areas by interactions with a summer low that develops over Argentina. In southeast Brazil, up to 63 in (1,600 mm) of rain is received annually, while in the southwest less than 23 in (600 mm) of precipitation may fall.

Geologic History. The pampas developed on fertile soils derived from wind-blown silts (loess) and fine sands rich in calcium interbedded with nutrient-rich volcanic material. The loess originated as sediments deposited in the Monte desert and in Patagonia by Pleistocene glaciers and streams flowing down the eastern slopes of the Andes. During the Holocene, the finest particles were picked up in the western drylands by prevailing westerly winds and carried eastward. As they reached more humid climate regions, they settled out, forming thick deposits of loess and sand seas. The loess is thicker, coarser, and younger in the western pampas; east of the Uruguay River thin layers of older loess are restricted to hilltops and fluvial terraces. In a few parts of the Argentine pampas, outcrops of Precambrian and Paleozoic crystalline rocks form isolated uplands. In Uruguay and southern Brazil, a variety of Precambrian granites, Carboniferous sandstones, and Jurassic basalts have been exposed to weathering and soil-forming processes, creating a mosaic of soil types.

Biota. Animals of the Pampas, like many of the native grasses, have declined or disappeared. The

Pampas deer is endangered and only remains in preserves. Rodents are prevalent and include the now very rare mara, large plains viscacha, wild guinea pig, various mice, and tuco-tucos. Opossums and armadillos also frequent the plains. Birds such as the Greater Rhea, tinamous, doves, and parrots live in the pampas. Large carnivores have been exterminated; and smaller ones, such as the pampas fox, grisón, pampas cat, and Geoffroys's cat, are vanishing.

Protected Areas. No large conservation areas exist, but many small preserves have been set aside in the more humid pampas. None occur in the semiarid portions.

Environmental Issues. Grazing altered the grasslands, eliminating the more palatable species and allowing for the invasion of woody plants, especially *chanar* or Chilean palo verde (*Geoffroea decorticans*) plus numerous exotic species.

Further Reading

Paruelo, José María, Estebán G. Jobbágy, Martín Oesterheld, Rodolfo A. Gollussscio, and Martín R. Aguiar. 2007. "The Grasslands and Steppes of Patagonia and the Rio del la Plata Plains." In *The Physical Geography of South America*, edited by Thomas T. Veblen, Kenneth R. Young, and Antony R. Orme, 232–248. New York: Oxford University Press.

Woodward, Susan L. 2009. *Grassland Biomes*. Greenwood Guides to Biomes of the World. Westport, CT: Greenwood Press.

Pamukkale

Turkey

Geographic Overview. Pamukkale is a natural hot springs site that includes Roman ruins. The snowy white travertine terraces of Pamukkale, which means cotton castle in Turkish, are some of the most beautiful in the world. Its mineral-rich waters, used for therapeutic purposes since Roman times, continue to draw people from all over the world to bathe in its warm spa waters. Although in ruins, the architecture and tombs of Hierapolis, a major Roman thermal center and cemetery, yield a wealth of information about the ancient cultures and customs.

Geographic Coordinates. 37°55'N, 29°07'E

Description. The hot springs of Pamukkale and the Roman ruins of Hierapolis are 22 mi (19 km) north of Denizli in southwestern Turkey. Pamukkale is one of several thermal springs, including Karahayit, Yenicekent, Akkoy, and Sarakoy, in the region. The water emerges and flows at approximately 105 gal/sec (400 liters/sec), at a temperature of 95°–133°F (33°–56°C) and a pH of 6. Total mineral content is 0.3 oz/gal (2,430 mg/liter). The travertine, deposited by the hot water saturated with calcium, magnesium, sulfate, and bicarbonate, is not stained by other minerals and remains snow white.

The hot water springs emerge from a plateau in the foothills of Cokelez Mountains, 330–650 ft (100–200 m) above the Curuksu River plain below. The slope is a series of travertine terraces, scallop-shaped or half-circle basins of water rimmed by "frozen" waterfalls and stalactite-like formations similar to those found in caves. The mineral-rich water spills from basin to basin as it flows downslope, forming several types of travertine terraces. With deposition and erosion, the terraces are constantly in a state of flux. The main hot springs location on the Pamukkale plateau is also the site of the Sacred Pool, Hierapolis ruins, and an archaeology museum. The travertine has enveloped part of the city of Hierapolis and the necropolis (cemetery). At Karahayit, the travertine is stained colorful greens, browns, and reds by minerals such as iron oxides in the water.

At the end of the second century B.C., the spa city of Hierapolis was built around a warm water spring Romans considered sacred to the gods. The city became cosmopolitan, with Anatolians, Graeco-Macedonians, Romans, Jews, and later Christians, all coming together to "take the waters." The city was abandoned after an earthquake in 1334. The site is significant for insight into various religious and funerary practices associated with the many temples, churches, and tombs. The sacred pool remains, open to swimming among the marble columns of the ruined Temple of Apollo.

The water is believed, including by some in the medical profession, to be beneficial treatment of many diseases and disorders, and the region is a major tourist attraction. The large necropolis, however, presents conflicting testimony to the healing properties of the water.

The beauty of the snow white travertine terraces and therapeutic benefits of the hot springs at Pamukkale in Turkey have attracted visitors since Roman times. (Daniel Boiteau/Dreamstime.com)

Geologic History. Pamukkale is in the West Anatolian sector of the Aegean extensional province, a tectonic region related to the subduction of the African and Adriatic plate and subsequent faulting and crustal extension. In its more than 400,000 years of activity, the springs have deposited approximately 4 mi^2 (10 km^2) of travertine. The water, from a source deep underground, emerges from open fissures and at least one fault zone. The source of the minerals is carbonate bedrock, Paleozoic marbles and Mesozoic limestones, beneath the surface. A complex network of fissures provides conduits for the water. As the water releases carbon dioxide on the surface, it loses its ability to hold calcium in solution and deposits it as travertine, first as a soft, jelly-like substance that hardens to hard, but brittle rock. More carbon dioxide is released in falling water, which in turn builds up the edges of the pools and terraces and promotes more waterfalls.

Protected Areas. Pamukkale National Park is the focal point for the Hierapolis–Pamukkale World Heritage Site.

Environmental Issues. Tourism and commercial activities have resulted in both physical damage and discoloration of the travertine. Terraces, pools, and formations are damaged by people walking on or bathing in the pools, especially with shoes, which are now banned. Algae discolor the travertine. Leakage from septic tanks at the base of the pools also fosters algal growth. In an attempt to maintain existing terraces, direction of thermal flow is now regulated. Hotels were removed from the Pamukkale plateau in the 1990s, replaced by luxury hotels with their own hot springs in Karahayit, 3 mi (5 km) north.

See also Anatolian Plateau

Further Reading

Altunel, E. and P. L. Hancock. 1993. "Morphology and Structural Setting of Quaternary Travertines at Pamukkale." *Turkey Geological Journal* 28: 335–346.

Sahin, Serap. 2006. *Pamukkale*. General Directorate of Information, Republic of Turkey Ministry of Culture and Tourism. http://www.goturkey.com/en/multimedia/brochure

Simsek, S. et al. 2000. "Environmental Protection of Geothermal Waters and Travertines at Pamukkale, Turkey." *Geothermics* 29: 557–572.

The Pantanal

Bolivia, Brazil, and Paraguay

Geographic Overview. The Pantanal is the largest wetland in the Neotropics and one of the largest wetlands in the world. It is located in the upper drainage basin of the Paraguay River between the Andes Mountains and the Brazilian Highlands. Roughly 62 percent lies in the Brazilian states of Mato Grosso and Mato Grosso do Sol, 20 percent in Bolivia, and 18 percent in Paraguay. Its name comes from the Portuguese word *pântano*, signifying swamp or marsh. It is known for its great diversity of plants and animals, many related to Amazonian forms.

Geographic Coordinates. Approximately 16°S–20°S, 55°W–60°W

Description. The Pantanal stretches for an estimated 54,000–81,000 mi^2 (140,000–210,000 km^2)—more area than the state of New York—over a flat, lowland at elevations of 250–660 ft (25–200 m) asl. It is a land of inland deltas and coalescing alluvial fans that merge with the floodplain of the Paraguay River, which is characterized by sand bars, oxbow lakes, and meander scars. Located in a tropical wet and dry climate region, the basin receives 32–48 in (800–1,200 mm) of rain a year; but most precipitation occurs during the rainy season in austral summer (October–March). Rainfall is highly variable from year to year and exceptionally wet and exceptionally dry periods may last for several years.

The annual flood dominates life in the Pantanal. The major tributaries create a flow from north to south and from east to west. Due to the low gradient of the basin, water moves slowly through the wetland, and the floodwaters of the upper Paraguay River take 6 months to get from Cáceras, Brazil, (16°11'S, 57°40'W) in the north to Concepción, Paraguay, (23°24'S, 57°26'W), in the south. Four distinct seasons are recognized, reflecting the importance of the flood in wetland ecology. *Enchente* begins in November with the start of the rainy season and rising waters. *Chera* occurs when the flood is at its maximum. The timing of this varies across the Pantanal. In the north this may occur as early as February; in the south it may be as late as June. The tributary streams, because of latitudinal differences, flood sequentially and extend the flood season. Nearly the entire region is inundated as floodwaters rise up to 16 ft (5 m). Only scattered islands and natural levees remain above water. Sediments settle out of the nearly still water, and clear water allows for the rampant growth of submerged and emergent aquatic plants and an explosion of aquatic invertebrates and their predators. During *vazante*, the floodwaters rapidly recede and aquatic plants become exposed. They die off to be replaced by terrestrial forms. Finally, the *seca* marks the low water period during the cool, dry season. Water retreats to deep channels and shallow pools, confining fish and other aquatic animals and, as oxygen levels drop, causing major die-offs. Such concentrations of food attract thousands of birds to the Pantanal and provide a time of abundance for other predators and scavengers. With the return of the summer rains, the cycle begins anew.

The natural levees and other places that are always above water support gallery forests, often with palms and kapok trees or semideciduous or deciduous tropical forest related to cerrado vegetation. Seventy percent of the region is a mosaic of grassland, wet meadows, palm savannas, and park savanna that is underwater during part of each year, but during the dry season, they must endure fire. Large areas are dotted with termite mounds. Lakes and ponds from a few feet to a few miles in diameter have floating mats of water hyacinth, eared water moss, and water lettuce and emergents such as of giant bulrush, flats edge, and cattail. The undersides of floating plants are rich in microcrustaceans such as isopods and amphipods and insect larvae.

Geologic History. The vast, seasonally flooded region occupies a flat-bottomed pre-Andean depression that formed as the Andes rose and filled with stream and lake deposits over the millennia.

Biota. The species-rich invertebrate fauna includes nearly 500 kinds of lepidopteran, numerous species of lunged and gilled snails, mussels, clams, freshwater crabs, and prawns. Fish are also diverse, with characins particularly numerous. Many are Amazonian in origin. Amphibians are related to cerrado species; half the toads and frogs are arboreal. The more than 170 reptilian species include the yellow anaconda and jacare caiman that hunt in the water. The Pantanal is famous for its huge congregations of migratory water birds, some of which roost in colonies numbering in the thousands. Among them are the iconic jabiru stork, wood storks, cormorants, herons, grebes, rails, bitterns, and kingfishers. The large, rare, and endangered Hyacinth Macaw lives in palm groves, and 29 species of hummingbirds contribute to the great diversity of birds, estimated at somewhere between 400 and 800 species. More than 100 mammal species are known from the Pantanal, including the capybara, the world's largest rodent, collared and white-lipped peccary, marsh deer, South American tapir, giant anteater, howler monkey, brown capuchin monkey, and carnivores such as maned wolf, jaguar, puma, and giant otter.

Protected Areas. The Pantanal Conservation Complex, a UNESCO World Heritage Site, consists of four relatively small areas in the northeast part of the wetland, including Pantanal Matogrossense National Park (520 mi² or 1,350 km²) established in 1981 and the nearby Pantanal Private Natural Heritage Reserve set aside in 1998. Both are Ramsar Wetlands of International Importance.

Environmental Issues. The Pantanal is under threat from drainage for pasture and cropland, deforestation, fragmentation by roads as development and the human population in the region increase, poaching, and water pollution. It has been compared to the much smaller Florida Everglades of 50 years ago, thought to be a healthy, invulnerable ecosystem in part due to its size, but actually on the brink of collapse.

Further Reading

"Information Sheet for a New Ramsar Wetland in the Pantanal." 2003. Wetlands International. http://sites.wetlands.org/reports/ris/6BR008en_RIS_2003.pdf

Roth, Richard A. 2009. *Freshwater Aquatic Biomes*. Greenwood Guides to Biomes of the World. Westport, CT: Greenwood Press.

Páramo

Colombia, Costa Rica, Ecuador, Guatemala, Panama, and Venezuela

Geographic Overview. In the Northern Andes of South America and in high elevations in Central America is a moist montane grassland called *páramo*, a Spanish word meaning "barren" or "treeless." Occurring between treeline and snow line in the *Tierra Helada* of tropical mountains, páramo is found primarily in Colombia, Ecuador, and Venezuela, but pockets of this uniquely Neotropical vegetation can also be found in Panama, the Talamanca Range of Costa Rica, and Guatemala.

Description. Páramo is a moist, alpine vegetation type occurring mainly in the Andes Mountains. At elevations between 9,800 ft (3,000 m) and 15,000 ft (4,500 m), thin air and low oxygen concentrations, intense solar radiation, cold winds, and below freezing temperatures every night prevail. During the day, temperatures may reach into the low 70°s F (ca. 23°C), but upslope winds carry moist air from the Pacific Ocean and the Amazon River basin (South America) or Caribbean Sea (Central America), and by noon the highlands may be enveloped in fog that suddenly drops the temperature to near freezing. Plants must be able to tolerate or find ways to avoid freezing with no time to prepare by hardening off, as plants in seasonal climates of the temperate zone do. Depending upon latitude and aspect, precipitation ranges from 27 in (685 mm) to 75 in (1,900 mm). Rains generally occur April–June in the Northern Hemisphere and August–November in the Southern Hemisphere.

A rich flora with many endemic genera and species has developed on isolated peaks in this environment; most derive from local lowland species. Growth forms characteristic of páramo vegetation are tussock grasses; ground-hugging mats, rosettes, and cushions; and giant rosettes—in particular, frailejones

(*Espletia* spp.) and puyas—which are terrestrial bromeliads. Patches of *Polylepis* forest also occur. *Polylepis* or *quenua* is usually a contorted tree that grows 10–30 ft (6–10 m) tall. On windward slopes that receive the most moisture, the reddish papery bark is thought to reduce the number of epiphytes that could grow on the tree. *Polylepis* is one the highest-growing trees in the world, often reaching elevations above 13,000 ft (4,000 m). Today groves are above the general treeline, but this may be the product of centuries of forest clearance and burning to expand páramo pastures downslope for livestock grazing.

Páramo consists of a number of different plant communities, each characterized by different growth forms. The giant rosette plants do not grow in all places, but where they do they dominate the landscape. They have counterparts in the afroalpine zone of high tropical mountains in Africa and on the Canary Islands, where convergent evolution has resulted in different taxa assuming the same growth form in adaption to similar environments. The frailejones of the Andes have thick trunks 3–10 ft (1–3 m) tall, depending upon species and habitat, draped in dead leaves and topped by a large rosette of long, elliptical fleshy, silvery living leaves covered in fine hairs. Large yellow daisy-like flowers adorn them in season. The dead leaves insulate the stem and keep it from freezing. They also provide shelter for invertebrates, small birds, and rodents. Frailejones are usually found in large numbers with an understory of tussock grasses and low rosettes and mats. Wet páramo dominated by tussock grasses, mostly *Calamagrostis* and *Festuca*, is the most extensive community. Slow decomposition in the mountain cold creates a wet spongy surface of dead plant material. Dwarf bamboo, low shrubs, low rosettes, cushion plants, sedges, mosses and lichens thrive in this habitat, as does puya. Puya has a large basal rosette of leaves but sends up an inflorescence 3–4 ft (1 m) high. The flower stalk of *Puya clava-hércules* is covered with a white wool that protects its blue-bracted blossoms from the cold. Other plants exhibit different adaptations to cold. Jata or candlebush (*Loucaria ferruginea*) is protected by a thick, but flammable wax. *Valeriana plantagenea* produces a natural antifreeze in its tissues. In drier areas low shrubs such as the flower of the Andes or Churaquiragua and low rosettes of daisies, gentians, and buttercups are prevalent. Rocky areas may host orchids, while boggy areas (*patonales*) support cushion plants. In a narrow zone just below snowline on loose scree slopes and sands, a sparse cover of small rosettes and *Azorella* cushions form the superpáramo community. Wind erosion may leave the cushions sitting atop earthen pedestals.

Biota. Mammals of the páramo tend to have compact bodies, short limbs, and dense, dark-colored hair. A larger number of red blood cells than normal enables them to absorb and store oxygen in the thin air. Small herbivores such as rabbits and rodents are most numerous. Larger herbivores include white-tailed deer, little red bracket deer, pudu, mountain tapir, and, on the dry páramo near Volcan Chimborazo in Ecuador, vicuña. The rare spectacled bear, an omnivore, leaves adjacent forests to eat the flower stalks of puya. Among carnivores, shrews are abundant and the long-tailed weasel fairly common. Hummingbirds are important pollinators on the páramo and survive because they go into torpor when at rest.

Protected Areas. Several national parks, especially in Ecuador, have been established to protect the páramo.

Environmental Issues. The páramo has long been disturbed by overgrazing by cattle and sheep; burning to improve pasture, and clearing for indigenous agriculture based on Andean root crops such as potatoes, oca, and melloca. Warming of the climate now threatens to diminish its geographic extent and push some of its plant and animals species to extinction.

Further Reading

"Paramo El Angel—Eerie Land of Frailejones." 2012. Wondermondo. http://www.wondermondo.com/Coun tries/SA/Ecuador/Carchi/ElAngelParamo.htm

Patzelt, Erwin. 1996. *Flora of Ecuador*. Quito: Banco Central del Ecuador.

Quinn, Joyce A. 2009. *Arctic and Alpine Biomes*. Greenwood Guides to Biomes of the World. Westport, CT: Greenwood Press.

Woodward, Susan L. 2003. *Biomes of Earth: Terrestrial, Aquatic, and Human-Dominated*. Westport, CT: Greenwood Press.

Paraná Plateau

Brazil

Geographic Overview. The southernmost section of the Brazilian Highlands, the Paraná Plateau, is covered with a mantle of basalt some 6,500 ft (2,000 m) thick. It is the largest continental lava flow on Earth. The states of Paraná and São Paulo lie wholly on the plateau, which also extends northward into southeastern Mato Grosso do Sul and south and southwestern Minas Gerais and southward into Santa Catarina and Rio Grande do Sul.

Geographic Coordinates. Approximately 21°S–33°S, 50°W–56°W

Description. Elevations on the Paraná Plateau section of the Brazilian Highlands vary from 1,600 to 4,300 ft (500–1,300 m). The surface is flat to gently rolling, but with deeply incised rivers. Rifting events that opened the South Atlantic Ocean uplifted the margins of southeastern Brazil, and the plateau now lies west of the Central and Southern Serras physiographic unit of the Brazilian Highlands. Most of it drains to the Paraná and Paraguay rivers and eventually into the estuary of the Rio de la Plata. Iguazu Falls, on a tributary of the Paraná River, plunges over the western edge of the plateau, and the largest two canyons on the continent (Itaimbezinho and Fortaleza canyons) are deeply incised into the plateau near its southeastern margin.

The climate grades from humid subtropical in the north to temperate in the south, where during winter months killing frosts occur. The warmest months, December to February, average in the upper 60s to low 70s°F (low 20s °C), while during the winter months the average drops to 59°F (15°C) in São Paulo and 54°F (12°C) in Curitiba. Precipitation is year-round and averages 55 in (1,400 mm) annually. Winter rains derive from mid-latitude cyclonic storms off the South Atlantic; summer precipitation is a result of convectional uplift induced by the heating of the land. Total annual amounts tend to decrease toward the west and toward the north, where a 3–4 month long winter dry season occurs between April and September.

The humid climate has helped decompose the basaltic bedrock and produce some of Brazil's most fertile soils, the reddish-purple *terra roxa* soils. These soils supported 19th-century coffee-growing, the source of southeast Brazil's early wealth. Before widespread human disturbance, the region was forested. In the east-central parts of the plateau, a distinctly Southern Hemisphere evergreen forest, the Araucaria Forest, dominated. This now highly fragmented vegetation is an evergreen coniferous forest of Paraná pine (*Araucaria angustifolia*) and podocarps (*Podocarpus* spp.). These trees have Gondwanan origins. The pines have tall straight trunks that stand more than 100 ft (30 m) high. Branches reach out, candelabra fashion, near the top and end in tufts of dark green needles. On the western plateau, in the valleys of the Paraiba and Paraná drainage systems, is the semideciduous broadleaf Alto Paraná forest, an inland expression of the Atlantic rainforest.

Geologic History. The outpouring of these flood basalts anticipated the Mesozoic Era rifting that fractured West Gondwana and separated the South American plate from the African plate.

Environmental Issues. Today the Paraná Plateau is the industrial center of Brazil and home to the largest and wealthiest city in the Southern Hemisphere, São Paulo. Other urban centers include Londrina, Curitiba, and Porto Alegre. Agriculture remains important; coffee continues to be grown here, joined now by citrus, soybeans, dairying, and beef cattle production. The natural vegetation is greatly reduced. According to some estimates less than 5 percent remains.

See also Atlantic Forest (Mata Atlântica); Brazilian Highlands; Iguazu Falls (Iguassu Falls, Foz do Iguaçu, Cataratas del Iguazú); Itaimbézinho and Fortaleza Canyons

Further Reading

Caviedes, César and Gregory Knapp. 1995. *South America.* Englewood, NJ: Prentice-Hall.

Kent, Robert B. 2006. *Latin America: Regions and People.* New York: Guilford Press.

Orme, Antony R. 2007. "The Tectonic Framework of South America." In *The Physical Geography of South America*, edited by Thomas T. Veblen, Kenneth R. Young, and Antony R. Orme, 3–22. New York: Oxford University Press.

"Umas Visão de Biodiversidade da Ecorregião Florestas do Alto Paraná—Bioma Mata Atlantica: Planejando a Paisagem de Conservação do Biodiversidade e Estabelecendo Prioidades para Ações de Conservação," 2003. Washington, D.C.: World Wildlife Fund. http://d3nehc6yl9qzo4.cloudfront.net/downloads/altoparana_versao_completa_portugues.pdf

Paricutín

Mexico

Geographic Overview. Paricutín is a volcano that suddenly appeared around 4 P.M. in a cornfield in Michoacán, Mexico, on February 20, 1943, and by the end of that year had attained a height of 1,000 ft (330 m) above the surface. It continued to erupt until March 4, 1952, by which time it stood 1,353 ft (424 m) above the surrounding land. This cinder cone has been dormant since and is probably extinct. Paricutín was the first volcano scientists were able to study firsthand from its birth to its death. It was such a marvel that some people list it as one of the Seven Natural Wonders of the World.

Geographic Coordinates. 19°30'N, 102°15'W

Description. Paricutín is one of 1,400 vents in the Michoacán–Guanajuato volcanic field, part of the Trans-Mexican Volcanic Axis. The field is a cluster of mostly young cinder cones, but contains other volcanic landforms such as small shield volcanoes, maars, tuff rings, lava domes, and lava flows. Paricutín is the youngest cinder cone in the field and, indeed, in the Americas. The initiation of activity at Paricutín was witnessed by the farmer who owned the cornfield in which it arose. A few days earlier, rumblings from deep earthquakes had been heard in the area; and then a 6 ft (2 m) high swell formed on the ground, causing a crack about 8 ft (2.5 m) long to open. What looked like smoke and smelled like rotten eggs hissed out of the fissure. A few hours later, an undeniable volcano sat in the field. Within 24 hours, the new cinder cone was 165 ft (50 m) high, a pile of volcanic bombs and cinders from the size of peas to that of walnuts. A week later, the cone had grown to more than 300 ft (100 m) above the ground. Explosive eruptions sent columns of ash and other volcanic material a mile or higher into the air. In April, lava flows began. On June 12, lava from a vent on the northeast flank

of the cone began a slow advance toward the village of Paricutín, and residents began to evacuate the area. Throughout the remainder of the year, explosive eruptions continued and the mountain reached a height of more than 1,000 ft (330 m).

In early 1944, another lava flow spread at a rate of 30 mi (48 km) a day toward the larger village of San Juan Parangaricutiro, which was abandoned. By August, the two villages were buried beneath ash and lava. Paricutín lay beneath as much as 650 ft (200 m) of black, jagged lava; only the church towers at San Juan protruded above the blanket of lava. Mostly quiet eruptions of lava continued until 1952, when on March 4, the volcano had one final spasm. Today the volcano's oval base is covered with nearly 40 ft (12 m) of ash. A circular crater forms the summit, which stands 14,400 ft (3,170 m) asl. Plumes of steam continue to rise from fumaroles, but the volcano is dormant. Most cinder cones have a single period of activity and then never erupt again. Paricutín is not expected to be any different.

See also Trans-Mexican Volcanic Axis (Eje Volcánico Transversal)

Further Reading
Burton, Tony. 2013. "Paricutin Volcano in Mexico Celebrates Its 70th Birthday." Geo-Mexico. http://geo-mexico.com/?p=8716
"The Eruption of Paricutin (1943–1952)." n.d. How Volcanoes Work, San Diego State University. http://www.geology.sdsu.edu/how_volcanoes_work/Paricutin.html
Krystek, Lee. 2012. "Paricutin: The Volcano in a Cornfield." Seven Natural Wonders of the World. The Museum of Unnatural Mystery. http://www.unmuseum.org/7wonders/paricutin.htm
"Michoacán-Guanajuato." n.d. Global Volcanism Program, Smithsonian Institution. http://www.volcano.si.edu/volcano.cfm?vn=341060

Patagonian Ice Fields

Argentina and Chile

Geographic Overview. Two large icefields remain on the South American continent in the Patagonian Andes of Chile and Argentina. They are remnants of a much larger ice sheet that had formed during the last

Pleistocene glaciations. The icefields and their outlet glaciers are very sensitive to contemporary climate changes, and currently most are losing volume at their outlets and thinning at higher elevations.

Geographic Coordinates. Northern Patagonian Ice Field: 47°00'S, 73°30'W; Southern Patagonian Ice Field: 49°55'S, 73°32'W

Description. The Northern Patagonian Ice Field (NPI) is the smaller of the two, covering 1,620 mi^2 (4,200 km^2) and extending some 70 mi (124 km) from 46°30'S to 47°30'S. Twenty-eight outlet glaciers flow from it. Its ice today has a maximum thickness of 4,600 ft (1,400 m). The San Rafael Glacier reaches the Pacific Ocean and has the global distinction of being the sea level glacier closest to the equator. The Southern Patagonian Ice Field (SPI) covers 5,020 mi^2 (13,000 km^2) and is the second largest non-polar icefield in the world (the largest lies along the Alaska–Canada border) and the largest in the Southern Hemisphere outside of Antarctica.

The SPI is over 3,300 ft (1,000 m) thick and extends through three degrees of latitude (48°15'S—51°30'S) with a length of about 224 mi (360 km); it has an average width of about 25 mi (40 km). More than 50 outlet glaciers, most with areas of 15–62 mi^2 (40–160 km^2), flow from the SPI. Outlet glaciers from both icefields flow either west into the fjords of the Chilean coast or east into Argentine lakes. North of 49°S, the SPI is a smooth ice plateau with only a few nunataks rising above the icefield, the surface elevation of which averages about 4,900 ft (1,500 m) asl. Between 49°S and 50°S, three discontinuous north–south mountain ranges interrupt the field. The highest peaks, the active Volcán Lautaro and Cerro Francisco Moreno, rise to elevations of 11,089 ft (3,380 m) and 11,600 ft (3,536 m), respectively. To the east of the icefield are

Perito Morena Glacier, which empties into Lago Argentino, Argentina's largest lake, is neither advancing nor retreating, but does undergo cycles of advance and retreat. This photograph dates to February 2009. (Michael Hutchinson/Nature Picture Library/Corbis)

the high needles of the Torres del Paine in the Paine Cordillera and Mount Fitz Roy. The part of the international border between Argentina and Chile passing through this part of the SPI is still undefined and disputed. At 50°24'S, fjords penetrate the icefield from both sides, constricting it and almost cutting it in two. To the south, the icefield narrows and large ice plateaus are absent.

The Patagonian Ice Fields are fed by mid-latitude weather systems that bring abundant precipitation to the windward (western) side of the Andes at these latitudes. Under a marine west coast climate, western slopes receive some 145 in (3,700 mm) of rain at sea level. On the icefields, 235–295 in (6,000–7,500 mm) of precipitation falls mostly as snow. Little data exists for the eastern slopes, but it is visibly much drier. The relatively mild temperatures translate into high ablation rates—the rates at which ice mass is lost through sublimation, melting, and calving—that counteract the high amounts of precipitation. Today only one glacier, Brüggen Glacier, the largest western outflow from the SPI, is advancing. Between 1945 and 2001 it added 23 mi² (60 km²) of ice and moved 6.2 mi (10 km) downslope. Perito Morena Glacier, which empties into Lago Argentino, Argentina's largest lake, is in a state of equilibrium, neither advancing nor retreating, but undergoing cycles of advance and retreat. Other glaciers of the SPI are retreating, as are all glaciers of the NPI. The SPI lost mass 1.5 times faster in 2000–2012 than in 1975–2000.

Protected Areas. The NPI is fully contained in Chile's Laguna San Rafael National Park, named for the fjord (lagoon) left by the retreating San Rafael glacier. Three national parks contain parts of the SPI: Los Glaciares National Park in Argentina—a UNESCO World Heritage Site—and Bernardo O'Higgins and Torres del Paine national parks in Chile.

See also Torres del Paine

Further Reading

Glasser, Neil F., Michael J. Hambrey, and Krister Jansson. n.d. "The Patagonian Icefields: Landforms, Sediments and Glacier Fluctuations." Institute of Geography & Earth Sciences, Aberystwyth University. http://www.aber.ac.uk/en/iges/research-groups/centre-glaciology/research-intro/patagonia/

Lliboutry, Louis. 1999. "Glaciers of the *Wet Andes*." USGS. http://pubs.usgs.gov/pp/p1386i/chile-arg/wet/index.html

"Southern Patagonian Ice Field (Lat 48°15' to 51°30'S.)." 1999. USGS. http://pubs.usgs.gov/pp/p1386i/chile-arg/wet/southpat.html

Patagonian Plateau

Argentina

Geographic Overview. The Patagonian Plateau is one of the four exposed shields in South America. Supposedly Ferdinand Magellan referred to the region as *pâtagon* or land of giants after the tall native Tehuelche people, a nomadic group of hunters and fishers.

Geographic Coordinates. Approximately 46°00'S–51°30'S, 71°30'W–73°30'W

Description. The Patagonian Plateau is a series of *mesetas* or plateaus appearing as steps, descending in elevation from the eastern foothills of the Andes to the Atlantic Ocean between 39°S and 50°S. Each level ends at an escarpment some 300 ft (100 m) high. Typically the surfaces are strewn with pebbles and gravel of glacial or glacio-fluvial origin, the product of Pleistocene glaciation and called by the naturalist Charles Darwin, who explored the region during his famous voyage on *HMS Beagle, rodadas patagónicos*. Reworked by Holocene stream action and by wind, the finer materials have been removed. (Some reappear as loess deposits in the Pampa region of Argentina and Uruguay.)

A number of large rivers cross Patagonia from west to east, including the Rio Chubut, Rio Mayo, and Rio Descado. Other west–east trending depressions hold large lakes, such as Lago Musters and Lago Colhue Huapi. Patagonia lies in the rain shadow of the Southern Andes and therefore has an arid to semiarid climate. The strong, constant westerlies of the Roaring Forties dominate and bring in Pacific airmasses that dry as they descend the eastern slopes of the mountains. Almost half the precipitation falls during austral winter, when the subpolar low pressure system intensifies and the ocean is warmer than the land. In the north and in the south, Atlantic air masses also contribute moisture, making these parts somewhat more humid than the central plateau. While the north receives up to 24 in (600 mm) a year and the south up to 14 in (350 mm), the central area receives less than 8 in (200 mm), some as snow. Latitude determines that temperatures are low, but proximity to the sea in this narrowing cone of South America makes them less extreme than in similar latitudes of the Northern Hemisphere. At 45°S in Chubut Province, Argentina, the coldest month of the year, July, has a mean temperature of 33°F (2°C) and the warmest month, January, a mean of 57°F (14°C). Even in summer, however, the wind chill factor is pronounced so sensible air temperatures average 40°F (4.2°C).

Vegetation reflects the west–east gradient in moisture and topography. In the most humid belt next to the mountains, the subandean zone, a grass-steppe of tussock fescue grasses occurs. Eastward as the climate becomes semiarid, a shrub-steppe with feather grasses and cushion plants dominates. In the most arid parts of the central plateau is a semidesert with a sparse cover of dwarf shrubs less than a foot (30 cm) high. Another area of shrub-steppe is found on the coast surrounding Golfo San Jorge, where Atlantic sea breezes and westerlies crossing large lakes add more moisture to the air. Throughout Patagonia, along rivers and creeks, near springs, and in valleys are flood meadows (*mallines*) and prairies with 100 percent cover of grasses, rushes, and sedges.

Biota. The Patagonian fauna exhibits low diversity but high endemism in most groups. Larger mammals include guanaco, mara or Patagonian hare, viscacha, foxes, Patagonian weasel, and puma. Fewer than 250 bird species are recorded from the steppes, including the Lesser or Darwin's Rhea, Patagonian Tinamou, Patagonian Mockingbird, and Patagonian Yellow-Finch. All 33 lizard, 11 snake, and the single turtle species are either restricted to Patagonia or shared with the Andes. The ten amphibian species are mostly endemic to the region.

Environmental Issues. Sheep and cattle were introduced to the Patagonian steppe in the early 20th century. Overgrazing has led to a decline in tussock grasses, less plant cover overall, and encroachment of shrubs in western Patagonia. Today continued sheep grazing and, increasingly, the extraction of oil are causing desertification and rapidly changing the landscape.

Further Reading

Paruelo, José María, Estebán G. Jobbágy, Martín Oesterheld, Rodolfo A. Gollussscio, and Martín R. Aguiar. 2007. "The Grasslands and Steppes of Patagonia and the Rio del la Plata Plains." In *The Physical Geography of South America*, edited by Thomas T. Veblen, Kenneth R. Young, and Antony R. Orme, 232–248. New York: Oxford University Press.

Woodward, Susan L. 2009. *Grassland Biomes*. Greenwood Guides to Biomes of the World. Westport, CT: Greenwood Press.

Patos Lagoon (Lagoa dos Patos)

Brazil

Geographic Overview. Patos Lagoon is a major feature of the southern Brazil coastal plain and, with a surface area of 4,000 mi² (10,360 km²), the largest choked lagoon in the world. Most believe the name comes from indigenous peoples, but since it translates from the Portuguese as "lake of the ducks," some maintain that the name refers the ducks raised by 16th century Jesuit settlers along its shores.

Geographic Coordinates. 31°06'S, 51°15'W

Description. As typical of coastal lagoons, Patos Lagoon is a shallow body of water oriented parallel to the coastline. A 20-mile (32 km) wide sand bar almost completely separates it from the Atlantic Ocean. Only a single, narrow inlet, the Río Grande, connects it to the open sea. This entrance to the lagoon is about 50 ft (15 m deep) and half a mile (800 m) wide. At its mouth at 32°S is the port city of Río Grande in the Brazilian state of Río Grande do Sul. Patos Lagoon measures about 180 mi (290 km) long and 40 mi (64 km) wide. Fresh water enters from Jacuí River and from Mirim Lagoon, another sizeable lagoon, by way of the São Gonçalo Channel, which is navigable by small boats. Roughly 80 percent of Patos Lagoon is fresh water most of the time. The inlet has brackish water. Its constriction greatly reduces both outgoing fresh water and incoming salt water, that is, it "chokes" the lagoon and causes water to be retained in the lagoon for a relatively long time. It also serves to eliminate tidal influences in both Patos and Mirim lagoons. Salinity in Patos Lagoon varies, sometimes rapidly, with changes in wind direction and rain or drought. In winter, the lagoon may be entirely fresh water, but southerly winds generated at the polar front can drive seawater into the Río Grande and the lower lagoon. During La Niña years, salt water may intrude 125 mi (200 km) or farther into the lagoon.

Biota. A variety of habitats is found in Patos Lagoon making it a prime area for spawning, feeding, nesting, and roosting. Much of the lagoon is less than 5 ft (1.5 m) deep; but deeper open water does exist to depths of 16 ft (5 m), and channels may be more than 20 ft (6 m) deep. Fringing salt marshes are inhabited by terrestrial isopods, amphipods, insects, and spiders; crabs are abundant in the lower marsh. The dense salt marsh grasses offer safe breeding areas for Red-gartered Coot, Black-necked Swan, Snowy Egret, and Green Heron, as well as Brown-hooded Gull and Trudeau's Tern. Seagrass beds offer food and protection for the larvae and juveniles of fish and numerous invertebrates. The leaves and shoots of the wigeon-grass are encrusted with epiphytes, dominated by diatoms, and an epifauna of grazing invertebrates. Tidal flats and subtidal soft-bottomed areas without vegetation are dominated by burrowing invertebrates. Rock jetties at the inlet offer the only stable hard substrate in 435 mi (700 km) of sandy beach between 32°S and 34°S and occur at a biogeographic mixing zone between tropical and cold-temperate species. Barnacles and encrusting algae on the rocks provide food not otherwise available at these latitudes.

Patos Lagoon provides critical habitat for the reproduction of some aquatic organisms and the larvae, juveniles, and subadults of both estuarine residents and marine species, some of which are of commercially important species. It is a nursery area for whitemouth croaker, black drum, mullets, and the flatfish *Paralichthys orbygnianus*. Bottlenose dolphins and sea lions come into the lagoon to hunt fish.

Environmental Issues. Overfishing led to the collapse of croaker and drum fisheries in the 1970s. High-nutrient loads from urban sewage can lead to toxic blooms of cyanobacteria. Dredging to allow ships to pass into the ports of Rio Grande and Porto Alegre, the state capital located at the head of the lagoon, has changed patterns of water circulation and deposition. Rising sea level, a consequence of global climate change, threatens to flood the lagoon with seawater.

Further Reading

Knoppers, Bastiaan and Björn Kjerfve. 1999. "Coastal Lagoons of Southeastern Brazil: Physical and Biogeochemical Characteristics." In *Estuaries of South America: Their Geomorphology and Dynamics*, edited by Gerardo M. E Perillo, M. Cintia Piccolo, and Mario Pino-Quivara, 35–66. Berlin: Springer.

Seeliger, U. 2000. "Patos Lagoon Estuary." In *Coastal Marine Ecosystems of Latin America*, edited by U. Seeliger and B. Kjerfve, 167–183. Berlin: Springer.

Peloponnesus

Greece

Geographic Overview. The Peloponnesus peninsula, including the Greek city states of Mycenae and Sparta, played a significant role in ancient Greece. Prominent ruins include Olympia, which was the site of the Greek Olympic Games, and remnants of ancient Byzantine civilizations, as well as medieval Venetian, Frankish, and Turkish sites. The natural landscape includes sandy beaches, rocky shores, caves, and both bare and forested mountains.

Geographic Coordinates. 36°26'N–38°20'N, 21°05'E–23°28'E

Description. The Peloponnesus is an irregular, hand-shaped peninsula connected to the rest of Greece by the narrow and low Corinth Isthmus, 4 mi (6.4 km) wide and 200 ft (6 m) asl, southwest of Athens. The peninsula, covering 8,278 mi² (21,439 km²), lies in the Mediterranean Sea between the Ionian Sea to the West and the Aegean Sea to the east. The Corinth Canal through the isthmus, connecting the Gulf of Corinth on the west with the Saronic Gulf on the east, was completed in 1893. Its small size, 70 ft (21.3 m) wide, however, prevented it from making an economic impact on transportation, and it is used primarily for tourist vessels.

Most of the Peloponnesus is a dissected mountain landscape, primarily limestone and marble, with a deeply indented coastline. The Aroania Mountains (also called Chelmos) run east–west south of the Gulf of Corinth. The tallest mountain in the Peloponessus, Profitis Ilias, 7,897 ft (2,407 m), is in the Taygetus Mountains, which comprise the central peninsula in the south, between Kalamata and Sparta, and terminate at Cape Matapan, the Peloponnesus's southernmost point. The Parnon Mountains form the southeastern peninsula, which terminates at Cape Maleas.

Caves are plentiful in the limestone rocks. Diros Caves, an area of approximately 355,225 ft² (33,000 m²) on the coast near Areopolis in the southern Taygetos peninsula, is flooded with seawater and can be toured by boat.

The Peloponnesus has a typical mediterranean climate, with hot summers and mild winters. Summer temperatures usually hover around 85°F (30°C), but can rise to 104°F (40°C). Winter temperatures average 50°–65° F (10°–18° C) and rarely drop below freezing. Both winters and summers are cooler in the mountains, with winter snow at higher elevations. Precipitation, 16–24 in (400–600 mm) falls in winter. The region is prone to wildfires during the hot, dry summers.

Geologic History. The Peloponnesus consists of a variety of imbricated thrust sheets of marine sedimentary rocks pushed together and upward during the Alpine Orogeny. They were subsequently reworked by extension and normal faulting. The thrust sheets are composed of different north–south trending zones of marine rock layers that were deposited in a geosyncline from the Jurassic to the Tertiary. On the west is the Ionian zone, tracing an arc that includes Crete, Rhodes, and Cypress. It is composed of several layers of limestone overlying a 5,000 ft (1,500 m) gypsum base (from the Messinian Salinity Crisis). The Gavron–Tripolitza is a 60 mi (100 km) wide zone in the Central Peloponnessus, separated into two sections by the Pindus zone. It consists of limestone topped by thick flysch (clastic marine deposits). The Pindus zone is cherty limestone and radiolarites, which have a high silica content. The Sub-Pelagonian zone in the eastern Peloponnesus has several layers, flysch-overlying limestone, which in turn overlies ophiolite (oceanic crust) and dolomite.

Two structural zones currently affect Peloponnesus physiography. The outer, or southern, zone, between the Peloponnesus and Crete, where it overlies the Hellenic trench and subduction of the African oceanic crust beneath the Aegean plate, is compressional, resulting in uplift of mountains. The inner, or northern, zone, where the Aegean plate is being pulled apart and is subjected to tensional forces, affects the majority of the peninsula. The Gulf of Corinth is a series of rifts forming a complicated graben. A complex pattern of normal faulting and shearing due to extension of crust is responsible for the peninsulas that project into the Mediterranean Sea. The region remains seismically active along many of these faults.

Biota. Natural vegetation is maquis, consisting of sclerophyllous shrubs and scrubby trees, both evergreen and deciduous. Windward western slopes retain remnants of oak, fir, and pine forests, but much of the landscape is under cultivation, including olives, citrus, and other fruits.

See also Aegean Sea; Mediterranean Sea

Further Reading

Greeka. "Peloponnese Geography." http://www.greeka.com/peloponnese/geography.htm

Karpodini-Dimitriadi, E. 1988. *The Peloponnese, A Traveller's Guide to the Sites, Monuments and History.* Athens: Rkdotike Athenon S.A.

Persian Gulf

Indian Ocean

Geographic Overview. With an estimated two-thirds of the world's oil and one-third of the world's natural gas reserves, the Persian Gulf region in the Middle East is the richest petroleum province in the world. Tanker traffic from ports in several countries transports both crude and refined oil through the Strait of Hormuz to the Indian Ocean and the rest of the world. The region played a significant role in the historical development of civilization and continues to be a controversial region because of the value of the oil fields.

Geographic Coordinates. 24°00'N–30°30'N, 48° 00'E–56°25'E

Description. The Persian Gulf, also called the Arabian Gulf, is approximately 615 mi (990 km) from Iraq in the northwest to the Strait of Hormuz at Oman in the southeast. It is 125–210 mi (200–340 km) wide, narrowing to 35 mi (55 km) at Hormuz, and covers approximately 93,000 mi² (241,000 km²). The gulf is bordered on the north by Iran, on the northwest by Iraq and Kuwait, and on the south and southeast by

Saudi Arabia, Bahrain, Qatar, United Arab Emirates, and Oman. A shallow body of water overlying continental crust, the Persian Gulf has a mean depth of 115 ft (35 m). The western part is 33–100 ft (10–30 m) deep, while the Iranian side is deeper. Except for the entrance, which is 360 ft (110 m) deep, the deepest parts are 300 ft (90 m).

The gulf is almost enclosed in the east by the northward extension of the Oman Mountains at the Musandam Peninsula. The southern shoreline is interrupted by a slight arch that produces the Qatar peninsula. Except for cliffs at Qatar and Musandam, the west coast, on the stable Arabian Shield is characterized by low relief, sandy beaches, and small lagoons. The northern shore in Iran is mountainous, often with cliffs extending down to a narrow coastal plain with sandy beaches, intertidal flats, and small estuaries. The broad delta of the Tigris, Euphrates, and Karun rivers occupies the northwest shore. High salinity and evaporation create extensive coastal salt flats called sebkhas.

The majority of fresh water entering the gulf comes from the Shatt al-Arab (Arvand River), which begins at the confluence of the Tigris and Euphrates in Iraq, and from the Karun in Iran. A few ephemeral streams and springs also flow from Iran, but no fresh water enters the gulf from Arabia. Because evaporation exceeds inflow, salinity is 37 to 41 ppt. The water is rich in calcium carbonate, which often encrusts mud or sands. Water from the Arabian Sea enters through the Strait of Hormuz at the surface, and saltier water exits at depth. General circulation in the gulf is counterclockwise. The tidal range, 4–11 ft (1.2–3.4 m), varies with location.

The dry, subtropical climate is hot, but humid, with frequent dust storms and little rain. Summer temperatures may rise to 122°F (50°C), and winter minima drop to 37°F (3°C). Surface water temperature is generally 75–90°F (24–32°C), but may drop to 60°F (16°C) in the northwest.

Geologic History. The Persian Gulf is part of a larger sedimentation basin, which includes the Mesopotamia area of the Tigris and Euphrates Rivers, from northern Syria to eastern Oman. Beginning in the Paleozoic (545 mya), the northeastern continental shelf of the Arabian Plate accumulated sediments of limestone, marls, evaporites, and organic matter. As the Arabian Plate moved toward and eventually collided with Eurasia, the leading edge of the Arabian Plate subducted and pulled down seafloor with it, which continued to accumulate sediments and depressed even further. Sediment deposition is asymmetrical, hundreds of feet thick just northeast of the Arabian Shield increasing to more than 59,000 ft (18,000 m) in the northeastern basin. The northern part of the gulf, adjacent to the mountains in Iran, remains seismically active.

When sea level was lower during Pleistocene glacials, the gulf was land, probably dotted with lakes and swamps. During the last glacial maximum (70,000–17,000 years ago), the gulf was a valley crossed by one river, formed by the convergence of the Tigris, Euphrates, and Karun, which drained to the Strait of Hormuz. As sea level rose at the close of the Pleistocene, the Gulf was flooded with seawater. Sediment deposits indicate that at its peak, 3,000 years ago, the gulf waters extended inland to Nasiriyya on the Euphrates River and past Qurnah on the Tigris River, approximately 125 mi (200 km) northwest of its present shoreline. Deltaic deposits from the Tigris and Euphrates rivers filled in the head of the gulf, creating today's marshes and lakes

Biota. High temperatures and salinity limit flora and fauna to fewer species than found in the Indian Ocean. Coastal zones support mangroves and corals. The gulf has over 700 species of fish, most of which are native and approximately 80 percent associated with coral reefs. Marine life includes sea turtles, whales, dolphins, and a large population of dugongs. Several species of migratory birds use the Persian Gulf.

Protected Areas. Harra Protected Area in the Strait of Khuran near the Iranian coast, a Ramsar Site and a Biosphere Reserve, is being considered as a World Heritage Site for protection of its gray mangroves, the largest stand in the Persian Gulf. Several areas in Saudi Arabian waters have been proposed as Marine Protected Areas. Qarnein Island, a combination of sand, rock, and coral habitats, was declared a Marine Protected Area by the United Arab Emirates.

Environmental Issues. The multitude of traffic and offshore installations dealing with petroleum products presents potential hazards. Artificial island

and real estate developments and oil spills have serious negative implications for local habitats, including those of mangrove and dugongs. Coral populations are declining due to careless dumping of waste. The Collared Kingfisher (*Todiramphus chloris kalbaensis*) is extremely rare and endangered. Detrimental effects of prolonged war continue.

See also Arabian Peninsula; Mesopotamia, Tigris River, and Euphrates River; Zagros Mountains

Further Reading

Goudie, Andrew S. 2002. "The Middle East." In *Geomorphological Landscapes of the World, 1. Great Warm Deserts of the World, Landscapes and Evolution*, 215–253. Oxford: Oxford University Press.

Konyuhov, A. and B. Maleki. 2006. "The Persian Gulf Basin: Geological History, Sedimentary Formations, and Petroleum Potential." *Lithology and Mineral Resources* 41: 344.

The Petén

Guatemala

Geographic Overview. The Petén region of northern Guatemala, together with Belize and Mexico's Yucatán Peninsula, forms the largest expanse of karst topography on the North American continent. The Petén itself comprises two Central American physiographic provinces, the Petén lowlands in the north and the northern part of the Maya Highlands in the south. Like Belize and the Yucatán, the Petén was home to Classic Mayan civilization.

Geographic Coordinates. 15°54'N–17°50'N, 89°10'W–91°26'W

Description. The northernmost section of the Petén, now included in the Maya Biosphere Reserve, is an extension of the Yucatán Peninsula. Elevations range from 650 to 1,130 ft (200–400 m) asl. Elevations are lowest in the west, but rise onto a plateau in the east as the Maya Mountains are approached. Classic karst features such as lack of surface streams, sinkholes, and cave systems have developed since the area was raised above sea level.

The southern edge of the gently rolling lowlands is marked by an east–west chain of lakes that includes Laguna Perdida, Lago Petén Itzá, and Lago Yaxhá. Immediately to the south is the Lacandón Range, a series of low ridges and valleys marking the northern edge of the Maya Highlands. The mountains do not exceed 2,600 ft (800 m) in elevation and form a broad arc running from the Sierra Madre de Chiapas in Mexico across the Petén to the Maya Mountains of Belize. The limestone and dolomites of the Lacandón Range are tightly folded and have developed into a rugged karst terrain with sinkholes, mogotes, and occasional towers. It is particularly rugged in the east, where steep escarpments more than 300 ft (100 m) high edge long fault-controlled depressions. In the Maya Mountains, the ancient granite basement rock of the Maya Block is exposed. They reach their maximum elevation, about 3,940 ft (1,200 m) asl, in Belize. The southern Petén of the Maya Highlands is higher than the Petén lowlands

Most of the Petén was originally covered with a semideciduous tropical rainforest. In central Petén, savanna occupies lower areas while forest grows on the limestone hills. The savanna may or not be natural. (It could be the product of long-term disturbance during the Mayan period.) The forests of southern Petén have been largely cleared in recent times as land use practices favor subsistence agriculture and cattle raising.

Geologic History. The Petén lowlands are on the Yucatán Platform and are underlain by thick beds of carbonate rock that accumulated on the Maya Block while it was submerged under a warm shallow sea 150–60 mya.

Protected Areas. The tropical forest is best preserved in the north in the Maya Biosphere Reserve, which contains several national parks and other preserves, including Tikal National Park. Much of this forest may be only 1,000 years old, however. The great Mayan city-states of Tikal, Uaxactún, and Caracol and numerous smaller cities were located here and the forest was cleared for agriculture, settlements, and monumental ceremonial centers. Tikal, at its height (A.D. 700–800), had a population of 90,000; and other dwelling sites have discovered scattered throughout the park area. More than 3,000 buildings dating from 600 B.C.–A.D. 900 were reclaimed by the forest and remained largely hidden until the 19th century.

Flooded savanna and marsh, a Ramsar Wetland of International Importance, occurs in the northwestern corner of the Petén in the Lagunas del Tigre National Park within the Maya Biosphere Reserve.

Environmental Issues. Deforestation as land is cleared for agriculture continues to threaten remaining natural areas.

See also Central American Isthmus; Yucatán Peninsula

Further Reading

Herrera-MacBryde, Olga and Jane Villa-Lobos. n.d. "Peten Region and Maya Biosphere Reserve Data Sheet." Department of Botany, National Museum of Natural History, Smithsonian Institution. http://botany.si.edu/projects/cpd/ma/ma13.htm

Marshall, Jeffrey S. 2007. "The Geomorphology and Physiographic Provinces of Central America." In *Central America: Geology, Resources and Hazards*, edited by Jochen Bundschum and Guillermo E. Alvarado, 75–122. New York: Taylor & Francis.

"Tikal National Park." 2013. World Heritage Centre, UNESCO. http://whc.unesco.org/en/list/64

Wallace, David Rains. 1997. "Central American Landscapes." In *Central America: A Natural and Cultural History*. Edited by Anthony G. Coates, 72–96. New Haven, CT: Yale University Press.

Philippine Islands

Pacific Ocean

Geographic Overview. The 7,107 islands comprising the Republic of the Philippines lie at the edge of converging plates on the western side of the Pacific Ring of Fire and at the crossroads between the Asian and Australian faunal regions. A megadiversity country as defined by Conservation International, the islands have unsurpassed degrees of vertebrate endemism and are exceptionally species-rich in terms of both plants and animals. Even with taxonomic inventories incomplete, the Philippine islands host the largest number of species per unit area anywhere on Earth.

Geographic Coordinates. 21°10'N to 4°40'N, 116°40'E to 126°34'E

Description. The Philippine islands lie south of Taiwan and northeast of Borneo in the western Pacific Ocean. To their east is the Philippine Sea and to the west the South China, Sulu, and Celebes seas. The archipelago has two large islands, Luzon in the north and Mindanao in the south. Between them is a swarm of smaller islands known collectively as the Visayas. The elongate island of Palawan, the only land area that is not an oceanic island, stretches southwestward from the main island groups nearly to Borneo. Palawan serves as the southeastern limit of the South China Sea, separating it from the Sulu Sea. The Sulu Archipelago, another group of Philippine islands reaching southwestward, divides the Sulu and Celebes seas.

The Philippines are mountainous islands with narrow coastal plains. Most are part of a chain of stratovolcanoes some 745 mi (1,200 km) long. Among the 22 active volcanoes are Mayon, Canaloan, Bulusan, Taal, Hibok-Hibok, and Mount Pinatubo. Pinatubo, in western Luzon, erupted in June 1991 after 460 years of dormancy. Its ash plume rose 18.6 mi (30 km) into the air and cooled global temperatures by 0.9°F (0.5°C). Taal, also in Luzon, is identified by the International Association of Volcanology and Chemistry of the Earth's Interior as one of 16 Decade Volcanoes, volcanoes close to populated areas and with a history of destructive eruptions. Taal is unusually low for a stratovolcano, standing only 1,030 ft (311 m) asl. Mt. Apo, a stratovolcano on Mindanao, is the highest peak in the Philippines, rising 9,692 ft (2,954 m) asl. Large north–south trending basins filled with marine, fluvial, and deltaic sediments form lowlands on many of the larger islands.

The Philippines have a wet, tropical climate influenced by the Asian monsoon. Heaviest rains occur with the summer monsoon from May through October. The winter monsoon brings cooler and drier air, but only the western parts of Luzon, the Visayas, and Palawan experience a true dry season from December to February. On mountain slopes on the east coast as much as 197 in (5,000 mm) of rain is received annually. In sheltered valleys less than 39 in (1,000 mm) of rain falls. The islands are in the Pacific typhoon belt, and typhoons are a major natural hazard—along with earthquakes and volcanic eruptions—in the Philippines.

Most islands were originally covered with tropical rainforest. Higher peaks host up to five altitudinally determined vegetation zones from lowland rainforests to montane forests to summit scrublands.

The mountainous Philippine Islands are comprised of several stratovolcanoes caused by both converging and subducting plates. The area remains seismically active and hazardous. (Simon Gurney/Dreamstime.com)

Geologic History. Palawan is a microcontinent that separated from mainland Asia during the Mesozoic Era, about 50 mya. Later rifting created new oceanic crust that became the seafloor of the South China Sea beginning about 20 mya. The other islands were a volcanic arc developed between the converging Eurasian–Sunderland Plate and the Philippine Plate. The islands are bounded by oceanic trenches to the east and west. On the west, the oceanic crust beneath the South China Sea is subducting into the Manila Trench system, giving rise to a chain of stratovolcanoes that includes Pinatubo and Taal. In the east, oceanic crust on the Philippine Plate has been subducting into the Philippine Trench system for 3–5 million years. The two opposing subduction zones run for 934 mi (1,500 km) and have created a 250 mi (400 km) wide deformed zone known as the Philippine Mobile Belt, a seismically active area traversed its entire length by a major strike-slip fault, the Philippine Fault Zone. The

Philippines experience as many as 20 earthquakes a day, although most are not felt. Some, however, are catastrophic; between 1968 and 2003 there were 12 earthquakes of M 6.2–M 7.9.

Biota. The Philippines possess an extraordinary number of vertebrates and a high degree of endemism. Other life-forms are not well known, and continuing research may reveal equally high numbers of invertebrates and plants. Certainly the country has the highest rate of discovery of new species at this time. Currently, more than 15,000 plants and 38,000 animals are reported in the Philippines. Among the more than 100 endemic mammals are Philippine flying "lemurs"; the Philippine tarsier, on the world's smallest primates; cloud rats, spiny rats, and other rodents; five species of maned pig; and the tamaraw, a dwarf water buffalo. The Philippine Eagle is the world's largest eagle in terms of length; one of over 170 endemic birds, it is the national bird of the Philippines. There are a number of endemic frogs, including fanged frogs, litter frogs, and stream frogs; four endemic genera of snakes, and flying lizards. Endemic plants include several species of *Rafflesia*, parasitic plants with enormous flowers that smell like rotten meat.

The high biodiversity of the Philippines is explained by its long and complex geologic history. Most recently, falling sea levels during the mid- to late Pleistocene (350,000–12,000 years ago) repeatedly connected individual islands into what are called Pleistocene Aggregated Island Complexes (PAICs); subsequent sea level rises separated and isolated the islands again and again. This process permitted evolutionary diversification during periods of isolation to be followed by colonization and the accumulation of species during times of lower sea level. The variety of habitats due to elevational and climatic gradients facilitated ecological specialization and adaptive radiation in many groups.

Protected Areas. The Philippines has a number of national parks, natural parks, wildlife sanctuaries, and protected landscapes and seascapes that protect almost 12 percent of the land area. Puerto Princesa Subterranean National Park on Palawan protects a karst landscape with an underground river as well as natural habitats running from sea level to mountaintops. Mt. Apo Natural Park is a UNESCO World Heritage Site protecting a variety of vegetation zones and endemic plants and animals.

Environmental Issues. The Philippines lost about half of their rich tropical forests during the 20th century as a result of war, industrialization, and plantation agriculture (hemp, bananas, sugar, and copra). Commercial logging and mining (gold, copper, sulfur, nickel cobalt, iron, etc.) also degraded forests. Current estimates are that 4–8 percent of old-growth forests remain.

Natural hazards and their mitigation are major issues. Communities must be prepared for earthquakes, volcanic eruptions, typhoon, and landslides.

See also Puerto Princesa Subterranean River National Park

Further Reading

Brown, Rafe and Arvin C. Diesmos. 2009. In *Encyclopedia of Islands*, edited by Rosemary G. Gillespie and David A. Clague, 723–732. Berkeley: University of California Press.

Yumul, Graciano, Jr., Carla Dimanlata, Karlo Queaño, Edanjarlo Marquez. 2009. "Philippines, Geology." In *Encyclopedia of Islands*, edited by Rosemary G. Gillespie and David A. Clague, 732–738. Berkeley: University of California Press.

Pico de Orizaba (Citlatépetl)

Mexico

Geographic Overview. The dormant, snowcapped stratovolcano Pico de Orizaba on the southeastern edge of the Mexican Plateau is Mexico's highest peak and North America's highest volcano and third highest mountain. In terms of local relief (the difference in elevation between the summit and the base), Orizaba is second only to Mt. Kilimanjaro in Tanzania. Reports give different figures, but in general agree that it rises at least 14,435 ft (4,400 m) above the surrounding landscape.

Geographic Coordinates. 19°02'N, 97°16'W

Description. Pico de Orizaba or Citlatépetl lies 68 mi (110 km) inland from the Gulf of Mexico on the border of the Mexican states of Veracruz and Puebla. Figures given for its elevation vary, but the summit stands somewhere around 18,619 ft (5,675 m) asl. The sunrise alpenglow is clearly visible from the sea well before the lowlands of the coastal plain receive the morning light. This massive cone is at the eastern end of the Trans-Mexican Volcanic Axis and is superimposed upon the collapsed edifices of two earlier stratovolcanoes built up on the site.

The summit bears a steep-walled oval crater almost 1,000 ft (300 m) deep and 1,300–1,640 ft (400–500 m) in diameter. Surrounding the crater is Mexico's largest ice cap and firn field (Gran Glaciar Norte), the source of several outlet glaciers on the northern and western flanks of the mountain. A single, separate niche glacier (Glaciar Oriental) occupies a small, funnel-shaped valley on the eastern flank. Gran Glaciar Norte is about 165 ft (50 m) thick and has a surface area of 3.5 mi^2 (9.0 km^2). It descends 2.2 mi (3.5 km) down the north side of the volcano to an elevation of approximately 16,000 ft (5,000 m), where it divides into two outlet glaciers, Lengua del Chichimeco and Jamapa. The former flows another 1.2 mi (2 km) down the mountain, terminating at 15,550 ft

(4,740 m) asl; while Jamapa continues for 0.9 mi (1.5 km) to end in two ice fans at 15,260 ft (4,650 m) and 15,520 ft (4,640 m) asl respectively. The other five outlet glaciers leave the west side of Gran Glaciar Norte; two of these—Glaciar del Toro and Glaciar de la Barba—become icefalls on giant lava steps at 16,170 ft (4,940 m) and 16,700 ft (5,090 m), respectively. They end as ice blocks at the heads of stream valleys 660–990 ft (200–300 m) below. The three other western glaciers are Glaciar Noroccidental, Glaciar Occidental, and Glaciar Suroccidental. With the recent loss of the glaciers on Popocatépetl, Pico de Orizaba and Iztaccíhuatl are the only two mountains in Mexico where glaciers remain.

A mountain this high has distinct altitudinal zonation of climate and vegetation. Elevational differences are magnified by the prevailing trade winds, which bring in moist air masses from the Gulf of Mexico. In the east, a humid tropical climate at the foot of the volcano gives way to a cool subtropical highland climate type with a dry winter at about 10,500 ft (3,200 m). The northern slopes experience a cool subtropical highland climate all the way to 10,500 ft (3,200 m), while the southern slopes at these elevations are also essentially subtropical in their temperature patterns but warmer and more humid than on the opposite side of the mountain.

Downslope winds on the western flanks create a rain shadow effect and a cool semiarid climate occurs below 8,500 ft (2,600 m). At higher elevations the mountain climate tends to be similar on all exposures: between 10,000 and 14,000 ft (3,200–4,300 m) asl a cool continental climate prevails with a closed coniferous forest of the cold-tolerant Hartweg's pine (*Pinus hartwegii*) as evidence. Treeline occurs around 13,450 ft (4,100 m) and an alpine vegetation with scattered, shorter pines continues until snowline near 14,000 ft (4,300 m), where the year-round cold of tundra and ice cap climates leads to heavy snowfall throughout the year. The snow melts rapidly on the southern and southeastern sides of the peak, but it persists and replenishes glaciers on the northern and northwestern sides.

Geologic History. The first phase in the history of Orizaba occurred between 650,000 and 250,000 years ago, with the construction of Torrecillas Volcano, the collapse of which resulted in a huge debris avalanche that surged through gaps in the surrounding limestone foothills. The second volcano to occupy the site, Espolón de Oro, developed during another phase of volcanic activity 210,000–16,000 years ago. A remnant of its edifice appears today as a knob on the northwest flank of Orizaba. The contemporary cone dates to eruptions beginning about 16,000 years ago and continuing to the present. A number of eruptions were recorded during the Spanish colonial period in the 16th and 17th centuries. The last activity took place in 1846.

Environmental Issues. The volcano is not extinct and continues to present a hazard to nearby towns and cities, including the city of Orizaba at its base and for which it is named. At the same time, the mountain and its glaciers serve as a vital source of fresh water for the people of both states.

See also Popocatépetl and Iztaccíhuatl; Trans-Mexican Volcanic Axis (Eje Volcánico Transversal)

Further Reading
"Pico de Orizaba." n.d. Global Volcanism Program, Smithsonian Institution. http://www.volcano.si.edu/volcano.cfm?vn=341100

White, Sidney E. 2002. "Glaciers of North America—Glaciers of México." In *Satellite Image Atlas of Glaciers of the World*, edited by Richard S. Williams, Jr. and Jane G. Ferrigno. U.S. Geological Survey Professional Paper 1386-J-3, J384–J388. http://pubs.usgs.gov/pp/p1386j/mexico/mexico-lores.pdf

The Pilbara

Australia

Geographic Overview. The Pilbara region of west-central Western Australia lies on the Pilbara craton, where some of Earth's oldest rocks are exposed. Archaean microfossils of bacteria and large stromatolites dating back 3.4 billion years have been recovered from the North Pole Dome in the northern Pilbara. Enormous deposits of banded iron in the Hamersley Ranges of the southern Pilbara supply half the iron ore imported by Asian countries.

Geographic Coordinates. Approximately 20°S–24°S, 114°E–120°E

Description. The Pilbara is a sparsely inhabited oval-shaped upland in west-central Western Australia developed atop the ancient Pilbara craton. It extends from the Indian Ocean east to the Great Sandy Desert. The Ashburton River flows intermittently along its southern border. The Pilbara is cut through by the Fortescue River—also intermittent, which divides it into two distinct landscapes and geologic regions. On the northern Pilbara, sedimentary rocks and flood basalts blanket the greatly deformed basement greenstones of the craton. In places heaps of granitic boulders indicate the remnants of batholiths intruded into the greenstones 3.5–2.8 bya. Today their smooth, orange to deep purple faces are often covered with Aboriginal petroglyphs of unknown age. These rock piles are major surface features. Iron-rich flood basalts covered much of the Pilbara 2.8–2.7 bya. At the southern edge of the northern Pilbara, remnants appear as the flat-topped mesas and buttes of the Chichester Range. The highest point stands 2,027 ft (618 m) asl.

South of the Fortescue River, a banded iron formation originally deposited onto an ancient seabed, forms the 160 mi (258 km) long, northwest–southeast trending Hamersley Ranges. Alternating horizontal layers of red hematite (Fe_2O_3) and black magnetite (Fe_3O_4) are exposed in steep-sided gorges cut into the mountains. Four layers of impact ejecta containing telltale iridium have also been identified in these rocks. Mt. Meharry, the highest point in the Hamersley Range (and in Western Australia), reaches 4,100 ft (1,250 m) asl.

The Pilbara ends at the Indian Ocean as a coastal plain composed of young sediments from the Ashburton and DeGrey Rivers. Only near Dampier do outcrops of Precambrian rocks form headlands.

Pilbara region has a tropical, arid–semiarid climate with annual precipitation ranging between 7 and 12 in (180–300 mm). The wettest areas are found along the coast and in the Hamersley Ranges. Prolonged droughts interrupted by tropical cyclones are characteristic. Runoff is usually of short duration, but pools remain in many watercourses throughout the year. Spinifex grasslands cover much of the area with snappy gum (*Eucalyptus leucophloia*) steppe on the mountains. Red river gum (*Eucalyptus camaldulensis*) lines some drainages. The abundance of iron-rich rock results in a deep red regolith cover across the entire Pilbara region.

Geologic History. The Pilbara craton consists of primordial crust, a greenstone rich in magnesium and iron. It was repeatedly reworked, deformed, and intruded by plumes of magma and became a permanent crustal block about 2.9 bya and had assembled with other cratons to form Rodinia about 1.5 bya. Flood basalts, perhaps related to asteroid impacts, covered the deformed greenstones and granites of the Pilbara 2.8–2.7 bya. The banded iron formation of the Hamersley Ranges resulted from the erosion of iron-rich bedrock on the land being deposited in a shallow sea sometime after the origin of oxygen-producing cyanobacteria. The scenario proposed is that iron(II) oxide (ferrous oxide or FeO) needed abundant oxygen from living organisms to be changed into hematite and magnetite.

Biota. The Pilbara is best known for its fossil biota. Giant stromatolites, layered dome structures constructed by cyanobactaria, up to 6.5 ft (2 m) tall have been discovered at the North Pole Dome in the northern Pilbara that date to 2.7 bya. Half-mile (1 km) size remnants of an even older stromatolite carbonate platform (3.43 billion yrs) have been found in the Strelley Pool Chert formation. Cyanobacteria were the first photosynthetic life-forms on Earth. The oxygen they produced polluted the water and led to the first mass extinction on the planet, with the loss of 90 percent of the microbial species that preceded them. Microscopic spherules in the chert have been interpreted as the fossils of some of these early sulfur-based bacteria and thus the earliest evidence of life on Earth.

Of conservation importance among the living biota is a highly diverse community of subterranean life-forms including amphipods, copepods, isopods, and ostracods.

Protected Areas. Millstream-Chichester National Park is located in the Chichester Range and Karijini National Park in the Hamersley Ranges.

Environmental Issues. Parts of the Pilbara are threatened by the expansion of iron ore mining, which currently supplies half of the iron ore imported by Asia. With it will come an expansion of infrastructure needed for its export.

See also Shark Bay

Further Reading

Johnson, David. 2009. *The Geology of Australia*, 2nd ed. New York: Cambridge University Press.

Morrison, Reg. n.d. "The Pilbara, Evolution's Turning Point." http://regmorrison.edublogs.org/files/2011/01/lifes-turningpoint-253mwf3.pdf

Plitvice Lakes National Park

Croatia

Geographic Overview. Plitvice Lakes in the Dinaric Alps of central Croatia is a karst landscape of lakes, travertine terraces, caves, waterfalls, and forest. Travertine, or tufa, of biogenetic origin, facilitated by the growth of mosses and algae, is characteristic of Plitvice. The national park not only preserves the unique travertine and lake landscape, but also provides protection for several rare and endangered plant and animal species.

Geographic Coordinates. 44°05'N, 15°37'E

Description. Approximately 85 mi (140 km) south of Zagreb, Plitvice is located on a plateau between two mountain areas in the Dinaric Alps. Mala Kapela Mountain, 4,200 ft (1,280 m), forms the western boundary of the park, and Plješevica Mountain, 5,380 ft (1,640 m), forms the eastern boundary, as well as the border with Bosnia and Herzegovina. Plitvice is the largest national park in Croatia, covering 72,850 ac (29,482 ha) and ranging in elevation from 1,338 ft (408 m) to 4,528 ft (1,380 m) asl. In the center of the park is a series of 16 step-like lakes, separated by natural dams of travertine and linked by waterfalls. The 12 upper lakes are generally large, occupying a dolomite valley and surrounded by thick forest, while the four lower lakes are smaller, enclosed within a deep limestone canyon and surrounded by sparse underbrush vegetation.

Various streams and underground drainage from the forested mountains feed the upper lakes. Within its 7.5 mi (12 km) length, lake elevations drop 436 ft (133 m). The tallest waterfall is in the downstream end of the lake system, where Plitvice River falls 256 ft (78 m) at Veliki Waterfall, becoming the Korana River. The distinctive colors of the lakes—azure, green, gray, or blue—change according to mineral and organism content and to angle of sunlight.

Geologic History. The carbonate rocks of the Plitvice Lakes region are dolomite and limestone. The less permeable dolomite of the upper lakes allowed water to accumulate in large lake basins. The small lakes in the limestone canyon to the northeast may be the remains of collapsed caverns. Faults that coincide with the barriers between lakes may have facilitated the growth of travertine. Calcium carbonate ($CaCO_3$), dissolved from the carbonate rocks by carbonic acid (carbon dioxide and water), is deposited when the water can no longer hold the mineral in solution. As $CaCO_3$ deposition builds above the water surface, mosses, *Cratoneuronum commutatum* and *Bryum pseudotriquetum*, grow on the barriers. $CaCO_3$ crystals adhere to bacteria and blue-green algae living on the mosses, coating and petrifying them and building the barrier higher. Most travertine is deposited around the spill points, especially the high falls, where the water is oxygenated and carbon dioxide is released. Growth may be 0.5–7.5 in (1–3 cm) each year, until overflow or the waterfall shifts to another location. The travertine system is dynamic, as sediments are carried away, new calcium is dissolved, and falls change position. The travertine dams formed in the last 4,000–10,000 years, although there are remains of pre-Pleistocene travertine.

Biota. The park has more than 1,000 species of plants, 75 of which are endemic. It preserves some of the last virgin beech (*Fagus sylvatica*), spruce (*Picea abies*), and fir (*Abies alba*) forests that formerly covered much of Europe, including trees more than 165 ft (50 m) tall and more than 5 ft (1.5 m) in diameter. Riparian communities include black alder (*Alnus glutinosa*), willow, reeds, and bulrush. The mosaic of meadow communities is anthropogenic, as forest was cleared for agriculture. Rare plants include two orchids (*Lingularia siberica* and *Cyprepedium calceolus*) and globeflower (*Trollius europaeus*).

The rich fauna is typical of preindustrial Europe, including European brown bear, wolves, eagle, chamois, deer, fox, lynx, and badger. The park counts 150 species of birds, including cuckoos, tits, warblers, and woodpeckers, 70–90 of which nest in the area. Rare and endangered birds include Black Stork (*Ciconia nigra*), Capercaillie (*Tetrao urogallus*), Western Barbastelle (*Barbastella barbastellus*), and Eurasian

Eagle-owl (*Bubo bubo*). Eurasian Otter (*Lutra lutra*), long-fingered bat (*Myotis capaccinii*), and European brown bear (*Ursus arctos*) are examples of rare mammals.

Protected Areas. Plitvice Lakes was declared a national park in 1949 when the region was part of Yugoslavia and remains a park under the Croatian government. It was inscribed as a World Heritage Site in 1979.

Environmental Issues. Plitvice Lakes National Park was the site of the first battle between Croatians and Serbians in 1991 and suffered damage from rebel fighter occupation.

See also Dinaric Alps

Further Reading

Markowska, Joanna. 2004. "The Origins of the Plitvice Lakes (Croatia)." In *Miscellanea Geographica*, Vol. 11, translated by Małgorzata Mikulska. Warsaw, Poland: University of Warsaw. *http://msg.wgsr.uw.edu.pl/?page_id=103*

UNESCO. n.d. "Plitvice Lakes National Park." http://whc.unesco.org/en/list/98

Popocatépetl and Iztaccíhuatl

Mexico

Geographic Overview. Popocatépetl (smoking mountain) and Iztaccíhuatl (white lady) are Mexico's second and third highest mountains, respectively—stratovolcanoes in the Trans-Mexican Volcanic Axis. They are linked physically by a high saddle and also linked in legends wherein "Popo" is always male and "Iztaccíhuatl" female. However, they have separate geologic histories and distinctly different edifices.

Geographic Coordinates. Popocatépetl: 19°01'N, 98°38'W; Iztaccíhuatl: 19°11'N, 98°38'W

Description. Popocatépetl is a massive, active volcano with a nearly perfect cone, the most recent in a series going back 730,000 years. A remnant of one of its predecessors (Nexpayantla) appears as a sharp peak called El Ventrillo on one side of Popo. Earlier cones at the site were pulled down during the Pleistocene by gravitational forces that created huge debris avalanches. El Ventrillo, too, has suffered

slumps; they expose the layered structure of stratovolcanoes. The summit of Popo is a deep, elliptical crater with its highest point (on the WSW rim) standing 17,802 ft (5,426 m) asl. The northeastern part of the rim is 558 ft (170 m) lower. The crater measures 1,300 × 2,000 ft (600 × 840 m) across, and its almost vertical walls descend some 1,450 ft (450 m). Prior to 1994, a small lake occupied the floor of the crater, and sulfurous gases were emitted from fumaroles on the crater walls. Water temperatures rose from 84°F (29°C) to 149°F (65°C) in 1994, just before the volcano came back to life after 50 years of dormancy. The lake was lost in the subsequent 1996 eruption, when three new craters appeared on the east wall. Glaciers on the summit began to recede rapidly after 1994, largely the result of being covered by ash that absorbed sunlight and warmed the surface. By 2001 the glaciers were gone, although some patches of ice remain. Since 1996, several lava domes have formed in the crater only to be explosively destroyed. Popo has been active continuously since the 1990s, usually emitting ash plumes and sometimes hurling lava into the air.

Snowcapped Iztaccíhuatl is an extinct volcano north of Popo. It has an elongated summit composed of four overlapping cones. The high point has an elevation of 17,160 ft (5,230 m) asl. A Spanish nickname for the mountain is La Mujer Dormida, the sleeping woman; and the cones, aligned in a north-northwest–south-southeast direction are called La Cabeza (the head), El Pecho (the breast), Las Rodillas (the knees), and Los Pies (the feet). They are constructed upon an ancient shield volcano that formed 900,000–600,000 years ago. Later volcanism produced lava flows and pyroclastics and the string of cones. All volcanic activity ended about 80,000 years ago. Glaciers remain on Iztaccíhuatl, but they have been retreating since the 1890s.

Popocatépetl and Iztaccíhuatl are joined by Paso de Cortés, a 12,073 ft (3,680 m) high ridge. It was from this vantage point that the Spanish conquistador, Hernán Cortés, first saw Tenochtitlan, the capital of the Aztecs, in 1519. The two mountains and their connecting saddle separate the Valley of Mexico from the Puebla basin.

Various legends are attached to the two peaks but follow generally similar lines. One has Popocatépetl

Popocatépetl ("smoking mountain") is a massive, active stratovolcano in the Trans-Mexican Volcanic Axis. (Jesús Eloy Ramos Lara/Dreamstime.com)

as a warrior in love with Iztaccíhuatl. Her father, not wanting her to marry, tells her that he has been killed in battle; and she dies of grief. When Popocatépetl returns and finds her dead, he kills himself. God then covers them in snow and changes them into mountains. The angry Popocatépetl becomes a raging volcano.

Environmental Issues. Popocatépetl is a major hazard to the 19 million inhabitants of Mexico City only 43.5 mi (70 km) away.

See also Trans-Mexican Volcanic Axis (Eje Volcánico Transversal)

Further Reading

"Iztaccíhuatl." n.d. Global Volcanism Program, Smithsonian Institution. http://www.volcano.si.edu/volcano .cfm?vn=341082

"Iztaccihuatl, Mexico." n.d. Volcano World, Oregon State University. http://volcano.oregonstate.edu/iztaccihuatl
"Popocatépetl." n.d. Global Volcanism Program, Smithsonian Institution. http://www.volcano.si.edu/volcano .cfm?vn=341090

Prince Edward Islands

Indian Ocean

Geographic Overview. The Prince Edward Islands comprise two small subantarctic islands, Marion Island and Prince Edward Island, in the southern Indian Ocean. Largely uninhabited except by researchers, they are administered by the Republic of South Africa. Marion Island is South Africa's only historically active volcano. It lies about 1,000 mi (1,770 km) southeast of Port Elizabeth.

Geographic Coordinates. 46°46'S, 37°51'E

Description. Marion Island is the larger of the two Prince Edward islands with an area of 112 mi² (290 km²). It has a low profile since it is composed of two shield volcanoes. Its highest point, Mascarin Peak (previously known as State President Swart Peak), rises 4,035 ft (1,230 m) asl and is permanently covered in ice and snow. Many lower hills—cinder cones, scoria cones and tuff cones—surround the peak. Intermittent lakes dot the landscape. A'a and pahoehoe lava flows cover much of the island. Some flows are covered by peat 4,000 years old, which creates a boggy terrain. Other flows, perhaps only a few hundred years old, remain unvegetated. The first known historical eruption occurred in 1980, when explosions and lava flows took place along a 3 mi (5 km) fissure extending from the western flank of Mascarin Peak to the coast. The peak erupted again in 2004, this time on the south side of the mountain.

Prince Edward Island has an area of only 17 mi² (45 km²). It consists of the remnant of a single shield volcano measuring 15.5 mi × 10 mi (25 km × 17 km). Its highest point is Van Zinderen Bakker Peak at 4,074 ft (1,242 m) asl. Cliffs up to 1,600 ft (490 m) high line its southwestern coast.

The two islands are in the Roaring Forties and affected by nearly constant, strong northwesterly winds. They are one of the cloudiest places on Earth and receive precipitation 320 days each year. Total annual precipitation on Marion Island, where a meteorological station is manned, ranges between 94.5 in (2,400 mm) on the drier eastern side and 118 in (>3,000 mm) on Mascarin Peak. Temperatures are low year round, but a maritime influence means freezing temperatures are rare in the lowlands. The daily mean for February, the warmest month of the year, is 45.9°F (7.7°C); the daily mean for August, the coldest month, is 38.7°F (3.7°C).

Geologic History. The islands rise from a flat-topped submarine platform. The shield volcanoes are believed to be of Holocene age, but actual dates of formation are unknown.

Biota. The Prince Edward Islands are part of the Southern Indian Ocean tundra ecoregion. The vegetation is mainly lichens, mosses, and grasses, with some cushion plants such as azorella. There are native mites, flies, weevils, and moths; some exhibit flightlessness, a relatively common adaptation to an island habitat. King and Macaroni Penguins breed on the islands, as do five species of albatross and a number of petrels. An estimated 44 percent of the world's Wandering Albatrosses return to these islands to nest. Two fur seals and the southern elephant seal also breed here. One of the biogeographical peculiarities of the Prince Edward Islands is the co-occurrence of both antarctic and subantarctic petrels and seals on the breeding grounds.

The house mouse is the only introduced species on the islands. Domestic cats were introduced in 1947 to control them, but the cat population exploded and preferred to prey on burrowing petrels, extirpating some species on Marion Island. Cats have since been eradicated from the islands.

Protected Areas. South Africa has designated the Prince Edward Islands a Special Reserve. As such, the only activities allowed on the islands are research and conservation management.

Environmental Issues. Climate change is a major threat to the island communities. Rising temperatures may make the islands more vulnerable to the invasion of alien species, which could displace native plants and decimate nesting birds. Linefishing for Patagonian toothfish (*Dissostichus eleginoides*), which is marketed as Chilean sea bass in the United States and Canada, is dangerous for scavenging sea birds, especially albatrosses, which get caught on baited hooks.

See also Kerguelen Islands (Desolation Islands)

Further Reading

"Antarctic Islands in the Southern Indian Ocean." n.d. World Wildlife Fund. http://worldwildlife.org/ecoregions/an1104

Cooper, John. 2006. "Antarctica and Islands." Background Research Paper Produced for the South Africa Environment Outlook Report on Behalf of the Department of Environmental Affairs and Tourism. http://soer.deat.gov.za/dm_documents/Antarctica_and_Islands_-_Background_Paper_1DXK5.pdf

"Marion Island." n.d. Global Volcanism Program, Smithsonian Institution. http://www.volcano.si.edu/world/volcano.cfm?vnum=0304-07-

Puerto Princesa Subterranean River National Park

Philippines

Geographic Overview. Puerto Princesa Subterranean River National Park, on the west-central coast of Palawan island in the Philippines, preserves one of the most impressive cave systems in the world and the world's largest underground estuary. The mountain-to-sea ecosystems have old growth forests, distinctive wildlife, and several endemic species.

Geographic Coordinates. 10°10'N, 118°55'E

Description. Puerto Princesa Subterranean River Park is also known as Saint Paul's Underground River Cave. The park covers approximately 78 mi^2 (202 km^2), including surface land, cave system, and a small marine component. Elevations range from sea level to 3,373 ft (1,028 m) at the summit of Mount Saint Paul. A total of more than 15 mi (24 km) of passageways, at a minimum of two levels in the cave system, have been discovered, as well as several other caves higher in the ridge, 650–1,325 ft (200–400 m) asl, and unrelated to the underground river.

The Cayayugan River rises at approximately 330 ft (100 m) asl southwest of Mount Saint Paul on the western slope of the St. Paul Mountain ridge. It soon disappears underground into Daylight Hole, which is 197 ft (60 m) high and 330 ft (100 m) wide, and the entrance to the cave where the river begins its underground passage. The river passes beneath the Saint Paul Range west of the summit, and after 5.1 mi (8.2 km), exits into the South China Sea at St. Paul's Bay, approximately 31 mi (50 km) northeast of Puerto Princesa city. Tides bring salt water as far into the cave as Rock Falls, 3.7 mi (6 km), creating a large subterranean estuary where fresh water and salt water mix. Beyond that point, the water is fresh. The river's maximum depth is 26 ft (8 m).

Many older long passages, which run parallel to the active river, are 165–330 ft (50–100 m) above it. Some passages have collapsed into the lower level and created large rooms, such as Italian's Chamber, which is 1,180 ft (360 m) long and 459 ft (140 m) wide. The cave has many examples of unique speleothems. Although the cavern is navigable 2.9 mi (4.5 km) from the sea, tourist boats travel only 0.75 mi (1.2 km) inland.

Although known to locals for centuries, scientific study of the cave and karst region began in 1911. The first documented exploration was in 1973, followed by several expeditions mounted by Australians, Americans, and Italians. The park is predominantly mountainous, with the karst area covering 13.5 mi^2 (35 km^2). On the surface, the thick layers of limestone have developed into a tropical karst landscape, which includes pinnacles, domes, sinkholes, shafts, and additional caves. Surface exploration is difficult or impossible due to the sharp edges in the karst landscape.

The Palawan region is subject to monsoon wind flows. The dry season is from November through April. Annual mean precipitation of 80–188 in (2,000–3,000 mm) falls during the wet season, May through October. Air temperature averages 80°F (27°C).

Geologic History. The dark gray massive limestone dates from the early Miocene, 20–16 mya, is more than 1,640 ft (500 m) thick, and is rich in fossils. It overlies Oligocene mudstone, marls, and volcanics. The ridge that forms the Saint Paul Mountain Range trends northeast–southwest (the alignment of the island), dips northwest, and is bordered by faults. It is mainly a tower and cockpit landscape, with approximately 90 percent being sharp limestone ridges around Mount Saint Paul, which is a series of rounded limestone peaks.

Biota. Because Palawan is a remnant of a land bridge to Borneo, the island's biota is more similar to that in Borneo than to the adjacent Philippine islands. The park preserves almost pristine ecosystems that range from mountain top to sea, with a rich forest biodiversity and both local and regional endemics. The park supports more than 800 plant species, including at least 295 species of trees. The Palawan moist forest, with the richest tree forest in Asia, is dominated by *Diptocarpus grandiflora, Instia bijuga,* and other hardwoods. Forest in the karst landscapes can only grow where small pockets of soil have developed. Coastal ecosystems include mangroves, seagrass beds, and coral reefs.

The fauna is moderately diverse, with one primate, the long-tailed macaque (*Macaca fascicularis*). Endemic mammals include Palawan species of tree shrew (*Tupaia palawanensis*), porcupine (*Hystrix pumilus*), and stink badger (*Mydaus marchei*). Of the 19 reptile species, eight are endemic. Amphibian species number 10, with one endemic. With 165 species and 15 endemics, birds are the largest group of vertebrates. Dugongs, monitor lizards, and marine turtles can be found in the marine component of the park. Subterranean fauna is not well studied, but includes fish, prawns, snakes, and insects. The cave tunnels and chambers are home to many swiftlets and nine species of bats.

Protected Areas. Puerto Princesa Subterranean River is a World Heritage Site, a Biosphere Reserve, a Ramsar site, and one of the New Seven Wonders of the World.

Environmental Issues. Although the entire catchment area of the Cayayugan River is within park boundaries, pollution from activities, such as forest clearing and agriculture, in adjacent watersheds may pose problems. Tourist activities are currently limited to 600 persons per day.

Further Reading

De Vivo, Antonio, Leonardo Piccini, and Marco Mecchia. 2009. "Recent Explorations in the Saint Paul Karst (Palawan, Philippines)." *Proceedings 15th International Congress of Speleology, Kerville, Texas* 3: 1786–1792. http://www.laventa.it/index.php?option=com_content&view=article&id=73&Itemid=69&lang=en

UNESCO. 2013. "Puerto-Princesa Subterranean River National Park." World Heritage Centre. http://whc.unesco.org/en/list/652

Puget Sound

Pacific Ocean

Geographic Overview. Puget Sound is a marine inlet occupying a structural trough in northwestern Washington, between the Cascade Mountains and the Olympic Mountains. Within this fjord-like estuary system, beaches, rocky shores, cliffs, and tidal flats provide productive habitats for a rich variety of plant and animal species, many of which are genetically distinct or are the world's largest. The surrounding area is home to approximately 3.6 million people.

Geographic Coordinates. 47°36'N, 122°45'W

Description. Puget Sound is part of the larger Georgia Basin, 6,550 mi² (17,000 km²), which includes the Strait of Juan de Fuca, between Vancouver Island and the Olympic Peninsula, and the Strait of Georgia, between Vancouver Island and British Columbia. Puget Sound proper, from Deception Pass, north of Whidbey Island, south to Olympia, Washington, covers approximately 1,000 mi² (2,600 km²) and has approximately 2,500 mi (4,000 km) of shoreline. Although averaging 450 ft (135 m), depth is extremely variable, from 33 ft (10 m) to approximately 1,200 ft (360 m). The deepest basins are in the Strait of Juan de Fuca and around the San Juan Islands. Maximum depth in Puget Sound proper is 930 ft (283 m), just north of Seattle.

The estuary system of interconnected basins is a series of valleys and ridges, called basins and sills. The major feature in the Northern Puget Sound, which extends from the U.S.–Canada border south to Admiralty Inlet and then west to the Pacific, is the Strait of Juan de Fuca 100 mi (160 km) long and 13–27 mi (22–44 km) wide. The Main Basin extends from Admiralty Inlet, which is 19 mi (30 km) wide, south to Tacoma Narrows, and is separated by sills at both ends. Whidbey Basin is on the eastern side of Whidbey Island, from Deception Pass in the north to the southern end of the Island. South Puget Sound is the narrow inlets and many islands south of Tacoma Narrows. Hood Canal, 56 mi (90 km) long and 0.6–1.2 (1–2 km) wide extends southwest from the Main Basin just south of Admiralty Inlet. It is a closed basin with no major inflow of fresh water and is partly isolated by a sill at its entrance. The Strait of Georgia is approximately 137 mi (220 km) long and 11.5–34.0 mi (18.5–55 km) wide. Both its north and south outlets are constricted by narrow straits, islands, and shallow sills.

Several rivers contribute fresh water to Puget Sound. The major ones in Washington are the Skagit and Snohomish entering the Whidbey Basin, but the Fraser River, entering the Strait of Georgia, adds the majority of fresh water for the whole system. Water circulation is influenced by tides, wind, freshwater inflow, and configuration of the inlets, islands, and bottom, particularly the sills at Admiralty Inlet, the Tacoma Narrows, and the mouth of Hood Canal. Puget Sound proper is connected to the Pacific in only two places, Admiralty Inlet and narrow Deception Pass. Fresh water flows out through Admiralty Inlet at the surface, while salt water flows in through the Strait of Juan de Fuca at depth.

Geologic History. Puget Sound is believed to be a continuation of the downfaulted basin of the Willamette Valley. Piedmont glaciers, up to 3,600 ft (1,100 m) thick, from the British Columbia Coast Mountains funneled into and deepened the preexisting lowlands. The sandy or muddy bottom is thickly covered with glacial debris over bedrock, which is probably oceanic crust.

Biota. The combination of fresh water, salt water, and physical configuration of the sound creates a very rich biological system with several major habitats, including kelp beds, eelgrass meadows, intertidal mudflats, rocky reef, and salt marsh. The Puget Sound region supports approximately 3,000 species of marine invertebrates. Macroinvertebrates, such as Dungeness crab (*Cancer magister*), several species of shrimp, the nonnative Pacific oyster (*Crassostrea gigas*), and clams, are widely distributed. The North Pacific Giant Octopus (*Enteroctopus dofleini*), giant Pacific chiton (*Cryptochiton stelleri*), a barnacle (*Balanus nubilis*), plumrose anemone (*Metridium senile*), and burrowing clam (*Panopea abrupta*) are among the world's largest. Marine mammals include harbor seal, Steller sea lion, California sea lion, grey whales, humpback whales, and killer whales.

Of the 230 species of marine and anadromous fish, including five species of salmon and three species of trout, there are also 25 species of rockfish.

Approximately 165 bird species depend on the marine environment, including large populations of seabirds that nest in Protection Island National Wildlife Refuge. On the Olympic Peninsula south of Admiralty Inlet, the refuge has one of the world's largest nesting populations of Rhinoceros Auklets (*Cerorhinca monocerata*).

Environmental Issues. The surrounding area has a mixture of urban and industrial development, forest, and agriculture, resulting in potential shoreline modification and contamination.

Further Reading

Gustafson R. G. et al. 2000. "Environmental History and Features of Puget Sound." In *Status review of Pacific Hake, Pacific Cod, and Walleye Pollock from Puget Sound, Washington.* U.S. Dept. Commerce, NOAA Tech. Memo. NMFS-NWFSC- 44.

Puna (Vegetation)

Argentina, Bolivia, Chile, and Peru

Geographic Overview. The cold, high-altitude grassland of the Central Andes of South America is called the *puna*, not to be confused with the southern section of the Altiplano, the Puna. Puna grasslands extend south from northern Peru through western Bolivia into northernmost Chile and Argentina at elevations of 9,850–16,400 ft (3,000–5,000 m) asl—above treeline and below permanent ice and snow.

Geographic Coordinates. Approximately 03°S–22°S, 65°W–80°W

Description. Major plant communities are distinguished as High Andean Puna, Wet Puna, Wet Montane Puna, and Dry Puna, reflecting topographic and climatic differences. These steppes dominate the landscape, but forests of endemic *Polylepis* trees also occur. They typically grow above normal treeline, although it is not known if this is the product of human manipulation of the vegetation over millennia. Today they are disappearing.

The High Andean Puna occurs on the Altiplano at elevations above 13,800 ft (4,200 m), where temperatures drop below freezing every night. Precipitation (less than 28 in [700 mm] a year] falls mostly as snow or hail. Tussocks of Peruvian feather grass, fescues, and reed grass grow 3 ft (1 m) in diameter and equally tall. Rosettes and cushion plants are also common. In *bofedales* or cushion bogs, the vegetation consists of floating and submerged cushions of grasses and sedges.

Wet Puna dominates the Altiplano at elevations between 12,000 and 13,800 ft (3,700–4,200 m). This is a landscape of snowcapped peaks, high lakes, and grass-covered plateaus and mountain slopes. Tussock grasses, mostly ichu grass, and shrubs form vast pastures, while sedges, rushes, and bulrushes grow in the less well-drained areas. Dramatic inflorescences of *Puya raimondii* rise 30 ft (10 m) from giant rosettes and create a stunning contrast to the otherwise low vegetation. The Wet Puna transitions into the Sechura desert to the west and the wet Peruvian Yungas to the east. Precipitation varies from 20 to 28 in (500–700 mm). A four-month long dry season characterizes the northern parts around Lake Titicaca, but becomes increasingly longer farther south. Near the southern margins, the dry season extends for 8 months of the year. Nighttime frost occurs from March through October. At the eastern margins, in the steep mountains and glacial valleys of the Cordillera Real, lie the grasslands of the Wet Montane Puna.

Dry Puna, a shrub-steppe, cloaks the slopes of the Cordillera Occidental in Bolivia and northernmost Chile and Argentina at elevations of 11,500–16,400 ft (3,500–5,000 m) asl. In the west it descends toward the Atacama Desert, finding its lower limits around 6,500 ft (2,000 m) in tropical latitudes and 11,500 ft (3,500 m) south of Antafagasto, Chile. Much of this area, which receives 2–16 in (50–400 mm) of precipitation annually and experiences an eight-month dry season, is covered by alpine herbs and dwarf shrubs, largely of the daisy family. Yareta (*Azorella compacta*) forms conspicuous, bright green cushions on well-drained slopes. In poorly drained areas, *bofedales* have floating and submerged cushion plants of *Plantago rigida, Distichia muscoides*, and other forbs.

Geologic History. Volcanic bedrock dating to after the rise of the Andes Mountains underlies most of the region, although in northern Peru loess up to 3 ft (1m) deep is present. There and elsewhere glacial moraines and other landforms of alpine glaciation can be found.

Biota. Plants and animals of the puna must be well adapted to a high-altitude environment where oxygen is limited, drought is prolonged, and every day is summer and every night is winter. Both native camelids, the vicuña and the guanaco, live at these heights, as do viscacha, chinchillas, and the Andean hairy armadillo (*quirquincho*). Andean fox, Andean cat, and puma are the main predators. Darwin's Rhea, a flightless bird, also inhabits the puna. Most other birds in the region are found near lakes or in the *Polylepis* forest.

Protected Areas. A number of small preserves protect specific animals or habitat. Sajama National Park in Bolivia's dry puna protects *Polylepis* forest and several mammals. National Faunal Reserve Ulla-Ulla in western Bolivia protects that country's largest vicuña herd.

Environmental Issues. The puna may be the most altered biome in Peru and Bolivia, the product of centuries of grazing llamas, alpacas, sheep, and goats. Added to the impacts of overgrazing are the pollution of lakes and poorly drained areas by mining, firewood collection, and road building.

See also Altiplano-Puna; Páramo

Further Reading

Locklin, Claudia. n.d. "Central Andean Dry Puma. Montane Grasslands and Shrublands, South America: Argentina, Bolivia, and Peru." World Wildlife Fund. http://world wildlife.org/ecoregions/nt1001

Quinn, Joyce A. 2009. *Arctic and Alpine Biomes*. Greenwood Guides to Biomes of the World. Westport, CT: Greenwood Press.

Salcedo, Juan Carlos Riveros. n.d. "Puna. Montane Grasslands and Shrublands, South America: Argentina, Bolivia, and Peru." World Wildlife Fund. http://world wildlife.org/ecoregions/nt1002

Salcedo, Juan Carlos Riveros and Claudia Locklin. n.d. "Central Andean Wet Puna. Montane Grasslands and Shrublands, Western South America: Peru and Bolivia." World Wildlife Fund. http://worldwildlife.org /ecoregions/nt1003

Pyrenees Mountains

Spain, France, and Andorra

Geographic Overview. The Pyrenees Mountains, a straight, narrow range, form a natural border between France and Spain. Their glaciated peaks retain remnants of valley glaciers, and several valleys are glacial troughs. The range is a climate divide between more humid France and the drier Iberian Peninsula. Because they are topographically isolated from other European mountains, the Pyrenees harbor many endemic species.

Geographic Coordinates. Approximately 42°N–43°N, 02°W–02°E

Description. The Pyrenees extend 270 mi (430 km) from the Bay of Biscay on the west to the Mediterranean Sea on the east and are generally 40–80 mi (65–130 km) wide. The crest is a succession of peaks over 9,500 ft (2,900 m) asl, and few passes are lower than 6,500 ft (1,980 m). The core of the Pyrenees, Paleozoic crystalline Hercynian rocks and batholiths that originated in Gondwana, are bordered by two fold belts (interior and exterior) on both the northern and southern sides. The axial range (the core) is wider in the eastern and central part of Pyrenees, where the Aneto-Maladeta Massif has the highest peaks, including Aneto, the highest at 11,169 ft (3,404 m). On either side of the Hercynian core is an interior zone of Mesozoic and Cenozoic sedimentary rocks, predominantly limestone, overlying ancient rock. Some Paleozoic crystalline massifs, such as Pic de St. Barthelemy at 7,707 ft (2,349 m), are locally exposed on the French side. In Spain's interior zone, limestone and sandstone summits are more than 8,200 ft (2,500 m) asl, higher and more continuous than the equivalent on the French side. Some peaks, including Monte Perdido at 11,007 ft (3,355 m), are higher than many in the core. This zone is also wider with more variety, from simple folds to complex folding and thrust nappes. Much of the strata remains fairly horizontal with deep canyons. The two exterior zones are marginal troughs of thick late Mesozoic and Cenozoic sediments that are less intensely folded. They form two minor ridges, the Little Pyrenees in France and the Sierras Zone in Spain.

Hot springs occur along the many faults and fractures, and the eastern Pyrenees are volcanic.

Major drainage is the Garonne River in France, flowing to the Bay of Biscay, and several tributaries to the Ebro in Spain, which flows to the Mediterranean Sea. Many rivers, fed by snowmelt, run north or south, at right angles to the mountain axis. The western part

The high, narrow range of the Pyrenees Mountains forms a climatic barrier between France and Spain. The northern French side is lushly vegetated, while the southern Spain side is in rain shadow. (Bjulien03/Dreamstime.com)

of the range is wetter because of the Atlantic influence, while the eastern end is more mediterranean, with dry summers. The mountains are an orographic barrier to northern cyclonic storms and receive more rain and snow on the northern slope, placing the Iberian plateau of Spain in rain shadow.

Glaciation was more evident on the northern slopes, especially over 8,200 ft (2,500 m), because of higher precipitation. Much of the core was glacially carved, and many deep river valleys, such as Ordessa with 3,300 ft (1,000 m) high walls, are glacial troughs. Most remnant glaciers, which are rapidly disappearing, are in cirques or high valleys.

Geologic History. Geologically, the Pyrenees are an extension of the Alps, separated by the northern Mediterranean Sea. An older Hercynian mountain chain, folded and metamorphosed slate, schist, and marble with granite intrusions, was replaced by the newer Pyrenees in the same location. With the breakup of Pangaea in the early Cretaceous, a rift developed between the Iberian microplate and the European Plate, opening the Bay of Biscay and separating the two plates, creating a new part of the Tethys Sea. Sediments accumulated along the southern edge of the European plate. The continental crust north of the break, the site where the Pyrenees would develop, was stretched and faulted. In the late Cretaceous to mid-Tertiary, plate movement reversed and Iberia and Europe converged. As the oceanic crust of the Tethys Sea subducted beneath the European Plate, eventually pulling down some of the European continental crust as well, folding and thrusting caused nappes to pile up over the thinned broken crust. The Hercynian massifs, which form the axial core of the mountains, were pushed toward the surface where erosion exposed them. Thrusting of folds and nappes was northward in France and southward in Spain, squeezed outward from the uplifted center. The Pyrenees are the sutured boundary between the Iberian plate and the European plate.

Stretching and thinning of the continental crust on the eastern end of the Pyrenees caused by movements of the Iberian Plate caught between the African and Eurasian plates, allowed alkaline magma to surface, forming a zone of explosive volcanoes in the eastern Pyrenees north of Barcelona. The last eruption occurred 11,500 years ago.

Biota. Plant communities vary with slope exposure. Broad-leaf deciduous forest is found at lower levels where there is Atlantic influence and is replaced by broad-leaf evergreen chaparral vegetation where there is Mediterranean influence. Vegetation zonation with increasing elevation changes from broad-leaved woodlands to needleleaf conifers to subalpine and alpine pastures. The Pyrenees are rich in large herbivores and predators. Endemic species include Pyrenean brown bear, a chamois, a lynx, and a rare ibex.

Protected Areas. Much of the Pyrenees is protected in three major national parks—Pyrenees National Park in France, Ordessa and Monte Perdido National Park, and Garrotxa National Park in Spain.

See also European Alps; Mediterranean Sea

Further Reading

Ager, Derek V. 1980. "Outer Arcs." In *The Geology of Europe*, 323–364. New York: John Wiley & Sons.

Sala, M. 1984. "Pyrenees and Ebro Basin Complex." In *Geomorphology of Europe*, edited by Clifford Embleton, 268–293. New York: John Wiley & Sons.

Q

Qattara Depression

Egypt

Geographic Overview. Qattara Depression is the largest of several major depressions in the Western Desert of Egypt. Its lowest point is 436 ft (133 m) bsl. The geologic development of the feature is debated, as is the idea of creating a hydroelectric project by diverting water from the Mediterranean Sea or Nile River into the basin.

Geographic Coordinates. 28°35'N–30°25'N, 26°20'E–29°02'E

Description. Qattara Depression is a large basin in northwestern Egypt within which is the second lowest point on the African continent (after Lake Assal in the Danakil Depression in the Afar Triangle). Shaped like an inverted comma, the depression is oriented northeast–southwest, with the tail in the northeast. Its full northeast–southwest length is about 177 mi (285 km), while it extends 84 mi (135 km) from north to south. The limits of the depression are placed at the contour line indicating current mean sea level, giving it a total area of 7,570 mi^2 (19,605 km^2). The western and northern sides rise steeply almost 920 ft (280 m) to the El Diffa Plateau, which separates Qattara from the Mediterranean Sea, as little as 34 mi (55 km) away. Most of the floor is below sea level; the deepest point lies near the western edge and is 436 ft (133 m) bsl. In the south, the basin gradually ascends to the general level of the Western or Libyan Desert, 650 ft (200 m) asl.

The Qattara Depression is a hyperarid region receiving on average 1–2 in (25–50 mm) of rainfall a year and even lower amounts in the southernmost section. Brackish to saline groundwater seeps out at the surface and evaporates, leaving salt pans (sabkhas) and other evaporites on the surface. Salt pans cover about one quarter of the surface. Salt marshes occur beneath the northern escarpment and along the southern edge of the basin. Moist sands persist in the eastern end, but intense salt weathering in the west has resulted in fine-grained materials easily eroded by the wind. Shallow, sandy deflation pits often host *Acacia* groves. Isolated, wind-abraded hills shaped like pinnacles or mushrooms or small mesas dot the floor of the depression, particularly near the western escarpment. They stand 15–100 ft (5–30 m) tall. Small oases have formed around the edges, including Ain El Qattara in the north, from which the name of the depression derives; Moghra Oasis in the eastern tip, which bears a small, brackish lake and reed marshes; and Qara Oasis in the west, the only permanently inhabited spot in the depression. A large wetland supporting salt marsh, grassland, palm groves, and shrubs across an area of 350 mi^2 (900 km^2) occurs in the southwestern corner. Sand dunes moving into the depression from the south are encroaching upon some wetlands.

Geologic History. How Qattara formed is still debated. It is the largest of seven major depressions in the Western Desert (the others are Fauym, Baharuya, Farfra, Dakhla, and Kharga). All may be parts of an ancient drainage system. A variety of processes, including fluvial, karstic, deflation, and mass-wasting have been shaping the basins since the late Miocene–Pliocene. Salt weathering and wind erosion appear to be major agents of landscape formation since the beginning of a dry climate during the Quaternary Period.

Biota. A small number of cheetahs still inhabit the sparsely vegetated Qattara Depression, which is also home to Cape hare, fennec fox, Rupelle's fox, Egyptian jackal, Dorcas gazelle, and the endangered slender-horned gazelle.

Protected Areas. The southwestern wetlands are included in the Siwa Protected Area, which is focused on preserving rare wildlife and cultural resources at Siwa Oasis.

Environmental Issues. Since 1912, a major hydroelectric project has been proposed to utilize the elevational drop well below sea level by diverting seawater by canal or pipeline from the Mediterranean or fresh water from the Nile River near Rosetta, Egypt, into the basin.

Some engineers propose letting evaporation remove the water; other foresee a large inland lagoon. More recently, the Qattara Depression has been proposed as a reservoir for excess waters from the Mediterranean Sea as sea level rises in response to global warming.

Further Reading

Aref, M. A. M., E. El-Khoriby, and M. A. Hamdam. 2002. "The Role of Salt Weathering in the Origin of the Qattara Depression, Western Desert, Egypt." *Geomorphology* 45: 181–195. Abstract available at http://www.sciencedirect.com/science/article/pii/S0169555X01001520

Saundry, P. 2013. "Qattara Depression." *The Encyclopedia of Earth.* http://www.eoearth.org/view/article/169468

R

Rancho La Brea Tar Pits

United States (California)

Geographic Overview. Rancho La Brea Tar Pits, covering 23 ac (9.3 ha) in Hancock Park in urban Los Angeles, is world famous for its fossil assemblage of animals that became trapped in ponds filled with viscous, sticky asphalt, commonly called tar. The Page Museum, part of the Natural History Museum of Los Angeles County, displays fossils, and visitors can view tar pits on the grounds of the park.

Geographic Coordinates. 34°04'N, 118°21'W

Description. The Native American Chumash used the natural tar as a water sealant on baskets and boats or canoes. Early settlers mined the tar for roofing material in the nearby village of Los Angeles. Because the area was originally part of a Spanish Land Grant and a working ranch, any bones found were believed to be from cattle. In the early 1900s, bones of a giant ground sloth were discovered and an oil geologist recognized bones of La Brea coyote (*Canis orcuttii*) as fossils. Initial excavations took place during 1913–1915. More than 100 pits were dug, but only Pit 91, the richest site, is still being excavated. In 2006, however, 16 new fossil deposits were discovered during the construction of an underground parking garage for the adjacent Museum of Art. These new deposits, called Project 23, were carefully extracted and wrapped in 23 large tree boxes and stored on site at the Page Museum. Construction of the garage continued, and the deposits are undisturbed for future excavation.

The fossils date from approximately 40,000 to 8,000 years ago. Merely preserved by the asphalt, which also turned the bones a dark brown or black color, the fossils are not petrified. Scientists found that the bone protein had degraded very little, and DNA could be extracted, to compare the fossils with living relatives. More than 660 species have been found, including at least 59 mammal species and over 135 bird species, as well as fossils of plants, mollusks, seeds, insects, and pollen grains. Most of the fossil animals, such as *Canis lupus furlongi*, a subspecies of the gray wolf (*Canis lupus*), are similar to modern species, and some, such as coyote (*Canis latrans*) and mule deer (*Odocoileus hemionus*), are the same.

Fossils of extinct animals from the last glacial period include mammoths, mastodons, longhorned bison, horses, camels, dire wolves, short-faced bears, ground sloths, and sabre-toothed cats. Approximately 90 percent of the large bones are from predators or scavengers, including vultures, condors, eagles, and stork-like birds called teratorns. Scientists believe that dead or dying prey species attracted predators in large numbers. Only one human skeleton has been found. A small dig into one box of Project 23 has yielded a large variety of animals. A major find in Project 23 is a nearly complete skeleton of a Columbian mammoth, significant because the other mammoth skeletons were disarticulated.

Animals coming to feed or drink at the ponds became mired in the asphalt and were unable to escape. The asphalt was stickier in warm weather, and the surface of the ponds was frequently disguised by a surface layer of dust, leaves or water. The tar pits continue to trap unwary animals, such as pigeons and lizards, and are fenced off from visitors. The Page Museum, designed for both research and displays of the animal finds, opened in 1977. Scientists believe that more deposits may be found.

Geologic History. For tens of thousands of years, crude oil seeped upward through fissures in the rock from the underground Salt Lake oil field, forming pools at the surface. The lighter fractions of the petroleum degraded or evaporated, leaving heavy, sticky asphalt, the lowest grade of crude oil. The pits seen in the park today are not natural but are human-made holes left from excavations. Except for Lake Pit, which was originally an asphalt mine, the pits were dug during the early excavations. Asphalt and water continue to seep upward, as much as 12 gal (45 l) a day, to fill the pits. The asphalt often appears to be boiling, due to methane gas released when bacteria eat the tar. In 2007, scientists discovered 200–300 different bacteria previously unknown to science.

Protected Areas. Rancho La Brea Tar Pits is a National Natural Landmark.

Further Reading

Page Museum. n.d. *La Brea Tar Pits*. http://www.tarpits.org/
Waggoner, Ben M. and Dave Smith. 2011. *The La Brea Tar Pits, Los Angeles*. University of California Museum of Paleontology. www.ucmp.berkeley.edu/quaternary /labrea.php

Red Sea

Indian Ocean

Geographic Overview. The Red Sea rift, separating Africa from the Arabian Peninsula, is part of a group of tectonic phenomenon in east Africa and the Middle East that provides scientific clues to understanding the breakup of continental crust and generation of new oceanic crust. The sea's coral reef ecosystem, with many endemic species, is the northernmost on Earth and a major tourist attraction. The Red Sea–Suez is one of the world's busiest shipping routes, especially for petroleum products.

Geographic Coordinates. Approximately 12° 30'N–29°57'N, 32°22'E–43°30'E, including Gulf of Suez and Gulf of Aqaba

Description. The Red Sea, more than 1,250 mi (2,000 km) long, from the Strait of Bab El Mandeb at the southern end where it connects with the Gulf of Aden and the Indian Ocean north to the southern tip of the Sinai peninsula, covers approximately 177,100 m² (458,620 km²). The majority of the Red Sea is 112 mi (80 km) wide, but its maximum width is 217 mi (350 km). At the southern strait, the southwestern tip of Arabia comes within 19 mi (30 km) of Africa. At the northern end, the Red Sea rift splits around the Sinai Peninsula. The Gulf of Suez to the west, separating the African plate from the smaller Sinai plate, is no more than 33 ft (100 m) deep. The Gulf of Aqaba to the east, part of the Dead Sea Transform fault and separating Sinai from the Arabian plate, is 6,070 ft (1,850 m) deep. In the center of the Red Sea is a deep trough, following the northwest–southeast axis of the rift, the bottom of which is very rugged with volcanic features and young basalt volcanoes. Although this axial trough is more than 3,300 ft (1,000 m) deep and with three places more than 6,550 ft (2,000 m) deep, most of the Red Sea is much more shallow. Almost half is less than 330 ft (100 m) deep, and 25 percent is less than 164 ft (50 m) deep. The sea floor has very little sediment deposition.

The Red Sea coast is characterized by mountains and scarps. The Yemen Mountains in the southwestern part of the Arabian Peninsula rise more than 10,000 ft (3,000 m) asl. The sea is also bounded by volcanics. The lava in the Yemen Mountains and across the Red Sea in Africa in Ethiopia and Eritrea erupted 25–5 mya, while younger lava (less than 5 mya) lines the western side of the Arabian peninsula, where many dikes parallel the Red Sea.

Surface water flows from the Indian Ocean into the Red Sea in winter, a flow which reverses in summer. Within the narrow basin, circulation is generally counterclockwise. High evaporation and low precipitation create one of the world's saltiest seas (42.5 ppt). No significant rivers drain into the Red Sea. Turnover time is 6 yrs for surface water, and 200 yrs for the entire basin.

The Red Sea is a tropical desert region. Air temperatures rise to more than 100°F (38°C) in summer, dropping to 60–70°F (15–21°C) in winter. Mean temperature of the surface water in summer is 79–86°F (26–30°C), with a 3.6°F (2°C) drop in winter. Annual precipitation is less than 2.5 in (64 mm).

Geologic History. The Red Sea is one of a series of rifts in East Africa, including the Gulf of Aden, East African Rift system, Afar Depression, Suez, and Dead Sea Transform Fault. These rifts separate four

The Red Sea, occupying a graben between Africa and Arabia and the Sinai Peninsula (the land seen here), provides evidence of continental rifting and sea-floor spreading. (Mildax/Dreamstime.com)

rigid plates—Arabian, African, Sinai, and Somalian. Both the northern and southern ends of the system have a junction of three rifts, Suez-Red Sea-Aqaba in the north and Red Sea-Afar-Aden in the south. Rifting occurred along these faults at various geologic times, from the Oligocene (30 mya) to the present. The result is a display of different stages in continental rifting and seafloor spreading, a valuable geologic laboratory illustrating breakup of continents and development of new ocean basins. The triple angle intersections of the rifts complicate plate movements. The Red Sea axial trough is traversed by many transform faults that trend consistently north–south, offsetting the trough in several places and indicating different rates of seafloor spreading. The rift remains geologically active. New crusts are forming around volcanic vents at depths of 6,550 ft (2,000 m), and mineral-rich thermal vents may be as warm as 144°F (62°C).

At various times when the Red Sea was beginning to open (30–25 mya), it was connected to the Mediterranean Sea. In contrast, the connection to the Indian Ocean is more recent, approximately 5 mya. Periodic inundations alternating with evaporation left massive salt deposits. Plastic movement of the salt pushes up islands, such as those around Hurghada, Egypt.

Biota. Although the Red Sea was periodically connected to the Mediterranean Sea in the geologic past, its biota has more similarities with the Indian Ocean. Periodic drying phases eliminated sea life from the Mediterranean. Varied habits in the Red Sea support a great variety of species, and endemism is high, especially in reef fishes and invertebrates.

Coastal zones may be covered with seagrass meadows, which support rays and echinoderms, such as starfish, sea urchins, and sea cucumbers. Mangrove swamps, dominated by white mangrove (*Avicennia marina*), are important nursery grounds. Four species of sea turtle (green, loggerhead, hawksbill, and leatherback) live in the Red Sea, and many wading birds use the shorelines.

In spite of a narrow coastal shelf and steep drop-offs, the Red Sea and the Gulf of Aqaba have a large and complex reef ecosystem, primarily fringing reefs in a narrow band close to shore. The colder Gulf of Suez has few reefs. The best reef development is in the northern and central Red Sea, with a wide range of habitats and species, including more than 250 species of hard coral as well as algae, sponges, jellyfish, anemones, octopuses, shellfish, nudibranchs, crabs, lobster, shrimp, starfish, sea urchins, moray eels, and tunicates. The sea has many endemics.

The Red Sea supports approximately 1,200 species of fish, in geographically diverse habitats. Fishing is mainly subsistence or small scale, with some commercial endeavors. Food fish include tuna, bonitos, billfishes, herring, sardines, and anchovies. Lobster and crab are also taken. Open water species also include sharks and dolphins.

Protected Areas. The Regional Organization for the Conservation of the Environment of the Red Sea and Gulf of Aden (PERSGA) was established in 1995 under the umbrella of the Arab League, to coordinate conservation in the Red Sea area.

Environmental Issues. Because the Red Sea is a relatively small and semienclosed system, it is vulnerable to environmental damage. Lack of regulations threatens sustainable fishing. Shark species have been exploited for their fins, and turtles, dugongs, and dolphins are frequently killed in nets. Uncontrolled development and tourism, urban and industrial discharge, oil pollution, and destruction of spawning or nursery grounds are all major threats to Red Sea biota and ecosystems. Ballast water discharge is a potential pollutant as well as carrier of exotic species. Dredging and landfill operations stir up silt that damages corals, which have also been affected by coral bleaching and outbreaks of crown-of-thorns starfish (*Acanthaster planci*) and other detrimental species.

See also Afar Triangle and Danakil Depression; Arabian Peninsula; Dead Sea; Sinai Peninsula

Further Reading

Goudie, Andrew S. 2002. "The Middle East." In *Geomorphological Landscapes of the World, 1. Great Warm Deserts of the World, Landscapes and Evolution*, 215–253. Oxford: Oxford University Press.

PERSGA. n.d. *The Regional Organization for the Conservation of the Environment of the Red Sea and Gulf of Aden*. http://www.persga.org/inner.php?mainid=1

Redwood National and State Parks

United States (California)

Geographic Overview. Stretching 40 mi (64 km) along the Pacific coast in northern California, Redwood National and State Parks protect the largest remnant of a once widespread coastal redwood forest. Coastal mountains, up to 3,000 ft (915 m) asl, support redwood and other forests, while the rocky cliff and beaches are home to a variety of marine and intertidal species. The parks protect many threatened and endangered species.

Geographic Coordinates. Approximately 41° 05'N–41°05'N, 123°51'W–124°09'W

Description. The majority of the parks' land area is covered with lush forests of towering trees with an undergrowth of tall ferns and scattered shrubs. Sea cliffs, seastacks, beaches, tide pools, and lagoons characterize the rocky coast. Estuaries at the mouths of the Klamath River and Redwood Creek are almost separated from the ocean by long baymouth bars. The Smith River flows through the northern part of the park. The Klamath River, the largest, crosses the middle of the park, and Redwood Creek is in the southern part.

Coastal redwoods (*Sequoia sempervirens*) are the tallest trees in the world, frequently 200 ft (60 m) tall and sometimes reaching more than 300 ft (91 m). The world's tallest, 367.8 ft (112 m) and 14 ft (4.3 m) in diameter at its base, is in the Tall Trees Grove. The fire and insect resistant redwood trees were exploited for lumber by early settlers. By 1964, only 15 percent of the original 2 million acres (809,400 ha) of redwood forest remained, and only 50,000 ac (20,235 ha) were protected in state parks. As of today, 39,982 ac (16,180 ha) of Redwood National Park's total extent of 131,983 ac (53,414 ha) preserve old-growth redwood forest, a small remnant of the original cover. The remainder under protection is cut over forest and other vegetation types. Reclamation of logged watersheds will limit damage to forests downstream. Approximately 42 percent of all remaining old-growth redwoods are within park boundaries. The significance of old-growth forest is highlighted in that two threatened species, Northern Spotted Owl (*Strix occidentalis caurina*) and Marbled Murrelet (*Brachyramphus marmoratus*), need old-growth forest for nesting sites.

The coastal climate is mild, with temperatures ranging 37°F (3°C) to 70°F (21°C). Winter is the wet season, with 70 in (1,780 mm) of rain. Summers are dry, but fog occurs year-round. Redwood forests extend inland as far as the fog.

Geologic History. Widespread in the Cretaceous, redwoods became confined to a narrow belt, approximately 35 mi (56 km) wide and 500 mi (805 km) north-to-south along the northern California coast and southern Oregon due to climate change during and after the Pleistocene.

Biota. The park has several habitats with distinct assemblages of plants and animals. Redwoods and Douglas fir (*Pseudotsuga menziesii*) dominate old-growth forests. The best stands grow in protected valleys and along streams. Associated species vary, but may include tanoak (*Lithocarpus densiflorus*), madrone (*Arbutulus menziesii*), and big-leaf maple (*Acer macrophyllum*). Sword fern (*Polystichum munitum*) and redwood sorrel (*Oxalis oregona*) are the most common understory plants, but rhododendron (*Rhododendron macrophyllum*) and azalea (*Rhododendron occidentale*) are prominent. At higher elevations or further inland where conditions are hot and dry, redwoods are replaced by a mixed evergreen forest that includes chinquapin (*Chrysolepis chrysophylla*), canyon live oak (*Quercus chrysolepis*), and Jeffrey pine (*Pinus jeffreyi*). Tolerant of wind and salt spray, sitka spruce (*Picea sitchensis*) grows on exposed seaside sites. Drier inland areas support grassland with Roosevelt elk (*Cervus elaphus* ssp. *roosevelti*) and black-tailed deer (*Ococoileus hemionus*).

Threatened and endangered birds include Brown Pelican, Southern Bald Eagle, and Western Snowy Plover.

Estuaries provide nurseries for juvenile fish and habitat for both freshwater and saltwater species. Several bird species, including pelicans, osprey, and gulls, nest on offshore seastacks. More than 40 percent of California's seabird population, and thousands of individuals, use these sites. Threatened Steller's sea lions (*Eumatopias jubatus*) may also be seen.

Protected Areas. The area became a national park in 1968, incorporating three existing California state parks, Jedediah Smith, Del Norte, and Prairie Creek, and adjacent privately owned land. It was enlarged in both 1978 and 2005, largely by the annexation of adjacent watersheds upstream from redwood groves. The park is both a World Heritage Site and part of California Coastal Ranges Biosphere Reserve. The Smith River, a Wild and Scenic River, is California's last major free-flowing river.

Further Reading

National Park Service. n.d. *Redwood National and State Parks, California*. www.nps.gov/redw/
UNESCO World Heritage Centre. n.d. *Redwood National and State Parks*. http://whc.unesco.org/en/list/134

Rhine River

Switzerland, Liechtenstein, Austria, France, Germany, and the Netherlands

Geographic Overview. The Rhine, Europe's longest river, flows through a densely populated river basin and provides drinking water for millions of Europeans. Major industrial sites, including petrochemical, pharmaceutical, steel, potassium mines, and coal mines, are situated along its banks. At the Rhine's outlet to the North Sea, Rotterdam is a major port for continental Europe. The river has been a strategic location since Roman times and has served as both a boundary between and a corridor linking political entities. The river has played a significant role in mythology, literature, and music. It is called Rhine in French and English, Rhein in German, and Rijn in Dutch.

The Rhine River, seen here at St. Goar and St. Goarshausen near Loreley in Germany, is a major thoroughfare through an industrial region in Europe. (Europhotos/Dreamstime.com)

Geographic Coordinates. Source: 46°50'N, 09°25'E, Mouth: 51°58'N, 04°05'E

Description. The Rhine River drains an area of approximately 71,500 mi² (185,000 km²) and flows 820 mi (1,320 km). Its route takes it from the high Alps in Switzerland, through deep gorges, and across broad plains to the North Sea. Mean discharge is 77,700 ft³/sec (2,200 m³/s). Water volume is stable year-round because alpine streams contribute maximum flow in early summer, while lower basin rivers contribute maximum flow in winter.

Two mountains streams in the eastern Swiss Alps, the Vorder Rhine from a lake and the Hinter Rhine from a glacier, merge at Reichenau to form the Rhine. At Chur, the river turns north to form the border between Switzerland and Liechtenstein before widening and flowing into Lake Constance on the Swiss–German border. Because sediments settle out in the lake, clear water emerges at the outlet, where it soon drops 75 ft (23 m) over Rhine Falls near Schaffhausen, Switzerland. When the river reaches Basel, Switzerland, it has flowed 230 mi (370 km) and dropped approximately 7,000 ft (2,100 m). From Basel, the river turns north and enters the Rhine Graben, between the Vosges in France on the west and the Black Forest in Germany on the east. Further north in Germany, two major tributaries enter the Rhine from the east, the Neckar River at Mannheim and the Main River at Mainz. Just north of Mainz is the Rheingau, a vineyard region where the river flows west for 25 mi (40 km) through the Taunus Mountains. At Bingen, the river turns north to Bonn, flowing 90 mi (145 km) in a narrow, winding gorge through slate mountains. Cliffs, castles, and vineyards line the river, where medieval lords demanded tolls for passage and the mythical Lorelei lured sailors to their deaths. The Mosel River enters from the west at Coblenz. Below Bonn, the river widens to 3,000 ft (900 m) and begins to cross the North German Plain, where it serves the Ruhr industrial region, including the cities of Dusseldorf and Essen. The Rhine and Meuse rivers merge in the Netherlands to build a large delta, which has been diked, channeled, and drained since Roman times. Waal Channel leads past the seaport of Rotterdam and into the North Sea.

To facilitate shipping, the Rhine River has been highly altered from its natural state and is linked by canals to both west European rivers and to the Danube, which provides water access from the North Sea to the Black Sea. The principal seaport is Rotterdam. Duisberg is head of deep-sea navigation, and ocean-going vessels go upstream to Cologne, where cargoes are transferred to barges. The limit of barge traffic is Basel, Switzerland, approximately 500 miles (800 km) from the North Sea.

Biota. The Rhine River was once a fertile fishing ground but is now the most ecologically stressed river in Europe with a drastic decline in aquatic species. Of 47 native fish, seven are no longer present. Environmental damage to the river, primarily during 1890–1950, is due both to channel alterations and to pollution (agricultural, industrial, chemical, and municipal).

Environmental Issues. Clear water from the Alps becomes polluted downstream as it passes industrial areas, particularly the Ruhr district. Dredging of shipping channels to accommodate ships recirculates polluted bottom sediments. After the Convention of the International Commission for the Protection of the Rhine (ICPR) was created in 1963, conditions were improving until the Sandoz Accident in 1986. During a fire, a large amount of dangerous chemicals was released from a storage facility at a Swiss pharmaceutical company. A 125 mi (200 km) stretch of river became ecologically dead and 500,000 fish were killed. In response, ICPR developed the Rhine Action Program (RAP), an international commission with a goal of improving water quality to enable the return of migratory fish. Levels of pollution have dropped by one-half, and salmon were thriving by 1997.

See also Black Forest and Vosges; European Alps

Further Reading

De Villeneuve, Carel H. V. 1996. "Western Europe's Artery: The Rhine." *Natural Resources Journal* 36: 441–454.

Penn, James R. 2001. *Rivers of the World*. Santa Barbara, CA: ABC-CLIO.

Raith, Sarah. 1999. "The Rhine Action Program: Restoring Value to the Rhine River." *Restoration and Reclamation Review*. University of Minnesota Digital Conservancy. conservancy.umn.edu/bitstream/59277/1/4.2.Raith.pdf

Rhone–Saone River System

Switzerland and France

Geographic Overview. The Rhone–Saone river corridor is a historically significant route linking the Mediterranean Sea with the Paris Basin and northern Europe. The river is a major contributor of fresh water to the Mediterranean Sea and continues to be economically important for transportation, irrigation, hydroelectric power, industrialization, and tourism.

Geographic Coordinates. Rhone Source: 46° 36'N, 08°23'E; Saone Source: 48°05'N, 06°10'E; Mouth: 43°20'N, 04°50'E

Description. The Rhone River, 505 mi (813 km) long from the Swiss Alps to the Mediterranean Sea, drains approximately 37,850 mi² (98,000 km²). The source of the Rhone River is the Rhone Glacier, at 5,740 ft (1,750 m) in the southern Swiss Alps. It empties into the Mediterranean Sea. The Saone River, the major tributary, merges with the Rhone at Lyons.

The alpine upper Rhone flows first south through steep-sided valleys in structural troughs, then turns southwest to flow 80 mi (128 km) through the Plain of Valais, a wide glacial valley between the Bernese Alps to the north and the Pennine Alps to the south. Tributaries join the Rhone as waterfalls from hanging valleys or via deeply incised gorges. After Martigny, the river turns abruptly north, cutting through the 12 mi (19 km) long St. Maurice gorge. Upon reaching a large flat valley, the former floor of a larger Lake Geneva, the Rhone's turbid waters, milky from glacial meltwater, enter the east end of Lake Geneva. After exiting the western end of the lake through the city of Geneva, the Rhone takes a zigzag course through the Jura Mountains in eastern France, flowing in valleys between ridges and in gorges cutting through ridges.

West of the Jura, the river crosses the Plain of Bresse, is joined by the Saone River at Lyons, and turns south. The Saone River rises in the Vosges Mountains in east-central France and flows southwest for 268 mi (431 km) in both a structural and glacial trough to Lyons. The Doubs, flowing between the Jura Mountains and the Vosges, is the major tributary. Water from the Saone almost doubles the flow of the Rhone.

South of Lyons, the Rhone's 130 mi (109 km) course to the Mediterranean Sea is defined by the linear Rhone rift, or graben, between the Massif Central to the West and the Jura and pre-Alps to the east. The river's course alternates between open basins and narrow gorges according to the underlying geologic structure, steep-sided gorges through limestone or crystalline rocks contrasted with broad basins and river terraces in softer rocks. From Lyons to Arles, several tributaries, including the Iser, Drome, and Durance, enter from the east, contributing water and sediment from the Alps, especially during early summer snowmelt. Shorter tributaries, such as the Ardeche, from the Massif Central contribute little water in summer, but may cause flooding in autumn and winter.

The delta begins at Arles, where the river channel splits into the Grande Rhone flowing southeast and the Petit Rhone flowing southwest. Between the two channels are the Camargue wetlands, characterized by brackish lagoons, marshes, shallow channels, sand spits, and coastal dunes. Sediment deposits continue to extend the delta of the Grande Rhone into the Mediterranean. A canal connects the Mediterranean port of Marseilles to the Rhone.

Varied topography and climatic influences give the Rhone a complex hydrology. Natural flow is irregular. Over a period of 400 years, the river's channel has been modified, and current flow is regulated by several dams and reservoirs on both the Rhone and its tributaries for hydroelectric power, flood prevention, and irrigation. The water is also used for cooling in several nuclear plants. The Rhone–Saone corridor is densely populated and industrialized. In spite of a natural tendency to flooding, steep gradient, strong current, changing depths, extensive sand and gravel banks, many gorges, and other natural impediments that should indicate poor navigability, the Rhone is a major transportation route and gateway from the Mediterranean Sea to northern Europe. A canal system connects the Rhone–Saone system to the North Sea and several northern European rivers, including the Moselle and Loire.

Biota. The biotic diversity of the Rhone River, related to temperature, can be divided into a cold alpine region, a cool and humid Saone corridor, and a hot and dry Mediterranean region in the south. Because of historical canal connections with other European river systems, the species assemblage is a combination of indigenous and non-native. Many fish, such as ruffe (*Gymnocephalus cernua*) and nase (*Chondrostoma nasus*), are accidental introductions from the canal system, while a few, such as mosquito fish (*Gambusia affinis*) and largemouth bass (*Micropterus salmoides*), were deliberate introductions. Over 400 species of birds use the Camargue. The wetlands provide wintering grounds for several duck species, nesting sites for flamingoes and nine species of herons, and resting and feeding sites for migratory birds.

Protected Areas. Several sites along the Rhone–Saone corridor and its tributaries are protected in some fashion, and some are part of the NATURA 2000 network. The Camargue is a Wetland of International Importance and a Special Protection Area.

Environmental Issues. Modifications to the river have altered the river's morphology, lowered the groundwater, changed riparian vegetation, polluted the water, and reduced biodiversity. Fish are contaminated with polychlorinated biphenyls (PCBs) and other pollutants. Efforts are underway to rehabilitate the river and restore its natural ecological state.

See also European Alps; Jura Mountains; Lake Geneva

Further Reading

Embleton, Clifford. 1984. "Hercynian Europe." In *Geomorphology of Europe*, 165–230. New York: John Wiley & Sons.

Olivier, Jean-Michel and Others. 2009. "The Rhone River Basin." In *Rivers of Europe*, edited by Klement Tockner, Urs Uehlinger, and Christopher T. Robinson, 247–295. London: Academic Press.

Penn, James R. 2001. *Rivers of the World*. Santa Barbara, CA: ABC-CLIO.

Río de la Plata

Argentina and Uruguay

Geographic Overview. The Río de la Plata (River Plate) is a shallow estuary located between Uruguay and Argentina at 35°–36°S latitude. Formed by the convergence of the Paraná and Uruguay rivers, it collects fresh water from a watershed that drains nearly 20 percent of the South American continent. The Río de la Plata drainage basin is the second largest in South America after the Amazon basin. It contains parts of five countries: 45 percent of the basin lies in Brazil, 30 percent in Argentina, and the remainder in Paraguay (13 percent), Bolivia (7 percent), and Uruguay (5 percent). Buenos Aires and Montevideo, the capital cities of Argentina and Uruguay, respectively, are situated on opposite banks of the Río de la Plata.

Geographic Coordinates. 35°40'S, 55°47'W

Description. The 180 mile (290 km) long Río de la Plata estuary is funnel-shaped, widening toward the Atlantic Ocean into which it empties. At its head the estuary is 1.2 mi (2 km) wide. At its mouth, measured from Punta Rosa, Argentina, across to Punta del Este, Uruguay, it is 140 mi (230 km) wide, which according to some makes it the largest estuary in the world. Upper reaches of the Paraná River system include its main tributary, the Paraguay River, and the Pantanal. Feeding into the Paraguay is the Pilcomayo River, which begins high in the Andes near Sucre, Bolivia, and forms an inland delta in the Gran Chaco that gives rise to a vast wetland, the estero Patiña, 170 mi (280 km) upstream from Asunción, Paraguay. The Pilcomayo disappears below into its own sediments for a time, but resurfaces before entering the Paraguay. Another tributary of the Paraguay is the Bemejo River, the only permanent stream to cross the Gran Chaco. The Paraná River itself begins in the Brazilian Highlands and carries the heavy sediment load contributed by its tributaries to the Rio de la Plata, where it has built up a delta at the head of the estuary. The Río de la Plata is brown with silt. Its main shipping channels must be continually dredged to allow sea-going vessels access to the ports at Buenos Aires and Montevideo.

Shallow shoals, the Barra del Indio, stretch between Punta Piedra, Argentina, and Montevideo, where the estuary abruptly flares to its maximum width. The shoals divide the estuary into two sections. Upstream of this point the water is fresh (salinity 0.2–5) and 3.3–16 ft (1–5 m) deep; downstream it is brackish (salinity 13–31) and 16–82 ft (5–25 m) deep. This is a salt-wedge estuary: outgoing fresh water floats on a wedge of incoming salt water that moves along the bottom with little mixing of the layers. Two distinct layers of water exist along a 60-mile (100-km) stretch downstream from the head of the salt wedge at Barra del Indio. Any particles settling out of the upper fresh layer tend to be carried upstream at depth and deposited at the tip of the wedge. This process helps retain the eggs and larvae of aquatic life-forms in the estuary, but also any pollutants that might be introduced. The salt wedge also serves as a barrier to the exchange of fish and plankters between two sections.

The Río de la Plata is in a humid subtropical climate region that receives 40–50 in (1,010–1,270 mm) of precipitation distributed throughout the year. The Argentine side tends to be cooler and somewhat drier than the Uruguayan side. At Punta del Este, Uruguay, January (austral summer) temperatures average 71°F (21°C), while the July temperatures (austral winter) average 53°F (11.5°C).

Biota. The Río de la Plata estuary is an important spawning ground and nursery area for fish and other aquatic life-forms. The muddy bottoms of Samborombón and Montevideo bays are rich in clams, snails, and crabs. Some of South America's rare salt marsh habitat occurs along the shores of Samborombón Bay, a major nursery area. The estuary is home to a rare, long-beaked river dolphin, the La Plata dolphin (*Pontoporia blainvillei*), that prefers brackish and saltwater habitat to freshwater. Sea lions live on rocky and sandy coasts along the estuary and hunt in the coastal waters of the Atlantic. South American fur seals inhabit steeper rocky areas along the estuary and feed at sea in the deeper waters above the continental shelf. Both consume fish, squid, and shrimps and are themselves prey for orcas.

Environmental Issues. The Río de la Plata is affected by land use in its drainage basin and activities in its waters. Much of the watershed is under agricultural use, both subsistence and commercial farming and cattle ranching. Urban sewage discharge, port activities, and industrial activities associated with the two large cities on its shores pollute the water. Overfishing by the mostly bottom-trawling industrial whitemouth croaker fishery has depleted its target fish. The loss of commercial mussel and red crab fisheries may be due to industrial effluent from Montevideo, which is located near the head of the salt wedge. Dredging channels and disposing of sediments destroys the bottom habitats of the estuary.

Further Reading

Cordeiro, Newton V. 1999. "Environmental Management Issues in the Plata Basin." In *Management of Latin American River Basins: Amazon, Plata, and São Francisco*, Part II. *The Plata River Basin*, edited by Asit K. Biswas, Newton V. Cordeira, Benedito P. F. Braga, and Cecilia Tortajada, 148–173. New York: United Nations University Press.

Mianzan, H., C. Lasta, E. Acha, R. Guerrero, G. Macchi, and C. Bremec. 2000. "The Rio de la Plata estuary, Argentina-Uruguay." In *Coastal Marine Ecosystems of Latin America*, edited by U. Seeliger and B. Kjerfve, 185–204. Berlin: Springer.

Rio Grande (Rio Bravo del Norte)

United States (Colorado, New Mexico, and Texas) and Mexico

Geographic Overview. The Rio Grande, flowing 4,554 mi (2,830 km) from southwestern Colorado to the Gulf of Mexico and draining approximately 36,000 mi^2 (870,000 km^2), is the fifth longest river in the United States. It is an important source of water for irrigated agriculture and urban areas in the arid Southwest. Both quantity and quality of water have been seriously impacted.

Geographic Coordinates. Source: 37°48'N, 107°32'W; Mouth: 25°57'N, 97°09'W

Description. From its headwaters in springs and snowmelt along the continental divide in the San Juan Mountains at approximately 12,140 ft (3,700 m) elevation, the Rio Grande and its highland tributaries flow down forested mountain slopes. From the

arid San Luis Valley in south-central Colorado south through New Mexico, the river's path is closely associated with the Rio Grande Rift Valley, a series of north–south trending grabens. For 70 mi (113 km), the river is confined by lava walls in a canyon as deep as 820 ft (250 m). Below its impoundment by Cochiti Dam north of Albuquerque, it continues to flow south, bisecting New Mexico until it reaches Elephant Butte Reservoir, the largest reservoir in New Mexico. Slightly downstream is Caballo Reservoir. North of El Paso, the river follows the border between Texas and New Mexico for a short distance. At El Paso, it begins to form the border between Texas and Mexico. At Presidio, Texas, the river is joined by the Rio Conchos from Mexico and enters a more mountainous region, including Big Bend National Park where the Rio Grande flows through three major canyons, 1,500–1,700 (455–520 m) deep. After turning northeast at Big Bend, the river then flows east to Amistad near Del Rio, where the river is impounded for irrigation and flood control, and is joined by the Pecos River, which flows into Amistad Reservoir. In the Rio Grande's southeast route to the Gulf of Mexico, it is impounded again at Falcon Dam. The lower Rio Grande is a flat agricultural plain. Minimal water reaches the Gulf of Mexico near Brownsville.

Before reaching Cochiti Reservoir, the upper reaches of the river are gravelly with clear, fast-flowing water from the mountains. From Cochiti Reservoir to Elephant Butte, the river's naturally low gradient formerly produced a slowly flowing alluvial river with floodplains and marshes, attractive to migrating waterfowl. Most of the river is now channelized from Cochiti Reservoir to El Paso. From El Paso to Laredo, the river's route is steeper, resulting in faster flow, especially through Big Bend. With the lower gradient near the coast, the river again becomes depositional.

From southern Colorado to Presidio, the volume of the river decreases, due to withdrawal for municipalities and irrigated agriculture and evaporation from reservoirs. Withdrawal for irrigation is especially heavy in the San Luis Valley in Colorado, the middle reaches in New Mexico, and the lower reaches in Texas. Withdrawals from Cochiti Dam to Elephant Butte sometimes cause the river to run dry in this region. Most river flow downstream from El Paso is wastewater and irrigation return. Spring snowmelt dominates the flow upstream from Cochiti Dam, where discharge averages 1,518 ft³/sec (43 m³/s). Above the confluence of the Rio Conchos, mean discharge has diminished to106 ft³/sec (3 m³/s). Peak flows downstream coincide with late-summer thunderstorms in the drainage basin of the Rio Conchos, which historically added 1,060 ft³/sec (30 m³/s) to the Rio Grande, but is now much less. Flow increases past Amistad Reservoir, a mean of 2,295 ft³/sec (65 m³/s), increasing to 3,355 ft³/sec (95 m³/s) at Falcon Reservoir. After water is withdrawn from the lower reaches, the river may reach the Gulf of Mexico with approximately 1,305 ft³ (37 m³/s), primarily from flood events such as hurricanes, but in 2002 and 2003, no Rio Grande water reached the Gulf for several months.

Between the mountain headwaters and humid Gulf coast, most of the Rio Grande's path is through arid or semiarid landscapes with local basins of interior drainage. About one-half of the watershed contributes water to the Rio Grande. After the alpine and forested San Juan Mountains, vegetation is pinyon and juniper woodlands and sagebrush in Colorado and New Mexico, changing to Chihuahuan Desert in southern New Mexico, western Texas, and adjacent Mexico.

The Pecos River originates in the southern Rocky Mountains north of Santa Fe, New Mexico, and flows south on the western edge of the Great Plains, passing through Carlsbad, New Mexico, and entering the Rio Grande at Amistad Reservoir. Through much of its route, it flows in deep gorges carved into limestone. It adds little to the flow of the Rio Grande because of the aridity of its drainage basin and several impoundments and water diversions, particularly upstream of Pecos, Texas.

Headwaters of the Rio Conchos are high along the continental divide in the Sierra Madre Occidental in northwestern Mexico. From pine forests in the mountains, it first flows east, then northeast through basin and range landscape of the Chihuahuan Desert, reaching the Rio Grande at Presidio. The upper sections are incised into narrow, volcanic rock canyons, while the lower reaches are alluvial,

meandering or braided. Several dams and diversions in Mexico for irrigated agriculture and grazing land now leave little river water. A mean discharge of 725 ft³/sec (20.5 m³/s) prior to 1995 decreased to a mean of 134 ft³/sec (3.8 m³/s) in 1995–2003, and discharge at times is zero. The basin has several endemic fish and herpetofauna.

The Rio Salado and its main tributary, the Rio Sabinas, originate in the northern Sierra Madre Oriental and join the Rio Grande at Falcon Reservoir between Laredo and Brownsville. Because the Rio Salado drains arid country and water is withdrawn for irrigation, the main stem is sometimes dry. The intermittent Rio Puerco, which begins north of Grants, New Mexico, contributes a heavy sediment load on the occasions it joins the Rio Grande north of Socorro, New Mexico.

Biota. The Rio Grande basin has six freshwater ecoregions—Upper Rio Grande, Lower Rio Grande, Pecos, Rio San Juan, Rio Salado, and Rio Conchos. None of the rivers have been well studied. Disconnection from floodplains and fragmentation by dams and diversions have altered riparian habitats.

Protected Areas. Two sections are designated Wild and Scenic Rivers, Rio Grande Gorge in northern New Mexico, noted for its narrow canyons, and Rio Grande in Texas, which includes the river's route through Big Bend National Park. Bosque del Apache National Wildlife Refuge, near Socorro, is a major wintering ground for waterfowl, especially Snow Geese and Sandhill Cranes.

Environmental Issues. Water quality is compromised by pesticides and fertilizers in agricultural return and by municipal waste.

See also Basin and Range Physiographic Province

Further Reading

Dahm, Clifford N., Robert J. Edwards, and Frances P. Gelwick. 2005. "Gulf Coast Rivers of the Southwestern United States." In *Rivers of North America*, edited by Arthur C. Benke and Colbert E. Cushing, 180–228. Amsterdam: Elsevier Academic Press.

Hudson, Paul F. et al. 2005. "Rivers of Mexico." In *Rivers of North America*, edited by Arthur C. Benke and Colbert E. Cushing, 1030–1103. Amsterdam: Elsevier Academic Press.

Rocky Mountains

United States (Alaska, Montana, Idaho, Wyoming, Utah, Colorado, and New Mexico) and Canada

Geographic Overview. The Rocky Mountains, stretching from northern Alaska southeast across Canada and the United States, is an almost continuous mountain barrier between eastern and western North America. The Rocky Mountain system is not just one mountain mass but several ranges and regions separated by valleys, with a variety of structures and landscapes. The mountains are important sources of water and minerals, provide significant recreation opportunities, and are also home to a variety of vegetation and wildlife.

Geographic Coordinates. Approximately 35° 30'N–69°30'N, 105°15'W–162'30'W

Description. The majority of the Rocky Mountains is a very rugged landscape, characterized by both high elevations and high relief. Many peaks stand more than 14,000 ft (4,250 m) asl, and local relief from mountain tops to adjacent valleys may be 5,000–7,000 ft (1,500–2,125 m). The region also includes deep gorges and alluvial basins. Generalities can be described in three major subdivisions. The Northern Rocky Mountain region, from the Brooks Range in Alaska south to western Montana and Idaho, is characterized by relatively horizontal sedimentary and metamorphosed sedimentary rocks, which were faulted and thrust eastward over the Great Plains. The major mountain mass in Idaho is composed of massive granitic intrusions. The Middle Rockies, primarily in Wyoming and including the Wyoming Basin, consist of isolated mountain ranges of various rock types and structures, including anticlines, fault-block mountains, and volcanics, separated by flat alluvial basins.

The forested landscapes and high glaciated mountains and alpine tundra in Colorado are typical of the Rocky Mountains in the United States. (Welcomia/Dreamstime.com)

The Wyoming Basin, although encompassed by the Rockies, is not mountainous and resembles the Great Plains. The general landscape of the Wyoming Basin is flat alluvial plains, with occasional low, rounded rock masses of exposed mountain tops. The Southern Rocky Mountains, primarily in Colorado with extensions into southern Wyoming and northern New Mexico, consist of several general north–south trending ranges separated by a large structural valley.

All of the higher areas were extensively sculpted by alpine glaciers, which left a rugged landscape of cirques, horns, arêtes, and glacial troughs. The Cordilleran Ice Sheet covered the Canadian Rockies during the Pleistocene, and many icefields, such as the Columbia Icefield, remain in the high mountains.

Geologic History. The various ranges within the Rocky Mountain system, which was uplifted due to interactions between the Pacific and North American plates, share a common geologic history. Although not all at the same time, the entire Rocky Mountain region occupied several geosynclines in the geologic past. During the Precambrian, isolated geosynclines developed in western Montana and in northeastern Utah. From the mid to late Mesozoic (160–130 mya), a long geosyncline, from the Gulf of Mexico to Alaska, rested on the continental shelf of western North America. During its 100 million years of existence, as much as 30,000 ft (9,000 m) of sedimentary rock was deposited. In the early Cretaceous, nonmarine sediments were still being deposited in a basin stretching from British Columbia south to New Mexico. Many of the sedimentary rock layers that were deposited in the geosynclines, such as the Dakota sandstone and Morrison shale, can be seen on both the eastern and western sides of the mountains, particularly in the Southern Rockies. These sedimentary layers were subsequently uplifted as the Rocky Mountains began to rise during the Laramide Orogeny in the late Cretaceous (70–40 mya). Mountain building, which included folding, faulting, granitic intrusions, and volcanism, lasted 30 million years, ending in the Tertiary.

Uplift was generally higher in Colorado and parts of Wyoming, which explains the higher elevations of those mountains today. From Alaska south to western Montana, tectonic movements were primarily horizontal—folding, faulting, and thrusting rock layers up and over younger rocks to the east. South of Montana, uplift was more vertical. Tectonics deformed the underlying craton, pushing the Precambrian rocks into anticlines surrounded by tilting Paleozoic sedimentary rocks. More Precambrian rock was pushed upward in the southern Rockies, where the geology becomes more complex. Broad basins between individual mountain ranges, especially in the Wyoming area, were covered with Cenozoic alluvium, which was eroded from adjacent mountains.

The Northern Rocky Mountain region was a geosyncline from the Paleozoic (500 mya) to the early Mesozoic (240 mya). Western Montana, in the vicinity of Waterton–Glacier International Peace Park, was a geosyncline for a longer period, beginning in the Precambrian (600 mya). During this long episode of geologic time, thick layers of sediments were deposited, which were compressed into both sedimentary and metamorphic rocks. In the Cretaceous (100 mya), magma intrusions pushed up the overlying layers of sedimentary and metamorphic rock, which were faulted in many places and thrust eastward over younger sedimentary strata. A prime example is the Lewis Overthrust fault in Montana, a 280 mi (452 km) long north–south block of rock, which moved 40 mi (64 km) eastward onto the edge of the Great Plains. The Rocky Mountain Trench is an 870 mi (1,400 km) long valley trending northwest–southeast in the Northern Rocky Mountains. The trench in British Columbia lies along a transform fault, while in Montana, it forms a graben, the site of Flathead Lake. The trench marks a boundary between rock type and structure. East of the Rocky Mountain Trench, the Rockies are a series of overlapping thrust faults and folds in Paleozoic limestones and quartzites that were thrust eastward into Mesozoic and Cenozoic sandstones and shales. West of the trench, mountains are characterized by granitic intrusions, such as the Idaho Batholith, into Paleozoic strata. The block west of the trench in Canada has moved 250–450 mi (400–750 km) along the fault and continues to move northwest. The sedimentary rock layers in the Brooks Range in Alaska are Paleozoic and early Mesozoic, folded and faulted in Laramide Orogeny.

The Middle Rockies have a variety of structures and rock types. The Bighorn Mountains is a long anticline with a Precambrian core. The Grand Tetons is a large west-tilting fault-block mountain with a Precambrian crystalline core. The granite core of the Wind River Range was pushed up and westward by a thrust fault. The Wasatch Range is a tilted fault block of deformed Paleozoic rocks. Low-elevation thrust faults and folded mountains lie on the border between Idaho and Wyoming. The Uinta Mountains, the only major east–west mountain range in the Rocky Mountains, is a folded and upfaulted core of ancient rocks dating from a Precambrian geosyncline. Tertiary lava flows formed the Absaroka Range and parts of Yellowstone. The Yellowstone Plateau is a large caldera, the remains of an explosive volcano. It is currently a hotspot, where a magma pool is close to the surface, heating water that subsequently surfaces in hot springs and geysers. In much of Wyoming, sediments eroded from the early uplift of the Rockies were deposited so thickly that they completely covered some of the anticlinal mountains, which had not been uplifted as high as others. With subsequent uplift, the mountain tops were partially exhumed, and rivers incised gorges, such as Devil's Gate, through the hard Precambrian rock.

While most of the rest of the Rocky Mountain region was still a geosyncline during the late Paleozoic, ancestral Rockies were uplifted in Colorado and northern New Mexico, particularly in the Front Range region on the east side of the current mountains and the Uncompaghre region, which covered a major portion of the southwestern part of the state. Erosion from these mountain masses contributed sediments to the adjacent Paleozoic basins, and to the later Mesozoic and Cretaceous seas, which covered the eroded mountains. The Southern Rockies were uplifted in the late Cretaceous, subjected to erosion, and uplifted again in the late Tertiary. The relatively level, undulating surfaces at high elevation in areas such as Rocky Mountain National Park's Trail Ridge Road are believed to be old erosion surfaces. Alluvium was carried to the Great Plains and to the Wyoming Basin.

The last uplift was complex, but was basically two arches of a large anticline with a basin between. The arches developed into the East Slope and West Slope ranges in Colorado. North Park, Middle Park, South Park, and the graben of the San Luis Valley form an almost continuous high elevation, 7,000–10,000 ft (2,125–3,000 m) central lowland from northern Colorado south to northern New Mexico. Under the large anticlinal uplift that formed the Southern Rockies is a variety of mountain types, including volcanism. Many of the mountain ranges, such as the Front Range and the Medicine Bows, in the Southern Rockies have Precambrian granite cores. The Mosquito Range and Sangre de Cristo Mountains are tilted sedimentary rocks, and the Sawatch is complexly folded and faulted. The San Juan Mountains is a complex volcanic dome, the Elk Mountains are a laccolith, basalt flows filled part of the San Luis Valley, and the Valles Caldera occupies the summit of the Jemez Mountains in New Mexico. The Spanish Peaks, surrounded by an extensive system of radiating dikes, are igneous intrusions that failed to reach the surface.

Many major rivers exit the Middle and Southern Rocky Mountains through deep gorges, indicating that the streams were antecedent, developing initially on sediment before eroding into the buried underlying mountains. Examples are the Arkansas River through Royal Gorge, the Green River through Ladore Canyon, and the Big Horn River through the Big Horn Mountains.

Biota. In general, both summer and winter temperatures decrease, and precipitation increases with elevation. Although the ecological zones of the Rocky Mountains follow elevational patterns, elevation limits are not precise because temperatures and precipitation also change with latitude. Ecological zones occupy lower elevations in higher, colder latitudes. Windward, generally the western side of the Rockies, and leeward, generally the eastern side, cause further complications, with the western slopes being wetter and the eastern slopes being drier. Because they are based in more southerly, warmer latitudes, the Southern Rockies have the most life zones. The mountains generally rise from plains or deserts, where both winter and summer temperatures are highest, precipitation the least, and short grasses and various forbs or sparse shrubs dominate. The montane zone, a transition from drier environments to wetter forests, are pinyon pine and juniper scrub forests with shrubs such as sagebrush at the lower elevations, changing to ponderosa pine, Douglas fir, and white fir, at higher elevations.

The subalpine zone is a closed forest dominated by Engelmann spruce and subalpine fir. Aspen is a common deciduous tree in both montane and subalpine zones, usually in wetter meadows. Close to the alpine zone, where conditions become difficult for tree growth, the forest trees become stunted and deformed often due to harsh winter winds, until they finally give way to short-stature plants of the alpine tundra. This seemingly barren landscape supports a number of short plants, including forbs, sedges, and ground-hugging shrubs, all adapted to harsh winters and short, cool summers. Montane forests in the Northern Rockies, especially in Canada, are dominated by Douglas fir, and white spruce. Wetter regions support a more lush forest, which also includes western red cedar and western hemlock. The subalpine zone grades from spruce-fir into the high-latitude taiga or boreal forest of black spruce and white spruce.

Animal life is varied. Rodents are plentiful, including marmots, beaver, and ground squirrels (*Spermophilus* spp.), as are showshoe hares. Coyote, wolf, grizzly bear, lynx, bobcat, and mountain lion are major predators, although not found throughout the Rocky Mountains. Black bears are common. Bison prefer open areas because they are grazers. Birds include eagles, jays, ravens, chickadees, water birds such as Canada Goose, and many others. Willow Ptarmigan is a common tundra bird. Ungulates include moose, elk, mule deer, and in the north, caribou. Mountain goats are native to the northern Rockies, while bighorn sheep are more wide spread. Reptiles and amphibians are more common at lower elevations because of their inability to regulate their body temperatures in cold climates.

See also Columbia Icefield; Gates of the Arctic National Park and Preserve; Grand Teton National Park; Greater Yellowstone Ecosystem; Waterton–Glacier International Peace Park

Further Reading

Elias, Scott. A. 2002. *Rocky Mountains*. Washington, D.C.: Smithsonian Institution Press.

Kummel, Bernhard. 1970. *History of the Earth*. San Francisco: W. H. Freeman and Company.

National Audubon Society. 1999. *Field Guide to the Rocky Mountain States*. New York: Knopf Doubleday Publishing Group.

Ross Ice Shelf

Antarctica

Geographic Overview. The Ross Ice Shelf is one of the 47 named ice shelves on the Antarctic continent and the largest in the world. It covers much of the coastal zone of the Ross Sea, which borders it on the north. The Transantarctic Mountains form the western and southern borders, while King Edward the VII Peninsula defines its eastern edge. The ice shelf and the Ross Sea are named for British explorer Captain James Clark Ross, who discovered the region in 1841.

Geographic Coordinates. 78°–86°S, 155°–160°E

Description. The Ross Ice Shelf floats upon the Ross Sea, although most of its volume lies beneath sea level. A vertical cliff of ice 50–200 ft (15–60 m) high marks the above surface portion of a mass of ice 182,000 mi^2 (472,000 km^2) in area. This sheer face extends for about 500 mi (800 km) between Ross Island and King Edward the VII Peninsula. The front extends as much as 280 mi (450 km) from the coast. Total thickness of the ice near the ice front is 820 ft (250 m); it increases landward to 2,600 ft (800 m). This huge mass rises and falls with the tides.

Eight outflow glaciers, primarily from the West Antarctic ice sheet, feed into the Ross Ice Shelf. Ice also accumulates from below as sea water freezes and accretes to the mass. New ice from the sea, however, is rather minor and only accounts for a basal veneer 16–20 in (40–50 cm). The glaciers push the shelf seaward at a rate of 3,000 ft (900 m) a year. This advance is compensated for by calving of large tabular icebergs along the ice front. Fissures and cracks develop along the outer shelf. They can fill with meltwater, which expands when it freezes and serves as a wedge to split the ice apart. The world's largest recorded iceberg, Iceberg B-15, calved near ice-covered Roosevelt Island in March 2000. This flat chunk of ice measured 170 mi (275 km) long and 25 mi (40 km) wide and had an area of 4,250 mi^2 (11,000 km^2).

Geologic History. Ice has covered the Antarctic continent for 14 million years.

Protected Areas. All of Antarctica is protected by the Antarctic Treaty System. If a Ross Sea Marine

Protected Area is established, as proposed, the ice shelf would be included.

Environmental Issues. Climatic warming is the greatest threat to the Ross Ice Shelf. Elsewhere in Antarctica ice shelves have been collapsing, and it is feared that this massive shelf may eventually follow suit. The ice shelf acts as a break on glaciers. Once they are gone glaciers speed up. While the melting of floating ice does not raise sea level directly, the melting of land-based glaciers will. For now, the fissuring of the Ross Ice Shelf does not appear other than normal.

See also Antarctica; Ross Sea; Southern Ocean

Further Reading

"Quick Facts on Ice Shelves." 2013. National Snow and Ice Data Center. http://nsidc.org/cryosphere/quickfacts/iceshelves.html

Saundry, Peter. 2011. "Ross Ice Shelf." *The Encyclopedia of Earth.* http://www.eoearth.org/article/Ross_Ice_Shelf

Ross Sea

Southern Ocean

Geographic Overview. The Ross Sea is a large bay between Victoria Land and Marie Byrd Land in Antarctica and is the southernmost extending body of water on Earth. Most of its coast is covered by the Ross Ice Shelf, the world's largest expanse of floating ice. The sea is the most productive region of the Southern Ocean and remains in nearly pristine condition. The Ross Sea Polynya (see below) is Earth's largest polynya (pool of open water surrounded by sea ice) and source of dense sea-water that flows down the continental slope to collect as Antarctic Bottom Water, a driver of global oceanic circulation and global climate patterns.

Geographic Coordinates. Approximately 70°S–85°S, 150°W–160°E

Description. The Ross Sea, the southernmost extending body of water on Earth, is a large bay between Victoria Land and Marie Byrd Land in Antarctica. It covers one of the two broad stretches of continental shelf along Antarctica's margins. (The other is beneath the Weddell Sea.) It has an areal extent of 370,000 mi² (960,000 km²). The continental shelf ends at a depth of about 985 ft (300 m), where a steep continental slope descends nearly 10,000 ft (3,000 m) to the sea floor. The shelf contains troughs gouged by ice streams during previous glaciations; these separate several banks. The Ross Sea is shallower in the north than in the south due to the presence of a broad submarine ridge, likely a terminal moraine, extending between Cape Colbeck and Pennel Bank. The shelf and slope are important marine habitats supporting a variety of organisms in what is regarded a biodiversity hotspot in the polar regions of Earth.

The Ross Ice Shelf, an extension of the West Antarctic ice sheet, forms an imposing wall 50–200 ft (15–60 m) high and 500 mi (800 km) long at its southern edge. Sea-ice covers much of the sea's surface during the summer. The northwest coastline, however, is generally ice-free in summer and allows the passage of cargo ships to McMurdo Station, the staging area for supplies going to other bases and camps on Antarctica, including the South Pole.

Winter sea-ice in the Ross Sea contains patches where open water appears (polynas), however briefly. Strong winds off the continent blow the sea-ice away from these areas, which are constantly refreezing, only to have the ice cover removed again. The huge and persistent Ross Sea Polynya, with a surface area of 9,650 mi² (25,000 km²), is the largest in the world. These openings in the ice allow penetration of sunlight and contribute to an earlier than expected spring production of phytoplankton in the surrounding sea.

Circulation and Major Currents. A clockwise gyre circulates in the Ross Sea between the Antarctic Circumpolar Current and Antarctica's continental shelf. Driven by the polar easterlies streaming from the Antarctic Plateau, Southern Ocean surface water enters the gyre near Cape Colbeck as a strong boundary current. It passes westward along the Ross Ice Shelf, collecting sea-ice, icebergs, and meltwater from the ice shelf. The resulting low salinity seawater then enters the Ross Sea Polynya, where constant refreezing in winter locks up water and concentrates dissolved salts in the remaining seawater, increasing its salinity and hence density. Dense shelf water slides down the continental slope to join the Antarctic Bottom Water, which moves along the Pacific Ocean

Pack ice and icebergs in the Ross Sea, Antarctica. (eeilers/iStockphoto.com)

seafloor into the Northern Hemisphere as an integral part of the global oceanic conveyor belt. Surface waters of the Ross Sea gyre continue westward along the coast of Victoria Land to mix with the Antarctic Circumpolar Current beyond the continental slope.

Biota. The continental shelf ecosystem is particularly rich in species. It also has a high rate of endemism due to isolation from other shelf areas and the fact that the northwest part of the shelf has never been scoured by major glaciations and thus preserves more ancient lineages. A high production of phytoplankton, aided by the presence of polynyas, supports an abundance of zooplankters, which in turn feed krill and Antarctic silverfish, the main prey for top predators such as Antarctic toothfish (*Dissostichus mawsoni*), penguins, albatrosses, and seals. On rocky substrates below the depth at which winter ice scours the bottom, is a zone harboring more than 230 species of sponge. The sponges themselves are microhabitats for other sessile invertebrates, as well as some mobile ones. The shelf community is rich in bryozoans, polychaetes, mollusks (gastropods, bivalves, and nudibranchs), as well as echinoderms. The lack of crabs, sharks, and barnacles, as well as the presence of few fish, may explain the diversity and abundance of these forms.

Ninety-five species of fish have been recorded in the Ross Sea, the ichthyofauna dominated by 61 species of icefish (notothenioids). One of the icefish, the Antarctic toothfish, fills the niche of sharks as predators. Toothfish commonly grow nearly 4 ft (127 cm) long and weigh 175 lb (80 kg).

A large variety of predators is a chief characteristic of the Ross Sea community. In addition to the toothfish, the world's largest squid—indeed largest invertebrate, the colossal squid (*Mesonychoteuthis hamiltoni*), lives in these waters; it reaches lengths of 32–46 ft (10–14 m). Its tentacles are equipped with sharp hooks as well as suckers. Six penguin species, five seals, six kinds of baleen whales, and six toothed whales are among other top carnivores that prowl the waters over the continental shelf and slope.

Protected Areas. The Commission for the Protection of Antarctic Marine Living Resources (CCAMLR), created as part of the Antarctic Treaty System in 1982, regulates the marine environment of the Ross Sea. The Antarctic Ocean Alliance advocates the creation of a network of marine protected areas and no-take marine reserves in 19 special areas in the Southern Ocean around Antarctica, including the Ross Sea. The United States and New Zealand announced a joint proposal for a Ross Sea Marine Protected Area in 2013.

Environmental Issues. The Ross Sea is the least impacted open sea area on Earth. Major threats come from commercial fishing for Antarctic toothfish in the deep waters above the continental slope and from climate change. The toothfish is a long-lived species that reproduces slowly. Already declines in fish size are reported in a fishery only begun in 1996. Unlike other areas off Antarctica, in the Ross Sea sea-ice is increasing, reducing the length of time open water and sunlight are available to phytoplankters and the food webs that depend upon them. However, warming of the climate, melting of the Antarctic icefields, and warming of the Southern Ocean will continue; and eventually this ice too will disappear. Currently, the Ross Sea is the last place in the Southern Ocean with sea-ice all year and hence will, for a time, be a refugium for ice-dependent Antarctic life.

See also Antarctica; Ross Ice Shelf; Southern Ocean

Further Reading

Cameron, Anna, Stephen Campbell, Claire Christian, and Robert Nicoll. 2012. "Antarctic Ocean Legacy: A Marine Reserve for the Ross Sea." Antarctic Ocean Alliance. http://antarcticocean.org/wp-content/uploads/2013/03/AOA-Ross-Sea-Report-ENGLISH.pdf

Hogan, Michael C. 2011. "Ross Sea." *The Encyclopedia of Earth.* http://www.eoearth.org/article/Ross_Sea?topic=49523

Smith, W.O. Jr., P. N. Sedwick, K. R. Arrigo, D. G. Ainley, and A. H. Orsi. 2012. "The Ross Sea in a Sea of Change." *Oceanography* 25(3): 90–103. http://www.tos.org/oceanography/archive/25-3_smith_w.pdf

Rupununi Savanna

Guyana

Geographic Overview. The Rupununi Savanna is a small tropical grassland in the southwest quadrant of Guyana. It is a good example of fire subclimax community.

Geographic Coordinates. 03°00'N, 59°30'W

Description. Measuring about 5,000 mi^2 (13,000 km^2) in area, the Rupununi has two distinct sections separated by the Kanuku Mountains. The North Rupununi Savanna is a flat to gently rolling lowland between the Rupununi River on the east and the Ireng River on the west. It has developed on sedimentary rocks that overlie the granitic basement rock of the region. Porous laterites form scattered ridges and domes that support forest. The South Rupununi occurs east of the Takutu River on basement rocks of Precambrian granite. The Rupununi River flows through this section, nearly bisecting it. The South Rupununi is dotted with granitic inselbergs. These boulder-strewn outcrops have steep slopes and sandy soils on which trees grow. A partially impermeable laterite has developed in depressions. Soils tend to be acidic and nutrient-deficient. Elevations in the Rupununi run approximately 500–1,000 ft (150–300 m) asl.

The Rupununi receives 60–78 in (1,500–2,000 mm) of rain year, most of it falling during a rainy season that lasts from May into August. During this time rivers flood, and water may stand on the grassland for several months wherever clay pans prevent downward percolation. Temporary ponds and lakes are frequent in both the north and the south. Most of the rivers of the regions are part of the Essequibo River drainage system; but the Ireng and Takutu rivers flow into the Amazon system. During seasons of flood the two drainage systems become connected.

The Rupununi grasslands are largely a fire climax, as the savanna is burned once a year to improve pasture for cattle and to keep the vegetation in and around settlements low. Regular burning promotes the growth of fire-tolerant and fire-adapted plants such as the small tree *Curatella americana*, which has a thick corky bark and often gnarled trunk. Grasses, too, are fire-adapted since their growing buds are near the ground and protected from the heat. After a burn they resprout and take advantage of a supply of nutrients provided by the fresh layer of ash. Many herbs that have woody stems buried beneath the soil only bloom after a fire, contributing to a flush of regrowth in the savanna. Other herbs, including those with bulbs, bloom only after summer rains begin. In addition to grasslands, a unique rock flora exists on the inselbergs, stands of buriti palm are conspicuous on the landscape, and gallery forests with trees no taller than 35 ft (10 m) line the rivers. Oxbow lakes beside the meandering Rupununi River harbor aquatic plants, including the giant Amazon water lily, *Victoria amazonica*, with its huge circular leaves with upturned edges. Air trapped between the ribs on the purplish-red underside of the leaves makes them strong and buoyant; they can support up to 100 lb (45 kg).

Toward the south, the grasslands increasingly merge with the Amazon rainforest of southern Guyana. Trees begin to become important as patches of forest locally called "bush islands," in the South Rupununi. These contain trees less than 35 ft (10 m) tall. Bush islands gradually coalesce and become larger patches and eventually a full-fledged forest.

Environmental Issues. The Rupununi has been relatively undisturbed until recently. It lies adjacent to Brazil's rapidly growing state of Roraima, and a bridge across the Takutu River has been constructed, connecting the two areas. Rapid development threatens to spread across the international border.

Rwenzori Mountains

Democratic Republic of the Congo and Uganda

Geographic Overview. The Rwenzori (formerly Ruwenzori) are high crystalline fault-block mountains on the side of the Albertine Rift, the western branch of Africa's Great Rift Valley. They sit nearly on the equator and separate two of the East African Great Lakes, Edward and Albert. Among the highest mountains on the continent, the Rwenzori's tallest three peaks still bear remnant glaciers. They also have classic afro-alpine vegetation with moss-draped giant heathers,

giant lobelias, and tree senecios. Ptolemy called them the Mountains of the Moon in AD 150, a name that persists until today. The current name means "rain maker."

Geographic Coordinates. 00°23'N, 29°52'E

Description. The Rwenzori Mountains include the third, fourth, and fifth highest peaks in Africa, after Mount Kilimanjaro and Mount Kenya. The central part of the massif has 25 peaks rising above 14,760 ft (4,500 m) asl. Margherita Peak, one of the twin peaks of Mount Stanley, reaches an elevation of 16,762 ft (5,109 m) asl. The other peak, Alexandra, is 16,677 ft (5,083 m) asl. Next in height is Mount Speke at 16,043 ft (4,890 m) and Mount Baker at 15,899 ft (4,843 m). These three high mountains are named for explorers who sought the source of the Nile River in the mid-19th century.

Unlike the two higher mountains (Kilimanjaro and Kenya), the Rwenzori are not volcanoes, but an uplifted, tilted block of Precambrian intrusive and metamorphosed igneous rocks (gneiss, schist, quartzite, and amphibolite) that perches on the side of the Albertine Rift, the western branch of the Great Rift Valley, where it separates Lake Edward from Lake Albert, both elongate rift valley lakes. The range extends 120 km north–south and 50 km east–west. The jagged, bare rock summits were carved by alpine glaciers and freeze–thaw activity. Snowfields survive on Mounts Stanley, Speke, and Baker, but are rapidly shrinking. In the early 1990s, the surface areas of glaciers totaled roughly 2 mi^2 (5 km^2), an estimated 40 percent of their 1955 expanse and less than 25 percent of what they had covered in 1906. The mountains also have numerous alpine wetlands, lakes, and streams.

The massif rises out of tropical rainforests on its western side and tropical savanna on the east and displays discrete altitudinal zones before reaching snowline at 14,436 ft (4,400 m) asl. Montane forest occurs from about 6,000–10,000 ft (1,800–3,000 m). A belt of African mountain bamboo (*Arundinaria alpina*) and *Mimulopsis* forest exists within the higher elevations of the montane forest. From 10,000 to 12,500 ft (3,000–3,800 m) a belt of moss- and lichen-draped giant heathers (*Erica* spp.) and small trees of *Hagenia abysinnica* and *Rapanea rhododendroides* occurs. The heathers attain heights of over 33 ft (10 m). Woolly-leaved shrubs of *Helichrysum guilelmii*, scattered tree groundsels (*Senecio longeligulatus*), and giant lobelias (*Lobelia stuhlmannii*) also grow in this zone. An afroalpine moorland extends above the heather zone to snowline. In this belt are giant lobelias (*Lobelia wollastonii*) and stands, sometimes dense, of tree senecios (*Dendrosenecio adnivalis*), which can grow 20–33 ft (6–10 m) tall. Above snowline, the rock surfaces of the jagged high peaks in the nival zone are covered with lichens.

The Rwenzori are wetter than other East African mountains, receiving 78–118 in (2,000–3,000 mm) of precipitation annually, depending upon elevation. Nighttime frosts can occur above 10,000 ft (3,000 m) in the heather zone, and are frequent (80–90 percent of nights) above 13,000 ft (4,000 m). In the afroalpine and nival zones, daily temperatures can range between freezing at night to 68°F (20°C) during the day.

Geologic History. The Rwenzori represent ancient basement rock that was uplifted during crustal extension 2–3 mya. Most of the uplift appears to have occurred after 2.5 mya. A horst block, they are the highest rift mountains in the world. To the north is the graben containing Lake Albert and to the south the graben holding Lake Edward. Prior to uplift, this section of the East African Rift Valley held Lake Obweruka, which was divided by the rise of the Rwenzori into the two great lakes just mentioned.

Biota. The woody plants in the afroalpine zone show a high rate of endemism, with 81 percent restricted to East Africa and 19 percent to that particular vegetation zone. Several primates occur in the range, including the eastern chimpanzee, Angolan colobus monkey, Rwenzori colobus monkey, L'Hoest's monkey, and the blue monkey. The Rwenzori duiker and the Rwenzori ottershrew (*Micropotamogale ruwenzorii*) are endemic to the region. The strange-nosed chameleon (*Bradypodion xenorhinis*) is an endemic reptile.

Protected Areas. Two national parks protect the Rwenzori: Rwenzori Mountains National Park in Uganda and Parc National del Virunga in the Democratic Republic of the Congo. The former is a UNESCO World Heritage Site.

Environmental Issues. Soil erosion, landslides, and gullying related to poor agricultural practices on mountain slopes are problems.

See also Mount Kenya; Mount Kilimanjaro

Further Reading

Barr, Jane and Arshia Chander. 2012. "Africa without Snow and Ice." UNEP Global Environmental Alert Service. http://www.unep.org/pdf/UNEP-GEAS_AUG_2012 .pdf

Bauer, F. U., U. A. Glasmacher, U. Ring, A. Schumann, and B. Nagudi. 2010. "Thermal and Exhumation History of the Central Rwenzori Mountains, Western Rift of the East African Rift System, Uganda." *International Journal of Earth Science* (Geologische Rundschau) 99: 1575–1597. http://ypeysson.free.fr/data/voyages/divers/Bauer-Rwenzori-2010.pdf

"Introduction of Rwenzori National Park." n.d. Institute of Tropical Forest Conservation. Mbarara University of Science and Technology. http://www.itfc.org/Rwenzori%20Mountains%20National%20Park.htm

Linder, H. Peter and Berit Gehrke. 2006. "Common Plants of the Rwenzori, Particularly the Upper Zones." Institute of Systematic Botany, University of Zurich.

S

The Sahara

Algeria, Chad, Egypt, Libya, Mali, Mauretania, Morocco, Niger, Sudan, and Tunisia

Geographic Overview. The world's third largest desert, surpassed in size only by the polar deserts of Antarctica and the Arctic region, the Sahara stretches across North Africa from the Atlantic Ocean to the Red Sea and from the Mediterranean Sea to the dry savanna of the Sahel. In area it is comparable to the contiguous United States plus Alaska. Much of the Sahara consists of plateaus with surfaces of bare rock (hamada) or gravel (reg). Sand seas (ergs) only cover about 25 percent of it. Biodiversity is low, especially for such a large area. "Sahara" is Arabic for desert.

Geographic Coordinates. Approximately 35°N–14°N, 14°W–40°E

Description. The Sahara is an immense, sparsely vegetated expanse of drylands covering most of North Africa. With an area of 3,532,448 mi² (9,149,000 km²), the Sahara reaches 3,100 mi (5,000 km) in an east–west direction from the Atlantic coast of Morocco and Mauritania to the Red Sea coast of Egypt and Sudan. It is part of the great subtropical arid zone that continues eastward across the Arabian Peninsula and southern Iran into Pakistan. The Sahara extends 930 mi (1,500 km) in a north–south direction from the Mediterranean Sea or piedmont of the Atlas Mountains to the edge of the semiarid Sahel near the latitude of the great Niger River bend and northern shores of Lake Chad. Much of the Saharan landscape is made up of escarpment-edged plateaus of sedimentary rock topped with hamadas (bare rock surfaces) and regs (gravelly desert pavement). Among the largest

plateaus developed on flat or slightly tilted strata are Tanezrouft, Tassili-n-Ajjer, Tademaït, and Tinrhert, all in Algeria. The 13 major ergs (sand seas) generally occur in topographical basins between the plateaus. Although vast fields of sand dunes may be the popular image of the Sahara, all ergs combined cover only about 25 percent of the total area. The Sahara is typically a low relief landscape except for some mountains in the central desert such as the volcanic Ahaggar (Hoggar), Tibesti, Aïr, and Ennedi massifs that reach heights of 10,000 ft (3,300 m), and the lower Jebel Uwienat at the junction of the Egypt–Libya–Sudan international boundaries. The highest point in the Sahara is Emi Koussi (19°48'N, 18°33'E), a shield volcano with two nested craters on its summit located at the southern edge of the Tibesti Mountains in northern Chad. Emi Koussi is an ultra prominence rising 7,546 ft (2,300 m) above the desert's surface to an elevation of 11,204 ft (3,415 m) asl. The lowest point in the Sahara is Qattara Depression, Egypt, where the land descends to 440 ft (134 m) bsl.

The vast Sahara is subdivided into several smaller deserts, including the Atlantic Coastal Desert, the Western Sahara, the Ténéré Desert, Libyan Desert, the Western Desert of Egypt, and the Arabian or Eastern Desert between the Nile and the Red Sea. The several massifs are also considered distinct regions.

Wind has played a major role in shaping the contemporary landscape of the Sahara. Aeolian processes of erosion and deposition have removed sand from one part of the desert and transported it to other parts. Erosional landforms include hamadas, regs, and deflation basins, where small particles have been removed. Blowing sand has left wind-sculpted yardangs and sand-abraded ridge and swale systems. Vast

Umm al-Ma Lake and oasis in the Awbari Sand Sea in the Sahara, Libya. (Patrick Poendl/Dreamstime.com)

fields of bedrock yardangs are found west of the Nile in Egypt and in the Tibesti region of Chad and Libya. Deposition has resulted in sand sheets and large sand seas. The thickness of sand deposits can be 65–330 ft (20–100 m), and some of the ergs have dunes almost 1,000 ft (300 m) tall. A most unusual feature in the Sahara is the Richat structure or "Eye of the Sahara." This nearly 30 mi (50 km) wide eroded dome in west-central Mauretania (21°07'N, 11°24'W) appears as three concentric circles of ancient sandstone and quartzite cuestas surrounding a flat interior of limestone intruded by volcanic rocks. Its formation has yet to be explained.

The Nile and Niger Rivers, along with some small rivers flowing from the Atlas Mountains, are the only permanent streams in the Sahara today. From the Pliocene well into the Pleistocene and even Holocene the region was well-watered, and ancient river courses from fossil fluvial systems can be traced by modern technology beneath the sand. Fossil groundwater is an important legacy of wetter times and is being tapped in large, regional aquifers such as the Bas Sahara artesian system underlying parts of Morocco, Algeria, Tunisia, and Libya, and the Nubian aquifer beneath Egypt, Libya, the Chad Basin, and northern Sudan. Oases exist in areas where groundwater intercepts the surface. Some of the larger oases are Bahariya, Dahkla, Farfara, Kharga, and Siwa in the Western Desert of Egypt, Ghardaia and Timimoun in Algeria, and Kufra in Libya.

Now, much of the Sahara is hyperarid, receiving less than 4 in (100 mm) of rain a year and exposed to high temperatures, low humidity, and strong winds. Aridity is a product of the latitudinal position of a strong subtropical high pressure system and its descending, drying air and the Sahara's position in the interior of the great mass of the northern African continent, which allows minimal maritime influence. A mediterranean regime of winter precipitation characterizes the northern and far eastern Sahara, where westerlies and frontal precipitation can penetrate when the high pressure system has shifted several degrees southward. The southern Sahara receives largely summer rainfall under the influence of the Intertropical Convergence Zone (ITCZ), which in summer migrates poleward to 15°–20°N latitude and moisture from the Gulf of Guinea is drawn inland. The central Sahara, the Tanezrouft in particular, is the driest part, although orographic uplift produces higher amounts of precipitation locally. The central massifs may receive as much as 12 in (300 mm)/yr.

The world's highest recorded temperature is usually attributed to a site in the Sahara: El Azizia, Libya, with a temperature of 136.4°F (58°C) reported in 1922. However, for a number of reasons, the World Meteorological Organization has discounted that reading, and the honor now goes to Death Valley, California, where 134°F (56.7°C) was recorded in 1913.

Several vegetation regions are recognized within the Greater Sahara. The Atlantic Coastal Desert, edged by cliffs 65–95 ft (20–50 m) high at the shoreline and rising inland onto a plateau 650 ft (200 m) asl, is watered by mists coming off the cold Canary Current. Lichens drape low shrubs or grow on the ground. The interior hamada is sparsely vegetated with succulents and halophytes. Other ecoregions follow latitudinal belts. Northern Sahara Steppe and Woodlands form a zone between the Atlas Mountains and Mediterranean Sea and the hyperarid core of the Sahara. Rains occurring between October and April total 2–4 in (50–100 mm), with lesser amounts falling toward the south. A dry, deciduous shrubland dominates. The core of the Sahara has a sparse cover of small shrubs; grasses grow in dune areas. Most plant life occurs in the dry watercourses known as wadis. The Southern Sahara Steppe and Woodlands forms a narrow belt between the southern edge of the extreme desert and the northern edge of the Sahel. The ITCZ brings 4–8 in (100–200 mm) of rain in July and August and supports ephemeral streams and summer pastures of grasses and forbs. The 8 in (200 mm) isohyet marks the southern boundary of the Sahara. Dry montane forests and shrublands of doum palms, date palms, acacias, myrtles, oleander, and tamarix grow in the Tibesti Mountains and on Jebel Uweinat. Other dry forests occur on western peaks. Seasonally flooded, saline depressions fed by streams coming from the Atlas Mountains or by springs at oases have halophytic communities of saltwort and saltbush. Such habitats exist at Qattara Depression and Siwa oasis and in the large Tunisian and northern Algerian salt lakes or chotts.

Geologic History. The Sahara is underlain by the stable Precambrian West African craton. The separation of Proto-Laurasia from Gondwana in the late Silurian–early Devonian (ca. 400 mya) produced the initial structure of the basins and uplifts preserved today. These were modified by subsequent collisions of the Laurasian and Gondwanan supercontinents. A large area was submerged during the Mesozoic Era (251–65 mya) and covered by marine deposits. Later uplift exposed these sedimentary strata to erosion.

Until relatively recently, geologically speaking, the Sahara was moister than today. Climate has alternated between subhumid (Green Sahara periods) and arid since the Pliocene, apparently in response to the wobble of earth's axis. (The tilt varies between 22° and 25° in 41,000-yr cycles.) As recently as 10,000–4,000 years ago, the Sahara was a savanna with permanent streams and lakes and inhabited by people who left rock art depicting humans, cattle herds, antelopes, elephants, hippopotamuses, and crocodiles. Gradual drying of the climate began about 6,200 years ago. True desert ecosystems may have become established only about 3,900–3,100 years ago.

Biota. Biodiversity is low for such a vast area. The flora and fauna is generally Palearctic in their affinities. Desert-adapted antelopes include dama gazelle, Dorcas gazelle, Rhim or slender-horned gazelle, addax, and scimitar-horned oryx—albeit the addax is extirpated from much of the Sahara and the oryx is presumed extinct in the wild. Carnivores include fennec fox, pale fox, and Rüppell's fox. On some massifs, Barbary sheep, cheetah, and caracal may still be found.

Protected Areas. Most, if not all, countries have protected some natural areas. Among them are Bou Hedma National Park—with its introduced herd of scimitar-horned oryx, and Djebil and Senghar National Parks in the Grand Erg Oriental with remnant herds of Rhim gazelle and plans to reintroduce addax in Tunisia; Sahara Zellat Nature Reserve in Libya; Termit and Tin Toumma National Nature and Cultural Reserve and the Aïr and Ténéré National Nature Reserves (a UNESCO World Heritage Site) in Niger; Ouadi Rimé-Ouadi Achim Faunal Reserve in Chad; and the Ahaggar and Tassili-n-Ajjer National Parks in Algeria. The last is inscribed as a UNESCO World

Heritage Site for its geological (such as the permanent waterholes—gueltas—sheltered from the sun in narrow gorges) and ecological features (such as relict Mediterranean plants, including cypresses, wild olives, and myrtle that grow in wadis), as well as prehistoric cave paintings.

Environmental Issues. Civil war has been or is a problem in several Saharan countries. In Chad, many "protected" areas were destroyed or abandoned during recent conflict. Overgrazing by domestic livestock and hunting of rare desert antelopes (especially by motorized hunters) has decimated wildlife in most of the region. The Sahara expands during dry periods—as it did during severe droughts in the Sahel in the 1980s, and retreats during wetter phases. It currently appears to be entering a time of increased precipitation.

See also Atlas Mountains; Qattara Depression; Niger River; Nile River; The Sahel; Tibesti Mountains

Further Reading

Berrahmouni, Nora and Neil Burgess. n.d. "The Sahara." Desert and Xeric Shrublands, Terrestrial Ecoregions, World Wildlife Fund. http://worldwildlife.org /ecoregions/pa1327. (*Note*: The World Wildlife Fund provides good information on all the major ecoregions of the Sahara. See http://worldwildlife.org/ecoregions /pa1304, http://worldwildlife.org/ecoregions/pa1321, http://worldwildlife.org/ecoregions/pa1329, http:// worldwildlife.org/ecoregions/pa1332, http://world wildlife.org/ecoregions/pa1331, and http://worldwild life.org/ecoregions/pa0905.)

Laity, Julie J. 2008. *Deserts and Desert Environments.* Chichester, UK: Wiley-Blackwell.

Lancaster, Nicholas. 1996. "Desert Environments." In *The Physical Geography of Africa*, edited by William M. Adams, Andrew S. Goudie, and Antony R. Orme, 211–237. Oxford: Oxford University Press.

"The Sahara." 2011. Sahara Conservation Fund. http:// www.saharaconservation.org/?-The-Sahara-

The Sahel

Burkino Faso, Chad, Mali, Mauritania, Niger, Senegal, and South Sudan

Geographic Overview. The Sahel is a relatively narrow, semiarid belt stretching across North Africa from the Atlantic Ocean to the Red Sea. The position of its northern margin fluctuates with long-term drought cycles, but generally it is 250–375 mi (400–600 km) wide and forms a transition between the Sahara and the moister Sudanian savannas to its south. The Sahel became notorious in the 20th century for a series of severe and prolonged droughts accompanied by desertification, famine, and death. In Arabic, sahel means "shore," and the region is viewed as a coast of the vast Saharan desert "sea."

Geographic Coordinates. Approximately 12°00'N–17°00'N, 18°00' W–20°00'E

Description. The Sahel is an ecoregion characterized by low and highly variable annual precipitation and dry grasslands with scattered low trees and shrubs. Most of it lies on a low plateau with a level to gently rolling surface and elevations of 650–1,300 ft (200–400 m) asl. The area consists of large sedimentary basins and dry lake beds. Occasionally, massifs of ancient basement rock, rising to heights near 10,000 ft (3,000 m) asl, interrupt the flatness. A relict drainage system of now ephemeral streams exists; permanent waterholes and rivers are scarce, although the Niger, Nile, and Senegal rivers do cross the region.

The Sahel cuts a swathe across the northern bulge of Africa from the Atlantic Ocean at Senegal along the southern margin of the Sahara to the coast of the Red Sea in South Sudan. Its north–south extent is vague as the Sahel is a transition zone between the desert and the Sudanian savanna of West Africa. The boundary between the Sahara and the Sahel is usually delineated at the 8 in (200 mm) isohyet, but the position of this line fluctuates as much as 185 mi (300 km) in response to long-term climate changes. On average, the zone is 250–375 mi (400–600 km) wide. Some geographers mark the eastern edge of the Sahel at the Sudd wetlands; others have it continuing across Sudan and even into Eritrea to the coast of the Red Sea.

Climate in the Sahel is tropical and semiarid. Rainfall is less than 20 in (500 mm), with higher amounts in the south than in the north. It is highly seasonal and controlled by the northward migration of the Intertropical Convergence Zone (ITCZ) during summer. The 6–8 month long dry season is marked by penetration of the dry harmattan winds out of the Sahara. Extreme dry years are associated with El Niño when the ITCZ does not move as far poleward in the

Northern Hemisphere. Prolonged periods of reduced rainfall have occurred throughout the historic period and have caused epic droughts and famines. In the 20th century alone, severe conditions persisted in 1910–1916, 1941–1945, and from the late 1960s into the 1980s. The last saw widespread desertification as the Sahara expanded southward; the loss of grasses and shrubs was initially blamed on overgrazing by cattle and goats in a region where nomadic pastoralism was the traditional land use and the human population was rapidly growing. Later scientific investigation showed that the cause was exceptionally low rainfall. When the rains again increased, the vegetation began to recover. Drought and famine struck the Sahel again in 2012.

Aridity in the Sahel is exacerbated by highly permeable soils developed on fossilized dunes and the clay pans that result from former large lakes that existed in the wetter phases (pluvial) of the Pleistocene Epoch. High evaporation rates are characteristic of this hot, semiarid region where monthly mean maximum temperatures are 91°–97°F (33°–36°C) and mean minimum monthly temperatures are 64°–70°F (18°–21°C).

The grasslands of the Sahel have a continuous cover of annual grasses with scattered thorny acacia bushes and trees rarely more than 15 ft (5 m) tall. The woody plants are small-leaved and deciduous and comprised mainly of *Acacia tortilis, Acacia senegal*, and *Acacia laeta*. The natural vegetation has been greatly altered by millennia of cattle and goat grazing by nomadic pastoralists, dry-farming of millets and sorghums, and firewood collection. These human activities are especially destructive of vegetation and soils in times of drought, but continue to support people in one of the poorest regions of the planet.

Geologic History. The sedimentary basins on which much of the Sahel lies are post-Jurassic features formed between cratons as the Gondwanan supercontinent rifted apart. Massifs are uplifted blocks of crystalline, Precambrian basement rocks. Large lakes were products of pluvial periods during the Pleistocene. Some dried out only 20,000–12,000 years ago.

Biota. The Sahel was once home to large herds of scimitar-horned oryx, dama gazelles, Dorcas gazelles and red-fronted gazelles, as well as elephants and other large mammals. Today the oryx is believed extinct in the wild; the dama gazelle is an endangered species, and the other two gazelles are deemed vulnerable. Endemic mammals include six species of gerbil.

Protected Areas. Few conservation areas exist in the Sahel, although some wetland areas important as migratory bird habitats are Ramsar sites. Most areas listed as protected areas in the Sahel are actually in the better watered Sudanian savanna zone to the south.

Environmental Issues. Desertification is always a threat in the Sahel. For the people of the region periodic drought and famine seem to be constants. Global climate change could make matters worse. Overgrazing, dry-farming, and firewood collection have deleterious effects on native vegetation. Native large mammals, their populations already decimated, are further threatened by the introduction of rifles and four-wheel-drive vehicles.

See also Lake Chad; Niger River; The Sahara; The Sudd

Further Reading

Laity, Julie J. 2008. *Deserts and Desert Environments*. Chichester, UK: Wiley-Blackwell.

Magin, Chris. n.d. "Sahelian Acacia Savanna." Terrestrial Ecoregions, World Wildlife Fund. http://worldwildlife.org/ecoregions/at0713

Stewart, Robert. 2008. "Desertification in the Sahel." Environmental Geoscience, Environmental Science in the 21st Century—An Online Textbook. College of Geosciences, Texas A & M University. http://oceanworld.tamu.edu/resources/environment-book/desertification-insahel.html

Saint Helena

South Atlantic Ocean

Geographic Overview. Saint Helena, one of the world's most remote inhabited islands, is 500 mi (800 km) east of the Mid-Atlantic Ridge in the South Atlantic Ocean. The closest land is tiny Ascension Island some 800 mi (1,300 km) to the northwest. The coast of Africa (Angola) lies 1,120 mi (1,800 km) to the east; the coast of South America (Brazil) 2,025 mi (3,260 km) to the west. The island is best known as the place where the exiled Napoleon Bonaparte

(1769–1821) spent his last years. The record of the destruction of its native biota, which began in the 1600s, is preserved in correspondence of the British East India Company and has influenced ideas of human–nature relationships in Western thought and produced some of the early roots of environmentalism. Today Saint Helena is part of the British Overseas Territory of Saint Helena, Ascension, and Tristan da Cunha.

Geographic Coordinates. 15°58'S, 05°43'W

Description. Saint Helena is the eroded remains of two volcanoes rising 16,400 ft (5,000 m) from the seafloor. Its maximum elevation, 2,690 ft (820 m) asl, occurs on Diana's Peak on the central ridge of the island, which is only 10 mi (16 km) long and 6 mi (8 km) wide. Vertical sea cliffs less than 1,300 ft (400 m) high edge the coast except where interrupted by steep-sided valleys. A broad marine terrace formed by wave action extends out from the shore. Coastal areas are bare rock, but the interior is green even though the original forest is largely gone.

A subtropical maritime climate prevails and exhibits little seasonality. Influenced by the Southeast Trade Winds and elevation, some areas are arid and others quite humid. In the driest areas, total annual precipitation is less than 8 in (200 mm), while on windward slopes of the central ridge, 40 in (1,000 mm) may be received each year. The cool Benguela Current nearby moderates temperatures.

Prior to its discovery by the Portuguese navigator João de Nova in 1502, the island supported a variety of habitats. Semidesert or scrub formed an outer fringe. Inland, with increasing elevation, were an ebony gumwood thicket, dry gumwood woodland, and moist gumwood woodland. Gumwood (*Commidendrum* spp.) trees, endemic members of the aster family (Asteraceae), grow about 25 ft (7–8 m) tall and represent a fairly common feature of oceanic islands in which species that are forbs on continents evolve into arboreal forms. Above the gumwood woodlands grew cabbage trees, another island aster assuming arboreal dimensions. At elevations above 2,300 ft (700 m) on the central ridge, was a cloud forest of tree fern thickets and endemic trees and shrubs intolerant of drought. Ferns, mosses, and liverworts formed the ground layer. Goats put on the islands even before permanent settlement ravaged these forests. After

settlement, which began in 1659, trees were cut for timber, fuelwood, and lime production; most of the island was deforested by the early 1800s. Today the original forests are reduced to a few small stands of gumwoods and about 40 ac (16 ha) of cabbage tree woodland and tree fern thickets on the central ridge.

Geologic History. Saint Helena emerged above the waters of the Atlantic 14–12 mya, built up from two volcanic centers overlying a hotspot on the slow-moving African Plate. The northeast center was active during and for three million years after emergence. Most of this volcano has since disappeared. The exception is the level land in the northeast of the island. A second volcano to the southwest formed the remainder of the island 11–7 mya. Initially a shield volcano formed, but this eroded to form a large amphitheater open to the southeast at what is now Sandy Bay. Lava flows in the southern and western parts of Saint Helena issued from this volcano. About 7.5 mya, igneous rock intruded into the mass. No volcanic activity has occurred since.

Biota. As a result of its extreme isolation, few terrestrial plants or animals reached the island on their own. No native freshwater fish, amphibians, or land reptiles inhabit the island. The long time the island has been exposed above sea level, however, has allowed for evolution among the few species that did colonize naturally, and endemism among those groups is high. There are 37 endemic flowering plants (six are now extinct), 30 native ferns (13 endemic species), and a rich bryophyte flora. Invertebrates are diverse, with a total of 80 endemic genera and 400 endemic species (150 of which are beetles and 77 are weevils). The most famous endemic insect is the giant earwig (*Labiduna herculeana*), which, with a maximum length over 3 in (80 mm), is the world's largest dermapteran. It has not been collected for more than 50 years.

The only surviving endemic land bird is the St. Helena Plover or Wirebird. Others, known from the fossil record, included two rails, a cuckoo, a hoopoe, and a dove. Large seabird colonies once flourished on the island, but they were decimated by introduced pigs, dogs, cats, and rats.

Two endemic plants thought to be extinct have been rediscovered: St. Helena ebony (*Trochetiopsis ebenus*) and St. Helena boxwood (*Mellissia begonifolia*). The St. Helena olive (*Nesiota ellipsis*) went extinct in 2003.

Protected Areas. Diana's Peak National Park was established in 1996. A concerted effort to reconstruct the Great Wood on the eastern half of St. Helena is underway.

Environmental Issues. Introduced species continue to threaten the remaining native species. New Zealand flax (*Phormium tenax*) was brought in as a crop at the end of the 1800s, and widespread clearing of the central ridge forests was a consequence. Now escapes are invading forest remnants. In drier areas, the primary invasive plants are prickly pear cactus, a creeper (*Carpobrotus edulis*), and lantana.

Construction of the island's first airport, scheduled for completion in late 2015, is a major concern, not only for its destruction of habitats on rare flat land, but also because it will open the island to tourism and development.

See also Ascension Island; Tristan da Cunha and Gough Island

Further Reading

Ashmole, Philip and Myrtle Ashmole. 2009. "St. Helena." In *Encyclopedia of Islands*, edited by Rosemary G. Gillespie and David A. Clague, 870–873. Berkeley: University of California Press.

"St Helena Gumwood." 2008. Global Trees Campaign. http://globaltrees.org/threatened-trees/trees/bastard-gumwood/

Saint Lawrence River (Rivière Saint-Laurent)

Canada

Geographic Review. The drainage basin of the St. Lawrence River includes the entire Great Lakes and their short tributaries. In terms of discharge, the St. Lawrence River and Great Lakes system, when the Saguenay River is included, is the largest in North America. It drains water from nine states (Minnesota, Wisconsin, Illinois, Indiana, Michigan, Ohio, Pennsylvania, Vermont, and New York) and two Canadian provinces (Ontario and Quebec). The landscape of the St. Lawrence's watershed is relatively low elevation and flat, rising to 6,550 ft (2,000 m) asl in the east. Millions of people live near the river, especially in Montreal, Ottawa, and Quebec City. Used by Native Americans for centuries and settled by Europeans in the 1600s, the river and its commercial traffic continue to be significant to the economies of both Canada and the United States.

Geographic Coordinates. Source: 44°29'N, 75°48'W, Mouth: 49°10'N, 67°14'W

Description. Beginning at Lake Ontario and separating the provinces of Ontario and Quebec from New York State, the main stem of the St. Lawrence River flows northeast 5,996 mi (965 km) to the St. Lawrence Estuary. From Lake Ontario, the river drops 600 ft (184 m) before reaching the Atlantic Ocean. The Ottawa River is the first tributary, joining the St. Lawrence at Montreal. Not far downstream, the shorter Richelieu River enters from New York state, followed by the Saint-Maurice flowing south from the Canadian Shield. The Saguenay flows from the Shield to the St. Lawrence Estuary.

River characteristics can be described in four sections. The river in the fluvial section, 407 mi (655 km) from Lake Ontario to Cornwall-Massena, Quebec, is variable. It includes braided channels, constrictions, rapids and navigation locks, small floodplains, islands, and four natural lakes (St. Lawrence, Lac Saint-François, Lac Saint-Louis, Lac Saint-Pierre), some of which have been developed for hydroelectric power. The lakes are shallow, generally less than 20 ft (6 m) deep. Most of the shoreline has many large boulders, while the channel is sand and gravel. The river is 0.6–1.2 mi (1–2 km) wide where constricted, and 7.5 mi (12 km) wide at the lakes. A shipping channel at least 60 ft (18.2 m) deep is maintained for ocean-going ship traffic. The fluvial estuary section, 65 mi (105 km) from Lac Saint-Pierre to the east end of Île d'Orléans, near Quebec City, has tidal influence but the water is still fresh. The 93 mi (150 km) upper estuary, extending from Île d'Orléans to the mouth of the Saguenay River, is the transition zone between fresh and salt water. The river here is 10.5 mi (17 km) wide and as deep as 330 ft (100 m). The lower estuary extends another 186 mi (300 km) further downstream toward the Gulf of St. Lawrence and the Atlantic Ocean.

The St. Lawrence River, seen here flowing through Quebec, is the only outlet of the Great Lakes. It continues to be a commercially important waterway for both the United States and Canada. (Wangkun Jia/Dreamstime.com)

The Great Lakes contribute one-half of the discharge of the St. Lawrence River, which ensures a low amount of suspended sediment and maintains water clarity. Although peak flow occurs with spring snowmelt and the least is in January, the flow in the St. Lawrence varies little because of the constant input from the Great Lakes. The river is at minimum partially ice-covered in winter, and sometimes and some places it is totally ice-covered.

The major tributaries to the St. Lawrence originate on the Canadian Shield. The Ottawa River is the largest. It originates in Lake Temiskaming and flows through 790 mi (1,271 km) of boreal and deciduous forest on the Canadian Shield before reaching the St. Lawrence. Its channel is naturally constricted in part of its journey, but there are also islands and bays. Petri Islands Preserve, south of Ottawa is an island and wetland complex with a variety of aquatic habitats. Although there are several dams, most of the river is undeveloped. The Saguenay River is the second largest tributary and the last to enter the St. Lawrence. From headwaters in Lac St. Jean on the Canadian Shield, the river is 102 mi (165 km) long and approximately 0.4 mi (0.6 km) wide, flowing through a deeply incised channel. For 62 mi (100 km) before reaching the estuary, it flows through the largest fjord in the northwestern Atlantic. The Richelieu River drains from Lake Champlain between New York and Vermont. With its drainage basin in urban and agricultural areas, the water quality is poor. The Saint-Maurice River originates in upland Quebec.

The St. Lawrence is highly regulated for shipping and electricity. The St. Lawrence Seaway, a series of dams, locks, and diversions, allows ocean ships to travel between the Atlantic and the Great Lakes.

Biota. The river has one freshwater ecoregion, the Lower St. Lawrence, which includes the main stem and the tributaries below Lake Ontario. Dams, however, disrupt the movement of fish, and invasive species have spread since the 1980s. Habitat at the confluence of the Richelieu River with the estuary is significant to migrating birds.

Protected Areas. Much of the Saint-Maurice River watershed is in La Maurice National Park. Lac Saint-Pierre is a World Heritage Site because of its diversity of habitat for fish and waterfowl.

See also Great Lakes

Further Reading

Thorp, James H., Gary A. Lamberti, and Andrew F. Casper. 2005. "St. Lawrence River Basin." In *Rivers of North America*, edited by Arthur C. Benk and Colbert E. Cushing, 982–1028. Amsterdam: Elsevier Academic Press.

Salar de Uyuni and Salar de Atacama

Bolivia and Chile

Geographic Overview. South America is home to the world's two largest playas or salt flats (*salares*). Salar de Uyuni on the Puna of southwest Bolivia is the larger of the two, covering 4,086 mi² (10,582 km²). Salar de Atacama, in a high basin in the front range of the Andes in northern Chile, is less than half as large, encompassing some 1,864 mi² (3,000 km²). Both are some of the world's major sources of lithium, an element increasingly important in batteries, especially for electric vehicles.

Geographic Coordinates. Salar de Uyuni: 20° 08'S, 67°29'W; Salar de Atacama: 23°30'S, 68°15'W

Description. Salar de Uyuni, the largest salt pan in the world, lies near the southern end of the Altiplano-Puna at 12,000 ft (3,656 m) asl and is the lowest part of this internally drained plateau. The surface of the salar is extremely flat and composed of a cracked crust of salt that looks as though the playa is covered with white hexagonal tiles. Beneath the crust is a saturated brine of sodium chloride, lithium chloride, and magnesium chloride. The tops of ancient volcanoes fringed by fossil coral reefs protrude above

the surface in several places and host tall columnar cacti. During the rainy season (December–March), the salar is flooded with 6–20 in (15–50 cm) of water and acts like a huge mirror. Even when dry, the salt flat is highly reflective. This, combined with its size, stability, and very low relief, makes it a good reference surface for satellites that determine elevations on Earth (e.g., NASA's Geoscience Laser Altimeter System [GLAS], a space-based LIDAR that operated from 2003–2010).

Salar de Atacama is in a tectonic basin between the Western Cordillera of the Andes Mountains and the front range to its west, the Cordillera de Domekyo. The oval-shaped basin developed in a zone of active volcanism where the Andes bend slightly eastward and became filled with sediments from the surrounding mountains and with evaporites. The salar is 62 mi (100 km) long and 50 mi (80 km) wide. Its surface lies at 7,546 ft (2,300 m) asl, about 2,300 ft (700 m) below the rim of the basin. Unlike Salar de Uyuni, the salt crust has an extremely rough surface, since the 0.4–1.2 in (10–30 mm) of rain it receives each summer is not enough to cover it and temporarily dissolve the salts. It is the world's largest and purest source of lithium.

A number of smaller salares and shallow lagunas (salt lakes) also occur on the Altiplano-Puno plateau of Bolivia. Among the more unique ones are Laguna Colorada (red lake or lagoon) and Laguna Verde (green lake) in the Eduardo Avaroa Andean Faunal Reserve, an area of active volcanoes, hot springs, geysers, and fumaroles in southwest Bolivia near the Chilean border. It is also home to three endemic species of flamingo. The red waters of Laguna Colorada come from red sediments and the red algae. This salt lake is only 23 mi² (60 km²) and less than 3 ft (1 m) deep. At 14,035 ft (4,278 m) asl, it provides important habitat for the James Flamingo, in particular, and is a Ramsar Wetland of International Importance. Laguna Verde's color comes from copper-rich sediments. It sits at the foot of Licancabur volcano at an elevation of 14,000 ft (4,300 m) asl.

Geologic History. Salar de Uyuni's salt crust is a deposit of evaporites precipitated when a series of huge, deep lakes that had filled the basin during wet periods of the Pleistocene dried up. These lakes include Lake Ballivián, which reached its maximum height of 12,664 ft (3,860 m) asl—about 160 ft (50 m) above the current surface of Lake Titicaca—about 191,000 years ago and inundated the Altiplano from Lake Titicaca south to Salar de Uyuni; Lake Minchin, which at its maximum between 31,000–26,000 years ago, had a surface elevation of 12,335 ft (3,760 m) asl; and most recently Lake Tauca, which was at its maximum at 12,369 ft (3,770 m) asl 17,000–15,000 years ago. Both Minchin and Tauca also flooded the basins of Lake Poopó and Coipasa to the north.

See also Altiplano-Puna; Lake Poopó (Lago Poopó); Lake Titicaca

Samoan Islands

Polynesia, Pacific Ocean

Geographic Overview. The Samoan Islands are an east–west trending chain of nine main islands and several islets lying north of the Tonga Trench near the center of Polynesia. They constitute two political units: the independent country of Samoa (formerly Western Samoa) and American Samoa, an unincorporated territory of the United States.

Geographic Coordinates. Samoa: 13°35'S, 172°20'W; American Samoa: 14°18'S, 170°42'W

Description. The Samoan Islands lie near the center of Polynesia in the Pacific Ocean. Samoa, at the western end of the chain, consists of two sizeable islands, Savai'i and 'Upolu, and several volcanic islets. Savai'i, at 700 mi² (1,820 km²), is the largest island in the chain and the fifth largest island in the tropical Pacific. Its Mount Silisili rises to an elevation of 6,102 ft (1,860 m), the highest point in the Samoan Islands. 'Upolu has an area of 429 mi² (1,110 km²) and a high point of 3,609 ft (1,100 m) asl. American Samoa consists of five small volcanic islands and two coral atolls. Tutuila is the largest island in the territory with an area of about 49 mi² (124 km²). Its highest elevation is 2,139 ft (652 m) asl. Very close to it is the small island of 'Aunu'u, with just 1.0 mi² (2.6 km²) of land. The three Manu'a islands of Ofu, Olosega, and Ta'u, are 68 mi (110 km) east of Tutuila. Ofu is just 1.9 mi² (5 km²) in area; its volcanic peak stands 1,624 ft (495 m) asl. Olosega is even smaller at 1.15 mi² (4 km²), but

the summit of its main peak is 2,100 ft (640 m) asl. Ta'u is the youngest island in the chain and has an area of 15 mi² (39 km²) and maximum elevation of 3,100 ft (945 m) asl. The collapse of its shield volcano has left a 3,000 ft (915 m) high cliff on its north side. All the volcanic islands have steep slopes and fringing reefs. Rose Atoll lies east of the volcanic chain of islands and has a total area of 1.0 mi² (2.6 km²). Swain Island is another tiny, remote atoll, with 0.6 mi² (1.5 km²) total area, one of the smallest atolls on Earth.

Twenty-eight miles (45 km) southeast of Ta'u is a future Samoan island, Vailulu'u Seamount, an active volcano currently standing 14,764 ft (4,200 m) above the seafloor and coming to within 1,940 ft (590 m) of the ocean surface. In the summit crater of the Vailulu'u Seamount is a growing cone; the last known eruption occurred in 2003. The crater contains an unusual hydrothermal vent called Eel City, after its population of the eel *Dysommina rugosa*. The base of the cone is surrounded by the "Moat of Death," a dead zone caused from toxic emissions from the volcano and littered with dead fish, squid, and crustaceans.

The humid, tropical Samoan Islands are oriented nearly parallel to the Southeast Trade Winds, which bring them year-round rainfall with little distinction between windward and leeward sides. About 125 in (3,280 mm) of rain falls annually on the coastal plain of Tutuila, increasing with elevation to over 195 in (5,000 mm) a year in the mountains. Tropical rainforests cloak much of the high islands from shore to mountain summit. A cloud forest appears on the highest slopes of Ta'u.

Geologic History. The Samoan island chain has formed along the southwest edge of the Pacific Plate north of the Tonga Trench, where the Pacific Plate is subducting beneath the Australian Plate. They occur near the point where the generally north-northeast trending oceanic trench takes a sharp turn to the west and becomes a transform fault zone. Thus the islands are moving west parallel to the trench and are not themselves being subducted. The high islands appear to have formed as a result of two episodes of volcanism related to a semistationary hotspot currently located halfway between Ta'u and Rose Atoll where the Vailulu'u Seamount is now rising. The islands are all overlapping shield volcanoes resting on older submarine ridges constructed of lava flows that bend toward the trench. The oldest island, Savai'i, began to form about 5.0 million years old, 'Upola is approximately 3.5 million years old, and Tutuila is about 1.5 million years old. Vailulu'u Seamount is only 50 years old.

Biota. The Samoan archipelago has a flora second in diversity only to Hawai'i's among Pacific Ocean islands. Like much of the terrestrial biota, plants are related to Malesian forms; only about 30 percent are endemic to the Samoan islands. (Malesia is a floristic province stretching from Indonesia to New Guinea, the Philippines, and the Bismarck Archipelago.) The 94 native land snails have a higher rate (62 percent) of endemism. Native vertebrate species include seven skinks, four geckos, one snake, 24 land or freshwater birds (including five gallinules, two starlings, a number of pigeons, and several honeyeaters), and three mammals, all bats. The endemic and endangered Tooth-billed Parrot is the national bird of Samoa. *Didunculus*, the genus name of this ground pigeon, means "little Dodo," and the Samoan bird may be the more famous Dodo's closest surviving relative.

The reef fauna contains 890 fishes and more than 200 coral species.

Protected Areas. Three preserves in independent Samoa protect rainforest: Falealupo National Park and Tafua Peninsula Rainforest Preserve on Savai'i and 'O le Pupu-Pu'e National Park on 'Upolu. The National Park of American Samoa has sections on four of the main islands protecting rainforests, reefs, and traditional culture. It is administered by the U.S. Park Service and is the only U.S. national park south of the equator. Rose Atoll is a U.S. Marine National Monument.

Environmental Issues. Coral reefs are threatened by destructive fishing techniques such as dynamiting the reef, overfishing, pollution, and outbreaks of the crown-of-thorns starfish. Soil erosion related to forest clearing for timber on the western islands and for expanding agriculture on all the major islands is a problem on land and can cause sedimentation over fringing reefs. With most of the human population living within a few hundred meters of the shore, rising sea level is a major concern.

The most aggressive invasive animals are pigs, rats, and the carnivorous snail *Euglandia rosea*. Among the most problematic introduced plants are the African silk rubber tree (*Funtumia elastica*), which has invaded the rainforests; the Moluccan albizia (*Falcataria moluccana*), a large nitrogen-fixing tree; and the Brazilian strawberry guava (*Psidium cattleianum*), a small tree that rapidly forms single-species stands that inhibit the regrowth of native trees.

Further Reading

Medeiros, A. C. 2009. "Samoa, Biology." In *Encyclopedia of Islands*, edited by Rosemary G. Gillespie and David A. Clague, 799–802. Berkeley: University of California Press.

San Andreas Fault System

United States (California)

Geographic Overview. The San Andreas Fault, more than 800 mi (1,287 km) long, is one of the longest faults in the world. It forms the boundary between the Pacific Plate and North American Plate and is the main part of a much larger zone of associated, branching faults. More than just a line, it is a complex zone of broken rock, as much as a mile (1.6 km) wide. It and its splinter faults are responsible for many earthquakes in California.

Geographic Coordinates. Approximately 31° 35'N–40°25'N, 114°45'W–124°25'W

Description. For most of its extent, the fault shows a visible trace on the land. A continuation of the Mendocino Fracture Zone in the Pacific Ocean, the San Andreas Fault touches Cape Mendocino before passing south through the ocean a short distance offshore. From Point Arena, it takes a straight path southeast, through Tomales Bay in Point Reyes National Seashore, and passes the San Francisco area in the ocean to the west of the Golden Gate. Around San Francisco, the fault zone becomes wider and complex, with several more-or-less parallel faults. The Hayward Fault marks the east side of San Francisco Bay, and a few miles inland is the Calaveras Fault. The valley south of the Bay is riddled with several parallel faults, bounded by the Calaveras on the east and the San Andreas on the west. The fault system continues southeast for approximately 100 mi (160 km) through the Coastal Ranges, its path marked by a trough of linear valleys and ridges. Near Tejon Pass, approximately

The Carizzo Plains of southern California provide an excellent view of the straight line and offset features of the San Andreas fault. (Kevin Schafer/Corbis)

60 mi (96 km) northwest of Los Angeles, the fault intersects with the left-lateral Garlock Fault, which defines the southern edge of the Tehachapi Mountains. The San Andreas Fault continues southeast, cutting through the mountains in San Bernardino at Cajon Pass, the route of Interstate 5. South of Cajon Pass, the fault zone again becomes complex, with no distinctive single trace. The geologic configuration of the mountains east of Los Angeles and of the Salton Sea trough is due to the splinter faults of the San Andreas System. The fault line continues through the Gulf of California.

Geologic History. The San Andreas Fault developed in the mid-Tertiary (28 mya) when the westward moving North American Plate overrode the spreading center of an oceanic plate. This action sheared off pieces of the North American Plate, now the part of North America west of the fault line, and added them

to the Pacific Plate. The Pacific Plate is rotating counterclockwise, carrying the western side of California northwest relative to the North American Plate.

The San Andreas is a right-lateral, strike-slip fault, with minimal vertical displacement. The western side of California is not going to break off and fall into the Ocean; it's just going to continue slowly moving northwest. Movement along the fault line averages 2 in (5 cm) a year, but is variable. Some sections "creep," with constant slow movement. "Locked" portions, where no movement is taking place, may be building up stress until the strain becomes too much and the fault moves suddenly. Movement in one section may put stress on another section. The sudden breaking or movement sends out shock waves, which are felt as earthquakes.

Movement of the two plates along the fault can be judged by offsets, frequently inches, but sometimes a sizeable distance. The 1906 San Francisco earthquake caused roads and fences to be offset 20 ft (6 m) at the head of Tomales Bay. An 1857 quake near Fort Tejon caused features on the Carrizo Plain to be offset by almost 30 ft (9.0 m). Long-distance offsets take place over millions of years. The volcanics at Pinnacles National Monument, for example, originated east of Los Angeles directly on the San Andreas Fault. The western part of the volcano was carried 200 mi (320 km) northwest with the movement of the Pacific Plate. Total displacement of rocks along the fault is approximately 300 mi (480 km).

The fault is shallow, extending 4–10 mi (6.4–16 km) into the earth's crust, making it more prone to producing destructive earthquakes, but earthquakes remain unpredictable. The Parkfield Earthquake Experiment in California, a dense network of instruments on the San Andreas Fault and the most complete active fault observatory in the world, is attempting to find answers.

Further Reading

Hickman, Steve and John Langbein. 2005. *The Parkfield Experiment—Capturing What Happens in an Earthquake*, edited by Peter H. Stauffer. U.S. Geological Survey. http://pubs.usgs.gov/fs/2002/fs049-02

Schultz, Sandra S. and Robert E. Wallace. 2013. *The San Andreas Fault*. U.S. Geological Survey. http://pubs.usgs.gov/gip/earthq3/safaultgip.html

Stoffer, Philip W. 2005. The San Andreas Fault in the San Francisco Bay Area, California: A Geological Fieldtrip Guidebook to Selected Stops on Public Lands. U.S. Geological Survey Open-File Report 2005-1127. http://pubs.usgs.gov/of/2005/1127/chapter1.pdf

São Francisco River

Brazil

Geographic Overview. The São Francisco River, running some 1,675 miles (2,700 km), is South America's fourth longest river, after the Amazon, Paraná, and Madeira Rivers. It lies fully within Brazil and is an important water source for the semiarid Northeast. Historically it served as an important regional transportation link for the eastern part of the country, an area without roads and railroads. Rapids at Paulo Afonso near its mouth, where it drops off

the Highlands, prevented access to and from the sea. Amerigo Vespucci arrived at the mouth on October 4, 1501, the feast day of St. Francis of Assisi, and named the river in the saint's honor.

Geographic Coordinates. Source: 16°12'S, 45° 07'W. Mouth: 10°30'S, 36°23'W

Description. A perennial stream, the São Francisco River flows northward in the Brazilian Highlands just west of the Great Escarpment (Serra do Mar). At the northern end of Chapada Diamantina, it swings east and becomes one the few rivers to cut through the escarpment and enter the Atlantic Ocean. Headwaters in the humid Serra da Canastra in Minas Gerais and tributaries in the subhumid upper part of its basin maintain the São Francisco as a perennial stream. Tributaries entering farther downstream come from the semiarid regions of the Northeast, the so-called Drought Polygon, and are intermittent; they contribute water during the rainy season, often causing destructive floods, erosion, and sedimentation.

Physiography, vegetation, and climate vary along the course. Average annual precipitation decreases from 63 in (1,600 mm) near the source to 14 in (350 mm) in the driest part of the catchment area. Four distinct subbasins are recognized by hydrologists. The upper basin is a land of rolling hills, plateaus, and elevated mesas (*chapadas*) with elevations ranging from roughly 2,000 ft to 5,000 ft (600–1,600 m) asl. Forest and cerrado are the chief types of natural vegetation. A humid temperate to subtropical climate has mean monthly winter temperatures of about 64°F (18°C) and summer temperatures averaging 73°F (23°C). Rainfall averages close to 50 in (1,250 mm) a year. The largest population center in the entire river basin, the industrial city of Belo Horizonte, is located in this section. Tres Maria dam provides hydroelectric power.

The upper-middle basin, located in Minas Gerais and Bahia, is subhumid to semiarid. However, western tributaries receive runoff from the Serra Geral de Goiás, which experiences abundant orographic precipitation and are perennial streams. This section lies at elevations of 1,300–3,330 ft (400–1,000 m) asl and is covered by cerrado and caatinga vegetation. Summer rains predominate and total annual precipitation is about 35 in (900 mm). Winter temperatures average 73°F (23°C), while summer temperatures average

77°F (25°C). There are no dams on this stretch of the river.

The lower-middle basin forms the border between the states of Bahia and Pernumbuco and slopes from 1,600 to 650 ft (500 m–200 m) asl. Average monthly temperatures range from 70°F (21°C) in winter to 80°F (27°C) in summer. This is the driest part of the São Francisco basin; its average annual precipitation is less than 20 in (500 mm). Four major dams have been constructed on this section of the São Francisco River: Sobradinho, Itaparica, Paulo Afonso, and Xingo. Sobradinho Dam provides hydroelectric power for much of the Northeast. The reservoir behind it is one of the largest artificial lakes in the world. Its waters are used for irrigating an important agricultural strip along the river where fruits, including grapes, mangoes, and papayas, are grown for export. Here at 8°S, fine wines are produced closer to the equator than anywhere else on Earth.

The lower basin extends from Paulo Afonso falls to the river's mouth. It forms the border between the states of Sergipe and Alagoas before entering the Atlantic Ocean. The land is hilly with elevations ranging from 650 ft (200 m) to sea level. The inland part of the watershed was once cerrado-covered; the coastal plain—where precipitation may be more than 50 in (1,300 mm) a year—supported Atlantic forest (*mata atlântica*). This section historically was navigable and served the sugar-growers of the coastal plain.

Environmental Issues. Today the flow of the São Francisco River is largely regulated by dams. Effluent from Belo Horizonte's sewerage, ore-processing and steel mills, and chemical and agrochemical industries are problematic. Construction on a massive interbasin diversion of water, the São Francisco water transfer system, began in 2008 to support economic development in the Drought Polygon states of Ceará, Pernambuco, Paraiba, and Rio Grande do Norte. Its impacts are yet to be known.

Further Reading

de Andrade, José Geraldo Pena , Paulo Sergio Franco Barbosa, Luiz Carlos Alves Souza, Daniel Lucas Makino. 2011. "Interbasin Water Transfers: The Brazilian Experience and International Case Comparisons." *Water Resources Management* 25: 1915–1934. http://rd.springer.com/article/10.1007/s11269-011-9781-6

Simpson, Larry D. "The Rio São Francisco: Lifeline of the Northeast." 1999. In *Management of Latin American River Basins: Amazon, Plata, and São Francisco*, Part III. *The São Francisco River Basin*, edited by Asit K. Biswas, Newton V. Cordeira, Benedito P. F. Braga, and Cecilia Tortajada, 207–244. New York: United Nations University Press.

Sargasso Sea

North Atlantic Ocean

Geographic Overview. The Sargasso Sea lies west of the Mid-Atlantic Ridge within the subtropical North Atlantic gyre. It the only sea not bounded on any side by land. A unique open sea ecosystem occurs within and beneath a mat of floating brown algae, the *Sargassum*, for which the sea is named.

Geographic Coordinates. Approximately 20°–35°N, 40°–70°W

Description. The Sargasso Sea is that part of the open Atlantic between Florida and the Azores. It is bounded on the west by the Gulf Stream, on the north by the North Atlantic Current, on the east by the Canary Current, and on the south by the North Equatorial Current. The sea slowly circulates within the subtropical gyre in a clockwise direction. Rotational forces raise the sea surface more than 3 ft (1m) above the surrounding waters of the Atlantic Ocean. Warm water near 68°F (20°C) flows into the Sargasso from the Gulf Stream and the North Equatorial Current. Under the influence of the Bermuda-Azores High, evaporation is high and precipitation is low, creating relatively high salinity. The water is blue and exceptionally clear, with visibility down to 200 ft (61 m) below the surface. This is a generally low-nutrient environment, but supports floating mats of gold-colored *Sargassum* algae, which harbor some unique and threatened marine animals. Indeed, one-third of the Atlantic's phytoplankton is produced here. Both the *Sargassum* and the nutrients that support life in the seaweed mat originate in the Gulf of Mexico and along the continental shelf of the southeastern United States and are carried to the Sargasso Sea in cold-core eddies that break away from the Gulf Stream.

The New England Seamount chain penetrates the northwestern part of the sea; the Corner Rise

A patch of sargassum seaweed floats above a swimmer in the Sargasso Sea. (Shaul Schwarz/Getty Images)

seamounts stand above the seafloor to their east. Other seamounts occur along the Bermuda Rise in the west.

Sargassum is a drifting brown alga that clumps together to form patches, floating mats, and weed lines. It is buoyed by spherical, grape-like air bladders. Masses of the floating seaweed provide structural habitat for the spawning grounds and nursery areas of certain fish and sea turtles and foraging and resting areas for certain seabirds. The migration paths of several fishes cross the region. A globally unique ecosystem has developed in this area, which measures 700 mi × 2,000 mi (1,126 km × 3,219 km). The Sargasso Sea is well known as the place where American and European eels go to mate and spawn. The nearly transparent larvae spend three years in the Sargasso; when they are about 3 in (80 mm) long they migrate to the continents, where they mature in freshwater streams. At about 10 years of age, they migrate downstream and across ponds and wet meadows back to the sea.

Biota. Eight species of *Sargassum* occur in the Sargasso Sea; two dominate: *Sargassum natans* and *Sargassum fluitans*. Ten species of endemic mollusk, crustacean, and fish occur, camouflaged to blend in with the seaweed. These include the Sargassum snail (*Litiopa melanostoma*), Sargassum shrimp (*Latreutes fucorum*), Sargassum crab (*Planes minutes*), Sargassum pipefish (*Synthagnus pelagicus*), and the Sargassumfish (*Histrio histrio*), an anglerfish with fins modified to allow it to crawl through the seaweed. In addition to the eels, Porbeagle sharks come to give birth here, and flying fish make bubble nests in the mats. Hatchling hawksbill, green, and loggerhead sea turtles find refuge in the Sargassum. Shearwaters, tropicbirds, and boobies forage and roost on the mats. The migration paths of yellowfin tuna, Atlantic bluefin tuna, and the threatened Albacore tuna cross the Sargasso Sea.

Protected Areas. The Sargasso Sea lies outside the jurisdiction of any country, although Bermuda and some nongovernmental organizations are seeking some type of international protection for the region.

Environmental Issues. Plastic pollution is a major problem as plastic debris enters the sea in much the same manner as nutrients and collects in the gyre, making the Sargasso Sea a North Atlantic garbage patch. Rising sea levels and increasing acidification of the ocean could alter the ecosystem. Overfishing, marine traffic, and the overharvest of *Sargassum* are other threats.

See also Atlantic Ocean; Gulf Stream and North Atlantic Current

Further Reading

McKenna, Sheila and Arlo Hemphill. n.d. "The Sargasso Sea." Global Ocean Biodiversity Intiative. http://www.gobi.org/Our%20Work/rare-2

"Protecting the Sargasso Sea." n.d. Sargasso Sea Alliance and Government of Bermuda. http://www.cbd.int/cop/cop-11/doc/vtable/SargassoBrochure.-fin-cop11-iucn2.pdf

"The Sargasso Sea." n.d. The Lighthouse Foundation. http://www.lighthouse-foundation.org/index.php?id=131&L=1

Saryarka—Steppe and Lakes of Northern Kazakhstan

Kazakhstan

Geographic Overview. The wetlands of Saryarka consist of two groups of lakes on the steppes of northern Kazakhstan. The area is an important stopping point for birds, including rare and endangered species, on the Central Asian Flyway. The dry surrounding steppes give the region its name *Saryarka*, meaning "yellow range." The combination of wetlands and steppes gives the area a high biological diversity.

Geographic Coordinates. Korgalzhyn-Tengiz: 49°54'N–50°59'N, 67°53' E–71°01'E; Naurzum: 51°00'N–52°00'N, 64°15'E–64°45'E

Description. The Saryarka region, also called the Kazakh Uplands, in central and eastern Kazakhstan is characterized by low hills, depressions, and saline lakes. The region includes two groups of lakes, Korgalzhyn-Tengiz and Naurzum, 220 mi (350 km) apart. Both lake groups are on the watershed divide between the Aral Sea basin to the south and the Irtysh River to the north, which drains to the Arctic Ocean via the Ob River. The shallow lakes are a combination of fresh water, brackish, and salty.

Korgalzhyn-Tengiz lakes, 90 mi (145 km) southwest of Astana, are the largest group, covering 639,889 ac (258,963 ha). They provide feeding grounds for 15–16 million birds, including 2.5 million geese, and nesting ground for 350,000 waterfowl. The lakes, with a mean depth of 5.3 ft (1.6 m), are deltas of the Nura and Kulanuptes rivers, which have no outlet to the sea. Lake sizes vary with input, but water levels are artificially stabilized. Most lakes, except Tengiz, have extensive reed beds. The largely untouched steppe at Korgalzhyn is elevated plains and hills, 1,000–1,080 ft (304–329 m) asl with low local relief. The Naurzum lakes area, 125 mi (200 km) south of the town of Kostanay, covers 472,896 ac (191,381 ha), and supports 500,000 nesting waterfowl. The Naurzum lakes are 8.2–9.8 ft (2.5–3 m) deep and dependent on spring floodwaters. The Naurzum region is part of the temperate forest grassland, at elevations of 375–820 ft (115–250 m) asl.

The continental climate is arid to semiarid, with 4–12 in (100–300 mm) of annual precipitation, very cold winters, and hot summers. January temperatures average 1°F (–17° C), but may go as low as –49°F (–45°C). June means are 68°F (20°C), but may rise to a maximum of 107°F (42°C). The sparse river network is ephemeral, with water flowing only in spring.

Biota. The lake and steppe regions provide refuge for the region's steppe flora, as well as threatened bird species and the endangered saiga antelope. More than 60 species of animals and plants are rare and endangered. Fescue and feather grass steppe in the north merges into semidesert in the south. The wetter Naurzum region includes some woodland and scrubby pine forests with birch and aspen. The steppes support approximately 350 species of plants, of which 90 percent are grasses, but also shrubs, such as *Spirea hypericifolia*, and ephemeral bulbs, such as tulips. *Artemisia pauciflora*, *Atriplex cana*, and *Salicornia europaea* are common on salty soils. Approximately one-third of the bird species on the steppes are rare or endangered, including Black Lark, Great Bustard, Gyrefalcon, and Steppe Wind Hover. The Naurzum region has a greater variety of mammals, including marmots and

Corsac fox, due to its greater variety of habitats. Occasional visitors from nearby forests include lynx, roe, and elk.

Birds from Africa, Europe, and South America, including several which are globally threatened, such as Steppe Eagle, Pallas's Sand Grouse, Demoiselle Crane, bustards, Dalmatian Pelican, and the extremely rare Siberian White Crane, stop at Saryarka en route to breeding grounds in Siberia. The region has one of the largest populations of wild fowl in Asia, including 112 species of waterbirds, representing 87 percent of all waterbird species found in Kazakhstan. The most numerous birds include several species of geese, swans, and ducks. Korgalzhyn has the most northern population of nesting pink flamingoes, 50,000–60,000 birds, which are resident in spring and summer. Approximately 700 insect species have been identified, and the number may reach 3,000. Wild boars forage in the reed beds. Fish, including crucian, ide, pike, tench, perch, and roach, live in the lakes.

Protected Areas. Two state nature reserves, Naurzum and Korgalzhyn, which have been under long-term legal protection, are included in Saryarka—Steppe and Lakes of Northern Kazakhstan Biosphere Reserve. Both regions are listed as Ramsay Wetlands of International Importance.

Environmental Issues. The Korgalzhyn area has a population of more than 12,000 people engaged in agriculture, and prior unsustainable use is now being ameliorated.

See also Aral Sea; Ob–Irtysh River System

Further Reading

BirdLife International. 2013. *Important Bird Areas Factsheet: Korgalzhyn State Nature Reserve.* http://www.birdlife.org/datazone/sitefactsheet.php?id=20852

UNESCO. 2013. *Saryarka—Steppe and Lakes of Northern Kazakhstan.* http://whc.unesco.org/en/list/1102

Sea of Japan (East Sea)

North Pacific Ocean

Geographic Overview. The Sea of Japan is a nearly enclosed marginal sea of the Pacific Ocean bounded by the Korean Peninsula, China, and Russia on the west and Sakhalin and the Japanese archipelago on the east. The name "Sea of Japan" is recognized internationally and by the U.S. government, but Koreans prefer the designation "East Sea." The International Hydrographic Organization, which sets the official parameters of oceans and seas, will likely review the name in 2017. The main port is Russia's Vladivostok, the terminus of the Trans-Siberian Railway.

Geographic Coordinates. 51°45'N–34°35'N, 127°30'E–141°28'E

Description. The Sea of Japan is nearly enclosed by the Asian mainland and the Japanese archipelago and connected to neighboring bodies of water only by five shallow straits less than 330 ft (100 m) deep. The sea has no large islands, no large bays, no large capes, and few rivers discharging into it. Several small islands, however, are high enough to create turbulent cloud patterns known as Von Karman vortices on cloudy days. Since it is enclosed, away from the straits it experiences very small tidal ranges.

The Strait of Tartary in the north between the island of Sakhalin and the Asian mainland connects the sea to the Sea of Okhotsk, as does Soya (La Pérouse) Strait between Sakhalin and Hokkaido. The Tsugaru Strait between Hokkaido and Honshu provides passage to the Pacific. Kanmon Strait between Honshu and Kyusu leads into the Philippine Sea; while at the southern end of the sea, Korea Strait between South Korea and Kyushu links the Sea of Japan to the East China Sea.

The Sea of Japan has a surface area of 377,600 mi^2 (978,000 km^2) and maximum depth of 12,276 ft (3,742 m) bsl. It narrows to the north from its maximum width of 665 mi (1,070 km) just south of the 40°N parallel. The sea is subdivided into three basins. Tsushima Basin in the southwest is the shallowest with a wide continental shelf underlying its eastern side. The Yamota Basin in the southeast contains the deepest point in the sea. These two basins are formed on thinned continental crust. The Japan Basin in the north lies on oceanic crust.

Climatic conditions are influenced by the East Asian monsoon. Summer's southeasterly monsoon off the Pacific ushers in the rainy season, while the winter monsoon brings cold dry air off the Asian continent. Total precipitation varies latitudinally: the northwestern part of the basin receives 12–20 in (310–500 mm), while the southeastern part receives

59–79 in (1,500–2,000 mm) annually. Due to higher rainfall amounts, average salinity in the southern part of the sea of Japan is 33.8, although snow melt can reduce salinity in the north to 31.5 in the spring. With an overall average salinity of 34, the Sea of Japan is less saline than the open Pacific Ocean. Sea ice forms along the Siberian coast and in the Strait of Tartary 4 or 5 months each year.

Geologic History. The Sea of Japan may lie in a back-arc basin formed some 55–40 mya, when the Indian plate collided with and subducted under the Eurasian Plate, a process that led to the uplift of the Himalaya Mountains near the contact zone. Under some scenarios, the sea opened during the Miocene Epoch 32–15 mya, and the Japan arc began to develop. The continental crust beneath both the Tsushima and Yamoto basins was extended, thinned, and rifted into basin-and-range topography by a rising magma plume formed as a result of subduction. Rifting in the Japan Basin fractured the crust completely and allowed magma to flow through and form new oceanic crust. The straits are much more recent developments.

Circulation and Major Currents. Circulation in the Sea of Japan occurs counterclockwise. The Tsushima Warm Current is an extension of a branch of the Kuroshio Current that enters through Korea Strait. The current forks at Tsushima Island in the strait; the western branch flows along the east coast of South Korea and into the center of the sea as the East Korea Warm Current. Both forks merge into the Tsugaru Current and exit to the North Pacific Ocean through the Tsugaru Strait or to the Sea of Okhotsk through Soya Strait. The Liman and North Korean cold currents flow south along the Asian coast.

Biota. The meeting of cold and warm currents creates nutrient-rich waters in the Sea of Japan that support important squid, scad, Japanese sardine, and yellowtail tuna fisheries. Seaweed production is important in coastal ones.

Environmental Issues. Some fish stocks have been depleted. Rapid industrialization in Japan in the 1960s caused water pollution, including mercury and cadmium contamination in two rivers. Development on coasts in the south has damaged mangroves and coral reefs in some locations. Sea-level rise is a problem causing saltwater intrusion of aquifers in Japan.

The former Soviet Union may have discarded radioactive wastes in the sea.

Further Reading

"Geological and Oceanographic Setting of the Japan Sea and Northern East China Sea." 2013. Scientific Prospectus, Integrated Ocean Drilling Program, Expedition 346. http://publications.iodp.org/scientific_prospectus/346/346sp_8.htm

NOAA. 2008. "Sea of Japan Large Marine Ecosystem." *The Encyclopedia of Earth.* http://www.eoearth.org/view/article/155943/

The Sechura and Peruvian Deserts

Peru

Geographic Overview. An extremely arid coastal desert extends along the west coast of South America for 2,300 mi (3,700 km). The Sechura and Peruvian Deserts occur in the northern reaches of this dry zone.

Geographic Coordinates. Sechura Desert: 04°20'S–06°50'S, 70°20'W–81°00'W. Peruvian Desert: 06°50'S–18°25'S, 70°20'W–79°40'W

Description. The Sechura Desert is the northernmost part of the coastal desert of western South America. It is a fog-free region. An area of sandy plains and active dunes, the desert begins near the Ecuador–Peru border and ends at the Peruvian Desert. Located on the coastal plain, the Sechura extends from the Pacific Ocean some 300 miles east to the foothills of the Andes Mountains. River valleys cross the plain. Many parts of the Sechura lack vegetation altogether. However, salt-tolerant plants (halophytes) grow in saline soils near the coast, and coastal dunes are stabilized by salt grasses and some woody plants. Inland dunes may be stabilized by woody shrubs and short trees; columnar cactus, and terrestrial bromeliads can be found on the lower slopes of the Andes. River valleys crossing the coastal plain once had thickets of trees on their banks, but most have been removed to allow agricultural land uses.

The Peruvian Desert is a fog desert and the middle section of South America's west coast desert, with the Sechura to its north and the Atacama to its south. The Peruvian Desert is a particularly narrow strip of arid land 12–60 mi (20–100 km) wide that stretches from the Pacific coast inland to elevations of about 3,000 ft (1,000 m) on the western flanks of the Andes. Fog formed over the cool Humboldt Current offshore provides the main source of moisture in this desert, but its penetration inland is blocked by the Andes Mountains, the western cordillera (Cordillera Occidental) of which lies right along the coast in Peru. The total area of the Peruvian Desert varies from 80,000 km² to 114,000 km², depending upon where its eastern limits are drawn on the foothills of the Andes.

From Chiclayo, Peru, south to Trujillo, alluvial fans extend from dry river valleys in the mountains. The fans have deep alluvial soils and are home to some of Peru's richest agricultural land. The plain itself is flat with some isolated hills less than 2,000 ft (600 m) high near the coast. The plain continues to narrow to the south until between Lima and Pisco it disappears; and the Andes, cut by deep valleys, descend directly to the sea. These valleys once supported ancient population centers and today are important agricultural areas. The coast has been uplifted since the valleys were incised in the Late Miocene Epoch, so that sea cliffs and marine terraces are encountered as far south as the Paracas Peninsula near Pisco.

The coastal plain reappears in southern Peru and continues to the Chilean border, but it is only 12–18 mi (20–30 km) wide and interrupted by steep ridges emanating from the Andes Mountains. The ridges funnel the fog inland, where it becomes less dense and loses its ability to provide much life-giving moisture.

The fog, or *garua* as it is known in Peru, moves onshore on westerly winds and controls climate patterns in the Peruvian Desert. Where it is blocked by the Andes, it becomes quite dense and the intensity of sunlight is diminished, cooling temperatures well below what might be expected in a tropical desert. Although little rain falls, the coastal areas are rather humid. This reduces the amount of water lost from plants due to transpiration and also prevents heat from escaping during the night, maintaining small diurnal temperature ranges. Much of the region receives only 0.1– 0.8 in (2–20 mm) of rain a year. The *garua* is most frequent during the austral winter and least frequent in summer.

Fog drip and drizzle wets the surface enough in some areas to allow moisture to seep into the soil, where it can be taken up by shallow-rooted plants. Other plants, such as lichens and terrestrial *Tillandsias* (a bromeliad), are able to absorb moisture directly from the air. The foliage of *Tillandsias* is covered in short, fine hairs (trichomes), structures that allow them to direct fog drip into the leaf itself, making them especially well adapted to the fog desert. Their roots merely serve to anchor them to the ground. Tillandsias and lichens grow in unique plant communities known as *lomas*. One of the best described *lomas* communities is near Lachay, about 35 mi (60 km) north of Lima. Two plant zones occur. From 300–1,000 ft (100–300 m) asl, a crust of cyanobacteria (mostly *Nostoc*) grows with a variety of foliose and fruticose lichens. Above them is a zone of higher plants. The communities on dry rocky slopes are dominated by terrestrial bromeliads, while on moister slopes low shrubs and perennial herbs can survive. *Lomas* communities near Pisco and Ica have unexplained stripes of shrubs amidst a ground cover of terrestrial *Tillandsias*. Above the *lomas* vegetation, as high as the fog reaches, is a zone of columnar cactus.

From southern Peru into northern Chile, cactus *lomas* occur in sandy areas. The chief plant is a columnar type of cactus (*Haagocereus* spp.) that lies prostrate on the ground, only its tip held erect. Lichens may grow on the long stem. Another interesting plant is the soil cactus (*Pygmaeocereus rowleyanus* in Peru and *Eriosyce* [=*Neochilenia*] spp. in Chile), which is unique to this desert. These small, globular cacti have thick, succulent tubers from which fine roots grow near the surface to trap any moisture seeping into the soil. During long periods of drought, the above ground part of the plant shrivels and shrinks down into the soil.

See also Atacama Desert

Further Reading

Laity, Julie J. 2008. *Deserts and Desert Environments.* Chichester, UK: Wiley-Blackwell.

Quinn, Joyce A. 2009. *Desert Biomes.* Greenwood Guides to Biomes of the World. Westport, CT: Greenwood Press.

Rundel, P. W., P. E. Villagra, M. O. Dillon, S. Roig-Juñent, and G. Debandi. 2007. "Arid and Semi-Arid Ecosystems." In *The Physical Geography of South America*, edited by Thomas T. Veblen, Kenneth R. Young, and

Antony R. Orme, 158–183. New York: Oxford University Press.

Woodward, Susan L. 2003. *Biomes of Earth: Terrestrial, Aquatic, and Human-Dominated.* Westport, CT: Greenwood Press.

Serengeti Plain and Maasai Mara

Tanzania and Kenya

Geographic Overview. The Serengeti Plain and Maasai Mara are parts of the same ecosystem in East Africa. On a high plain east of Lake Victoria, this vast savanna is renowned for the great migration cycle of wildebeest, zebra, and Thomson gazelle that occurs annually in response to seasonal rainfall. Long-term studies of the interrelationships among vegetation, herbivores, predators, and disturbances in this region informed much of modern ecology. Serengeti comes from a Maasai word often translated as "endless plain," while mara refers to the nature of a landscape dappled by shadows cast by clouds and by patches of trees and bush.

Geographic Coordinates. 01°15'S–03°30'S, 34°E–36°E

Description. The Serengeti Plain (Tanzania) and its northern extension, the Maasai Mara (Kenya), lie between Lake Victoria and the Albertine Rift at a general elevation of 3,000 ft (900–1,200 m) asl. The flat to gently rolling surface tilts westward toward the great lake from a high point of 6,000 ft (1,850 m) in the Gol Mountains at the edge of the rift to a low point of 3,018 ft (920 m) close to Speke Gulf in Lake Victoria. The northern limits are defined by the Isuria Escarpment and Loita Plains in Kenya; the southern border, 250 mi (400 km) away, is delineated by the Lake Eyasi escarpment in Tanzania. The plains end in the east in Kenya at the Loita Hills and Nguruman Escarpment and in Tanzania at the Gol Mountains and the Crater Highlands, the mountainous rim of Ngorongoro Crater. On the west, the plains' savannas extend almost to Lake Victoria, separated from the lake by dense miombo woodland and fertile lands converted to agriculture.

The rainfall pattern on this equatorial plateau has a double maximum, with long rains from March–May and short rains October–November. Precipitation amounts decrease from northwest to southeast. Near Lake Victoria annual rainfall averages 47 in (1,200 mm); while in the southeast, in the rain shadow of the Crater Highlands, it falls to 20 in (508 mm). Most of the region receives 23–31 in (600–800 mm) annually.

Vegetation patterns reflect the moisture regime but are modified by soil type and grazing/browsing pressures. Much of the region is covered by *Acacia-Commiphora* savanna, a grassland with patches of woodland containing 16 species of thorny acacia and other trees that shed their leaves during the long dry season. On the fine volcanic soils of the southeast, including in Ngorongoro crater, a treeless, short-grass vegetation with diverse forbs occurs. Wildebeest are a keystone species maintaining, by their grazing, the short grass plains. One of the early findings of studies in the Serengeti was the role of herbivores in determining the plant composition of an area. A seasonal succession of browsers and grazers (and sometimes fire) maintained a mosaic of habitats that allowed for the great diversity of large mammalian herbivores for which the Serengeti is famous. A simplified scheme has migrating zebra arriving earliest and consuming the coarse grass stems of the previous year's growth. They are followed by wildebeest, which prefer softer, shorter grasses and forbs made accessible by the removal of taller growth by zebra. Finally, Thompson's gazelles arrive to graze the new shoots responding to grazing pressures and a new rainy season.

The so-called Great Migration entails a clockwise, circular route of some 500 mi (800 km) from the southern Serengeti (and the Ngorongoro region) north to the Maasai Mara and back. Hundreds of thousands of Burchell's zebras and Thomson's gazelles and more than a million blue wildebeest participate. Their predators—lions, hyenas, jackals—accompany them. During the rainy season, peaking in February, the herds are on their calving grounds on the southeastern grasslands. As the dry season begins in late May, waves of animals begin to move north and west into the *Acacia-Commiphora* woodland savanna near the Grumeti River at about the midway point in the trek. By late June, they are on the move again, arriving at the Mara River on the Kenyan border by late July.

They then make the treacherous crossing of the Mara River onto the Maasai Mara, forced to swim across a river full of waiting crocodiles. The herds remain on the Mara through the dry season, starting their southward return journey at the beginning of the short rains in early November. They reach the short-grass region again by early December.

Geologic History. The Serengeti and Maasai plains are underlain by Precambrian metamorphic rocks (primarily gneiss and quartzite) covered by now-eroded younger sedimentary rocks, remnants of which appear as occasional hills. Outcrops of the Precambrian basement rock form isolated kopjes (inselbergs). Volcanic materials, including lava, tuff, and tephra from nearby volcanoes, blanketed the area during the late Pliocene–Pleistocene and are useful in dating early hominin remains. Ash deposits, probably from Lemagrut volcano, are nearly 40 ft (12 m) thick and, when wet, preserved the 3.8 million year old footprints of *Australopithecus afarensis* at Laetoli. Layers of volcanic ash from the younger but now dormant Ngorongoro and Kerimasi volcanoes as well as still active Ol Doinyo Lengai have developed into fertile soils supporting nutritious grasses.

Biota. The Serengeti–Mara ecosystem supports 70 species of large mammals, among them elephant, hippopotamus, black rhinoceros, buffalo, a large suite of antelopes, giraffe, warthogs, baboons, patas monkey, hyraxes, aardvark, aardwolf, mongooses, pangolin, lion, civet, genet, serval, and so on. Five hundred species of birds are known from the region as are numerous reptiles, including crocodile, monitor lizard, spitting cobra, and rock python. The richness of the Serengeti fauna is sometimes regarded as an analog of the world's fauna prior to the mass extinctions of the Pleistocene Epoch.

Protected Areas. Much of the nearly 11,900 mi^2 (30,000 km^2) Serengeti–Mara region is protected. In Kenya, the Maasai–Mara National Reserve covers 583 mi^2 (1,510 km^2). In Tanzania, Serengeti National Park encompasses 5,700 mi^2 (14,763 km^2), while the Ngorongoro Conservation Area extends over another 850 mi^2 (2,200 km^2). Several sizeable game reserves abut or are close to Serengeti National Park.

Environmental Issues. Poaching of game continues to be a problem. Grazing rights of native Maasai pastoralists are an unresolved issue, as are the destructive habits of elephants in agricultural plots on the western margins of the region. Protection and growth of the black rhinoceros population remains a significant management concern.

See also Ngorongoro Crater

Further Reading

Saundry, Peter and World Wildlife Fund. 2012. "Serengeti." *The Encyclopedia of Earth.* http://www.eoearth.org /view/article/155980/

Sinclair, A. R. E., Simon A. R. Mduma, J. Grant C. Hopcraft, John M. Fryxell, Ray Hilborn, and Simon Thirgood. 2007. "Long-Term Ecosystem Dynamics in the Serengeti: Lessons for Conservation." *Conservation Biology* 21: 580–590. http://ib.cbs.uoguelph.ca/pdfs /Sinclair_2007_ConsBiol.pdf

Seychelles

Indian Ocean

Geographic Overview. The Seychelles comprise more than a hundred small islands north of Madagascar in the western Indian Ocean. Arranged in clusters, the northern group is unique among oceanic islands in being granitic and ancient. Southern islands are coralline. The islands are known for the giant tortoises of Aldabra Atoll and the coco-de-mer, a palm that produces the largest seed in the plant kingdom.

Geographic Coordinates. 04°S–10°S, 46°E–54°E

Description. The Seychelles extend over 500,000 mi^2 (1.3 million km^2) of the Indian Ocean north of Madagascar and some 930 mi (1,500 km) east of Africa. Two main groups are recognized: 42 northern high granitic islands in the north and 115 low coral islands in the south. Most islands are small and uninhabited. (Although granitic, the high islands are generally considered oceanic islands because they are not on a continental shelf and had only distant connections with a contemporary continental landmass. They are not, however, true oceanic islands, yet neither are they true continental islands.) The largest island is granitic Mahé (4°40'S, 55°28'E), which is about 15 mi (25 km) long and 5 mi (8 km) wide and has an area of 59 mi^2 (153 km^2). Its steep boulder-strewn hills

View of island of La Digue, one of the granitic islands in the Seychelles. (Simon Hack/Dreamstime.com)

and mountains rise abruptly from the sea to reach the highest point in the Seychelles, 2,969 ft (905 m) asl, on Morne Seychellois. The area of the second largest, Praslin Island, 19 mi (30 km) northeast of Mahé, is only 11 mi² (28 km²). The granitics are Earth's oldest oceanic islands.

Twenty-nine coral islands form the Amirantes group west of the granitics. Southwest of them is the Farquhar group of 13 coral islands, and the 67 raised coral islands of the Aldabra group lie west of the Farquhars. All stand less than 26 ft (8 m) asl; many are less than 3 ft (1 m) asl. The Aldabra Atoll (09°42'S, 47°03'E) is one of the world's largest atolls and the least disturbed major island in the Indian Ocean. Its four main islands are built of raised coral limestones and separated by narrow passages. They enclose a lagoon and are themselves surrounded by an outer fringing reef. The limestone has weathered into a rough,

pitted surface. Undercut limestone cliffs and perched dunes occur on the windward (southern) side of the atoll. The atoll's isolation and general inaccessibility have prevented settlement and protected a number of endemic species including the famous giant tortoises.

These tropical islands lie outside the cyclone paths of the Indian Ocean and rarely experience high winds. Temperatures show little variation and are warm all year, ranging from 75°–86°F (24°–30°C). Total annual precipitation can be 114 in (2,900 mm) or more on the slopes of Mahé, but as less than 20 in (500 mm) on the low coral islands. The granitics have or had forests in which palms were a major component. Most of the diverse fauna are small, inconspicuous animals adapted to live in the leaf litter or in narrow spaces among the palm fronds. Mangroves line the shores of the coralline islands. Giant tortoises were the major herbivore on numerous islands, but two of the four species are now extinct. Plants evolved spines and other strategies to cope with their browsing.

Geologic History. Precambrian granite, 750 million years old, forms the core of the granitic islands. At one time this continental crust was part of Gondwana. Either as a fragment of that supercontinent or as a distinct microcontinent, the Seychelles block, attached to India, moved away from Africa some 150 mya. About 65 mya, the Seychelles separated from India, perhaps due to rifting as the block passed over the Réunion hotspot. While India continued to move rapidly northward toward Eurasia, the Seychelles remained off the coast of Africa and slowly eroded and subsided until only the mountain tops remained above sea level. Later tectonic movement and associated volcanic activity gave rise to other islands. Fringing reefs grew along their shores. As these islands subsided the reefs remained as cays and atolls.

Biota. The high granitics are home to diverse plants and animals with affinities to Asia and Madagascar. Of the 300 plant species, 40 percent are endemic, including six species of palm, carnivorous pitcher plants in the genus *Nepenthes*, and the jellyfish tree, sole member of an endemic family, Medusagynaceae. Insects such as a carrion-eating caddisfly and a terrestrial diving beetle demonstrate niche-changes common among oceanic island endemics. Unique mollusks include 10 species of carnivorous snails in six genera, and other Gondwanan ground and tree snails. Insect diversity is high, with some 6,000 species identified. Among vertebrates, four species of frog belong to the endemic family Sooglossidae, related to an Indian species. These frogs have no free-living tadpole stage but develop in the egg or on the back of an adult. Gardiner's frog (*Sooglossus gardineri*), 0.3–0.4 in (8–11 mm) long, is one of the world's smallest frogs. Froglets 0.1 in (3 mm) in length hatch directly from the egg. Other endemic amphibians include six caecilians with Gondwanan origins. Reptiles are the dominant vertebrates, and include chameleons, geckos, skinks, and snakes as well as giant tortoises. A bizarre sucker-tailed gecko lives in caves. The world's largest population of giant tortoise thrives on the Aldabra Atoll, where 152,000 Aldabra tortoises live in a natural state. Endemic birds are closely related to species in Madagascar. The Aldabra Rail is the last of the Indian Ocean's large flightless birds. The Seychelles separated from Gondwana before the rise of modern mammals. Only two endemic mammals are known from the Seychelles, both flying mammals: the sheath-tailed bat and a flying fox. People have introduced rats, mice, cats, tenrecs, and goats to the islands.

On the fringing reefs, over 1,200 fishes have been identified. Unfortunately the corals were severely damaged by coral bleaching in 1998 and 80 percent of corals were lost. Recovery has been slow.

Protected Areas. Nearly half of the land in the Seychelles is protected in national parks and nature preserves. Vallée de Mai, on Praslin Island, is a World Heritage Site protecting coco-de-mer and the five other endemic palms, as well as numerous endemic reptiles, the Black Parrot, and other island endemics. Aldabra Atoll is another World Heritage Site; more than 400 endemic species and subspecies are protected here, as well as the world's second largest breeding colony of frigate birds and one of only two populations of oceanic flamingos. Silhouette Island, the third largest and most scenic of the granitic islands, has been nominated for World Heritage Site inscription to protect the last known roosts of the sheath-tailed bat and other endemic species.

Environmental Issues. All the low islands are threatened with rising sea levels associated with global climate change. Except for Aldabra, most islands were modified by human activity in the 19th century, in part by conversion to extensive coconut and cinnamon plantations. Today tourism is altering landscapes in major ways as hotels and resorts are constructed. Introduced species are a continuing problem as invasive plants such as cinnamon, Chinese guava, and Koster's curse spread.

See also Indian Ocean; Mascarene Islands

Further Reading

Gerlach, Justin. 2009. "Seychelles." In *Encyclopedia of Islands*, edited by Rosemary G. Gillespie and David A. Clague, 829–833. Berkeley: University of California Press.

UNESCO. n.d. "Aldabra Atoll." http://whc.unesco.org/en/list/185

UNESCO. n.d. "Vallée de Mai Nature Reserve." http://whc.unesco.org/en/list/261

Shark Bay

Australia

Geographic Overview. Shark Bay is a large, semi-enclosed embayment on the westernmost part of Australia. It is best known for the living stromatolites in Hamelin Pool at the southeastern end of the bay, one of two known marine examples of these structures, fossils of which have been found all around the world. The bay also harbors the largest and most diverse seagrass meadows on Earth, a rare beach composed entirely of cockle shells, and a large population of dugongs. Most islands and bays are named after members of a French expedition that surveyed the Bay in 1800.

Geographic Coordinates. 24°44'S–27°16'S, 112°49'E–114°17'E

Description. Shark Bay is a 5,000 mi² (13,000 km²) shallow embayment on Australia's Indian Ocean coast. It is located on the westernmost bulge of the continent, where it stretches for 125 mi (200 km) in a northwest–southeast direction. The Peron Peninsula reaches into the Bay from the southeast and for 68 mi (110 km) divides it into two sections: Denham Sound–Freycinet Harbor on the west and L'Harodin Bight and Hamelin Pool on the east. A chain of narrow barrier islands—Bernier, Dorre, and Dirk Hartog and the Edel Peninsula separate the Bay from the Indian Ocean.

Vast seagrass beds trap sediment and impede the flow of seawater into Shark Bay, especially along the eastern side of the Bay at Wooramel Seagrass Bank. The only inflow of ocean water occurs through passages between Dorre and Dirk Hartog Islands and between Dirk Hartog and Steep Point on the tip of the Edel Peninsula. Two intermittent streams on the eastern shore discharge fresh water into the bay when they flow; saline groundwater also seeps into the Bay. Strong summer winds push surface water out of the Bay and contribute to the counterclockwise circulation from west to southeast to northwest. The bay has an average depth of 29.5 ft (9 m) and a maximum depth of 95 ft (29 m). Tidal range is 2–5.5 ft (0.6–1.7 m). A noticeable salinity gradient exists, with northern and northwestern bay water being close to that of seawater (35–40 ppt) and that in L'Haridon Bight and Hamelin Pool being hypersaline (56–70 ppt). Hypersalinity is a result of low tidal flushing—in part due to blocking seagrass beds, low precipitation, and high evaporation rates at the southeastern end of Shark Bay.

The seaward margin of Shark Bay consists of 10–100 ft (3–30 m) high cliffs and narrow sandy beaches. The exceptional Zuydorp Cliffs in the south reach heights of 650 ft (200 m) and are among the highest sea cliffs in Australia. Behind the limestone escarpment in the east is a low plain. The three barrier islands and the Edel Peninsula on the west side have long, north-trending sand dunes cemented and stabilized by loose limestone. Peron Peninsula is a sandy plain with salt and gypsum pans. In the south, it constricts to become the narrow Taillefu Isthmus, which, on the east, forms the southern end of L'Haridon Bight and the location of 75 mi (120 km) long Shell Beach. Constructed of the snow-white shells of the cockle *Fragum eragatum*, the beach deposit is 23–33 ft (7–10 m) deep. The cockles thrive in the hypersaline waters of the Bight because their predators do not tolerate such conditions.

Hypersalinity contributes to the formation of carbonate banks by the seagrasses, because limestone sands are precipitated from the seawater under these conditions and trapped by the plants. Such a structure is Fauré Sill near Monkey Mia on Peron Peninsula, which cuts Hamelin Pool off from the main body of water. Wooramel Seagrass Bank on the east side of the Bay is the world's largest seagrass meadow, covering nearly 400 mi² (1,030 km²).

The main attraction of Shark Bay, the living stromatolites of Hamelin Pool, also exists as a consequence of hypersalinity. These dome-shaped, layered mounds are constructed by cyanobacteria that trap and bind detritus in a sticky outer covering. Photosynthesis by these microbes depletes the water of carbon dioxide and increases pH, initiating the precipitation of carbonate minerals. As sediments cover the colony, the microbes move to the surface to form a new mat or layer; the rock-like mound grows upward at rate of less than 0.04 in (1mm)/yr. Most are less than 1.5 ft (0.5 m) high. The cyanobacteria descend from forms that lived on Earth 1.9 million years ago; although the stromatolites of Shark Bay are only 2,000–3,000 years old. They serve as analogs for a one-celled life-form that dominated shallow seas for 3.5 billion years during the Precambrian and became rare after the Cambrian explosion, presumably because grazers evolved. The hypersaline waters of Hamelin Pool prevent the establishment of invertebrates that would graze them. Fossil stromatolites are found all over the world. Living stromatolites are rare today, inhabiting shallow lakes, streams, and springs. The only other major occurrence of marine stromatolites is at Lee Stocking Island in the Exuma Cays of the Bahamas.

Shark Bay is in a semiarid to arid region with hot, dry summers and mild winters. Annual precipitation varies from 15 in (400 mm) in the west to 8 in (200 mm) in the east. Sea surface temperatures within the bay range from 63°F (17°C) in winter (August) to 75°–79°F (24°–26°C) in summer (February), with a maximum of 81°F (27°C) in Hamelin Pool.

Geologic History. Shark Bay is a product of changing sea levels during the Quaternary Period. Sea level 125,000 years ago was lower than today, and sand dunes developed on dry land. Rising seas at the end of the last glacial, about 10,000 yrs ago, flooded the low-lying coast and produced the bay, leaving high points as islands and peninsulas.

Biota. Twelve species of seagrass grow in Shark Bay. Most common are sea nymph (*Amphibolus antarctica*) and fiberball weed (*Posidonia australis*). Marine animals include 323 fish species including whale shark, tiger shark, basking shark, and scalloped, great, and smooth hammerhead sharks. A number of ray species, including the rare manta ray, also inhabit the Bay. Endangered green and loggerhead sea turtles nest on beaches on Peron Peninsula and Dirk Hartog Island. The endemic Shark Bay sea snake (*Aipysurus pooleorum*) is one of six sea snake species found there. Marine mammals include population of 11,000 dugongs, southern right whales and humpback whales, and the popular Indo-Pacific bottlenose dolphins that come to be fed at Monkey Mia.

Four globally threatened marsupial species inhabit the barrier islands: burrowing bettong, rufous hare wallaby, banded hare wallaby, and western barred bandicoot. One native rodent, the Shark Bay mouse (*Pseudomys fieldi*), also occurs on these islands. These animals once were widespread across Australia, but today are restricted to these small islands that have been kept free of feral cats and other predators.

Protected Areas. Shark Bay is a UNESCO World Heritage Site composed of several national parks, marine reserves, and other conservation areas.

Environmental Issues. Climate change could alter the aquatic environment to the detriment of its significant communities. Fire is a threat to small animal populations on islands.

Further Reading

"Nature of Shark Bay." 2009. Shark Bay World Heritage Area, Western Australia. http://www.sharkbay.org/default.aspx?WebPageID=117

"Shark Bay, Western Australia." n.d. World Heritage Centre, UNESCO. http://whc.unesco.org/en/list/578

Shetland Islands

Atlantic Ocean

Geographic Overview. The Shetland Islands, 62 mi (100 km) north of mainland Scotland, are the northernmost remnants of the Caledonian Mountains, now eroded to rolling hills. The islands' rocky cliffs, home to thousands of nesting seabirds, preserve several ancient Precambrian rocks from the former continent of Laurentia. Many archaeological sites preserve cultural development from the Neolithic through the Iron Age and into the Viking Age.

Geographic Coordinates. 59°30'N–60°50'N, 00°44'W–02°07'W

Description. The approximately 100 islands of the Shetland complex include small uninhabited islets and skerries. The major islands are Mainland, the largest, and Yell, Unst, Fetlar, Bressay, Whalsay, and Burra. Bedrock in the Shetland Islands is a variety of ancient gneisses and granites, which was scoured into an undulating hilly landscape by Pleistocene glaciation. The general trend to the islands is south-southwest to north-northeast. Rocks with varying resistance, along with several north–south trending faults, determine the topography, which is dominated by lines of almost parallel hills, valleys, and inlets. River valleys and subsequent glaciers followed the faults. The very irregular and indented coastline, fringed by cliffs, inlets, and beaches, totals 1,697 mi (2,702 km). The western side of the Shetlands feels the full force of the Atlantic Ocean, which carves the hard rocks into

The rocky Shetland Islands provide safe nesting sites for a variety of seabirds, such as the gannet colony shown here on Muckle Flugga, the northernmost point of the British Isles. (Orion9nl/Dreamstime.com)

cliffs, coastal arches, and stacks. The highest elevations of most islands are 165–330 ft (50–100 m) asl. Ronas Hill, comprised of granite on Mainland, is the highest at 1,476 ft (450 m).

Fair Isle, halfway between the Shetlands and the Orkney Islands, is predominantly Devonian sandstone, conglomerate, and mudstone. Fault zones that cut through the island were conduits for lava, now eroded away by waves and contributing to the indented coastline. The island, reaching 712 ft (217 m) asl, is characterized by sea cliffs, stacks, and moorland.

The Shetlands have many Iron Age sites called brochs, 2,000-year-old multistory rock towers as tall as 42.5 ft (13 m) associated with multiroom dwelling sites. Other significant archaeological sites document the transition from Iron Age or Pictish villages to Viking villages.

The Shetland Islands are bathed by the North Atlantic Drift, which moderates temperature extremes. Summer temperatures average 58°F (14°C), and winters average 38°F (3°C), with little frost or snow. The region is frequently cloudy, and annual precipitation is 44 in (1,220 mm). Fog and wind are common.

Geologic History. The Lewisian gneiss of the Shetland Islands, a complex group of metamorphosed gneiss and schists from various periods of mountain building and erosion in the Precambrian (15,000–3,000 mya), were initially part of the continental shield of Laurentia, the ancient continent west of the Iapetus Ocean. When Laurentia collided with Baltica, during the Caledonian Orogeny, part of the ocean floor rocks were thrust west over Laurentia. The overlying rocks eroded away, exposing peridotite and gabbro on Unst and Fetlar, oceanic crust, and mantle rarely found on Earth's surface. With closure of the Iapetus Ocean, granite and some gabbro were intruded into the older Precambrian rocks. During the Devonian (400 mya), sand, silt, mud, and gravel were deposited in a large freshwater basin at the base of the Caledonian mountains. Collectively, the 5,000 ft (1,500 m) thick deposits are called the Old Red Sandstone. At the end of the Devonian, the lake dried, the sediments were folded and faulted and intruded by lava flows. Most of these deposits were eroded away, but some remain in the southeast, Bressay and Lerwick, and in the west, Walls Peninsula. When the North Atlantic opened with the breakup of Pangaea, a piece of ancient Laurentia was carried eastward with Eurasia, to become the Shetland Islands. The tensional forces that opened the Atlantic Ocean in the Tertiary also affected the North Sea. Although a gorge, called the Viking Graben, opened, no magma spewed out. The chasm filled with sediments, which became the trap for extensive oil and gas deposits.

Several north–south faults separate rocks of different ages and origins. The Walls Boundary Fault, an extension of the Great Glen Fault that runs through the western mainland island, is the main fault in Shetland, with many offshoots or splinter faults. The shatter zone along the fault was weakened, allowing erosion. To the east, the Nesting Fault and its splinter faults run through the eastern Mainland and Yell.

Biota. The variety of habitats in the Shetland Islands, including sandy beaches, coastal cliffs, meadows, and alpine environments, support 400 species of plants. The unique flora on Unst, such as sea plantain, scurvy grass, stone-bramble, northern rock-cress, Norwegian sandwort, and the endemic Edmondston's chickweed (*Cerastium nigrescens*), is related to the chemical composition of the oceanic and mantle rocks. Small pockets of machair, lime-rich habitats on broken shells, support unique plants and meadows, which are home to many birds, including denlin, twite, redshank, and corncrake.

The Shetlands are a major area in the North Atlantic for seabirds. More than a million birds breed in very large colonies. Fair Isle has an internationally important seabird population, 100,000 breeding pairs of fulmar, hag, Arctic Skua, Great Skua, kittiwake, razorbill, puffin, and guillemots, and an endemic subspecies of wren (*Troglodytes trolodytes fridariensis*). Common seal, gray seal, otters, and porpoises are often seen marine animals, with an occasional dolphin or whale.

Protected Areas. A National Scenic Area incorporates most of the Shetlands and Fair Isle, and the Shetlands have several Sites of Special Scientific Interest and Special Protection Areas. The Shetlands are part of the European Geoparks Network. Iron Age brochs, Mousa, Old Scatness, and Jarlshof are being considered for inscription as a World Heritage Site.

Environmental Issues. Sullom Voe, on Shetland's mainland, is a large oil and gas terminal serving the North Sea. The Shetland Oil Terminal Environmental Advisory Group oversees and keeps the environmental impact at a minimum.

See also Loch Ness and the Great Glen; Orkney Islands

Further Reading

McKirdy, Alan. 2010. *Orkney and Shetland, A Landscape Fashioned by Geology*. www.snh.org.uk/pdfs/publications/geology/orkneyshetland.pdf

Shetland Amenity Trust. 2013. http://www.shetlandamenity.org/

Ship Rock

United States (New Mexico)

Geographic Overview. Ship Rock (also spelled Shiprock), in northwestern New Mexico, is one of about 80 volcanic necks in the Navajo Volcanic Field in the Four Corners Area. It is a rugged spire of igneous rock, with winglike dikes, above the adjacent land. In the Navajo language, it is called *Tse Bi dahi*, or the "Rock with Wings." In Navajo legend, Ship Rock is the bird which transported the Navajo to this land and is sacred to the Navajo Nation. First climbed in 1939, Ship Rock remains attractive to technical climbers. Because the monolith is sacred to the Navajo Nation, however, climbing has been prohibited since 1970.

Geographic Coordinates. 36°48'N, 108°41'W

Description. Ship Rock is on Navajo Nation reservation land, approximately 11 mi (18 km) southwest of the town of Shiprock. At an elevation of 7,178 ft (2,188 m) asl, this steep rock, approximately 1,640 ft (500 m) in diameter, towers approximately 1,968 ft (600 m) above the surrounding plain. It is a type of solidified core of the conduit, called a diatreme, which fed a volcano approximately 30 mya during the Oligocene. Evidence suggests that Ship Rock may have developed as much as 3,280 ft (1,000 m) deep underground, indicating that the volcano and its surrounding landscape was at least that high above the current surface. Radiating from Ship Rock are three large dikes, 1.9–5.6 mi (3–9 km) long and 2–15 ft (0.6–4.6 m) wide. Three smaller dikes, each shorter than 0.6 mi (1 km), run parallel to the northeastern dike, which is segmented into 35 smaller sections.

Geologic History. Ship Rock is associated with both the Navajo Volcanic Field and the Chuska Volcanic Field. The mineral composition of the rocks indicates that the magma was derived from deep within the continental crust. Minette is a rare type of dense intrusive igneous rock that has fine crystals, primarily alkali feldspar, phlogopite mica, and diopside pyroxene. The rock color is dark brown because it lacks plagioclase feldspar, the pink variety of the mineral.

The overlying rock layers of shale, through which Ship Rock extends were not deformed and remain essentially horizontal. The composition of Ship Rock, a fused breccia of volcanic rocks intermixed with the shale country rock, indicates that the eruption was explosive. Rising magma may have incorporated abundant ground water, causing an explosive eruption to occur fairly close to the surface, creating a maar, which is a surface crater blown out by the explosion. Cracks through the breccia are filled with minette, the rock that also comprises the dikes, indicating that the explosive eruption occurred first, the relatively quiet magma intrusion without gas came second.

Volcanic activity in New Mexico may be related to a rifting or stretching of the crust, allowing magma to surface. The extensive volcanics in the region as well as the horsts and grabens associated with the Rio Grande Valley are strong evidence of such crustal deformation.

See also Colorado Plateau

Further Reading

Crumpler, Larry. 1999–2012. *Navajo Volcanic Field: Ship Rock*. New Mexico Museum of Natural History and Science. http://nmnaturalhistory.org/chuska-shp-rock-navajo-field-ship-rock.html

Kuss, Lawrence. 2004. *Shiprock*. Emporia State University. http://academic.emporia.edu/aberjame/student/kuss1/shiprock.html

Rakovan, John. 2006. "Diatreme." *Rocks and Minerals* 81: 153–154. www.cas.muohio.edu/~rakovajf/WTTW%20Diatreme.pdf

Sierra Madre del Sur

Mexico

Geographic Overview. The Sierra Madre del Sur comprises several small, discontinuous mountain ranges in two states in southwestern Mexico, Guerrero and Oaxaca. Their steep slopes have tended to make the higher elevations inaccessible and thereby protected humid montane forests known for their rich diversity of plant and animal species. In the high basin known as the Valley of the Oaxaca, monumental Monte Albán, one of the earliest cities in Mesoamerica, developed; it was to thrive from 500 BCE to AD 750, when it was abandoned.

Geographic Coordinates. 15°42'N–18°52'N, 95°09'W–103°43'W

Description. The Sierra Madre del Sur comprises several small, discontinuous mountain ranges, including the Sierra de Atoyac in the west, the Sierra de Yucuyacua at the Guerrero–Oaxaca border, and the Sierra de Miahuatlán in southern Oaxaca. The eastern section, in Oaxaca, is wider and sometimes called the Mesa del Sur. Together the two parts are referred to as the Southern Highlands. The mountains extend 745 mi (1,200 km) along the Pacific coast of the country from the Balsas Depression to the Isthmus of Tehuantepec and form some of the most rugged terrain in Mexico.

Summits frequently reach 7,000–8,000 ft (2,000–2,400 m) asl, but a few exceed 10,000 ft (3,000 m). This is a former plateau deeply incised by streams, which may carve V-shaped valleys 3,000–4,000 ft (900–1,200 m) deep and leave knife-edged ridges. The mountains descend abruptly to the Pacific along a steep escarpment that forms rugged sea cliffs north of Cabo Corrientes. South of this cape, a narrow coastal plain separates the mountains from the Pacific Ocean. Level land is scarce, but in the Mesa del Sur the flat, high basin of the Valley of Oaxaca, covering more than 1,300 mi² (3,375 km²), nurtured the agriculture and civilization of the Zapotec people for more than

4,000 years. The Valley of Oaxaca is a Y-shaped system of rift valleys (grabens) 5,000 ft (1,550 m) asl. Monte Albán was built at the fork in the Y.

The slopes facing the Pacific Ocean have high humidity and support temperate forests at higher elevations. They are a continuation of the biodiverse Madrean forests that begin at the U.S.–Mexican border and extend the length of the Sierra Madre Occidental and Sierra Madre Oriental. Semideciduous lower montane forests occupy the slopes between 2,000 and 4,600 ft (600–1,400 m) asl. Oak forests occur from 6,200 to 8,200 ft (1,900–2,500 m) asl. A cloud forest of broadleaf trees as tall as 100 ft (30 m) grows on the wettest slopes 7,500 ft (2,300 m). Cloud trees are covered with epiphytes and joined by tree ferns. At still higher elevations from 7,900 to 8,200 ft (2,400–2,500 m), the biologically rich Madrean pine-oak forests are found, and firs dominate at elevations above 9,800 ft (3,000 m).

Geologic History. The Southern Highlands region is formed of ancient volcanic and plutonic rocks. Particularly in the southern area, the plutons are exposed. Mesozoic limestones and Tertiary volcanic rocks occur as remnants of a plateau surface on the higher peaks. The bedrock was folded and faulted during the Mesozoic Epoch as a consequence of the subduction of the Cocos and a couple of smaller plates beneath the North American plate. The region remains seismically active today; earthquakes are frequent.

Biota. More than 350 species of orchid and 160 species of butterfly are found in the Sierra Madre del Sur, about half of them in the montane and cloud forests. These high elevation forests also house about 50 percent of the region's amphibians and 34 percent of its endemic reptiles, together with a large number of avian species.

Protected Areas. Few reserves exist to protect this biodiversity, which until recently was defended by rugged terrain.

Environmental Issues. Clearing for agriculture—citrus in the north, and coffee plantations in the south, removal of pine and fir for timber, and clearing for livestock production threaten the natural vegetation, as well as the native fauna. Hunting for game meat puts pressure on deer, paca, tapir, and monkeys. Predator control by farmers and ranchers threatens such wild cats as ocelot and puma.

See also Sierra Madre Occidental; Sierra Madre Oriental

Further Reading

"Endemic Bird Area factsheet: Sierra Madre del Sur." 2013. BirdLife International. http://www.birdlife.org/datazone/ebafactsheet.php?id=12

"Sierra Madre del Sur Pine-oak Forests (NT 0309)." n.d. WildWorld ecoregion profile. WildWorld, National Geographic. http://web.archive.org/web/20100308075013/http://www.nationalgeographic.com/wildworld/profiles/terrestrial/nt/nt0309.html

Valero, Alejandra, Jan Schipper, and Tom Allnutt. n.d. "Mexico: States of Guerrero and Oaxaca." Terrestrial Ecoregions, Tropical and Subtropical Coniferous Forests. World Wildlife Fund. http://worldwildlife.org/ecoregions/nt0309

Sierra Madre Occidental

Mexico

Geographic Overview. The Sierra Madre Occidental is the western edge of the Mexican Plateau. A 750-mi (1,250-km) long mountain range, the Sierra runs from northwest to southeast starting near the U.S.–Mexico border in the state of Sonora and continuing through Chihuahua, Sinaloa, Durango, Nayarit, and southwestern Zacatecas to its southern limit in Jalisco, where it converges with Mexico's Transverse Volcanic Axis. Carved into it by tributaries of the Fuerte River is Copper Canyon (Baranca del Cobre), often compared to the Grand Canyon in the United States.

Geographic Coordinates. 20°30'N–31°20'N, 103°30'W–110°00'W

Description. The Sierra Madre Occidental is about 190 mi (300 km) from the Gulf of California in the north then more closely approaches the Pacific Ocean to the south, where the coastal plain is only 30 mi (50 km) wide. Summit elevations reach more than 10,000 ft (3,000 m) asl, the highest points being in the Sierra Tarahumara of Chihuahua and Durango. Western slopes, especially in the north, are deeply incised by a number of rivers, including the Yaqui, Humayo, and Fuerte.

The Sierra Madre Occidental loom above prehispanic Los Guachimontones, a World Heritage Site in Jalisco, Mexico, remarkable for its circular stepped pyramids. (Joe Ferrer/Dreamstime.com)

Much of the range experiences two wet seasons (summer and winter) and two dry seasons (spring and fall), under the same climatic influences as the nearby Sonoran Desert. Temperatures are mild, but at higher elevations frost and snow can occur in winter.

The Sierra Madre Occidental is one of the most biologically rich areas in North America. Both biodiversity and endemism rates are high. Its elevational range allows for a variety of environmental conditions and vegetation types, but most significant is the Madrean pine-oak forest found at roughly 4,000–7,350 ft (1,220–2,240 m) asl. It contains 23 species of pine and as many as 200 different oaks. Lower slopes on the western side of the mountains are drier and host different plant associations. In the northwest, the Sonoran Desert occupies the lowlands. A deciduous thornscrub occurs in the foothills then gives way to tropical dry forest with tree-like cactus at 1,600–5,000 ft (500–1,160 m) asl. Oaks dominate at

3,500–5,550 ft (1,050–1,700 m). Above the pine-oak forest is a mixed conifer forest with tall Douglas fir and several pines. This last vegetation type occurs on the highest peaks and is a continuation of the Madrean Sky Island coniferous forest found on the small isolated mountain ranges of southern Arizona occurring between the edge of the Colorado Plateau (Mogollon Rim) and the Sierra Madre Occidental.

The mountains are important wintering grounds for migratory birds from the United States and Canada. Very little of the forest remains intact after more than a century of logging.

Geologic History. Precambrian granite and gneiss, continental crust from Old North America, underlie the Sierra in the north. They are buried beneath a vast sheet of ignimbrite, deposits resulting from pyroclastic flows rich in pumice and ash and dating to the Oligocene Epoch, 34–23 mya. Lava flows are also common. All were associated with the final, low-angle subduction of the former oceanic Farallón Plate under the North American Plate. Ten calderas, three of which occur in Copper Canyon, are remains of this mid-Tertiary ignimbrite flare-up, which created one of the world's largest volcanic provinces. Some geologists identify this period of magmatism as the precursor of poorly understood tectonic forces, which subsequently pulled the region in an east-northeast direction, creating the widespread basin and range topography on either side of the Sierra Madre Occidental prior to the opening of the Gulf of California. Only the core of the region was not so stretched and faulted, and this undeformed bedrock became the Sierra.

Biota. The rich diversity of species in the Sierra Madre Occidental attests not only to altitudinal variation but also to the range's function as a biogeographical corridor that has allowed the intermingling of temperate and tropical plants and animals. At the same time, mountain habitats are isolated by the more arid conditions on both sides; and this promotes local evolution and endemism. Over half of the amphibians and 25 percent of reptiles are unique to the ecoregion, as are about 10 percent of the birds. Mammals such as the Mexican gray wolf and Mexican grizzly have already been extirpated; and the world's largest woodpecker, the Imperial Woodpecker, is probably extinct, the endemic Thick-billed Parrot nearly so.

See also Mexican Plateau (Mexican Altiplano); Sonoran Desert

Further Reading

Ferrari, Luca, Martín Valencia-Moreno, and Scott Bryan. 2007. "Magmatism and Tectonics of the Sierra Madre Occidental and Its Relation with the Evolution of the Western Margin of North America." *Geological Society of America, Special Paper* 422. http://www.geo ciencias.unam.mx/~luca/Ferrari%20et%20al%202007 .pdf

"Sierra Madre Occidental Pine-Oak Forests." 2006. *The Encyclopedia of Earth*. http://www.eoearth.org/article /Sierra_Madre_Occidental_pine-oak_forests

Van Devender, Thomas. 2013. Research in the Sierra Madre Occidental of Eastern Sonora, Mexico (Yécora region): Introduction. Conservation Education and Science Department. Arizona-Sonora Desert Museum, http:// www.desertmuseum.org/programs/yecora_index.php

Sierra Madre Oriental

Mexico

Geographic Overview. The Sierra Madre Oriental is the eastern edge of the Mexican Plateau, rather unimposing when viewed from the plateau but a major mountain range when encountered from the Gulf Coastal Plain. The Sierra comprises a group of long, folded, and faulted parallel ridges running some 840 mi (1,350 km) from the Chisos Mountains in southern Texas south to the Mexican state of Veracruz. The mountains terminate where they meet the Trans-Mexican Volcanic Axis near Pico de Orizaba, the highest peak In Middle America.

Geographic Coordinates. 27°47'N–18°50'N, 100° 30'W–96°55'W

Description. The Sierra Madre Oriental is composed of sedimentary rocks of marine origin, primarily limestones and shales. Eroded anticlinal and synclinal structures create the steep-sloped mountainous terrain. In the north, the ridges are sharp and separated by deep, narrow valleys. Toward the southern extreme the valleys are shallower and wider. Mountain crests are generally 7,000–8,000 ft (2,100–2,400 m) asl, but the highest mountains are more than 12,000 ft (3,650 m) asl. Cerro de Potosí in Nuevo Leon (12,208 ft or 3,721 m) is the highest, closely rivaled by Cerro San Rafael in Coahuila (12,205 ft or 3,720 m).

The Sierra Madre Oriental is an ecologically diverse range, with arid habitats in the north and subhumid to humid environments in the south. Deep canyons and valleys have isolated populations of plants and animals and allowed the accumulation of endemic species. Nearctic pine-oak forest communities occur between elevations of 3,300–10,000 ft (1,000–3,000 m), habitat islands in the dry, desert-like conditions of lowlands in the north and in the midst of more humid tropical forests in the south. Pines include *Pinus arizonica*, *Pinus cembroides*, the endemic and endangered *Pinus nelsoni*, and *Pinus pseudostrobus*, distributed according to substrate and moisture regimes. Oaks include the leathery-leaved *Quercus castanea* and evergreen, lanceolote-leaved *Quercus affinis*. Agaves are also well represented in this forest, which occurs along ridgelines, in high valleys, and in patches on isolated summits and slopes. In Coahuila, especially, the forest provides important roost areas for migrating monarch butterflies.

The wettest slopes, mostly south of 25°N latitude on steep slopes and in sheltered ravines between 5,000 and 8,000 ft (1,500 – 2,500 m) asl support cloud forests. Here the moisture in rising air condenses and bathes the slopes in near constant mist and fog. This is a dense, multilayered forest 65–130 ft (15–40 m) high. The canopy consists of deciduous trees, the lower layer of evergreen species. Some trees also occur in the eastern deciduous forest of the United States; these include sweet gum, American hornbeam, basswood, and dogwood. Trees with neotropical affinities occur too, as do tree ferns, orchids and bromeliads.

In the northern part of the range, environments of lower slopes in the west grade into the Chihuahuan Desert. Elevations below 6,500 ft (2,000 m) on the east-facing slopes support Tamaulipas matorral, an arid scrubland of mesquite, yuccas, mimosa, jatropha, and succulents that extends onto the Gulf Coastal Plain. In this region where annual precipitation averages 18–35 in (450–900 mm), the dominant shrubs are 10–15 ft (3–5 m) tall. Succulents are abundant and include a large number of endemic cacti and agaves. It is also home to the endangered Mexican prairie dog. This habitat is largely intact, but threatened by conversion to agricultural land uses, urban expansion, and overcollection of rare plants and animals.

The southern part of the Sierra Madre Oriental is flanked on the east by a Neotropical forest, the Veracruz moist forest. This is a subhumid tropical broadleaf forest with trees close to 100 ft (30 m) tall. On this karstic surface, it rains 7 months of the year and total annual precipitation is 43–63 in (1,100–1,600 mm). Dominant trees include Mayan breadnut, sapodilla, *Celtis monocia*, and *Bursera* sp. Epiphytes, including orchids, are abundant. Very little of this forest remains unmodified by logging or subsistence farming and cattle raising.

Environmental Issues. Most of the pine-oak forest has been degraded or cleared by logging operations. Although some of the largest tracts of the biologically rich cloud forest that remain are in the Sierra Madre Oriental, as elsewhere they are threatened by deforestation and climate change. The dry vegetation of the northern Sierra is largely intact, but threatened by conversion to agricultural land uses, urban expansion, and overcollection of rare plants and animals. Most of the pine-oak forest has been degraded or cleared by logging operations.

Very little of the Veracruz tropical forest remains unmodified by logging or subsistence farming and cattle raising.

See also Chihuahuan Desert; Mexican Plateau (Mexican Altiplano)

Further Reading

Valero, Alejandra, Jan Schipper, and Tom Allnutt. n.d. "Southern North America: Northeastern Mexico." Terrestrial Ecoregions. World Wildlife Fund. http://world wildlife.org/ecoregions/na1311

Valero, Alejandra, Jan Schipper, and Tom Allnutt. n.d. "Veracruz Moist Forests." Terrestrial Ecoregions. World Wildlife Fund. http://worldwildlife.org/ecoregions/nt0176

Valero, Alejandra, Jan Schipper, Tom Allnutt, and Christine Burdette. n.d. "Southern North America: Eastern Mexico into Southwestern United States." Terrestrial Ecoregions. World Wildlife Fund. http://worldwildlife.org/ecoregions/na0303

Sierra Nevada

United States (California)

Geographic Overview. The Sierra Nevada in California is a scenic and rugged mountain region presenting an almost unbroken east–west barrier through most of the state. With a windward side contrasting with a rain shadow side and an elevational change of more than 10,000 ft (3,050 m), the range has a variety of climates, vegetation zones, and habitats. The range has 11 peaks more than 14,000 ft (1,220 m) asl, including Mount Whitney, the highest peak in the lower 48 states. Few roads cross the Sierra Nevada, and none exists between Tioga Pass, 9,943 ft (3,031 m) in Yosemite, and Nine Mile Canyon road to Pine Pass, 7,200 ft (2,195 m), northeast of Bakersfield. Most roads are closed in winter, and snow occasionally closes Interstate 80 through Donner Pass. The mountains are an important source of water for adjacent valleys, provide many recreational opportunities, and are world-renown for sight-seeing.

Geographic Coordinates. Approximately 35°N–40°N, 118°W–121°W

Description. The Sierra Nevada extends approximately 430 mi (690 km) from the Feather River in northern California south to the Garlock Fault south of Bakersfield, with an east–west extent of 50 mi (80 km). The western slope is a gently tilting surface, eroded into deep valleys. The east side is an abrupt fault scarp, dropping steeply from more than 14,000 ft (1,220 m) at the crest to 4,000–5,000 ft (1,220–1,525 m) in the Owens Valley. While rivers draining the east slope are short, those on the western slope run in a relatively parallel pattern for miles down the dip slope of the fault block. Lake Tahoe occupies a downfaulted valley at 6,224 ft (1,897 m) within the major fault block and is drained by the Truckee River, which flows east into Pyramid Lake. South of Lake Tahoe, the eastern crest is almost continuous, with no passes below 10,000 ft (350 m). The upland slope in the northern Sierra Nevada has been severely dissected by large rivers, such as the Sacramento, Feather, Yuba, and American, flowing west. In the southern part of the Sierra, the uplands are not as dissected and retain broad highland expanses, such as Kern Plateau, between deep canyons, such as the Kern River, Kings River, and Merced River. The South Fork of the Kings River is 4,000–8,000 ft (1,220–2,440 m) deep, below the alpine landscape. Rocks in the Sierra are dominated by a form of granite, but several types of sedimentary rocks and metamorphic rocks also occur. Basalt and other volcanics are found on the eastern side of the range.

The mountains were heavily glaciated in the Pleistocene, evidenced by cirques on the high peaks and sharp mountain ridge arêtes. Valley glaciers moved far down the western slope, where they carved deep U-shaped valleys, such as Yosemite Valley and Kings Canyon. Other prominent glacial features include glacial polish, striations, and grooves. Moraine deposits are visible in some places, and outwash was deposited in many valleys. The floor of Yosemite Valley, for example, is flat because it contains a deep sediment fill.

While thunderstorms occasionally occur in the higher mountains in summer, the majority of the precipitation falls in winter. Precipitation increases with elevation, heaviest on the western slope and less on the eastern slope. Annual totals in the north exceed 60 in (1,525 mm), decreasing to 40 in (1,015 mm) in the south. Mean snow pack in the mountains is 37 ft (11 m), providing much of the water supply for many California cities and farms.

Geologic History. The Sierra Nevada is a product of the convergence of the Pacific Plate with the North American Plate. The sedimentary and meta-sedimentary rocks covering the granite batholith on the western slope are a series of terranes developed from pieces of oceanic crust and continental sediments deposited in oceanic trenches along the subduction zone. In the early Paleozoic (500 mya), the western edge of North America was in the current Sierra foothills, just east of the Central Valley. As the Pacific plate moved toward the North American plate, these terranes were pushed into and accreted onto what is now the western Sierra Nevada, building the west coast further west. The terranes are several huge slabs of metamorphosed rock units trending north–south and separated by faults, with the oldest terranes on the east and the youngest ones on the west. Gold deposits in the Sierra Nevada Mother Lode are associated with a 130 mi (200 km) long zone along the Melones Fault between two terranes. Mineralized water from the molten granite was injected into the overlying metamorphic rock as quartz veins containing gold. Most of the gold was eroded from its original position and accumulated in the sands and gravels of stream beds, both modern waterways and ancient Tertiary drainages. These placer deposits were the impetus for the California Gold Rush in 1849.

As the oceanic plate subducted during the Mesozoic (140–65 mya), volcanoes erupted and plutons of granite were emplaced. Some of the rocks high on the Ritter Range and the Minarets are metamorphosed volcanics, part of a caldera. The granite solidified from magma that cooled several miles below the base of the volcanoes. Millions of years of erosion obliterated the volcanoes and exposed the granite. The granite, actually several different plutons with slight variation in mineral composition, is the core of the Sierra Nevada. The deepest part of the batholith is exposed in the south, but it is still buried under other plutons in the northern part of the range. The White Mountains and Inyo Mountains to the east are geologically part of the Sierra Nevada, separated by the fault of the Owens Valley. The Klamath Mountains in northwestern California are also part of the batholith, now detached 60 mi (100 km) to the northwest. Roof pendant is the term for the remnants of older meta-sedimentary rocks into which the granite intruded. These rocks formerly covered the batholith but have mostly been eroded away, with remains found between the individual plutons and capping some of the high peaks.

Beginning in the early Tertiary (65 mya), the surface of the Sierra Nevada region underwent a long erosional process and became a rolling lowland. The Tertiary (30 mya) also saw renewed volcanic activity, which has continued to the present, on the east side of the Sierra. The eastern side of the region, or the western side of the Owens Valley, was faulted approximately 25 mya, and the broad upland began slowly uplifting and tilting toward the west, ultimately to become the Sierra Nevada. Most of the renewed volcanic activity occurred close to the eastern fault scarp that raised the mountain range. By 2 mya, the mountains were rising more rapidly and the tilt toward the west became more severe. In this giant fault-block mountain, the highest peaks are on the east side where uplift was greater and the eastern side is a steep descent down to the Owens Valley.

Biota. Vegetation varies with elevation and windward or lee side of the range. The western foothills have oak woodland and chaparral, replaced by sagebrush and pinyon pine and juniper woodlands at similar elevations on the eastern slope. Higher elevations on both slopes support yellow pine forest, either ponderosa pine or Jeffrey pine, which give way to lodgepole pine and red fir forests with increased elevation. Only alpine meadows or sparse vegetation survive at the highest elevations.

Scattered within the yellow pine forests on the western slope, at 5,000–7,000 ft (1,524–2,135 m), are 75 groves of giant sequoias, which are the largest trees in the world in terms of volume. Four of the five largest trees in the world, including the largest, 2,000- to 3,000-year-old General Sherman, are in Giant Forest, within Sequoia National Park. General Sherman is 225 ft (68.6 m) tall, with a base diameter of 36 ft (11 m). Its largest limb is 7 ft (2.1 m) in diameter.

Protected Areas. Many areas of the Sierra Nevada are protected in several national forests, wilderness areas, three national parks, national monuments, several state parks, and recreational areas. Sequoia and Kings Canyon National Parks in the southern part of the range preserve mountain landscapes, canyons, and high alpine areas as well as giant sequoias. Mount Whitney, 14,505 ft (4,421 m) asl, is on the eastern side of Sequoia National Park. Yosemite National Park is a landscape of high mountains, deep glacial valleys, waterfalls, and exfoliation domes. The General Grant grove of sequoias is in Kings Canyon National Park.

See also Devils Postpile National Monument; Mount Whitney; Yosemite National Park

Further Reading

Alt, David and Donald W. Hyndman. 2000. *Roadside Geology of Northern and Central California*. Missoula, MT: Mountain Press.

Michaelsen, Joel. n.d. *Sierra Nevada Physical Geography*. http://www.geog.ucsb.edu/~joel/g148_f09/readings/sierra_nevada/sierra_nevada.html

National Park Service. n.d. "Geology." Devils Postpile National Monument. http://www.nps.gov/depo/naturescience/geology.htm

Sinai Peninsula

Egypt

Geographic Overview. The Sinai Peninsula is a triangle of desert between Egypt in northeastern Africa and Israel in Eurasia. Geologically a part of Africa, the Sinai in the 20th century has been disputed between Egypt and Israel. Largely a barren region dotted with few oases, the Sinai played a significant role in biblical times.

Geographic Coordinates. 27°45'N–31°10'N, 32°20'E–35°00'E

Description. The Sinai Peninsula is bounded on the north by the Mediterranean Sea, on the west by the Gulf of Suez, on the south by the Red Sea, and on the east by the Gulf of Aqaba (Gulf of Eilat) and by the Negev Desert in Israel. Covering approximately 23,500 mi² (61,000 km²), the peninsula is

130 mi (210 km) east-to-west and 240 mi (385 km) north-to-south.

The Sinai has three distinct topographic regions. The northern coastal plain is dominated by sand dunes that are 60–90 ft (18–27 m) tall, with a few interspersed brackish wells or oases. The dune region is wider in the west, where it is called the Desert of Shur, and narrower in the east. The central region of the peninsula is the Tih Plateau, limestone and chalk layers intersected by valleys and ridges and pinnacles. The plateau surface, which slopes north to the coastal plain, is both sandy and rocky, with few oases. The sedimentary rocks on the northern edge of the plateau are folded into mountains 2,000–3,200 ft (600–1,000 m) asl. The southern edge of the Tih is characterized by sheer whitish limestone cliffs and a zone of deep valleys and wadis, including Wadi Feiran. The rugged and mountainous region of the southern Sinai consists of exposed granitic massifs and pinnacles scored by deep wadis and gorges. Peaks include Gebel Musa (also called Mount Sinai or Mount Horeb) at 7,500 ft (2,286 m) asl. A cluster of three peaks in the Saint Catherine area includes Gebel Katarina at 8,652 ft (2,637 m) and Gebel Zebir, the highest point on the peninsula at 8,671 ft (2,642 m). Winter snows support oases at the base of the mountains. The massif extends north along the west coast and is a continuation of similar mountains in eastern Egypt, west of the Red Sea.

Most of the peninsula receives less than 4 in (100 mm) of annual precipitation, and one-half receives 1–2 in (25–50 mm). Precipitation is influenced by the mediterranean trend, wet in winter and dry in summer.

The peninsula has a long history and has been a trade and invasion route since prehistoric times. According to biblical stories, Moses wandered through the Sinai, primarily the Tih Plateau, with the Israelites, settling occasionally to spend years at oases. Mount Sinai is believed to be the mountain where Moses received the Ten Commandments, but the site may have been another mountain. Traditionally part of Egypt, the peninsula has been contested by Israel and Egypt since Israel's establishment in 1948. Since the Camp David Peace Accords in 1979, the Sinai has been under Egyptian control. The economy of Bedouin populations is being replaced by tourism, especially along the Red Sea.

Geologic History. The Sinai was part of the African plate and has a long geological history. In the late Precambrian (620–580 mya), granite plutons were emplaced, which are now exposed as the rugged mountain core in the Saint Catherine, Serbal, and Um Shower groups in the southern peninsula. During the Cambrian (540 mya), Syenite ring dikes were intruded into the granite. Periodic inundation by the Tethys Sea left Mesozoic and Tertiary sedimentary rocks of sandstone, limestone, and chalk, which still cover much of the northern and central part of the peninsula. Africa (Gondwana) began to break apart in the late Mesozoic, and the rifting of the Red Sea and Gulf of Aqaba gave the peninsula its characteristic triangular shape. Rifting in the Miocene (21–19 mya) was accompanied by intrusions of basaltic dikes seen on the surface today.

Biota. The Sinai Desert is primarily barren, inhospitable reg, with only a few oases. Vegetation is primarily ephemeral or desert scrub on slopes and the plateau. Even though the southern mountains have very little vegetation, they are a local center of plant diversity. The St. Catherine region has 28 endemic species. Limestone bedrock supports a few shrubs of bushy bean-caper (*Zygophyllum mandavillei*), *Reaumuria* species, and *Gymnocarpus decander*. Regs and salty areas, such as coastal plains, may have a few scattered berry-bearing glassworts (*Anabasis articulata*). Oases support date palms and limited agriculture.

Large animals, mostly rare, extinct, or in preserves, may include sand fox, Nubian ibex, hyrax, gazelles, wildcats, jackals, hares, hedgehogs, and moles. Birds include falcons, eagles, quail, partridge, and grouse.

Protected Areas. Three national parks—Ras Mohammed, Abu Galum, and St. Catherine Monastery—along with Nabq Managed Resource Protection Area are all in the southern Sinai.

See also Arabian Peninsula; Red Sea

Further Reading

Geographica.com. n.d. "Sinai, Egypt." http://www.geographia.com/egypt/sinai/index.html

Goudie, Andrew S. 2002. "The Middle East." In *Geomorphological Landscapes of the World, 1. Great Warm Deserts of the World, Landscapes and Evolution*, 215–253. Oxford: Oxford University Press.

Greenwood, Ned. 1997. *The Sinai: A Physical Geography*. Austin: University of Texas Press.

Snake River

United States (Idaho and Oregon)

Geographic Overview. Originating in northwestern Wyoming and traversing the southern part of Idaho in a wide arc, the Snake River is the largest tributary to the Columbia River. In places on the Snake River Plain, the river has developed steep waterfalls over layers of basalt. Underground drainage through the porous basalt feeds the river through a number of springs along its banks. Prior to regulation, the river supported thousands of salmon and steelhead. Water is now important for hydroelectric power, irrigation, and recreation.

Geographic Coordinates. Source: 44°08'N, 110° 13'W, Mouth: 46°11'N, 119°02'W

Description. With a drainage basin covering 108,500 mi^2 (281,000 km^2) and 36 percent of the Columbia River Basin, the Snake River drains primarily southern Idaho, but also parts of northwestern Wyoming, southeastern Oregon, and small parts of adjacent Utah and Nevada. It flows 870 mi (1,400 km) before joining the Columbia River.

At Shoshone Falls in southern Idaho, the Snake River drops 212 ft (65 m) over the edge of a basaltic lava flow. (Aliaksandr Nikitsin/Dreamstime.com)

From the Yellowstone Plateau at approximately 9,800 ft (3,000 m) asl, the Snake River flows south for 100 mi (160 km) (passing the Grand Tetons) before turning west into Idaho, where it curves south on the basalt lava plain around the Idaho Batholith. In the eastern part of the Snake River Plain, the river runs on top of the most recent lava flows. After a series of waterfalls, including 50 ft (15 m) American Falls, 180 ft (55 m) Twin Falls, and 212 ft (65 m) Shoshone Falls, it then flows in deep gorges through older lava flows. From Twin Falls to Weiser, Idaho, the canyon is as much as 600–700 ft (180–210 m) below the lava plain. At the Oregon border, the river turns north through 70-mi (113 km) long Hells Canyon, the deepest gorge in North America, 7,900 ft (2,405 m) from Devil Peak to the river. The Snake River turns west in southeastern Oregon, joining the Columbia near Pasco.

Because the majority of the Snake River flows through arid landscapes, most of the river's discharge, averaging 55,267 ft³/sec (1,565 m³/s) where it enters the Columbia River, is from mountain snowmelt, especially April through June. Along the border of Idaho with Washington and Oregon, the Snake River is joined by several tributaries draining off the Idaho Batholith. The most important are the Salmon and Clearwater, which contribute almost one-half of the Snake River's flow. The Owyhee River and Grande Ronde River enter the Snake River from the south. The lava plain north of the river is permeable, causing drainage to be underground, through pores and lava tubes. The water reemerges from 185 ft (56 m) above the river on the north side of the gorge, especially at Thousand Springs between Twin Falls and Bliss. Some water from Thousand Springs is diverted for hydroelectric power generation, irrigation, and fish hatcheries.

At the close of the Pleistocene, water from Glacial Lake Bonneville, the forerunner to Great Salt Lake, spilled north via the Portneuf River at Pocatello, Idaho, into the Snake River drainage and contributed to carving the river's deep canyons through the lava flows. Outwash and sediment accumulated upstream from the constriction at Hells Canyon, forming broad islands or gravel bars in the river, which are now Deer Flats National Wildlife Refuge near Boise.

With the exception of a 37 mi (60 km) stretch below Hells Canyon where the Snake is free-flowing, the Snake River is regulated from Yellowstone to the Columbia River. Water from a number of dams and diversions is used in hydroelectric power generation and in elaborate irrigation systems. Above Milner Dam, between American Falls and Twin Falls, almost all the water is diverted, leaving a dry river until it is recharged by Thousand Springs. Dams and locks, in conjunction with the Columbia River, enable barge traffic to travel upstream to Lewiston, Idaho, 465 mi (750 km) from the Pacific Ocean. The Salmon River is the only free-flowing tributary.

Biota. More than 20 fish species are found in the Upper Snake River drainage basin, above Shoshone Falls, which is a barrier to upstream travel. Only two-thirds of those are also found downstream. The Lower Snake is included in the Unglaciated Columbia River ecosystem. River regulation, especially Hells Canyon Dam, has severely impacted populations of anadromous fish, such as salmon and steelhead.

See also Columbia River; Grand Teton National Park; Great Salt Lake; Greater Yellowstone Ecosystem; Snake River Plain

Further Reading

Northwest Power and Conservation Council. n.d. "Hells Canyon Dam." Columbia River History. www.nwcouncil.org/history/HellsCanyon.asp

Stanford, Jack A. et al. 2005. "Columbia River Basin." In *Rivers of North America*, edited by Arthur C. Benke and Colbert E. Cushing, 591–653. Amsterdam: Elsevier Academic Press.

Snake River Plain

United States (Idaho)

Geographic Overview. The Snake River Plain occupies an arc-shaped structural trough skirting the southern edge of the Idaho Batholith in southern Idaho. Although the region appears to be dominated by basaltic lava, a thin veneer of basalt covers a deep accumulation of older rhyolite related to eruptions at Yellowstone. The dark lava flows appear fresh because the basalt erodes very slowly. Young basalt lava flows and cinder cones occur in the eastern region. Columnar jointing, lava tubes, and the vesicular nature of the rock allow water to permeate rather than run off.

Geographic Coordinates. Approximately 42°20'N–45°00'N, 110°W–118°W

Description. The Snake River Plain, covering 8,000 mi² (20,700 km²), extends 400 mi (645 km) east to west and 30–125 mi (48–200 km) north to south. The flat plain gently slopes from 6,000 ft (1,830 m) elevation in the northeast to 3,500 ft (1,065 m) in the west. Two sections of the Snake River Plain, east and west of the vicinity of Twin Falls, differ in structure, age and source of volcanic activity, and types of surface deposits. The eastern Snake River Plain is a structural downwarp, depressed by the weight of the overlying volcanic rocks. The underlying layers of rhyolite, ash, and flow tuffs are thicker while the surface basalts are thinner than similar deposits in the western plain. The surface of the eastern Snake River Plain, extending from Yellowstone west to Boise, is 95 percent late Tertiary or Quaternary basalt. Very fluid lava, mostly pahoehoe, originated from small shield volcanoes averaging 10 mi (16 km) in diameter, fissures, tubes, and cinder cones. Compound flows, averaging 5,000 ft (1,525 m) thick, were built up layer by layer, each 3–30 ft (0.9–9.0 m) thick.

Trending northwest to southeast across the eastern Snake River Plain, the Great Rift is a series of cracks or fissures, extending about 50 mi (80 km) from Craters of the Moon National Monument almost to American Falls. At the northern end, the fissures are filled with basalt. Farther south, open cracks are as deep as 800 ft (245 m). These fissures and eruptions appear to be due to crustal stretching related to Basin and Range faulting, which allows basaltic crust beneath to melt and rise to the surface. Most shield volcano centers of eruption and cinder cones are aligned along Great Rift fissures. Three major lava fields, Craters of the Moon, King's Bowl, and Wapi Lava Field, line the rift.

Because the scoriaceous basalt is porous, drainage from the Rocky Mountains, notably Lost River, sinks into the rock and flows southward underground through pores and lava tubes. The water reemerges in springs from the north side of the Snake River Gorge, especially at Thousand Springs between Twin Falls and Bliss.

The western Snake River Plain, from Twin Falls in south-central Idaho northwest to the Oregon border, is geologically related to the Columbia Plateau and Basin and Range. It is a northwest-trending graben, approximately 30–45 mi (48–72 km) wide, filled with layers of basalt interbedded with fluvial and lacustrine sediments and thick layers of rhyolitic tuffs and ash flows. Although the rhyolitic ash drifted in from volcanoes on the eastern Snake River Plain, the basalt flows are from Basin and Range faulting and not related to the Yellowstone hotspot. Columbia Plateau lava flows impounded lakes several times, evidenced by sediments interbedded between basalt layers. During the Pliocene, the area was occupied by Lake Idaho, the source of more sediments, and some valley fill was contributed by interior drainage. Northwest of Boise is an extensive area of fluvial deposits.

Geologic History. North America is moving southwest over the Yellowstone hotspot at a rate of approximately 1–2 in (2.5–5 cm) a year. Rhyolite eruptions began when northeastern Nevada was over the hotspot (17–13 mya), and the volcanic centers along the Snake River Plain are successively younger eastward. The hotspot currently sits beneath the Yellowstone caldera. Each of the volcanic centers erupted violently, spilling out ash, which solidified into tuff. Several small rhyolite domes stand out as hills above the younger layers of basalt. Much later, in the Quaternary and not associated with the hotspot, fissures developed, from which cinder cones erupted and basalt flowed.

Biota. Areas not converted to agriculture support sagebrush steppe with *Artemisia* species and grasses along with greasewood (*Sarcobatus vermiculatus*) and saltbush (*Atriplex* spp.). Much of the landscape surface is bare basalt.

Protected Areas. Craters of the Moon National Monument is a 618 mi² (1,600 km²) area of pahoehoe and a'a lava flows, cinder cones, cinder fields, small shields, spatter cones, pressure ridges, and lava tubes. Eruptions occurred periodically from 15,000 to 2,000 years ago. The site has more than 25 cinder cones, as many as 65 vents, and approximately 60 flows. The second group of *Apollo* astronauts that went to moon studied volcanic geology at Craters of the Moon.

See also Basin and Range Physiographic Province; Columbia Plateau; Greater Yellowstone Ecosystem; Snake River

Further Reading

Alt, David D. and Donald W. Hyndman. 1998. *Roadside Geology of Idaho*. Missoula, MT: Mountain Press.

Digital Atlas. n.d. *Digital Geology of Idaho*. Idaho State University. http://geology.isu.edu/Digital_Geology_Idaho/Module11/mod11.htm

Dunham, Sarah. 2007. "Craters of the Moon." *Volcano World*. http://volcano.oregonstate.edu/craters-moon

Socotra Archipelago

Indian Ocean

Geographic Overview. The Socotra Archipelago is a group of four islands and two limestone islets in the Arabian Sea off the Horn of Africa. Long isolated from Africa and the Arabian Peninsula but at the crossroads of three biogeographic provinces (Ethiopian, Palearctic, and Oriental), they are globally significant for their high biodiversity and plant and animal relicts, such as the emblematic dragon's blood tree. Socotra is politically part of Yemen.

Geographic Coordinates. 12°30'N, 53°55'E

Description. On a map, the islands of the Socotra Archipelago appear as an extension of the Horn of Africa, lying about 60 mi (100 km) off Cape Guardafui, Somalia, and 240 mi (380 km) southeast of Yemen. They stretch for 155 mi (250 km) from Abd al Kuri in the west to the largest island, Socotra, at the eastern end of the chain. Samha and Darsa, much smaller than the other two, lie in between.

Socotra Island is roughly 80 mi (130 km) long and 25 mi (40 km) wide, with an area of 1,000 mi² (2,600 km²). Of continental origins, it has a granitic core exposed in the Haggeher Mountains (Jabal Haggeher) at the eastern end of the islands. The jagged peaks of these mountains reach a maximum elevation of 5,006 ft (1,526 m) on Jabal Skand. Slopes rise steeply on the north side; more gentle slopes and six parallel valleys occur on the south side of the Haggehers. Surrounding the peaks on the east, south-central and western flanks is a limestone plateau 1,000–2,300 ft (300–700 m) asl. The limestones have eroded into a karstic landscape with large solution caves. West of the mountains are interior plains. On the north side of the island, the coastal plain consists of several small fertile valleys separated by headlands. On the south side, the limestone plateau descends over a 1,300 ft (400 m) high escarpment to a long, narrow, and dry coastal plain.

Abd al Kuri is a little less than 46 mi² (120 km²) in area and consists of a low, limestone-capped granitic range reaching a maximum elevation of 2,437 ft (743 m). Raised beaches edge the north coast; sea cliffs line the south coast.

Socotra's climate is tropical and arid, influenced by the Asian monsoon and topography. June–September, hot, dry winds of the southwest monsoon blow off the African continent and strong winds up to 68 mph (110 kmph) cause high waves and upwelling that brings cool nutrient-rich water up from the depths. Hot winds also descend from the mountains. October–April brings the moist northeast monsoon and rain falls, especially on the north coast and north-facing cliffs. Total annual precipitation is about 6 in (150 mm) on the coast, but may be close to 40 in (1,000 mm) at the highest elevations. Temperature highs near sea level range from 80°–100°F (27°–38°C); lows from 63°–80°F (17°–27°C). In the mountains it is cooler, and the temperature may drop to 46°F (8°C).

Mangrove thickets up to 16 ft (5 m) high occur in places along the shore. Coastal vegetation typically has low succulent shrubs 4 ft (1.5 m) high with patches of taller shrubs emerging above them. The coastal plain is covered with a deciduous shrubland with a few of the bottle-trunked cucumber trees (*Dendrosicyos socotranus*) endemic to the island protruding to heights near 20 ft (6 m). Limestone cliffs and escarpments and other rocky areas support a succulent shrubland with emergent trees. The limestone plateau is where relict woodlands of the Socotran dragon's blood tree (*Dracaena cinnabari*) and eight kinds of frankincense trees (*Boswellia* spp.) grow. At elevations above 3,000 ft (950 m) on the peaks, cliffs, and ravines of the Haggeher Range, a mosaic of vegetation types occurs that includes dense evergreen woodlands and thickets, dwarf shrublands, and cushion plants. Dragon's blood tree grows there, too.

Geologic History. The Socotra Archipelago sits on the submerged Socotran Platform, Precambrian continental crust that was part of Gondwana until Eastern Gondwana began to break up 700–800 mya.

It was attached to the Arabian Plate until rifting began to open the Gulf of Aden 34–23 mya. Since that time, seafloor spreading increased the distance between Socotra and the Arabian Peninsula and uplift raised the islands above sea level.

Biota. Great age, long isolation, a location at the crossroads of three global-scale biogeographic regions, and diverse habitats allowed Socotra to develop a rich and distinct flora and fauna. Thirty-seven percent of the 825 native species of higher plants and ferns are endemic, as are 95 percent of land snails and 90 percent of the 34 native reptiles. All are adapted to arid conditions. Some of the strange-looking tree succulents that contribute to Socotra's unique landscape are archaic and limited in distribution. These include *Euphorbia arbuscula*, a leafless pencil-stemmed tree that serves as dry season fodder for livestock; the Socotran desert rose (*Adenium socotranum*), its large swollen trunk having stubby branches clustered at the top and adorned with pink flowers; the cucumber tree—the only tree in the squash family; eight species of frankincense; and the Socotran dragon's blood tree, its branches forming an umbrella-shaped canopy of rosettes of long, stiff leaves growing from their tips. The dragon's blood tree has become the symbol of the island, its red resin collected since antiquity for medicinal use and for use as a dye. Its only close relatives are in the Mascarene Islands.

Studies on the coral reefs offshore reveal 253 species of hard corals, 730 fishes, and 300 crustaceans (crabs, lobsters, and shrimps).

Protected Areas. A group of land-based nature preserves, national parks, and areas of special botanical interest protecting the Socotra's natural treasures and covering 75 percent of the island were inscribed as a UNESCO World Heritage Site in 2008. The island is also a UNESCO Biosphere Reserve, a World Wildlife Fund Global 200 Ecoregion, and a Plant International's declared Center of Plant Diversity. Detwah Lagoon on the western end of Socotra is a designated Ramsar Wetland of International Importance. Management and enforcement remain challenges, however.

Environmental Issues. Expanding human settlement, increasing tourism, and changing ways of life are problems confronting a place that was relatively pristine until about 20 years ago. Pollution from urban wastes and agriculture, poorly planned urban development and road construction conflict with conservation goals, as do the increasing consumption of firewood and overgrazing by goats that accompany changes to traditional economies. Among troublesome invasive species are the Indian House Crow, Norway rat, and mesquite. Warming of the climate has meant a reduction in precipitation and may be related to the poor reproduction seen in dragon's blood tree populations.

Further Reading

Quinn, Joyce A. 2009. *Desert Biomes*. Greenwood Guides to Biomes of the World. Westport, CT: Greenwood Press.

"Socotra Archipelago, Yemen." 2008. World Heritage Sites, United Nations Environmental Programme, World Conservation Monitoring Centre. http://www.socotraproject.org/userfiles/files/UNEP_Socotra_for_UNESCO.pdf

Van Damme, Kay. 2009. "Socotra Archipelago." In *Encyclopedia of Islands*, edited by Rosemary G. Gillespie and David A. Clague, 846–851. Berkeley: University of California Press.

Solomon Islands Archipelago

Melanesia, Pacific Ocean

Geographic Overview. The Solomon Islands archipelago consists of the high volcanic islands and low atolls of the nation of Solomon Islands and the islands of Bougainville and Buka, an autonomous region of Papua New Guinea. The largest of the Solomon Islands, Guadalcanal, was the scene of a fierce battle during World War II that was waged from August 1942 to February 1943 and marked the first Allied offensive against the Empire of Japan in the Pacific.

Geographic Coordinates. 05°S–12°S, 152°E–170°E

Description. The Solomon Islands archipelago lies east of New Guinea and northeast of Australia and stretches to the southeast for 900 mi (1,450 km) from Buka Island, Papua New Guinea, to just north of Vanuatu (formerly the New Hebrides). Bougainville is the largest island in the archipelago with an area of 3,978 mi^2 (9,318 km^2) and has several volcanoes rising to elevations of about 7,875 ft (2,400 m) asl. Southeast of Bougainville is the western and central part of the Solomon Islands, six high volcanic islands and numerous smaller islands arranged in a double chain that extends for 530 mi (850 km). The northern chain consists of three islands: Choiseul, Santa Isabel, and Malaita. The southern chain contains the largest of the Solomon Islands, Guadalcanal—with an area of 2,050 mi² (5,310 km²)—as well as the New Georgia group of islands north of Guadalcanal and Makira to its south. Set off 230 mi (375 km) to the east of Makira is a separate group of medium-sized islands, the Santa Cruz Islands, which are geologically related to Vanuatu. The raised limestone islands of Bellona and Rennell sit 155 mi (250 km) south of Guadalcanal. The atoll of Ontong Java, one of the world's largest and the northernmost point in the Solomon Islands, lies 280 mi (450 km) north of Santa Isabel Island.

The double chain of islands rises above a submarine ridge bounded to the southwest and northeast by oceanic trenches, the convergent boundaries of the Pacific Plate and the Australian and Woodlark plates. South of the islands is the Makira (or South Solomons) Trench and to the northeast the Kilinailau–North Solomons Trench. The entire archipelago is part of the Outer Melanesian Arc, a broken chain of volcanic islands reaching from the Bismarck Archipelago in the northwest to Fiji and Tonga in the southeast.

The Solomon Islands archipelago has a maritime tropical wet climate with little variation in temperature throughout the year. It comes under the influence of the northwest Asian monsoon from December through March and the Southeast Trade Winds from May into October. Average annual precipitation is about 120 in (3,050 mm). Mangrove forests and freshwater swamps are found along the coasts. Lowland rainforests and dry forests cover the high islands at elevations below 2,295 ft (700 m). Above them, montane rainforests cloak the upper slopes. On windward slopes at the highest elevations cloud forests grow, the trees covered with epiphytic orchids; gingers, bamboos, and pandans form an understory. The rainforests are species-poor, but the mangroves, with 26 species, are quite rich.

The coral reefs and atolls of the Solomons are within the Coral Triangle, a global marine biodiversity hotspot within the species-rich Indo-West Pacific region.

Geologic History. Volcanism in the area began with the development of the vast Ontong Java Plateau (OJP) 122 mya. This submarine plateau is a thickened piece of oceanic crust standing 8,000 ft (2,500 m) above the surrounding seafloor that probably has its origins in flood basalts produced at a mantle plume far to the southeast of its current position. A volcanic island arc formed with the subduction of the Pacific Plate at Kilinailau Trench during the Eocene (56–34 mya). Continued west-northwest movement and subduction of the Pacific Plate transported the OJP to the trench, but it was too massive (as much as 20 mi [30 km] thick) to be subducted. As a consequence a new subduction site, the Makira Trench, formed southwest of the island arc where the Pacific and Australian plates converged. Volcanism was again active 10–8 mya. Makira and other islands in the southeastern part of the double chain are the oldest islands; the New Georgia group and Bougainville are the youngest. Volcanoes are still active on Bougainville and on Tinakulu Island in the Santa Cruz group.

Biota. The flora of the rainforests of the Solomons shows low rates of diversity and endemism. This pattern is not repeated in the fauna. Although not well studied, there are 200–270 species of land snail. Amphibians are represented by 17 frog species and three endemic genera. The 61 terrestrial reptiles (lizards and snakes) include a large prehensile-tailed skink. Among birds, 44 percent are endemic species, including the Fearful Owl, Solomons Sea Eagle, and Megapode. Native mammals include 44 species of bat—26 of which are flying foxes, and eight arboreal rats, some weighing as much as 2 lb (1 kg).

Species diversity among corals is second only to Indonesia, with at least 485 species of coral in 76 genera. More than 1,000 fishes have been identified; single reefs may support more than 200. Commercially important invertebrates include sea cucumbers sold as "bêche-de mer," pearl oysters, trochus shells, and green marine snails. Marine reptiles include five species of sea turtle, one sea snake, and a saltwater crocodile. The most common of 11 species of cetacean inhabiting the waters of the Solomons are spinner, pan-tropical, and common bottle nose dolphins. Dugongs live in lagoons and estuaries where there are sea grasses.

Protected Areas. At least 30 Marine Protected Areas exist in the Solomon Islands, although most are informally designated. The three Arnavon Islands between Santa Isabel and Choiseul in the northern group of islands in the Solomons's double chain conserve nesting hawksbill sea turtles, coral reefs, and lagoons.

Environmental Issues. Habitat loss and fragmentation related to a growing human population and its demand for more agricultural land have increased in the last five decades. Trees have been overharvested for the timber export business, and forests have been converted to oil palm and copra plantations. Also overexploited and exported to foreign markets are saltwater crocodiles, pearl oysters, sea turtles, trochus shells, bêche-de mer, and green marine snails.

As on most oceanic islands, invasive plants and animals are major problems. In the Solomons, species with negative impacts are pigs, cats, rats, and little fire ants.

Further Reading

Davies, Hugh L. 2009. "Solomon Islands, Geology." In *Encyclopedia of Islands*, edited by Rosemary G. Gillespie and David A. Clague, 854–857. Berkeley: University of California Press.

Steele, Orlo C. 2009. "Solomon Islands, Biology." In *Encyclopedia of Islands*, edited by Rosemary G. Gillespie and David A. Clague, 851–854. Berkeley: University of California Press.

Sonoran Desert

United States (Arizona and California) and Mexico

Geographic Overview. The Sonoran Desert extends north from the central part of the Baja peninsula and the state of Sonora, Mexico, into southeastern California and southwestern Arizona, a latitudinal range of 23 degrees. Its basin and range landscape is rich in plant life due to the biseasonal distribution of rainfall. Some plants are adapted to summer rain, while others require winter moisture. Frost and snow are rare in this warm or subtropical desert. Tree-size cactus, many short tree species, and many succulent plants are characteristic of the Sonoran Desert. The desert is known for the saguaro (*Carnegiea gigantea*), which can reach 50 ft (15 m) tall and weigh more than 10 tons.

Geographic Coordinates. Approximately 27°N–35°N, 109°W–116°W

Description. The Sonoran Desert, covering approximately 120,000 mi^2 (310,000 km^2), lies in the southern part of the Basin and Range, where the topography consists of eroded fault-block mountains alternating with broad alluvial valleys and extensive bajadas. Rocks in this region are primarily Precambrian granite and gneiss. Paleozoic and Mesozoic sedimentary rocks are not widespread. Mesozoic and Cenozoic granite, however, are common and may be reworked Precambrian rocks, melted and recrystallized during orogenies (mountain-building episodes). Granite batholiths, emplaced during the Laramide Orogeny, form the core of several of the larger mountains in south-central Arizona and adjacent Sonora, Mexico. Volcanic mountains, including plugs and basalt-capped mesas, are found throughout the desert. The Baja peninsula is basically a large fault-block mountain of granite, faulted on the east and tilted west toward the Pacific Ocean. Most mountains, especially west of Phoenix and into California, are extensively eroded. Approximately 80 percent of the landscape consists of basins filled with both coarse and fine alluvium. The valley floors hold playas, many of which were lakes during the Pleistocene.

Parts of the desert are drained by the Gila River, and its tributary the Salt River, which joins the Colorado River near Yuma, Arizona. Most of the basins, however, have interior drainage. Rivers in Mexico, the Sonoita, the Sonora, Rio Yaqui, and Rio Magdalena, rarely reach the coast. Most of the structural valleys are less than 2,000 ft (600 m) asl, and the mountain ranges stand only 2,000 ft (600 m) higher.

Because of the low latitude and low elevation, winters are mild 50°–68°F (10–20°C), although slightly cooler in southern Arizona than in Mexico. Frost is rare, and the northern limit of the desert is marked by areas that experience 36 continuous hours of freezing temperature, a limiting factor for many desert plants. Summer days are consistently warmer than 100°F (38°C), often for 90 consecutive days. The exception is the west coast of Baja, where the desert is frequently foggy and temperatures are mild due to the influence of the cold California current offshore.

Although the saguaro symbolizes the Sonoran Desert in southwestern United States and adjacent Mexico, the region is home to a rich variety of other cacti, succulents, grasses, shrubs, trees, ephemerals, and associated wildlife. (Anton Foltin/ Dreamstime.com)

The region, especially south of Arizona, lies in the rain shadow of the Sierra Madre Occidental, which blocks moisture-bearing winds originating in the Gulf of Mexico. Precipitation is biseasonal, averaging 3–12 in (75–300 mm), driest in the west and at lower elevations. Cyclonic storms from the north bring gentle winter rains, particularly in the northern and western reaches, while heavy thunderstorms develop in all regions in summer.

Biota. The desert has a variety of growth forms, including grasses, shrubs, short trees, and cacti. Widespread indicator plants are blue paloverde (*Cercidium floridum*), foothill paloverde (*Cercidium microphyllum*), and ironwood (*Olneya tesota*), all small trees. Creosote bush (*Larrea tridentata*), bursage (*Ambrosia* spp.), brittlebush (*Encelia farinosa*), and wolfberry (*Lycium andersonii*) are common and conspicuous shrubs. Paloverde, mesquite (*Prosopis* spp.), cottonwood (*Populus fremontii*), willow (*Salix* spp.), and the introduced salt cedar (*Tamarix* spp.) are all phreatophytes, growing along dry stream channels to tap underground moisture. Plants from the pea family (Fabaceae), such as mesquite (*Prosopus* spp.) and acacia (*Acacia* spp.) are abundant, and ocotillo (*Fouquieria* spp.) is widespread. Some plants, such as ocotillo, creosote, and paloverde, are drought deciduous, losing their leaves not because of cold weather but due to a dry season. Because of the rainfall pattern, winter annuals dominate in the north and west, while spring and summer annuals become more numerous in the south.

The substrate texture and physiography, particularly variation from fine or salty sediment in the valleys to coarse gravel and boulders at the top of alluvial fans, strongly influences plant distributions.

While the saline centers of the valleys are often encrusted with salt deposits and lifeless, saltbush (*Atriplex* spp.) grows on the fine-textured soil at the edge of the playas. Widely spaced creosote bush and white bursage normally cover the lower slopes of the fans and bajadas, and the plant assemblage becomes more complex with increasing slope and coarser texture.

Scientists recognize several subdivisions based on differences in climate, species composition, and plant growth form. The Lower Colorado River Valley, at the head of the Gulf of California from Phoenix, Arizona, west past the Salton Sea and north to Needles, California, has little rainfall. The landscape is primarily flat gravelly plains, sand dunes, or salt flats, most of which are dominated by a sparse cover of creosote and white bursage. Stunted acacia and paloverde are restricted to water courses. Native desert fan palms (*Washingtonia filifera*) can be found in moist canyons near the Salton Trough and in Baja.

The Arizona Upland, in south-central Arizona from Tucson west to Phoenix and extending south into north-central Sonora, Mexico, is the classic example of the Sonoran Desert. Higher in elevation and with more precipitation, the desert here appears crowded with shrubs, small trees, and both small and tall cacti. The creosote-bursage community is joined by some acacias and chollas (*Opuntia* spp.). Mid- to upper-bajada slopes are dominated by saguaro, tall ocotillo, and 10–20 ft (3–6 m) tall paloverde, mesquite, catclaw acacia, and ironwood trees. Brittlebush is common in the shorter shrub layer, alongside barrel cactus (*Ferocactus* spp.) and several species of cholla and prickly pear (both *Opuntia* spp.). Two additional tall columnar cacti, senita (*Lophocereus schottii*) and organ pipe cactus (*Lamaireocereus thurberi*), are locally dominant in southern Arizona and adjacent Sonora. Grasses, such as grama (*Grama* spp.), tobosa (*Hilaria* spp.), and sacaton (*Sporobolus* spp.), may be scattered among the trees and cactus.

Temperatures in the Central Gulf section, centered on the island of Tiburon and restricted to the Gulf of California coast in both Baja and Sonora, are modified by the adjacent water. In spite of unreliable precipitation, the region supports a distinctive community. Widely spaced shrubs of sangre de drago

(*Jatropha cuneata*), jatropha (*Jatropha cinerea*), and ocotillo grow with small trees and large cardon columnar cactus (*Pachycereus pringlei*). Cardon is the largest cactus in the world, reaching 70 ft (21 m) tall and weighing as much as 25 tons. Sangre de drago and elephant trees (*Bursera* spp.) are prevalent in this subdivision. Creosote is less common, with teddy bear cholla (*Opuntia bigelovii*) joining the sparse understory shrub layer. The flatter plains and base of the bajadas have a sparse cover of ocotillo, sangre de drago, creosote, barrel cacti, and cholla.

With more rainfall, as much as 15 in (380 mm), the Plains of Sonora, centered on Hermosillo, Mexico, and transitional to the more humid thorn scrub grasslands to the south, is the least diversified. Trees, including ironwood, paloverde, and mesquite, reaching 13–33 ft (4–10 m) tall, dominate, while creosote, white bursage, and cacti are scarce.

Although the Vizcaino region in central Baja shares many species with the rest of the Sonoran Desert, low rainfall (less than 4 in, 100 mm), fog, and its flora make it distinct. This area is dominated by large leaf succulents, including several species of *Agave, Yucca*, and *Dudleya*. More than 20 percent of its plant species are endemic. Lichen communities are well developed in fog zones along the coast. The broad sandy valleys and gently sloping bajadas support a uniform vegetation of several agave species. Visual dominants because of their size include cardon, boojum (*Fouquieria columnaris*), elephant tree, and datillo (*Yucca valida*). Except for a small stand on the Mexican Gulf of California coast, boojums are endemic to Baja. Elephant trees are short and squat, with fat trunks and peeling bark, while datillo is a tree size yucca, 23–33 ft (7–10 m) tall. Plants communities further inland are more typical of the Sonoran Desert in general.

Most animal species, such as pronghorn, mule deer, coyotes, desert bighorn sheep, and javalinas, are shared with other North American deserts. Common small animals include kangaroo rats, wood rats, cottontails, jack rabbits, and ground squirrels. Elf Owl, Gambel Quail, Roadrunner, Phainopepla, Cactus Wren, and Curved-bill Thrasher are frequently seen. Gila Woodpeckers (*Melanerpes uropygialis*) and Ladder-backed Woodpeckers (*Picoides scalaris*) are endemic.

Reptiles, including western whiptail, horned lizards, desert spiny lizards, desert iguana, and chuckwalla, are plentiful. Poisonous creatures include five species of rattlesnake, the Arizona coral snake, Gila monster, and scorpions. Nonpoisonous snakes include western shovelnose, desert rosy boa, and Sonoran gopher snakes. Arizona coral snake and Sonoran gopher snake are endemic.

Protected Areas. Several areas are protected in some way. Saguaro National Park, Sonoran Desert National Monument, Organ Pipe National Park, Kofa National Wildlife Refuge, Superstition Wilderness, and Cabeza Prieta National Wildlife Preserve are in Arizona. Joshua Tree National Park in California is includes part of the Sonoran Desert. El Pinacate y Gran Desierto de Altar Biosphere Reserve and El Vizcaíno Biosphere Reserve are in Mexico.

See also Altar Desert (Gran Desierto de Altar) Baja California; Basin and Range Physiographic Province

Further Reading

Quinn, Joyce A. 2009. *Desert Biomes*. Greenwood Guides to Biomes of the World. Westport, CT: Greenwood Press.

Turner, Raymond M. and David E. Brown. 1982. "Sonoran Desertscrub." In *Special Issue: Biotic Communities of the American Southwest—United States and Mexico*, edited by David E. Brown, 181–221. *Desert Plants* Volume 4. Tucson: The University of Arizona for Boyce Thompson Southwestern Arboretum.

Soufrière Hills Volcano

Montserrat

Geographic Overview. Soufrière Hills volcano is the youngest of three volcanic centers on Montserrat, an island in the Lesser Antilles, where the Atlantic oceanic crust is subducting beneath the Caribbean Plate.

Geographic Coordinates. 16°43'N, 62°11'W

Description. Monserrat is only 10 mi (16 km) in north–south extent. The oldest volcanic center is in the north, Silver Hills. In the middle of the island, the Centre Hills mark the next oldest volcano to build the island, and the southern part of the island is composed of the restless Soufrière Hills volcano, which came to life again in 1995 after a 350-year period of quiescence.

The current summit of this andesitic stratovolcano stands 3,300 ft (1,050 m) asl, but this elevation is ever-changing as the newest lava dome continues to rise and sink. The summit actually consists of an east-southeast trending series of lava domes in English's Crater, a 0.6mi (1km) wide caldera formed 4,000 years ago when a former summit collapsed. At the northwest edge of the crater are the oldest lava domes, Gages lava dome and Chances Mountain, both formed during the late Pleistocene Epoch. Until 1995, Chances Mountain was the highest peak on the mountain, rising to 3,000 ft (915 m). Between them is Gages Ghaut, the valley down which moved the pyroclastic flow that destroyed the capital city of Plymouth in 1995. Castle Peak lava dome formed ca. 1630 during the only historic eruption of Soufrière Hills volcano prior to 1995.

Volcanic activity at Soufrière Hills is characterized by ash eruptions followed by lava dome growth and pyroclastic flows. In 1995, activity began with steam rising from vents on English's Crater and Castle Peak and small earthquakes rattled the southern end of Monstserrat. In July, an ash plume rose from the lava dome in English's Crater. Explosions of ash-laden gases known as Vulcanian eruptions followed and continued for 18 weeks. The first eruption occurred in August, where a new crater formed on the northwest side of Castle Peak. A second crater later formed on the southwest side. Over the next few years, three lava domes were built only to collapse, leading to pyroclastic flows. Incandescent lava rock falls lit the night and block-and-ash flows streamed down the volcanoes flanks in December 1996. The largest pyroclastic flow occurred on August 3, 1997, when hot gas and rock ran down Tar Valley and covered central Plymouth with ash and blocks as large as 3–6.5 ft (1–2 m) in diameter. Plymouth had been constructed on debris from an older pyroclastic flow and was the island's largest city. The death toll was low, however, because residents had heeded warnings and evacuated the city.

Vulcanian explosions, earthquakes, occasional ash venting with ash clouds reaching 3,000–4,000 ft (900–1,200 m) into the air, and small pyroclastic flows continue as the youngest lava dome grows and collapses. Some volcanologists believe the long period of near constant activity may be related to the mountain's having two connected magma chambers beneath it, one at a depth of 3.7 mi (6 km) and the other at a depth of 7.5 mi (12 km). The southern half of the island remains uninhabitable, and up to two-thirds of the pre-eruption population has emigrated. However, the island is now home to the Montserrat Volcano Observatory, perhaps the world's most modern volcano-monitoring facility, complete with a live webcam watching the activity on Soufrière Hills from about 3.7 mi (6 km) away.

See also Lesser Antilles

Further Reading

"Soufrière Hills." n.d. Global Volcanism Program. Smithsonian Institution. http://www.volcano.si.edu/volcano.cfm?vn=360050

"Soufriere Hills Volcano." n.d. Volcano Discovery. http://www.volcanodiscovery.com/montserrat.html

South America

Geographic Overview. South America is Earth's fourth largest continent with 12 percent of the planet's land area. Triangular in shape, South America has a prominent bulge into the South Atlantic Ocean in tropical latitudes, narrowing that ocean significantly and reflecting the former Gondwanan connection to Africa. While much of the land mass has a tropical climate, the region south of the Tropic of Capricorn (the "Southern Cone") is temperate. The Andes Mountains, the longest and second highest chain in the world, has environmental zones based on elevation and exposure to prevailing winds.

Table 1 Geographic Parameters of South America

Area: 6,900,000 mi² (17,800,000 km²)

Northernmost point: Punta Gallinas (12°28'N, 71°40'W) on the Guijara Peninsula of Colombia

Southernmost point: Aguila Islet (56°32'S) in the Diego Ramierez Islands south of Chile

Easternmost point: Ponta do Seixas (07°09'S, 34°48'W) on Cabo Branco, Brazil

Westernmost point: Punta Pariñas (04°41'S, 81°20'W) in Peru

Highest point: Cerro Aconcagua, Argentina: 22,837 ft (6,960 m) asl

Lowest point: Laguna del Carbon, Argentina: 344 ft (105 m) bsl

Geographic Coordinates. 12°28'N–56°32'S; 34°48'W–81°20'W

Description. The various geologic forces working on the South American continent (see "Geologic History" section below) are reflected in the major landform regions recognized today. At the simplest level, from west to east, are the Andes Mountains, Central Lowlands, and Eastern Highlands or Shields.

Andes Mountains. From a single low range at their southern terminus in Tierra del Fuego, the Andes quickly gain elevation to the north. Glaciers have carved the mountains into sharp peaks and U-shaped valleys, and many lakes are scattered throughout. Ice fields persist between 45°S and 57°S. Near the Bolivian border, two distinct ranges appear with cold, dry intermontane basins and plateaus, the largest of which is the Altiplano, at elevations of 10,000–12,000 ft (3,000–3,600 m) asl. The world's highest navigable freshwater lake, Lake Titicaca, occurs here. To its south and east is Lake Poopó, a shallow, highly saline lake that is a relict of wetter periods during the Pleistocene. Elsewhere numerous *salares* (playas or dry lake beds) dot the floor of the Altiplano, further evidence of the desiccation that followed the end of the last Ice Age. North of Peru, a series of small intermontane valleys have formed. They supported major population centers in Pre-Columbian times and do so today.

Three parallel ranges appear in Colombia, and major cities again are located in the high valleys between the mountains. A fourth range, the Cordillera of Chocó, is separated from the main three branches of the Andes by the Pacific coastal plain. The easternmost cordillera bends northeast toward Venezuela, where it divides into two more ranges which extend toward the Caribbean Sea and Atlantic Ocean on either side of the oil-rich Maracaibo basin. (Trinidad's mountains are, geologically speaking, the northeastern end of the Andes.)

The Central Lowlands. The Central Lowlands, between the Andes and the Eastern Highlands, are largely alluvial plains built of sediments from the surrounding uplands. Four units are recognized: (1) the Llanos, a flat grassland savanna on the floodplain of the Orinoco River; (2) the Amazon Basin; (3) the Gran Chaco, site of the Pantanal, the largest tropical freshwater wetland in the world; and (4) the Pampa, a temperate grassland growing on rich soils derived from loess-covered alluvium and volcanic ash.

Eastern Highlands. Three of the four highland regions are shields, the ancient crystalline cores of the continent, uplifted, exposed by erosion, and deeply weathered and leached. As a consequence they typically have infertile soils. The Brazilian Highlands are a series of erosional surfaces that range in elevation from 1,500 to 6,500 ft (450–1,980 m) asl and are separated by escarpments. Some of the world's richest deposits of gold, diamonds, titanium, chromium, molybdenum and iron are here. The Guiana Shield north of the Amazon basin is highly eroded. Tepuis—flat-topped erosional remnants of older, higher surfaces—are capped by sandstones and have high, sheer cliffs. Angel Falls, the world's highest waterfall, cascades from the top of Auyántepui. The Patagonian Plateau in southern Argentina, at an elevation of about 5,000 ft (1,500 m), is a region where sedimentary rocks cover the granitic basement rock.

The Paraná Plateau, the youngest of the four highlands, is formed of flood basalts that spilled out with the opening of the Atlantic Ocean and contains some of the most fertile soils (*terra roxa*) in tropical South America. Four-mile-wide Iguaçu Falls thunders over the western edge.

Because the bulk of the South America land mass lies in the tropics, it experiences relatively little difference in temperatures month to month. Elevation determines the actual temperatures, so in equatorial regions it is hot in the Amazon Basin but "eternal spring" in the Quito basin of Ecuador nearly 10,000 ft (3,000 m) asl. South of the Tropic of Capricorn (23°26'S), however, there is seasonal variation in temperatures, and frost occurs. Tierra del Fuego experiences cool temperatures year-round, but because of the tapering of the continent and its proximity to the open sea, it is not nearly as cold as comparable latitudes (e.g., in Montreal or Moscow) in the Northern Hemisphere. The cool Humboldt Current pulls the temperate climate equatorward on the west coast as far as Lima, Peru (12°S), whereas the warm Brazil Current off the east coast draws the tropical regime southward to 30°S.

Altitudinal zones in the Andes are based on temperature. In general, temperatures decrease 3.5°F with every increase of 1,000 ft (6.4°C/1,000 m) elevation. At the equator, average annual temperatures in the lowest zone, *tierra caliente*, are warm all year, decreasing from 82°F (28°C) at sea level to 72°F (22°C) at the upper limit, approximately 3,000 ft (1,000 m). *Tierra templada*, where temperatures average between 72° and 59° F (22°–15°C), ranges from 3,000 ft (1,000 m) asl to about 6,000 ft (2,000 m). Mild temperatures dominate and frost does not occur. *Tierra fria*, where frosts occur occasionally, extends from 6,000–12,000 ft (2,000–4,000 m) and is the home of traditional Andean crops such as potatoes, oca, tarwi, and quinoa. *Tierra helada*, where frost occurs every night, occurs from 12,000 to 18,000 ft (4,000–6,000 m). Treeline is encountered at about 15,000 ft (5,000 m). In the uppermost zone, *tierra nevada*, beginning at 18,000 ft (6,000 m), average temperatures are below freezing; and snow or ice is permanent.

Rainfall is a better indicator of seasons than is temperature. In the tropics rain occurs when the Intertropical Convergence Zone (ITCZ) is overhead, causing heavy downpours. Tropical areas are also affected by the easterly flowing trade winds that carry moisture inland off the Atlantic Ocean. The release of moisture through evapotranspiration enables rainforest trees to recycle water and helps produce year round rainfall in the central Amazon basin. Dry seasons in the tropics occur when the ITCZ is in the opposite hemisphere and the region is dominated by the subtropical high pressure (STHP) system. In temperate South America, south of the Tropic of Capricorn, the Prevailing Westerly Winds carry moist air off the Pacific Ocean. Wet and dry seasons south of the tropics are related to seasonal shifts of the STHP cell and westerly winds that cause summers to be dry and winters to be wet on the west coast. These general precipitation patterns are interrupted by both the Andes and the escarpments of the Eastern Highlands. The windward sides of these land barriers receive more precipitation, while the leeward or rain shadow sides have less. The sertão of Brazil, the Atacama and Peruvian deserts, the Monte, and the Patagonian steppe in Argentina all lie in rain shadows.

The cool Humboldt and Peruvian currents moving equatorward along the Pacific Coast of the continent modify the arid climate, causing condensation from maritime air masses to form fog banks over the ocean. Some places in the Atacama have never recorded rainfall, but plants and animals exist, surviving on water droplets formed when upright structures intercept the fog as it blows inland. Changes in atmospheric circulation over the Pacific some years drive warm water toward the west coast of South America during the winter, resulting in El Niños. Subsequent heavy rains may then fall on the western deserts and western slopes of the Andes and cause devastating floods.

Much of the continent is drained by one of three large river systems: the Amazon, Orinoco, and Paraguay-Paraná. The Amazon is the second longest river in the world and the largest river when discharge is measured; its discharge accounts for 20 percent of the fresh water entering the ocean each year. The drainage patterns of the Amazon and other South American rivers are largely controlled by the geological structure of the continent. Much of the Amazon system, for example, is contained in a downwarped basin; it empties through a rift valley into the Atlantic Ocean. Rivers and lakes on the Brazilian Highlands usually follow fracture systems. The Magdalena River in Colombia flows in a rift valley between two ranges of the Andes.

Rivers in the Amazon system are identified as whitewater (actually brown, from sediments), blackwater (stained with tannins), or clearwater (bearing few sediments/nutrients) streams. Streams flowing from the Andes carry heavy sediment loads, while those coming the shield areas are deficient in sediments and hence nutrients for aquatic life. Widespread annual flooding allows water to be stored in vast wetlands. The Pantanal on the upper Paraguay River is under water 6 months a year. The Llanos receive water from the Orinoco River, which leaves water standing on its floodplain, inland delta, and coastal delta for several months each year. The seasonally flooded forests along the Amazon provide food, habitat, and dispersal opportunities for a variety of river and rainforest organisms. Annual flooding is also significant along smaller rivers such as the Magdalena and on the southern llanos of Bolivia and Peru.

The interplay of bedrock, soils, climate, and tectonically derived connection or isolation has allowed distinctive vegetation types to develop. South America is famous for its rainforest, the Amazonian forest being the largest and most species-rich in the world. Two other tropical rainforest regions occur: the mata atlântica or Atlantic rainforest and the Chocó on the Pacific coast of northern South America. Tropical savannas and dry forests occur in the Llanos of Colombia and Venezuela, the cerrado of Brazil, and the Gran Chaco. Semiarid shrublands, the caatinga, dominate on the Brazilian Highlands of Northeast Brazil.

Subtropical semideciduous forests with Gondwanan genera such as *Araucaria* and *Podocarpus* can be found in temperate Brazil. Temperate rainforests (Valdivian, North Patagonia, and Magellanic) dominate the cool, wet regions of the southern coast of Chile and occur in small patches on the eastern slopes of the Andes in Argentina. The dominants are evergreen species of Gondwanan origin and include broadleaved southern beeches (*Nothofagus*), and needle-leaved conifers such as *Fitzroya cupressoides*.

The mattoral of central Chile is a mediterranean type of woodland and shrubland comparable to the chaparral of southern California and developed under a similar subtropical dry summer–wet winter climates.

Desertscrub extends along the west coast of the continent in the fog deserts of Peru and Chile, and also east of the Andes, in the rain shadow of the Andes, in Patagonia.

Higher elevations of the Andes support unique vegetation types. Cloud forests occur at elevations where moisture in air rising over the mountains condenses to form low clouds or dense fog. Above treeline in the Ecuadorian and Colombian Andes, the wet tundra-like paramo occurs. From Peru southward, under drier conditions, puna grassland covers the high elevation landscape.

Geologic History. The continent lies wholly on the South American tectonic plate, the northern boundary of which is the Atrato Valley in Colombia, site of a former oceanic trench that once separated South and Central America and a transform fault along which the Caribbean Plate shears eastward. The eastern edge of the South American plate is a passive margin pushed westward by seafloor spreading at the Mid-Atlantic Oceanic Ridge, whereas the western margin is an active zone of subduction where the Nazca and Antarctic plates descend into the Peru–Chile Trench. This convergence of plates promotes active volcanism and mountain-building along the Andean Cordillera. At the southern margin of the South American Plate is another zone of eastward shearing, in this instance where the Scotia plate moves past the South American and Antarctic plates.

The contemporary landmass of South America has been shaped by tectonic activity including the convergence of major and minor plates to form the supercontinent of Gondwana during the Cambrian Period; the assembly of Pangaea beginning in the late Paleozoic; the rifting of Gondwana and formation of the South Atlantic Ocean between Africa and South America beginning in the Mesozoic; several episodes of mountain-building that led to not only to the formation of the Andes Mountains as plates collided on the western side of the continent, but also the uplift of eastern shield areas and related igneous intrusions; and the shearing associated with the Caribbean and Scotia plates during the Cenozoic Period.

For 100 million years after splitting from Africa and the other parts of Gondwana, South America was an island, unconnected to any other landmass. The beginning of that time was the Age of Reptiles, although marsupial mammals also inhabited the Earth. During its long isolation, species, genera, and even the families of plants and animals evolved to add to the flora and fauna common to Gondwanan lands. Today South America is species-rich in most taxonomic groups and endemism is high, even though connections with North America that arose with the formation of the Central American isthmus 3–2 mya greatly affected species composition of the fauna.

The core of the continent consists of Precambrian igneous and metamorphic rocks. Some today are buried beneath overlying rocks of younger ages; others are exposed as shields, such as the Guiana Shield and the Brazilian Highlands. During the formation of Gondwana, tectonic pressures resulted in the sagging of some cratons, creating large basins such as the Amazonas, Parnaíba, and Solimões basins in northern Brazil and the Paraná and Chaco-Paraná basins to the south. Structural arches separating these basins influence drainage patterns to this day. The basins filled with sediments 9,800–23,000 ft (3,000–7,000 m) thick over millennia, and some collected fossils as well. The

Permian shales of the Paraná Basin, for example, contain the remains of the Gondwanan *Glossopteris* flora as well as the Gondwanan reptile *Mesosaurus*. The interior of the supercontinent, distant from sources of atmospheric moisture, saw widespread accumulations of windblown sands and the formation of "red beds" as desert conditions prevailed. The rifting of West Gondwana ruptured connections between Africa and South America and left similar rocks, fossils, and geologic structures on opposite sides of the Atlantic Ocean, providing strong, early evidence in support of the theory of plate tectonics.

The Andes, the longest and second highest mountain range on Earth, is the product of plate convergence, which caused folding and faulting, accretion of volcanic arcs once offshore, volcanism, and intrusions of magma that cooled and solidified within the continental rocks some 8–5 mya, forming granodioritic batholiths. The intrusions left veins of metallic ores such as gold, silver, tin, and copper. The cordillera extends more than 5,000 mi (8,500 km) from 12°N to 56°S, sometimes forming two, three, and even four parallel ranges separated by high plateaus. Volcanic activity has long been and continues to be an important and often scenic aspect of the Andes. Part of the "Ring of Fire" encircling the Pacific Ocean, four active volcanic zones occur along that range wherever the slope of the subducting plates is 30° or greater. Many massive snow-covered stratovolcanoes stud the Andean landscape. Nevado Ojos de Salado (6,887 m), on the Chile–Argentina border at 27°N, is the highest active volcano in the world. However, it is not the highest peak in the Andes. Cerro Aconcagua at 22,837.3 ft (6,960.8 m) asl is. Indeed, it is the highest peak in all of the Americas.

Glaciers have carved the highest Andean mountains into rugged peaks. Present snowline lies between 14,400 (4,400 m) and 16,400 ft (5,000 m) asl depending upon latitude and mountain mass. Although most alpine glaciers are currently retreating in face of a warming climate, large ice fields still persist in Patagonia. Most Andean lakes formed when terminal and recessional moraines dammed meltwaters from retreating glaciers.

Volcanism has been a significant part of the shaping of the South American land surface in other areas

South America and Western Science

During the Middle Ages maps depicted a world divided into three parts: Europe, Africa, and Asia. Yet geographers and mapmakers believed a fourth part had to exist beyond the ocean to balance these landmasses. Voyages of discovery by Columbus and others at the very end of the period discovered this fourth part: the Americas. When, in 1507, the German cartographer Martin Waldseemüller showed this still largely unexplored New World for the first time on a map of the world, he named it after Amerigo Vespucci, whom he believed was the first to find a continent there. The name was printed in what is now Brazil. It would be centuries before the map of South America was filled in and North America would be discovered as a continent in its own right.

Nineteenth-century surveys and exploration were especially important in the development of western science, especially the life sciences. Among the most famous and influential naturalist-explorers was Alexander von Humboldt, whose travels in northern South America (1799–1803) with the French botanist Aimé Bonpland set the foundations of biogeography. Charles Darwin's time in South America (1832–1835) and especially on the Galápagos Islands helped him frame the theory of evolution by natural selection. The co-founder of the theory, Alfred Russel Wallace, had spent several years (1848–1852) in the Amazon collecting plants and animals for English museums before embarking on the trip to Malaysia, which inspired his thoughts on how species and their distributions change over time. Henry Walter Bates was with Wallace in the Amazon in 1848 and remained for more than a decade, collecting butterflies and other insects and formulating ideas on how unrelated species come to resemble each other, what is now known as Batesian mimicry.

The shape of the eastern edge of the South American continent that makes it "fit" the western margin of Africa like two pieces of a puzzle, as well as similar geologic formations on the two continents, supported early theories of "continental drift" by Alfred Wegener (1912) and others. Wegener's ideas later evolved into the theory of plate tectonics, a concept which now informs thoughts on how continents and ocean basins are shaped and how their changing positions on the planet have influenced climate, plant and animal distribution patterns, and landscape transformation through geologic time.

also. The rifting of Gondwana and opening of the Atlantic Ocean allowed flood basalts to pour forth and form the Paraná Plateau during one of the largest lava flows in geologic history. Offshore in the Pacific Ocean, Ecuador's Galápagos Islands continue to form over a hot spot where a mantle plume rises near the boundary of the Cocos and Nazca plates.

Biota. South America, occupying the major part of the Neotropical Zoogeographic Province, is species-rich in most animal groups, including vertebrates. Approximately 30 percent of the Earth's freshwater fish, amphibian, and bird species are found here, many of them endemic at family, genus, or species level. Nearly 20 percent of all the reptiles and mammals in the world occur on this relatively small continent.

The Andes, Amazon, and Atlantic forest host the greatest diversity of amphibians. Reptiles are most diverse in the three tropical rainforest regions. Species richness of birds is highest in humid mountain habitats, where the natives are joined seasonally by Neotropical migrants (especially warblers, vireos, and flycatchers) that breed in North America during the Northern Hemisphere spring and summer. Northern hawks, waterfowl, and shorebirds also spend Northern Hemisphere winter in South America, but tend to prefer non-montane shrublands and wetlands.

Mammals include 71 species of marsupials, 30 kinds of xenarthans (anteaters, armadillos, and sloths); 104 primates (monkeys, tamarins, and marmosets), 219 species of bat, and 522 species of rodent. New World mice and rats and caviomorphs such as chinchillas, guinea pigs, agoutis, and capybaras are especially well represented among the rodents. Mammal diversity is high in the Amazon, cerrado, mata atlântica, Gran Chaco, caatinga, and Pantanal. New species continued to be identified at a rate of 40–45/yr.

See also Amazon River; Andes Mountains; Brazilian Highlands; Guiana Shield and Its Tepuis; The Llanos; Orinoco River; The Pampas; Paraná Plateau; Patagonian Plateau; Tierra del Fuego

Further Reading

Caviedes, César and Gregory Knapp. 1995. *South America*. Englewood Cliffs, NJ: Prentice-Hall.
Dunne, Thomas and Leal Anne Kerry Mertes. 2007. "Rivers." In *The Physical Geography of South America*,

edited by Thomas T. Veblen, Kenneth R. Young, and Antony R. Orme, 76–90. New York: Oxford University Press.

Meserve, Peter L. 2007. "Zoogeography." In *The Physical Geography of South America*, edited by Thomas T. Veblen, Kenneth R. Young, and Antony R. Orme, 112–132. New York: Oxford University Press.

Orme, Antony R. 2007. "Tectonism, Climate, and Landscape Change." In *The Physical Geography of South America*, edited by Thomas T. Veblen, Kenneth R. Young, and Antony R. Orme, 23–44. New York: Oxford University Press.

Orme, Antony R. 2007. "The Tectonic Framework of South America." In *The Physical Geography of South America*, edited by Thomas T. Veblen, Kenneth R. Young, and Antony R. Orme, 3–22. New York: Oxford University Press.

South China Karst

China

Geographic Overview. The limestone and karst landscapes of southern China are world famous, often depicted in Chinese paintings, for their tall and steep limestone hills towering over green rice paddies. The karst region is among the largest in areal extent, with some of the best developed karst topography in the world. South China contains the world's reference sites for tropical karst.

Geographic Coordinates. Approximately 23°N–29°N, 103°E–111°E

Description. The limestone area of southern China, covers 115,850–193,000 mi^2 (300,000–500,000 km^2), primarily in Guangxi, Guizhou, and eastern Yunnan provinces. The region has prime examples of three major types of karst. The best development is in hot, humid Guangxi province, which has pure Devonian and Permian age limestone. Karst is less developed on the Guizhou Plateau, which is higher in elevation and cooler than Guangxi. The Guizhou plateau is a Tertiary erosion surface cut by deep valleys. It merges with the Yunnan Plateau to the west, which is limestone, sandstone, and shale. The surface is dry, with few rivers, and most drainage is underground.

In eastern Yunnan and Guizhou, the upper Paleozoic limestones and other carbonate rocks are 9,850–16,400 ft (3,000–5,000 m) thick. The limestone here erodes into a sharp-peaked landscape of smooth, grooved spires known as stone forests. The stone forests of Shilin, in Yunnan 75 mi (120 km) east of Kunming have a wide range of pinnacle shapes.

The Libo area in southern Guizhou on the border with Guangxi, has both cone and tower karst, as well as deep dolines, sinking streams, and long river caves. Guilin, in northeastern Guangxi Province, illustrates the classic karst tower landscape, famous for its steep limestone towers rising from a flat alluvial base with green agricultural fields. Local relief in the karst tower landscape of the Zhujiang (Hongshui) River valley is 985–2,300 ft (300–700 m). The Wulong region in Chongqing is cone karst with giant dolines (sinkholes), or collapse depressions called tiankengs, and very high natural bridges.

The carbonate rocks are riddled with caves, occupied by flowing rivers at the water table or inactive if they are above the water table.

Geologic History. Southern China and its thick limestone strata was uplifted and fractured when India collided with Eurasia in the Tertiary Alpine Orogeny.

Tropical karst develops in three stages. Full development requires pure carbonate rocks (limestones) at least 655–985 ft (200–300 m) thick and wet climates where rivers are deeply entrenched. Solution of the limestone begins in a series of crisscrossing vertical joints. Cockpit karst is the initial stage, where the surface becomes pitted with conical depressions, supposedly resembling open cockpits of airplanes. As solution of the limestone continues, the cockpits deepen and widen, leaving a landscape of cone-shaped hills—cone karst. Relative relief is 300–500 ft (100–150 m), hill diameter is usually 1,000 ft (300 m), and slopes are 30–40 degrees. When solution dissolves the intervening limestone down to the level of the water table, lateral solution steepens the hills into isolated vertical towers. Tower karst consists of very steep-sided, almost vertical, hills separated by a flat-floored lowland.

Tiankengs, more than 330 ft (100 m wide) and deep, are usually formed by underground water that dissolves the limestone and causes the surface to collapse. Tiankengs develop in cone karst with extensive cave river systems. The cave river systems dissolve the limestone, causing the surface to collapse, giving the doline close to vertical walls, with a gap between the walls and the floor. Natural bridges are remnants of cave roofs.

The stone forests are formed from rainwater penetrating vertical joints in the thickly bedded rock, dissolving the limestone and separating it into discreet spires. Over time, even minimal precipitation will continue to carve vertical grooves or furrows, called lapies, into the bare rock.

Biota. Natural vegetation in south China karst is broadleaf evergreen and deciduous forest. Once the forest is destroyed, reestablishment is difficult, and the plant cover deteriorates to sparse shrubs. Biodiversity is limited due to thin soil, drought, and alkaline conditions. Mosses and algae are important pioneer species on limestone rocks. Although ground water may be abundant, surface water is scarce.

Protected Areas. South China Karst World Heritage Site is comprised of three disjunct clusters, Shilin, Libo, and Wulong, which illustrate the diversity of karst landscapes.

Environmental Issues. The ecosystems are ecologically fragile, subject to drought, flood, soil erosion, surface collapse, and rock desertification. Rock desertification is the transformation of vegetation and soil-covered karst into a bare rocky landscape through unsustainable agricultural practices, which may include burning and wood gathering.

Further Reading

Knez, Martin, Hong Liu, and Tadej Slabe, editors. 2011. *South China Karst II*. Ljubljana, Slovenia: ZRC Publishers.

Xiaoping, Chen, Franci Gabrovsek, Huang Chuxing, Jim Yuzhang, Martin Knez, Jania Kogovek, Liu Hong, Metka Petaric, Andrej Mihevc, Bojan Otonikar, Shi Mengxiang, Tadej Slabe, Stanka Sebela, Wu Wenqing, Zhang Shouyue, and Nadja Zupan Hajna. 1998. *South China Karst I*. Ljubljana, Slovenia: ZRC Publishers.

Xuewen, Zhu and Chen Weihai. 2006. "Tiankengs in the Karst of China." *Speleogenesis and Evolution of Karst Aquifers* 4(1): 1–18.

South China Sea

North Pacific Ocean

Geographic Overview. The South China Sea is the Pacific Ocean's largest marginal sea and Earth's sixth largest body of water after the five oceans. It extends from near the equator north to the Tropic of Cancer and lies within the Indo-West Pacific region of high biodiversity. Claims on tiny islands, the Spratly Islands in particular, are contested by surrounding countries in a sea through which one fourth of the world's trade passes, which is a major international communications center, and which may sit on rich reserves of petroleum and natural gas. Among nations claiming territory are the People's Republic of China, Vietnam, Taiwan, Malaysia, and Philippines. Brunei extends its exclusive economic zone (EEZ) into the South China Sea.

Geographic Coordinates. 02°30'N–23°30'N, 99° 10'E–121°50'E

Description. The tropical waters of the South China Sea extend about 1,120 mi (1,800 km) south from mainland China and the island of Taiwan to the north coast of Borneo. On the west the sea is bounded by Vietnam and the Malay Peninsula and 600 mi (900 km) away on the east the Philippine Islands separate it from the Philippine Sea. It is connected to neighboring bodies of water mostly by narrow and shallow straits. The Taiwan Strait links to the East China Sea to the north, while the Karimata Strait connects it to the Java Sea located between Borneo and the Indonesian island of Java. Balabac Strait leads to the Sulu Sea between the Philippine islands of Palawan and Mindanao. The South China Sea is linked to the Indian Ocean by the Strait of Malacca between the Malay Peninsula and the Indonesian island of Sumatra. The only deep water channel in and out of the South China Sea is Bashi Channel in the Luzon Strait south of Taiwan, which connects to the Philippine Sea.

The western and southern sides of the sea cover a broad continental shelf that accounts for about half of the basin's floor. Most of this is part of the Sunda Shelf, which, when sea levels fell during Pleistocene glacial periods, became a land bridge connecting Borneo to mainland Asia. In the central and northeastern parts of the sea, a wide abyssal plain reaches depths of 17,640 ft (5,377 m) bsl.

Over 750 islets, small islands, coral reefs, atolls, cays, and seamounts dot the sea in the north. The islands occur in four clusters: the Spratly Islands (Nansha Islands) west of Palawan (which according to some includes the seamount Reed Tablemount or Reed

Bank), the Paracel Islands (Xisha Islands) between Vietnam and Luzon, the Pratas Islands (Dongsha Islands) southeast of Hong Kong, and the Macclefield Bank (Zhongsha Islands), a submerged atoll east of the Paracel Islands. A poorly charted area of seamounts, submerged reefs, and atolls that includes many of the Spratly Islands is known as the "Dangerous Ground" because of the navigational hazards these landforms present.

Along the coast of northern Vietnam the South China Sea extends inland as the Gulf of Tonkin. This body of water is semienclosed by Vietnam, China, and the Chinese island of Hainan. In the southwest, an arm of the sea forms the shallow Gulf of Thailand between the Malay Peninsula and Indochina.

Freshwater input to the sea comes from several major Asian rivers, including the Chao Phraya, Mekong, Red, and Xi (Pearl) Rivers. The entire basin is under the influence of the Asian monsoon with southeasterly summer flows bringing rain and the northwesterly winter monsoon creating a dry season. Surrounding lands are generally classified with tropical monsoon, tropical wet and dry, or subtropical wet and dry climates.

Geologic History. The South China Sea began to open 45 mya when rifting in the continental crust at the margin of the Asian landmass caused the block underlying the Dangerous Ground to break away from China. Subsequent seafloor spreading 30–18 mya widened the basin. Eventually the seafloor was covered in deep sediments that may hold significant deposits of oil and natural gas.

Circulation and Major Currents. Circulation, not well studied, is controlled by the monsoons, with a counterclockwise gyre developing in winter and reversing in summer. Overall, Pacific water enters via the Java Sea and flows northward to exit into the East China Sea via the Taiwan Strait. During what is known as a Kuroshio intrusion, a branch of the warm Kuroshio Current, sometimes enters through the Balintang Channel in the Luzon Strait. Most of this water leaves again through the Bashi Channel, but some can flow westward into the South China Sea, especially in winter.

Biota. The marine fauna of the South China Sea is essentially tropical in origin. The southern coast of Hainan and the southern and eastern coasts of Taiwan are at the northern limit of coral reef development. The variety of aquatic habitats from sandy shores to shallow coastal waters to deep sea, from seagrass meadows to mangroves and reefs, supports an enormous diversity of Indo-West Pacific marine life that is still largely unexplored.

Environmental Issues. Pollution from increasing industrial development and overfishing are major problems. The South China Sea was one of the world's great fisheries. Since 2000, populations of Chinese shrimp have decreased to the point where this once important commercial fishery is on the verge of extinction. In the Gulf of Tonkin, horseshoe crabs have also recently become endangered. Most commercially important fishes are overexploited as well.

South Georgia and the South Sandwich Islands

South Atlantic Ocean

Geographic Overview. South Georgia and the South Sandwich Islands are two clusters of subantarctic islands. Administered as a British overseas territory, the islands lack permanent settlers; a handful of researchers from the British Antarctic Survey (BAS) and government officials stay on South Georgia and Bird islands during summer months. Argentine claim to the islands in part fueled the Falklands War in 1982.

Geographic Coordinates. South Georgia Island: 54°15'S, 36°45'W; South Sandwich Islands: 56°18'–59°27'S, 26°23'–28°02'W

Description. South Georgia Island is 104 mi (167 km) long and less than 25 mi (37 km) wide. A string of 11 peaks above 6,560 ft (2,000 m) form its backbone. Mt. Paget, the highest, rises to 9,626 ft (2,934 m) asl. Composed of gneiss and schist, these mountains may be extensions of South America's Andes Mountains. Most of the island is ice-covered, and alpine glaciers extend down the mountain slopes, but the surrounding seas typically remain free of pack ice during the winter. A number of sheltering bays grace the north coast of the island, where low-lying areas are snow-free in summer.

Although most of uninhabited South Georgia Island is ice-covered, low-lying areas on the north coast are ice-free in summer and are visited by King Penguin and other seabirds. Pack ice rarely forms in the surrounding ocean. (Monkeygreen/Dreamstime.com)

South Georgia Island has several small satellite islands and rocks. Most noteworthy is Bird Island, 0.3 mi (500 m) off its northwest tip. Here the BAS maintains a research station and collects environmental data. Bird Island is 3 mi (4.8 km) long and less than 0.5 mi (800 m wide). Sheer cliffs and sea stacks line the north shore, but the southern coast has small bays, beaches, and rock platforms exposed at low tide. Lying south of the polar front, the island is open to Antarctic storms, but temperatures, though low, are moderated by the ocean. In winter temperatures are usually at the freezing point, but in summer rise to about 39°F (4°C). Summer weather is typically misty with low clouds. Gales from the southwest or north are frequent. Annual precipitation on South Georgia Island is 59 in (1,500 mm). Land below 500 ft (150 m) is covered in tussac grass. Higher elevations are boggy and have small lakes where it is flat; steeper areas are rocky with scree slopes.

The South Sandwich Islands lie 350–500 mi (560–800 km) southeast of South Georgia at the edge of the Southern Ocean. They comprise 11 islands in a north–south oriented island arc 220 mi (355 km) long just east of the Scotia Sea. Each is the top of a volcano rising from the ocean floor. Customarily they are divided into three groups: a northern cluster made up of the Traversay and Candlemas island groups; the three largest islands together as a central group; and the southern cluster known as Southern Thule. Six passages separate the islands and island groups. The largest island is Montagu, 7.5 mi (12 km) long and 6.2 mi (10 km) wide, with an area of 42 mi² (110 km²). The highest point in the South Sandwich Islands, Mount Belinda, is on this island. An active shield volcano, Mount Belinda stands 4,490 ft (1,370 m) asl.

The South Sandwich Islands have a polar climate characterized by highly variable weather conditions. The maximum temperature in winter (August) is 32°F (0°C), but temperatures rarely go below 14°F (−10°C). The islands are surrounded by sea-ice from mid-May until late November. Icebergs can be seen offshore throughout the year. The summer (January) high is 46.4°F (8°C). Precipitation averages 59 in (1,500 mm) a year and usually occurs as sleet or snow. Summer snowline is at 980 ft (300 m) asl. The island landscape is largely one of bare rock, lava flows, and ash deposits. Coasts are cliff-lined, with small dark beaches of volcanic sands and stones.

Geologic History. South Georgia is a fragment of continental crust on the Scotia Plate which probably became separated from South America during the opening of the Drake Passage and the Scotia Sea beginning about 100 mya. It consists of sediments metamorphosed into gneiss and schist.

The South Sandwich Islands lie on the small South Sandwich Plate abutting the eastern margin of the Scotia Plate. The South Sandwich Trench, where the South American Plate is subducting beneath the Scotia Plate, is 60 mi (100 km) farther east. Active volcanism is a feature of most of the islands, especially the largest three. Montagu Island became active again in 2001. Lava flows, ash plumes, and lava lake activity continued through 2007. The northernmost volcano in the island arc is the seamount Protector Shoal, which comes to within 90 ft (27 m) of the sea surface.

Biota. Ice-free areas support vegetation similar to that of Tierra del Fuego and southern Patagonia. Grasses, mosses, and lichens dominate. Tussac grass (*Parodiochloa flabelleta*) grows on South Georgia Island. Bird Island has some of the densest concentrations of breeding seabirds and seals in the world, with one bird or seal every 16 ft² (1.5 m²). They attest to the richness of the nearby marine ecosystem. Since no rats have been introduced to this island, burrowing petrels and prions are abundant. Estimates of animals breeding on this small island include 50,000 breeding pairs of penguins, 14,000 pairs of albatross, 700,000 pairs of nocturnally feeding petrels, and 65,000 fur seals. Macaroni Penguins, Black-browed Albatrosses, Wandering Albatrosses, and Southern Giant Petrels are some of the more common seabirds. The endemic South Georgia Pipit is the Antarctic's only songbird. Other birds unique to the islands include the South Georgia Shag and the South Georgia Pintail.

There are no native terrestrial mammals, but mice, brown rats, and reindeer have been introduced on South Georgia Island.

Protected Areas. The islands are recognized as Important Bird Areas by Birdlife International and have been designated a Special Protected Area by the British government. In 2012, the territorial government established the South Georgia and South Sandwich Islands Marine Protection Area, an area of 656,374 mi² (1.7 million km²), making it the world's largest protected area.

Environmental Issues. The islands are vulnerable to the introduction of alien species. Already rats and mice have been accidentally introduced, as have dandelions. Rats have decimated populations of burrowing birds and take albatross eggs on South Georgia. Ten reindeer were introduced to South Georgia Island in 1911 to serve as a meat supply. The population had grown to 5,000 by the early 21st century, trampling and overgrazing the tussac grasslands.

Management is aimed at eliminating nonnatives and preventing the arrival and establishment of new species. Eradication of reindeer began in 2013 and will be completed in 2014. Eradication of rats is planned for 2011–2015. Path management along routes repeatedly used by scientists is also a recognized need.

Further Reading
"Bird Island Research Station. 2011. "British Antarctic Survey." http://www.antarctica.ac.uk/living_and_working/research_stations/bird_island/
"South Georgia and South Sandwich Islands." 2013. Kew Royal Botanical Gardens. http://herbaria.plants.ox.ac.uk/bol/southgeorgia
"South Sandwich Islands." 2010. Island Encyclopedia, Oceandots.com.http://web.archive.org/web/20101223021450/http://oceandots.com/southern/south-sandwich/

Southern Ocean

Geographic Overview. The Southern Ocean is that part of the world ocean encircling Antarctica. Unlike the other four oceans, it is not contained in a distinct basin, but in a series of deep basins occurring between the continental shelf of Antarctica and the spreading ridges at the edge of the Antarctic Plate, which were initiated when Gondwana split apart and the other southern continents moved away from the Antarctic core. The International Hydrographic Organization defines the northern boundary of the Southern Ocean as the 60°S parallel, but this definition has not been ratified by all members. In fact, some scientists (and the National Geographic Society) do not recognize the existence of a Southern Ocean at all, but declare the waters are simply the southern extensions of the Atlantic, Indian, and Pacific oceans.

Description. When considered as a separate body of water, the Southern Ocean is the fourth largest of Earth's oceans with a surface area of 7,834,000 mi² (20,327,000 km²); only the Arctic Ocean is smaller. The ocean includes a number of seas including the Ross, Weddell, and Bellinghausen seas along the Antarctic Coast and parts of the Drake Passage and Scotia Sea at the northern limits of the ocean. Beyond Antarctica's narrow continental shelf, depths range from 13,000 to 16,000 ft (4,000–5,000 m). Shelf waters are unusually deep since the weight of the great ice sheets has depressed the continental crust. Whereas off most continents the shelf only extends to depths of about 436 ft (133 m), the Antarctic continental shelf lies some 2,600 ft (800 m) bsl. The deepest part of the Southern Ocean is in the South Sandwich Trench, where it extends poleward of 60°S northwest of the South Sandwich Islands. Here, the maximum depth is 23,737 ft (7,235 m) bsl.

Sea surface temperatures vary seasonally from 28° to 50°F (–2°–10°C). During the austral winter almost the entire ocean freezes over; sea-ice extends northward to 65°S in the Pacific sector and to 55°S in the Atlantic sector. Ice shelves attached to 44 percent of the continent's coast and to some adjacent islands are permanent masses of ice continually renewed by glaciers. The largest is the Ross Ice Shelf, approximately the size of Spain. The Ronne Ice Shelf is only slightly smaller. Sometimes enormous icebergs calve from the shelves and float into the Southern Ocean.

Circulation and Major Currents. Circulation in the Southern Ocean is dominated by the Antarctic Circumpolar Current (ACC or West Wind Drift), a 6,500 ft (2,000 m) thick layer of seawater that moves eastward around Antarctica, driven by the strong and constant Prevailing Westerly Winds of the Southern Hemisphere. In terms of the volume of water transported, this is largest ocean current on the planet. The ACC is strong enough to separate much of the cold

Southern Ocean water from warmer water in neighboring oceans and thereby prevent warming of Antarctica. Along its northern margin at roughly 55°S is the Antarctic Convergence, where cold water, moving equatorward, sinks beneath the relatively warm subantarctic waters of the Atlantic, Indian, and Pacific Oceans. Temperature and water chemistry change abruptly at this interface and act as a barrier to many marine organisms. It is also a region of upwelling, where nutrients rise to the surface. The Antarctic Convergence is only 20–30 mi (20–50 km) wide but, with the ACC, serves to make the Southern Ocean a distinct body of water even though it is not hemmed in by landmasses as are other oceans.

A narrow coastal current, the East Wind Drift, moves counter to the Antarctic Circumpolar Current just off the Antarctic coast. It is driven by the polar easterly winds blowing from the South Pole region.

Antarctic Bottom Water is the densest water mass in the world and the coldest bottom water. It develops near the coast of Antarctica. Dense water accumulates over the continental shelf and then slides down the continental slope and then northward along the floors of all adjacent oceans. Dense surface water forms in summer as a result of the low temperatures caused by melting ice. In winter, the freezing of sea ice leaves highly saline and hence dense water on the surface. Strong winds blowing off the Antarctic Plateau further aggravate the situation, as they can blow sea-ice away and leave pools of open water (polynyas), which then immediately refreeze only to have the ice pushed off again. As the process is repeated, the water becomes more saline and denser and it too sinks to the bottom. At the surface the cold water is oxygenated, and the Antarctic Bottom Water transports oxygen to the deep sea abyss, which otherwise would be without this element vital to life. Together with the North Atlantic Deep Water Current, Antarctic Bottom Water drives the global conveyor belt of oceanic circulation, which moves seawater around the world at great depth; it rises to the surface again at upwelling zones off the west coasts of continents. Antarctic Bottom Water reaches into the Northern Hemisphere and is a major player in the global climate system.

Biota. Life thrives in and under the ice and in the waters of the Southern Ocean. Photosynthesis can occur within the top 6.5 ft (2 m) of ice. Bacteria and diatoms, grazed upon by protozoa, turbellarians (flatworms), and copepods, may live trapped between ice crystals or in brine channels within the ice. They impart a brown color to most sea-ice; only the fresh snow on the surface is white. Feeding on these organisms along the edge of the pack ice are other copepods, amphipods, krill, and Antarctic icefish or notothenioids, a nearly endemic suborder of fish. The icefish live in these cold, oxygen rich waters without red cells or hemoglobin, oxygen dissolving freely in their blood. Body fluids contain glycoproteins that act as antifreeze.

Under the ice along the coast at depths greater than 45 ft (15 m) are several habitats supporting a surprising variety of life-forms. (The first 45 ft [15 m] are scoured clean by ice each winter.) Coastal zonation is evident off areas free of ice in summer. In the zone reached only by high tides, black lichens grow. The tidal zone has a felt of annual diatoms and filamentous green algae. Lower down annual red and green algae encrust the rocks. Limpets are the dominant grazers on rocky coasts, but are joined by small bivalves, amphipods, a chiton, and turbellarians. On hard surfaces under fast ice macroalgae and sessile suspension-feeders can be found. Below 80 ft (25 m) large Antarctic kelps grow. At these depths are also sea anemones, soft corals, tunicates and hydroids. Farther down, between 150 and 600 ft (45–180 m), is the sponge zone, where sponges assume various shapes more common to tropical hard corals.

In the seasonally open waters off Antarctica, krill form the base of the food chain. About 85 species of these shrimp-like creatures range in length from 0.4 to 5.5 in (1–14 cm). There are no large fish, skates, rays or sharks, but seabirds, penguins, and marine mammals are abundant. Six penguin species from three genera feed on krill in Southern Ocean waters: Adélie, Chinstrap, Gentoo, Macaroni, King and Emperor penguins. The misnamed crab-eating seal filters krill from the sea, using its serrated teeth as sieves much in the manner of feeding baleen whales. Among other Antarctic pinnipeds is the Weddell Seal, the mammal with the southernmost range on Earth. It can found as far south as 80°S feeding on icefish and Antarctic cod. The leopard seal is an ambush hunter of young seals and penguins. So many crab-eating seals bear scars from their attacks that they were never a target of the fur seal trade. The largest seal in the world, the southern elephant seal, also inhabits this region. Baleen whales consuming krill and small fish include the Minke, southern humpback, and blue whales. Toothed whales include the orca, which takes both seals and penguins.

Protected Areas. In 2009, a high-seas Marine Protected Area (MPA) was established near the Antarctic Peninsula south of the South Orkney Islands by the Commission for the Conservation of Antarctic Marine Living Resources (CCAMLR). At that time a network of 11 other MPAs in critical areas of the Southern Ocean were recommended by 2012, but to date this has not been realized.

Environmental Issues. Commercial fisheries for Antarctic cod, Antarctic toothfish, and krill occur in these waters. Overfishing is affecting seabirds and marine mammals as their food supply is diminished. Another major threat to life in the Southern Ocean is climate change. Retreating glaciers threaten penguin nesting areas and feeding grounds.

See also Antarctica; Ross Sea

Further Reading
Anderson, Genny. 2003. "Marine Mammals in Antarctica." Marine Science, MarineBio. http://www.marinebio .net/marinescience/04benthon/AAmammals.htm
Anderson, Genny. 2004. "Penguins in Antarctica." Marine Science. http://www.marinebio.net/marinescience /04benthon/AApenguins.htm
Bostock, Helen and Emmanuelle Sultan. 2013. "The Formation of Antarctic Bottom Water." Coasts and Oceans Science Centre, NIWA. http://www.niwa.co.nz/blog /the-formation-of-the-antarctic-bottom-water
"Southern Ocean." 2013. *The World Factbook*. Central Intelligence Agency. https://www.cia.gov/library/pub lications/the-world-factbook/geos/oo.html
Woodward, Susan L. 2009. *Marine Biomes*. Greenwood Guides to Biomes of the World. Westport, CT: Greenwood Press.

Spiny Forest

Madagascar

Geographic Overview. The spiny forest of Madagascar is an arid region of globally distinctive and unique plants that evolved similarly to several types of cacti and succulents in the Americas but are woody rather than succulent. Dominated by the Didiereaceae family, 95 percent of the plant species are endemic to the region. The spiny forest also harbors a unique assemblage of animals, including lemurs, chameleons, and geckos.

Geographic Coordinates. 21°26'S–25°37'S; 43°13'E–46°44'E

Description. The spiny forest of Madagascar covers approximately 17,100 mi² (44,000 km²) in the southwestern corner of the island, from the Mongoky River on the west coast south and east past Cap Sainte Marie to the western slopes of the Anosyennes Mountain chain and the Mandrare River west of Tolanaro. Topography of the region is relatively flat, increasing from sea level to 180–650 ft (55–200 m) inland. In the east and south, the region is drained by the Mandrara, Manambovo, and Linta Rivers, all flowing south. The Onilahy and Fiherenana Rivers flow west, and the Mangoky River flows northwest. Substrate is generally of two types, Tertiary limestone on the Mahafaly Plateau and unconsolidated red sands in the south-central and southeast regions. The sandy soils are dominated by tall dense, dry forest with *Didieria madagascarensis*, while the limestone plateau is characterized by dwarf species.

Southwestern Madagascar is in the rain shadow of the island's mountainous spine and the trade winds that hit the east coast. Although as much as 18 in (450 mm) of annual rainfall falls between October and April, it is sporadic and localized. Little moisture is retained by the porous limestone and sandy soils. Clear skies and intense solar radiation can cause surface temperatures to reach 158°F (70°C). Although driest in terms of rainfall, less than 14 in (350 mm) with a 9- to 11-month dry season, the littoral strip has relative humidity of 60 percent, resulting in dew and fog. Maximum air temperatures are over 100°F (38°C), while minima average 60–70°F (15–21°C).

Geologic History. As Madagascar was moving north after the breakup of Gondwana, it passed beneath the subtropical high-pressure cell. The whole of the island was subjected to desert conditions, which caused extinction of all plants which were not drought tolerant. As the majority of the island continued north into the wet tropical zone, new rainforest flora developed, leaving the southwestern end of the island as a relict community of plants adapted to arid conditions.

Biota. Knowledge of the biota in the spiny forest is limited. The spiny forest has a high rate of endemism, 50 percent of the genera and 95 percent of the species are unique. This desert area coincides with the range of the endemic family Didiereaceae and many Euphorbia species. The region also has several small centers of local endemism.

Although variations exist among the several different habitats and communities, the basic vegetation is consistent—a sparse tree layer, a dense shrubby thicket, and a sparse ground layer. The area is dominated by a deciduous thorn forest, dense thickets of succulents and thorn bushes as tall as 10–20 ft (3–6 m), with emergent tree succulents, primarily in the Didiereaceae or Euphorbiaceae families, which reach 33–50 ft (10–15 m) tall. Undergrowth consists of small stature leaf succulent euphorbias, such as *Euphorbia cylindrifolia* and *Euphorbia francoisii*, as well as plants in several other families, including begonia, mallow, Pedaliaceae, and Caesalpiniaceae. Groundcover is sparse, with few annuals, grasses, or bulbs. *Alluadia procera* and *Alluadia ascendens* dominate in the east. In the west and north, emergent *Alluadia* species are replaced by *Delonix madagascariensis*, dwarf baobabs (*Adansonia fony*), the large *Pachypodium geayi*, and *Delonix* species.

Drought adaptations include extensive root systems with enlarged tubers, thickened trunks (pachycauly), succulent or small leaves, green stems and bark, leaf-like shoots, thorns, and waxy or hairy surfaces. *Alluadia, Pachypodium, Mimosa,* and *Didieria* species are especially spiny. Several Euphorbia species have no leaves and depend on green stems for photosynthesis. Other types of succulents include bottle trees, such as baobab (*Adansonia* spp.), *Moringa drouhard, Commiphera spp.*, and *Pachypodium lamerei*, which have swollen stems or trunks as wide as 6 ft (1.8 m) in diameter. Plants in several other genera have a smaller, but still enlarged, base called a caudex. Major genera of leaf succulents are *Kalanchoe* and *Aloe*, both of which may be tree-like. The most dominant and diverse families are Burseraceae, Didieriaceae, Euphorbiaceae, Anacardiaceae, and Fabaceae.

The region has no large animals. Six lemur species—red-tailed sportive (*Lepilemur ruficaudatus*), ring-tailed (*Lemur catta*), fork-marked (*Phaner furcifer*), fat-tailed dwarf (*Cheirogaleus medius*), gray mouse (*Microcebus murinus*), and Verreaux's sifaka (*Propithecus verreauxi*)—are found only in the spiny thicket and adjacent succulent woodlands. Locally endemic animals include several geckos, Grandidier's mongoose (*Galidictis grandidieri*), white-footed sportive lemur (*Lepilemur leucopus*), grey-brown mouse lemur (*Microcebus griseorufus*). Other significant animals include the large-eared tenrec (*Geogale aurita*) and the lesser hedgehog tenrec (*Echinops telfairi*). Verreaux's Coua (*Coua verreauxi*), Running Coua (*Coua cursor*), Red-shouldered Vanga (*Calicalicus rufocarpalis*), and Lafresnaye's Vanga (*Xenopirostris xenopirostris*) are endemic birds. Reptiles endemic to the spiny forest include chameleons (*Furcifer belalandaensis* and *Furcifer antimena*), spider tortoise (*Pyxis arachnoides*), and radiated tortoise (*Geochelone radiata*). The boa (*Acrantophis dumerilii*) is present.

Protected Areas. Approximately 3 percent of the remaining spiny forest is under some form of protection, in several small reserves such as Tsimanampetsotsa National Park and Ramsar site, Beza-Mahafaly Special Reserve, Cap St. Marie Special Reserve, and Berenty Private Reserve.

Environmental Issues. Habitat destruction is the major threat to the spiny forest. Uncontrolled fires, cutting of wood for charcoal and construction, and clearing for agriculture or grazing continues to be a problem. Invasive prickly pear, agave plantations, and illegal collection of plants for the nursery trade and animals for the pet trade threaten local ecosystems and populations. Rare species or those with restricted ranges are especially vulnerable.

See also Madagascar

Further Reading

Crowley, Helen. 2013. *Madagascar Spiny Thickets*. World Wildlife Fund. http://worldwildlife.org/ecoregions/at1311

Fenn, M. D. 2009. "The Spiny Forest Ecoregion." In *The Natural History of Madagascar*, edited by Steven M. Goodman and Jonathan P. Benstead, 1525–1530. Chicago: University of Chicago Press.

Strait of Gibraltar

Atlantic Ocean/Mediterranean Sea

Geographic Overview. The Strait of Gibraltar has been an important strategic and economic site since ancient times and remains vitally important to southern Europe, northern Africa, and western Asia as a shipping route. The Pillars of Hercules, two large rock outcrops, at the eastern end of the strait were considered the western limit of the Classical World. The Gibraltar peninsula, including the Rock of Gibraltar, the southernmost tip of Europe, has been controlled by the British since 1713.

Geographic Coordinates. 35°47'N–36°11'N, 05°20'W–06°00'W

Description. The Strait of Gibraltar, 36 mi (58 km) long and lying between southern Spain and northwestern Africa, is the only marine connection between the Bay of Gibraltar in the Atlantic Ocean and the Alboran Sea in the Mediterranean Sea. At its narrowest, between Point Marroqui in Spain and Point Cires in Morocco, it is 8 mi (13 km) wide. On the western end, between Cape Trafalgar in Spain and Cape Spartel in Morocco, it is 27 mi (43 km) wide. The eastern end measures 14 mi (23 km) between the Pillars of Hercules. The Rock of Gibraltar is the northern pillar, but the southern one is disputed, either Mount Harbo near Ceuta, a Spanish enclave in Africa, or Jebel Moussa in Morocco. The Rock of Gibraltar, 1,396 ft (426 m) high, is part of the Baetic Cordillera and Apulian plate, a sliver of Africa. Depth of the strait is variable, approximately 980–3,000 ft (300–900 m), but with an average of 1,200 ft (365 m).

The strait is floored by continental crust of sedimentary rocks or sediments, including limestone, sands, and breccias. The large-scale shape of the strait is rectilinear, a flat bottom between steep sides, with two shallow sills, or impediments, on the Atlantic side of the strait. The Camarinal Sill is no deeper than 932 ft (284 m). Depth of the Spartel sill is approximately 1,150 ft (350 m). The rectangular shape of the channel extends west past the Spartel Sill into the Atlantic Ocean.

Tarifa Narrows is a deep channel in the middle of the eastern part of the strait, its elevation sloping east-northeast, from 2,460 ft (750 m) bsl in the west down to 3,150 ft (960 m) near Gibraltar and Cueta. This deep submarine canyon is divided into a northern and southern zone by a central crest only 1,475–2,460 ft (450–750 m) deep. The wider western strait is divided into two channels by the Majuan Ridge (Spartel Bank), with a summit only 165 ft (50 m) deep. The deeper southern channel, 2,135 ft (650 m), is a western continuation of Tarifa Narrows. The northern channel is only 985 ft (300 m) deep. The central section of the strait is the Camarinal Sill, a mosaic of trenches, 755–2,065 ft (230–630 m) deep, and hills, 265–885 ft (80–240 m) bsl.

Warm surface water flows into the Mediterranean from the Atlantic Ocean. Colder, saltier, and denser water flows back to the Atlantic at a depth below 400 ft (120 m).

Geologic History. In the late Tertiary (5.5 mya), the Mediterranean was a closed sea with little to no water exchange with the Atlantic. During a period called the Messinian Salinity Crisis, evaporation lowered the water level to almost nothing, which resulted in a deep accumulation of salt and gypsum in the Mediterranean basin until connection was reestablished.

The strait is not the plate boundary between Africa and Europe. Those faults cut both north and south of the strait, but not through the strait. A weakness in the rocks between the Baetic Mountains in Spain and the Rifian Mountains in Morocco became a saddle, which funneled drainage to its center, the low point on the rim between the Atlantic Ocean and the Mediterranean. Because rivers flowing into the lowered Mediterranean had a base level of 8,850 ft (2,700 m) lower than the Atlantic, they carved deep canyons, such as Tarifa Narrows, which are now submerged. The origin of the modern Strait of Gibraltar is a massive example of stream, or ocean, piracy. At the close of the Messinian Salinity Crisis, rapid, eastward flowing streams cut headward into the isthmus between Spain and Africa. Subsequently, eustatic sea level rise caused the ocean to overflow the isthmus and flow steeply down to the Mediterranean floor. The deep Tarifa channel widened with the collapse of its banks, forming the U-shaped canyon. Slumps or landslides from the north in the western part of the strait partially filled the channel closer to the Atlantic, forming both the Camarinal and

Spartel sills. The slumps and landslides help to explain the jumbled physiography of the strait floor. Geologic drilling related to a proposed tunnel revealed that the flood channel was 125 mi (200 km) long, 3.7–6.8 mi (–6–11 km) wide, and 985–2,135 ft (300–650 m) deep. The rate of flow must have been cataclysmic, estimated at more than 1 billion ft^3/sec (100 million m^3/s), as fast as 62 mph (100 kmph). Current estimates of the time required to refill the Mediterranean range from a few months to two years.

Protected Areas. El Estrecho National Park covers approximately 47,000 ac (19,000 ha) on the Spanish side of the strait. The upper area of the Rock of Gibralter is a nature reserve, home to approximately 250 Barbary macaque monkeys. The limestone contains more than 100 caves, including St. Michaels's.

Environmental Issues. Engineers have plans to construct a tunnel beneath the strait, 25 mi (40 km) of rail to move people and goods. Challenges include the depth of the sea, earthquakes, strong currents, and various rock layers.

See also Mediterranean Sea

Further Reading

Blanc, Paul-Louis. 2002. "The Opening of the Plio-Quaternary Gibraltar Strait: Assessing the Size of a Cataclysm." *Geodinamica Acta* 15: 303–317. www.sciencedirect.com/science/article/pii/S0985311102010951

Grossman, Lisa. 2009. *Strait of Gibraltar & Mediterranean Sea Saved by Monumental Flood.* http://tricorder.at?p=2377

Strait of Magellan, Beagle Channel, and Drake Passage

Argentina and Chile

Geographic Overview. The three treacherous passages around and through the southern tip of South America—the Strait of Magellan, Beagle Channel, and the Drake Passage—played important roles in voyages of discovery and trade in the days of sailing ships.

Geographic Coordinates. Strait of Magellan: 53°29'S, 70°47'W. Beagle Channel: 54°53'S, 68°08'W. Drake Passage: 58°35'S, 62°55'W

The Beagle Channel follows the south shore of Isla Grande de Tierra del Fuego and provides relatively sheltered passage through the tip of South America. (Steve Allen/Dreamstime.com)

Descriptions. The Strait of Magellan is a narrow channel, 2–20 mi (3–32 km) wide, between the southern end of the South American mainland and Tierra del Fuego. This relatively sheltered 350-mile (560-km) passage from the Atlantic Ocean to the Pacific Ocean takes a twisting path full of dead end bays and fjords. The eastern entrance is marked by a wide bay located between Cape Virgenes in Argentina, and Punta Catalina in Chile. The strait swings to the southeast through two narrows and then curves to the northwest around Cape Froward at the southern end of the Brunswick Peninsula. It reaches the Pacific Ocean north of Desolation Island, its direction controlled by the transform Magellanes–Fagnano fault at the boundary of the South American and Scotia plates. The strait is named for the Portuguese explorer, Ferdinand Magellan, whose fleet was the first European expedition to circumnavigate the globe. Magellan's ships first entered the strait on October 21, 1520, and reached the Pacific on November 28 after weeks of seeking the exit. Leaving behind the cold, foggy region of the strait and coming into the calm, blue ocean waters to its west, a grateful Magellan named the new ocean "La Mar Pacifico." Despite its inhospitable climate and limited room to maneuver a sailing vessel, mariners in small sailing ships preferred the Strait of Magellan to sailing around Cape Horn; Puntas Arenas, Chile, developed as the main port city. Only the Yankee clippers and New England whalers of the 19th century used the faster, stormier route through the Drake Passage (see later discussion). Both routes became obsolete with the advent of steamships and the opening of the Panama Canal in 1914.

Another narrow, more or less sheltered passage through the southern tip of South America is the Beagle Channel along the southern shore of Isla Grande de Tierra del Fuego. The eastern section of this 150-mile (240 km) long channel forms the boundary between Chile and Argentina; the western part lies entirely in Chile. Bifurcating around Gordon Island, the channel has two outlets to the Pacific. At its narrowest point, the Beagle Channel is 3 mi (5 km) wide. The largest settlement on the strait is Ushuaia in Argentine Tierra del Fuego, one of the southernmost towns in the world. The channel is named for the HMS *Beagle*, the British ship which, under Captain Robert Fitzroy, conducted the first hydrographic survey of southern South America, from 1826 to 1830. On its second expedition to the area, beginning in 1831, the ship carried the famous naturalist Charles Darwin.

Drake Passage is the open water between 56° and 62°S that separates South America from the South Shetland Islands and Antarctica. Through it flows the Antarctic Circumpolar Current, which circles the globe unhindered except for this constriction, which funnels wind and ocean currents in such a way as to increase their velocity and create the roughest seas in the world. At its minimum width, between Cape Horn and Livingston Island, the Drake Passage is 500 mi (800 km) across; this is the shortest distance between Antarctica and the rest of Earth's landmasses. Lying in the latitudes known as the Furious Fifties and Screaming Sixties, in days of sailing ships, the passage was infamous for its violent and sudden gales. Still, it was preferred by captains of larger clipper ships to the passage through the Strait of Magellan or Beagle Channel, both home to williwaws, sudden strong katabatic winds that stream down from the east–west trending Fuegian Andes that can easily dash ships onto the rocks in narrow waterways. "Rounding the Horn" was a treacherous ordeal that became legendary. The waterway was named for the British adventurer Sir Francis Drake, who discovered Cape Horn in 1578, but never actually crossed through the passage bearing his name.

See also Cape Horn (Cabo de Hornos); Tierra del Fuego

Further Reading

Murphy, Dallas. 2004. *Rounding the Horn, Being the Story of Williwaws and Windjammers, Drake, Darwin, Murdered Missionaries and Naked Natives—A Deck's Eye View of Cape Horn*. New York: Basic Books.

The Sudd

South Sudan

Geographic Overview. The Sudd is one of Africa's and the world's largest wetlands. It lies on the broad floodplain and inland delta where the Bahr al Ghazal joins the White Nile or Bahr al Jabal in South Sudan. The area has been inaccessible, in part due to prolonged civil wars, so information on this maze of meandering channels, marshes, and floating mats of vegetation (in Arabic, "sudd") is limited. Massive wildlife migrations rivaling those of the better known Serengeti take place annually across the Sudd—although different animals are involved.

Geographic Coordinates. Approximately 05°30'N–09°00'N, 31°00'E

Description. The Sudd is a vast wetland developed on the flat inland delta of the White Nile (Bahr al Jabal or river of the mountains) at an elevation of 1,250–1,475 ft (380–450 m) asl. The region extends some 310 mi (500 km) from north to south and a maximum 155 mi (250 km) from east to west on the floodplains of the Nile and a large tributary from the west, the Bahr el Ghazal (river of giraffes). Permanent open water, marsh, and floating mats of papyrus cover some 3,860 mi^2 (10,000 km^2), but during the flood season this expands to more than 35,520 mi^2 (92,000 km^2) as river water spills over the broad floodplain, which is up to 16 mi (25 km) wide on either side of the main channels. The wetland is fed by both local rains and the annual flood of the Nile. The outflow from Lake Victoria accounts for about 80 percent of the water submerging the floodplain, while water from Lakes Kioga and Albert make up the rest. Local rainfall, low in this part of the semiarid Sahel, fills the swamp before the channels overtop their banks. It takes about 4 months for the Nile flood to filter through the Sudd, which serves as a temporary storage area for water heading to Egypt. Under high evaporation rates, more than half of the Nile's discharge is lost in the Sudd. Little percolates to depth, since the wetland is underlain by an impermeable layer of black, clay-rich soil (vertisol).

The Sudd is under a seasonal precipitation regime, with rains occurring from April to September. It is wetter in the south, where average annual rainfall is 31 in (800 mm). In the north, precipitation decreases to 24 in (600 mm) a year. During the warmest months temperatures rise to 86°–91°F (30°–33 C); cool season high temperatures fall to 64°F (18°C).

Vegetation reflects the seasonal rhythms of rain and flood. The general pattern is as follows: fringing the center of a channel of flowing water or lake is a zone of submerged aquatic plants, beyond which are floating mats of papyrus backed by reeds and cattails. The first zone with plants rooted in the land consists of seasonally river-flooded marshes of wild rice and other aquatic grasses. Farther inland on the floodplain are seasonally rain-flooded grasslands of giant thatching grass. The outer edge of the floodplain will be marked by woodlands of thorny red acacia, *Balanites aegypticaca*, and other drought resistant trees. Enormous herds of antelope follow the seasonal flux of available forage in a migration covering more than 900 mi (1,500 km).

Geologic History. During the Tertiary, a group of closed basins in separate rift valleys existed where the Sudd is located today. The basins gradually filled with sediments. During a rainy period 120,000 years ago, the basins overflowed and became interconnected. Outflow from Lake Victoria did not occur until at least 12,500 years ago. At that time, the White Nile (and thus the Sudd) had enough flow to reach the Nile main stem.

Biota. The Sudd is home to huge numbers of migratory antelopes. Aerial surveys in 2007 revealed 800,000 white-eared kob (*Kobus kob*), 160,000 tiang (*Damaliscus lunatus tiang*)—a subspecies of topi, and 250,000 Mongalla gazelle (*Gazella thomsonii albontata*)—a subspecies of Thomson's gazelle. Also counted were 4,000 endemic Nile lechwe (*Kobus megaceros*). Hippopotami and crocodiles swim in shallow water and shelter under the floating papyrus mats. In all, some 100 mammal species inhabit the Sudd, as do more than 400 resident and migratory avian species. Among the birds are Africa's largest population of Shoebill, a large heron-like bird with a bulbous beak, the Black-crowned Crane, and the endangered White Pelican, which migrates from eastern Europe and Asia for the winter.

Protected Areas. The Sudd was declared a Ramsar Wetland of International Importance in 2006. Areas legally set aside as protected areas were neglected and probably degraded during the civil war that lasted until 2005. Access is still difficult, so their status is largely unknown. On paper, at least, are Shambe National Park and Fanyikang and Zeraf game preserves. Boma National Park to the east is part of the migration route focused on the Sudd, as is the new (2011) Bandigalo National Park to the south.

Environmental Issues. The greatest threat to the Sudd is completion of the Jonglei Canal, a diversion canal planned since 1946 west of the wetlands to reduce evaporative loss and hasten the delivery of water downstream for irrigation projects. If the canal is finished, the Sudd might shrink, placing its biodiverse habitats in jeopardy. Regional climate, water quality, and groundwater recharge could also be affected; but actual impacts are unknown and may not be severe. Construction begun in 1978 was halted by civil war in 1984.

Civil war has plagued the region twice in recent decades, from 1955 to 1972 and again from 1983 to 2005. Conservation areas were neglected and it was feared that large mammals may have been hunted for meat (or tusks) to the point where the great herds were decimated. However, aerial surveys in 2007 revealed the mass migrations were still occurring, although numbers of elephants were down and buffalo were absent. A group of elephants was discovered on an island deep in the Sudd; hope remains that other groups also survived in isolated parts of the wetlands.

The most recent civil war introduced automatic weapons and motor vehicles to the region, so enforcement of antipoaching and antihunting policies may be more difficult now.

See also Nile River

Further Reading

"Massive Migration Revealed." 2007. Wildlife Conservation Society. http://www.wcs.org/news-and-features-main/massive-migration-revealed.aspx

Seymour, Colleen. n.d. "Saharan Flooded Grasslands." Terrestrial Ecoregions, World Wildlife Fund. http://world wildlife.org/ecoregions/at0905

Sundarbans

Bangladesh and India

Geographic Overview. The mangrove forest of the Sundarbans, which means "beautiful forests," is part of the world's largest delta, formed by the Ganges, Brahmaputra, and Meghna Rivers in Bangladesh and India. The Sundarbans are the largest contiguous intertidal mangrove forest in the world, with a high biodiversity of mangrove flora and fauna, including globally endangered species. The forest provides nursery grounds for fish and invertebrates, including commercially important tiger prawns, and forms a "wall," which blunts the intensity of cyclones and provides some protection to low-lying Bangladesh and northeastern India.

Geographic Coordinates. 21°30'N–22°50'N, 88°02'E–22°25'E

Description. The Sundarbans, in southwestern Bangladesh and northeastern India at the edge of the Bay of Bengal, is a complex cluster of islands, tidal waterways, mudflats, and salt-tolerant mangrove forests. They extend approximately 185 mi (300 km) between the two major outlets of the Ganges–Brahmaputra river delta, from the Hooghly River on the west to the Meghna River in the east, and reach at least 18 mi (30 km) inland. The forested area is bounded in the east by the Baleswar (Haringhata) River. This large block of mangrove forest, where land and water meet, is distinct from the rest of the delta due to the twice-daily incursion of saltwater tides. During high tide, the mangrove forests are flooded. Water level drops 6–7 ft (2 m) at low tide. The area has no roads or trails; all transportation is by boat during high tide or by foot during low tide. Although there are no permanent villages, the Sundarbans provide a livelihood for many people. Although the area is known for man-eating tigers; honey-collecting is an important economic activity. Honey collectors believe tigers won't strike if they see a human's face, so they wear masks on the backs of their heads.

The climate is hot and humid. Winter temperatures vary from 50 to 93° F (10–34° C). Summer highs reach 108°F (42°C). June through September monsoons bring a mean annual rainfall of 65–70 in (1,650–1,780 mm).

Biota. The Sundarbans, which support a wide diversity of terrestrial, aquatic, and marine habitats, are critical to globally endangered species, such as tigers, dolphins, and crocodiles. The forest is dominated by sundari trees (*Heritiera fomes*) (a type of mangrove), Gewa trees (*Excoercaria agallocha*), and patches of nypa palm (*Nypa fruticans*), and other species of mangrove, according to salt tolerance. The total flora includes 334 plant species in 245 genera.

The region is home to a diverse fauna, approximately 49 mammal species, 59 reptile species, 8 amphibian species, 315 bird species, and many fish and shellfish. Mammals include chital or spotted deer (*Axis axis*), wild boar (*Sus scrofa*), otter, and three species of wild cats. The Indian Sundarbans house the world's last population of Bengal tigers (*Panthera tigris*) adapted to saline water in mangrove swamps. Barking deer are limited to Holiday Island. Rhesus monkeys (*Macaca mulatla*) and jackals (*Canis aureus*) may be seen. Common reptiles include various lizards, saltwater crocodile (*Crocodylus porosus*), king cobra (*Ophiophagus hannah*), rock python (*Python molurus*), and water monitor (*Varanus salvator*).

Avian life includes jungle fowl, snipe, pochards, redshanks, storks, kingfishers, egrets, herons, coots, yellowlegs, sandpipers, migratory Siberian ducks, fish eagles, and many colorful tropical birds. Masked Finfoot (*Heliopais personatus*), Mangrove Pitta (*Pitta megarhyncha*), and Mangrove Whistler (*Pachycephala cinerea*) are rare. Aquatic life includes the Ganges River dolphin (*Platanista gangetica*), the Irrawaddy dolphin (*Orcaella brevirostris*), the finless porpoise (*Neophocaena asiaeorientalis*), Ridley sea turtle (*Lepidochelys olivacea*), crabs, and many fish species. The endangered river terrapin (*Batagur baska*) is found on Mechua Beach. Giant honeybees (*Apis dorsata*) are common, their honey collected by residents.

Environmental Issues. The region is densely populated and the mangroves are heavily used for timber, pulpwood, and fuel. The ecosystem is threatened by sewage, industrial pollution, deforestation, and expanding agriculture. In spite of the Environmental Conservation Act of 2010, which prohibits industries within 6 mi (10 km) of the mangrove forest, Indian government agencies are allowing industrial development in the buffer zone around the Sundarbans. The potential for oil spills from ships and release of nonbiodegradable waste threatens the mangrove ecosystem.

Protected Areas. The entire Sundarbans region was protected as a reserved forest by the Indian Forest Act of 1878. Sundarbans World Heritage Site includes parts of both India and Bangladesh. Sundarbans National Park in India, covering 1,650 mi^2 (4,264 km^2), is the largest tiger reserve and national park in that country. The Sundarbans Reserve Forest (UNESCO), straddling the India–Bangladesh border and covering 3,860 mi^2 (10,000 km^2), has three wildlife sanctuaries, which are core breeding areas for endangered species.

See also Brahmaputra (Tsangpo) River; Ganges River

Further Reading

Roy, Pinaki. 2013. "Sundarbans Threatened." *The Daily Star*, London. www.thedailystar.net/beta2/news/sundarbans-threatened/

World Heritage Centre. 2013. *The Sundarbans*. UNESCO. http://whc.unesco.org/en/list/798

World Heritage Centre. 2013. *Sundarbans National Park*. UNESCO. http://whc.unesco.org/en/list/452

Surtsey

Atlantic Ocean

Geographic Overview. Surtsey is the youngest and outermost of the Westman Islands (Vestmannaeyjar), a chain of 14 islands and rocks (skerries) that lies off the southern coast of Iceland. A volcanic island, it suddenly appeared above the waves on November 14, 1963, and remained active until 1967. Iceland immediately protected the new island and only permitted scientists to visit it. Surtsey became a natural laboratory for the study of volcanic islands and their colonization by plants and animals. It is named for the fire giant Surtur the Black, a figure in Nordic mythology.

Geographic Coordinates. 63°18'N, 20°36'W

Description. Surtsey is a small, teardrop-shaped island on the Mid-Atlantic Ridge 20 mi (32 km) southwest of mainland Iceland. When eruptions ended in 1967, it had reached its maximum size of 1.0 mi^2 (2.7 km^2); at its highest point it stood 574 ft (175 m) asl. Since that time it has been eroded by wave action, losing about 7.5 ac (3 ha) per year. By 2008, it had been reduced to almost half its original size and had an area of 0.54 mi^2 (1.4 km^2). Subsidence due to the settling and compaction of loose tephra, the compaction of sediments on the ocean floor, and downwarping of the lithosphere under the weight of the island has reduced the height of the island. The high point currently stands 505 ft (154 m) asl. It is estimated that the island will disappear entirely by the end of this century.

Surtsey has two craters, Surtungar and Surtur, aligned west to east, respectively. The southern rims of both have been destroyed. Most of the islands rocks consist of loose or consolidated tephra, primarily brown volcanic glass; about 30 percent of the island is formed of black lava. In the south, both the rough a'a and ropy pahoehoe lava can be found. Where lava flows cap loose tephra, as in the south and east, the easily eroded loose tephra is protected. Along the north coast, tephra consolidated into palagonite tuff and became more resistant to erosion; wave action there has created cliffs nearly 400 ft (120 m) high. Lower sea cliffs edge the southwestern coastline, where the lava is fractured and erodes more easily. Waves and currents have transported erosional debris northward and created a sand and boulder spit on the northeast side of the island.

Surtsey has a subpolar maritime climate characterized by wind and rain. Wind, sea, and birds transported seeds and spores to the islands soon after its formation. Fungi, mosses, lichens, grasses, forbs, and willows have become established. Seabirds began to breed on Surtsey in 1970 and currently number 13 species. Pioneering invertebrates, including insects and earthworms, became established when the gull populations expanded in the early 1980s. A number of higher plants also became established in the gull

Surtsey Island, off the south coast of Iceland, was created by undersea volcanic eruptions in 1963. Strong wind and wave action are expected to reduce it to sea level or below in the next 100 years. (Arctic-Images/Corbis)

colonies after 1986. The black lava sands and pumices in the colonies supported patches of lush grass and forbs.

Geologic History. Construction of Surtsey began with an eruption 426 ft (130 m) bsl along the Vestmannaeyjar submarine fissure, part of the Mid-Atlantic Ridge. Within 24 hours, on November 14, 1963, an island formed. Initially tephra spewed forth in explosive eruptions, but in 1964 eruptions became less explosive and lava flows and lava fountains covered the earlier loose material. Eruptions ceased on June 5, 1967. Most volcanoes of this type are active only once, and Surtsey is now considered extinct. In the Westman Islands, most other islands have quickly eroded and disappeared. They survive only as submarine hills. The consolidation of the tephra on Surtsey to form a resistant rock known as palaganite and the lava cap give the island a longer projected lifespan, but it is expected to be gone in 100 years.

Biota. Scientists have kept a close record of the arrival and establishment (colonization) of Surtsey's biota. First to arrive were diatoms (algae), found on a sandy beach in 1964. Seeds and other plant parts washed ashore during the first spring after the initial eruption. The first higher plant to become established was sea rocket (*Cakile arctica*); it was followed by sea sandwort (*Hokena peploides*), sea lyme grass (*Leymus arenarius*), and oyster plant (*Mertensia maritima*). All likely came as seeds from neighboring Heimay Island, the largest of the Westman Islands. Floating clumps of grass and root debris brought living plants and invertebrates from nearby islands. By summer seeds and fruits with various adaptations for wind dispersal began to arrive from Iceland. Some early arrivals, such as cottongrass and common groundsel, never became established; but dwarf willow, tea-leaved willow and woolly willow, as well as common dandelion and others, did. The spores of fungi, ferns, horsetails, and lichens were also transported to Surtsey on the wind, some from Iceland and others from Europe.

Birds carried seeds in their feathers and on their feet as well as in their digestive tracts. Early colonizers favored the nitrogen-rich areas where birds rested and left their droppings. As gull colonies became densely populated after 1986, a number of forbs and grasses appeared, including crowberry, meadow buttercup, smooth meadowgrass, Bering's tufted hairgrass, and northern dock. By the summer of 2004, scientists had collected 60 species of vascular plant. Surtsey validated the theoretical relationship between area and species: Heimay, seven times larger than Surtsey has 150 species, while the much smaller islands of Geirtaglasker and Sulnasker have fewer than 10 each. However, Surtsey, as it erodes away, can be expected to resemble its small neighbors more and more. Among lower plants, 71 lichens, and 75 mosses and liverworts have successfully colonized as have 24 fungi.

The first invertebrates were reported in 1967, arriving in the same ways seeds and living plants did. Only a few species were successful colonizers. A diverse soil fauna dominated by springtails and mites developed in gull colonies. About 150 species are now established, mostly flying insects. A rare wingless beetle (*Ceutorrhyncus insularis*), two land snails, a slug, and 10 tiny sheet-weaver spider species are among other inhabitants.

Black Guillemots and Northern Fulmars began breeding on Surtsey in 1970. The Lesser Black-backed Gull arrived in 1981, to be joined later by Greater Black-backed and Herring gulls. The increasing density of gull breeding colonies changed the island ecosystem by enriching soils with nitrogen derived from guano. Today the most common seabird is the Atlantic Puffin.

The only mammals on the island are common and gray seals. They have been breeding on Surtsey since 1983.

Protected Areas. The entire island is protected by Iceland. Since its appearance in 1963, access has been prohibited to anyone other than scientists. Surtsey has been nominated as a UNESCO World Heritage Site.

Environmental Issues. The major concern is being able to continue the control and protection of the island in the face of outside human influence.

See also Iceland; Mid-Atlantic Ridge

Further Reading

Fridriksson, Sturla. 2009. "Surtsey." In *Encyclopedia of Islands*, edited by Rosemary G. Gillespie and David A. Clague, 883–888. Berkeley: University of California Press.

Fridriksson, Sturla and Borgþor Magnússon. 2007. "Colonization of the Land." Surtsey—The Surtsey Research Society. http://www.surtsey.is/pp_ens/biola_1.htm

Jakobsson, Sveinn P. 2007. "Geology: Erosion of the Land." Surtsey—The Surtsey Research Society. http://www.surtsey.is/pp_ens/geo_2.htm

Svalbard Archipelago

Arctic Ocean

Geographic Overview. Svalbard Archipelago lies halfway between the northern coast of Norway and the North Pole. Spitsbergen is the largest island in the group. The relatively warm water of the North Atlantic Current usually keeps the coast ice-free throughout the year, but fjords freeze over in winter. This is a rugged polar land with glaciers and permafrost and, where it is vegetated at all, arctic tundra. Svalbard is part of the Kingdom of Norway.

Geographic Coordinates. Approximately 74°N–81°N, 10°E–35°E

Description. Svalbard is a cluster of arctic islands situated between the Greenland and Barents seas north of Norway and east of Greenland. The largest island, Spitsbergen, has an area of 23,561 mi² (61,022 km²), more than 60 percent of which is covered in permanent ice. Much of the remaining land is barren; tundra only covers about 10 percent of the total area. Ice-free areas are underlain by permafrost which thaws to depths of 1–5 ft (30–150 cm) each summer. Freeze–thaw activity gives rise to a variety of periglacial landforms, including pingos, rock glaciers, thermokarst, and patterned ground (rock stripes and circles) on flatter surfaces.

Much of Spitsbergen is mountainous; the highest peak, Newtontoppen, stands 5,633 ft (1,171 m) asl. A broad strandflat, a uniquely polar landform, surrounds the island. This is a low coastal plain, partly submerged and characterized by raised beaches and marine terraces. The inland margin occurs at the foot of steep cliffs, favored nesting areas for seabirds. The coast is cut by deep fjords, the longest of which, Wijdefjorden, cuts almost directly south for 67 mi (108 km) into the northern coast.

Svalbard lies at the contact zone between cold, dry polar air masses and warmer, wetter maritime airmasses from the south. The interaction of the two produces frequent cyclonic storms and frequent fogs. April and May tend to be the sunniest and calmest months. The proximity of the North Atlantic Current keeps the coast ice-free all year, but the many fjords freeze over in winter. July temperatures average 39°–43° F (4°–6°C); January temperatures average –10° to –3°F (–12° to –16°C). At 78°N, the latitude of the capital city, Longyearben, the midnight sun shines from April 20 to August 22, and darkness envelops the land from October 26 to February 15. Total annual precipitation at Longyearben is 11 in (270 mm), most falling as snow. The western side of the island where Longyearben is located is drier than the eastern side, which may receive as much as 39 in (1,000 mm) a year.

The tundra vegetation is composed of ground-hugging perennial plants, mosses, lichens, and fungi. It is richest beneath the bird cliffs, where it benefits from bird droppings rich in nutrients obtained at sea. Salt marshes edge lagoons and river deltas.

Geologic History. Svalbard contains a vast record of Earth's history in its rocks. Granitic and metamorphic rocks more than 570 million years old form the basement rock of Svalbard and are exposed along the west coast of Spitsbergen, where they give evidence of several mountain-building episodes at a time when Svalbard was located near the equator. The Caledonian Orogeny of the Silurian Period (434–410 mya) folded and faulted the bedrock as the Baltica and Laurentia continental masses converged. These geologic structures are revealed in the Hekla Hoek peaks in the northwest. Newtontoppen is the product of an intrusion of granite that occurred at that time. The Devonian (400–360 mya) was a period of erosion resulting in the deposition of over 26,000 ft (8,000 m) of sandstone, shales, and conglomerates. Later, in the Carboniferous, tropical swamps grew that were to become seams of coal. During the Mesozoic Era, Svalbard was covered by a warm shallow sea; marine deposits from that time contain fossils of ammonites, squid, and bivalves as well as *Plesiosaurus*, a medium-sized marine reptile up to 11 ft (3.5 m) long.

Between 65 and 60 mya, Svalbard converged with Greenland with folding of rock layers and the development of a deep basin as consequences. The basin collected sediments and supported swamps that later became coal deposits. The islands of Svalbard attained their current configuration late in the Tertiary and then were sculpted by ice sheets during the Quaternary Period into an array of glacial features, including cirques, arêtes, and fjords.

Biota. Some 178 species of vascular plant have been collected in the Svalbard archipelago along with 373 mosses, 606 lichens, and 705 fungi. Three vascular plants are endemic to the islands. The tundra vegetation supports an impoverished fauna that includes only the Svalbard reindeer as a grazing mammal. (There are no lemmings or other rodents native to the islands.) This endemic subspecies has distinctly shorter appendages and a thicker coat than populations elsewhere in the Arctic. A thriving population of arctic fox, the only mammalian predator on the land, feeds on the eggs and chicks of eider, geese, and seabirds on the bird cliffs and on ptarmigan, geese, and wading birds in the interior. The Svalbard Rock Ptarmigan is the only year-round avian resident. The Snow Bunting is the only songbird nesting on the islands.

Marine mammals of Svalbard include polar bears, narwhal, white and bowhead whales, ringed, bearded and harbor seals. A walrus population is shared with Franz Josef Land. The harbor seal population is the world's northernmost.

Protected Areas. About two-thirds of Svalbard's land and nearshore waters are protected in seven national parks, 23 nature preserves, and 15 bird sanctuaries. There is also a geotype preserve at Festningnen at the mouth of Grønfjorden along the west coast that protects an array of unique geologic features as well as dinosaur tracks from 130 to 125 mya and fossil remains of *Plesiosaurus, Ichtyosaurus*, and *Pliosaurus funkei*—discovered in 2006 and reputedly one of the largest marine predators ever.

Environmental Issues. A warming climate may facilitate the spread of alien species. It may also allow for expansions in the range of native species such as dwarf birch, arctic holy grass, crowberry, and polar bilberry, plants now rare in the archipelago. Increased tourism is a threat to the fragile tundra also, since trampling of moist tundra vegetation can result in an increase in the depth of the active zone and accelerate erosion.

See also Gulf Stream and North Atlantic Current

Further Reading

Ingólfsson, Ólaffur. 2008. "Outline of Physical Geography and Geology of Svalbard." Department of Geology and Geography, University of Iceland. https://notendur.hi.is/~oi/svalbard_geology.htm

Øverein, Oystein. 2009. "Svalbard's Wildlife." Cruise Handbook for Svalbard. http://cruise-handbook.npolar.no/en/svalbard/wildlife.html

Øverein, Oystein and Lennart Nilsen. 2009. "Svalbard's Vegetation." Cruise Handbook for Svalbard. http://cruise-handbook.npolar.no/en/svalbard/vegetation.html

Swedish Lakeland

Sweden

Geographic Overview. The large lakes in southern Sweden, some of the largest bodies of fresh water in Europe, are remnants from a lake that formed in a larger Baltic Sea area at the close of the Pleistocene. They are part of a band of lakes stretching across southern Finland and into western Russia.

Geographic Coordinates. Approximately 57° 40'N–59°45'N, 12°E–18°E

Description. The area in southern Sweden, between Stockholm on the east and Goteborg on the west, is known for its exceptionally large lakes, four of which exceed 385 mi^2 (1,000 km^2). They are connected by canals. Vänern, 2,184 mi^2 (5,655 km^2), with a mean depth of 86 ft (27 m), is the largest lake in Sweden and the third largest in Europe. The northwestern and northeastern shores of Lake Vänern are bounded by faults. Vättern, 735 mi^2 (1,900 km^2) and 135 ft (41 m) deep, fills a rift valley, giving it its long, slender shape. Mälaren, 440 mi^2 (1,140 km^2) and 210 ft (64 m) deep, is third in size and the deepest lake in Sweden. It drains northeast to the Baltic Sea via the Sodertalje Canal, and its easternmost bay, Riddarfjarden, is close to Stockholm. The much smaller

Hjälmaren, 187 mi^2 (485 km^2) and 20 ft (6 m) deep, is joined by the Hjälmare Canal to Stockholm and also drains east into Lake Mälaren. The general elevation of the region is less than 330 ft (100 m) asl, and the surface elevation of the lakes is approximately 144 ft (44 m). Smaller lakes related to continental glacial deposition extend out in all directions from the main water bodies.

The landscape in Southern Sweden that houses the large lakes is a complex area of valleys outlined by faults, called fissure valleys, and often surfaced with sedimentary rocks. The surficial deposits are various types of glacial drift, and the substrate of the Lakeland area is a combination of rolling hills and minor crystalline rock outcrops. Local relief is 165–330 ft (50–100 m).

Geologic History. Southern Sweden bedrock is predominantly crystalline rocks of the Baltic Shield, primarily Precambrian granites and gneisses but complicated by many faults and residual Cambrian and Silurian marine sandstones, limestones, and shales. The less resistant sedimentary rocks are preserved in and form flat land in downfaulted areas. These younger rocks also outcrop on Bornhold Island, Gotland Island, and the floor of the Gulf of Bothnia before forming Åland Island and extending into southern Finland. Most of the shield rocks were subjected to long periods of erosion, leaving a peneplain.

Scandinavia and the Baltic area were the source of the continental glacier that covered northern Europe in the Pleistocene, which blanketed the shield rock with a veneer of moraines, kames, and eskers. A major recessional moraine crosses the lake region. During the Pleistocene, the Baltic region was depressed as much as 2,130 ft (650 m) because of the weight of the ice. As the ice melted, sea level rose and the land slowly began to rise, or rebound, but much more slowly than sea level rose. Water flooded the southern Baltic area, first as a lake from meltwater, then as an arm of the ocean, covering the southern part of both Sweden and Finland. With continued rebound, the water drained from the land, but not before waves and currents had rearranged some of the glacial drift. The lakes are remnants of the freshwater lake that covered the southern part of the Baltic region after the glacial ice melted. Very old crystalline rocks are juxtaposed with very young glacial drift that in some areas was modified by wave action.

Biota. The lakes are surrounded by coniferous forests of Scots pine and Norway spruce, with scattered stands of broadleaf birch and aspen. Most fish in the lake district, including perch, bream, pike, roach, whitefish, eel, and rainbow trout, are typical of other Swedish lakes as well. Fish species also include pike-perch, salmon, smelt, and vendace. Seabirds, such as terns, gulls, and cormorants, are common around the lakes. Sea eagles are a frequent raptor.

Protected Areas. Viking settlements, Birka on the island of Bjorko, and Hovgarden on the island of Adelso, both in Lake Malaren, were declared World Heritage Sites in 1993. Djuro National Park is an island group in the middle of Lake Vanern.

See also Baltic Sea; Europe; Finnish Lakeland

Further Reading

Bridges, E. M. 1990. "Europe." In *World Geomorphology*, 188–240. Cambridge: Cambridge University Press.

Embleton, Clifford. 1974. "Caledonian Highlands." In *Geomorphology of Europe*, 92–131. New York: John Wiley and Sons.

Swedish and Norwegian canals. 2010. "Sweden's Largest Lakes." www.sverigesochnorgeskanaler.com/lakes/

T

Talamanca Range

Costa Rica

Geographic Overview. The Talamanca mountain range is the only nonvolcanic segment of the cordilleras that form the backbone of the Central American isthmus. The Talamancas are also the only part of southern Central America where elevations approach 13,000 ft (4,000 m) and are one of only two places in Central America that were likely glaciated during the Pleistocene Epoch. (The other is on the high limestone plateau of the Altos de Cuchumantes massif in Guatemala. Evidence for glaciations there is not nearly as strong as in the Talamancas, however.) Cerro Chirripó at 12,533 ft (3,820 m) is the highest peak in Costa Rica. The Talamanca Range is the site of largest tract of virgin montane rainforest in Central America, a large part of which is conserved in La Amistad–Talamanca International Park on the Costa Rica–Panama border.

The Talamancas are a biodiversity hotspot within the highly diverse Central American region.

Geographic Coordinates. 08°40'N–09°40'N, 83° 38'W–82°00'W

Description. Although there are no glaciers in Central America today, at elevations above 10,000 ft (3,000 m) the Talamancas have many erosional and depositional landforms derived from alpine glaciation. These are best expressed in Chirripó National Park. U-shaped valleys gouged by alpine glaciers occur above 10,200 ft (3,100 m) and give way to V-shaped fluvial valleys below that elevation. At the head of valleys are cirques, well-defined arêtes, and cols. Glacier-scoured basins in the cirques now bear tarns, some 65 ft (20 m) or more deep. Lateral, terminal, and medial moraines 65–80 ft (20–25 m) high have been deposited in the glacial valleys. Much of the area above 10,000 ft (3,000 m) was smoothed by Pleistocene ice fields, and the bedrock on mountaintops was grooved, striated, or polished. High elevation slopes today have low angles. Periglacial features such as frost-cracked boulders and block fields of angular rocks also have been identified in some places. Much is yet to be discovered or confirmed in this remote park, where research has frequently relied on the interpretation of aerial photography and not on-the-ground surveys.

Vegetation types grade from lowland tropical forest at the foot of the mountains into a lower montane rainforest that at about 8,200 ft (2,500 m) becomes a rare upper montane forest of mixed oaks. The upper montane forest covers the main crest line of the range, but higher peaks, such as Cerro Kamuk (and Cerro Cirripó to the north), also have cloud forests, subalpine paramo, and high elevation bogs.

Geologic History. Intrusive igneous rocks, mostly granodiorites, form the core of the range, which was rapidly folded and uplifted about 1 mya as the Cocos Plate subducted beneath the western margin of the Caribbean Plate. Overlying volcanic rocks eroded away after uplift. Glaciation sculpted the massif during the Pleistocene Epoch.

Biota. The Talamanca Range is the site of the largest tract of virgin montane rainforest in Central America. Plant diversity is extremely high due to a geographic location where North American and South American species converge and also due to the varied microclimates and edaphic conditions in mountains.

Faunal diversity is similarly high, and animal life exhibits a high rate of endemism, especially in Lepidoptera, amphibians, and birds. The Talamanca forests in general are home to an estimated 4 percent of the terrestrial species on Earth.

Protected Areas. UNESCO declared La Amistad–Talamanca International Park and three adjacent natural areas as a Biosphere Reserve in 1982 and inscribed the Costa Rican portion of the park as a World Heritage Site in 1983, expanding this to include the Panamanian part in 1990. Located in the foothills of the Talamancas and contiguous with Cirropó National Park, La Amistad encompasses land ranging in elevation from 650 to 11,644 ft (200–3,549 m) asl, the high point being the summit of Cerro Kamuk. The elevational range supports rare birds such as the Resplendent Quetzal, Bare-necked Umbrella Bird, and Three-wattled Bellbird, which migrate vertically in their search for food. The forests also serve as important wintering grounds for migratory North American songbirds, including the Wood Thrush and some wood warblers. In addition to its geological and biological assets, the park is home to four indigenous groups who follow traditional subsistence lifeways based on hunting, gathering, and gardening. The Bribri, Cabécar, Guaymí or Ngäbe , and Naso or Teribe peoples utilize the buffer zone surrounding La Amistad as well as other areas in the Talamancas.

Further Reading

"La Amistad/Talamanca Highlands, Costa Rica." n.d. The Nature Conservancy. http://www.nature.org/ourinitia tives/regions/centralamerica/costarica/placesweprot ect/amistad.xml

Lachniet, Matthew S. 2007. "Glacial Geology and Geomorphology." In *Central America: Geology, Resources and Hazards*, edited by Jochen Bundschum and Guillermo E. Alvarado, 171–184. New York: Taylor & Francis.

"Talamanca Range-La Amistad Reserves / La Amistad National Park." n.d. World Heritage Centre, UNESCO. http://whc.unesco.org/en/list/205

"World Heritage Nomination—IUCN Summary 552: La Amistad International Park and Volcan Baru National Park (Panama)." 1990. World Conservation Monitoring Centre, United Nations Environmental Programme. http://whc.unesco.org/archive/advisory_body_evalua tion/205.pdf

Tallgrass Prairie National Preserve

United States (Kansas)

Geographic Overview. Tallgrass Prairie National Preserve was designed to protect and provide interpretation not only for the prairie ecosystem, but also for the heritage of American ranching. The property, known as Spring Hill Ranch since the 1870s and more recently as the Z Bar Ranch, lies west of Emporia in the Flint Hills of Kansas and preserves 10,894 ac (4,409 ha) of tallgrass prairie lands. The ranch house, built with native stone in 1881, and the three-storied barn provide a glimpse into ranching in the 1800s and early 1900s. The area incorporates a formerly missing element, tallgrass prairie ecosystem, into the National Park System and protects some of the last remaining tallgrass prairie in North America.

Geographic Coordinates. 38°26'N, 96°34'W

Description. The native tallgrass prairie ecosystem originally stretched from southern Manitoba in Canada to central Texas in the United States. It covered the eastern edge of the Great Plains States and extended through southwestern Minnesota, Iowa, northern Illinois, and into Indiana. Because the soils were ideally adapted to agriculture, less than 4 percent of original tallgrass prairie remains. Although 35 in (890 mm) of precipitation yearly would normally sustain tree growth, periodic burning, by natural causes or by Native Americans, coupled with the grazing of bison promoted the growth of tall grasses. The prairie is maintained to preserve natural conditions, including prescribed burns and cattle grazing, to maintain the ecosystem. Because grass roots may extend 10–15 ft (3.0–4.5 m) deep, 75–80 percent of the biomass is underground, and plants resprout after the aerial portions are burned or grazed.

The Flint Hills, a rolling landscape characterized by limestone capped hills and deep valleys, are rich in nodules of chert, a hard, flinty rock embedded in the limestone. Unsuited for plowing, the Flint Hills retain the largest remnants of tallgrass prairie. Maximum elevation is 1,640 ft (500 m), with local relief as much as 330 ft (100 m).

Biota. Biota in the tallgrass prairie is diverse, especially in plants. Over 500 species of plants, almost

A remnant of a formerly widespread ecosystem is maintained at Kansas Tallgrass Prairie Preserve, as is the history of American ranching. (Ricardo Reitmeyer/Dreamstime.com)

150 bird species, 39 reptile and amphibian species, and 31 mammal species can be found in the preserve. Approximately 80 percent of the grassland is composed of 40–60 species of grasses, while the remaining 20 percent is forbs. There are also lichens and liverworts, and woody trees and shrubs along the creeks. Major grasses include switch grass (*Panicum virgatum*), Indian grass (*Sorghastrum nutans*), little bluestem (*Schizachrium scoparium*), and big bluestem (*Andropogon gerardi*). Big bluestem and Indian grass, major sod-forming grasses, can be 8 ft (2.4 m) tall by September. The tall grasses grow together with shorter grasses, such as side-oats grama bunchgrass (*Bouteloua curtipendula*) and many perennial forbs, such as yarrows (*Achillea* spp.), coneflowers (*Echinacea* spp.), and various sunflowers (*Helianthus* spp.). The prairie has many microhabitats depending on moisture, soil depth, and slope. Prairie cordgrass (*Spartina pectinata*) may grow in wet seeps, while drier hilltops may support hairy grama (*Bouteloua hirsuta*).

Animals formerly found on tallgrass prairie include bison (*Bison bison*), pronghorn (*Antilocapra americana*), elk (*Cervus canadensis*), and wolf (*Canis lupus*). Several bison from Wind Cave National Park were recently reintroduced to the range, the first wild bison in the area in more than 100 years. Small mammals include Eastern cottontail rabbit (*Sylvilagus floridanus*), white-tailed jackrabbit (*Lepus townsendii*), thirteen-lined ground squirrel (*Spermophilus tridecemlineatus*), grasshopper mouse (*Onychomys leucogaster*), and pocket gopher (*Geomys bursarius*). Coyotes (*Canis latrans*) and red foxes (*Vulpes fulva*) are the main carnivores.

Birds include the rare Greater Prairie Chicken (*Tympanuachus cupido*), Upland Sandpiper (*Bartamia longicauda*), Eastern Meadowlark (*Sturnella major*), Dickcissel (*Ammodramus savannarum*), Grasshopper Sparrow (*Eremophila alpestris*), Common Poorwill (*Phalaenoptilus nuttallii*), Common Nighthawk (*Chordeiles minor*), Red-tailed Hawk (*Buteo jamaicensis*), Northern Harrier (*Circus cyaneus*), American Kestrel (*Falco sparverius*), and Burrowing Owl (*Speotypto acunicularia*).

Protected Areas. Designated a National Historic Landmark in 1997, Tallgrass Prairie National Preserve is a joint endeavor, owned primarily by The Nature Conservancy and managed by the National Park Service. The preserve is on the Flint Hills National Scenic Byway in Kansas.

Further Reading

National Park Service. n.d. *Tallgrass Prairie National Preserve, Kansas.* www.nps.gov/tapr/

Woodward, Susan L. 2008. *Grassland Biomes.* Greenwood Guides to Biomes of the World. Westport, CT: Greenwood Press.

Tarim Basin and Takla Makan Desert

China

Geographic Overview. The Tarim Basin is an oval depression surrounded by high mountains in northwestern China. In the center of the Tarim Basin, the Takla Makan Desert, roughly translated from the Uigur language as "place from which there is no return," is the second largest region of shifting sand in the world. Although its sand dunes may be a forbidding place, oases skirting the edges of the basin were important stops on the Silk Road for camel caravans between China and the Greek and Roman empires.

Geographic Coordinates. Approximately 36°N–42°N, 75°E–96°E

Description. The Tarim (Sinkiang) Basin in North-Central Asia, approximately 1,250 mi (2,000 km) east-to-west and 325 mi (520 km) north-to-south, covers approximately 193,000 mi² (500,000 km²) in Xinjiang Province. It is almost completely surrounded by high mountains—the Tian Shan in the north, the Pamirs in the west, and the Karakoram and Kunlun

Mountains in the south. To the east, the Hexi (Gansu) corridor connects the Tarim Basin with the Alashan Plateau in the southwestern Gobi Desert and with the Huang He River. The basin is higher in the west, 4,500 ft (1,400 m) asl, gently sloping east to 2,500 ft (780 m). There is also a general slope from south to north. The general topographic zonation is gravelly alluvial fans near the mountains, oases and agriculture at the base of the fans, and the sandy interior. Several oases, such as Kashgar and Yarkand in the southwest, Kuqa in the north, and Dunhuang in the East, developed into cities. A few small oases dot the rivers that manage to penetrate north into the dunes.

All rivers originate in the surrounding mountains, but most of the flow sinks into the gravel or sand without connecting into a network. The western and northern edges of the basin are watered by the Tarim River, which begins in the western basin at the convergence of three streams—the Yarkant and Hotan Rivers, which rise in the Karakoram Range and the Kun Lun Shan and the Aksu River from the Tian Shan. The Hotan may terminate in the central sands before reaching the Tarim River. From the confluence at 4,265 ft (1,300 m) asl, the Tarim River flows east into Lop Nor salt lake, a barren salt crust and lowest point in the basin at 2,560 ft (780 m) asl in the east. The Tarim River has a wide floodplain, with shifting, braided channels. Its depth may be 33 ft (10 m).

Large mobile sand dunes of the Takla Makan Desert, extending approximately 600 mi (960 km) west-to-east and 260 mi (420 km) north-to-south, cover 85 percent of the basin, 123,550 mi² (320,000 km²). Sand dunes are generally 330–660 ft (100–200 m) high, but they may reach 1,000 ft (300 m) high.

The continental midlatitude desert climate is characterized by temperature extremes, from summer monthly means of 75–80°F (24–27°C) to winter monthly means of 15–20° F (–7 to –10°C). Summer maxima may be 105°F (41°C) and winter lows may drop to –4° F (–20°C). Winter and spring are dry due to dominance of the Siberian high pressure. Wind brings sparse summer rain from the east, and the base of the Pamirs in the west receives some orographic precipitation. Mean annual precipitation is 2.2 in (55 mm) at Kashgar, decreasing to less than 0.5 in (12 mm) in the east. The relatively narrow gap between mountains in the east, the Hexi Corridor, often creates a wind tunnel, subjecting the region to wind storms strong enough to disrupt transportation and lift dust 13,000 ft (4,000 m) into the atmosphere. Wind speeds can reach almost 1,000 ft/sec (300 m/s), and dust storms can last for weeks. Much of the dust is deposited as loess on the low mountain slopes in the west. Prevailing northeast winds move the sand south, burying many ancient oases and tracks of the Silk Road north of the Kun Lun Mountains.

The Tarim Basin was one of several routes along the Silk Road. Mummies, as old as 4,000 years, with Caucasian features and western dress indicate an even older connection between European and Asian cultures.

Geologic History. The Tarim Basin is an ancient massif, encircled and demarcated by many deep faults. Shield rocks are buried beneath 5–7.5 mi (8–12 km) of porous Mesozoic and Cenozoic sediments. The basement complex was uplifted during the Alpine Orogeny in the Tertiary, which folded the surrounding mountains and faulted the basins in Central Asia.

Biota. The Tarim Basin has low plant diversity, with 120 species and no endemics. Many of the same species also occur in the Central Asian Deserts (Karakum and Kyzylkum), but no species are shared with the Gobi Desert. Four vegetation types are common. Gravelly alluvial fans support a sparse cover, less than 5 percent, of dwarf shrubs of joint pine (*Ephedra*, not a pine tree), bean-caper, *Gymnocarpus, Sympegma*, glasswort, and *Reaumuria*. The shifting dunes are largely barren, with sporadic salt cedar or black saksaul trees, occasional shrubs of *Nitraria schoeberi, Calligonum reboroski*, and boxthorn, and a few herbs and grasses where the water table is 5–15 ft (1.5–5.0 m) below the surface. Vegetation in old river channels with salty soils is similar to that of dunes but joined by halophytes, such as seepweed. River floodplains and oases have sufficient water for continuous forests of poplar and elm, with seaberry, salt cedar, Russian olive, and even reeds, but most floodplain areas have been converted to irrigated agriculture.

Small populations of wild Bactrian camels, approximately 500, and onager (Asian wild ass) exist east of Lop Nor. Most animals in the basin, including Tarim red deer, desert beaver, wild boar, and goitered gazelle, and smaller mammals such as long-eared hedgehog, gerbils, jerboas, and the endemic Tarim hare, are found on the periphery, close to rivers. Predators include red fox and corsac fox. The most common birds are Tufted Lark and Tarim Jay. Others frequently seen include Rufous-tailed Shrike, Common Starling, Collared Turtle Dove, and White-browed Chinese Warbler. Steppe Eagle is a common raptor. Qinghai sand lizard is common.

Protected Areas. Talkimakan Desert *Populus euphratica* Forests along the Tarim River have been nominated for a World Heritage Site. Considered to be "living fossils" from the Tertiary, these poplars are the oldest in the world.

See also Asia; Central Asian Deserts—Karakum and Kyzylkum; Gobi Desert; Karakoram Mountains; Kunlun Shan; Pamirs; Tian Shan; Turpan Depression

Further Reading

Quinn, Joyce A. 2009. "Cold Deserts." In *Desert Biomes*. Greenwood Guides to Biomes of the World, 103–148. Westport, CT: Greenwood Press.

Songqiao, Zhao. 1986. "Temperate and Warm-Temperate Desert of Northwest China." In *Physical Geography of China*, 167–184. New York: John Wiley & Sons.

UNESCO. 2010. Taklimakan Desert—*Populus euphratica* Forests. World Heritage Centre. http://whc.unesco.org/en/tentativelists/5532/

Tasman Sea

Pacific Ocean

Geographic Overview. The Tasman Sea lies between Australia and New Zealand at the southwestern edge of the Pacific Ocean. Locally referred to as "The Ditch," it is influenced in the north by tropical waters flowing in from the Coral Sea and in the south the subpolar waters of the Southern Ocean. Currently, the Tasman Sea is warming at a rate three times greater than the world ocean average. The sea is named for the Dutch explorer Abel Tasman, who discovered the sea in 1642. Sydney, Australia, is the largest city on the Tasman Sea.

Geographic Coordinates. Approximately 32°S–45°S, 150°E–175°E

Description. The Tasman Sea is a marginal sea in the southwestern part of the Pacific Ocean. Covering an area of 890,000 mi² (2,300,000 km²), it extends south from the tropical Coral Sea some 1,700 mi (2,800 km) to the Antarctic Circumpolar Current at the northern edge of the Southern Ocean. Warm waters from the Coral Sea flow into the Tasman Sea and produce a subtropical climate in the north. Norfolk Island, at the boundary between the Coral and Tasman seas, is encircled by the planet's southernmost coral reef. Cold water enters the sea through the windy Bass Strait between Australia and Tasmania and produces a temperate climate over the southern Tasman Sea. The subantarctic water is cooler and saltier and sinks to depths of 1,300–2,260 ft (400–800 m) in what is known as the Bass Strait Cascade. This water can remain undiluted in eddies for months. In 2011, one such eddy was 650 ft (200 m) thick and 25 mi (40 km) in diameter.

The western portion of the seafloor is an abyssal plain reaching depths of 19,500 ft (5,945 m) bsl. To its east is a broad submarine plateau almost 1,240 mi (2,000 km) long, the Lord Howe Rise. The rise, some 250–370 mi (400–600 km) wide, extends northward into the Coral Sea and ends in the south at the Challenger Plateau, another large submerged piece of continental crust just west of New Zealand. Both Lord Howe Rise and Challenger Plateau are fragments of the Australian continent called Zealandia that broke away during the breakup of Gondwana (see later discussion). The Lord Howe Rise is about 3,330 ft (1,000 m) bsl. Lord Howe Island and Ball's Pyramid on the western edge of the rise are extinct, eroded shield volcanoes and the youngest members of the Lord Howe seamount chain, which continues along the northern section of the underwater plateau as a series of coral-capped guyots.

Geologic History. The Tasman Sea opened 85–52 mya when rifting of Gondwana detached a large piece of continental crust from eastern Australia and created a now largely submerged microcontinent now called Zealandia. The northern seamount chain probably resulted from the passage of Zealandia over the Lord Howe hotspot.

Circulation and Major Currents. The generally counterclockwise circulation in the Tasman Sea is marked by the inflow of warm water from the South Equatorial Current, which enters the Coral Sea and then exits it as the southward-moving warm East Australian Current. This, the western boundary current, turns east off Tasmania and then north-northeast off the west coast of New Zealand. Between New Zealand and Norfolk Island, warm waters return to the Pacific Ocean. Cold subpolar water enters the loose gyre through Bass Strait and as a cold, northward-flowing coastal current along South Island, New Zealand.

Biota. The cold waters of the southern Tasman Sea support marine mammals and seabirds. Doubtful Sound, a large fjord in southwestern New Zealand, is home to whales and dolphins, the New Zealand fur seal, and the threatened Fiordland Crested Penguin (*Eudyptes pachyrhynchus*). In the shallow waters of the sound are also black corals, more commonly found in deep-sea environments.

Protected Areas. Elizabeth and Middleton Reefs Marine National Nature Reserve (Australia) in the northern Tasman Sea protect two isolated coral platform reefs on the Lord Howe Rise as well as the rare and endangered Black Cod (*Epinephelus daemelli*).

Environmental Issues. Rapid warming of the Tasman Sea has resulted in more than a 3.6°F (2°C) increase in sea surface temperatures in the past 60 years, three times the average warming of Earth's oceans. The rise appears to be related to strengthening wind systems pushing the East Australian Current farther to the south. On land, exotic mammals such as cats and rats are a threat to breeding Fiordland Crested Penguins.

See also New Zealand

Further Reading

CSIRO Australia. 2012. "Warming in the Tasman Sea, Near Australia, a Global Warming Hot Spot." ScienceDaily. http://www.sciencedaily.com/releases/2012/01/120130102538.htm

Tasmania

Australia

Geographic Overview. Tasmania is a continental island located on the Australian Plate 125 mi (200 km) off southeastern Australia. It is mountainous and forested, unlike the mainland. During the Pleistocene it experienced two major glaciations that helped to shape the contemporary landscape. Having shared Australia's long isolation, Tasmania is home to a number of relict and endemic plants and animals, though overall biodiversity is much less than on the continent. Tasmania is a state in the Commonwealth of Australia.

Geographic Coordinates. Approximately 40°S–43°S, 145°E–148°E

Description. Tasmania is a medium-size, heart-shaped island across the Bass Strait from the southeast tip of Australia. The east and north are the products of faulting and characterized by plateaus bounded by escarpments at the edges of grabens and hills that are erosional remnants of higher surfaces. Much of the bedrock is Permian and Triassic sedimentary rock capped by Jurassic age dolerite, an intrusive igneous material, and containing rare plant and amphibian fossils. The western and southern parts of the island are rugged and mountainous, formed of Precambrian quartzite and schist and Jurassic dolerite that have been folded along north–south axes and glaciated. A dramatic landscape of horns, arêtes, cirques, mountain lakes, and U-shaped valleys is the result. Within this region is Tasmania's highest peak Mount Ossa, elevation 5,305 ft (1,617 m) asl. Below 2,000 ft (600 m), depositional landforms associated with alpine glaciations such as moraines and outwash plains are common. Periglacial activity has produced talus and solifluction deposits. The coasts of the island are considered classic examples of drowned shorelines. Bathurst Harbor in the southwest is a ria coast, while the alternating headlands and bays in the south were produced by the differential erosion of bedrock of varying hardness (i.e., a discordant coastline).

Tasmania has a cool, temperate maritime climate. The weather is often cloudy, windy, and wet. The island lies in the zone of the Roaring Forties, and the Prevailing Westerlies blowing off the Southern Ocean can bring more than 78 in (2,000 mm) of precipitation annually to the southwestern mountains. The east, however, lies in a rain shadow and typically receives 20 in (500 mm) or less each year. Northerly winds from Australia can bring in hot, dry air masses during summer. Southerly and southwesterly squalls bring rain and snow. Above 1,000 ft (300 m), frosts can occur at any time of year.

Western Tasmania, below 3,300 ft (1,000 m), is cloaked in a temperate rainforest of Gondwanan relicts. The southern beech *Nothofagus cunninghamii* is usually dominant. Emerging above the main canopy may be one of two eucalypts, messmate stringybark or Smithton peppermint. Lianas are absent, and mosses and lichens are the main epiphytes. In the east, sclerophyllous forests dominated by eucalyptus prevail. They grade from tall closed forests in the wetter areas to savannas in drier areas. The Tasmanian oak or stringy gum (*Eucalyptus regnans*), the world's tallest flowering plant, reaches heights of 200–374 ft (60–114 m) and stands high above the general canopy of the wet sclerophyll forest, which is but 30–65 ft (10–20 m) above the ground.

Large areas in the west have peaty soils and are covered by tussocks of button grass sedge (*Gymnoschoenus sphaerocephalus*) surrounded by heaths and other shrubs, including ti-trees (*Leptospermum* spp.) and paperbarks (*Melaleuca* spp.). Alpine habitats above treeline (at 2,600 ft [800 m] near the coast and above 3,900 ft [1,200 m] in the interior) are dominated by shrubs. In poorly drained areas cushion plants and dwarf conifers are common; in well-drained areas Tasmania's only deciduous southern beech, *Nothofagus gunni*, grows with heaths and coniferous shrubs in these moorlands.

Geologic History. Tasmania's oldest rocks date to 1,290 mya and are exposed in the west and on King Island in Bass Strait. Precambrian rocks were uplifted during the Cambrian, roughly 500 mya, and folded when Tasmania was compressed in an east-west direction during the Devonian Period, some 420–360 mya. Massive intrusions of magma about 165 mya, during the Jurassic, produced the greatest expanse of dolerite (diabase) in the world, which affected not only much of Tasmania but also parts of South Africa (Karoo), Argentina, and Antarctica, all part of the Gondwanan supercontinent at the time. Dolerite was deposited primarily as sills up to 1,650 ft (500 m) thick. The columnar jointing of this subvolcanic rock and its blue-gray color make Tasmania's mountains distinctive.

During the Cretaceous Period, the crust at Bass Strait was extended and thinned to form several basins inundated by the sea while Tasmania was still attached to Antarctica. The connection was severed about 45 mya as faulting associated with the breakup of Gondwana continued. During the Pleistocene Epoch (2 mya to about 12,000 years ago), about half the island was covered by a sizeable ice cap and valley glaciers, a rare occurrence on landmasses of the Southern Hemisphere. Tasmania's latitudinal position and relatively high elevations allowed ice to accumulate and also led to periglacial activity. During glacial episodes, when sea level was lowered, Bass Strait was dry land, a land bridge between Tasmania and the Australian continent. During interglacials, sea level rose and cut the island off from the mainland. Tasmania was separated for the last time about 10,000 years ago. The ocean attained its current levels about 6,000 years ago.

Biota. Tasmania's flora is a mix of Australian and Antarctic elements and has affinities to the temperate rainforests of South America and New Zealand. Antarctic species include Gondwanan relicts found in alpine moorlands and in the rainforest, among them endemic coniferous genera such as *Athrotaxis* (e.g., King Billy and pencil pines), *Diselma* (a cypress), and *Macrocachrys* (a podocarp). Australian eucalypts dominate the sclerophyll forests, which include species such Morrisby's gum (*Eucalyptus morrisbyi*) now extinct on the mainland.

The fauna is depauperate compared to Australia's but has a high degree of endemism. Its best known marsupials are the wolflike thylacine (now extinct) and the Tasmanian devil (*Sarcophilus harrisii*), currently threatened by a contagious facial tumor. Two catlike quolls (*Dasyrus viverrineus* and *Dasyrus maculatus*) are other carnivorous marsupials. Several herbivorous species extinct or threatened on mainland Australia find refuge in Tasmania, among them the barred bandicoot, long-nosed potoro, and the Tasmanian pademelon. The platypus and echidna, both monotremes, are widespread.

Tasmania has one endemic flightless bird, the Tasmanian Nativehen (*Gallinula mortierii*), a rail. In contrast to the diversity of reptiles on the Australia continent, only 17 skink species, one agamid lizard, and three snakes inhabit Tasmania.

Invertebrates of note include the giant freshwater crayfish, more than 3 ft (1 m) long and weighing up to 4 kg. This is the largest freshwater invertebrate on Earth. Gigantism is also seen in other invertebrate

groups. The Tasmanian mountain shrimp (*Anaspides tasmaniae*) is a living fossil and one of the most ancient representatives of the subphylum Crustacea; it appears unchanged after 250 million years of existence.

Protected Areas. The Tasmanian Wilderness Area protects about 20 percent of the island and is a UNESCO World Heritage Site. National parks, nature preserves, and other types of conservation areas protect many more hectares.

Environmental Issues. Few wild rivers remain; most major streams have been dammed for hydroelectric power. Habitat loss and fragmentation, climate change, and introduced species are current challenges.

See also Australia

Further Reading

Richardson, Alastair M. M. 2009. "Tasmania." In *Encyclopedia of Islands*, edited by Rosemary G. Gillespie and David A. Clague, 904–907. Berkeley: University of California Press.

UNESCO. n.d. "Tasmanian Wilderness." World Heritage Centre. http://whc.unesco.org/en/list/181

Thar Desert

India and Pakistan

Geographic Overview. The Thar Desert, in northwestern India and adjacent Pakistan, is the seventh largest and one of the most populated deserts in the world. It is dominated by rivers, notably the Indus, that rise high in the Himalayan mountain complex and are the source of abundant alluvial deposits. The Thar is also significant for its system of parabolic sand dunes.

Geographic Coordinates. Approximately 24°N–30°N, 68°E–75°E

Description. The Thar Desert, also called the Great Indian Desert, is on the eastern edge of the dry belt of northern Africa and southwestern Asia. The larger arid region, which includes the Thar, extends east from highlands of Baluchistan in Pakistan, crosses the Indus River valley and ends in the foothills of the Aravalli Range in central Rajasthan state in India. From north to south, it extends from the foothills of the Himalayan system and the Punjab region of Pakistan and India south to the Arabian Sea. It covers approximately 170,000 mi^2 (440,000 km^2) and averages 650 ft (200 m) asl. Some definitions of the desert include the Rann of Kutch, a salty plain in Gujarat state in India.

Although 90 percent of the desert is rocky plateaus or gravel plains, it is also characterized by mobile dunes, sandy plains, salt pans, and saline marshes. The sand-dune-covered portion of the Thar, primarily in western Rajasthan state in India, is called the *Marusthali*, meaning "place of death." Although driest, the region is densely inhabited. The dune field is dominated by parabolic dunes, 33–100 ft (10–30 m) high. Northern desert extensions of the Thar, with similar sand dune topography, are the Cholistan in the Punjab region on the border between India and Pakistan and the Thal between the Indus River and the Jhelum River in Pakistan.

The hills at the base of the Aravalli Range, at the eastern margin of the Thar, stretch from northern Gujarat state across Rajasthan state to Delhi. While the roots of these eroded Precambrian mountains are a continuous range in the south, the northern part consists of disconnected hills and ridges that rise above the sand. The slightly higher elevations receive more rainfall and are less sandy.

The state of Rajasthan, in both the Thar proper and in the Aravalli Range, has many seasonal lakes, formed by disrupted river flow or merely depressions between dunes. Lake Sambhar, west of Jaipur, is the largest, approximately 22 mi (35 km) long and covering approximately 90 mi^2 (233 km^2). It is only 3 ft (1 m) deep and completely dries out in the dry season. Most lakes are saline, containing sodium chloride or gypsum, but some are fresh water, where headwater tributaries are blocked by sand.

Irrigation systems have attracted increased population and agriculture to the desert. The Sukkar Barrage on the Indus River, completed in 1932, brings irrigation water to the southern Thar in Pakistan. The Gang Canal from the Sutlej River carries water to the northwest. The Indira Gandhi Canal begins at the confluence of the Sutlej and Beas rivers in the Indian Punjab and carries water southwest.

Average annual precipitation is 4–20 in (100–500 mm), least in the west, increasing toward the Aravalli Range. Because of southwestern monsoon flow, 90 percent of the rain falls in intense storms in late summer, promoting runoff rather than infiltration. Temperatures are extreme, from 5–10°F (41–50°C) in winter, with possible frost, to more than 122°F (50°C) in summer. The upper Indus plains near Lahore, Pakistan, are plagued by frequent dust storms but overall, the Thar is not known for excessive wind.

Geologic History. The bedrock of the desert is Precambrian gneiss and sedimentary rocks overlain by river alluvium. The Indus River, which flows through an enormous alluvial plain, and its tributaries have shifted widely in the past. Considerably wetter in the Tertiary (54–25 mya) when the Indian Plate was on the Equator, the climate became drier as the plate drifted north. A network of old river beds dating from historic times indicate that a major channel flowed parallel to the modern Indus River through what is now the Thar. That river moved steadily northwest, pushed by sand dunes, until it joined the Indus. Some of the old routes serve as irrigation canals or channels for flood water.

Biota. The region is a crossroads of Palearctic, Oriental, and Saharan biogeographic realms with a unique biota. It has more taxa associated with Asia, especially India, than with Africa. Sparse vegetation consists of xeric grasses or a desert thorn scrub of low trees and shrubs. Vegetation also varies with the water-holding capacity of the substrate. Solid rocky areas and sandstone plateaus tend to be barren. Alluvial fans and hills support a sparse population of acacia trees (*Acacia* spp.), caper shrubs (*Capparis decidua*), and cactus-like euphorbias (*Euphorbia caducifolia*). Dune and sand plain vegetation is dominated by hackenkopf (*Calligonum polygonoides*) and rattlebox (*Crotalaria burbia*) shrubs with a scattering of gum acacia (*Acacia senegal*) and ghaf (*Prosopis cineraria*) trees.

Typical small animals include mice, shrews, and Indian species of hare, gerbil, and desert jird. Large mammals, such as mountain gazelle, onager, blackbuck, and nilgai, are more common in the Indus River valley. Carnivores include striped hyena, caracal, wolves, Bengal fox, and sand cat.

The desert is under a flyway to the Rann of Kutch. More than 300 birds have been identified, an increase since the construction of irrigation canals. Grassland and desert birds include francolins (a partridge), quail, bustards, Cream-colored Courser, Hoopoe Lark, sandgrouse, raptors, wheatears, larks, and pipits. Migratory birds include sandgrouse, ducks, and geese. Reptile species are associated with India biota.

Protected Areas. Although the desert region has 11 officially designated protected areas, primarily wildlife preserves covering a total area of 17,000 mi² (44,000 km²), most of them contain numerous villages and are grazed by livestock. Desert National Park, Nara Desert, the Rann of Kutch, and Cholistan are the largest.

Environmental Issues. The Thar Desert, especially the Indus Valley plain, is densely populated, with scattered villages and large herds of camels, cattle, goats, and sheep. Grazing pressure has degraded native forage. Salt pans developed for commercial production may negatively affect Sambhar Lake.

See also Indus River

Further Reading

Goudie, Andrew S. 2002. "The Deserts of India and Pakistan." In *Geomorphological Landscapes of the World, Great Warm Deserts of the World: Landscapes and Evolution*, 254–289. Oxford: Oxford University Press.

Rawat, Gopal S. and Erid D. Wikramanayake. n.d. *Southern Asia: Western India into Pakistan*. World Wildlife Fund Ecoregions. http://worldwildlife.org/ecoregions/im1304

Singh, Panjab, Asad R. Rahmani, Sonam Wangchuk, Charudatta Mishra, K. D. Singh, Pratap Narain, K. A. Sing, Sanjay Kumar, G. S. Rawat, and Raghunandan Singh Chundawat. 2012. *Report on the Taskforce on Grasslands and Deserts*. Government of India Planning Commission, New Delhi.

Tian Shan

China, Kyrgyzstan, and Kazakhstan

Geographic Overview. The Tian Shan, primarily straddling the borders of China, Kazakhstan, and Kyrgyzstan, is one of the largest mountain ranges in the world and the largest mountain chain rising from a mid-latitude arid region. Its glaciers are the source of several rivers, such as Syr Darya, that feed the cities and fields of adjacent deserts.

Geographic Coordinates. Approximately 38°30'N–45°30'N, 67°E–94°E

Description. An amalgam of several mountain ranges generally trending west-to-east, the Tian Shan extends 1,500 mi (2,500 km) from the Amu Darya River west of Dushanbe, Tajikistan, east to the Bogda range north of the Turpan depression in China. Its north–south width is 220–300 mi (350–500 km), and the mountain mass covers approximately 386,000 mi² (1,000,000 km²). With the exception of its southwestern boundary with the Pamir Mountains, it is distinct from its low-elevation desert or semi-desert surroundings. The Tian Shan are bounded on the north by the Dzungarian (Jungar) Basin and the southern Kazakhstan Plains. To the south is the Tarim Basin and Turpan depression. To the southwest, in Tajikstan and Kyrgyzstan, is the Gissar-Alay (Trans-Alai) fault, which geologically separates the Tian Shan from the Pamirs to the south. Elevations are uniformly high, with many peaks more than 18,000 ft (5,500 m) asl. Although generally arid, the mountains were sculpted by glaciers and many areas above 13,125 ft (4,000 m) asl retain permafrost and are covered with ice.

Most ranges and intervening valleys in the Tian Shan are oriented east–west. The Eren Habirga Mountains, west of Turpan, rise to 18,200 ft (5,550 m) asl. Further west, the Tian Shan branches. The Borohoro Mountains extend northwest and the Halik Mountains, more than 22,000 ft (6,700 m) asl, trend west, with the Ili River Valley in Kazakhstan between them. At the juncture of the China–Kyrgyzstan–Kazakhstan border, a number of ranges radiate from a cluster of the highest peaks of the Tian Shan. The tallest is Victory Peak (Tomur, Jengish Chokuso), 24,419 ft (7,443 m). Khan Tangiri Peak, 22,949 ft (6,995 m), in Kazakhstan, is the second highest. Several ranges of the main Tian Shan, including Terskey Alai, Kakshaal, and Atbashi, extend further west, forming the northwest border of the Tarim Basin. Those ranges and the Kungey Alai to the north enclose Lake Ysyk (Issyk-kul). In Kyrgyzstan and Uzbekistan, approximately north of Kashgar, China, the main mountain mass splits around Fergana Ridge and Fergana Valley. The Gissar–Alay Fault separates the Pamirs on the south from the western extension of the Tian Shan in

Although high in elevation, most of the Tian Shan Mountains are too arid to support forest. Oases, such as that seen here on the Assy Plateau in Kazakhstan, provide water. (Maxim Petrichuk/Dreamstime.com)

the north. North of Fergana Valley, elevations are generally 7,500–10,500 ft (2,300–3,200 m). South of Fergana, several peaks rise to more than 15,000 ft (4,575 m) and the maximum elevation is 18,441 ft (5,621 m) asl.

Glaciers cover approximately 3,900 mi² (10,100 km²), 80 percent of which is in Kyrgyzstan and Kazakhstan. The largest are in the Khan Tangiri and Victory Peaks, Eren Habirga Mountains areas, including Inylchek Glacier, 37 mi (60 km) long on the west slope of Khan Tangiri. The mountain region is extensively faulted, and the region is seismically active.

By creating windward and lee sides, the mountains control adjacent climates. The region is arid continental with little precipitation in lower elevations and abrupt horizontal and vertical changes caused by elevation and aspect. Because the source of most precipitation is the Atlantic, the western and northwestern slopes are wetter, 28–79 in (710–2,000 mm). The eastern slopes and interior are drier, 8–16 in (200–400 mm). The southern Tian Shan has a dry summer, while precipitation in the north is more evenly distributed. Temperatures vary with elevation, but annual temperature differences become more extreme eastward. Valleys are often colder than the adjacent hills because of strong temperature inversions. Foehns, strong downslope winds, frequently warm valleys above freezing and melt snow in winter.

Geologic History. The mountains of Central Asia were uplifted by the collision of India and Eurasia, with several microplates, such as the Afghan, Dzungarian, Tarim, Tibetan, Pamir, Fergana, and Tajik, sandwiched in between. The northern ranges, such as the Tian Shan, which were further from the contact zone, were only weakly folded. The initial collision in the late Cretaceous was intensified during the Alpine Orogeny in the Miocene. Those early mountains were eroded to a peneplain and rejuvenated in the Cenozoic. The result is the high-elevation, plateau-like topography, with a mean elevation of 10,170 ft (3,100 m), in parts of the Tian Shan.

Most of the rocks are Paleozoic (540–250 mya) crystalline and sedimentary. Basins between the mountains filled with sediment eroded from the rising mountains. The northern and eastern parts of the mountain were folded in the early Paleozoic, and the sedimentary cover has now been mostly obliterated by erosion (peneplanation), exposing granitic outcrops. In the southern and western Tian Shan, the rocks were folded in the late Paleozoic, resulting in meta-sedimentary rocks, with some volcanics.

Biota. Climatic diversity and complex orography are responsible for the variety and distribution of biota. Central Asian mountains are one of the world's centers of biodiversity because of habitat diversity, which provided refugia during climate changes. Indo-Himalayan, Mongolian, Central Asian, Mediterranean, and Eurasian elements coexist.

Altitudinal zonation, from desert foothills to alpine, is complicated by aspect, and most zones are a mosaic of communities. Bare rock on southern slopes often stands in stark contrast to northern slopes with forests and meadows. Although the northern Tian Shan has a forest belt, most ranges are too arid. Desert, with sagebrush and *Ephedra*, dominate the lower slopes, replaced at higher levels by feather grass steppe with rose and honeysuckle shrubs, flora which is related to the Kazakh plains. Forests of maple, aspen, and wild fruit trees in the northern Tian Shan are replaced by coniferous forests of *Picea schrenkiana*, *Abies semenovii*, and birch at higher elevations. Tall sedge and herb meadows, with *Juniperus siberica* woodlands, form the subalpine zone, which merges into a *Kobresia* spp.–dominated low-grass alpine at 9,500–13,450 ft (2,900–4,100 m). In the western Tian Shan, the woodland zone supports nut trees, such as pistachio and walnut. The more extreme climate in the Central Tian Shan is dominated by *Stipa* and *Festuca* grass steppes or deserts. A short growing season susceptible to frost and a thin snow cover for 1–6 months make the environment similar to arctic tundra, with a sparse cover of *Kobresia* on the flat expanses. Drought tolerant cushion plants are found on rocky slopes.

Animals include wolves, fox, and ermine, as well as distinctly Asian animals, such as snow leopards, Siberian ibex, and argali (Kyzylkum sheep) in the high mountains. The forest–meadow–steppe environments support bear, wild boar, badgers, voles, jerboas, and pikas. Lower zones are similar to deserts, with gazelle, Tolai hare, and gray hamster. Birds include Mountain Partridge, pigeon, Alpine Chough, crow, Mountain Wagtail, redstart, Golden Eagle, vulture, and Himalayan Snow Cock. Horned Lark, Lesser Sand Plover, Isabelline Wheatear, and Snow Finch are abundant in dry communities.

Protected Areas. Xinjiang Tianshan World Heritage Site, in the eastern Tian Shan, consists of four components—Tomur, Kalajun-Kuerdening, Bayinbukuke, and Bogda.

Environmental Issues. Drastic retreat of glaciers would be detrimental to adjacent desert areas that depend on meltwater. The steep slopes are highly unstable and prone to intensive mass movement, which may be triggered by earthquakes, intense precipitation, or human activities such as deforestation or overgrazing.

See also Aral Sea; Pamirs; Tarim Basin and Takla Makan Desert

Further Reading

Quinn, Joyce A. 2009. "Mid-Latitude Alpine Tundra." In *Arctic and Alpine Biomes*. Greenwood Guides to Biomes of the World, 83–156. Westport, CT: Greenwood Press.

Shahgedanova, Maria, Nikolay Mikhailov, Sergey Larin, and Aleksandr Bredikhim. 2002. "The Mountains of Central Asia and Kazakhstan." In *The Physical Geography of Northern Eurasia*, edited by Maria Shahgedanova, 375–402. Oxford: Oxford University Press.

United Nations Educational, Scientific, and Cultural Organization (UNESCO). 2013. Xinjiang Tianshan. World Heritage Centre. http://whc.unesco.org/en/list/1414

Tibesti Mountains

Chad

Geographic Overview. The Tibesti Mountains are the largest and highest of several massifs scattered across the Sahara. The center of the range consists of five inactive shield volcanoes, rare landforms in the middle of a continent. The highest peak, Emi Koussi, reaches 11,302 ft (3,415 m) asl. The higher slopes are somewhat moister and milder than the surrounding desert and support a dry woodland and a drought-adapted fauna.

Geographic Coordinates. Approximately 20°N–22°N, 16°E–19°E

Description. The Tibesti Mountains are an isolated, triangular massif in northwest Chad in the heart of the Sahara. The massif is about 250 mi (400 km) long on each of its three sides. More than half the region lies at elevations greater than 4,900 ft (1,500 m) asl. The center of the range is composed of five inactive shield volcanoes, each with a large crater at the summit. The highest is Emi Koussi at the southern apex; it stands 11,302 ft (3,445 m) asl and is the highest peak in the Sahara. The other volcanoes are Tarso Toon, Tarso Voon, Tarso Yega, and Tarso Toussidé. Four lava domes have elevations between 4,300 and 6,600 ft (1,300–2,000 m) asl. Especially at the eastern end of the massif, lava flows have produced plateaus, and stone spires and other jagged rock formations stand as erosional remnants of thick basalts. Lava fields and tephra deposits also occur in various places throughout the range. The Tibesti massif blocks sand movement across the desert, and a large sand sea (erg) has developed to the northeast.

The northern face of the Tibesti Mountains is a steep descent to desert pavement below, whereas the southern and eastern slopes are gentle. Narrow, steep-sided canyons have formed along fractures in the lava plateaus, some occupied by streams with intermittent flow. Dry valleys also appear on the north- and east-facing slopes. These wadis or enneris have ephemeral streams fed by occasional southwest monsoon rains; they vanish via seepage and evaporation upon reaching the desert. The longest, Enneri Tijitinga, extends southward for nearly 250 mi (400 km) from the western end of the range before disappearing north of the Bodélé Depression. The upper reaches of the wadis, above 6,500 ft (2,000 m), often contain a string of pools, rainfed wetlands known locally as gueltas. They contain fresh or slightly brackish water most of the year and are fringed with reeds and other macrophytes. Many contain fish.

Volcanic activity in the not too distant past is evidenced by gases still escaping from Tarso Toussidé, the Yi Yerra hot springs on the southern slopes of Emi Koussi, and the Soborom geothermal field on the northwest flank of Tarso Voon, where water temperatures are 72°–190°F (22°–88°C). A soda lake occurs in the crater of Emi Koussi; a deposit of sodium carbonate looks like a light cover of snow in the caldera of Trou au Natron southeast of the summit of Tarso Toussidé.

On average, 4–6 in (100–150 mm) of rain falls on the Tibesti peaks each year, making the mountains somewhat moister than the surrounding desert lowlands. Occasionally snow falls on the summits. Large areas are devoid of vegetation, but scattered acacias grow on some slopes and grasslands appear at elevations of 5,900–8,900 ft (1,800–2,700 m) asl. Shrubs less than 2 ft (60 cm) high occupy certain areas above 8,500 ft (2,600 m). Most plant life is found in and along the wadis, where doum palm, date palm, salt cedar, and acacias can extend their roots to groundwater.

Other massifs in the Sahara include Ahaggar (Hoggar) in southeast Algeria and Aïr, in Niger. Both, like the Tibesti Mountains, formed over hotspots above mantle plumes rising beneath continental crust. Ahaggar attains a maximum elevation over 9,500 ft (2,900 m) asl; Aïr reaches more than 6,500 ft (2,000 m) asl. Other prominent, isolated mountain ranges in the Sahara, such as Ennedi Massif in eastern Chad, Tassili n'Ajjer in eastern Algeria, and the Acacus Mountains in western Libya, are sandstone massifs displaying rare sandstone karstic landforms, including dolines, tubes, and karren.

Geologic History. The central uplands of the Sahara (Tibesti, Ahaggar, and Aïr) were uplifted during the late Cenozoic Era, at which time flood basalts similar to those of India's Deccan Plateau or the Columbia River Plateau in the United States poured forth layer by layer until 980 ft (300 m) thick. From the Oligocene Epoch into the Holocene (35–0 mya), hotspots above mantle plumes lying beneath the basement rocks of Africa gave rise to the shield volcanoes, continental analogs to the Hawaiian Islands in the Pacific. Tarso Toussidé has been active during the last 2,000 years.

Biota. The dry woodland vegetation of the region is considered part of an ecoregion that encompasses Tibesti and Jebel Uweinat in northeast Sudan. The mammalian fauna consists of arid land herbivores such as addax, Barbary sheep, Dorcas gazelle, and Rhim gazelle, as well as numerous rodents including gerbils, jerboas, spiny mouse, jird, and desert hedgehog. Baboons, rock hyrax, and Cape hare also inhabit the mountains. Among carnivores are striped polecat, golden jackal, fennec fox, Rüppell's fox, and striped hyena. Fishes, amphibians, and reptiles are poorly represented. Birds are more diverse, finding nesting and roosting sites in the mountains.

Protected Areas. None. An area to protect Rhim's gazelle and Barbary sheep has been proposed.

Environmental Issues. The Tibesti are an inaccessible and forbidding place to most people. Camel caravans and nomadic herdsmen stop at gueltas for water. Land mines left from war between Chad and Libya are a major hazard.

See also The Sahara

Further Reading

Burdette, Christine. n.d. "Tibesti-Jebel Uweinat Montane Xeric Woodlands." Terrestrial Ecoregions, World Wildlife Fund. http://worldwildlife.org/ecoregions/pa1331

Tibetan Plateau

China

Geographic Overview. With a mean elevation of more than 13,125 ft (4,000 m) asl, the Tibetan Plateau is the youngest, largest, and highest plateau in the world. Along with the Himalayas, the Tibetan Plateau is called the "Roof of the World." Tibet and the Himalayas provide water for 20 percent of the world's population.

Geographic Coordinates. 27°35'N–39°45'N, 78°30'E–104°00'E

Description. The Tibetan (Qinghai-Xizang) Plateau, approximately 2,175 mi (3,500 km) east-to-west and 930 mi (1,500 km) north-to-south, covers almost 1 million mi² (2.5 million km²) in southwestern China, including all of Xizang Autonomous Region and Qinghai Province and parts of Xinjiang Uigur Autonomous Region and Gansu, Sichuan, and Yunnan provinces. Elevations in the southeast are 1,000 ft (300 m), rising to 14,750–16,400 ft (4,500–5,000 m)

in the northwest. Most of the plateau is surrounded by mountains 23,000–26,250 ft (7,000–8,000 m) asl. The southern boundary of the plateau is the north face of the Himalayas; the northern boundary is the Kunlun and Qilian ranges. On the west, the plateau abuts the Karakoram Mountains. On the eastern side, it drops to the lower Yunan and Guizhou plateaus and the Hengduan Mountains. Most mountain ranges on the plateau trend east–west, but they turn to a north–south orientation on the eastern edge. The southern plateau is drained by the Tsangpo (Brahmaputra) River. The eastern part is drained by the headwaters of the Huang He (Yellow), Irrawaddy (Salween), Mekong, and Chang Jiang (Yangtze) rivers. Elsewhere on the plateau, drainage is interior.

The central plateau, between the Kunlun Mountains to the north and the Gangdise–Nysingentanglha mountains to the south, occupies the largest area. It stands 14,750–15,750 ft (4,500–4,800 m) asl and is characterized by interior drainage lakes, such as Nam and Siling, which contain carbonate and sulfate salts in the northern regions and chloride salts in the south. Northeast of the central plateau, the Altun and Qilian mountains split from the Kunlun and extend north to enclose the lower elevation Qaidam (Tsaidam) Basin, 6,550 ft (2,000 m) asl and covered with sand dunes in the west and swamps in the east. Qinhai (Tsing Hai) Lake, on the east side on the basin at 10,500 ft (3,200 m) asl in the folds of the Qilian Mountains, is the largest lake in China, covering 1,700 mi² (4,400 km²). The southern plateau, between the Gangdise–Nysingentanglha mountains and the Himalayas, is characterized by high ridges, 5,000–6,000 m (16,400–19,700 ft), valleys, and gorges. The rivers flow in broad open valleys at 11,500–13,100 ft (3,500–4,000 m) before dropping into deep gorges 6,500–13,100 ft (2,000–4,000 m) asl. The largest river, the Tsangpo, occupies a graben. On the southeast border of Tibet and China, the plateau is separated from the low plateaus of eastern China by the Yungling fault. The mountain ridges of Amne Machen and Bayan Karsa, at 16,400–19,650 ft (5,000–6,000 m) in the northeastern plateau, are drained by the headwaters of the Huang He, Yalung, Chang Jiang (Yangtze), Mekong, and Irrawaddy rivers. As the mountain trend changes to north–south, the ridges decrease in elevation to become the Hengduan Mountains in western Yunan Province.

Because of its high elevation, the Tibetan Plateau is very cold in both winter and summer, with no frost-free season at elevations over 13,125 ft (4,000 m). Because of intense solar radiation, temperature differences between sun and shade are extreme, and freeze–thaw action occurs almost daily. The plateau has periglacial features and well-developed permafrost, 262–295 ft (80–90 m) thick with an active layer of 3.3–13.1 ft (1–4 m). Glaciers cover approximately 18,150 mi^2 (47,000 km^2). The predominantly east–west ranges are a barrier to southern monsoon moisture. Precipitation decreases from more than 40 in (1,000 mm) in the southeast to less than 4 in (100 mm) in the northwest.

Geologic History. The Tibetan Plateau is composed of several distinct terranes (microcontinents) accreted to southern Asia in the Paleozoic and Mesozoic during the closure of the Tethys Sea. Suture zones cross the middle and southern plateau, and overthrust faults are common in the north. The plateau, with rocks from the late Mesozoic (135–65 mya), is a late Tertiary erosion surface uplifted 11,500–13,125 ft (3,500–4,000 m) in the Alpine Orogeny. It continues to rise 5.1–5.5 in (13–14 cm) every 100 years. When Gondwanaland broke up approximately 140–100 mya, India moved rapidly (in geological time) north as the oceanic part of the plate subducted beneath Asia. Approximately 55 mya, the Indian continental crust began to push into Asia, piling up continental crust from both plates to become both the Himalayan Mountains and the Tibetan Plateau. The continental crust underlying the plateau is the thickest on earth, 44–62 mi (70–100 km). Since its initial collision, India has moved 1,865 mi (3,000 km) north into Asia.

Biota. The central and northern parts of the plateau are in the Palearctic biogeographic realm, with no forests, only dwarf shrubs. The southeastern part is in the Oriental realm and Chinese Himalayan forests, with large stands of needle leaf forests. The Himalayas were a barrier to tropical or subtropical Indian biota. Because the Kunlun–Altun–Qilian mountains form a less effective barrier between the plateau and northwest China, the plateau has many species of flora and fauna in common with central Asian deserts. In contrast, the north–south ridges and valleys in the southeast serve as corridors. Parts of the plateau served as refugia during Quaternary glaciations, conserving pre-Tertiary relict species.

Because of its expanse and elevation, the plateau has both latitudinal and vertical zonation, related to temperature and moisture. In the humid and subhumid southeast, montane needleleaf forest is dominated by one or more species of pine, hemlock, spruce, fir, or larch. At treeline, approximately 14,750 ft (4,500 m) which is the highest in the world, forest is replaced by alpine scrub, consisting of rhododendron, willow, and *Caragana* shrubs, and alpine meadows dominated by herbaceous *Kobresia, Polygonum,* and *Saussurea* species.

No forest belt exists in the arid and semiarid regions that cover most of the plateau. Montane steppe and desert are dominated by *Stipa, Aristida,* and *Pennisetum* grasses and a few shrubs, such as *Sophora.* Above 16,400 ft (5,000 m) are alpine meadows of *Kobresia* and *Carex* with small *Caragana* shrubs and cushion plants. The center of the plateau, between the Gangdise–Nyainqenianglha and the Kunlun Mountains, is a desolate upland with sparse alpine steppe and meadow, characterized by *Stipa, Carex,* and *Kobresia* species. The deserts shrubs of *Ephedra, Salsola,* and *Artemisia* in the Qaidam Basin are transitional to the northwestern deserts.

Protected Areas. China has established several nature preserves in the Tibetan Plateau region, including 10 in Qinghai Province and 24 in Tibet Autonomous Region.

See also Brahmaputra (Tsangpo) River; Chang Jiang (Yangtze River); Himalayan Mountains; Karakoram Mountains; Kunlun Shan; Mekong River

Further Reading

Bridges, E. M. 1990. "Asia." In *World Geomorphology,* 123–165. Cambridge: Cambridge University Press.

Songqiao, Zhao. 1986. "The Qinghai-Xizang Plateau." In *Physical Geography of China,* 185–197. New York: John Wiley & Sons.

Sorkhabi, Rasoul, Allison Macfarlane, and Jay Quade. 1996. "Roof of the Earth Offers Clues about How Our Planet Was Shaped." *Eos Transactions American Geophysical Union* 77: 385–387. http://wayback.archive

Tierra del Fuego

Argentina and Chile

Geographic Overview. Tierra del Fuego is an archipelago at the southern end of South America, separated from the mainland by the Strait of Magellan. It consists of one large triangular-shaped island, Isla Grande de Tierra del Fuego, and many smaller islands, including Hornos Island, on which Cape Horn is located. Both Argentine Ushuaia and Chilean Puerto Williams (on Isla Navarino) claim to be the world's southernmost city. This "land of fire" was named by Ferdinand Magellan, the first European to find and sail through the strait that now bears his name. Presumably, he saw smoke from fires built onshore by the native peoples, the Yaghan and Selk'nam (or Ona), nomadic hunters of marine mammals.

Geographic Coordinates. 52°28'S–56°00'S, 54°45'W–70°28'W

Description. The Tierra del Fuego archipelago consists of four physiographic and structural regions arranged from north to south as they arc west–northwest to east–southeast and create north–south bands of natural landscapes. The archipelago has an area of 28,500 mi² (73,815 km²); Isla Grande de Tierra del Fuego, South America's largest island, accounts for 18,750 mi² (48,100 km²) of it. The eastern part of the main island and a few small islands in the Beagle Channel belong to Argentina, while the remaining 61 percent of the land is Chilean territory. The international border passes through Isla Grande de Tierra del Fuego along the 68°36'W meridian, and then proceeds eastward through the Beagle Channel. The southwestern islands, including Hornos Island, have the Patagonian batholith as their cores. Immediately to the north are the east–west trending Fuegian Andes, which end at Peninsula Mitre, the easternmost part of the main island and form the north coast of the Beagle Channel. This region includes the eastern part of Isla Hoste, Isla Navarino, and other small islands stretching to and including Isla de los Estados (Staten Island). The highest point is the summit of Mount Darwin (8,163 ft or

2,448 m) in the Darwin Cordillera. To the north is the Magallanes Fold-and-Thrust Belt, with the long Lake Fagnano filling a glacially enlarged rift valley on its southern edge. The northeastern section of the main island is part of the Magallenes foreland, a basin filled with Cenozoic sediments.

A transect through Argentine Tierra del Fuego from Ushuaia in the south to Rio Grande, Argentina, (53°46'S, 67°42'W) on the Atlantic Coast in the north would begin in windswept subantarctic tundra where peat bogs cover wide swathes of land. Rising into the Andes, where some mountain peaks reach nearly 5,000 ft (1,500 m) asl, U-shaped hanging valleys are encountered that still contain glaciers. A forest of *lenga*, a deciduous southern beech (*Nothofagus pumilo*), mixed with *guindo*, an evergreen beech, *Nothofagus betuloides*, grows to treeline at 2,100 ft (650 m). Boglands occupy some of the deeper valleys. North of Lake Fagnano the land is hilly with patches of a dwarfed beech, *ñire* (*Nothofagus antarctica*) forest, lakes, ponds, and streams. Peat bogs occur in small valleys, and drowned landscapes produced by the invasive North American beaver are evident. The northern region is a flat plain covered by Magellanic steppe, a tussock grassland with scattered low shrubs. The wetter areas or *vegas* are now prime pastures for sheep and cattle. The coast provides important wintering grounds for Arctic shorebirds, including the Hudsonian Godwit and Red Knot. The Atlantic Coast Natural Reserve is set up to protect these migratory birds and has been designated a Ramsar Wetland of International Importance.

Tierra del Fuego has a very short summer, cool maritime climate. Precipitation declines rapidly in an eastward direction from a high of 118 in (3,000 mm) or more a year along the Pacific coast to less than 12 in (330 mm) a year in the northeast. The mean annual temperature at Ushuaia, Argentina (54°48'S, 68°19'W), which is located on the Beagle Channel, is 41.5°F (5.3°C), with January having an average monthly temperature of 48°F (9.1°C) and July 34°F (1.0°C). The highest recorded temperature there is 85°F (29.4°C); the lowest –5.6°F (–21°C). Average annual sea surface temperature is 43°F (6.3°C).

Chilean Tierra del Fuego includes the western areas with high amounts of precipitation. Its

Magellanic subpolar rainforests host the world's southernmost conifer, the cypress *Pilgerodendron uvifera*. Furthermore, its *lenga* and *guindo* forest at 55°S has the distinction of being Earth's southernmost old-growth forest, and on Hoste Island grow the southernmost trees in the world, the *ñire*.

See also Cape Horn (Cabo de Hornos); Strait of Magellan, Beagle Channel, and Drake Passage

Further Reading

"How Much Do You Know about Tierra del Fuego?" n.d. Official Site of the Province of Tierra del Fuego, Antarctica, and South Atlantic Islands (Argentina). http://www.tierradelfuego.org.ar/v4/_eng/index .php?seccion=4

Menichetti, M., E. Lodolo and A. Tassone. 2008. "Structural Geology of the Fuegian Andes and Magallanes Fold-and-Thrust Belt—Tierra del Fuego Island." *Geologica Acta* 6:19–42. http://www.raco.cat/index.php /GeologicaActa/article/view/83442/108425

Tongass National Forest

United States (Alaska)

Geographic Overview. Tongass National Forest, in the Alaskan Panhandle, is the largest national forest in the United States. Designated primarily for its forest ecosystems, the Tongass boasts a variety of landscapes. Alaskan natives, such as Tlingit, Haida, and Tsimshian who have lived in the region for more than 10,000 years, continue to maintain subsistence living. Native corporation lands are private enclaves within the National Forest.

Geographic Coordinates. Approximately 54° 42'N–59°40'N, 129°58'W–139°52'W

Description. Tongass National Forest is a region of temperate rainforest, towering trees, muskegs, alpine meadows, caves, islands, sandy beaches, deep fjords, rocky cliffs, ice fields, and glaciers. Elevations range from sea level to more than 13,000 ft (3,960 m). Approximately 75,000 people live in several communities within the forest's boundaries, including the state capital Juneau.

Tongass National Forest surrounds the Inland Passage, from the southern tip of Prince of Wales Island north to Yakutat, approximately 80 percent of the Alaskan panhandle, but does not include Glacier Bay National Park. The entire region was covered by ice in the Pleistocene, and many glaciers remain, from high elevations down to sea level. The Mendenhall Glacier, 13 mi (21 km) from Juneau, is part of the 1,500 mi² (3,885 km²) Juneau Icefield along the Alaska–British Columbia border. It flows into Mendenhall Lake. LeConte Glacier, 25 mi (40 km) east of Petersburg, is the southern most tidewater glacier in North America. At 76 mi (122 km) long, Hubbard Glacier, 30 mi (48 km) north of Yakutat, is the longest tidewater glacier in the world. Currently very active, it has crossed and blocked Russell Fjord many times, most recently in 2008. The Stikine Icefield on the crest of the Coast Mountains is 2,900 mi², stretching 120 mi (193 km) from Whiting River to Stikine River.

Approximately 850 mi² (2,200 km²) in the Ketchikan area has dramatic karst and extensive cave systems, an unusual location in temperate rainforest, peatlands, subalpine, and alpine zones. The caves, significant to archaeology and paleontology as well as to natural history, contain evidence of human occupation dating from 10,500 years ago and animal bones more than 45,500 years old.

Geologic History. The Alaska panhandle's geology is a complexity of terranes, accreted onto North America when the Pacific Plate converged with the North American Plate. The panhandle also has granitic intrusions and extrusive volcanics. The Alexander Archipelago is a limestone terrane from the Tropical Pacific.

Biota. Tongass National Forest preserves the largest temperate rainforest in the world, covering approximately 500 mi (800 km) north-to-south between the Pacific Ocean and the Coast Mountains. Because the forest is managed for multiple use, some has been clear-cut, and logging of old-growth remains controversial. The cool, coastal climate with more than 100 in (6,450 mm) of annual rainfall promotes growth of tall hemlock, spruce, red and yellow cedar, covered with moss, ferns, and lichens. Western hemlock (*Tsuga heterophylla*) is the most common tree, followed by Sitka spruce (*Picea sitchensis*). They are the largest trees, and together they make up most of the rainforest. Hemlock can be 100–150 ft (30–45 m) tall, 2–4 ft (0.6–1.2 m) in diameter, and 200–500 years old. Sitka spruce is larger, 150–225 ft (45–68 m) tall, 5–8 ft (1.5–2.4 m) in diameter, and 500–700 years old. Smaller trees, 40–100 ft (12–30 m) tall and 1–2 ft (0.3–0.6 m) in diameter, include mountain hemlock (*Tsuga mertensiana*) and western redcedar (*Thuja plicata*). Shore pine (*Pinus contorta* var. *contorta*), often small and scrubby, grows from sea level to alpine regions and is often found in muskegs, with yellow-cedar (*Chamaecyparis nootkatensis*).

The area has high concentrations of black bears and brown bears. Sitka blacktail deer (*Odocoileus hemionus sitkensis*) is the smallest subspecies of mule deer. Marine mammals include sea lions, porpoises, hair seal, sea otters, and whales. Ocean and rivers teem with fish, including salmon. Bald eagles are common.

Protected Areas. Originally preserved in 1902 as Alexander Archipelago Forest Reserve, the region was renamed Tongass National Forest and expanded in 1908 to roughly 16.8 mil ac (6.8 mil ha). One-third of the Tongass, 19 units comprising approximately 5.8 mil ac (2.3 mil ha), including Admiralty Island and Misty Fjords in national monuments, is officially designated Wilderness Area.

See also Glacier Bay National Park and Preserve

Further Reading

Prince William Network. n.d. *Tongass National Forest. America's Rain Forests, A Distance Learning Adventure*. Prince William County Public Schools. Manassas, Virginia. http://rainforests.pwnet.org/americas_rain forests/tongass.php

Schulte, Priscilla, Karalynn Crocker-Bedford, and Gregg Poppen. 1998, revised 2002. *Karst and Caves in Southeastern Alaska, A Teachers' Resource*. University of Alaska, Ketchikan Campus and Cultural Heritage Research. http://www.fs.fed.us/outdoors/naturewatch/implementation/Curricula/Karst-Caves-Curriculum.PDF

Torres del Paine

Chile

Geographic Overview. Torres del Paine (the Paine Towers) have become almost iconic examples of landscapes produced by alpine glaciation. Located at the southern end of the Southern Patagonian Ice Field, the three granitic spires are just some of the spectacular features of the Cordillera del Paine, an eastern spur of the Andes Mountains near their southern terminus on the South American continent. The name *Paine* is believed to come from a Tehuelche Indian word meaning "blue."

Geographic Coordinates. 51°10'S, 73°00'W

Description. Torres del Paine is a land of jagged peaks, many above 6,500 ft (2,000 m), with near vertical rock walls as well as glaciers, large lakes in glacial troughs, small tarns in mountain cirques, and waterfalls all emanating from the ice field and its meltwaters. The highest peak is Paine Grande, the summit of which is close to 10,000 ft (3,050 m) asl. Sources do not agree on the actual elevations of the summits of the Torres del Paine, and modern global positioning system (GPS) technology is revising older figures. Commonly cited elevations for the three peaks are: South Tower 8,202 ft (2,500 m); Central Tower 8,070 ft (2,460 m); North Tower 7,415 ft (2,260 m). When first described in 1880, the three towers were called "Cleopatra's Needles." Among the nearby Cuernos del Paine (Paine Horns), elevations also reach near or above 8,000 ft (2,500 ft).

The high peaks of the Cordillera del Paine are separated by narrow valleys that allow visitors access to breathtaking scenery. The head of Valle del Francés (French Valley) is a large cirque above the steep walls of which are peaks anchored in the west by Cerro Catedral and Cerro Cota 2000 and in the east by the knife edge (arête) of Aleta de Tiburón (Shark's Fin). The eastern flank of the valley consists of numerous high peaks whose names reflect their shapes. They include—from north to south—Forteleza (The Fortress), La Espada (The Sword), La Hoja (The Blade), Las Máscara (The Masquerade), Cuerno Norte (North Horn), and Cuerno Principal (Main Horn). Valle del Ascencio is popular with hikers and leads to Valle del Silencio (Silent Valley), northeast of Cerro Forteleza. On this valley's southern side are the Torres del Paine.

The Cordillera del Paine possesses a range of habitats from sea level at Seno de Última Esperanza (Last Hope Sound) to the top of Paine Grande. Four main vegetation zones are recognized along

Torres del Paine are the three granitic spires seen at the left edge of the skyline. The Cordillera del Paine is an eastern spur of the Andes Mountains in Patagonia, Chile. Guanacos graze in the foreground. (Dmitry Pichugin/Dreamstime.com)

this altitudinal gradient: dry Patagonian steppe at the lowest elevations, pre-Andean heath or shrublands above the steppe, then Magellanic subpolar forest, and—above treeline—Magellanic tundra. Much of the western part of the park is covered by the Southern Patagonian Ice Field, from which several large glaciers flow. The longest is Grey Glacier, which descends a little more than 9 mi (15 km) into Lago Grey, a large lake filling the trough the glacier gouged along a fault zone during the Pleistocene. Grey Glacier splits into two branches; one is 0.75 mi (1.2 km) wide and the other is 2.2 mi (3.6 km) across. Lago Grey, and two other large lakes, Lago Nordenskjöld and Lago Pehoé, arc around the southern edge of the massif.

Geologic History. The Cordillera del Paine is part of the Paine Massif, an exposed granitic laccolith that intruded overlying sedimentary rocks of Cretaceous age some 13 mya. The sedimentary layers were folded and faulted during the formation of the Andes Mountains, as the massif lies near the triple junction of the Nazca, Antarctic, and South American tectonic plates. On the Torres del Paine, the sedimentary rocks have been completely removed by erosion, especially by glacial activity, so that only bare granite peaks remain. On the nearby peaks of the Cuernos del Paine, the summits are formed of remnants of dark sedimentary rocks, which produce a banded effect with the lighter-colored granite beneath them.

Protected Areas. Torres del Paine National Park was established in 1959 and became part of Chile's National System of Protected Forest Areas. UNESCO declared the park a Biosphere Reserve in 1978. To its west is Bernardo O'Higgins National Park, Chile's largest national park; and to its north, in Argentina, lies Los Glacieres National Park. Torres del Paine is a sister park of Yosemite National Park in the United

States, with which it shares resource management techniques.

See also Patagonian Ice Fields

Further Reading

"Geological Localities: Torres del Paine." 2009. The Andean Geotrail. http://www.georouteandine.fr/English/expedition/geological_localities.php?date=paine

"Torres del Paine-Chile (map)." n.d. 210 Countries. http://www.210countries.com/destinations/good-old-destinations/torres-del-paine-chile/

"Trekking Torres Del Paine." n.d. About.com. Travel South America. http://gosouthamerica.about.com/od/topdestpatagonia/a/Torrestrek.htm

Trans-Mexican Volcanic Axis (Eje Volcánico Transversal)

Mexico

Geographic Overview. The Trans-Mexican Volcanic Axis crosses south-central Mexico from the Colima volcanic complex in the west to the Pico Orizaba in the east. Many of Mexico's highest peaks are found here, some snowcapped throughout the year. Low passes between the mountain edifices have allowed relatively easy access to the southern parts of the Mexican Plateau—defended by steep escarpments on the east and west—prehistorically and historically. Fertile soils derived from volcanic materials and moist air penetrating through the low passes from both the Pacific and Gulf of Mexico permitted the growth of Mexico's densely settled basins near the southern edge of Plateau.

Geographic Coordinates. 19°30'N–19°02'N, 97°16'W–103°37'W

Description. The Trans-Mexican Volcanic Axis is a seismically active belt of volcanic peaks crossing south-central Mexico for a distance of approximately 500 mi (800 km). Also known as the Transverse Volcanic Axis, Neovolcanic Range, or (locally) the Sierra Nevada, this 30-mi (50 km) wide zone trends in an east–west direction from the Colima volcanic complex near the Pacific coast to Mexico's highest mountain, Pico de Orizaba (Citaltépetl) near the Gulf Coastal Plain. To the west and south, the volcanic peaks rise high above the low, dry hills of the Balsas Depression, which separates the volcanic belt from the Sierra Madre del Sur.

Thirteen of Mexico's highest mountains are located in this belt. From west to east they include the following. At the western margin, in Jalisco, are the two edifices of Colima, the older cone of Nevado de Colima (13,800 ft/4,200 m asl) and the slightly lower but still active stratovolcano Fuego de Colima (13,450 ft/4,100 m). Fuego de Colima erupted as recently as January 2013, when an explosion destroyed the lava dome formed in 2007 and created a new crater, sending an ash column 10,000 ft (3,000 m) into the air. Paricutín (9,186 ft/2,800 m asl), in the state of Michoacan, is a cinder cone and, though lower than the massive stratovolcanoes, it is perhaps more famous: it suddenly appeared as a fissure in a cornfield in 1943; and before its eruptions ceased in 1952, it had risen 1,390 ft (424 m) above the ground. Nevado de Toluca (15,016 ft/4,577 m asl), is a dormant stratovolcano 50 mi (80 km) west of Mexico City. Snowcapped Popocatéptl (17,900 ft/5,426 m asl), an active stratovolcano and Mexico's second highest peak, is about 40 mi (70 km) southeast of the city, visible on clear days. A high saddle, the Paso de Cortés, connects it to its dormant neighbor on the east, Iztaccihuatl (17,300 ft/ 5,230 m asl). Matlalcuetl (14,636 ft/4,461 m asl), also a stratovolcano, lies still farther east in the chain, which culminates in the east with Pico de Orizaba (18,491 ft/5,636 m asl). North of Pico de Orizaba is a shield volcano, Cofre de Perote (14,049 ft/4,461 m asl), named for the boxlike (coffer) prominence on its summit. A number of other stratovolcanoes, low cinder cones, lava flows, and crater lakes appear across the zone.

Peaks in the Trans-Mexican Volcanic Axis are forested and some are high enough to have arctic-alpine communities. Pine forests occur at 7,500 ft–8,500 ft (2,275–2,600 m); pine-oak forests are found in the upper part of this altitudinal belt. Above 8,800 ft (2,700 m) a pine-fir forest grows. In Michoacán, these high elevation coniferous forests are vital wintering grounds for monarch butterflies, which congregate in pine and firs in enormous numbers in 12 distinct locations.

Geologic History. The reason for the geologically recent (< 25 mya: from the Pliocene until today) magmatic seismic activity in the Trans-Mexican Volcanic

Axis is somewhat puzzling. A large number of normal faults run parallel to the line of volcanoes and in the west have formed three main rift valleys or grabens: Colima, Chapala, and Zacoalco. Many geologists believe the area is influenced by the oblique subduction of the Rivera and Cocos tectonic plates at a low angle beneath the North American Plate. Not only are volcanoes such as Colima and Popocatépetl stirring and threatening major population centers, but in places small mud pots spit out a hot slurry, small geyser fields spew hot water, and hot springs attract the development of spas.

Biota. The region in general has one of the greatest diversities of reptiles in Mexico, including the Mexican beaded lizard, and also a great number of amphibians, including the axolotl or Mexican salamander, a species that even as an adult maintains a gilled juvenile morphology (neotony) and lives its entire life in intermontane lakes. Endemic mammals in the pine-oak forest include the volcano rabbit and the Mexican volcanic mouse.

Protected Areas. The Monarch Butterfly Biosphere Reserve on the border between the states of Mexico and Michoacán protects about 200 mi^2 (520 km^2) of habitat and was inscribed as a UNESCO World Heritage Site in 2008.

Environmental Issues. Forests have been heavily logged and also burned to promote the new growth of grasses for cattle, threatening the survival of endemic animals. A number of small reserves work to protect monarch butterfly roosts.

See also Colima Volcano (Volcán Colima de Fuego); Mexican Plateau (Mexican Altiplano); Paricutín; Pico de Orizaba (Citlatépetl); Popocaétpétl and Iztaccìhautl

Further Reading

Burton, Tony. 2012. "Mexico's Volcanic Axis." Geo-Mexico: The Geography and Dynamics of Modern Mexico. http://geo-mexico.com/?p=6242

"Road Log of Sea of Cortex Field Trip, 1997." 1997. Michigan Tech. http://www.geo.mtu.edu/volcanoes/research/djsofiel/cortez/roadlog.html

Valero, Alejandra, Jan Schipper, Tom Allnutt, and Christine Burdette. n.d. "Southern North America: Southern Mexico." Tropical and Subtropical Coniferous Forests. Terrestrial Ecoregions. World Wildlife Fund. http://worldwildlife.org/ecoregions/nt0310

Tristan da Cunha and Gough Island

Atlantic Ocean

Geographic Overview. The Tristan da Cunha archipelago and Gough Island, 218 mi (350 km) to the southeast, are the only cool temperate islands in the Atlantic Ocean. Located almost half way between the southern tip of Africa and the east coast of South America, Tristan boasts the most remote human community on Earth. These islands are part of the British Overseas Territory of St Helena, Ascension, and Tristan da Cunha.

Geographic Coordinates. Tristan: 37°07'S, 12°17'W; Gough: 40°18'S, 09°54'W

Description. Tristan da Cunha consists of three small volcanic islands 12–20 mi (20–30 km) apart: Tristan, Nightingale, and Inaccessible. Each is separated from the others by deep trenches; waters more than 1,600 ft (500 m) deep lie between Nightingale and Inaccessible, while they are separated from Tristan by water more than 6,500 ft (2,000 m) deep. The three islands differ in age, size, and elevation. Tristan is the youngest and largest and indeed is still volcanically active. This circular island has a surface area of 37 mi^2 (96 km^2); the summit of Queen Mary's Peak, at 6,760 ft (2,060 m) asl, is the highest point in the archipelago. Cinder cones dot the lower slopes, while the mountain has a summit crater close to 1,000 ft (300 m) across. Inaccessible is next in age, size, and elevation, having an area of 5.4 mi^2 (14 km^2) and rising 2,000 ft (600 m) asl. Tiny Nightingale Island is the oldest and smallest, having been eroded to its core of highly resistant rock. Its area is only 1.5 mi^2 (4 km^2) and maximum elevation about 1,150 ft (350 m) asl. Vertical cliffs with high waterfalls plunging over the side edge the coasts of these islands.

Distant Gough Island is similar in age to Inaccessible Island, but considerably larger and higher. It has an area of 25 mi^2 (65 km^2) and is mountainous with a high plateau rising to 3,000 ft (910 m) asl. The only low land is in the south. Steep cliffs line the coast and numerous stacks and islets occur offshore.

The climate is cool and temperate with abundant rainfall. On Tristan, the average high temperature in austral winter (July–September) is 57°F (14°C), while average lows are near 40°F (4°C). During the summer, highs average 70°F (21°C) and lows 63°F (17°C). Gough Island is cooler than the Tristan da Cunha archipelago. On average there are 252 days each year when some rain is recorded. Every month, the island receives between 4 and 7 in (90–175 mm) of rain; total annual precipitation averages 66 in (1,681 mm). Gough Island lies in the Roaring Forties and has higher amounts of precipitation (118 in or 3,000 mm) and is windier and cooler than Tristan. Snow falls in the highlands during winter.

The vegetation pattern on Tristan and Gough is one of concentric bands rising to the summits at the centers of the islands. Coastal tussock grasslands give way to a narrow zone of bogfern heath, above which is fern bush, dominated by a cycad-like fern and a tree, *Phylica arborea*. Above this a belt of wet heath with fewer ferns but more mosses, sedges, and other flowering plants. The highest elevations are covered with the dwarf cushion plants of the "Feldmark." Two types of bogs are widespread on the islands, *Sphagnum* moss bogs and pools of water covered with floating mats of bog grass (bulrush). Most native species have been replaced by introduced pasture plants.

Geologic History. Tristan is a high shield volcano 310 mi (500 km) east of the Mid-Atlantic Rise. It is the southwestern end of string of seamounts forming the Walvis Ridge. They are products of the slow northeast migration of the African Plate over the Walvis Hot Spot. Nightingale emerged about 18 mya and had its final eruption about 200,000 years ago. Inaccessible emerged 3–4 mya and remained active until 50,000 years ago. Gough Island rose from a separate volcanic center some 3–5 mya and was active until 100,000 years ago. Tristan only emerged about 200,000 years ago. It last erupted on October 10, 1961, leading to the evacuation of island residents. Activity ceased in mid-March of the following year; resettlement began in September 1962.

Biota. Most species that naturally colonized Tristan da Cunha and Gough Island came from South America. Postarrival evolution has led to a high degree of endemism: 27 of the 50 native flowering plants are endemic as are 16 of the 35 ferns, approximately 100 invertebrates, all seven land birds. Among the last group are buntings (*Nesospiza* spp.) that have radiated

into small-billed generalists and large-billed specialists exploiting the woody fruits of the native *Phylica* trees. Two species coexist on Nightingale and three on Inaccessible. A number of seabirds nest on the island, although their numbers are much reduced due to introduced predators and human collection of eggs and nestlings. Of note are three species of albatross and the Great Shearwater, which after nesting during austral summer migrates to the North Atlantic waters off Newfoundland and Greenland to feed during June and July.

Protected Areas. Gough and Inaccessible islands are UNESCO World Heritage Sites. Tristan protects nearly half of its land surface.

Environmental Issues. Overharvesting of subantarctic fur seals and southern elephant seals is a thing of the past, but only the fur seal populations on western Gough Island are recovering. Invasive species have been a major problem since 1790, when sealers stocked the islands with pigs and goats. Before they died out, pigs nearly eliminated the Spectacled Petrel and Tristan Wandering Albatross from Inaccessible. Only two to three pairs of the albatross still breed on Inaccessible; critically endangered, another 1,500 pairs nest on Gough. The house mouse invaded Gough Island in the 1800s and preyed on the eggs and chicks of the Gough Bunting. Rats invaded Tristan after an 1882 shipwreck and threatened many nesting birds. Human collection of eggs and nestlings of seabirds also decimated populations. This practice was eliminated from Tristan and Gough when nature preserves were set aside in the 1970s. On Nightingale, only the eggs of Great Shearwaters and Rockhopper Penguins may now be collected legally. Plans exist to eradicate rats and mice from Tristan and mice from Gough. Control programs against alien plants focus on New Zealand flax on Inaccessible and Nightingale and procumbent pearlwort on Gough.

See also Ascension Island; Saint Helena

Further Reading

"Gough and Inaccessible Islands." n.d. World Heritage Center, UNESCO. http://whc.unesco.org/en/list/740

Ryan, Peter G. 2009. "Tristan da Cunha and Gough Island." In *Encyclopedia of Islands*, edited by Rosemary

G. Gillespie and David A. Clague, 929–932. Berkeley: University of California Press.

"Tristan da Cunha." n.d. Global Volcanism Program, Smithsonian Institution. http://www.volcano.si.edu/world/volcano.cfm?vnum=1806-01=

"The Tristan da Cunha Website." 2013. Tristan da Cunha Government and the Tristan da Cunha Association. http://www.tristandc.com/index.php

Tsingy de Bemaraha National Park

Madagascar

Geographic Overview. The Malagasy word, *tsingy*, meaning "walking on tiptoes," is an apt description for the inhospitable but striking labyrinth of limestone needles and spires in Tsingy de Bemaraha National Park. The park also contains canyons, gorges, forests, lakes, and mangrove swamps. The rich flora and fauna includes a variety of drought tolerant plants, lemurs, and chameleons, and many endemic species.

Geographic Coordinates. 18°12'S–19°09'S; 44°03 04'E–44°57'E

Description. Located in west-central Madagascar, 45 mi (70 km) inland from the west coast, Tsingy National Park covers 608 mi^2 (1,575 km^2). The eastern edge of the plateau is marked by the abrupt Bemaraha Cliffs, 985–1,300 ft (300–400 m) above the north–south Manambolo River valley. Rounded hills slope more gently toward the west. In the north, rolling hills alternate with limestone outcrops. The most extensive limestone pinnacle formations are in the southern region, where several hanging bridges facilitate visitor access. Untouched forests line Manambolo Gorge, which houses lemurs and waterfalls as it crosses east-to-west through the southern Bemaraha Plateau. Some rock faces in the gorge rise 1,300 ft (400 m) from the river's edge. A large cave system, complete with stalactites and stalagmites, has developed in the soluble limestone.

The complex karst hydrology of springs and rivers is the water source for rice fields in western Madagascar and for the forest and lake ecosystems to the west, including estuary mangroves and coastal forests.

The region has a subarid climate with strong contrasts between the hot, rainy season (November–March), which renders the park inaccessible, and the cool, dry season (April–October). Annual rainfall averages 39–59 in (1,000–1,500 mm). Mean temperatures are 79°–82° F (26°–28° C).

The cave system has sheltered humans for centuries, especially the Vazimba, reputedly the first human inhabitants of Madagascar. Tombs and archaeological relics abound, and the region is still used for rituals. As the land of ancestors, the tsingy is a sacred place to the local ethnic group, the Sakalava.

Geologic History. The Jurassic (200 mya) limestone of the Bemaraha Plateau developed while Madagascar was part of Gondwana. The limestone seabed was uplifted to become the plateau approximately 6 mya. In the purest limestone, rainwater sculpted a dense network of deep crevasses, separated by fluted ridges and sharp tipped spires. The grooves dissolved by rainwater are called lapies, which developed very sharply on a grand scale at Tsingy de Bemaraha.

Biota. The mosaic of habitats supports a rich biota with many endemics. Approximately 85 percent of the biota is endemic to Madagascar, and 47 percent is locally endemic to the tsingy. Difficulty of access limits discovery and description of species.

Of the more than 450 plant species in 81 families, 84 percent are endemic and many are unique to the tsingy. The dry, deciduous, and semideciduous forest is typical of western Madagascar, while the eastern side has grassy savannas and lowland bushes. Major plants are rosewood (*Dalbergia*), *Commiphora*, and *Hildegardia*. Zones with little lapies development exhibit a flat surface with high solar radiation and little soil, characterized by bushy xerophytic plants as tall as 26 ft (8 m). Almost all of the plants are deciduous and have various adaptations to drought, including few to no leaves, thickened stems, and spines. Bare rock surfaces include a variety of drought-tolerant plants, such as *Kalanchoe gastonisboniri*, bulbs, and spiny bushes such as *Pachypodium rutenbergianum*. Trees include bottle trees in the genus *Delonix*. Small areas of dense tropical forests dominated by *Pandanus* and ferns occupy deep, narrow canyons which trap humidity and limit direct sunlight.

The park supports 11 lemur species. Decken's sifaka (*Propithecus deckenii*), red-fronted lemur (*Eulemur rufifrons*), brown lemur (*Eulemur fulvus*), fat-tailed dwarf lemur (*Cheirogaleus medius*), grey mouse lemur (*Microcebus murinus*), Cleese's wooly lemur (*Avahi cleesei*), and Sambirano lesser bamboo lemur (*Hapalemur occidentalis*), are all endemic to this area. Small carnivores include the falanouc (*Eupleres goudotii*), ring-tailed mongoose (*Galidia elegans*), and several species of bats. Other notable mammals include fossa (*Cryptoprocta ferox*) and lowland red forest rat (*Nesomys lambertoni*).

The 94 species of birds include the critically endangered Madagascar Fish Eagle (*Haliaeetus vociferoides*), Crested Ibis (*Lophotibis cristata*), Madagascar Woodrail (*Canirallus kioloides*), Giant Coua (*Coua gigas*), and Coquerel's Coua (*Coua coquereli*). Many of the 16 amphibian species and 59 reptile species are endemic to Madagascar. Those found only in Tsingy de Bemaraha include Madagascar iguana (*Chalarodon madagascariensis*), Antsingy leaf chameleon (*Brookesia perarmata*), a dwarf chameleon (*Brookesia exarmata*), and Nicosia's chameleon (*Furcifer nicosiai*). Crocodiles are found in the rivers.

Protected Areas. Preserved as an Integrated Natural Reserve since 1927, the region was redesignated in 1997. The reserve was limited to the northern 610 mi² (1,578 km²) and remains off-limits to visitation, while the southern 279 mi² (723 km²) opened to ecotourism as a national park. In 1990, Tsingy was inscribed as a World Heritage Site. West of the park, a Ramsar site for protection of endemic species, such as fish eagles, freshwater turtles (*Erymnochelys madagascariensis*), Berniers Teal (*Anas bernieri*), and many other water birds, was designated in 1999.

Environmental Issues. As elsewhere in Madagascar, habitat destruction is the most serious threat. Forests are devastated by cutting of trees and setting of fires to stimulate growth of grass for Zebu. Some lemurs are hunted for food. Illegal export trade in wild animals, especially chameleons for the pet trade, threatens local populations.

See also Madagascar

Further Reading

Rasoloarison, V. and F. Paquier. 2003. "*Tsingy de Bemaraha.*" In *The Natural History of Madagascar*, edited by Steven M. Goodman and Jonathan P. Benstead, 1507–1512. Chicago: University of Chicago Press.

UNESCO. 2013. *Tsingy de Bemaraha Strict Nature Reserve*. World Heritage Centre. http://whc.unesco.org/en/list/494

Tubbataha Reef National Marine Park

Pacific Ocean

Geographic Overview. Tubbataha Reef, in the Sulu Sea west of the Philippines, is a significant location in the Coral Triangle of the Pacific Ocean, which is the global center of tropical marine diversity. The park is almost totally submerged. The reef itself is a biodiversity hotspot.

Geographic Coordinates. Approximately 08°36'N, 119°49'E

Description. Tubbataha Reef National Marine Park sits in the middle of the Sulu Sea, approximately 93 mi (150 km) southeast of Puerto Princesa City on the Philippine island of Palawan. Although a few sandy islands exist, most of the park is submerged. The park covers approximately 390 mi² (1,000 km²) of high-quality marine habitats, including three atolls and a large area of deep sea, with a mean depth of 2,500 ft (750 m).

The park consists of two large shallow reef platforms, each enclosing a sandy lagoon. North Reef is a large, oblong platform 2.5–3 mi (4–5 km) wide, completely surrounding a center sandy lagoon. A small part of this shallow reef is emergent at very low tides. South Reef is smaller, a triangle 0.6–1.2 mi (1–2 km) wide, also surrounding a sandy lagoon. Its southern tip is a sandy island, South Islet, which provides nesting sites for birds and turtles and a base for a lighthouse. The park area is uninhabited. The park's shallow areas are extensive reef flats, at 50–80 ft (15–25 m) depth, with their outer edges descending in almost vertical walls that plunge to depths of more than 330 ft (100 m). Jessie Beazley Reef, 12 mi (20 km) north of the atolls, is a coral island, emergent at low tide.

Its healthy coral reef ecosystem serves as a nursery area for reproduction and dispersal of species, supporting fisheries elsewhere in the Sulu Sea. Both the reefs and the deep sea provide habitat for threatened and endangered species. With visibility often 100 ft (30 m) and an abundance of life, the marine park is an increasingly popular site for scuba diving, which can only be visited on live-aboard ships making the overnight trip from Puerto Princesa.

The climate is influenced by monsoons, with a southwest air flow June–October and a northeast air flow December–June. Seas are calmest March–June, and air temperatures are 82°–86°F (28°–30°C).

Geologic History. The Sulu Sea is a marginal deepwater sea west of the Philippine Plate and separated from the South China Sea on the northwest by a narrow strip of Eurasian continental crust, Palawan Island. It is separated from the Celebes Sea to the southeast by Sulu Archipelago, a string of Philippine islands. To the southwest is the continental craton of Borneo. The reefs lie on top of Cagayan Ridge, a string of extinct underwater volcanoes in the center of the Sulu Sea. The reefs are classic atolls, coral reefs which developed upward, building upon themselves around the shoreline of eroding and submerging volcanic island.

Biota. The Coral Triangle, extending east from Java to the Solomon Islands and north to the Philippines, is known for its rich coral biological diversity. Covering just 2 percent of the world's oceans, it supports 40 percent of the world's fish species and 75 percent of its coral species. The park has approximately 375 species of coral, half of all species in the world, and approximately 600 species of fish. Remote and undisturbed, the park retains large marine fauna, including 11 shark species and 13 cetacean species (whales and dolphins). The reef manta ray (*Manta alfredi*) is a rare species that frequents the reef rather than the deep sea. Large pelagic fishes, such as jacks, barracuda, tuna, and trevallies are common. The threatened Napoleon wrasse, which occupies the reef, is also a key large species. The presence of top predators, such as tiger sharks and hammerhead sharks, indicates a healthy, balanced ecosystem.

The park counts 100 species of birds. The emergent islands, Bird Islet and South Islet, offer nesting sites for the few colonies of breeding seabirds remaining in Southeast Asia. The Christmas Island Frigatebird (*Fregata andrewsi*) is a regular visitor, and the islands are the only nesting site for the endemic Philippine Black Noddy (*Anous minutus worcestri*). Endangered green turtles and hawksbill turtles also nest on the islands.

Protected Areas. Through the 1970s, Tubbataha Reef was naturally protected from exploitation because it was far from land and lacked fresh water. Motorized boats in the 1980s allowed fishermen to fish further from home, and they often used destructive practices, such as dynamite and cyanide. Large fishing vessels from China and Taiwan also occasionally fished the Sulu Sea. At the urging of divers and conservationists, the national marine park was declared in 1988. The park is now a strictly no-take zone. Tubbataha Reefs Natural Park is a World Heritage Site and a Ramsar Wetland of International Importance.

Environmental Issues. Increasing pressure from dive operations require strict regulation. Outbreaks of crown-of-thorns starfish (*Acanthaster planci*), first seen on the reef in 2007, do severe damage to coral. The park has had two major coral bleaching episodes, in 1998 and 2010, both due to an El Niño event that raised the water temperature. Although the reef has recovered well, climate change remains a threat to the health of the coral. Illegal fishing and taking of shellfish, such as *Trochus niloticus* to be made into buttons and jewelry, continues in spite of a ranger station on North Reef. Trash, especially plastic and discarded fishing nets, is hazardous to marine life.

Further Reading

"Tubbataha Reefs National Park." 2012. http://www.tubba tahareef.org/home

UNESCO. 2013. *Tubbataha Reefs Natural Park.* http://whc.unesco.org/en/list/653

Turpan Depression

China

Geographic Overview. The Turpan Depression, in northwestern China, is the lowest point in China and one of the lowest elevations in the world. Although it is the hottest and driest location in China, the basin, with the aid of an ancient and efficient irrigation system, produces an abundance of fruit.

Geographic Coordinates. Approximately 41°00'N–43°20'N, 88°E–95°E

Description. The Turpan Depression, or Turpan-Hami basin, is slightly northeast of the Tarim Basin and approximately 125 mi (200 km) southeast of Urumqi. It is a long, narrow downfaulted basin in northeastern Xinjiang Autonomous Region, 300 mi (500 km) east-to-west and 37–60 mi (60–100 km) north-to-south, covering 20,650 mi² (53,500 km²). It lies in the eastern part of the Tian Shan between the Bogda Mountains to the north and the Kuruktag (Kurultag, Jueluotage) Mountains to the south. Local relief between the perpetually snow-covered northern mountains and the green oases in the depression is 16,400 ft (5,000 m). The lowest point is Lake Ayding, where the salt surface is 508 ft (155 m) bsl. It vies with Lake Assal in Djibouti for being the world's second lowest point of land. The combined depression includes the Liaodong Uplift between Turpan to the west and Hami to the east. The basin is filled with more than 23,000 ft (7,000 m) of sediments.

The Turfan–Hami Oil Field in both basins produces oil and natural gas, and the Shihongtan uranium ore deposit is on the southwest margin of the depression.

The region is a well-watered oasis that produces a wide variety of fruits, including stone fruit, melons, pomegranates, figs, walnuts, and grapes. The fruit is naturally processed in ventilated drying structures. Crops are irrigated by extensive underground water projects, called karez, a system of wells linked by underground tunnels, similar to the qanats in the Middle East. Wells collect snowmelt from the mountains as it percolates through the alluvial fans. Tunnels connecting the wells channel the water underground, using the natural slope, to fields—an efficient method that reduces evaporation in the desert climate. The system, with 1,100 wells and 3,100 mi (5,000 km) of channels in the Turpan and Hami Depression, has been in use for 2,000 years.

The Turpan Depression, dry and sunny all year, is characterized by continental temperature extremes. January mean temperature is 14°–18°F (–8° to -10°C). July mean temperature is 90°F (32°C). The region holds the records for both the highest and lowest temperatures in China, 118°F (48°C) and –62°F (–52°C).

Mean annual precipitation is 0.4–1.2 in (10–30 mm), and it often fails to rain for months at a time.

The region was a significant political center in China's dynastic past, with many sites and ruins. The town of Gaochang, near modern Turpan oasis and now in ruins, was an important stopover on the Silk Road 2,000 years ago. Astana-Karakhoja, near Gaochang, is the site of ancient tombs for nobles and officials. Thousand Buddha Caves at Bezeklik in the Flaming Mountains' Mutou Valley, has 57 grottoes dating from 581–420. The caves were excavated out of the red sandstone rock, and murals, primarily depicting Buddhist tales, cover the walls.

Geologic History. Published geologic studies of the Turpan Depression are few. The Turpan–Hami Depression is bounded by faults, especially on the north, and is a partial graben. A shear zone formed in the late Paleozoic between two plates, which was further deformed in the Tertiary when India collided with Eurasia. The Flaming Mountains, with a high peak of 2,729 ft (832 m), is a thrust fault belt in the center of the basin. Little is known about Turpan volcano, a cinder cone which reputedly erupted between AD 960 and 1279.

Biota. The salty shores of Lake Ayding support reeds, salt cedar, and saxsaul trees, but areas without water are barren. The irrigation system, however, has brought abundant agricultural life to the desert.

Protected Areas. The karez well system and several sites along the Silk Road, including Gaochang, Astana cemeteries, and the Bezeklik Buddha Caves, are being considered as World Heritage Sites.

See also Asia; Tarim Basin and Takla Makan Desert; Tian Shan

Further Reading

Shao Leia, Karl Statteggerb, Wenhou LI, and Bernd J. Haupt. 1999. "Depositional Style and Subsidence History of the Turpan Basin (NW China)." *Sedimentary Geology* 128: 155–169.

Songqiao, Zhao. 1986. "Temperate and Warm-temperate Desert of Northwest China." In *Physical Geography of China*, 167–184. New York: John Wiley & Sons.

U

Uluru/Ayers Rock

Australia

Geographic Overview. The red Uluru monolith is one of the most iconic landscapes of Australia, recognized by people all over the world. Located near the geographic center of the continent, Uluru is a deep-rooted inselberg, a remnant of ancient sandstone layers tilted nearly vertically and rounded by weathering and erosion. It was named Ayers Rock in1872 in honor of Sir Henry Ayers, premier of the former colony of South Australia from 1863 to 1873. In the 1993, the name was officially changed to Uluru/Ayers Rock, giving precedence to the name given it by the local Aboriginal people. Uluru is a sacred site for the Anangu people, and caves and rock overhangs at the base preserve their distinctive rock art.

Geographic Coordinates. 25°21'S, 131°02'E

Description. Uluru or Ayers Rock is a red sandstone inselberg at the southern edge of the Amadeus sedimentary basin, which lies between the MacDonnell Ranges to the north and the Petermann and Musgrave ranges to the south. This region is Australia's Red Centre, covering a large portion of southern Northern Territory. The monolith is 2.2 mi (3.6 km) long and 1.2 mi (1.9 km) wide. Its summit is 1,141 ft (346 m) above the red plains west of the Simpson Desert and 2,830 ft (865 m) asl. Most of the ancient sandstone block lies below surface, where it is estimated to continue to a depth of 19,685 ft (6,000 m). The sandstone beds are nearly vertical, dipping to the southwest at angle of 85°. The sandstone is a type known as arkose and high in feldspar, suggesting its source is ancient granite. Arkose is gray; oxidation of iron minerals in the rock gives Uluru its red coloration. The massive rock lacks joints that might have eroded into talus slopes. The absence of talus deposits and presence of exfoliation sheets 3–10 ft (1–3 m) thick contribute to its smooth, rounded profile and steep flanks. Differential erosion of beds of varying resistance has produced distinct grooves in the surface. The summit is nearly flat. Around the base of the inselberg, chemical weathering and sand blasting have created caves and overhangs, some containing Aboriginal rock art.

Uluru is in a semiarid region receiving about 12 in (300 mm) of rain annually. In summer (November–March) daily low temperatures average 72°F (22.3°C), highs are near 100°F (37.8°C). In winter daily lows average 40°F (4.7°C) and highs around 68°F (20.2°C). Frost can occur from June into August. Surface water only exists in ephemeral pools fed by small streams flowing from the rock after summer rains.

The surrounding landscape is one of level to gently rolling terrain of red sands and soils. The monolith is nearly bare rock that changes color with the season and time of day, becoming a deep, glowing orange-red at sunrise and sundown and after a rain. Uluru's sparse vegetation consists of perennial grasses, sedges, and scattered hummocks of spinifex (*Triodia* spp.) and individuals of Uluru mulga (*Acacia ayersiania*), Australian fig (*Ficus platypoda*), and bloodwood (*Eucalyptus terminalis*).

About 20 mi (32 km) west of Uluru are the 36 rock domes of Kata Tjuta. This cluster of steep-sided inselbergs, also known as the Olgas, are composed of conglomerate but are geologically related to Uluru. The highest stands 1,791 ft (546 m) above the surrounding plain and 3,507 ft (1,069 m) asl. Much larger than

Aerial view of iconic Ayers Rock (Uluru), a red sandstone inselberg in Australia's Northern Territory. (Venomize/Dreamstime.com)

Uluru is Mount Augustus (Burringurrah) in Western Australia. This monolith rises 2,820 ft (860 m) above its surroundings to an elevation of 3,629 ft (1,106 m) asl. Claims are that Burringurrah is the largest monolith in the world, and Uluru second largest; but these assertions, good for tourism, are unsubstantiated by geologists.

Geologic History. Uluru is formed of Paleozoic marine sediments. The sands had likely eroded from granitic mountains to the south of the Amadeus basin during the early Cambrian (550–530 mya). The basin was probably uplifted 400–300 mya, tilting the sandstone layers to near vertical.

Protected Areas. Uluru is protected in Uluru–Kata Tjuta National Park. The park was inscribed as a World Heritage Site in 1997.

Environmental Issues. Tourism is a threat to the integrity of the rock and the cultural and spiritual landscape of its Aboriginal owners. All tourist facilities are located outside the national park. Climbing the rock, a popular tourist activity, can be treacherous;

35 recreational climbers have died trying to make the ascent. The single trail is closed whenever high winds buffet the summit and may soon be closed permanently to prevent desecration of the Dreamtime track of the Ananga people. Local Aborigines do not ascend sacred Uluru and request visitors also not do so.

Further Reading
"Uluru-Kata Tjuta National Park." n.d. World Heritage Centre, UNESCO. http://whc.unesco.org/en/list/447

Ural Mountains

Russia

Geographic Overview. Although the Urals are the conventional boundary between Europe and Asia, they are not a topographic barrier for humans, weather systems, or plants and animals. They are among the world's oldest mountains, now eroded primarily to high hills. The Urals are well-known for their gemstones and mineral deposits and have been an industrialized region in Russia since the late 16th century.

Geographic Coordinates. Approximately 48°00'N–77°00'N, 51°20'E–67°04'E, including Novaya Zemlya

Description. The Ural Mountains are a nearly linear range of parallel ridges of folded strata. They extend approximately 1,865 mi (3,000 km) from the island of Novaya Zemlya in the Arctic south to central Asia near the Aral Sea in Kazakhstan. The range is 60–250 mi (100–400 km) wide and most often 3,000–4,000 ft (900–1,220 m) asl but with summits rising to 6,000 ft (1,830 m). Rocks on the western slope are limestones, dolomites, sandstones, and shales. Most of the high mountains are exposed quartzite, schist, and gabbro. The eastern slope has prominent horsts of uplifted crystalline basement and ultrabasic seafloor rocks. The Urals are rich in mineral wealth, including gems and semiprecious stones, such as emerald, beryl, amethyst, topaz, diamonds, and sapphire. Other deposits include coal, iron, copper, gold, platinum, silver, nickel, aluminum, manganese, lead, zinc, magnesium, chromium, and potash. The Ural River rises on the east slope of the southern Urals and flows 1,570 mi (2,527 km) south to the Caspian Sea.

The Polar, Subpolar, and Northern Urals extend from the island of Novaya Zemlya southward. On the continent, they make an eastward arc before continuing due south along the 58°–60°E meridians to the city of Perm. Most of the region is 3,300 ft (1,000 m) or higher, and includes the highest peak, Mount Narodnaya at 6,214 ft (1,894 m). The Polar and Subpolar Urals were repeatedly glaciated in the Pleistocene, by continental, alpine, and piedmont glaciers, and retain typically sharp alpine features. Ice still covers more than one-quarter of Novaya Zemlya. There is a notable lack of glaciation southward. The Middle Urals, from Perm south to Chelyabinsk, are the lowest, less than 3,300 ft (1,000 m) asl, and narrowest section. This region is very industrialized because of its mineral wealth. The Murzinsko–Aduiskii Belt contains precious stone deposits. The Southern Urals is the widest part of the range, extending south from Chelyabinsk to the Ural River valley near Orsk. The highest peak is Mount Yamantau, 5,380 ft (1,640 m), and the western slope has many karst features. Folds here

have been eroded down to Precambrian quartzites and other metamorphic rocks. South of Orsk, elevation of the Kazakh Urals, which includes the Mugodzhars, decreases and the range becomes more arid.

Climate in the Urals is zonal, including latitudinal belts ranging from tundra and subarctic to humid continental and desert. The northern and central regions are affected by cyclonic storms bringing precipitation, while the southern and Kazakh Urals are dominated by high pressure and experience greater continentality, with hot, dry summers and cold, dry winters. Mean January temperatures range from –9°F (–23°C) on the Polar Ural coast to 3°F (–16°C) in Kazakhstan. Mean July temperatures are 43°F (6°C) in the polar region to 70°F (21°C) in Kazakhstan. The mean annual precipitation is 20 in (500 mm) in the Polar Urals, 32 in (800 mm) in the Northern Urals, 20–24 in (500–600 mm) in the Middle and Southern Urals, and less than 12 in (300 mm) in the Kazak Urals.

Geologic History. The Urals were built by repeated orogenies from the Precambrian to the Hercynian in the late Paleozoic. Prior to the collision of the East European Platform and Siberian Plate, which contributed to the formation of the supercontinent Pangaea, the Ural region was a geosyncline. The convergence of the major plates, with related microcontinents and volcanic arcs, occurred in the late Paleozoic (300–250 mya) and lasted 90 million years. The Main Uralian Fault, extending along almost the entire length of the Urals, separates continental rocks in the western part of the range from an island arc of volcanics and deep sea deposits in the eastern part. Renewed tectonics in the Jurassic uplifted the northern sections of the Urals and created Novaya Zemlya. The region has been subjected to erosion since the end of the Jurassic.

In the middle of the range, 54°–59°N, the mountain chain curves eastward in a circular pattern of faults. The majority of the mineral fields in this section of the Urals may stem from a giant impact crater in the Precambrian.

Biota. The Urals are at the juncture of tundra and taiga vegetation zones, with a unique mixture of European and Asian species. Tundra extends south to 64°N, where it is replaced by sparse forest and taiga. Dominant trees in the taiga include Siberian spruce

(*Picea obovata*), Siberian larch (*Larix russica*), Russian larch (*Larix sukaczewii*), and Siberian fir (*Abies sibirica*). South of 56°N, forests are broadleaf deciduous trees, such as oaks, linden, and maples, most of which have been replaced by agriculture. The extreme south has steppe grasslands.

Typical Siberian animals include reindeer, sable, elk, brown bear, wolf, wolverine, and lynx. European species include hare, polecat, and mink. Reintroduced European beaver is now common. Bird species, including Eurasian Dipper, Golden Eagle, Chaffinch, Eurasian Dotterel, Northern Black Grouse, and Ural Owl, are representative of both European and Siberian taigas.

Protected Areas. The Urals have several national reserves. Bashkir Ural, a World Heritage Site in the Southern Urals, includes the Paleolithic cave drawings in Kapova. Reserves in the Middle Urals include a famous ice cave, Kungurskaya.

Environmental Issues. The Urals are a region for nuclear research, and also the site of several nuclear accidents.

Further Reading

Burba, G. A. 2003. "The Geological Evolution of the Ural Mountains: A Supposed Exposure to a Giant Impact." *Microsymposium 38 MS011*. www.lpi.usra.edu/meetings/largeimpacts2003/pdf/4117.pdf

Shahgedanova, Maria, Veniamin Perov, and Yury Mudrov. 2002. "The Mountains of Northern Russia." In *The Physical Geography of Northern Eurasia*, edited by Maria Shahgedanova, 284–313. Oxford: Oxford University Press.

V

Venice Lagoon

Italy

Geographic Overview. The City of Venice, Italy, is a world cultural site that is sinking into Venice Lagoon because of human interference with the natural lagoon geomorphological system. In order to fortify the city environs, Venetians began diverting the silt-bearing rivers 600 years ago, which initiated the subsidence that continues today.

Geographic Coordinates. 45°26'N, 12°20'E

Description. Venice Lagoon is on the northeast coast of Italy on the northern edge of the Adriatic Sea. Bounded on the north by the Sile River and on the south by the Brenta River, the lagoon is 31 mi (50 km) long and 5–8.7 mi (8–14 km) wide, covering approximately 212 mi^2 (550 km^2). Within the lagoon are shallows, tidal flats, salt marshes, islands, and a network of channels. The mean depth is 3.3 ft (1 m), while channel depths are 3.3–49 ft (1–15 m). In addition to the city of Venice, the lagoon has several other inhabited and uninhabited islands. The lagoon is enclosed by baymouth bar islands. Between the islands, three coastal inlets, Lido, Malamocco, and Chioggia, allow water exchange with the Adriatic Sea. Due to alterations in the hydraulics of the lagoon, the city of Venice and other areas of the lagoon have been subsiding into the sea for centuries.

Geologic History. The lagoon and the island of Venice originally underwent a natural subsidence due to tectonic processes related to the uplift of the Alps and the Appennines. Sea level also rose. Natural subsidence during the Quaternary is estimated to have been 0.5–1.3 mm per year. Sediment supply from several rivers, including the Adige, Bacchiglione, Brenta, Sile, and Piave, offset the natural subsidence and eustatic sea level rise and proceeded to fill in the lagoon. The Venetians, however, wanted to maintain the lagoon for security against enemies. They diverted the rivers and developed hydraulic works to prevent sediment buildup. Since 1800, more intensive changes were made to the geomorphology, further reducing sedimentation and accelerating erosion.

Exploitation of groundwater aquifers was a more recent development. Groundwater withdrawal became a major problem with post–World War II industrialization, peaking from 1950 to 1970. Withdrawal of water caused compaction of sediment and increased subsidence. Between 1930 and 1970, groundwater extraction caused a net loss of 4.7 in (120 mm) of height. Upon realization of the causal link between groundwater extraction and subsidence, the wells were closed and the rate of subsidence slowed. Land levels even slightly rebounded following closure of the wells.

Over the course of the 20th century, the city of Venice lost 9 in (23 cm) of height, of which 4.7 in (12 cm) was caused by land subsidence (both natural and human-induced) and 4.3 in (11 cm) was attributable to natural sea level rise. This loss of elevation caused increased flooding in the city and changed the hydrodynamics within the lagoon, causing both erosion and channel silting. The changes also weakened the littoral system of the baymouth bars, which protect the lagoon from storm damage, making them more susceptible to being overtopped by storm waves. Flooding, in both frequency and intensity, has increased in the last 50 years.

Due to natural sediment compaction exacerbated by human diversion of rivers and groundwater withdrawal, the city of Venice has been sinking into Venice Lagoon for centuries. Former streets are now flooded canals. (Gunaleite/Dreamstime .com)

Although a survey in 2000 indicated that the city was no longer subsiding, new satellite evidence confirms that Venice is sinking 0.04–0.08 in (1–2 mm) per year, and the Adriatic Sea continues to rise. Numbers vary with location, study, and date, but subsidence continues. Based on accurate historical paintings, the city has sunk more than 2 ft (60 cm) since 1727.

Environmental Issues. Although attempts exist to refill the aquifers with seawater, subsidence is irreversible. In addition to subsidence, changes to the lagoon have decreased the extent of natural salt marsh and seagrass meadows ecosystems, which are used by over 60 species of birds and are critical for fish, shellfish, and crustaceans. Venice has never had a sewer system. Waste is released into the canals. Now, however, there are a few septic tanks and plans for treatment and dispersing effluent directly into the Adriatic Sea. The water quality is poor, not due solely to human waste, but also to heavy metal and chemicals from industry as well as pesticides from both the city and the watershed, which is heavily used for agriculture and livestock. Corrosive seawater, motor boat wakes, and soil erosion beneath building foundations are additional problems. Climate warming and glacial melt will further increase sea level rise in the Adriatic. Modulo Sperimentale Elettromeccanico (MOSE) is a flood protection system, scheduled to be completed in 2014. Mobile gates across the inlets between the baymouth bars are designed to close and prevent flooding when high tides reach a certain level. Currently, that could happen as many as 200 times a year. While the city may be protected from flooding, the lagoon ecosystem will suffer without the exchange of water with the Adriatic.

Further Reading

Scearce, Carolyn. 2007. *Venice and the Environmental Hazards of Coastal Cities.* CSA Discovery Guides. ProQuest Information and Learning. www.csa.com /discoveryguides/discoveryguides-main.php

Victoria Falls (Mosi-oa-Tunya)

Zambia and Zimbabwe

Geographic Overview. Victoria Falls, on the Zambezi River along the border between Zambia and Zimbabwe, is considered the world's largest waterfall even though it is neither the highest nor the widest. Nonetheless its combined height and breadth produce the largest curtain of falling water anywhere, rivaled only by Iguazu Falls on the Argentina–Brazil border. The native name for the falls, Mosi-oa-Tunya, translates as "the smoke that thunders" in tribute to the great spray that produces rainbows even in moonlight. The English name was given by David Livingstone when, in 1855, he became the first European to see the falls; it honors Queen Victoria of England.

Geographic Coordinates. 17°55'S, 25°51'E

Description. Victoria Falls is the latest in a series of massive cascades in the Zambezi River that over geologic time have dropped off a high plateau formed of horizontal layers of basalt nearly 1,000 ft (300 m) thick. The contemporary falls are more than a mile wide (5,604 ft [1,708 m]) and at their highest point, 355 ft (108 m) high. Iguazu Falls (Argentina and Brazil) is wider and Angel Falls (Venezuela) is higher, but Victoria Falls is regarded as the world's largest waterfall by virtue of the size of the sheet of falling water produced. Above the falls, at an elevation of 3,000 ft (915 m) asl, the Zambezi flows through a broad, shallow valley bounded by low sandstone hills and then abruptly plunges vertically into a deep and narrow chasm (First Gorge) running east–west, perpendicular to the river's course. During the rainy season, the crashing water produces spray that rises as much as 1,640 ft (500 m) above the river and can be seen from the plateau 18–30 mi (30–50 km) away.

The waters falling into the chasm along the entire breadth of Victoria Falls collect in the plunge pool known as the Boiling Pit and then exit via a short, narrow north–south running passage into another long east–west chasm (Second Gorge). The Zambezi River proceeds in this manner through a zigzagging course of a total of eight, deep steep-sided canyons (counting First Gorge) known collectively as the Zambezi

or Bakota Gorges. Each canyon represents the former position of a large waterfall that has been retreating upstream for perhaps 5 million years.

The rim of Victoria Falls has two permanent islands. On the west, in Zimbabwe, is Boaruka Island, "the divider of waters." It separates the Devil's Cataract from the rest of the water flowing over the falls. Devil's Cataract has the lowest drop, 197 ft (60 m), of any of the streams plunging into First Gorge, but has cut a 30 ft (10 m) deep notch into the rim, which may represent the place where the Zambezi will next cut headward, intercept, and erode another east–west fracture in the basalt, and form—some 20,000 years from now—a new great waterfall. The other permanent island is Livingstone Island, the site of David Livingstone's first view of the falls he named Victoria in November 1855. These two islands are joined by a few others during low water periods in the dry season. They create other major streams of water falling over the rim: from west to east Main Falls, Rainbow Falls (where the highest drop occurs), and the Eastern Cataracts. Livingstone Island at times of low water is between Main Falls and Rainbow Falls.

Victoria Falls lies in a tropical wet and dry climatic region. The summer rainy season begins in October and continues through April, with December and January being the wettest months. The rains produce high water from February to May with peak flow in April. Winters are dry and flow rates drop significantly so that minimum flows, usually in November, may be one-tenth that of April. Maximum monthly flow is almost equal to that at Iguazu Falls, but because of the dry season the mean annual flow is lower than at either Niagara or Iguazu.

Most of the area surrounding the falls and gorges on the Zimbabwe side is covered with mopane woodland. On the Zambia side, beyond the basalt formation, a woodland savanna of Zambezi teak, bushwillow, and miombo (*Brachystegia* spp.) developed on red Kalahari sands. A riparian forest with trees such as palms, African ebony, figs, and sausage tree line the Zambezi upstream. An extension of this forest occurs in a small area that is watered by the spray from the falls and is often referred to as rainforest. This "rainforest" has an abundance of flowering shrubs and forbs, as well as trees. On the steep slopes of the gorges, fever trees (*Acacia*) and corkwoods (*Commiphora*) grow with aloe and shrubs.

Geologic History. Flood basalts poured forth, layer by layer, beginning about 180 mya when the region lay in Gondwana. Cooling magma formed a system of joints in which major fractures ran east–west and minor ones ran north–south, intersecting them. These joints deepened when Gondwana began to break up and filled with clayey sediments. Roughly 15 mya, the upper Zambezi was part of the paleo-Limpopo River system and drained into large Lake Makgadikgadi. Tectonic forces associated with the breakup of Gondwana uplifted the region centered on present-day Makgadikgadi Pan some 5 mya, accelerating downcutting by a then separate "lower Zambezi" drainage system. This river, with its mouth at the coast of the Indian Ocean, extended headward into the lake, emptying it. The outflow of water created the first "Victoria Falls" and linked the upper and lower Zambezi systems to form the modern Zambezi River. The river was able to erode the softer clay materials in the large east–west fractures and create a succession of deep gorges into which the Zambezi would flow. Weak spots at the intersections of north–south fractures allowed the river to continue to erode headward in a zigzag fashion across the basalt plateau, and the plunge line of the Zambezi retreated slowly but surely upstream. There have been eight "Victoria Falls" so far. The current one probably developed 250,000–100,000 years ago. The next one is expected to form as the notch at Devil's Cataract deepens and cuts into either of two east–west fracture lines just upstream from the magnificent waterfall of today.

Biota. Victoria Falls acts as biogeographic barrier for fishes in the Zambezi River. Above the falls some 89 species have been recorded; below the falls only 39.

Protected Areas. Two national parks flank Victoria Falls. Mosi-oa-Tunya National Park in Zambia is on the left bank between the Sinde River and one of the lower gorges (Songwe). Victoria National Park lies on the right bank in Zimbabwe and reaches 3.7 mi (6 km) upstream and 7.5 mi (12 km) downstream from the falls. Above the falls, Zambezi National Park (Zimbabwe) is adjacent to the river. Mosi-oa-Tunya and

Victoria Falls national parks are part of a UNESCO World Heritage Site that also includes a 5.5 mi (9 km) strip along the river in Zambezi National Park. UNESCO's inscription deems it "significant worldwide for its exceptional geological and geomorphological features and active land formation processes."

Environmental Issues. The main issues revolve around the development of tourist facilities and services and urban infrastructure in the vicinity of Victoria Falls.

See also Zambezi River

Further Reading

Berger, Leon and Brett Hilton-Barber. 2010. "The Geology of Victoria Falls." Guide to Exploring Victoria Falls. Prime Origins and Siyabona Africa Travel Ltd. http://vicfalls.zimbabwe.co.za/Climate,_Geology,_Flora-travel/explore-victoria-falls-geology.html

"Mosi-oa-Tunya/Victoria Falls" 2013. World Heritage Center, UNESCO. http://whc.unesco.org/pg.cfm?cid=31&id_site=509

Virgin Islands

Caribbean Sea/Atlantic Ocean

Geographic Overview. The Virgin Islands are made up of several sizeable islands and many smaller islets and cays. Although sometimes included in the Leeward Islands and hence Lesser Antilles—perhaps because of their size and position, they are geologically an eastward extension of the Greater Antilles. They are located on the same microplate that holds Puerto Rico. With the exception of Anegada, which is a coral island, these islands are volcanic and consist of an old, deformed island arc overlain with sedimentary deposits and intruded by younger igneous rocks. Two zones, separated by the deep Virgin Islands trough, are recognized. To the north lie St. Thomas and St. John of the U.S. Virgin Islands, as well as all of the British Virgin Islands. South of the trough, on a submarine ridge running parallel to it, is St. Croix. The islands were named by Christopher Columbus in honor of Saint Ursula and the 11,000 virgins supposedly martyred with her.

Description. Two islands, Isla de Vieques and Isla de Culebra, are part of the U.S. Commonwealth of

Puerto Rico and designated herein as the Puerto Rican Virgin Islands. Vieques lies about 10 mi (16 km) off the eastern end of Puerto Rico. It stretches east–west for about 21 mi (34 km) and is about 4 mi (6 km) wide. Until 2003, much of the island served as a test range for the U.S. Navy, and this protected it from the usual types of agricultural and tourism development found on many Caribbean islands. In 2003, the Navy's property became Vieques National Wildlife Refuge. The rolling hills are covered by subtropical dry forest. The highest point is Monte Pirata, 987 ft (300 m) asl. No permanent streams exist on Vieques. Its coastline is fringed with white coral sand beaches, lagoons, mangrove swamps, salt flats, and coral reefs. On the south side is one the world's brightest bioluminescent or phosphorescent bays, Mosquito Bay.

Culebra is an archipelago consisting of one main island and 22 smaller islets located 17 mi (27 km) east of Puerto Rico. Smaller than Vieques, the main island is 7 mi (11 km) long and has a maximum width of 5 mi (8 km). It is also a volcanic island lacking permanent streams. The highest point, Mount Resaca, rises 650 ft (198 m) asl and hosts most of the island's remaining dry forest, here a unique community known as a boulder forest, since the trees grow on steep, boulder-covered terrain. Culebra's long, indented coastline has cliffs, white coral sand beaches, and mangrove swamps.

U.S. Virgin Islands. This island group is a territory of the United States. St. Thomas is the westernmost of the three islands. It has a long central ridge of forested hills running east–west across much of its 13-mi (21-km) length. Smaller ridges branch off from it leaving little flat land on the island. The highest point is Crown Mountain at 1,556 ft (474 m) asl. The island is famous for its white beaches, large natural harbor, and many protected bays. St. John lies 4 mi (6.5 km) east of St. Thomas. It is also a hilly place with little flat ground and many sheltered bays. Cliffs along the island's coasts often drop off into deep water. Dry forest covers most of the island and is particularly thorny at the top of cliffs. At higher elevations in the interior and on the north coast, a moist forest with evergreen and deciduous trees attaining heights of 75 ft (23 m) dominates. Water courses may be devoid of vegetation because of frequent flash floods. Moist forest areas

Table 1 The Virgin Islands

	Area	Geographic Coordinates
Puerto Rican Virgin Islands, "Spanish" Virgin Islands or Passage Islands		
Isla de Culebra	11.6 mi² (30 km²)	18° 19' N, 65° 17' W
Isal de Vieques	134 mi² (348 km²)	18° 07' N, 65° 25' W
U.S. Virgin Islands		
Saint Croix	83 mi² (215 km²)	17° 44' N, 64° 44' W
Saint John	20 mi² (51 km²)	18° 20' N, 64° 44' W
Saint Thomas	31 mi² (81 km²)	18° 20' N, 64° 55' W
British Virgin Islands		
Anegada	15 mi² (38 km²)	18° 44' N, 64° 20' W
Jost Van Dyke	3 mi² (8 km²)	18° 27' N, 64° 44' W
Tortola	21.5 mi² (56 km²)	18° 25' N, 64° 35' W
Virgin Gorda	8 mi² (21 km²)	18° 29' N, 64° 23' W

receive 45–55 in (1,140–1,400 mm) of rain annually, whereas dry forest areas in the east and southeast parts of the island only get 25–35 in (635–900 mm). Cactus, agave, and thornscrub occur in the driest areas. This island at the eastern edge of the Greater Antilles measures 7 mi (11 km) × 3 mi (5 km); its high point is Bordeaux Mountain at 1,277 ft (390 m).

St. Croix lies 40 mi (65 km) south of St. Thomas. Twenty-two miles (35 km) long and 6 mi (10 km) across at its widest point, St. Croix is constructed of soft sedimentary rocks and extensive coral reefs. The western end has the highest hills, including the highest point, Mount Eagle, which reaches 1,088 ft (332 m) asl. Slopes are forested and descend to flat land in the south. The eastern half is also hilly but arid and covered with grasses and clumps of cacti. A discontinuous bank-barrier reef lies about 0.5 mi (0.8 km) offshore. The southwestern part of the island is a broad marine platform but has no reef due to strong easterly currents and waves that have covered the platform with sand.

British Virgin Islands. These four main islands and 50 smaller islets and cays are an Overseas Territory of the United Kingdom. Most have hills rising only a few hundred feet above the sea, but three of the four larger islands are rugged and mountainous. The exception is Anegada, a low and flat limestone island with a maximum elevation of 28 ft (8.5 m) asl. The western half of Anegada is taken up by large salt ponds. An 18-mile (29 km) long barrier reef extends along the entire northern coast of Anegada, curving southward toward Virgin Gorda in the east. Many a ship has wrecked and many a sailor's life has been lost on Anegada Horseshoe Reef.

Virgin Gorda is crowned by Gorda Peak and Gorda Peak National Park, which protects the Caribbean dry forest growing on the mountain slopes. Gorda Peak rises 1,370 ft (418 m) asl. The island's most famous attraction is The Baths, a jumble of large granitic boulders, weathered in place, at Virgin Gorda's southern tip.

Tortola is largest of the British Virgin Islands; it is 13.5 mi (km) long and has a maximum width of 3 mi (5 km). Another of the volcanic islands, Tortola has the highest elevation in the island group, Mount Sage, which is 1,710 ft (521 m) asl. Jost Van Dyke is the smallest of the main islands, measuring 4 mi (6.5 km) × 3 mi (4.8 km). It, too, has rugged hills, the remnants of extinct volcanoes, which culminate in the island's highest peak, Majonny Hill, 1,054 ft (321 m) asl. All three of the volcanic islands are known for their white sand beaches and sheltered bays.

Located on an active plate boundary between the North American Plate and the northeastern corner of the Caribbean Plate, the Virgin Islands are highly vulnerable to earthquakes. Twelve major earthquakes of M 7.0 or greater have been recorded near the islands in the past 500 years. The threat of tsunamis generated by large earthquakes, submarine slope failures in the Puerto Rico Trench, undersea volcanic eruptions, or landslides is real. A tsunami higher than 23 ft (7 m) occurred in 1867. The most recent earthquake in the region, an M 8.1 in 1946, generated a tsunami that killed an estimated 1,600 people in Hispaniola. The Virgin Islands are also vulnerable to tropical storms and hurricanes that are generated off the coast of Africa and follow the general circulation westward.

Biota. Biological diversity in the Virgin Islands is highest in the sea in reefs and other littoral habitats. At least 400 reef fishes are known as well as some 50 corals and a variety of gorgonians and sponges. Sea turtles nest on some beaches, which are also visited by numerous shorebirds.

Protected Areas. Vieques National Wildlife Refuge, a preserve that now encompasses the eastern half of Vieques as well as its western tip and is the largest wildlife reserve in the Caribbean. Culebra National Wildlife Refuge was established by President Theodore Roosevelt in 1909 and is one of the oldest such preserves on U.S. territory. It harbors several seabird nesting colonies and sea turtle nesting grounds. Two-thirds of St. John, in the U.S. Virgin Islands (USVI), is protected in Virgin Islands National Park. Adjacent to it is Virgin Islands Coral Reef National Monument. Together the park and monument protect habitats ranging from steep forested slopes to mangrove, seagrass meadows, natural salt ponds, and coral reefs. About 20 percent of the land in the USVI is in parks, preserves, and bird sanctuaries; large areas of littoral and marine reserves aim to protect coastal waters and reefs. In the British Virgin Islands, about 18 percent of the land is protected in national parks and other preserves. The Western Salt Ponds of Anegada were declared a Ramsar Wetland of International Importance in 1999. One of them, Flamingo Pond, once had a huge colony of Greater Flamingos, but the bird was extirpated as a consequence of the feather trade of the 19th and early 20th centuries. Today flamingos have been reintroduced and are gaining in numbers.

Environmental Issues. Major issues focus on protection of the coral reefs from coastal development, overfishing, and careless boating. Warming water temperature from climate change also threatens coral viability. Solid waste management is a problem on these small islands with little room for landfills. The availability of potable water is a concern aggravated by frequent drought, since all fresh water comes from rainfall. As on most islands in the world, invasive species threaten to displace native flora and fauna. Particularly significant are plants such as rubber vine, coral vine, guinea grass and neem trees, and animals such as small Asian mongoose, black and brown rats. Feral goats and donkeys also occur on some islands.

See also Bioluminescent Bays; Lesser Antilles

Further Reading

Birdlife International. n.d. "Anegada: Western salt ponds and coastal areas." Important Bird Areas. http://www.birdlife.org/datazone/sitefactsheet.php?id=19790

Dengo, G. and J.E. Case, editors. 1990. *The Caribbean Region.* The Geology of North America, Vol. H. Boulder, CO: Geological Society of America.

National Parks Conservation Association. 2008. "Virgin Islands National Park, Virgin Islands Coral Reef National Monument, A Resource Assessment." http:// www.npca.org/about-us/center-for-park-research /stateoftheparks/virginislands/viis_lo.pdf

Rankin, Douglas W. 2002. "Geology of St. John, U.S. Virgin Islands." U.S. Geological Survey Professional Paper 1631. http://pubs.usgs.gov/pp/p1631/P1631-tag.pdf

Uhler, John William. 1995–2007. "Virgin Islands National Park Information Page." http://www.virgin.islands .national-park.com/info.htm

U.S. Fish and Wildlife Service. n.d. "Culebra National Wildlife Refuge." http://www.fws.gov/southeast/pubs /facts/cbrcon.pdf

U.S. Fish and Wildlife Service. n.d. "Vieques National Wildlife Refuge." http://www.fws.gov/caribbean/Re fuges/PDF/vieques_factsheet.pdf

U.S. Geological Survey. 2013. "Caribbean Tsunami and Earthquake Hazards Studies." http://woodshole.er .usgs.gov/project-pages/caribbean/ (*Note*: Includes good animated maps of tectonic history of region)

VINow.com. 2013. "Virgin Islands Geography." http:// www.vinow.com/general_usvi/geography/

Virunga Mountains

Democratic Republic of the Congo, Rwanda, and Uganda

Geographic Overview. The Virunga Mountains are an east–west running chain of volcanoes associated with the Albertine Rift and located between the rift valley lakes of Edward and Kivu. They consist of eight major peaks with summits higher than 10,000 ft (3,000 m) asl. Most are dormant, but the westernmost two are Africa's most active volcanoes. The mountains are best known for their population of critically endangered mountain gorillas, the group studied by the late Dian Fossey. The volcanoes occur where the boundaries of Rwanda, Uganda, and the Democratic Republic of the Congo (DCR) converge.

Geographic Coordinates. 00°25'S, 29°33'E

Description. The Virunga Mountains are a small chain of volcanoes just south of the equator that extend east–west for 50 mi (80 km) across the western or Albertine Rift of Africa's Great Rift Valley. The group consists of eight major stratocones plus the numerous cinder cones, fissures, and vents on their flanks. The highest peak is Mount Karisimbi in Rwanda, which

rises to 14,787 ft (4,507 m) asl. It is dormant, as are Mount Sabyinyo (11,923 ft or 3,634 m asl) on the Uganda–Rwanda border; Mount Mikeno (14,560 ft or 4,437 m asl) in the DCR; Mount Muhuabura (13,540 ft or 4,127 masl) on the Rwanda–Uganda border; Mount Bisoke—or Visoke—12,180 ft or 3,711 m asl) on the Rwanda–DCR border; and Mount Gahinga (11,400 ft or 3,474 m asl) on the Rwanda–Uganda border. However, the two westernmost cones are the most active in Africa. Both Mount Nyiragongo (11,358 ft or 3,462 m asl) and Mount Nyamuragiva (10,049 ft or 3,063 m asl) are in the DCR and have erupted in 2006 and 2010. Nyamuragiva has erupted 30 times since 1900.

Mount Nyirangongo has central cone with a crater 0.8 mi (1.3 km) across. It sits 12 mi (20 km) north of Lake Kivu and 9 mi (15 km) north of the city of Goma, DCR. It is classified as a Decade Volcano, one of 16 in the world that pose multiple hazards to large populations nearby and a high probability of eruption. Nyirangongo has a semipermanent lava lake in its central crater that periodically empties, sending very fluid lava downslope into Goma. The lake formed in 1928 and emptied in 1977. It developed again in 1994, sending up a lava fountain about 200 ft (60 m) high, and emptied again in 2002. In addition to eruptions and lava flows, Nyirangongo produces earthquakes and emits toxic gases. Lava flows in both 1977 and 2002 resulted in many human fatalities. The lava lake has again formed; it showed signs of activity in July 2013.

The Virungas are in a humid tropical climate region where it rains throughout the year. Still, a double maximum of precipitation is evident, with the heaviest rains from March through May and another very wet period from mid-September to mid-December. Climatic differences induced by elevation account for zonation of habitats in a pattern rather typical of high mountains in equatorial Africa. Although much disturbed by settlements and agriculture, the general scheme is a semideciduous montane broadleaf forest from the base of a volcano to an elevation of about 8,200 ft (2,500 m). Above this is a narrow bamboo zone extending to about 9,000 ft (2,800 m). From 9,000 to 10,500 ft (2,800–3,200 m) is a subalpine *Hagenia-Hypericum* woodland with an understory of shrubs, mosses, and lichens. This grades into a higher subalpine zone between 9,800 and 12,500 ft (3,000–3,800 m) dominated by tree heathers festooned with *Usnea* lichens, giant groundsels, and giant lobelias, a community best developed on Mount Muhabura. Alpine moorland begins above treeline, which occurs at roughly 11,000 ft (3,400 m) asl on these equatorial mountains.

Geologic History. The geologic history of the Virunga volcanoes is poorly documented, in part due to inaccessibility related to political turmoil in the region. Each volcano has formed independently of the others in the Virunga Volcanic Province since the Miocene. Mount Sabyinyo is the oldest cone. Magmatism in the region is associated with uplift and crustal extension that contributed to the formation of the East African Rift system.

Biota. The Virunga Mountains are home to about 200 of the world's 700 critically endangered mountain gorillas (*Gorilla beringei beringei*). The only other population is found in Uganda's Bwindi Impenetrable Forest. Other primates in the area are the endangered golden monkey (*Cercopithecus kandt*) and the blue monkey (*Cercopithecus mitis*). In all, 86 mammals are known from the region, many of them endemic to the Albertine Rift. Of the 878 plant species identified to date, 124 are limited to the Rift.

Protected Areas. Three national parks serve to protect the Virunga Mountains: Parc National des Virungas, DCR (the oldest wildlife reserve in Africa, having been established in 1925); Mgahinga Gorilla National Park, Uganda; and Parc National des Volcans, Rwanda. The Karisoke Research Center, where Dian Fossey famously studied gorillas, is situated between Mount Karisimbi and Mount Bisoke.

Environmental Issues. Most attention has focused on protecting the mountain gorillas, which have been threatened by poaching, disease, habitat loss, and war. Mitigating the hazards of the active volcanoes is being studied as part of the UN-sponsored Decade Volcano program.

Further Reading

Owiunji, I., D. Nkuutu, D. Kujirakwinja, I. Liengola, A. Plumptre, A. Nsanzurwimo, K. Fawcett, M. Gray, and A. McNeilage. 2004. The Biodiversity of the Virunga Volcanoes. World Conservation Society, Dian Fossey Gorilla Fund International, ICCN, ORTPN, UWA, International Gorilla Conservation Programme. http://programs.wcs.org/portals/49/media/file/volcanoes_biodiv_survey.pdf

Wafula, M. D., N. Zana, M. Kasereka, and H. Hamaguchi. n.d. "The Nyiragongo Volcano: A Case Study for the Mitigation of Hazards on an African Rift Volcano, Virunga Region, Western Rift Valley." International Union of Geodesy and Geophysics, GeoRisk Commission. http://iugg-georisk.org/presentations/pdf/Wafula_volcano_Africa.pdf

Vizcaino Whale Sanctuary

Mexico

Geographic Overview. The El Vizcaino Whale Sanctuary protects breeding and calving grounds of the eastern gray whale in west-central Baja California Sur, Mexico. It is part of the El Vizcaino Biosphere Reserve, which stretches across the Baja peninsula, incorporating strips of coastal habitat in both the Pacific Ocean and the Gulf of California as well as in the arid hills in between. The Biosphere Reserve is the largest protected area in Latin America.

Geographic Coordinates. 27°48'N, 114°14'W

Description. El Vizcaino Whale Sanctuary consists primarily of two warm, shallow lagoons. Laguna Ojo de Liebre (formerly Scammon's Lagoon) extends inland from Bahía Sebastián Vizcaíno on the north side of Desierto Vizcaino, which forms a prominent, triangular spur west of the mountainous spine of Baja California. This hypersaline body of water is 30 mi (48 km) long, 6 mi (9 km) wide, and 15–40 ft (5–12 m) deep. Tidal flats with tidal channels edge the area. A large marsh borders the lagoon in the east. Two lakes adjoin the lagoon: Guerrero Negro and Manuela.

The smaller Laguna San Ignacio penetrates Baja's west coast 60 mi (100 km) southeast of Laguna Ojo de Liebre on the south side of the Desierto Vizcaíno spur. This inlet is brackish and measures 22 mi (35 km) long, 4 mi (6 km) wide, and 6.5–13 ft (2–4 m) deep. Broad tidal flats occur and a lake is present at the northern end. The mangroves (*Rhizophora mangle*) lining the margins of the lagoon are at the northern limit of mangroves in the North Pacific.

These two lagoons, together with a few smaller ones farther south along Baja's west coast and at the southern end of the Gulf of California, are the main breeding grounds of the eastern gray whale

(*Eschrichtius robustus*). Some 300–400 of these baleen whales come each winter from the Arctic to find mates, breed, and calve. They leave the Chukchi and Bering seas in November–December and migrate southward close to shore, traveling about 115 mi (185 km) each day. The whales are segregated according to gender, age, and reproductive status, with females in the late stages of pregnancy leaving first. The earliest migrants swim alone, but those departing later travel in pods of two or more animals. The first arrive at El Vizcaino in late December–early January; pregnant females enter the lagoons ahead of the others in order to calve. More than half calve in Laguna Ojo de Liebre. Most other whales spend the winter in Bahia Sebastian Vizcaino and Bahia de Ballenas outside the lagoons.

These large (43–50 ft or 13–15 m long) benthic feeders apparently eat little while on their wintering grounds and lose 20–35 percent of their body weight. The northbound migration begins in mid-February; males and females without calves leave first and by April some are already back on the summer feeding grounds in the Bering Sea, having completed a 5,000 mi (8,000 km) trip. Females with calves linger longer at El Vizcaino, tending to depart between late March and mid-April.

The gray whale was on the verge of extinction in the late 1880s, when only 160 were counted passing by San Simeon, California. International protection of the species began in the 1930s, when it was no longer allowed to be taken by commercial whalers. This protection has continued under the auspices of the International Whaling Commission since 1946. Most recently, the population of eastern gray whales was estimated at 26,000 animals (the western gray whale has not recovered). In 1994 the species was removed from the U.S. Endangered Species list, but it still protected under the Marine Mammal Act and international whaling conventions.

The west coast of Baja California is a fog desert next to the cool California Current. Inland is the Vizcaino region of the Sonoran Desert, where hills reach 6,500 ft (1,985 m) asl. With very little precipitation and intense solar radiation, a distinct vegetation has evolved, dominated by leaf succulents, cacti, boojum trees, and elephant trees. Fan palms grow where springs occur. In this land, an endemic subspecies of pronghorn and the desert bighorn sheep find refuge.

Protected Areas. The El Vizcaino Whale Sanctuary and El Vizcaino Biosphere Reserve are refuges for gray whales and other animals as well. These include resident northern elephant seals, California sea lions, common seals, and common bottlenose dolphins. Orcas, blue whales, and humpback whales are seasonal visitors. Four sea turtles (green, loggerhead, olive ridley, and hawksbill) are also protected here. The marshes and mangroves are important nursery areas for marine fish and provide significant winter habitat for migratory shorebirds and waterbirds that breed in Canada and the United States.

Environmental Issues. Threats to the lagoons and the whales largely stem from development to support a large salt evaporation industry at Guerrero Negro on Laguna Ojo de Liebre. Problems include disposal of wastes, domestic and industrial; and increasing traffic by vessels transporting salt and by whale-watchers' boats. On land, development of resorts and airstrips, grazing by cattle, illegal hunting of bighorn, pronghorn, and other mammals, and off-road vehicles threaten the rare and valued natural assets of El Vizcaino.

See also Baja California Peninsula; Sonoran Desert

Further Reading
"El Vizcaino Biosphere Reserve." 2004. Park Profile, Parks Watch. http://www.parkswatch.org/parkprofile.php?l=eng&country=mex&park=vibr
"Gray Whale, *Eschrichtius robustus*." 2012. Office of Protected Resources, NOAA Fisheries. http://www.nmfs.noaa.gov/pr/species/mammals/cetaceans/graywhale.htm
Rice, Dale W., Allen A. Wolman, and Howard W. Braham. 1984. "The Gray Whale, *Eschrichtius robustus. Marine Fisheries Review* 46: 7–14. http://spo.nmfs.noaa.gov/mfr464/mfr4643.pdf
"Whale Sanctuary of El Vizcaino." 2011. World Heritage Centre, UNESCO, http://whc.unesco.org/en/list/554

Volcanic Highlands of Central America

Guatemala, El Salvador, Nicaragua, Costa Rica, and Panama

Geographic Overview. The spine of the Central American isthmus consists largely of a 680-mi (1,100-km) chain of volcanoes running from the

Mexico–Guatemala border into Panama. It is interrupted by the granitic Talamanca Range of Costa Rica 110 mi (175 km) between Volcán Turrialba in Costa Rica and Volcán Barú in Panama. Some 40 centers of volcanism are arranged approximately 16 mi (26 km) apart along this part of the Pacific Rim of Fire; it is one of the densest areas of active volcanism in the world.

Geographic Coordinates. 08°30'N–15°35'N, 80° 38'W–92°03'W

Description. The 50 active or potentially active edifices in the Volcanic Highlands vary in height, type of eruption, composition, and morphology. Constructive features such as cinder cones, andesitic shield volcanoes, stratovolcanoes, maars, and lava domes all occur, as do calderas and other destructive volcanic features. Guatemala's volcanoes are the highest and most active. Tajumulco near the border with Chiapas,

Mexico, is a stratovolcano, as are all 14 of the country's volcanoes. At 13,845 ft (4,220 m) asl, Tajumulco is the highest peak in Central America. Volcán Fuego (12,346 ft or 3,763 m asl), overlooking the former capital city of Antigua, has been erupting almost constantly since records began to be kept in 1524. Typically it displays fiery strombolian activity, with plumes of incandescent lava fragments, bombs, and ash. It is the most active volcano on the isthmus. Guatemala is also home to the large Atitlán caldera, which first collapsed about 11 mya, then again 8 mya ago, and underwent its last stage of development about 84,000 years ago. Today the northern half of the youngest caldera is filled with Lake Atitlán, the deepest lake in Central America. Three post-caldera stratovolcanoes (Tolimán, San Pedro, and Atitlán) were constructed over the rims of the second and third calderas.

The Volcanic Highlands of Central America are a chain of stratovolcanoes forming the spine of the Central American isthmus and part of the Pacific Rim of Fire. Lago Atitlán, shown here, fills a caldera and is the deepest lake in Central America. (Ben Pipe/Robert Harding World Imagery/Corbis)

El Salvador's stratovolcanoes also have explosive eruptions. They are lower than Guatemala's, reaching heights of about 6,500 ft (2,000 m) asl. The country's youngest volcano, Izalco, lies on the edge of the Coatepeque caldera. It appeared as a smoking fissure in a field in 1770 and today is a stratocone standing 2,132 ft (650 m) above the local surface and 6,398 ft (1,950 m) asl. It was active almost continuously until 1966.

There are six stratovolcanoes in Nicaragua's Maribios Cordillera, but the base of the range is composed of three shield complexes. The El Hoyo stratocone is the active vent of the latter structure. Two low flat craters called maars are other features on the shield area of the Maribios range. One, Laguna Asososca, is filled with water; the other, Malpaisillo, is only partially filled. In the Sierras of central Nicaragua, southwest of Lake Managua, is another broad shield with calderas. The Mombacho stratovolcano sits on the northwest side of Lake Nicaragua and rises to an elevation of 4,409 ft (1,344 m) asl. Two other volcanoes, Concepción at 5,280 ft (1,610 m) asl and the extinct Maderas at 4,574 ft (1,394 m) asl, make up Ometepe Island in the lake itself. Nicaragua has the lowest volcanic peaks in Central America, in part because they have formed along fault lines in the Nicaraguan Depression.

Costa Rica's Arenal volcano is unique in that it is an isolated twin peak, while the country's other volcanoes are clumped together in massifs. Arenal, a relatively low stratovolcano at 5,358 ft (1, 633 m) asl and the youngest in Costa Rica, is famous for its 1968 eruption in which 78 people in surrounding villages died from ejected lava, pyroclastic flows, and hot gases. The mountain has remained active since then. Volcanoes of the Central Cordillera of Costa Rica have the greatest volume among the Central American volcanos and all rise at least 3,500 ft (1,067 m) above their bases. Turrialba, standing 10,958 ft (3,340 m) asl at the southeast end of the chain, has three craters and remains active. It is the last stratovolcano until Panama due to the presence of the non-volcanic Talamanca range.

In Panama, near the Costa Rican border is one of that country's two major volcanic landforms, the Cerro Barú complex. The young namesake stratovolcano rises to an elevation of 11,397 ft (3,474 m) asl and is located just southeast of the continental divide. It may have been active within the last 500 years, but the last eruption documented by archeological evidence occurred about AD 700. Smaller peaks continue as far as the Canal Zone. The other major volcanic feature in Panama is a broad massif, the El Valle caldera, just east of Panama City.

See also Central American Isthmus; Lake Atitlán (Lago de Atitlán); Lake Nicaragua (Cocibolca or Mar Dulce); Talamanca Range

Further Reading

"Atitlán." n.d. Global Volcanism Program, Smithsonian Institution, Museum of Natural History. http://www.volcano.si.edu/world/volcano.cfm?vnum=1402–06=&volpage=photos

Ball, Jessica. n.d. "Arenal Volcano (Volcán Arenal), Costa Rica." Geology.com, http://geology.com/volcanoes/arenal/

"Barú." n.d. Global Volcanism Program, Smithsonian Institution, Museum of Natural History. http://www.volcano.si.edu/volcano.cfm?vn=346010

"Izalco Volcano." n.d. Volcano Discovery, http://www.volcanodiscovery.com/izalco.html

Marshall, Jeffrey S. 2007. "The Geomorphology and Physiographic Provinces of Central America." In *Central America: Geology, Resources and Hazards*, edited by Jochen Bundschum and Guillermo E. Alvarado, 75–122. New York: Taylor & Francis.

Van Wyk de Vries, Benjamin, Pablo Grosse, and Guillermo E. Alvarado. 2007. "Volcanism and Volcanic Landforms." In *Central America: Geology, Resources and Hazards*, edited by Jochen Bundschum and Guillermo E. Alvarado, 123–154. New York: Taylor & Francis.

Wallace, David Rains. 1997. "Central American Landscapes." In *Central America: A Natural and Cultural History*, edited by Anthony G. Coates, 72–96. New Haven, CT: Yale University Press.

Volga River

Russia

Geographic Overview. The Volga River, called Mother Volga by Russians, has been an important artery in eastern Europe since the Middle Ages. It is the longest river in Europe and the longest navigable waterway in Russia, providing access from the Baltic Sea to the Caspian Sea and Black Sea. The Volga provides more than 75 percent of the inflow to the Caspian Sea. Most of the rivers in the Volga drainage basin, including the major tributaries, are highly regulated, primarily for hydroelectricity, flood control, and irrigation.

Geographic Coordinates. Source: 57°09'N, 32°36'E, Mouth: 45°50'N, 47°58'E

Description. Draining approximately 560,000 mi^2 (1,450,000 km^2), the Volga River flows 2,300 mi (3,700 km) from its source, northwest of Moscow, southeast to the Caspian Sea. In its course, the river drops only 830 ft (253 m) elevation, from 738 ft (225 m) asl at its source to 92 ft (28 m) bsl at the Caspian Sea. The major western tributary, the Oka River, flows 918 mi (1,478 km) from the Central Russia Upland south of Moscow and drains 94,600 mi^2 (245,000 km^2). The Kama River, 1,262 mi (2,031 km) long, drains 201,500 mi^2 (522,000 km^2) and joins the Volga from the Ural Mountains to the east.

The source of the Volga is a chain of small lakes in the northern forests of the Valdai Hills, a glaciated district of lakes, marshes, and low moraines midway between Moscow and St. Petersburg. The river enters the 34-mi (55 km) long Ivankovo Reservoir below Tver, the first of many dams and reservoirs, and is linked by canal to Moscow. The river flows northeast to Rybinsk Reservoir before bending abruptly southeast. It passes Nizhniy Novgorod where it is joined by the Oka on the right bank. Much of the river's course from Nizhniy Novgorod to Volgograd is characterized by contrasting bank topography. One bank is generally broad, flat and swampy, while the other is a steep slope with high bluffs. The Volga flows east to Kazan, doubling in volume, and enters the 370 mi (595 km) long, 25 mi (40 km) wide Kuibyshev Reservoir, which covers 2,500 mi^2 (6,500 km^2). The Kama River, the largest tributary and an important waterway from the Urals to the Volga, flows into the reservoir from the northeast. At the southern end of the reservoir, the Volga loops eastward, in the Samara Bend, around the Zhiguli Hills and is joined the Samara River on the left bank. The Volga continues south-southwest to Volgograd where it turns abruptly southeast to the Caspian Sea. The river begins forming its delta 100 mi (160 km) before reaching the Caspian Sea. The delta, covering approximately 4,600 mi^2 (12,000 km^2), is the largest estuary in Europe, with many distributary channels, freshwater and saline bays, dunes, algae flats, and swamps.

The Volga is predominantly a lowland river fed by snowmelt. The source region is 738 ft (225 m) asl, and most of its tributary drainage basins are below 1,000 ft (300 m). Originally characterized by slow currents, sand bars, and meandering channels, and formerly subject to seasonal flooding from snowmelt, the river is now a chain of reservoirs connected by navigable stretches of river. The middle and lower Volga is a heavily industrialized river corridor, with oil and gas, chemical, and diversified industries. It is linked by canal to Moscow, the Baltic Sea, the White Sea, and via the Don River to the Sea of Azov and the Black Sea. Although frozen for 3 months, the river remains a significant transportation route for bulky goods.

Biota. The Volga's course begins in the taiga and mixed forests of northern Russia. As it flows generally south to the Caspian Sea, it enters successively drier climates of steppe and desert.

Approximately 70 fish species, 40 of commercial value, including Caspian roach, herring, pike, and sturgeon, live in the Volga drainage. Dams and reservoirs have affected all fish species. Typical riverine fish, such as dace and chub, adapted to shallow water and strong currents are replaced by fish, such as smelt and burbot, adapted to deeper water. Dams are obstacles for migrating fish, especially sturgeon and whitefish from the Caspian Sea. The Volga whitefin gudgeon (*Romanogobio albipinnatus*) is endemic. Nutrients from upstream make the delta productive, a spawning area for semianadromous fish and a wintering area for Volga sturgeon. The delta supports approximately 400 vertebrate species, including 127 species of fish and 260 species of birds, including swans, ducks, herons, terns, ibis, and pelicans. Unusual species include Dalmatian Pelican (*Pelecanus crispus*), Great White Egret (*Egretta alba*), and Penduline Tit (*Remiz penduculinus*).

Protected Areas. The migratory bird habitat of the Volga Delta is a Ramsar Wetland of International Importance.

Environmental Issues. Water lost from reservoirs through withdrawal for irrigation and by evaporation has decreased the discharge of the Volga River, reducing the level of the Caspian Sea. Unregulated industrial, urban, and agricultural waste has resulted in much pollution, and the deforested watershed has altered the flow.

See also Baltic Sea; Black Sea and Sea of Azov; Caspian Sea; Don River

Further Reading

Bogutskaya, Nina. 2013. "Volga—Ural." *Freshwater Ecoregions of the World*. The Nature Conservancy. www.feow.org/ecoregions/details/volga_ural

Litvinov, Alexander S. et al. 2009. "Volga River Basin." In *Rivers of Europe*, edited by Klement Tochner, Urs Uehlinger, and Christopher T. Robinson, 23–58. London: Academic Press.

Vredefort Structure (Vredefort Dome)

South Africa

Geographic Overview. Commonly called the Vredefort Dome, this feature is the largest and one of the oldest meteorite impact structures known on Earth. Located 75 mi (120 km) southwest of Johannesburg, South Africa, the structure marks the site of the largest energy release event experienced on the planet, one which may have been implicated in the evolution of cyanobacteria and later, indirectly, multicellular life.

Geographic Coordinates. 26°52'S, 27°16'E

Description. The Vredefort Structure, the largest known impact structure on Earth, is visible today as concentric arcs of hills surrounding a nearly circular core of ancient granitic basement rock. It resembles an eroded geological dome and was once thought to be one, but strong evidence now confirms that it is an eroded meteorite impact crater (astrobleme) of tremendous size. Dating methods using zircon show that the impact occurred 2.023 billion years ago, making the Vredefort Structure the second oldest known impact crater after Suavjärvi Crater in Karelia, Russia, which had formed 300 million years earlier.

The remains of the Vredefort crater visible today include the central raised dome of granite 3.2 billion years old at the center of the crater and the northwestern section of the innermost of three concentric rings of sedimentary rocks uplifted and overturned when the core rock rebounded after impact. Erosion over millions of years has exposed the core, shaped like an inverted bowl, and worn away most of the encircling rows of hills, now revealed only in geologic maps. The original crater was 190 mi (300 km) in diameter. The innermost circle of hills had a diameter of some 112 mi (180 km), and the core (dome) is about 56 mi (90 km) across. The southeastern section of the structure was buried by Karoo sediments during the Mesozoic Era; all traces of it at the surface are gone.

For comparison, the second largest impact structure is the Sudbury Basin in Ontario, Canada. It is 160 mi (250 km) in diameter and dates to 1.85 bya. Suavjärvi Crater, in Russia, is the oldest, but only 10 mi (16 km) across and filled by a lake. Chicxulub impact crater on the Yucatán peninsula of Mexico is 110 mi (180 km) across, but much younger. Its asteroid struck 65 mya and is believed to have resulted in the extinction of the dinosaurs. Surface features are so subtle they were only revealed by a 1978 airborne magnetic survey of the Gulf of Mexico north of Yucatán and aerial photography taken from the Space Shuttle *Endeavor*.

The meteorite that struck South Africa is estimated to have been 6 mi (10 km) across and moving at a speed of 22,369 mph (36,000 kmph). Impact released an estimated 87 million megatons of energy and vaporized 15 mi^3 (70 km^3) of rock. The domed structure itself formed some 10.5 mi (17 km) below the surface of the Kaapvaal craton in basement rock of the Earth's crust. Horizontal layers of younger volcanic and sedimentary rocks were deformed as the dome pushed upward, forcing them upright and then over backwards so that now they dip toward the center of the crater. The oldest of the overlying rocks (which were the lowest strata in the sequence) formed the innermost ring of encircling hills, a collar around the granite core. The outer rings—now eroded to surface level—are composed of progressively younger rock.

The meteorite struck at a time in Earth history when only single-celled organisms existed. The great pressure and high temperatures generated by impact altered rock and released large amounts of oxygen into the atmosphere. The appearance of cyanobacteria in the geologic record coincides with the time of impact, but it is not clear whether the presence of these oxygen-producing organisms predates or postdates the powerful meteorite strike. The time is also close to the evolutionary boundary between Prokaryotes and Eukaryotes, including the rise of multicellular organisms. Cyanobacteria are credited with making the oxygen needed by multicellular life available, but the Vredefort meteorite may also have played a role.

Small-scale geologic features also prove the Vredefort Structure was an impact crater. Shockwaves produced by the hit created shatter cones and breccias. Shatter cones are small triangular formations appearing in rock as stacked ice cream cones or fir trees. Larger fractures a yard (meter) wide and several yards (meters) long cut deeper into surrounding rock and filled with molten rock melted by impact. Cooled and solidified, this material formed hard dark granophyre dikes that have since weathered, but persist on the surface as lines of angular blocks. Breccias formed during impact have a dark, glassy matrix and are known as pseudotachylite; Vredefort Dome is the type locality for this rock type.

The Vredefort Structure is in a savanna woodland complex, wherein five different plant communities are recognized, reflecting different edaphic conditions: dolomite grasslands, gold reef mountain bushveld, andesite mountain bushveld, Vredefort Dome granitic grasslands, and Vaal riverine bushveld, The Vaal River traverses the northern part of the structure. Rural and natural landscapes prevail.

Protected Areas. The Vredefort Dome was inscribed as a World Heritage Site in 2005. The land is privately owned, but landholders are forming conservation groups to protect the structure from development.

Environmental Issues. Tourists' removal of shatter cones for souvenirs or otherwise defacing rocks has been a problem. Development of tourist facilities could become an issue.

See also Chicxulub Crater; Monturaqui Crater

Further Reading

Fleminger, David. 2006. *World Heritage Sites of South Africa: Vredefort Dome*. Southbound Pocket Guide. Johannesburg, South Africa: 30° South Publishers.

Mayer, Joe. 2007. "The Vredefort Structure-Misconceptions and Facts." http://www.vredefortstructure.org/vrede01.htm

"Visit Deep Impact-The Vredefort Dome." n.d. Hartebeesthoek Radio Astronomy Observatory. http://www.hartrao.ac.za/other/vredefort/vredefort.html

"Vredefort Dome, South Africa." 2005. World Heritage Evaluation–IUCN Technical Evaluation. UNESCO. http://whc.unesco.org/archive/advisory_body_evaluation/1162.pdf

Wadden Sea

Atlantic Ocean

Geographic Overview. Bordering northern Netherlands, Germany, and Denmark at the southern edge of the North Sea, the Wadden Sea is a large, natural intertidal ecosystem. In the path of the East Atlantic Flyway and African–Eurasian migration routes, the Wadden Sea influences ecosystems from the Arctic to southern Africa. Breeding and wintering birds number in the millions. The region is one of the best studied depositional coastlines in the world and has scientific importance for coastal and wetland management

Geographic Coordinates. Approximately 52° 58'N–55°36'N, 04°40'E–09°01'E

Description. The Wadden Sea, including the offshore barrier islands, extends approximately 280 mi (450 km) from Den Helder in the Netherlands east along the coast of Germany and north past Esbjerg in Denmark. The relatively flat coastal wetland environment covers 5,000 mi² (13,000 km²). The Dutch word *wad,* for "mudflat," perfectly describes the Wadden Sea, which is typified by tidal mudflats and low islands. The Wadden Sea Islands are called the Frisian Islands off the Netherlands and Germany and the North Frisian Islands off Denmark.

The region is a large depositional coastline, a barrier bar system on a low-lying coastal plain reacting to rising sea level conditions. The general elevation is less than 164 ft (50 m) asl, and water depth rarely exceeds 164 ft (50 m). More than 50 islands, some very small and some inhabited, parallel the coastline of all three countries. Dunes and broad sandy beaches face the North Sea, while the flat tidal coast faces the continent. The configuration of some islands changes with waves, currents, and tides. Inhabited parts of islands are protected from flooding by dikes. Uninhabited areas are generally subject to natural processes. Sediments and nutrients are washed through tidal inlets between islands into the Wadden Sea, and shallow water alternates with mudflats as the tide changes.

The area has a marine west coast climate. Mild winters average 39°F (4°C) and cool summers average 59°F (15°C). The average water temperature is 48°F (9°C). Precipitation is 27–31 in (700–800 mm).

Biota. The Wadden Sea has many habitats that are transitional between land, sea, and fresh water, including tidal channels, sandy shoals, seagrass meadows, mussel beds, sandbars, mudflats, salt marshes, estuaries, beaches, and dunes. Both the sea and islands are rich in plant and animal species, which are adapted to the daily changing flood and ebb tides, which alter salinity, light, oxygen, and temperature. Productivity of the biomass, including fish, shellfish, and birds, is one of the highest in the world. The region has more than 10,000 species of plants and animals. Approximately 2,300 species can be found in the salt marshes, the primary terrestrial habitat. Salt marsh species, including glasswort (*Salicornia* spp.), sea lavenders (*Limonium* spp.), and cordgrass (*Spartina angelica*), form a mosaic according to salinity and water levels. The sandy islands hold a freshwater lens (from rainfall) overlying the heavier salt water, supporting plants less tolerant of salt. Grasses such as marram grass (*Ammophila arenaria*) trap sand grains, maintaining both the dunes and the coastlines. Plant communities from sandy shore to inland dunes include various grasses, low herbaceous plants, mosses, lichens, and dwarf-shrub heathlands. Mixed stands of sea grasses thrive on tidal flats.

The Wadden Sea is a staging, molting, nesting, and wintering area for many birds. More than 6 million birds, primarily waterbirds, may be seen gathered at one time, and 10–12 million pass through yearly. Autumn and spring migrations see birds with breeding grounds in Siberia, Scandinavia, Greenland, or northeastern Canada, and birds that winter in Europe or Africa. Several species of ducks and geese overwinter, and the majority of the nesting birds are gulls.

Of the approximately 4,200 species of animals, most are invertebrates, such as shellfish, crustaceans, and worms. Marine mammals include harbor seal, gray seal, and harbor porpoise. The Wadden Sea is a nursery area for North Sea fish, such as plaice and herring, and a staging area for fish and lampreys migrating between rivers and oceans for spawning. Approximately 20 fish species, such as bottom dwellers eelpout and bull rout, are residents.

Protected Areas. The World Heritage Site, designated in 2009, covers 66 percent of the Wadden Sea region. National parks include Lower Saxony and Schleswig–Holstein in Germany and the Dutch islands of Schiermonnikoog and Texel. The Trilateral Wadden Sea Plan outlines policies and projects, and the entire region is a conservation area.

Environmental Issues. Although the extensive human uses of the Wadden Sea area are well regulated, threats remain from fisheries, harbors, industrial facilities, maritime traffic, residential and tourism development, alien species, and climate change. Sea level changes may alter the dynamics of natural erosion and deposition. Recently increased populations of the Pacific oyster (*Crassostrea gigas*) have overgrown many native blue mussel (*Mytilus edulis*) beds, changing the environment on tidal flats. The effect on other benthic species and mussel-eating birds is as yet unknown. According to a 2010 study, the major food, a clam (*Macoma balthica*), for two subspecies of knots (*Calidris canutus*) has become rare, potentially threatening their survival.

See also North Sea

Further Reading

Birdlife International. 2014. Important Bird Areas Factsheet: Wadden Sea. http://www.birdlife.org/datazone/sitefactsheet.php?id=1179

Bungenstock, Friederike and Dirk Enters. 2010. *The Wadden Sea*. Niedersachsisches Institut fur historische Kustenforschung, Wilhemshaven. www.archaeobotany.org/download/excursion_guide1.pdf

"Waddensee Worldheritage." 2013. www.waddensea-world heritage.org

Wadi Al-Hitan (Whale Valley)

Egypt

Geographic Overview. Wadi Al-Hitan is a dry river bed in the Western Desert of Egypt that contains a rich and significant Eocene Epoch fossil record of early whales. Nearly complete and articulated skeletons document the transition from land mammals to marine mammals. Early sirenians and primitive proboscidians are also represented.

Geographic Coordinates. 29°15'N–29°24'N, 30°01'E–30°10'E

Description. A dry river valley in Egypt's Western Desert, Wadi al-Hitan preserves fossilized skeletons of the earliest suborder of whales, the Archaeoceti. Along a distance of more than 6 mi (10 km) over 400 skeletons, many articulated and nearly complete, have eroded from sandstones formed in ancient seabed. The presence of many infant skeletons suggests the shallow sea along the southern coast of the Tethys Sea had been a calving ground.

The largest specimen is a 68.9 ft (21 m) long *Basilosaurus isis*, which possesses hind legs, feet, and toes, but has the streamlined body of a modern whale. Another species, *Dorudon atrox*, is more dolphin-like and has only vestigial hind limbs. In addition, three species of early sirenian (sea cow) have been identified in the fossil bed, as well as a primitive elephant, *Moeritherium*. The number and concentration of ancient whale fossils and their excellent state of preservation, as well as their relative accessibility makes Wadi al-Hitan a globally significant site. Furthermore, the presence of other vertebrate and invertebrate materials allows reconstruction of Late Eocene environments.

Wadi al-Hitan is about 90 mi (150 km) southwest of Cairo in a sub-basin known as Wadi el-Rayan on the western edge of the Fayum Depression, just

Fossilized remains of the ancient dolphin-like whale *Dorudon atrox* lie exposed in Wadi Al-Hitan, Egypt. (Peter Langer/Design Pics/Corbis)

west of the Nile River. The landscape is flat and sand-covered, with pillars and other bizarre rock formations sculpted by blowing sand. Dunes, cliffs, and low shale and limestone hills, remnants of a former plateau, surround the wadi. Areas in Wadi el-Rayan are strewn with great spheres of conglomerate called "Water Melons," which formed in former Lake Moeris, a lake that came into existence from the flood of the Nile about 5,000 years ago during the time of Ancient Egypt and is the predecessor of today's smaller Lake Qarün.

Less than 0.4 in (10 mm) of rain falls in this hyperarid desert each year, generally during the mild winter season. Summers are hot and dry; mean temperature is 83°F (28.5°C), daily highs can reach 119°F (48.4°C). In contrast, mean winter temperature is 57°F (13.7°C), with daily lows down to 34°F (1.2°C). Prevailing winds are from the north and cause both

erosion and deposition of sand, revealing and burying whale skeletons. The land is generally barren; a few salt cedars and halophytic shrubs grow here and there. Animal life is also sparse.

Geologic History. The Eocene bedrock consists of thick layers of sandstones, limestones, and shales. The oldest (41–40 mya) is a white, marly limestone containing fossilized skeletons of archaic whales and sirenians. The youngest unit dates to the Late Eocene, 39 mya, and contains fossils of marine invertebrates indicative of shallow seas. Whale evolution began about 55 mya; both toothed and baleen whales had appeared by 33 mya. The Wadi al-Hitan fossils represent a key period as terrestrial ancestors transitioned to the marine mammals of today. The sedimentary beds were raised above the level of the ancient Tethys Sea from the southwest, giving rise to an ancient drainage system that now is buried beneath sand. Later, with the onset of aridity, wind removed sand, exposing fossils on the desert floor and releasing them from cliffs. Windblown sand sculpted the rocks into an array of strange shapes.

Protected Areas. Wadi al-Hitan is a Special Protection Zone within the Wadi el-Rayan Protected Area. No vehicular traffic is allowed and visitation is permitted only with a guide. A 2 mi (3 km) footpath leads to the fossil site.

Environmental Issues. Exposed skeletons are fragile and vulnerable to illegal collection. Wind continues to expose them and to bury them. Significant damage has occurred from 4WD vehicles running over fossils; and the surrounding landscape is marred by 4WD tracks, despite the prohibition on vehicles.

Further Reading

"Wadi al-Hitan (Whale Valley)." n.d. World Heritage Centre, UNESCO. http://whc.unesco.org/en/list/1186a

"Wadi el Rayan: Gateway to the Western Desert. 2002. Wadi el Rayan Protected Area Project. http://issuu .com/ziomimmo/docs/wadielrayan

Walcott Quarry

Canada

Geographic Overview. Walcott Quarry, high in the Rocky Mountains of British Columbia, is considered one of the world's most important fossil discoveries. The site preserves a wide variety of soft-bodied invertebrate fossils representing an ecosystem just after the Cambrian Explosion, which was a rapid evolution of many complex animals. The 200,000-year record provides a glimpse into the nature of evolution, particularly rapid diversification and extinction. The fossils are significant for their age, exceptional preservation, and diversity.

Geographic Coordinates. 51°26'N, 116°28'W

Description. Walcott Quarry is an outcropping of Burgess Shale in Yoho National Park. The site, on Fossil Ridge between Wapta Mountain and Mt. Field, was discovered in 1909 by Charles D. Walcott, Secretary of the Smithsonian Institution. More than 65,000 specimens are housed in the Smithsonian National Museum of Natural History. Raymond Quarry, higher in the stratigraphic column and higher on the mountain wall, has similar fauna but different concentrations. The area of both quarries is strictly protected and accessible only by guided hikes. Only scientific collecting is allowed, and research continues. Similar fossil deposits have subsequently been found in China, Greenland, Siberia, Europe, and the United States.

The Burgess Shale has yielded more than 170 different species of plants and animals and contains samples of all 32 phyla in the animal kingdom. The majority of the fossils are in the phyla Arthropoda, animals with external skeletons, segmented bodies, and jointed appendages. Extinct classes of arthropods include Trilobita and Dinocarida, the latter class being predators described in 1966 based on Burgess Shale fossils. Fossil life-forms representative of still living classes include Uniramia (modern centipedes), Chelicerata (spiders and scorpions), and Crustacea (crabs, lobster, and shrimp). Other phyla and their modern examples include Onychophora (velvet worms), Annelida (earthworms and leeches), Porifera (marine sponges), Cnidaria (jellyfish, coral, and sea anemones), Echinodermata (starfish and sea urchins), and Chordata (vertebrates). Fossils range in size from approximately 0.4 in (1 cm) to 24 in (60 cm).

Geologic History. In the middle Cambrian (505 mya), this location was a coral reef in an Equatorial sea. A 330 ft (100 m) high limestone cliff, now the Cathedral Formation, stood at the edge of the continental shelf. Mudflows carried the organisms from the shallow water on top of the reef over the limestone cliff, depositing them at its base, where the mud turned to shale. The fine mud, which penetrated and filled space inside the bodies of the organisms as well as surrounding them, was a significant factor in preserving the shape of soft parts and rarely seen detail.

Protected Areas. The quarry has been part of a Rocky Mountain Parks World Heritage Site since 1984.

Further Reading

Morris, Simon Conway and Stephen Jay Gould. "Showdown on the Burgess Shale." *Natural History* 107 (10): 48-55. The Unofficial Stephen Jay Gould archive. http://www.stephenjaygould.org/library/naturalhistory_cambrian.html

Walcott-Rust Quarry

Walcott-Rust Quarry is a small site along Gray's Brook in north-central New York. Although fossils from the site were being sold by William Rust, an area resident, the site was brought to the attention of science in 1870 by Charles D. Walcott. The site, Upper Ordovician lime mudstone deposited by landslides or storm events approximately 455 mya, is rich in well-preserved trilobites, especially *Ceraurus pleurexanthemus* and *Flexicalymene senaria*. Walcott was the first to identify appendages, such as gills, legs, and other soft parts, on the trilobite fossils. Many of his specimens remain in collections at the Museum of Comparative Zoology at Harvard. Louis Agassiz, the founder of the museum, purchased Walcott's 325 trilobites, along with 190 crinoids, 6 starfish, approximately 15 cystoids, and corals and brachiopods, for the museum. The quarry fell into disuse for 60 years until interest was rekindled by Thomas Whiteley, a fossil collector who worked and documented the site for 20 years and published his findings. Whiteley donated many of his finds.

Parks Canada. 2013. "The Burgess Shale." Yoho National Park of Canada. www.pc.gc.ca/pn-np/bc/yoho/natcul/burgess/apprenez-learn.aspx

Smithsonian. 2013. "The Burgess Shale." Smithsonian National Museum of Natural History. http://paleobiology.si.edu/burgess/index.html

Waterton–Glacier International Peace Park

United States (Montana) and Canada

Geographic Overview. Waterton–Glacier International Peace Park in the Rocky Mountains of northwestern Montana and southwestern Alberta, Canada, was deeply sculpted by alpine glaciers into spectacular scenery. The sheer rock walls exhibit a long record of Precambrian rocks. The park has an unusual juxtaposition of prairie and high-mountain ecosystems, resulting in a diverse biotic assemblage. Several hiking trails follow routes over the mountain passes which have been used by Native Americans for centuries.

Geographic Coordinates. Approximately 48° 14'N–49°12'N, 113°14'W–115°02'W

Description. The alpine landscape of Waterton–Glacier park, primarily horizontal metamorphosed sedimentary rock, is rugged with many glacial landforms, including horns, arêtes, cols, tarns, troughs, lakes, cirques, hanging troughs, and waterfalls, primarily carved during the Pleistocene. The glacial features are large scale. McDonald Lake, 1.5 mi (2.4 km) wide, 464 ft (141 m) deep, and occupying a glacial trough, is the largest lake. Bird Woman Falls cascades a total of 960 ft (293 m), including a single drop of 560 (171 m), from a hanging trough into Logan Valley, a much larger U-shaped valley. Triple Divide Peak drains to three major watersheds and three seas—the Pacific Ocean, Hudson Bay, and the Gulf of Mexico. The park is well watered, with 762 lakes and 563 rivers and streams. Mt. Cleveland, at 10,500 ft (3,200 m) and the highest peak in the park, is of moderate height for the Rocky Mountains. Going-to-the-Sun road, hugging cliffs and skirting lake shores, crosses Glacier National Park and the continental divide at 6,645 ft (2,025 m) high Logan Pass. The road extends 50 mi (80 km) and was completed in 1932.

Geologic History. Sediments deposited in a broad, shallow sea during the Precambrian (1,600–800 mya) later solidified to become sandstone, siltstone, and limestone. Uplift of the Rocky Mountains at the end of the Cretaceous (60 mya) caused a huge block of crust, extending 300 mi (483 km) from Canada into the United States, to be pushed 40–50 mi (64–80 km) east along a low-angle thrust fault over the Great Plains. Although lightly metamorphosed to quartzite, argillite, and marble, the Precambrian rocks remained relatively horizontal. The excellent preservation of ancient strata, including details of sedimentation, such as ripple marks, mud cracks, and fossil algae called stromatolites, provides information regarding the physical and chemical conditions on earth more than a billion years ago. The Lewis Overthrust Fault is one of the largest in the world. Chief Mountain in Montana on the eastern side of the park is an erosional remnant of the Lewis Overthrust block.

Morning sun lights the Prince of Wales Hotel in Waterton Lakes National Park in Alberta, Canada. Upper Waterton Lake sits below Goat Haunt Mountain and snow-capped Mount Cleveland rising from adjacent Glacier National Park in Montana in the United States. (milehightraveler/iStockphoto.com)

Biota. With 1,132 vascular plant species, 79 animal species, and 277 bird species, the park is the most ecologically diverse of any protected area in the Rocky Mountains. Pacific Northwest, mountain, and prairie ecosystems converge in this narrow part of the Rocky Mountain chain. Mountains and valleys create habitat for a mosaic of communities, including old-growth cedar and hemlock forests, subalpine fir, aspen, prairie grasses and forbs, and wetlands. Animal life is equally diverse, including mountain goat, bighorn sheep, grizzly bear, moose, golden eagle, and beaver.

Protected Areas. Waterton–Glacier International Peace Park includes Glacier National Park, 1,584 mi^2 (4,100 km^2), and Waterton Lakes National Park, 195 mi^2 (505 km^2). Waterton Lakes became a Canadian national park in 1895. Glacier was designated a U.S. national park in 1910. In 1911, officials from both parks concurred that the upper Waterton Valley, which crosses the U.S.–Canada border, should not be divided and that the two parks should be managed as one protected area because they share geology, climate, wildlife, and ecology. The combined efforts of Montana and Alberta Rotary Clubs bought this proposal to fruition, and the two parks became the world's first international peace park in 1932, partly to commemorate the longest unfortified border in the world, 5,525 mi (8,892 km) long between the United States and Canada. The joint park was designated an International Biosphere Reserve in 1974 and a World Heritage Site in 1995. Going-to-the-Sun road is a National Historic Civil Engineering Landmark.

Environmental Issues. In 1850, Glacier Park had 150 glaciers, remnants from the Little Ice Age. By 1990, the number had been reduced to 50, and in 2013, only 25 remained, all of which are small. The largest is Blackfoot Glacier, 0.7 mi^2 (1.8 km^2). Estimates indicate that all glaciers will disappear by 2030.

See also Rocky Mountains

Further Reading

Harris, Ann G., Esther Tuttle, and Sherwood D. Tuttle. 2004. "Waterton-Glacier International Peace Park." In *Geology of National Parks*, 6th ed., 357–371. Dubuque, IA: Kendall Hunt.

National Park Service. 2013. *Glacier National Park*. http://www.nps.gov/glac/index.htm

Parks Canada. 2012. *Waterton Lakes National Park*. http://www.pc.gc.ca/eng/pn-np/ab/waterton/intro.aspx

West Norwegian Fjords—Geirangerfjord and Nærøyfjord

Norway

Geographic Overview. Norway has one of the finest concentrations of fjords in the world, approximately 200 on the mainland, with more on adjacent islands. As well as being scenically outstanding, Geirangerfjord and Nærøyfjord are among the world's longest and deepest and are the type locality for fjord landscapes. The word *fjord* is Norwegian.

Geographic Coordinates. Geirangerfjord—62°07'N, 06°57'E; Nærøyfjord—60°55'N, 07°00'E

Description. Geirangerfjord and Nærøyfjord, in southwestern Norway northeast of Bergen, are part of a fjord landscape that stretches 310 mi (500 km) from Stavanger in the south northeast to Andalsnes. Steep sides rise 4,600 ft (1,400 m) from sea level and extend another 1,650 ft (500 m) below the surface. Many waterfalls cascade over the sheer cliffs, and the steep walls reveal geologic history. The uplands contain rugged mountains, deciduous and coniferous forests, free-flowing rivers, and many glacial lakes and glaciers. Many hanging glacial valleys are on the higher parts of the fjord walls. Valleys and steep grassy slopes contain remnants of old farmsteads. Fewer than 500 individuals reside in six settlements within this World Heritage Site.

The two regions are distinctive. Nærøyfjord, with its rounded mountain tops, covers 274 mi^2 (709 km^2). Geirangerfjord, with its glaciated peaks, some of which were nunataks, covers 200 mi^2 (518 km^2). Storfjord begins at the Norwegian Sea at Ålesund and extends 93 mi (150 km) inland to end in four tributary fjords—Norddalsfjord, Tafjord, Sunnylvsfjord, and Geirangerfjord. The water depth is 2,225 ft (679 m) in Storfjord, and 984 ft (300 m) in Geirangerfjord. At the coast, adjacent mountains are 1,640 ft (500 m) asl, increasing to more than 5,250 ft (1,600 m) asl at Geirangerfjord. Geirangerfjord narrows to 0.6 mi (1 km), with major waterfalls, such as Seven Sisters and The Suitor, cascading over steep cliffs. Nærøyfjord is one of the side fjords to Sognefjord. As much of 985 ft (300 m) of sediments cover the fjord floor, and the heads of many fjords have emergent flat land deltas.

The North Atlantic Drift, bringing warm water north from the Gulf of Mexico, modifies the high latitude climate. The coast remains ice-free as far north as Finland.

Geologic History. The dominant rock is Precambrian gneiss, mixed with sedimentary rocks that were altered and folded during the Caledonian Orogeny (400 mya). In the early Tertiary (65–40 mya), after the region was eroded to a low-lying peneplain of rolling plains and rounded hills and the Atlantic Ocean opened, Norway was uplifted, especially in the West. Increased precipitation associated with higher elevations caused large rivers to carve deep V-shaped valleys running steeply down to the Atlantic Ocean. Pleistocene ice sheets covered the landscape, all the way west to the ocean. As ice funneled through the river valleys, it gouged and eroded them wider and deeper, into U-shaped glacial troughs. When the ice melted, the rise in sea level flooded the seaward parts of the glacial valleys, often extending many miles inland.

With the release of the weight of glacial ice, the land rebounded and continues to do so. The heads of formerly flooded valleys emerge as flat, dry land covered with sediments. Water in Geirangerfjord, for example, was 300 ft (90 m) higher at the close of the Pleistocene.

Biota. Vegetational zonation, from a narrow coastal strip up to alpine habitats, provides a variety of terrestrial landscapes and species. Granite and gneiss are poor in nutrients. Slate, chalk, or olivine outcrops support more botanical diversity. South-facing slopes up to 2,800 ft (850 m) asl have a mixed woodland of birch, alder, willow, hazel, and some conifers. Forbs, such as red campion, buttercups, and cranesbill, grow in hay meadows. Dry stone ridges have harebell and alpine campion. Orchids, cloudberries, bog cotton, and mosses grow in bogs. The alpine region has dwarf shrubs, such as mountain birch, heather, and cranberries, as well as bare rocky areas.

Red deer and roe deer are common, but moose are rarely seen. Three herds of wild reindeer live within the World Heritage Site. Predatory animals include fox, bear, lynx, pine marten, and others. The variety of topography favors a rich diversity of birdlife, including many waterbirds. Approximately 100 species nest in the area. Agricultural land and mountains offer different habitats, for woodpeckers, nuthatches, thrushes, and others. Several rare and endangered insects, including a butterfly and beetles, are present.

A variety of fish, including salmon, eels, herring, cod, haddock, and mackerel, use the fjords. Larger marine species include Greenland shark and porpoises.

Protected Areas. Five areas are designated as Nature Reserves, and three others are designated Protected Landscape Areas. West Norwegian Fjords became a World Heritage Site in 2005.

Environmental Issues. The unstable fractured gneiss walls of the fjords are prone to rock falls and avalanches, which may generate large, but local, tsunamis. In 1934, a massive rock slide in Tafjord generated a wave as high as 203 ft (62 m), which crushed three villages and left 41 people dead. Snow avalanches occur annually in the Geiranger area.

Further Reading

Aarseth, Inge, Atle Nesje, and Ola Fredin. 2008. *UNESCO Fjords, 33 IGC Excursion No. 31*. IGC (International Geological Congress). www.iugs.org/33igc/coco/Lay outPage-c11459-p5062.html

Geiranger Turist-og Naeringslag. 2012. "Welcome to Geiranger." http://www.geiranger.no/index.php/

Verdsarv. n.d. "The Geirangerfjord." http://www.verd sarvfjord.no/index.php?searchword=søk%20.&or dering=&searchphrase=all&Itemid=94&option= com_search&lang=en

Western Ghats

India

Geographic Overview. The Western Ghats, an almost unbroken escarpment paralleling the west coast of India, are characterized by high summits, steep slopes, and deep gorges. The range is the drainage divide between eastern and western India, and the source of a large proportion of India's water supply. The Ghats support one of the best examples of nonequatorial monsoon forest in the world, with high levels of biological diversity and endemism. The region is significant in demonstrating speciation related to the breakup of Gondwanaland and the subsequent isolation of the Indian landmass.

Geographic Coordinates. Approximately 08°11'N–21°06'N, 72°45'E–77°25'E

Description. The Western Ghats extend approximately 1,000 mi (1,600 km) from the Tapti River north of Mumbai south to Cape Comorin at the southern tip off India and cover approximately 69,500 mi^2 (180,000 km^2). The range is a major scarp rising above a narrow coastal plain, without a break until Palghat Gap in southern India. The mountains, with a mean elevation of 3,000–5,000 ft (900–1,500 m) asl, are 6–37 mi (10–60 km) from the coast. On the east side, many spurs or lateral ranges run east–west, separating the east-flowing Godavari, Bhima, and Krishna river systems. The term "ghat" refers to a "stairstep," a description of the step-like levels of the eroded Ghats.

The northern part of the Western Ghats, stretching 375 mi (600 km) from the Tapti River south to Goa, is the crest of the northwestern edge of the basalt flows of the Deccan Trap. The scarp, with more than 3,300 ft (1,000 m) of successive lava layers, rises as a steep wall from the narrow coastal plain. The range is primarily flat-topped hills, often capped by laterite, with bare walls of basalt. The eastern side is eroded into giant steps. Flat-topped spurs average 2,300–3,300 ft (700–1,000 m) asl, with some higher pinnacles, such as Kalsubai at 5,400 ft (1,646 m) and Salher at 5,141 ft (1,567 m). Deep ravines and canyons with fast-flowing streams dissect the western scarp face and flow to the Arabian Sea. The width of the coastal plain is 20–30 mi (30–50 km).

South of Goa, the central region of the Western Ghats, composed of steeply dipping gneiss and schist capped by laterite and with some granite intrusions, are less abrupt and steep. Hill summits are mostly bare. The western scarp is considerably dissected by west-flowing streams, waterfalls are common at the heads of rivers, and the watershed divide between east and west India is pushed approximately 100 mi (160 km) eastward. Although a steep barrier, the ridge is irregular in height, with elevations generally 2,000–3,300 ft (600–1,000 m) and peaks such as Kodrachadri at 4,406 ft (1,343 m) and Kudremukh at 6,207 ft (1,892 m). Major rivers, such as the Kalinadi, Gangavali, and Sharavathy, have carved deep valleys. Near Goa, where the coastal plain dwindles to nothing, the Western Ghats extend down to the sea, with peaks standing as islands. Further south, the coastal plain widens to 20–50 mi (30–80 km).

The highest elevations are in the south, where mountains are composed of hard charnockites, a type of metamorphic rock or granite with unusual composition. The Western Ghats merge with the Eastern Ghats, the discontinuous group of hills lining the east coast of India, in the Nilgiri Hills south of Mysore. The Nilgiri Hills are a plateau more than 6,000 ft (1,800 m) asl, with two high peaks, Dodabetta at 8,652 ft (2,637 m) and Makurti at 8,403 ft (2,561 m). Palghat Gap, 20 mi (30 km) wide and 1,000 ft (300 m) asl, separates the Nilgiris massif to the north and the equally high Anaimalai to the south.

South of Palghat Gap, the Southern Ghats are a complex group of highlands, including the Cardamom Hills, all of which are composed mainly of charnockites. The Southern Ghats includes southern India's highest point, Animudi Peak, 8,841 ft (2695 m). The south is a narrow rugged ridge, steep on both east and west sides, reaching almost to Cape Comorin.

Geologic History. The Western Ghats are part of the Indian shield, or craton, most of which is highly metamorphosed Precambrian sedimentary and igneous rocks. The younger (67–65 mya) lava flows of the Deccan Plateau overlie older Precambrian rock in the Northern Ghats. The western scarp may be faulted. Evidence indicates a series of northwest–southeast striking faults that parallel the coast, punctuated by several hot springs. The Nilgiri and Cardamom Mountains are plateaus and horsts, which may represent an old eroded Gondwana surface.

Biota. The region has a diversity of ecosystems, from tropical wet evergreen forests to montane grasslands, all of which contain medicinal plants and wild relatives of grains, fruit, and spices. It is one of the eight most important biodiversity hotspots on Earth, with more than 5,000 species of flowering plants, 139 species of mammals, 508 species of birds, and 179 species of amphibians. At least 325 species—both flora and fauna—are globally threatened. Although covering only 6 percent of India, the Western Ghats support more than 30 percent of all plant, fish, reptile, amphibian, bird, and mammal species in the country, many of which are endemic or endangered. Endemic animals include Nilgiri tahr (*Hamitragus hylocrius*) and lion-tailed macaque (*Macaca silenas*). The southwestern Ghats harbor elephants, Bengal tigers, macaques, sloth bears (*Ursus ursinus*), tahrs, and many more species. The Nilgiri Hills are home to approximately 30 percent of the world's Asian elephants and 10–17 percent of the world's tigers. Other wildlife includes leopard, wild boar, sambar, black panther, and many bird species.

The Deccan Traps are significant for their fossil assemblages, most notably frogs and mollusks, between lava flows.

Protected Areas. The Western Ghats have several national wildlife sanctuaries, tiger reserves, and national parks, as well as two Biosphere Reserves. Nilgiri Biosphere Reserve, 39 parts in seven subclusters, is the largest, with both evergreen forest and deciduous forest.

Environmental Issues. Dense forest has largely been logged and converted to tea, rubber, oil palm or coffee plantations or to grazing. Habitat fragmentation, poaching, and human–animal conflicts are problems in or near protected areas.

See also Deccan Plateau

Further Reading

Mittermeier, R. A., N. Myers, C. G. Mittermeier, and P. Robles Gil. 1999. *Hotspots: Earth's Biologically Richest and Most Endangered Terrestrial Ecoregions*. Mexico City: CEMEX, SA, Agrupacion, Sierra Madre.

Pai, Mohan. 2009. *The Western Ghats—Topography*. http://creative.sulekha.com/the-western-ghats-by-mohan-pai-topography_387405_blog

Western Madagascar Wetlands

Madagascar

Geographic Overview. Wetlands in Western Madagascar contain extensive mangroves, freshwater lakes, and marshes, which provide breeding grounds for several globally threatened species. It is an important area for commercial fishing, and many families rely on the region for subsistence.

Geographic Coordinates. Tsiribihina and Manambolo Rivers—19°00'S–20°00'S, 44°15'E°–44°35'E; Lakes of Manambolomaty—19°01'S, 44°24'E; Lake Kinkony—16°08'S, 45°49'E; Lake Mandrozo—17° 32'S, 44°06'E; Lake Bedo—19°57'S, 44°36'E

Description. Wetlands occur in several different regions of western Madagascar. Coastal reaches of the Tsiribihina and Manambolo Rivers support the most extensive areas of mangroves in the country. Habitats also include deciduous forest and lakes. The Lakes of Manambolomaty are slightly north of the Manambolo River. The four lakes, three freshwater and one brackish, cover 18,510 ac (7,491 ha) and are surrounded by forest. Lake Kinkony, an important bird area and freshwater lake southwest of the Mahavavy delta, covers 43,100 ac (13,800 ha). Rice paddies along its banks and its fish populations support local communities. The Humid Zone of Lake Mandrozo, near the west coast approximately midway between the Tsiribihina and Mahavavy Rivers, covers 37,423 ac (15,145 ha). Lake Mandrozo, the fourth largest in Madagascar, is surrounded by marshes, irrigated rice fields, dry forest, and savanna. The region provides the livelihood for many local families. The Humid Zone of Lake Bedo, south of the Tsiribihina River, centers on shallow, open Lake Bedo and its surrounding marshes, which are rich in aquatic vegetation. A permanent river flowing through the forest feeds the lake and marshes, from runoff during the rainy season and springs during the dry season.

Biota. Mangrove forests of the Tsiribihina and Manambola Rivers provide breeding grounds for endangered species such as the Madagascar Teal (*Anas bernieri*) and the Madagascar Fish Eagle (*Haliaeetus vociferoides*). The waters of mangrove forests are also nurseries for many fish, crustaceans, and mollusks that support important local fisheries. The Tsiribihina River is one of the country's largest, and its delta has one of the most extensive blocks of mangroves, extending 12–31 mi (20–50 km) both north and south of the main delta. Mangroves in the Manambola estuary and neighboring rivers are also extensive. A series of lakes with adjacent mangroves is an important conservation area for aquatic birds. The Lakes of Manambolomaty support 20 birds endemic to Madagascar and include breeding sites for the Fish Eagle, Humblot's (or Madagascar) Heron (*Ardea humbloti*), and the big-headed turtle (*Erymnochelys madagascariensis*). The big-headed turtle (also called side-necked) is the only freshwater chelonian (in the family Testudines). With the development of commercial fishing since the 1970s, populations of this critically endangered turtle declined because they are caught in the fine mesh of fishing nets. One lake is the only known area to support the Madagascar Teal and White-backed Duck (*Thalassornis leuconotus insularis*).

Lake Kinkony is dominated by reeds (*Phragmites mauritianus*), which provide nesting grounds for 45 waterbird species, four of which are threatened, and for the endemic and endangered Sakalava Rail (*Amaurornis olivieri*). The lake's reeds also provide food and spawning grounds for 18 fish species, including endangered *Paretroplus dambabe* and the vulnerable *Paretroplus kieneri*, as well as the big-headed turtle. The Lake Mandrozo region supports a diversity of species, including Fish Eagle, big-headed turtle, Sakalava Rail, and several threatened reptiles. The Lake Bedo region supports at least 34 waterbirds, including the Madagascar Teal, Humblot's Heron, Madagascar Plover (*Charadrius thoracicus*), and the migratory Greater Flamingo (*Phoenicopterus roseus*) and Lesser Flamingo (*Phoenicopterus minor*). It also houses the big-headed turtle. The lake provides fish and prawns and grassy construction material for local villagers.

Protected Areas. The Tsiribihina delta is part of the Menabe Antimena Protected Area. Several sites—Lakes of Manambolomaty, Lake Kinkony, Humid Zone of Mandrozo, and Humid Zone of Bedo—are Ramsar Wetlands of International Importance. Lake Kinkony is part of Mahavavy Kinkony Protected Area.

Environmental Issues. Harvesting of timber for construction and charcoal, along with clearing for new agricultural land, threatens the effectiveness of mangrove forests to both harbor significant species and prevent coastal flooding. Lakes of Manambolomaty are used seasonally as rice paddies. Lake Kinkony is threatened by overfishing and unregulated fishing techniques, conversion of marshes to rice fields, and destruction of drainage basins for agriculture.

See also Madagascar; Menabe Antimena Protected Area

Further Reading

Ramsar. 1999. "The Annotated Ramsar List: Madagascar." The Ramsar Convention on Wetlands. http://www.ramsar.org/cda/en/ramsar-documents-list-anno-madagascar/main/ramsar/1-31-218%5E16534_4000_0_

World Wildlife Fund. 2009. *Mangrove Conservation in Western Madagascar: Vulnerability Assessment.* http://wwf.panda.org/who_we_are/wwf_offices/madagascar/?uProjectID=MG0933

White Sands

United States (New Mexico)

Geographic Overview. The snowy white dunes of southern New Mexico's White Sands, both in the national monument and in the missile range, is the largest gypsum dune field in the world. The site of the first atomic bomb test in 1945 is on the grounds of the military land. The pure gypsum, hydrous calcium sulfate ($CaSO_4.2H_2O$), is a rarely found form because it is soluble in water.

Geographic Coordinates. National monument: 32°47'N, 106°10'W. Missile range: 32°57'N, 106°25'W

Description. White Sands lies in the Tularosa Valley, a graben between the San Andres Mountains on the west and the Sacramento Mountains on the east. The dune field, including White Sands Missile Range, covers approximately 275 mi² (712 km²), of which 115 mi² (298 km²), or 40 percent is in White Sands National Monument. Different types of dunes develop according to wind strength and volume of sand. On the southwest side of the dune field, closest to the sand sources on the dry lake bed and where winds are strongest, there are low mounds of sand. Crescent-shaped barchan dunes develop under strong

winds and a limited sand supply. Where sand is abundant, barchans dunes join together into transverse dune ridges. Near the margins of the dune field where winds are weak, vegetation anchors the sand, causing parabolic dunes. Although the dunes are moving and sand is eventually moved out of the basin, the playas continue to supply gypsum that maintains the dune field.

Geologic History. The source of the gypsum is Permian (245 mya) rocks of the San Andres Mountains on the west side of the valley. In the Paleozoic (545–245 mya), this area was the site of a vast tropical sea, the same sea in which the limestones of Carlsbad Caverns and the Guadalupe Mountains were deposited. Gypsum, along with other salts, crystallized as water evaporated during a dry time period when the sea was shallow. The gypsum deposits alone are as thick as 500 ft (152 m). During the formation of the Rio Grande Rift in the Cenozoic (70 mya), the rock layers were upwarped into an anticline. With crustal stretching during the Miocene (10 mya), the anticline collapsed to become a graben. The strata of evaporite minerals on the side of the escarpment were exposed and carried in solution by rivers to the valley floor. The interior drainage and aridity of the Tularosa Valley play a major role in the development of the gypsum dunes. Under wetter conditions, the gypsum would be dissolved in water and carried to the ocean. During the Pleistocene, the valley was occupied by glacial Lake Otero, of which intermittent Lake Lucero is a remnant. The immediate source of the gypsum for the dunes is both the dry playa surface of Lake Otero and Lake Lucero, southwest of the dunes. Capillary action draws gypsum-saturated groundwater beneath Lake Otero toward the surface, where it crystallizes into selenite crystals, a form of gypsum. Although the fragile crystals may be initially 3 ft (0.9 m) long, they quickly deteriorate into sand.

Wind is not capable of carrying sand grains far above the land surface. The major movement of sand grains is due to saltation, a sort of jumping or bouncing of sand grains. Wind initially picks up the sand grain. When the grain falls back to the ground, it bounces upon impact and briefly again becomes airborne, an average of 4 in (10 cm) off the surface, where wind then carries it a short distance. The sand accumulates

The snowy white sand dunes of White Sands National Monument in southern New Mexico are composed of gypsum, eroded from high on the cliffs west of the valley. (Daniel Raustadt/Dreamstime.com)

in dune fields where the wind energy is reduced. Sand moves upslope in the dune by saltation, then cascades down the lee side, causing the dune to slowly migrate over the land surface.

Biota. Specialized plants and animals are adapted to the dune environment, cold winters, hot summers, little surface water, and highly mineralized ground water. A clay layer underlying Lake Otero and the dune fields creates a shallow perched water table that provides water for plants. As dunes advance, as fast as 30 ft (9 m) per year, they cover everything it their path. Plants, species typical of the northern Chihuahuan Desert, must grow rapidly enough to escape being buried. Although most life on the dunes has normal coloration, many small animals, such as lizards, insects, and spiders, evolved white coloration for camouflage.

Protected Areas. White Sands Missile Range, America's largest land military test range, was estab-

lished in 1945. The museum and military park, showcasing missiles and rockets, is open to the public, but the test range is not. White Sands was proclaimed a national monument in 1933.

Environmental Issues. The water-loving saltcedar tree (*Tamarisk* spp.) is a problematic invasive species in the monument. South African oryx, or gemsbok (*Oryx gazelle*), introduced for hunting, are currently fenced out of the Monument but may threaten the native habitat in the missile range.

Further Reading

Chronic, Halka. 1987. *Roadside Geology of New Mexico.* Missoula: MT: Mountain Press Publishing.

National Park Service. n.d. *White Sands National Monument.* http://www.nps.gov/whsa/index.htm

National Park Service. n.d. "White Sands National Monument, New Mexico." *Geology Fieldnotes.* www.nature.nps.gov/geology/parks/whsa/index.cfm

Wrangel Island

Arctic Ocean

Geographic Overview. Russia's Wrangel Island straddles the 180° meridian in the Chukchi Sea. It remained ice-free during the glacial periods of the Pleistocene Epoch, when it was part of the Bering Land Bridge, a corridor along which North American and Eurasian plants and animals migrated. As a result of never having been glaciated, it accumulated a relatively high number of plants for an Arctic island and developed unique tundra communities. Woolly mammoths persisted on Wrangel Island until about 3,700 years ago, later than anywhere else on Earth.

Geographic Coordinates. 71°14'N, 179°25'W

Description. Wrangel Island is located between the Chukchi and East Siberian Seas, approximately 87 mi (140 km) off the coast of Russia. The island stretches 78 mi (125 km) from east to west across the 180° meridian, so that it lies in both the Western and Eastern Hemispheres. (The International Date Line is adjusted so that the entire island is in the same time zone.) It has an area of 2,900 mi² (7,600 km²).

Wrangel's core is Precambrian continental crust that has been overlain with sedimentary rocks, folded, and faulted. In the south-central section, the east–west trending Tsentral'nye Range rises to a general elevation of 1,600 ft (500 m) asl. The highest peak, Sovetskaya Mountain, is 3,596 ft (1,096 m) asl. Low, highly dissected hills with scree-covered slopes and elevations of 650–1,970 ft (200–600 m) asl surround the range on all sides. To the north is the Akademia Tundra, a coastal plain about 16 mi (25 km) wide. A much narrower coastal plain stretches along the southern coast. The land is well-watered with many streams and myriad ponds and lakes, particularly in the Akademia Tundra. Sand and gravel bars and spits occur on both shores.

A species-rich arctic tundra covers low-lying areas of patterned ground on Wrangel Island in the Chukchi Sea. The land was ice-free and part of the Bering Land Bridge during the Pleistocene epoch. (Jenny E. Ross/Corbis)

Wrangel Island is under the influence of cold, dry polar winds most of the time. The frost-free period only extends for 20–25 days a year. Total annual precipitation is about 8 in (200 mm), usually occurring as snow. On the south coast, July temperatures average 36°–38°F (2.4°–3.6°C), while on the north coast they average 34°F (1°C). However, interior valleys are shielded from cold winds and often experience foehns (dry, warming downslope winds), raising summer temperatures to 46°–50°F (8°–10°C).

Tundra developed on patterned ground dominates areas below 575 ft (175 m) asl, while tundra-steppe is found over a large part of the west-central region. Talus and scree slopes in the hills and mountains host communities of dwarfed shrubs, herbs, and lichens. Steppe and meadow-steppe occur in a narrow belt at the interior edge of the southern coastal plain and in strips along a few rivers in the central and western hills, unique relicts of Pleistocene habitats and centers of floral richness.

Geologic History. Wrangel Island was part of the Canadian Shield in the Precambrian. During the Paleozoic it was submerged and sediments accumulated, but it has been above sea level since the Cretaceous. During the Pleistocene Epoch, it was part of the Bering Land Bridge (Beringia)—the exposed continental shelf linking Alaska and Siberia—during glacial periods and an island whenever sea level rose again during interglacial periods. As part of the ice-free land bridge, it was at the crossroads of the North American–Eurasian faunal interchange and home to some of the largest land mammals of the Pleistocene, including woolly mammoths, woolly rhinoceros, horse, steppe bison (*Bison priscus*), large muskoxen, and saber-toothed cats. Small woolly mammoths (*Mammuthus primigenius wrangelensis*) survived until 3,700 years ago. Wrangel, which became an island again at the end of the Wisconsin glacial period about 10,000 years ago, preserves a rich and important paleontological record of Ice Age Beringia.

Biota. The flora of Wrangel Island has more species than other Arctic island, including Greenland. To date, 417 vascular plants have been identified, including 23 endemic species. In addition there are 331 mosses and 310 lichens. Some plants are American species found nowhere else in Asia.

Among vertebrates, 62 bird species, including eight seabirds, nest here. The only large breeding colony of Snow Goose in Asia occurs on Wrangel, where many other migratory species have their northernmost nesting grounds.

Only three extant terrestrial mammals are native to the island: the arctic fox and two species of lemming. Reindeer and muskox were reintroduced in 1948 and 1975, respectively. However, the island has the highest density of family dens of polar bears anywhere in the Arctic and the world's greatest concentration of Pacific walrus (100,000 individuals), which haul out on Wrangel's shores.

Protected Areas. The entire island was protected by the Soviet Union in 1976, when it was declared a state nature reserve (zapovednik) along with nearby Herald Island. Access was limited to scientists. Wrangel Island was inscribed as a UNESCO World Heritage Site in 2004. In 2013, a 24-nautical-mile (45 km) wide buffer zone was established around the entire island to protect coastal and marine habitats and marine mammals.

Environmental Issues. The ruins of a Soviet radar station at Cape Hawaii and the defunct settlement of Ushakovskoe on the southern shore are littered with rusting oil drums and metal scrap. Clean up is part of the management plan, but difficult to achieve in Arctic conditions. A warming climate could give Wrangel Island geopolitical significance as it lies along the Northern Sea Route from Murmansk, Russia's easternmost ice-free port in the Arctic, through the Bering Strait to its key Pacific port of Vladivostok. Currently, the route is ice-free 2–3 months a year; but as Arctic sea ice continues to decrease, this could become a viable year-round link between the extreme ends of Russia, avoiding the present southern route around Asia, through the Suez Canal and Mediterranean Sea, into the Atlantic Ocean. Increased traffic increases the risk of oil spills and other forms of pollution that could circulate through the Arctic Ocean to the coasts of Alaska, Canada, and Europe.

See also Bering Sea and Bering Land Bridge

Further Reading

"Natural System of Wrangel Island Reserve." 2004. World Heritage Scanned Nomination, UNESCO. http://whc.unesco.org/uploads/nominations/1023rev.pdf

Xi (Pearl) River System

China

Geographic Overview. The Xi River system in southern China is known by several names in different parts of the river system. Xi, Hongshui, Zhujiang, and Pearl are best known. Most of the river's course is through mountainous or hilly terrain, in stark contrast with the flat agriculturally rich delta. The Xi is the third longest river in China and the second largest by volume. It is named for the pearl-colored shells on the river bottom near Guangzhou.

Geographic Coordinates. Source: 25°46'N, 103°55'E; Mouth: 22°44'N, 113°39'E

Description. The Xi River system and its tributaries drain an area of approximately 173,000 mi^2 (448,000 km^2), most of Guangdong and Guangxi provinces, parts of Yunnan, Guizhou, Hunan, and Jiangxi provinces, and extreme northeastern Vietnam. The river flows generally east 1,250 mi (2,012 km) from Yunnan Province to the South China Sea. The name Xi, or Pearl, is usually narrowly applied to its lower course, after its confluence with the Bei and Dong Rivers in Guangdong Province. More than half of the watershed is mountainous, with elevations of 1,650–9,900 ft (500–3,000 m) asl, and much of the rest is hilly, 330–1,650 ft (100–500 m). The delta lowlands are a small part of the drainage area. Most of the mountains are limestone, with the river flowing through deep valleys or gorges with steep walls and rapids. Because the river drains South China karst, much of the tributary drainage in its watershed is underground.

The major headstream is considered to be the Nanpan River, which rises in the Maxiong Mountains on the Yunnan–Guizhou Plateau of eastern Yunnan Province at 6,900 ft (2,100 m). The river drops rapidly, 5,900 ft (1,800 m) in the first 530 mi (850 km). After first flowing south, then northeast, the Nanpan River forms the border between Guizhou and Guangxi for 160 mi (257 km). After the Beipan River joins from the north, the Xi River's name changes to Hongshui. The river turns south and then again east, flowing through a narrow valley between mountains 850 ft (260 m) above the river. At Shilong, Guangxi, where the major left-bank tributary, the Liu River, joins the Hongshui from the north, the river name changes to Qian as it flows through narrow and rocky Dateng Gorge. Shortly after, the main river is joined at Guiping by the major right bank tributary, the Yu River, which rises in southeastern Yunnan and roughly parallels the Hongshui for approximately 400 mi (750 km). The name changes to the Xun River and continues 120 mi (190 km) to meet the Gui River from the north. Below the Gui and the city of Wuzhou, the main stem is officially called the Xi. It flows through gorges, such as narrow Lingyang, just prior to entering its delta near Guangzhou, Guangdong. Guangdong Province is also hilly, with shorter tributaries coming from the north. The delta, covering approximately 1,500 mi^2 (3,900 km^2), is in the Guangdong Highlands, where alluvial deposition has enveloped islands, incorporating hills into the delta. The triangular Pearl or Zhujiang delta, approximately 100 mi (160 km) on each side, is formed by the convergence of three rivers, the Xi from the west, the Bei from the north, and Dong from the east. The delta is a maze of canals, channels, and rice paddies. After 44 mi (70 km), the river enters the South China Sea between Hong Kong to the east and Macao to the west.

Except for the delta region, which is densely populated, the mountainous terrain along the river's course has few towns. Wuzhou is the most important, at the junction of the Xi with the navigable Gui River coming from Guilin and tower karst topography in northeastern Guangxi. Guangzhou (Canton) is a major port in southern China, and historically the only port when it was the first to open to westerners. Because of deep limestone gorges and rapids, ease of navigation is dependent on water levels and monsoon floods. Wuzhou is generally the upstream limit of large vessels, and the Lingqu Canal links the Li River, a tributary to the Gui, with the Chang Jiang (Yangzte).

The watershed is in a humid subtropical climate, with hot summers, mild winters, and heavy precipitation, 60–80 in (1,500–2,000 mm), primarily from summer monsoons. Mean discharge is 38,850 ft³/sec (1,100 m³/s), much less during the dry winter and much more during summer monsoons.

Biota. The river system supports more than 400 freshwater, brackish, and anadromous fish in 55 families, the majority in the family Cyprinidae. More than 90 fish species, primarily Cyprinidae and Balitoridae, are endemic, including cave fishes in the karst areas. Rare Chinese sturgeon (*Acipenser sinensis*) and two shads (*Tenualosa reevesii, Clupanodon thrissa*) may be found in the river. Detailed information is scarce.

Environmental Issues. The river in the city of Guangzhou has serious pollution problems, especially with effluent from blue jean factories. Many dams on the Xi and its tributaries threaten the integrity of its ecosystems.

See also Chang Jiang (Yangtze River); South China Karst

Further Reading

Penn, James R. 2001. *Rivers of the World*. Santa Barbara: ABC-CLIO.
Songqiao, Zhao. 1986. "Surface Water and Ground Water." In *Physical Geography of China*, 41–56. New York: John Wiley & Sons.

Y

Yenisey–Angara River System

Russia and Mongolia

Geographic Overview. The Yenisey River and its major tributary, the Angara River, combined have the largest discharge of all Russian rivers. The river system is one of the longest in Asia and is one of the 10 largest in the world. Spring floods are common for this north-flowing river. The Trans-Siberian Railway connects major cities and ports in central Siberia, Irkutsk on the Angara River, and Krasnoyarsk on the Yenisey, with the rest of Russia.

Geographic Coordinates. Yenisey—Source: 50° 44'N, 98°40'E; Mouth: 70°59'N, 82°52'E. Angara—Source: 51°52'N, 104°48'E; Mouth: 58°06'N, 93°00'E

Description. From the junction of the Great Yenisey and the Little Yenisey, near the city of Kyzyl in the Tuva Republic in Central Asia, the Yenisey River flows approximately 2,200 mi (3,550 km) to the Kara Sea in the Arctic Ocean. The total catchment area of the Yenisey–Angara is approximately 100,000 mi² (2,590,000 km²), making it one of the 10 largest in the world. The southern part of the drainage basin is mountainous, averaging 2,300–7,200 ft (700–2,200 m) asl, with deep valleys between high ranges. Most of the drainage basin is on the western part of the Central Siberian Plateau, at 1,640–2,300 ft (50–700 m) asl. The Yenisey flows south-to-north at the eastern side of the Western Siberian Lowland and along the western boundary of the Central Siberian Plateau, which is underlain by the Precambrian crystalline Angara shield. The major tributaries flow west from the Central Siberian Plateau; the swampy taiga in the lowland contributes little flow. The river floods annually in spring because the southern reaches thaw before ice melts in the northern, downstream regions, blocking the flow.

The two branches of the Yenisey begin in the high Eastern Sayan Mountains, one in Russia, the other in northern Mongolia. After their confluence in a deep mountain basin, the combined Yenisey flows through deep gorges and passes through the long, narrow Krasnoyarsk Reservoir, the site of a dam and hydroelectric power station. Below Krasnoyarsk, the Yenisey widens and flows more than 1,000 mi (1,600 km) north to the Kara Sea and the Arctic Ocean. The Angara joins the Yenisey near Yeniseysk.

The Angara River, draining more than 400,000 mi² (1,040,000 km²), flows approximately 1,150 mi (1,851 km) from Lake Baikal on the Central Siberian Plateau to its confluence with the Yenisey. Its flow out of Lake Baikal is strong and steady, with a steep gradient and fast current that prevents the river from freezing. The Angara is dammed at Irkutsk and at Bratsk where the river formerly flowed in rapids over basalt flows. After the Ilim River joins it, the Angara turns west to the Yenisey.

Below the Angara confluence, the river bed of the Yenisey widens and depth increases to 32–56 ft (10–17 m). Two additional major tributaries join from the Central Siberian Plateau, the Stony Tunguska and the Lower Tunguska. The width of the river valley increases from 23 mi (37 km) to 93 mi (150 km), and water depth varies from 16 to 80 ft (5–24 m). The broad delta, at the head of a long, sinuous estuary, begins at Ust-Port, and the Yenisey enters the Kara Sea through Yenisey Bay.

The climate is subarctic and tundra in the north and winter-dry continental in the south. Continentality fosters temperature extremes. Depending on latitude, summer temperatures may rise to 86°F (30°C), and winters may be colder than –22°F (–30°C). Annual precipitation is 16–30 in (400–750 mm) in the northern and central regions, increasing in the southern mountains. Most precipitation falls in summer.

Flow in the upper and middle Yenisey is irregular, fed by melting snow or rain. The upper course and its tributaries are turbulent. The flow below the confluence with the Angara is steady, due to waters from Lake Baikal. Spring melt discharge may be more than 4,500,000 ft³/sec (127,450 m³/s) at the delta. The river carries 10.5 mil tons of alluvium into the Kara Sea each year. Except for 6–9 months when frozen, the Yenisey is navigable from Abakan to the sea.

The dam at Irkutsk, on the Angara River, backs up water to Lake Baikal, where it has raised the lake level by 10 ft (6 m). The dam at Bratsk created the Bratsk Sea, a reservoir covering 2,125 mi² (5,504 km²), which backs up water approximately 300 mi (483 km) to Irkutsk. It is one of the largest hydroelectric stations in the world. A third major power plant is at Ust-Ilimsk, also on the Angara. The hydroelectric power is used primarily for pulp and paper mills and aluminum processing.

The mining center of Norilsk is linked to Dudinka, a port on the Yenisey near the delta, via a railroad. The Trans-Siberian Railway crosses the Yenisey at Krasnoyarsk.

Biota. Most of the watershed of both rivers is in taiga, with some tundra in the far north and minor amounts of steppe in Tuva.

The rivers have a rich variety of fish. Mountain streams support grayling, trout, lenok, roach, and dace. Middle reaches have sterlet, trout, goldilocks, and several whitefish species. Lamprey, sturgeon, char, carp, pike, and sterlet are found in the lower Yenisey.

Environmental Issues. Like other Siberian rivers, the Yenisey is polluted as a consequence of the industrial and military development of communist Soviet Union and the Cold War during the 1970s and 1980s. Pollutants include pesticides, herbicides, heavy metals, and radioactive sediment.

Further Reading

Hogan, C. Michael. 2012. "Yenisey River." *The Encyclopedia of Earth*. www.eoearth.org/view/article/175644/

Penn, James R. 2001. *Rivers of the World*. Santa /Barbara, CA: ABC-CLIO.

Yosemite National Park

United States (California)

Geographic Overview. Located in the central part of the Sierra Nevada range in California, Yosemite National Park is a landscape sculpted by alpine glaciers. The park, which has 800 mi (1,287 km) of hiking trails, includes glacial valleys, waterfalls, steep cliffs, alpine meadows, lakes, and giant sequoia forests.

Geographic Coordinates. Approximately 37° 30'N–38°11'N, 119°14'W–120°22'W

Description. Yosemite National Park covers 747,956 ac (302,698 ha), with a variety of features and ecosystems ranging from 1,800 ft (550 m) in the lowest foothills to over 13,000 ft (3,950 m) on the highest mountain peaks. As part of the Sierra Nevada granite fault-block mountain, the general elevation of Yosemite gently decreases westward toward the Central Valley of California, while the eastern slope is a steep drop down to the Great Basin. The road over Tioga Pass, 9,945 ft (3,031 m) asl, to the eastern side of the Sierra Nevada, takes a route through an almost barren landscape of granite exfoliation domes. Initially carved by the Merced River, Yosemite Valley was deepened and widened by an extensive alpine glacier during the Pleistocene. Granite cliffs, such as El Capitan, a favorite rock climbing site, rise 3,000–3,500 ft (915–1,065 m) higher than the floor of Yosemite Valley, which is 4,000 ft (1,220 m) asl. Half Dome, topping out at 8,842 ft (2,695 m), is another almost-sheer cliff. The steep cliffs are home to several waterfalls, the largest being Yosemite Falls, which drops a total of 2,425 ft (739 m) in three sections, making it the tallest waterfall in North America. In comparison, Bridalveil Fall, on the opposite side of Yosemite Valley, drops 620 ft (189 m).

Yosemite has a mediterranean climate, meaning that rain, or snow at higher elevations, falls primarily in winter. Average precipitation in Yosemite Valley is approximately 37 in (940 mm) a year. High elevations frequently have deep snowfalls, which provide water for the many waterfalls in spring, and snow is possible in the valley. Except for occasional thunderstorms

Classic view of Yosemite National Park, with the sheer cliffs of El Capitan to the left, Bridalveil Falls to the right, and Half Dome in the middle distance. (Hotshotsworldwide/Dreamstime.com)

at the high elevations, little to no rain falls in summer. Winter temperatures in the valley range from lows of 30°–35°F (–1° to 2°C) to highs of 50°–60°F (10°–16°C). Summer nights average 40°–55°F (4°–13°C), while summer days average 80°–90°F (27°–32°C). Higher elevations are cooler, and nighttime temperatures in the subalpine or alpine zones may drop below freezing even in summer.

Geologic History. The geologic history of Yosemite is similar to that of the larger Sierra Nevada range. Throughout the Paleozoic (545–251 mya), sedimentary rocks were deposited and metamorphosed. Most of these rocks were eroded away from areas within the park, but some layered metamorphosed sedimentary rocks remain in the western foothills and on some of the eastern peaks. These rocks are often referred to as roof pendants, remnants of sedimentary rocks that formerly covered the batholith before it was

faulted and uplifted. At various times during the Mesozoic (210–80 mya), dozens of granitic plutons intruded the subsurface to become the Sierra Nevada Batholith. Approximately 25 mya, in the Tertiary, after the granite core had been exposed by erosion, the area was faulted on the east and uplifted into a giant fault-block mountain, tilting toward the west. Rivers flowing westward cut long valleys into the dip slope, which were subsequently enlarged and deepened by valley glaciers.

Biota. Due to its topographic variation and elevation change, Yosemite National Park has a rich biodiversity. The foothills at 2,000 ft (610 m) asl are clothed in oak woodland or chaparral, giving way to montane forests of ponderosa pine and incense-cedar at 3,000 ft (915 m). Several groves of giant sequoia trees (notably the Mariposa Grove), which can be 25 ft (7.6 m) in diameter and 200 ft (61 m) tall, are located in the montane forest zone. Upper montane forest, beginning at 6,000 ft (1,830 m), with thick stands of red fir and lodgepole pine, is found at higher elevations. At approximately 8,000 ft (2,440 m), the upper montane forest merges into the subalpine forest of western white pine and lodgepole pine. Interspersed throughout the montane and upper montane forests are moist meadows that bloom with wildflower displays in summer. Tuolumne Meadows, at 8,575 ft (2,615 m), near Tioga Pass is an example. Near 9,500 ft (2,900 m), the forest trees become stunted, eventually being replaced by low-growing herbaceous plants in the alpine zone. The highest peaks, Mt. Lyell at 13,114 ft (3,997 m)—which is the tallest mountain in Yosemite—and Mt. Maclure at 12,960 ft (3,950 m), still have small alpine glaciers on their slopes. The park has 1,400 species of flowering plants and over 400 species of vertebrates, including fish, amphibians, reptiles, birds, and mammals.

Protected Areas. Although first deeded to the State of California in 1864, Yosemite was designated a U.S. national park in 1890. It became a World Heritage Site in 1984. Both the Merced and Tuolumne Rivers have been designated as Wild and Scenic Rivers, and almost 95 percent of Yosemite National Park is designated wilderness.

Environmental Issues. Because of its popularity, parts of Yosemite, especially the valley, which houses the majority of development such as hotels, campgrounds, and concessions, suffer from overuse. Almost 4 million people visited Yosemite in 2011. Thick smog from nearby urban areas is visible from many park viewpoints, and the air quality within the park itself may be poor due to both photochemical smog and campfires. Invasive species, such as Himalayan blackberry and yellow starthistle, threaten the natural vegetation. The Tuolumne River in Hetch Hetchy, a similar glacially carved valley in the northwestern part of the park, was dammed in the 1920s to provide water for San Francisco. Removal of the dam to restore Hetch Hetchy to its original state remains controversial.

See also Sierra Nevada

Further Reading

Alt, David and Donald W. Hyndman. 2000. *Roadside Geology of Northern and Central California*. Missoula, MT: Mountain Press.

Holing, Dwight, Len Jenshel, and Diane Cook. 1996. *The Smithsonian Guides to Natural America, the Far West, California and Nevada*. Washington, D.C.: Smithsonian Books.

National Park Service. 2013. *Yosemite National Park, California*. http://www.nps.gov/yose/index.htm

Yucatán Peninsula

Mexico

Geographic Overview. The Yucatán Peninsula separates the Gulf of Mexico and Caribbean Sea. This karstic region is perhaps best known for its large number of Mayan archaeological sites dating from AD 600–1200. These include the large city of Chichén Itzá with its pyramids, temples, grand ball court, and sacred cenote and Uxmal with its ornate ceremonial structures. Tens of thousands of people were able to live here in pre-Columbian times despite the lack of surface water and the presence of only thin soils. They developed a sophisticated civilization complete with a writing system, astronomy, and the concept of zero—otherwise developed in the ancient world only by Arab mathematicians. The Mexican states of Yucatán, Campeche, and Quintana Roo are located on the peninsula, which geologically extends southward into the El Petén region of Guatemala and into Belize.

Geographic Coordinates. Approximately 17° 50'N–21°30'N, 86°42'W–90°40'W

Description. The Yucatán Peninsula is a limestone plain projecting northward from southern Mexico, where it separates the Gulf of Mexico from the Caribbean Sea. Under humid, tropical conditions, the limestone has developed a karst topography with cenotes (water-filled sinkholes) on the surface and dry and underwater cave systems below ground. Along the northwestern part of the peninsula is an arc of cenotes marking the edge of the Chicxulub Crater, site of the asteroid impact implicated in the extinction of dinosaurs and other biota some 65 mya ago.

The Yucatán platform was submerged in a warm shallow sea for millions of years. Major development of karstic features began in the Pleistocene when a combination of slow uplift and lowered sea levels

Ik-Kil Cenote, a water-filled sinkhole near Chichén Itzá, Yucatán Peninsula, Mexico. (Subbotina/Dreamstime.com)

during glacial periods exposed the limestone to the atmosphere. Rainwater seeped through fractures and groundwater channeled through faults to dissolve the carbonate bedrock and form an intricate network of cave systems. Ceiling collapses created the cenotes, which became the primary source of water for early human inhabitants, since no perennial surface streams of any significance appear north of the Champotón River in central Campeche. Instead groundwater flows in subsurface streams and discharges into unusual brackish lagoons along the east coast or beneath Holocene sands and silts along the north coast.

Annual precipitation decreases northward with the region bordering Guatemala and Belize receiving upwards of 120 in (3,000 mm) a year and the northwest receiving less than 40 in (1,000 mm). Rainfall is seasonal; the wet season begins in May or June and peaks in September. A distinct dry season extends from February to April. Semideciduous tropical rainforest covers much of the peninsula that has not been disturbed by human activities. This rainforest grades into a low, deciduous thorn forest in the more arid northwestern corner of the Yucatán.

Geologic History. The Yucatán is an emergent carbonate platform that, to the north, slopes gently beneath the sea, forming a broad continental shelf. Elevations on much of the peninsula vary from 15–100 ft (5–30 m) asl. In the Sierrita de Ticul in Campeche, however, the land rises to between 200 and 330 ft (60–100 m) asl. The bedrock is mostly thick horizontal beds of Mesozoic- and Cenozoic-era limestones, dolomites, and anhydrites. The youngest materials are in the north, the oldest in the Sierrita de Ticul. Along the east coast, a ridge of lithified Pleistocene beach dunes parallels the shoreline about a mile (1–2 km) inland.

Protected Areas. The Sian Ka'an Biosphere Reserve south of Tulum protects some of the diversity of habitats on the eastern side of the peninsula including tropical forests, marshes, mangroves, lagoons, bays, and coral reef.

See also Chicxulub Crater; The Petén

Further Reading

"A Condensed Geological Chronicle of the Yucatan Platform." 2001. Quintana Roo Speleological Society. http://www.caves.org/project/qrss/geo.htm

Perry, Eugene, Guadalupe Velazquez-Oliman, and Richard A. Socki. 2003. "Hydrogeology of the Yucatán Peninsula." In *The Lowland Maya Area: Three Millennia at the Human-Wildland Interface*, edited by Arturo Gómez-Pompa, M.F. Allen, S. L. Fedick, and J. J. Jiménez-Osornio, 115–138. Binghamton, NY: The Haworth Press. http://www.reservaeleden.org.mx /publicaciones/libro_el_eden/Capitulos/Capitulo%207 .pdf

"Yucatan Peninsula." 2012. Yucatan Wildlife. http://www .yucatanwildlife.com/places/peninsula.htm

Yukon River

United States (Alaska) and Canada

Geographic Overview. The Yukon River is the fifth longest in North America and its drainage basin is the seventh largest on the continent. With only one dam on the main stem and one each on two tributaries, it is North America's longest wild and free-flowing river. Its path incorporates many environments, including mountain streams, glacial runoff, fast currents, boreal forest, tundra, and wetland flats. During the Pleistocene, the valley was a migration pathway significant to the biological history of North America. The river played a major role as a transportation route during the Klondike gold rush.

Geographic Coordinates. Source: 60°32'N, 134°31'W; Mouth: 62°36'N, 164°48'W

Description. The Yukon River basin covers 324,040 mi² (839,200 km²), 60 percent in Alaska and 40 percent in the Canadian Yukon. Originating less than 18.6 mi (30 km) from the Pacific Ocean in lakes between the Coast Range and the Rocky Mountains in extreme northwestern British Columbia, the Yukon River flows 1,988 mi (3,200 km) north and west to the Bering Sea. It flows first northwest through the Yukon, where it is joined by the White, Stewart, and Klondike rivers. After crossing the border into Alaska, it is joined by the Porcupine River at Fort Yukon. In central Alaska, the Yukon River receives its largest tributary, the Tanana River. After the Koyukuk River joins the main stem, the Yukon River turns south and then again west before entering the Bering Sea.

Although the ultimate source of the headwaters is considered to be the Llewellyn Glacier south of Atlin Lake, the Yukon River begins at the outflow from Marsh Lake, slightly upstream from Whitehorse in the Yukon. Downstream from a hydroelectric dam near Whitehorse, the Yukon River flows unimpounded for 1,926 mi (3,100 km) through boreal forests and tundra in a landscape of plateaus and lowlands. Because they drain from steep and high mountains, the headwaters of the Yukon and its major tributaries have a high gradient. The White River flows from the St. Elias and Wrangell Mountains at elevations reaching 20,000 or more ft (6,100 m) asl, and the Stewart River drains the west side of the Selwyn Mountains at approximately 9,840 ft (3,000 m). Both rivers join the Yukon south of Dawson, the White River on the left bank and the Stewart River on the right bank. From Whitehorse to Dawson City, the river has a moderate gradient and is a clear and fast-flowing mountain river. The Klondike River merges into the Yukon River at Dawson. Downstream from Dawson, the river is turbid with glacial input. West of the Alaska border, the gradient decreases as the river enters the Yukon Flats area of several channels and ponds. The Porcupine River joins on the right bank of the Yukon in this low-relief wetland. After the flats, the Yukon is crossed by the Trans-Alaska Pipeline and joined first by the Tanana River and then by the Koyukuk River. The Yukon delta is 62 mi (100 km) wide at the Bering Sea. Although discharge averages 223,895 ft³/sec (6,340 m³/s), it is highly variable, controlled by seasonal variation in temperature and precipitation, ice breakup, glacial melt, and permafrost.

As the largest tributary, the Tanana River drains 44,000 mi² (114,000 km²) on the north slope of the Alaska Range. From its headwaters in lakes and ponds in the Tetlin National Wildlife Refuge near the Alaska–Yukon border, the Tanana flows northwest approximately 620 mi (1,000 km) to the Yukon River. Other rivers from the Alaska Range contribute glacial meltwater to its flow. Except for some agricultural land near Fairbanks, most of the river passes through wilderness, in a wide valley through a broad plain. The Koyukuk is the last major tributary, draining 32,240 mi^2 (83,500 km^2) of Alaska. From its headwaters in the Endicott Mountains of the Brooks Range in Gates of the Arctic Wilderness Area, the river flows 497 mi (800 km) south through tundra and taiga to join the Yukon. Its eastern branch is the path of the Trans-Alaska Pipeline over the Brooks Range. Because it has little input from glacial meltwater, the water remains clear. The lower part of the river has gentle relief, similar to Yukon Flats and the delta.

The drainage basin is characterized by cool summers and very cold winters. The cold air and rain shadows limit precipitation. Permafrost is sporadic in the upper Yukon basin and discontinuous in the lower basin. It is continuous only in the delta area and the upper Porcupine basin.

Biota. The Yukon River basin was not covered by Pleistocene ice and formed a corridor between the alpine glaciers that capped the coastal mountains and the continental glaciers further inland in Canada. It served as a migration pathway from the Bering Land Bridge for both humans and animals.

Although the rivers are not well studied, the Yukon has one freshwater ecoregion. Its low biodiversity, including 30 native species of fish and two nonnative, is due to northern cold climate. Typical fish include Pacific salmon (*Oncorhynchus* spp.), char (*Salvelinus* spp.), and whitefishes (*Coregonus, Prosopium* spp.).

Protected Areas. Several headwaters and drainage basins of tributaries are within national parks or preserves. Yukon–Charley Rivers National Preserve is on the border of Alaska and the Yukon. Sites in Dawson and Whitehorse in the Yukon commemorate the Klondike gold rush. Yukon Flats is the site of Yukon Flats National Wildlife Refuge.

Environmental Issues. The Yukon River has suffered pollution from mining, waste dumps, and military installations.

Further Reading

Bailey, Robert C. 2005. "Yukon River Basin." In *Rivers of North America*, edited by Arthur C. Benke and Colbert E. Cushing, 774–802. Amsterdam: Elsevier Academic Press.

Yukon River Inter-Tribal Watershed Council. 2008. http://www.yritwc.org/

Z

Zagros Mountains

Iran and Iraq

Geographic Overview. The Zagros Mountains, which form the southwestern coast of Iran north and east of the Mesopotamia basin, were formed in the last 5 million years. They contain some of the world's largest oil reserves and are noted for numerous salt formations, many of which flow downhill like glaciers. The region is home to a variety of ethnic groups and is famous for hand-tied woolen carpets.

Geographic Coordinates. Approximately 26° 30'N–37°20'N, 43°15'E–57°00'E

Description. The greater Zagros Mountains extend approximately 930 mi (1,500 km) in a northwest–southeast orientation from the Taurus Mountains in southern Turkey through Iran to the Strait of Hormuz. A stricter definition has the range being 550 mi (900 km) long, from the Sirvan (Diyala) River northeast of Baghdad southeast to Shiraz, Iran. The mountains are a complex combination of rocks, generally corresponding with tectonic region.

The Zagros have three distinctive parallel tectonic and topographic zones. Adjacent to the Persian Gulf is a broad zone of simple parallel folds, uniformly spaced. Rocks are primarily carbonates and evaporites, with some overlying shale. Ridges and mountains rise 9,850–12,000 ft (3,000–3,650 m) asl. The many fertile, linear valleys between the anticlines are populated. Drainage in many valleys is interior, while other rivers cross the folds to enter the Persian Gulf or Mesopotamian plain. Salt intrusion features are numerous. The Asmari limestone in the folded Zagros is the principal oil-producing formation in southwestern Iran. Inland is the High Zagros, a narrow zone of imbricated thrusts, where nappes, or slices of Mesozoic limestone, radiolarites, and ophiolites, complicated by Eocene volcanics, were thrust southwest over one another onto the leading edge of the fold belt. The main suture zone between the plates is a metamorphic core of phyllites, ophiolites, and volcanics. On the eastern edge of the High Zagros is a complex linear zone of intrusive and extrusive igneous rocks, including granites, gabbros, rhyolites, and pyroclastic tuffs. Zard Kuh, 14,921 ft (4,548 m), is the highest peak.

The climate is mid-latitude semiarid. Annual precipitation, primarily falling in winter and spring, is 16–32 in (400–800 mm), increasing to 40 in (1,000 mm) on the highest peaks. Summers are hot and extremely dry. Winters are severe, with temperatures dropping below −13°F (−25°C). High peaks have permanent snow and glaciers.

Geologic History. The Zagros, well known due to oil exploration, are the result of the Arabian Plate's convergence with the Eurasian Plate and the Turkish Plate and the Arabian Plate's subduction beneath Eurasia. A thrust and transform fault suture zone joins Arabia and Eurasia. The Zagros are separated from the Turkish Plate by the East Anatolian transform fault. They are separated from their southeastern extension, the Makran Range, by a transform fault north of Oman. Geologically, the Zagros also include the Oman Mountains on the Arabian peninsula. The majority of what is now the Zagros Mountains originated as sediments deposited in the Tethys Sea, especially from the Cretaceous to Middle Tertiary (100–25 mya). The sedimentary deposits contain several sequences, from marginal platform to deep sea to shallow continental sea, which is reflected in the rocks, generally thick limestone layers covered with subsequently coarser classic rocks.

The region closest to the Persian Gulf underwent gentle folding in the early Tertiary, resulting in a series of anticlines. In the late Tertiary (5 mya), strong faulting and thrusting took place in the northern and eastern Zagros, without further deformation to the western folded region. Older rocks were thrust southwest over younger rocks of the folded belt as plates collided and the Arabian Plate subducted under Eurasia. Rocks in the thrust zone—marls, radiolarites, and ophiolites—were deposits from the deepest part of the Tethys Sea. Many of the nappes, or thrust blocks, are cored by metamorphic rocks, including schists and geneisses. Salt and gypsum beds may have facilitated the thrusting by acting as a lubricant. Basaltic flows, cones, and fumaroles form a linear zone of volcanics from Tabriz to Kerman. The mountain region is still seismically active and the site of many relatively shallow earthquakes.

Evaporite layers flow plastically under pressure, producing diapirs (intrusions of salt) and topographical bulges, which sometimes break the surface. Due to its very light weight, salt either rises through denser rocks or remains in place while heavier rocks sink around it. Exposed salt may dissolve, causing depressions called salt karst. Salt may be channeled upward through faults, and, if the extrusion rate exceeds the solution rate, the salt will flow downhill due to gravity, creating a salt glacier. The Zagros has many diapirs and salt glaciers. The biggest is Kuh-e-Gach, 2.9 mi (4.7 km) wide, 164 ft (50 m) thick, and covering approximately 9.0 mi^2 (23.5 km^2).

Biota. The Zagros Mountains are in a mountain forest-steppe ecosystem. The trend of the linear ranges served as corridors for north–south migration. The mountains are also the center of origin for several species and genera, including *Astralagus, Salvia,* and *Centaurea.* Forest-steppe consists of deciduous broadleaf trees or shrubs, dominated by oak or pistachio, with a diversified steppe ground cover. Lower elevations of the northern mountains are dominated by *Astralagus* and *Salvia* species, replaced at higher elevations by forests or forest remnants of *Quercus brantii* and *Quercus boissieri.* Above timberline,

approximately 6,250 ft (1,900 m), is a broad zone of subalpine vegetation. Southern regions are drier, with less forest but richer steppe ecosystems. Forest remnants are primarily *Quercus persica,* other oak species, hawthorn (*Crataegus*), almond (*Prunus amygdalus*), nettle tree (*Celtis*), and pear (*Pyrus* spp.) Lower elevations are covered by steppe shrubs.

Large mammals include brown bear, Asiatic black bear (*Ursus thibetanus*), wild goats (*Capra aegrarus*), sheep (*Ovis orientalis*), wolves, and leopards. Blandford's fox (*Vulpes cana*), found in the mountains near Kerman and Fars, is one of the rarest fox species in the world. Five taxa of lizards are endemic to the Zagros and adjacent Anatolian ranges. Steppe birds include Rock Partridge (*Alectoris chukar, Alectoris graeca*), See-see Partridge (*Ammoperdix griseogularis*), Little Bustard (*Tetrax tetrax*), Houbara Bustard (*Chlamydotis undulate*), Black-bellied Sandgrouse (*Pterocles orientalis*), and Black Vulture (*Aegypius monachus*).

The Persian fallow deer (*Dama dama* ssp. *mesopotamia*), formerly believed extinct, was rediscovered in the western foothills in 1950. Captive breeding programs were instituted, but the last wild population was disappearing by 1988.

Protected Areas. The Zagros contain many protected areas. Arjan Protected Area and Biosphere Reserve covers 162,466 ac (65,750 ha) on the southwestern side of the mountains. Mooteh Protected Area on the eastern side, covers 494,193 ac (200,000 ha).

Environmental Issues. Natural vegetation has been cleared for agriculture and grazing. As steppes and woodlands become overgrazed, woodlands are degraded or decreased.

See also Arabian Peninsula; Mesopotamia, Tigris River, and Euphrates River; Persian Gulf

Further Reading

Bourns, Julie. n.d. "Western Iran." World Wildlife Fund. http://worldwildlife.org/ecoregions/pa0446

Molnar, Mike. 2006. *Tertiary Development of the Zagros Mountains.* Geology 418—Earth History. www.uwec .edu/jolhm/Student_Research/Molnar/reports/zagros.pdf

Yamato, P. and others. 2011. "Dynamic Constraints on Crustal-scale Rhelogy of Zagros Fold Belt, Iran." *Geology* 39: 815–818.

Zambezi River

Angola, Botswana, Malawi, Mozambique, Namibia, Tanzania, Zambia, and Zimbabwe

Geographic Overview. The Zambezi River drains much of south-central Africa, some 40 percent of the entire African continent, to the Indian Ocean. Only the watersheds of the Congo, Nile, and Niger are larger. It ranks fourth in length among African waterways after those same three rivers. Most of the watershed lies on the high interior plateau of Southern Africa, and low gradient reaches are associated with large wetlands fed by the annual flood. The best known and most spectacular feature along the Zambezi is Victoria Falls, the world's largest single sheet of falling water.

Geographic Coordinates. Source: Approximately 11°00'S, 24°30'E; Mouth: 18°34'S, 36°28'E

Description. The Zambezi River begins in a rain-fed dambo (shallow, linear, seasonal wetland) in northwest Zambia, a short distance from a headwater stream of the Congo River. From its source, situated 4,920 ft (1,500 m) asl, it flows south and west into eastern Angola. After 150 mi (240 km) its course turns south and the river reenters Zambia, rushing over rapids at Chavuma on the border. The elevation there is about 3,600 ft (1,100 m) asl. When the Zambezi reaches Namibia's Caprivi Strip, the river turns eastward, following the Namibia–Zambia border to the confluence of the Chobe River, which enters from the south along the border between Namibia and Botswana. The Zambezi continues eastward as a broad, shallow river forming the border between Zambia and Zimbabwe. The next 500 mi (800 km) stretch of the river crosses a nearly level surface, and the river slows, descending only 500 ft (180 m) until it abruptly plunges some 330 ft (100 m) over Victoria Falls. The Zambezi then passes through a number of deep, narrow gorges, zigzagging for 150 mi (240 km) and dropping another 820 ft (250 m) before entering artificial Lake Kariba, one of the largest human-made lakes on Earth. The Kariba Dam was constructed in 1959. Before crossing into Mozambique, the river passes though another large reservoir, Lake Cohora Bassa, where a dam built in 1974 submerged the former Kebrabassa rapids. For the next 205 mi (330 km), the Zambezi is a broad, braided stream 3–5 mi (5–8 km) wide; but then it is forced between high hills into Lupata Gorge, only 720 ft (220 m) wide. Halfway between the gorge and the Indian Ocean, the Shire River enters from the north. This stream is the outlet of Lake Malawi. Another 100 mi (160 km) downstream, the Zambezi reaches sea level and flows through its triangular delta into the Indian Ocean, having completed a course 1,599 mi (2,574 km) long and drained an area of 540,000 mi^2 (1,390,000 km^2). The lower river is navigable 400 mi (650 km) inland by shallow-draft vessels. The four distributaries are obstructed by sand bars; only the Chinde branch, which is only 6.5 ft (2 m) deep at its entrance, is used by ships.

The watershed of the Zambezi, which covers parts of eight countries in tropical Africa, receives on average 37 in (950 mm) of precipitation annually, most of it during the hot summer months, when the Intertropical Convergence Zone (ITCZ) is overhead. Amounts are greatest in the north and west, where 55 in (1,400 mm) or more of rain falls and the rainy season is 4–6 months long. Other wet spots include the northern shores of Lake Malawi, in Tanzania, and along the Malawi–Mozambique border. The driest areas are in the extreme south and southwest, which receive only about 20 in (500 mm) of rain during a shorter rainy season. Only 10 percent of the rain that falls over the basin actually enters the river. The remaining 90 percent is lost through evaporation. The seasonal rainfall produced an annual flood, usually in March or April, prior to the construction of dams. Floodplain wetlands and coastal wetlands depended on the influx of nutrients and water that came during high water. The seasonality and the variability in precipitation from year to year have complicated water management in the large drainage basin.

The Zambezi can be subdivided into three sections. The Upper Zambezi extends from the headwater streams in Zambia to Victoria Falls. Much of the drainage basin here is covered by miombo woodland with trees 50–65 ft (15–20 m) tall. Deciduous species of *Brachystegia*, *Julbernardia*, and *Isoberlinia* dominate. Broadleaf deciduous shrubs and grasses provide an understory. The upper basin lies mostly on an ancient

The Zambezi River plunges over Victoria Falls (Mosi-oa-Tunya or the Smoke That Thunders), creating the world's largest single sheet of falling water. (Luca Roggero/Dreamstime.com)

Gondwana plateau 2,950–4,760 ft (900–1,450 m) asl with a cover of Kalahari sands and other sedimentary deposits, including former lake beds and alluvium deposited by the Zambezi.

The Middle Zambezi River runs from Victoria Falls to the Kebrassa rapids now submerged beneath Lake Cahora Bassa. This stretch of gorges and rapids more or less coincides with a large body of flood basalt that extends along the river from just east of the Caprivi Strip almost to Lake Kariba. Much of the land on either side of the river is covered in mopane woodland. This vegetation type also covers much of the Lower Zambezi basin downstream from Lake Cohora Bassa, where mopane grows with acacias, *Commiphora*, and occasional baobabs. A coastal flooded savanna, freshwater swamps, and *Borassus* fan palms savannas occur in the delta region. Mangroves line the distributaries and coast.

Geologic History. Geomorphic and geologic evidence supports the hypothesis that the Zambezi was once two separate drainages. Two million years ago the Upper Zambia River flowed through the region of today's Makgadikgadi Pan and entered the Limpopo system. Tectonic uplift is implicated in cutting off the link to the Limpopo and establishing an inland lake now referred to as Paleo-Lake Makgadikgadi, comparable in size to Lake Victoria. The ancient Upper Zambezi had, like many rivers of African Gondwana, an interior drainage pattern. Some 250,000–100,000 years ago, the lake may have overtopped its natural dam, causing a catastrophic flood that carried water with great erosive power into the Middle Zambezi 980 ft (300 m) below. An alternative hypothesis has the middle Zambezi eroding headward to drain the waters of Lake Makgadikgadi and capture the drainage of the Upper Zambezi.

Biota. The fish fauna of the Zambezi River, including the brackish waters of its delta, numbers about 190 species. This includes several eels, tigerfish, elephantfish, and bullhead shark. The delta region is home to dugong; many upper stretches of the river host hippopotamuses.

Protected Areas. In addition to national parks serving to protect Victoria Falls (Mosi-oa-Tunya National Park in Zambia; Victoria National Park and Zambezi National Park in Zimbabwe), Mana Pools National Park in northwestern Zimbabwe is a major wildlife conservation area and a UNESCO World Heritage Site. The pools are former channels of the Zambezi inundated during the annual flood and providing essential habitat for large mammals and resident and migratory birds. Six areas have been designated Ramsar Wetlands of International Importance, including the Barotse Floodplain on the upper Zambia River in western Zambia, considered one of the great wetlands of Africa. Busanga Swamps and Kafue Flats in Zambia are also Ramsar sites. The Kavango-Zambezi Transfrontier Conservation Area (KAZA) is planned as a five-country protected area embracing major sections of the upper Zambezi River basin as well as the Okavango Delta.

Environmental Issues. Major issues revolve around the artificial flood regime imposed by dams on the Zambezi. Transboundary management of water quality and quantity is difficult to coordinate. Floodplain and coastal wetlands are affected by the loss of nutrients, disrupting feeding and breeding grounds for fish, birds, and other wildlife as well as reducing floodplain pastures and traditional floodplain agriculture. Groundwater recharge is also reduced. Pollution from mines, agricultural, and municipal and industrial wastes is problematic at various points along the river. Annual floods once helped control invasive species. Today aquatic weeds such as water hyacinth and azolla clog intakes to power plants and water treatment plants as well as sewage outlets. They obstruct navigation and shade the river bottom, causing the demise of submerged plant life.

See also Victoria Falls (Mosi-oa-Tunya)

Further Reading

Hogan, C. Michael. 2012. "Zambezi River." *The Encyclopedia of Earth.* http://www.eoearth.org/view/article/174239/

Mott McDonald. 2007. "Rapid Assessment—Final Report." Integrated Water Resources Management Strategy for the Zambezi River Basin. South Africa Development Authority/Zambezi River Authority. www.icp-confluence-sadc.org/project/docs/publicfile?id=261

Roberts, Peter. 2012. "Formation of the Victoria Falls: The Formation of the Zambezi." To the Victoria Falls. http://www.tothevictoriafalls.com/vfpages/formation/zambezi.html

Zapata Swamp (Ciénega de Zapata)

Cuba

Geographic Overview. Zapata Swamp is the largest and best preserved wetland in the West Indies. The area has both freshwater and marine components, and a large variety of native plants, as well as animals endemic to Cuba and even to the swamp itself. It is an important stopover point for North American birds that winter in South America.

Geographic Coordinates. 22°24'N, 81°41'W

Description. Zapata Swamp occupies the Zapata Peninsula of southern Cuba, where it is divided into two sections by Bahía de Cochinas (the Bay of Pigs). The western section of the swamp is barely above sea level and flooded throughout the year. Shallow brackish lagoons averaging 20 in (50 cm) deep occur along the coast, and coral reefs are offshore. The area is dominated by marshes and mangrove swamps, but also has a swamp forest with palm groves and broadleaf trees up to 65 ft (20 m) tall. The eastern part of Zapata is higher, up to 32 ft (10 m) asl, with exposed limestone bedrock pitted by sinkholes, some containing lakes. The coast is rocky. The edaphic environment is drier than in the west and supports a semideciduous dry forest and coastal scrub. Sand dunes appear at the easternmost end of the Zapata Peninsula. This tropical area has a seasonal precipitation regime and receives about 50 in (1,200–1,300 mm) of rain during the wet season and another 10–12 in (250–300 mm) during the dry season.

Biota. The variety of ecosystems occurring at this freshwater–marine interface supports a great variety of plants and animals. At least 900 native plant species have been identified in the park area, 150 endemic to Cuba and five of them endemic to Zapata

Swamp. Among vulnerable animal species finding refuge in the reserve are 17 of Cuba's 20 endemic vertebrates. The largest wild population of the Cuban crocodile is found here, and the American crocodile also lives in the swamp. Among endangered endemic birds are the Zapata Rail (*Cyanolimnas cerverai*), Zapata Wren (*Ferminia cerverai*), and Zapata Sparrow (*Torreornis inexpectata*). Another Cuban endemic, the Bee Hummingbird (*Mellisuga helenae*), also nests in the swamp. A little more than 2 in (5–6 cm) in length and weighing 0.6 oz (1.6–2 g), this is the smallest living bird in the world. Mammals include representatives of three Cuban genera of hutia, a Neotropical caviomorph rodent. The West Indian manatee is also a resident. Offshore, the reefs and seagrass beds in lagoons are important nursery areas for commercially important crustaceans and fish. In addition the area is visited by at least 65 species of migratory birds.

One of the natural spectacles of Zapata Swamp is the spring migration of millions of female red land crabs to the Bay of Pigs to deposit their eggs. The crabs live in burrows and on the shaded forest floor and breed during spring rains. Laden with fertilized eggs, the females travel as many as 6 mi (9.7 km) to the sea in the evening, covering lawns and roadways and suffering many casualties when they are run over by passing vehicles. The eggs hatch almost immediately in the bay, and after a few weeks young crabs are making their way to the forest to repeat the cycle.

Protected Areas. The wetland is protected in the Ciénega de Zapata Biosphere Reserve, the core of which is the Ciénega de Zapata National Park. Zapata Swamp was declared a Ramsar Wetland of International Importance in 2001.

Environmental Issues. The swamp is threatened today by drainage projects, agricultural runoff carrying pesticides and fertilizers, and harvesting of trees for charcoal making.

Further Reading

"Ciénega de Zapata National Park." n.d. World Heritage Centre, UNESCO. http://whc.unesco.org/en/tentative lists/1801/

"Flooded Grasslands and Savannas: Cuba." n.d. World Wildlife Fund. http://worldwildlife.org/ecoregions/nt0902

Zion National Park

United States (Utah)

Geographic Overview. Zion National Park, in the southwestern part of the state, was Utah's first national park. Located in slickrock canyon country, Zion has many outstanding geologic features, including canyons, sheer cliffs, arches, seeps, and springs. The landscape is dominated by tall cliffs, and even the rocky slopes and ledges are steep. The White Cliffs in Zion are part of the Grand Staircase on the Colorado Plateau.

Geographic Coordinates. Approximately 37° 09'N–37°30'N, 112°52'W–113°14' W

Description. Zion National Park covers 229 mi^2 (593 km^2) of canyon country in the High Plateaus section of the Colorado Plateau. The main canyon, carved by the North Fork of the Virgin River, has eroded 3,000 ft (915 m) deep into the southern edge of the Markagunt Plateau. Rock formations include arches, alcoves, potholes, cliffs, and hoodoos. Alcoves and arches form when sections of rock cliffs are undermined, causing both large and small pieces to break off, leaving a shallow cave or overhang. Kolob Arch, in the northern section of the park is a sandstone slab 80 ft (24 m) thick and spanning 310 ft (94.5 m). With a window 330 ft (101 m) tall, Kolob Arch is one of the largest natural arches in the world. Checkerboard Mesa is frequently illustrated in textbooks as an example of cross-bedded sandstone and intersecting joints. Great White Throne, rising 2,450 ft (747 m) above the canyon floor, is a steep wall of Navajo sandstone. Angels Landing is a hanging tributary, a dry stream channel high above the valley floor. Water seeping out of the sandstone wall at Weeping Rock supports a hanging garden. In the Narrows, a slot canyon, the walls are 2,000 ft (600 m) high, but less than 20 ft (6 m) apart.

The Zion-Mt. Carmel Highway was completed in 1930, a significant engineering feat for the time. The road switchbacks from the canyon floor to the high plateaus to the east, running through two long, narrow tunnels blasted through the cliffs.

Geologic History. For millions of years during the Mesozoic (225–65 mya), this region was a large basin near sea level where sand, gravel, and mud were deposited in shifting environments, which included shallow seas, coastal plains, and deserts. More than 10,000 ft (3,050 m) of sediments solidified to become colorful layers of sandstone, conglomerate, shale, and limestone, many of which are widespread on the Colorado Plateau. The different layers form sheer cliffs or rocky slopes and ledges depending on the type of rock.

The Zion area was uplifted along with the Colorado Plateau in the Tertiary (20 mya), with little warping of the horizontal layers of rock. Two major north–south trending vertical faults outlined the uplifted Markagunt Plateau. Fast streams flowing toward the faulted western edge of the plateau created deep canyons, narrow in hard sandstone, and wider in softer shales and mudstones. With a steep gradient of 50–80 ft per mi (9–15 m per 1 km), the Virgin River continues to erode Zion Canyon. Today, as well as in the past, floods intensify erosion by empowering the river to carry more abrasive material, including large boulders. Because the few tributaries are predominantly intermittent, the canyon erodes far below their levels, leaving the tributary valleys "hanging" high on the canyon walls, sites of spectacular waterfalls during storms.

Although six rock formations are prominent in Zion, Navajo sandstone is the most spectacular rock layer because of its size, 1,500–2,000 ft (450–600 m) thick. It forms the temples, towers, cliffs, and canyon walls. The lower part of the Navajo was sand dunes deposited at the edge of a shallow sea, sometimes mixing with the Kayenta formation, which it overlies. The upper part is massive cross-bedded sand dunes from an inland desert. The Navajo sandstone forms vertical cliffs topped with rounded domes weathered from of the cross-bedded layers. The top is light tan to whitish, while the lower layer is reddish due to iron oxide staining. Beneath the Navajo sandstone is the more thinly bedded siltstone and sandstone of the Kayenta and the Moenave Formations, both forming slopes with ledges according to the resistance of individual layers.

Other formations include remnants of the Carmel, 200–300 ft (60–90 m) of limestone, the youngest sedimentary rocks found on top of high areas. Beneath the Moenave are the Chinle shale and the Moenkopi, a variety of shales, sandstones, and limestones. The Kaibab limestone underlies the Moenkopi and the Virgin River but is only exposed along the Hurricane Cliffs in the Kolob Section of the park. Cenozoic and mid-Tertiary lava flows cap the Kolob Terrace and parts of the Markagunt Plateau. More recent cinder cones and flows occur along the Hurricane Fault marking the western edge of the Colorado Plateau.

Biota. With elevations from less than 4,000 ft (1,220 m) to more than 8,000 ft (1,440 m) asl, the park has several life zones, from desert scrub to montane forest. Much of the park is typical Great Basin vegetation, pinyon pine and juniper woodlands with rabbit brush and sagebrush. Higher elevations support ponderosa pine, fir, aspen forests, and meadows. Ecosystems are not restricted by elevation, however, but can form a mosaic due to sheltered canyons and springs. Animal life is typical for those ecosystems and includes mule deer, coyote, ground squirrels, and black bear.

Protected Areas. Zion canyon was protected as a national monument in 1909 under the name of Mukuntuweap National Monument. The area was designated a national park in 1919.

Environmental Issues. Like many national park areas, increased visitation threatens the integrity of geologic formations and ecosystems, as well as severely impacting aging facilities. In response, Zion National Park closed the road into the valley to individual cars. With some exceptions, such as campers and the disabled, all visitors are required to board a free shuttle to visit the narrow canyon.

See also Colorado Plateau

Further Reading
Harris, Ann G., Esther Tuttle, and Sherwood D. Tuttle. 2004. "Zion National Park." In *Geology of National Parks*, 29–42. Dubuque, IA: Kendall Hunt.
National Park Service. 2013. *Zion National Park*. www.nps .gov/zion/

Appendix I

The Highest, Lowest, Biggest, Deepest Places: "Top Tens" and Other Global Comparisons

Note: Multiple sources were consulted to compile the following information; however, only a single source, if it provided most or all of the data, is cited. Actual figures vary from source to source, commonly as a consequence of exactly what is being measured, rounding, and the measuring techniques and instruments used. Scientists are continually updating data as discoveries are made or measurement methods are improved. We have made every effort to use the most current figures in individual entries in the encyclopedia and to adjust appendix data from outside sources to reflect these updates. Differences are usually not enough to alter rankings.

Global Dimensions

Equatorial circumference: 24,900 mi (40,075 km)

Meridional circumference: 24,860 mi (40,008 km)

Diameter, pole to pole: 7,900 mi (12,713 km)

Diameter, at equator: 7,926 mi (12,765 km)

Tilt of axis: 23° 26'

Total surface area: 197,000,000 mi^2 (510,100,000 km^2)

Total land area: 57,308,738 mi^2 (148,940,000 km^2) or 29.2%

Total surface area of oceans: 139,433,845 mi^2 (361,132,000 km^2) or 70.8%

Highest elevation (Mount Everest, Himalayan Mountains, Asia): 29,035 ft (8,850 m)

Point farthest from center of Earth: Summit of Chimborazo, Ecuador

Lowest elevation on land (Dead Sea shore, Israel and Jordan, Asia): 1,339 ft (408 m) bsl

Greatest known depth in ocean (Challenger Deep, Mariana Trench, Pacific Ocean): 36,070 ft (10,994 m) bsl

Mean temperature at surface: 59°F (15°C)

Source: Veregin, Howard, editor. 2010. *Goode's World Atlas*. 22nd ed. Englewood, NJ: Pearson Prentice Hall.

Land Area of Continents

	Square Miles	Square Kilometers
Asia	17,179,000	44,493,400
Africa	11,690,000	30,276,960
North America	9,442,000	24,454,670
South America	6,890,000	17,845,000
Antarctica	6,000,000	15,539,930
Europe	3,956,000	10,246,000
Australia	3,454,000	8,9458,820

Surface Area of Oceans

	Square Miles	Square Kilometers
Pacific Ocean	60,667,000	115,557,000
Atlantic Ocean	29,937,000	76,762,000
Indian Ocean	26,737,000	68,556,000
Southern Ocean	7,927,500	20,327,000
Arctic Ocean	5,482,000	14,056,000

Source: *The World Factbook*, Central Intelligence Agency. https://www.cia.gov/library/publications/the-world-factbook

Largest Seas, by Surface Area

	Square Miles	Square Kilometers
1. South China Sea	1,148,500	2,974,600
2. Caribbean Sea	971,395	2,515,900
3. Mediterranean Sea	969,116	2,510,000
4. Bering Sea	873,016	2,261,100
5. Gulf of Mexico	582,088	1,507, 600
6. Sea of Okhotsk	537,493	1,392,100
7. Sea of Japan	391,083	1,012,900
8. Hudson Bay	281,893	730,100
9. East China Sea	256,604	664,600
10. Andaman Sea	218,109	564,900

Source: *National Geographic Atlas of the World*, revised 6th ed.

Deepest Point in Each Ocean

	Feet Below Sea Level	Meters Below Sea Level
Atlantic Ocean: Milwaukee Deep, Puerto Rico Trench	28,230	8,605
Arctic Ocean: Litke Deep, Amundsen Basin	17,880	5,450
Indian Ocean: Sunda or Java Trench	23,377	7,125
Pacific Ocean: Challenger Deep, Mariana Trench	36,070	10,994
Southern Ocean: South Sandwich Trench	23,737	7,235

Ten Largest Islands

	Square Miles	Square Kilometers
1. Greenland	840,000	2,175,600
2. New Guinea	312,167	808,510
3. Borneo	287,863	745,561
4. Madagascar	226,657	587,040
5. Baffin Island, Canada	195,927	507,451
6. Sumatra, Indonesia	182,860	473,606
7. Honshu, Japan	87,805	227,414
8. Great Britain	84,354	218,476
9. Victoria Island, British Columbia, Canada	83,897	217,897
10. Ellesmere Island, Canada	75,767	196,236

Source: *National Geographic Atlas of the World*, revised 6th ed.

Ten Highest Mountains (elevation above sea level)

	Feet	Meters
1. Mount Everest (Himalayas)	29,035	8,850
2. K2 (Himalayas Karakoram Mountains)	28,251	8,611
3. Kangchenjunga (Himalayas)	28,169	8,586
4. Lhotse (Himalayas)	27,939	8,516
5. Makalu (Himalayas)	27,765	8,463
6. Cho Oyu (Himalayas)	26,906	8,201
7. Dhaulagiri (Himalayas)	26,794	8,167
8. Manaslu (Himalayas)	26,781	8,163
9. Nanga Parbat (Himalayas)	26,660	8,126
10. Annapurna (Himalayas)	26,545	8,091

Source: Melina, Remy. 2010. "The World's Tallest Mountains." *Live Science*. http://www.livescience.com/29627-world-highest-mountain-summits.html

The "Seven Summits": Highest Peaks on Each Continent (elevation above sea level)

	Feet	Meters
Asia: Mount Everest	29,035	8,850
Africa: Mount Kilimanjaro	19,340	5,895
Antarctica: Vinson Massif	16,066	4,897
Australia: Mount Kosciusko	7,310	2,228
Europe: Mount Elbrus	18,510	5,642
North America: Mount McKinley (Denali)	20,237	6,168
South America: Aconcagua	22,834	6,960

Source: "Highest Mountain on Each Continent." 2014. Geology.com .http://geology.com/records/continents-highest-mountains.shtml

Lowest Point on Each Continent*

	Feet Below Sea Level	Meters Below Sea Level
Africa: Lake Assal, Djibouti	502	153
Asia: Dead Sea, Israel and Jordan	1,401	427
Australia: Lake Eyre	52	16
Europe: Caspian Sea, Russia and Kazakhstan	92	28
North America: Badwater, Death Valley, California, United States	282	86
South America: Laguna del Carbon, Argentina	344	105

*Lake elevations refer to water surface.

Adapted from *National Geographic Atlas of the World*, revised 6th ed., with adjustments reflecting more recent data as reported in individual encyclopedia entries.

Ten Longest Rivers*

	Miles	Kilometers
1. Nile River, Africa	4,130	6,600
2. Amazon River, South America	3,900	6,200
3. Mississippi-Missouri River System, North America	3,740	6,000
4. Chang Jiang (Yangtze River), Asia	3,964	6,380
5. Ob–Irtysh Rivers, Asia	3,459	5,568
6. Huang He (Yellow River), Asia	2,900	4,650
7. Amur River, Asia	2,800	4,500
8. Congo River, Africa	2,700	4,367
9. Lena River, Asia	2,700	4,300
10. Mackenzie River, North America	2,635	4,200

*Figures vary considerably from source to source, and little consensus exists beyond the Nile being the longest and the Amazon the second longest river in the world. The rivers listed here make most top ten lists, however. Source: McKnight, Tom L. and Darrel Hess, 2000. *Physical Geography, A Landscape Appreciation*, 6th ed. Upper Saddle River, NJ: Prentice Hall.

Ten Largest Lakes, by Surface Area

	Square Miles	Square Kilometers
1. Caspian Sea* (Azerbaijan, Iran, Kazakhstan, Russia, Turkmenistan)	143,200	371,000
2. Lake Superior (United States)	31,820	82,414
3. Lake Victoria (Kenya, Tanzania, Uganda)	26,828	69,485
4. Lake Huron (United States)	23,000	59,600
5. Lake Michigan (United States)	22,000	58,000
6. Lake Tanganyika (Burundi, Democratic Republic of Congo, Tanzania, Zambia)	12,700	32,893
7. Lake Baikal (Russia)	12,200	31,500
8. Great Bear Lake (Canada)	12,000	31,080
9. Lake Malawi–Lake Nyasa (Malawi, Mozambique, Tanzania)	11,600	30,044
10. Great Slave Lake, Canada	11,170	28,930

*Sometimes discounted as a lake because it contains an oceanic basin. If the Caspian Sea is not considered a lake, then Lake Erie becomes Number 10 at 9,930 mi² (25,719 km²).

Source: "Largest Lakes (Area)." Lakes at a Glance. LakeNet. http://www.worldlakes.org/lakeprofiles.asp?anchor=area.

Ten Largest Saline (Endorheic) Lakes, by Area

	Square Miles	Square Kilometers
1. Caspian Sea* (Azerbaijan, Iran, Kazakhstan, Russia, Turkmenistan)	143,200	371,000
2. Lake Balkhash (Kazakhstan)	7,115	18,428
3. Lake Eyre (Australia)	3,669	9,500
4. Lake Turkana (Ethiopia, Kenya)	2,473	6,405
5. Lake Issyk Kul (Kyrgyzstan)	2,407	6,236
6. Lake Urmia (Iran)	2,000	5,200
7. Qinghai Lake (China)	1,733	4,489
8. Great Salt Lake (Utah, United States)	1,700	4,400
9. Lake Van (Turkey)	1,450	3,755
10. Dead Sea (Israel and Jordan)	394	1,020

*Caspian Sea is sometimes discounted as a lake because it contains an oceanic basin.

Source: "Ten Largest Endorheic (Salty) Lakes of the World." 2011. All Downstream. http://alldownstream.wordpress.com/2011/01/22/top-ten-largest-endorheic-lakes-of-the-world-by-area/.

Ten Largest Lakes, by Volume

	Cubic Miles	Cubic Kilometers
1. Caspian Sea* (Azerbaijan, Iran, Kazakhstan, Russia, Turkmenistan)	18,800	78,362
2. Lake Baikal** (Russia)	5,700	23,600
3. Lake Tanganyika (Burundi, Democratic Republic of Congo, Tanzania, Zambia)	4,500	18,900
4. Lake Superior (United States)	2,800	11,600
5. Lake Malawi–Lake Nyasa (Malawi, Mozambique, Tanzania)	1,853	7,725
6. Lake Vosto (Antarctica)	1,300	5,400
7. Lake Michigan (United States)	1,180	4,920
8. Lake Huron (United States)	850	3,540
9. Lake Victoria (Kenya, Tanzania, Uganda)	650	2,700
10. Great Bear Lake (Canada)	536	2,236

*Caspian Sea is sometimes discounted as a lake because it contains an oceanic basin.

**Lake Baikal is the largest freshwater lake, by volume.

Source: "Largest Lakes (Volume)." 2003–2004. Lakes at a Glance. LakeNet. http://www.worldlakes.org/lakeprofiles.asp?anchor=volume.

Ten Deepest Lakes (by Maximum Depth)

	Feet	Meters
1. Lake Baikal (Russia)	5,370	1,637
2. Lake Tanganyika (Burundi, Democratic Republic of the Congo, Tanzania, Zambia)	4,823	1,470
3. Caspian Sea* (Azerbaijan. Iran, Kazakhstan, Russia, Turkmenistan)	3,363	1,025
4. Lake Vosto (Antarctica)	1,770–3,000	510–900
5. O'Higgins-San Martin (Argentina, Chile)	2,742	836
6. Lake Malawi–Lake Nyasa (Malawi, Mozambique, Tanzania)	2,316	706
7. Lake Issyk Kul (Kyrgyzstan)	2,192	688
8. Great Slave Lake (Canada)	2,015	614
9. Crater Lake, Oregon (United States)	1,949	594
10. Lake Matano (Sulawesi, Indonesia)	1,935	590

*Caspian Sea is sometimes discounted as a lake because it contains an oceanic basin.

Source: "Deepest Lakes." 2003–2004. Lakes at a Glance. LakeNet. http://www.worldlakes.org/lakeprofiles.asp?anchor=deepest.

Ten Oldest Lakes

	Age (Millions of years)
1. Lake Eyre (Australia)	20–50
2. Lake Maracaibo (Venezuela)	>36
3. Lake Issyk Kul (Kyrgyzstan)	25
4. Lake Baikal (Russia)	20
5. Lake Tanganyika (Burundi, Tanzania, Zaire, Zambia)	9–20
6. Caspian Sea (Azerbaijan, Iran, Kazakhstan, Russia, Turkmenistan)	>5
7. Aral Sea (Kazakhstan, Uzbekistan)	>5
8. Lake Ohrid (Albania, Greece)	>5
9. Lake Prespa (Albania, Greece, Macedonia)	>5
10. Lake Lanao (Philippines)	3.6–5.5

Source: "Ancient Lakes." LakeNet. http://www.worldlakes.org/lakeprofiles.asp?anchor=ancient

Ten Tallest Waterfalls

	Feet	Meters
1. Angel Falls (Venezuela)	3,212	979
2. Tugela Falls (South Africa)	3,110	948
3. Las Tres Hermanas Cataracts (Peru)	3,000	914
4. Olo'upena Falls (Hawaii, U.S.)	2,953	900
5. Yumbilla Falls (Peru)	2,938	896
6. Vinnufossen (Norway)	2,822	860
7. Balåifossen (Norway)	2,788	850
8. Pu'uka'oku Falls (Hawaii, U.S.)	2,756	840
9. James Bruce Falls (British Columbia, Canada)	2,755	840
10. Browne Falls (New Zealand)	2,744	836

Source: "World's Tallest Waterfalls." 2014. World Waterfall Database. www.worldwaterfalldatabase.com/tallest-waterfalls/total-height.

Ten Largest Waterfalls, by Average Volume

	ft³/sec	m³/s
1. Inga Falls, Congo River (Congo and Democratic Republic of the Congo)	910,000	125,778
2. Livingstone Falls, Congo River (Congo and Democratic Republic of the Congo)	885,000	25,060
3. Wagenia Falls (Stanley Falls), Lualaba River (Congo and Democratic Republic of Congo)	600,000	16,990
*Salto del Guaíra, Paraná River (Brazil)	470,000	13,309
4. Khone Falls, Mekong River (Laos)	410,000	11,610
*Celilo Falls, Columbia River (Oregon, United States)	189,500	5,366
*Kettle Falls, Columbia River (Washington, United States)	165,340	4,682
5. Salto Pará, Rio Caura (Venezuela)	125,000	3,540
6. Cachoeira Paulo Afonso (Rio São Francisco, Brazil)	100,000	2,832
*Salto do Urubupunga, Paraná River (Brazil)	97,000	2,747
7. Niagara Falls, Niagara River (Ontario, Canada, and New York, United States)	85,000	2,407
8. Vermillion Falls, Peace River (Alberta, Canada)	64,000	1,812
9. Iguazu Falls, Rio Iguazu (Argentina, Brazil)	61,660	1,746
*Saltos dos Patos e Maribondo, Rio Grande (Brazil)	53,000	1,501
10. Victoria Falls, Zambezi River (Zambia and Zimbabwe)	38,430	1,501

* Those listed without numbers are now submerged behind dams, but are placed in their pre-inundation rank.

Source: "World's Largest Waterfalls." 2014. World Waterfall Database. http://www.worldwaterfalldatabase.com/largest-waterfalls/volume/

Ten Largest Waterfalls, by Width

	Feet	Meters
1. Khone Falls, Mekong River (Laos)	35,376	10,783
2. Salto Pará, Rio Caura (Venezuela)	18,400	5,608
*Salto del Guaíra, Paraná River (Brazil)	15,840	4,828
3. Kongou Falls, Ivindo River (Gabon)	10,500	3,200
4. Iguazu Falls, Rio Iguazú (Argentina and Brazil)	8,800	2,682
5. Saltos del Mocona, Rio Uruguay (Argentina)	6,775	2,065
*Saltos dos Patos e Maribondo, Rio Grande (Brazil)	6,600	2,012
*Salto do Urubupunga, Paraná River (Brazil)	6,600	2,012
6. Vermillion Falls, Peace River (Alberta, Canada)	6,000	1,829
*Celilo Falls, Columbia River (Oregon, U.S.)	5,800	1,768
7. Victoria Falls, Zambezi River (Zambia and Zimbabwe)	5,600	1,707
8. Wagenia (Stanley) Falls, Lualaba River (Congo and Democratic Republic of Congo)	4,500	1,372

(Continued)

Ten Largest Waterfalls, by Width (Continued)

	Feet	Meters
9. Niagara Falls, Niagara River (Ontario, Canada, and New York, U.S.)	3,950	1,204
10. Inga Falls, Congo River (Congo and Democratic Republic of Congo)	3,000	914

* Those listed without numbers are now submerged behind dams, but are placed in their pre-inundation rank.

Source: "World's Largest Waterfalls, by Overall Width." World Waterfall Database. http://www.worldwaterfalldatabase.com/largest-waterfalls/total-width/

Ten Deepest Caves (total vertical extent)

	Feet	Meters
1. Krubera-Voronja Cave (Abkhazia, Georgia)	7,188	2,191
2. Illuzia-Snezhnaja-Mezhonnogo (Abkhazia, Georgia)	5,751	1,753
3. Gouffre Mirolda (France)	5,685	1,733
4. Vogelschacht and Lamprechtsofen (Austria)	5,354	1,632
5. Reseay Jean Bernard (France)	5,256	1,602
6. Torca del Cerro del Ceuvon (Spain)	5,213	1,589
7. Sarma ((Abkhazia, Georgia)	5,062	1,543
8. Shakta Vjacheslav Pantjukhina (Georgia)	4,498	1,508
9. Sima de la Cornisa-Torca Magali (Spain)	4,944	1,507
10. Ceki2 (Slovenia)	4,928	1,502

Source: "10 Deepest Caves in the World." n.d. Scribol Outdoor Sports. scribal.com/outdoor-sports/10-deepest-caves-in-the-world

Ten Longest Known Caves

	Miles	Kilometers
1. Mammoth Cave, Kentucky, U.S.	405	652
2. Sistema Sac Actun-Sistema Dos Ojos, Quintana Roo, Mexico	193	311
3. Jewel Cave, South Dakota, U.S.	166	268
4. Sistema Ox Bel, Quintana Roo, Mexico	151	243
5. Optymistycha Cave, Ukraine	147	236
6. Wind Cave, South Dakota, U.S.	140	226
7. Lechuguilla Cave, New Mexico, U.S.	138	223
8. Hoelloch, Switzerland	125	200
9. Gua Air Jernih Clearwater System, Sarawak, Malaysia	122	197
10. Fisher Ridge Cave System, Kentucky, U.S.	121	195

Source: Gulden, Bob. 2014. "World's Longest Caves." The NSS Geo2 Long & Deep Caves Web Site. http://www.caverbob.com/wlong.htm

Ten Largest Drainage Basins (Watersheds)

	Square Miles	Square Kilometers
1. Amazon Basin, South America	2,772,213	7,180,000
2. Congo Basin, Africa	1,475,682	3,822,000
3. Mississippi River Basin, North America	1,243,635	3,221,000
4. Ob–Irtyush, Asia	1,148,654	2,975,000
5. Nile River Basin, Africa	1,112,360	2,881,000
6. Rio de la Plata Basin, South America	1,023,171	2,650,000
7. Yenisey River Basin, Asia	1,005,796	2,605,000
8. Lena River Basin, Asia	961,394	2,490,000
9. Niger Basin, Africa	807,726	2,092,000
10. Chang Jiang (Yangtze) Basin, Asia	760,621	1,970,000

Ten Largest Rivers, by Discharge

	Drainage Area mi² (km²)	Average Discharge ft³/sec (m³/s)	Outflow
1. Amazon–Marañón River, South America	2,669,896 (6,915,000)	7,380,765 (209,000)	Atlantic Ocean
2. Congo River, Africa	1,550,007 (4,014,500)	1,454,964 (41,200)	Atlantic Ocean
3. Ganges-Brahama-putra, Meghna River System, Asia	631,227 (1,635,000)	1,346,513 (38,129)	Bay of Bengal, Indian Ocean
4. Orinoco River, South America	339,770 (880,000)	1,271,328 (36,000)	Atlantic Ocean
5. Madeira River. South America	548,265 (1,420,000)	1,101,818 (31,200)	Amazon River
6. Chang Jiang (Yangtze), Asia	698,265 (1,808,500)	1,065,302 (30,166)	East China Sea, Pacific Ocean
7. Rio Negro, South America	266,797 (691,000)	1,002,937 (28,400)	Amazon River
8. Rio de la Plata-Paraná Rivers, South America	1,196,917 (3,100,000)	776,923 (22,000)	Atlantic Ocean
9. Yenisey, Asia	996,144 (2,580,000)	692,167 (19,600)	Kara Sea, Arctic Ocean
10. Brahmaputra, Asia	203,321 (526,600)	691,573 (19,300)	Padma River

The 34 Terrestrial Biodiversity Hotspots Currently Recognized by Conservation International

1. Tropical Andes
2. Mesoamerica
3. Caribbean Islands
4. Tumbes-Chocó-Darien-Magdalena (including Galápagos Islands and Malpelo)
5. Atlantic Forest
6. Brazilian Cerrado
7. Chilean Winter Rainfall–Valdivian Forests
8. California Floristic Province
9. Madagascar and Indian Ocean Islands
10. Coastal Forests of Eastern Africa
11. Eastern Afromontane
12. Cape Floristic Province
13. Succulent Karoo
14. Guinean Forests of West Africa
15. Mediterranean Basin (including the Azores and Cape Verde islands)
16. Caucasus Mountains
17. Sundaland
18. Wallacea
19. Philippines
20. Himalayas
21. Indo-Burma
22. Mountains of South-Central China
23. Western Ghats and Sri Lanka
24. New Caledonia
25. New Zealand (including Lord Howe and Norfolk islands)
26. Polynesia/Micronesia
27. Southwest Australia
28. Madrean Pine-Oak Woodlands
29. Maputaland–Pondoland–Albany
30. Horn of Africa
31. Irano-Anatolian Region
32. Mountains of Central Asia
33. Japan
34. East Melanesian Islands

Source: Norman Myers, Russell A. Mittermeier, Cristina G. Mittermeier, Gustavo A. B. da Fonseca, and Jennifer Kent. 2000. "Biodiversity hotspots for conservation priorities." *Nature* 403: 853–858.

Megadiverse Countries

Seventeen countries harbor more than 70 percent of Earth's species:

Australia, Brazil, China, Colombia, Democratic Republic of Congo (DRC), Ecuador, India, Indonesia, Madagascar, Malaysia, Mexico, Papua New Guinea, Peru, the Philippines, South Africa, the United States, and Venezuela.

Source: Department of the Environment, Australian Government. n.d. "Megadiverse Countries." http://www.environment.gov.au/topics/biodiversity/biodiversity-conservation/biodiversity-hotspots

Appendix 2

Opposing Viewpoints: Issues Related to Natural Features

Issue/Key Question

Should U.S. national parks be left to "wilderness" or be developed so that more visitors could be accommodated more comfortably?

Dilemma: Opening

Since founded in 1916, the National Park Service in the United States has been confronted with the dual problem of protecting national parks and providing means for visitation. Not all visitors, however, enjoy parks in an identical manner. Some prefer to "rough it" and backpack through backcountry, while others, either unwilling or unable, prefer to view the landscape and wildlife from the safety and comfort of vehicles or lodges. Can U.S. national parks be managed to accommodate all tastes, or must some sacrifices be made in order for parks to be available for the enjoyment of all Americans? Many national parks in other parts of the world (e.g., Manú in Peru and Greenland National Park), as well as more remote U.S. parks, are largely inaccessible and set aside primarily for the preservation of natural landscapes and native biota. In contrast, concessionaires at some parks (e.g., Death Valley and Yosemite) provide golf courses for the public's entertainment. How much development and accommodation is appropriate to national parks in the United States? In the first perspective, Dr. Whitney Snow, assistant professor of history, contends that roads, traffic, excessive visitation, and visitors flouting rules, in addition to a government policy of artificially managing wildlife, in Great Smoky Mountains National Park are destroying the very environment that people come

to experience. Although conjecturing that it may be too late, she suggests that less development be allowed within park borders and that more backcountry be set aside as wilderness. Alyssa Warrick, a doctoral candidate in American history, takes the viewpoint in the second perspective that more accommodations within the park might ease congestion on park roads, as hundreds of cars bearing visitors enter daily. In order to preserve what remains of the natural landscape, the park must improve facilities and infrastructure to accommodate, or channel the flow of, the ever-increasing number of visitors who visit Great Smoky Mountains National Park.

Perspective #1. Cherishing Wilderness? The Toll of Tourism on the Great Smoky Mountains National Park

At what cost can national parks and tourism coexist? From the inception of the National Park Service (NPS) in 1916, its mission was clear: "To conserve the scenery and the natural and historic objects and the wild life therein and to provide for the enjoyment of the same in such a manner and by such means as will leave them unimpaired for the enjoyment of future generations" (Pierce 2000). While the goal involved conserving "wilderness," the NPS also sought to attract tourists using scenery and animals. This begs the question: Is nature being protected or exploited? Tourism results in traffic jams, air pollution, wildlife endangerment, and questionable management practices, all of which can be seen in the following case sample.

Covering over 800 square miles, the 80-year-old Great Smoky Mountains National Park (GRSM) brings roughly $600 million in revenues and over 9 million visitors a year to cities in Tennessee and North Carolina. Observing auto-tourism on popular routes like Newfound Gap Road, Little River Road, and an 11-mile loop in Cade's Cove, the NPS has tried to prevent the creation of new streets like the North Shore Road. This controversy, a 1943 promise by the Department of the Interior to build a 34-mile road in Swain County, North Carolina, to replace one flooded by the creation of Fontana Dam, was finally put to rest in 2010 when the county settled for a $52 million trust instead. Seeking to deter traffic from current roads, the NPS worked with the Federal Highway Administration to initiate the formation of the Foothills Parkway along the outskirts of the park. Expected completion is 2016, but the NPS expects this "missing link" road to lessen auto-tourism inside the park (Simmons 2013). In another effort in 2002, the NPS teamed up with the Knoxville Regional Transportation Planning Organization to form the Regional Transportation Alternative Plan which included shuttles as a way to diminish overcrowding. While some tourists ride for-profit or nonprofit shuttles from neighboring areas, far more continue to drive their own vehicles so even if the GRSM established a park shuttle, comparatively few tourists would select that option. This is bad news for the park because the onslaught of automobiles has wrought havoc on its air quality.

Nitrogen oxide from car emissions and sulfur dioxide from neighboring coal-powered plants have made the GRSM very smoggy. Since 1950, visibility has plummeted from 113 to 25 miles (NPS 2002). In 2002, the park was deemed the most polluted national park in the country and since 1999 the National Parks Conservation Association has placed it on the list of America's Ten Most Endangered National Parks. While the NPS monitors factory output and violations of the Clean Air Act of 1970, chemicals cause the park to become hazier each year. Decreased air quality is just one problem plaguing the park because people pose constant threats.

Encouraging a Leave No Trace policy, park guidelines instruct tourists not to feed animals, get closer than 150 ft (45 m), or litter, but these rules are often ignored. Bears become conditioned to stand alongside the roads, may be struck by vehicles, and accustomed to humans, are more likely to be seen and killed outside the park. In order to deter them from roads and campsites, rangers shoot nuisance bears with paintballs or rubber bullets, relocate, or worst-case scenario, euthanize even though there is only one recorded bear-caused death in the history of the park. It seems the park should focus on managing people to protect wildlife rather than the other way around. This is unlikely to happen because the NPS tries to alter the park and its inhabitants in order to draw tourists.

Throughout the existence of the park, rangers have sought to shape the type and number of animals in its ecosystem and such efforts continue to this day. While introduced before the park's formation, rainbow trout were encouraged by the NPS to lure fishermen but this species competes with native brook trout. To their credit, rangers strove without success to reintroduce red wolves in the 1990s and did manage to reestablish elk in 2001, river otters in 1986, and to a far lesser extent, peregrine falcons in 1984. Historically, however, they also endeavored to decrease the population of so-called undesirable natives like snakes and kingfishers. This tampering may be well intentioned, but picking and choosing which animals have value demeans the concept of wilderness.

The Wilderness Act of 1964 allows Congress to declare parts of federal lands "wilderness" in order to prevent roads, logging, and machines in such areas. Of the roughly 106 million acres of wilderness throughout the country, over 44 million acres are in national parks but none are in the GRSM despite its having the most tourism. Congress defeated a bill to make 247,000 acres of GRSM wilderness back in 1966 and has continuously voted against declaring portions of the park wilderness ever since.

The GRSM, with its 384 miles of roads and 2,115 miles of streams, strikes tourists as an ideal place to witness nature but the allure is largely illusory. The roads and 150 hiking trails alter terrain and that, coupled with manipulated flora and fauna populations, exposes tourists to an artificial, human-made "synthetic" nature (Brown 2000). Travelers drive hundreds if not thousands of miles to witness "wilderness" without realizing that their car exhaust, even their very presence jeopardizes the wildlife they come to admire (Lewis 2007). This is all the more poignant considering that for many vacationers the park plays second fiddle to shopping malls and concerts in gateway cities like Pigeon Forge and Gatlinburg. Perhaps historian Margaret Lynn Brown correctly assessed the irony by asking, "If the mountains finally disappear from view, will anyone at Dollywood notice?" (Brown 2000)

Tourists do, in fact, leave a trace so can anything be done to alleviate their impact? The GRSM is one of the few national parks in the country to allow free entrance so its best hope may be initiating a small entrance toll to generate funds for upkeep. The NPS has no authority to do this so the Tennessee legislature would have to make this change. Historically, the state has vehemently opposed any charge so such a scenario is unlikely. Limiting the number of hiking trails and protecting the backcountry, which is estimated to have 390,500 acres of eligible wilderness, from human encroachment, are more feasible goals. Since February 2013, the NPS has been requiring backcountry campers to pay a fee of $4 a night with a cap of $20. Insisting national parks are free, tourists have responded with outrage even though the revenue is being used to improve customer service and provide more rangers in the backcountry. Rather than resist, backcountry campers should gladly pay because more rangers means more access to help in times of injury, illness, or hazard. Instead of complaining, these men and women need to prioritize and focus on helping conserve the park for future generations. Then again, perhaps such efforts are futile because as famed environmentalist Aldo Leopold explained, "All conservation of wilderness is self-defeating, for to cherish we must see and fondle, and when enough have seen and fondled, there is no wilderness left to cherish" (Leopold 1966).

Bibliography

Brown, Margaret Lynn. 2000. *The Wild East: A Biography of the Great Smoky Mountains*. Miami: University Press of Florida.

Keiter, Robert B. 2002. *To Conserve Unimpaired: The Evolution of the National Park Idea*. Washington, D.C.: Island Press.

Leopold, Aldo. 1966. *A Sand County Almanac with Essays on Conservation from Round River*. New York: Ballantine Books.

Lewis, Michael. 2007. "American Wilderness: An Introduction." In *American Wilderness: A New History*, edited by Michael Lewis, 3–14. New York: Oxford University Press.

Ludmer, Larry H. 2000. *The Great American Wilderness: Touring America's National Parks*. West Palm Beach: Hunter Publishing, Inc.

Miles, John C. 2009. *Wilderness in National Parks: Playground or Preserve*. Seattle: University of Washington Press.

National Park Service. 2002. "Great Smoky Mountains National Park—Threatened by Air Pollution." In *Air Quality in the National Parks*, 2nd ed., Chapter 4, 35–44. http://www.nature.nps.gov/air/pubs/pdf/aqNps/aqnpsFour.pdf

Pierce, Daniel S. 2000. *The Great Smokies: From Natural Habitat to National Park*. Knoxville: University of Tennessee Press.

Sellars, Richard West. 1997. *Preserving Nature in National Parks: A History*. New Haven, CT: Yale University Press.

Simmons, Morgan. 2013. "Parkway Progress: Missing Link's Longest Bridge Completed but Five More to Go." http://www.knoxnews.com/news/2013/jun/25/parkway-progress-missing-links-longest-bridge-to/

About the Author

Dr. Whitney Adrienne Snow is an assistant professor at Midwestern State University in Wichita Falls, Texas, specializing in southern history. Her articles have appeared in *The Alabama Review*, *The Journal of Mississippi History*, *The Journal of East Tennessee History*, and *Textile: The Journal of Cloth and Culture*. She received her Ph.D. from Mississippi State University.

Perspective #2. Preservation through Development: Great Smoky Mountains National Park and the Case for Tourism Infrastructure

Historians and preservationist-minded scholars have multiple ideas about what wilderness is and what it is not. The passage of the Wilderness Act in 1964 provides a working definition. For the purposes of preservation, the wilderness is "an area where the earth and its community of life are untrammeled by man, where man himself is a visitor who does not remain" (Harvey 2005).

In 1916, Congress passed the Organic Act creating the National Park Service, and charged this agency with a dual mandate "to provide for the enjoyment" of the national parks, "in such manner and means as will leave them unimpaired for the enjoyment of future generations" (Dilsaver 1994). This seemingly conflicting order for use and preservation has been debated for nearly one hundred years. The example of Great Smoky Mountains National Park (GRSM) provides a remarkable case to debate wilderness, but clearly shows the need for wise development in national parks.

Cherokee Indians altered the land of GRSM for hundreds of years before the encroachment of white settlement. By 1900, the Smokies were far from being a wilderness; they were "a patchwork" landscape of fields and homes "connected by spiderwebs of dirt roads" (Brown 2000). Still, the mountainous land contained enough potential as a national park that in 1926 the Southern Appalachian National Park Commission endorsed the Great Smokies to be suitable for inclusion into the growing system of national parks.

Great Smoky Mountains National Park proved remarkably successful. It is the most-visited national park in the system, drawing in 9 million visitors each year. The heavy visitation has provoked questions about the park's future development. Wilderness advocates have worked tirelessly to save the remaining wilderness of GRSM under the Wilderness Act, though their efforts have not led to such declarations from Congress (Turner 2012). Even without such declaration, these preservationists have fought against the construction of roads, hydroelectric dams, and other obvious forms of human impact on the environment (Pierce 2000). These preservationists have in mind the protection of thousands of species of trees, shrubs, wildflowers, birds, mammals, and fish that live in GRSM. This is surely a worthy and necessary goal if the National Park Service is to remain true to its mission.

However, wilderness advocates should consider the history and purpose of both parts of the mission. The language of preservation and enjoyment in the Organic Act stems in part from Frederick Law Olmsted's 1865 statement about future management of Yosemite:

The main duty with which the Commissioners should be charged should be to give every advantage practicable to the mass of the people to benefit by that which is peculiar to this ground and which has caused Congress to treat it differently from other parts of the public domain. This peculiarity consists wholly in its natural scenery. . . . The first point to be kept in mind then is the preservation and maintenance as exactly as is possible of the natural scenery . . . (Dilsaver 1994)

Olmsted even predicted that visitors, once they had a way to reach Yosemite, would come by the millions, and would need necessary provisions such as campgrounds, roads, and supplies (Dilsaver 1994). Furthermore, he warned that lack of development would lead to abuse of the environment and wildlife, as GRSM officials have recognized at the popular Cades Cove area (Cades Cove Briefing Statement 2007). While there are campgrounds and roads and trails available to visitors at GRSM, there are no lodges or resorts as in some of the western parks. Rather, park officials left accommodations to gateway communities like Gatlinburg, Tennessee.

This kind of planning works for the benefit of the hospitality industry and outfitters, but the enormous visitation to the park clogs the roads with traffic (and ensuing air pollution), inundates visitor centers and park facilities, and threatens the environment in the backcountry with horses (Air Quality Briefing Statement 2010). It would seem that there has been too much development outside the park in the form of interstates, hotels, restaurants, nonpark entertainment, and theme parks, but not enough development inside the park.

If the park is to continue serving visitors then it will have to develop more infrastructure or revise current policies, particularly as to private vehicles in the park. Yosemite, for instance, has implemented an extensive shuttle system in the valley and employs buses to popular recreational spots. The Smokies have the Cades Cove Heritage Tour, but it is only for 11 miles of road out of the park's total of more than 380 miles. Due to an agreement with the state of Tennessee, the park cannot charge an entrance fee without action from the state legislature, and instead relies on usage fees. Perhaps the park could implement parking fees or offer incentives for using the few public transportation options that exist from Gatlinburg and Cherokee, North Carolina.

From their inception, national parks have been preserved for the enjoyment of present and future generations. The national parks have proven not just "if you build it, they will come," but rather, "they" are coming anyway, so it is best to prepare to receive them. When President Franklin Roosevelt dedicated GRSM, he hoped that a hundred years in the future the park would still exist, owned by the people; that the trees would still stand; that roads would continue to be built "in the cause of the liberty of recreation"; and, importantly, that visitation would not be essentially rationed out (Roosevelt 1940).

As the National Park Service approaches its centennial, it must develop parks to receive those visitors eager to enjoy the splendor of places like GRSM. But the dual mandate does not have to necessarily be a conflicting one—development does not have to be everywhere, including wilderness areas, whether officially declared or not (Carr 1998). For all of their natural and historic wonders, parks are essentially creations of, by, and for the people. If they are not to perish under the weight of unrestricted enjoyment and use, parks like GRSM must upgrade facilities, develop new infrastructure, and address the challenges of the 21st century.

Bibliography

Brown, Margaret Lynn. 2000. *Wild East: A Biography of the Great Smoky Mountains*. Tallahassee, FL: University Press of Florida.

Carr, Ethan. 1998. *Wilderness by Design: Landscape Architecture and the National Park Service*. Lincoln: University of Nebraska Press.

Dilsaver, Lary M., ed. 1994. *America's National Park System: The Critical Documents*. Lanham, MD: Rowman & Littlefield Publishers.

Great Smoky Mountains National Park. 2010. "Briefing Statement: Air Quality Issues." http://www.nps.gov/grsm/naturescience/upload/Air%20Quality%20-%20Apr%202010.doc

Great Smoky Mountains National Park. 2007. "Briefing Statement: Cades Cove Management & Development Planning Process." http://www.nps.gov/grsm/parkmgmt/upload/Brief-Cades%20Cove%20Planning.pdf

Nash, Roderick. 1967. *Wilderness and the American Mind*. New Haven, CT: Yale University Press.

Pierce, Daniel S. 2000. *The Great Smokies: From Natural Habitat to National Park*. Knoxville: University of Tennessee Press.

Roosevelt, Franklin D. 1940. "Address at Dedication of Great Smoky Mountains National Park," September 2, 1940. Online by Gerhard Peters and John T. Woolley, *The American Presidency Project*. http://www.presidency.ucsb.edu/ws/?pid = 16002

Turner, James Martin. 2012. *The Promise of Wilderness: American Environmental Politics since 1964*. Seattle: University of Washington Press.

About the Author

Originally from the Missouri Ozarks, Alyssa D. Warrick graduated with a B.A. in history from Truman State University in Kirksville, Missouri. She is currently a Ph.D. candidate in U.S. environmental history at Mississippi State University. Her dissertation will examine the intersection of race, class, gender, and the environment in national parks in the South. In addition to her research, Alyssa has "rangered" at six national parks since 2004.

Issue/Key Question

Should underdeveloped countries, such as those on the island of Borneo, have the same opportunities to exploit their resources to better themselves that developed countries did before the "green" age, or should developed and developing countries be held to the same rules to protect the whole Earth?

Dilemma: Opening

For many developing countries worldwide, economic growth often comes at the expense of the environment. Borneo is no exception. Home to one of the oldest rainforests in the world, the island has seen a rapid depletion of its most valuable natural resource due to logging, oil palm cultivation, agriculture, and forest fires. Borneo's rainforest is valued for not only its tropical hardwoods, but also for its diversity of plants and animals, and as an essential element in the global carbon cycle. However, 50 percent of its rainforest has already disappeared. The fundamental problem is that Borneo's economy is driven by extractive industries. Can the island of Borneo, under three different national governments—Indonesia, Brunei, and Malaysia—slow the "rip and run" destruction of its environment? Advocating a complete stop to land clearing is essentially asking the island to remove itself from the global economy. What can realistically be done to both save Borneo's environments and enable it to join the developed world?

Donald Rallis, in the first perspective, argues that there is still hope for Borneo's forests and that a "middle road" of sustainable resource management can be taken, or a compromise made, that is supportive of the environment and supportive of industry. By virtue of inaccessible location and governments' dedication to moderation, exploitation can be balanced with preservation. In the second perspective, Bruce Johansen is pessimistic, arguing that the pull of the global market is too strong. Too much money is to be made in Borneo's environmental resources for any of the players to pay attention to sustainable resource management. Borneo's natural environments are being sacrificed to accommodate the developed world's "needs."

Perspective #1: Development Can't Be Stopped, but It Can Be Managed

The tropical island of Borneo is one of the most biologically diverse places on Earth. Its rainforests, rivers, coastlines, and coral reefs are home to tens of thousands of species of plants and animals, with more being identified each year. Over the past few decades, however, vast changes have come to Borneo. Tropical hardwoods have been cut down for the valuable timber they provide, and forests have been cleared to make way for profitable plantations, primarily oil palms. In many areas, forests may never return and numerous species have already become extinct. It is not too late, however, to save most of the considerable biodiversity that remains. By protecting remaining environments from further destruction, and by promoting sustainable resource exploitation, it is possible to not only preserve those natural environments that remain in

Borneo, but also to begin to reclaim some of the environments that have been lost.

A hundred years ago, the island of Borneo was virtually untouched by all but the members of its small population of indigenous inhabitants. By the beginning of the 21st century, its forests were being destroyed at an unparalleled rate, its indigenous people displaced from their traditional homelands, and the survival of its myriad species of plants and animals imperiled by the disappearance of their natural habitat. Devastating harm has already come to Borneo, and much of it cannot be reversed.

According to the Worldwide Fund for Nature (WWF), Borneo is the only part of Southeast Asia where rainforests can still be preserved "on a grand scale." There are three main reasons to be optimistic about the future of sustainable development in Borneo—the island's topography, its sparse and unevenly distributed population, and the recent establishment of the vast and ambitious Heart of Borneo conservation and development project.

Most of Borneo's remaining rainforest lies along the mountain spine that runs from the island's northern tip to its central region. Although the mountain range is not particularly high, its steep slopes mean that rivers are not navigable, and roads and rail lines are difficult and expensive to build. As a result, while Borneo's lowland forests have almost given way to palm oil plantations and farms, most of the forests in the upland areas—the Heart of Borneo—remain intact, and can continue to survive well into the future if they are protected and managed properly.

By comparison with some of its neighboring islands, Borneo is very sparsely populated. It is home to some 20 million people, and has an average population density of about 27 people per square kilometer. This average is misleading, however; the vast majority of Borneo's people live on or near the coasts, leaving the island's highland interior very sparsely populated. Many of the people living in the interior are Dayaks and other indigenous people who know the forests well and utilized it sustainably for tens of thousands of years. Low population density and an informed local population with an interest in maintaining the forest make sustainable development in Borneo a much more likely prospect than it would be in some of the more densely populated parts of Southeast Asia.

Sustainable development plans in Borneo were given a major boost in 2007 when the governments of Brunei, Indonesia, and Malaysia jointly committed to managing sustainably a large transnational area called the Heart of Borneo. The area was not to be a national park or conservation area; rather, it would be developed in a way that supported a green economy, where forest destruction would be stopped, greenhouse gas emissions would be reduced, and local people supported in making their living in an environmentally sustainable way. The project is a huge undertaking, and its success is far from certain. It does offer hope, however, and it represents an important recognition by the governments that control Borneo that one of the world's most important and diverse ecosystems is under their control, and that they have an obligation to ensure its survival for future generations.

Development cannot be stopped, but it can be managed in a way that makes it sustainable and minimizes environmental damage. Declaring Borneo's rainforests to be off limits to all development may well protect local ecosystems, but it would also deny governments, investors, and local inhabitants the chance to profit from resources they understandably regard as their own. Permitting unrestricted exploitation of resources, however, would certainly mean that they would be lost forever. Sustainable development is a middle path between those two options. It allows exploitation of natural resources for the benefit of inhabitants and investors, but only in ways that would not unduly harm the long-term future of the region's natural environment.

A great deal of Borneo's unique rainforest remains and it can be saved. It will take a concerted effort by local inhabitants, businesses, and governments. Consumers around the world will need to help too, by refusing to buy products manufactured unsustainably using resources from threatened environments. Students can help by making sure that they learn what these products are, and by sharing what they know with others. Sustainable development in Borneo is possible, but it will not be easy, and it will take a global effort to make sure that it succeeds.

About the Author

Donald Rallis was until 2013 an associate professor of geography at the University of Mary Washington in Fredericksburg, Virginia. He received his B.A. and B.Sc. (Hons) degrees at the University of the Witwatersrand in Johannesburg, South Africa, his M.A. from the University of Miami, and his Ph.D. from Penn State University. In 2014, Dr. Rallis was appointed professor at the American University of Phnom Penh, where he teaches courses on geography and world history. He is an avid traveler who tries whenever possible to visit the places he talks about in his regional geography classes, and uses his travels as a basis for writing about geography on his web site and blog.

Perspective #2: Progress, with an Environmental Price

Can Borneo develop sustainable economic growth without further destroying its environmental resources? For the most part, today, Borneo is serving as a resource plantation for the developed world. Sustainable development may be on some academics' lips, but down on the oil palm farm, in the gold mines, and across the logged-off forests, it's still mainly rip and run. The question of sustainable development has been raised, but mainly as an intellectual exercise.

Indonesia, which exercises jurisdiction over most of Borneo, has banned the export of raw logs. While that sounds commendable, it does not mean that devastation of Borneo's rainforests has stopped. It means that by developing a large timber-processing industry Indonesia has become one of the world's largest exporters of manufactured plywood. Massive logging feeds Asian markets, mainly in China, India, and Japan. Once milled In Japan, wood harvested from what used to be one of the oldest and richest rainforests in the world becomes furniture and packing crates. Much of it becomes construction material, primarily plywood cement forms that are used once or twice, then discarded.

Palm oil, as a biofuel, is being marketed as carbon-friendly. The problem is that to create its oil palm plantations (and other agriculture), Borneo has been burning enough subsurface peat, as thick as 66 ft (20 m), to alter the global carbon balance in a negative way. Susan E. Page and colleagues used satellite images of a 4.9 million ac (2.5 million ha) study area in central Borneo from before and after fires in 1997. According to their estimates, about 32 percent of the area had burned, of which peat land accounted for 91.5 percent. An estimated 0.19 to 0.23 gigatons of carbon were released to the atmosphere through peat combustion, with a further 0.05 gigaton released from burning of the overlying vegetation.

As several million hectares of forests also have been converted to oil palm plantations, many indigenous people have been evicted as their lands have been deforested by fire to develop these plantations. Traditional peoples in Borneo have survived by accommodating in several ways. Some former headhunters have turned their longhouses into bed-and-breakfasts for Japanese tourists. Of roughly 9,000 Penan people surviving in the rainforests of Sarawak (part of Malaysia in Northern Borneo), only a few hundred continue to live in the traditional way as nomads in the rainforest. While trying to live a traditional life, some Penan have tried to attack loggers with blowpipes, with little success. They also have erected blockades, and then been arrested or killed.

Seven indigenous people were killed on October 8, 2000, by the Indonesian Mobile Police Brigade after they erected a blockade of Unocal's Tanjung Santan Oil Refinery on the nearby island of Sulawesi that lasted two weeks. They were protesting pervasive air and water pollution in their homelands. In Kalimantan on Borneo, Rio Tinto's Kelian Gold Mine, which closed in 2005, had produced more than 400,000 troy ounces of gold per year using the cyanide heap-leaching process, producing cyanide-laced tailings. Local people cannot drink or bathe in the water because it causes skin lesions and stomach aches. In addition to other exploitation, homelands of indigenous peoples in Borneo have become sites for several hydroelectric dams.

On several fronts, Borneo (like many "developing" regions of the world) finds itself caught in a worldwide system that consumes natural resources, turning them into salable products, profits, and waste carbon dioxide. Increases in population and affluence

are making these problems worse around the world. Borneo's ecosystems are not likely to become sustainable until steps toward this goal are taken on a broader scale. In the meantime, Borneo has become a case study in just how quickly the resources of the Earth are being consumed by the industrial engines of capitalism. When considering development, one must ask: Sustainable for whom? At what price?

Bibliography

Page, Susan et al. 2002. "The Amount of Carbon Released from Peat and Forest Fires in Indonesia during 1997." *Nature* 420: 61–65.

Richardson, Michael. 2002. "Indonesian Peat Fires Stoke Rise of Pollution." International Herald-Tribune, December 13.

About the Author

Bruce E. Johansen is a professor of communication and Native American studies, University of Nebraska at Omaha. He has been teaching and writing in the School of Communications at UNO since 1982. He had authored 33 books as of 2010. Johansen's first academic specialty was the influence of Native American political systems on United States political and legal institutions; his best-known books in this area are *Forgotten Founders* and *Exemplar of Liberty*. He also writes as a journalist in several national forums, including the *Washington Post* and the *Progressive*. Johansen also writes frequently about environmental subjects.

Adapted from ABC-CLIO's World Geography Database by Joyce A. Quinn.

Issue/Key Question

Should examples of Earth's geological and geomorphic features be preserved?

Dilemma: Opening

The natural heritage of humanity includes geological and geomorphic features, some displaying the ongoing processes that shape Earth's surface, others specific landforms, still others the record of earth history in general and/or life history in particular. Svalbard, for example, has a "geotype preserve" on its west coast. Several UNESCO World Heritage Sites were inscribed to protect intact geological sites of outstanding aesthetic or scientific value. In the United States, a number of natural national landmarks recognize such places, and state and national parks try to protect them from use and abuse. In the first essay, Dr. Danny Vaughn, a physical geographer, argues that the United States is not doing as much as some other countries to protect these assets, in part because laws exist to protect property and compensate monetarily for its destruction or loss. He uses the specific example of vandalism in Utah's Goblin Valley as a case in point. In the second essay, Dr. John Conners, a geologist and geomorphologist, utilizes a broader scale and looks at the depositional features of continental glaciation and their economic, recreational, esthetic, and scientific resource value. He states that preservation and understanding of these features will help guide management and allow better land use planning in the future.

Perspective #1. An Attack on the Hoodoos of Goblin Valley State Park, Utah

In the fall of 2013, two Boy Scout leaders decided that a rock remnant (hoodoo) sculptured by natural weathering and erosional processes was unstable and could possibly tumble off its stand. The defense they asserted for pushing it over and breaking it off from its base was that it could cause serious injury to anyone visiting Goblin Valley State Park located in southeastern Utah. This essay will take the position that naturally occurring Earth surface features identified and set aside within local, state, national parks, and monuments should be protected from damage due to malicious human interventions. State and federal laws should reinforce park and monument rules, and vandals should be punished.

The Earth is about 4.5 billion years old, and energy exchanges have been shaping the planet since its inception. Rocks forming the crust of the earth have developed through a cycle of internal (volcanism

and tectonic activity) and external (weathering and erosion) processes. These processes are actions that also continuously change the surface expression of the planet and result in a unique assemblage of landforms. The Jurassic Period Entrada rock formation developed from sedimentary deposits weathered off ancient highlands bordering an inland sea about 170 million years ago. Streams transported and deposited the sediment onto tidal flats, which lithified into the sandstone currently exposed in the park. Although the Entrada formation dates back millions of years, the natural processes that created the ultimate surface expressions currently distributed throughout the park are continuously changing the overall size, shape, and distribution of all rock types forming the landscape; and they will do so as long as there is an exchange of energy on the planet. Since weathering and erosion are persistent throughout time, it is neither reasonable nor defensible to assert any geologic features will be permanently preserved. However, this should not imply earth surface features that have been identified as unique in their creation and forms are expendable due to damage and destruction by irresponsible acts of vandalism.

When viewed from a geologic perspective, humans are constantly altering the Earth's landscape for many purposes such as constructing roads, bridges, dams, and buildings. This is necessary for providing transportation networks, shelter, places to work, recreate, and live. Whenever any action is taken to disturb the earth's surface, an equal and opposite reaction will ensue. Physicists call this the law of action–reaction. This can result in disrupting the delicate balance of stability that had been attained over thousands of years of surface and subsurface processes. Any disturbed surface is vulnerable to mass movements of Earth materials such as slope failures, rock and debris falls, landslides, and massive flood events over unstable ground. The movement of a single boulder (or hoodoo in this case) can trigger a series of movements with extensive damage to a much larger area than a single formation. This should give pause to anyone contemplating the destruction or displacement of earth materials if for no other reason than the potential for massive property damage, potential injury, or ultimately a loss of life.

Let us assume that protection for these natural geologic features is both acceptable and necessary. In the case of Goblin Valley State Park, Eugene Swalberg, the public affairs coordinator for the Utah State Parks has declared that everyone entering the park is given a brochure that states, "It is unlawful to mutilate or deface a natural or constructed feature or structure." A few rather significant issues need to be addressed before rushing to judgment on a vandalism case such as what had occurred in Goblin Valley. Vandalism laws in Utah are written to protect property value, which is a monetary criterion. Since the hoodoos are an intrinsic feature associated with the entire exposed surface area of the Entrada formation, placing a monetary value on the cost to replace a small remnant is difficult, if not impossible. Fred Hayes, the director of Utah State Parks, has stated that Utah laws do not currently address natural conditions such as geologic formations in the same light as archaeological artifacts. At best only general vandalism and criminal mischief charges would be appropriate and defensible in a court of law. So when a state park posts rules prohibiting destroying or removing any of the natural features within the park boundaries, what actions are appropriate against those few citizens who violate these rules? What is a reasonable punishment, if any?

It would seem that if we value our geologic heritage as another means of understanding and preserving the planet, stricter laws need to be written to ensure actions of vandalism do not go unpunished. Marjorie Chan, a geologist from the University of Utah, has asserted there is an international effort to preserve scientifically significant geologic features for educational and reference purposes, yet the United States has not yet matched the protections offered by other countries. It seems good form and prudent judgment would dictate protecting any naturally occurring unique geologic feature that has formed over a time span that is practically inconceivable to most of the human species. When the amount of time required to develop these geologic features is explained, most people begin to appreciate why they should be protected. A genuine desire exists to add value to the unique shapes and manner in which these rock formations were created, although not everything in existence can be valued in terms of monetary significance or personal use.

Bibliography

Chan, M. 2009. "Protection Needed for Geologic Features." Inside Science News Service. http://www.inside science.org/content/protection-needed-geological-features/1081

"Goblin Valley State Park, Utah." 2013. Utah.com. http://www.utah.com/stateparks/goblin_valley.htm

Milligan, M. 1999. "The Geology of Goblin Valley State Park." Public Information Series 65, Utah Department of Natural Resources, Division of Parks and Recreation. http://books.google.com/books?id=eyqrTpWHzrcC&pg=PA21&lpg=PA21&dq=goblin+valley+damage&source=bl&ots=3YUe3TbxHQ&sig=AyGOOJqSiaN7Id bYm9jY6OLd0lo&hl=en&sa=X&ei=2ETVUrfrAqewy QH704GwDw&ved=0CFsQ6AEwBjgU#v=onepage&q=goblin%20valley%20damage&f=false

About the Author

Dr. Danny M. Vaughn received a Ph.D. in physical geography at Indiana State University. His research has been in fluvial geomorphology, catastrophic events, and the mapping sciences. He has taught, developed curriculum, directed programs, and conducted research at the university level for nearly 35 years.

Perspective #2. Depositional Glacial Landforms: Their Origin, Use, and Misuse. Are They Worth Preserving?

Loose gravelly sediments are in great demand as construction material for roads, foundations, and as aggregate in the manufacture of concrete and similar materials. In terms of tonnage, sand and gravel is the largest single mineral resource mined from the Earth. Good construction material is hard to find in many areas. Its weight and the high volumes required make long-distance transport economically unfeasible. Among the major sources of clean gravelly sediments are glacial outwash deposits.

Glaciers covered roughly 30 percent of Earth's land area during the glacial episodes of the Quaternary Period. Today, they cover only about 10 percent.

No other erosional or depositional agent so completely transforms a landscape as glaciers. In North America, for example, most of the area north of the Ohio and Missouri Rivers is a glacial landscape, as are many of the great mountain ranges and valleys of the west and nearly all of New York and New England, all products of continental glaciers.

Glaciers entrain and transport vast amounts of earth material. Where the ice melts, this material is deposited. At the end of a glacier, sediment from the glacial conveyor belt accumulates as a low range of hummocky deposits called moraines which parallel the glacial terminus. The longer the border of the glacier remained at the same location, the more sediment would accumulate and the larger the moraine would become. Other moraines formed when the retreating ice margin stabilized at one position for a number of years. The relief (height or depth) of these features varies greatly and can exceed 100 ft (30 m). Morainal landforms consist of either till—a poorly sorted conglomeration of sediment sizes unceremoniously dumped directly by the ice, or outwash—a fairly well sorted sand-and-gravel mixture deposited by glacial meltwater.

Outwash deposits filled many low places on top of, and alongside, the ice and buried large blocks of melting ice separated from the main mass. Imagine the terrain after the ice has melted. Left behind are deltas, terraces, kames, kettle holes, crevasse fillings, and eskers. Kames and crevasse fillings are hills and ridges of outwash deposited amidst masses of melting ice blocks, usually near the terminus of a stagnating glacier. Where ice blocks were buried (or partially buried) and later melted, depressions called kettles dot the outwash. Numerous small parks and preserves have been created to protect these features, both for their scenic interest and for the lakes, bogs, and varied habitats they host.

Eskers are sinuous ridges made of sediment deposited by a stream that flowed on, within, or beneath a glacier. When the ice melts, the sediment remains as an elongated, often discontinuous, ridge of outwash marking the path of the former stream. Eskers can be difficult to pick out from the ground but are easily identified on air photos and topographic maps. They are usually found in low-lying, flat terrains. Some wind across old lake beds, swamps, and even form ridges across present-day lakes. The largest eskers may exceed 100 mi (160 km) in length and 100 ft (330 m) in height, but most are much smaller. Being composed of clean sand and gravel, they provide an excellent foundation for buildings, roads, and, in years gone by, protective fortifications. Today their major use is as an easily exploited source of sand and gravel, and many have been destroyed or diminished as a result.

Deposition also occurs beneath moving glaciers. A glacier will either erode additional rock matter or it will deposit excess sediment in order to maintain a balance between the amount of material it can hold (capacity) and the amount it actually has (load). Ground moraine, till plains, and the smooth streamlined hills called drumlins are among the landforms formed from subglacial deposits. Drumlins are elongated in the direction of ice flow with the upcurrent side typically steeper than the downcurrent side. Most drumlins range from 10 to about 150 ft (3–45 m) in height and often occur in swarms. An estimated 10,000 drumlins lie between Lake Ontario and the Finger Lakes in upstate New York. Hill Cumorah (Mormon Hill) in New York and Bunker Hill in Massachusetts are two famous drumlins.

In addition to the direct mining of landforms made of glacial outwash, widespread scarification and degradation of glacial deposition features is occurring from poor agricultural practices, especially erosion from overgrazing and poor cultivation practices. Clear-cuts and other forms of lumbering, and the roads these operations require, also create excessive gullying and soil erosion of many glacial landforms. Off-road vehicle use has scarred attractive drumlins, eskers, and other landforms in many areas. Still other landforms have been defaced by billboards, ugly buildings and other poorly planned developments. Ironically, in many parts of the world, more sand and gravel deposits are being covered over and rendered inaccessible by urban and suburban sprawl than are being mined.

Preserving all eskers, kames, and related features is not feasible. But many glacial deposits have a unique, informative, and fascinating nature and are well worth setting aside for the use and enjoyment of future generations. Glacial landforms and their associated landscapes often have great scenic, recreational, historical, even spiritual, value to millions of people. Should they be set aside and preserved? The answer would appear to be an obvious "yes." Many geomorphic features are beautiful, providing us with pleasure and inspiration. Every year millions of people spend huge amounts of money and time to visit scenic places, which are special because of the geologic features they contain. Remarkable landforms and landscapes are often the dominant reason for establishing national parks and preserves around the world. In addition to their recreational and economic value, much knowledge remains to be gained by studying unaltered landforms and terrains. Improved knowledge of the characteristics and origins of landforms can yield better management of the habitats that have evolved upon them, allow more responsible planning of future development and human settlement, and increase understanding of basic earth processes.

Bibliography

Costa, J. E. and V. R. Baker. 1981. *Surficial Geology: Building with the Earth*, 138–140, 150–151, and 471–482. New York: John Wiley & Sons.

Hunt, C. B. 1986. *Surficial Deposits of the United States*, 93–117. New York: Van Nostrand Reinhold Company.

Sullivan, Walter. 1984. *Landprints*, 243–264. New York: Times Books.

Van Diver, B. B. 1980. *Field Guide: Upstate New York*, 12–15, 119–149, 227–239. Dubuque, IO: Kendall/Hunt Publishing Co.

Wyckoff, Jerome. 1999. "The Works of Glaciers." *Reading the Earth. Landforms in the Making*. Mahwah, NJ: Adastra West, Inc.

About the Author

Dr. John A. Conners received his masters from SUNY Binghamton in 1970 and his Ph.D. in geology from the University of Idaho in 1976. He has taught over 60 different college-level courses in geology, environmental science, geography, and related fields, and has also worked as an environmental consultant. His book *Groundwater for the 21st Century* was published in late 2013.

Issue/Key Question

How have Earth's natural features evoked the "power of place" in literature and other arts?

Dilemma

In geography, place is a central theme and is defined as a location with distinctive features that give the site meaning to the people who interact with it. In this sense, place differs from mere space and is the creation of human beings who give it a name, draw boundaries around it, and often define themselves based on their sense of this place. A leader in geographic education in the United States, Dr. Robert W. Morrill of Virginia Tech, has said a "substantial and essential part of being human involves deep attachment to places. Individual and group identities are inextricably tied to the meaning of places and a sense of place. People cannot easily empty themselves of early experiences of places. The characteristics of places help shape who we are. The experience of belonging somewhere is linked to a sense of place and fulfills a fundamental human need" (Morrill 2013). The writer Barry Lopez laments that Americans have lost their sense of place, in part because "to really come to an understanding of a specific American geography, requires not only time but a kind of local expertise, an intimacy with place few of us ever develop" (Lopez 1989). What Lopez terms "local geographies" were common among people living off the land and resulted in love and respect for that place. Many writers and artists, however, still take the time to develop and express such intimacy and love and become "the voice of memory over the land." The following essays are written by artists and reveal the artist's point of view. In the first Nick Fleck looks at the outer and inner landscapes of the writer. In the second, Margot Fleck shows how two landscape painters have different and very personal visions and interpretations of the power of the same place, Mount Washington in New Hampshire.

Bibliography

Lopez, Barry. 1990. "Losing our Sense of Place." *Teacher Magazine*. http://www.edweek.org/tm/articles/1990/02/01/5geo.h01.html

Morrill, Robert W. 2013. "The Meanings of Place: Who Are You and Where Are You from?" Unpublished essay. Quoted with permission of author.

Perspective #1. Literature and Place

I. Sense of Place

> *I wish to speak a word for Nature, for absolute*
> *freedom and wildness . . . to regard man as an*
> *inhabitant, or part and parcel of Nature. . . .*
> —Thoreau, from "Walking" (1851–1854)

Lame Deer, Seeker of Visions, *Oglala*, commented that the artist is the Indian of the White Man. Geary Hobson, Cherokee, in his essay *Remembering the Earth*, notes that "continuance" is essential for American Indian Writers and that "remembering is all." N. Scott Momaday, Kiowa, writes in his essay "Man Made of Words": "None of us lives apart from the land entirely, such *isolation is unimaginable*." Paula Gunn Allen, Laguna/Sioux, starts her essay, *"Inani: It goes this way": We are the Land. . . . The Earth is the Mind of the People*. This is not an identity with but an absolute equal to. She continues: *"The Earth is, in a very real sense, the same as ourself."* The artist/writer recognizes that there is no separation, no superiority, only natural harmony, that we are a "part and parcel of Nature."

II. Outer and Inner Places

The Pasture

> I'm going out to clean the pasture spring;
> I'll only stop to rake the leaves away
> (And wait to watch the water clear, I may):
> I sha'n't be gone long.—You come too.
> I'm going out to fetch the little calf
> That's standing by the mother. It's so young,
> It totters when she licks it with her tongue.
> I sha'n't be gone long.—You come too.
> —Robert Frost (1915)

For the novelist and poet, for the artist the outer landscape is a reflection of, a door into, or a representation of the inner landscape. Robert Frost's invocation to his poetry starts *I'm going out to clean the pasture spring . . . you come too*. Once a farmer and still a poet his call is both literal and figurative. Thomas Hardy devotes a whole chapter to the heath, which becomes alive and the most powerful character in *The Return of the Native*. Sarah Orne Jewett is under the influence of the land of Firs and Spruce along the Maine Coast. From Sappho to Dickinson to Jane Kenyon writers have become as one with their landscapes so as to express their inner being with the power of the Earth, the remembrance of and harmony with the Earth.

III. Landscape Not as a Symbol

> *When I walk alone along trails hardly worn*
> *I find a rhythm in my voice full of silence borne.*

I remember hiking the first section of the Appalachian Trail in Maine; a section reputed to be one of the most difficult sections. We prepared for them, but the difficulties we encountered—getting sick from gorging ourselves on Bilberries and Blueberries, coming to where beavers obliterated the trail for miles, and finding no shelter where indicated—were not the ones we had been warned about. In intimacy change dominates the landscape.

If we go into the woods or to a floodplain or to a mountain slope or onto the river itself and pick an area to become intimate with, we will soon learn that change dominates the area, that change makes our intimacy an exciting and endless process. So the writer enters both the outer and inner landscape to become intimate with herself and with the Earth we are an integral part of, not a world apart; so it is that the volumes of poems I have written find that the outer landscape is not a symbol, but a living aspect of my inner landscape. It is the interplay of these worlds that becomes the source and expression of my poetry. For William Wordsworth, the River Wye and the lake country are a source of all that is of value in his life; for Hemingway the mountains of Spain, the shores of the great lakes, and the Sea. Man is not so much tested by his settings but has as James Dickey writes a "supple inclusion" in the landscape of his being, of his Earth. For me the voices in the Northfield (Massachusetts) woods are a melding of Nature's outer and inner worlds.

IV. A Vision of Place

> *One impulse from a vernal wood*
> *May teach you more of man,*

Of moral evil and of good
Than all the sages can.
　　　—"The Tables Turned" 1798; Wordsworth

For the remainder of this essay I have chosen *An Essay on Kentucky's Red River Gorge*; text by Wendell Berry; photographs by Gene Meatyard.

Gene Meatyard's black and white photographs lead us to a vision of not the grand landscape, but the affinity of small sites, of a waterfall, of a small pool by a rock face, of an arch of rock, of dark trees arcing over dancing light, of the lines of black trees, and the delicate trap lines of a spider web. He clearly speaks of the spirituality that captured him during his three and half years of sauntering in the Red River Gorge. He writes that his photographs reveal places "to hide or be fully exposed," of the full width and length of human experience.

Most often Wendell Berry's verse is of the landscape of his farm and the Kentucky River. In his collection *The Timbered Choir* lyric after lyric brings him together with the heritage of the land and river, a parcel that was his grandfather's farm. But in his essay, "The Unforeseen Wilderness," he faces a wilderness not of his native farm and river. Here he discovers, learns with this "new experience" that place is not mark on a "map," but a process constantly changing so much like the inner landscape of his own being. Melville wrote in *Moby Dick or The Whale*, "It is not down on any map, true places never are." Wendell Berry also discovered that in an unknown wilderness only the present exists. There is no way to anticipate the obstacles of tomorrow. ". . . a river . . . or a home is not a place but a process, not a fact but an event. . . ." Later he identifies the Upper Gorge that the Red River passes through is a "grand and austere personage." And finally I note that he came to realize that the arrogance of humans is unwarranted and is merely *hubris*, the desire to be like a god. Wendell Berry has successfully met the challenge that Robert Bly sets for readers: a book is only worthwhile if it changes a reader. Human hubris is the attitude that caused the white man to dam up a stream in Darcy McNickle's *Wind from an Enemy Sky* thus causing the Meadowlark no longer to sing and to cause the world to end.

About the Author

Richard "Nick" Fleck, Jr. taught high school English for 40 years and is now retired. He lived alone in the Maine woods for a year, is a watcher of landscape, an amateur ornithologist, and a poet.

Perspective #2. Painting Mount Washington

The essential component of art-making is love. Skill and practice and diligence are necessary to express this love but even the most cynical and angry artist who depicts society's ills demonstrates his love, his love for humanity, by raging against the suffering humankind experiences under the auspices of tyrants, hypocrites, and restrictive systems of government.

Landscape artists become enamored of natural places. They became attached to mesas, lakes, seas, mountains and deserts either as a result of their childhood environs or an affinity for a place that develops unbidden and sometimes far from their homelands.

Mt. Washington inspires many people. One can visit the summit on any summer day and see travelers from all over the world breathing the mountain air and exclaiming at the beauty of the entire Presidential Range as they snap myriad photographs with which to remember their adventure.

Painters on the other hand are not casual lovers; they demand more time to absorb the moods and feelings that a place instills in them than the ordinary amateur photographer requires. The artists add their own personality to the images of a landscape. They make sketches to acquaint themselves with all the various natural characteristics of a place. Imagine an artist drawing over and over the rocks in the felsenmeer stretching across the Presidential Range and making 50 small oil sketches each of the White-throated Sparrow and the diapensia in the krummholz. Every detail is precisely rendered to enhance the artist's appreciation of his chosen place. He may spend weeks, months, or even years visiting the place he is learning to love before he attains the power and knowledge to express the complexity and depth of his affection.

John Frederick Kensett (1816–1872) was among the second generation of the American Hudson River School of painters who accentuated the grandeur of the new terrains discovered with westward expansion. In 1851, after studying in Germany and traveling extensively in the western United States, he presented the world with what has become the archetypal image of Mt. Washington, Mt. Washington from the Valley of Conway. Viewing this work one can see the stance the artist has toward this peak and the relative position of human beings and their activities within the natural world that the mountain dominates. Our eyes gravitate immediately to the great white massif. Snow covers the mountains and fills the ravines with a sparkling whiteness that is a sharp contrast to the lush but subdued greens of the valley and pale blue sky.

Kensett conjures a vision of the Conway valley as part of Eden itself; there is an innocence and virginity to the valley that he makes radiant with celestial light. The mountain king—cold, distant, unreachable—is both majestic and life-giving. Winter snows replenish the river that becomes the source of life for all the flora and fauna which thrive below.

Kensett was not immune to the ethos of his times. Few artists are. Transcendentalism had seeped into the consciousness of the educated and the philosophically minded folk of the early 19th century. An individually honed relationship with God, rather than one dictated by Christian orthodoxy was regarded as an ideal approach to a spiritual life. The separation of the divine and the human was obliterated through the contemplation of and reverence for the natural landscape. Though a widely circulated engraving of this painting helped to popularize the White Mountains as a tourist attraction, the initial passion is lost as it is in any copy. Copies, like most of the amateur snapshots of today, can inspire further investigation of a scene but the loss of the artist's choice of colors and evidence of the artist's moving hand always translates his feelings far less powerfully than the original does.

One of the best known landscapes artists is Albert Bierstadt (1830–1902). Born in Germany, Bierstadt painted innumerable scenes as he traveled throughout his adopted country and was particularly drawn to the spectacular scenery of the American West. His works epitomize the Romantic view of nature as he is a master in the use of scale and perspective to express the sublimity of the natural world in comparison to the human one. His western mountains are so monumental, the light on his lakes so mystical, that the viewer may question the probability of such phenomena existing.

Bierstadt painted Autumn in the Conway Meadows looking toward Mt. Washington, New Hampshire, in 1858. Again a personal vision of the primal Eden is presented. The colors are muted. Rich browns and wine hues predominate. There is a dirt pathway winding toward the tiny houses on the edge of the meadow. A herd of deer wander peacefully in the fields. Each tree, each fern, the burnished bush, and each late fall flower is exquisitely painted. The decaying stump has red highlights reflecting the light from an autumnal sun; and the granite outcroppings too are graced by the receding glow. One feels invited to wander in the quietude beneath Washington's presence.

An ethic is implicit in many of the landscapes of the nineteenth century. Human beings and their ambitions do not dominate nature. Progress may have obliterated that notion in the minds of many but, nonetheless, the truth of our insignificance remains. May the work of earlier painters, who through their skill and personal passion for the land gave embodiment to a philosophy of interdependence, influence our perspective on our own relationship to the natural features of our planet.

About the Author

Margot Fleck graduated from Middlebury College with a B.S. in biology. A retired reference librarian living in western Massachusetts, she is a portrait artist, printmaker, collagist, and poet. The best times of her childhood were spent at a summer camp close to the Conway, New Hampshire, valley.

Issue/Key Question

Can damage to natural landscapes in time of war be minimized? Who is responsible for rehabilitation or recompense, the victor or the vanquished, at the close of the war?

Dilemma: Opening

Wars destroy not only lives but landscapes. As civilization evolved, so did the development of weaponry and technology used in warfare. Increasingly more powerful weapons cause more intensive and wide-ranging environmental damage, both from the unintended consequences of battles and from deliberate destruction to weaken the enemy's ability to wage war. Europe suffered extensive damage during World War II, and Plitvice Lakes National Park (Croatia) was damaged in the Balkans War. Civil wars have ravaged parks and natural habitats in Africa, including the Somalia Afar Triangle and the Danakil Depression, the Limpopo River, and the Sahara. Vietnam's forests were devastated by Agent Orange, bombs, and fires. Environmental destruction, however, is not limited to the battlefields. Resources required to wage war also cause damage. The German and Russian armies poached wildlife from nature preserves in the Carpathian Mountains, and irreplaceable old-growth forests were cut for firewood. Pacific atolls, including Amchitka (Aleutian Islands), Enewetok and Bikini (Marshal Islands), and Tuamoto (French Polynesia), were used for nuclear weapons testing. Abandoned military installations with rusting equipment, leaking oil drums, etc. remain on Attus and Kiska (Aleutians) and on Novaya Zemlya.

In the first perspective, Dr. Joseph Hupy, associate professor of geography, contends that it is counterproductive to implement rules of warfare that would limit or deny access to resources necessary to overpower the enemy and win. Environmental damage is an unavoidable consequence. Using Vietnam as an example, however, he states that the strategy of deliberate destruction of forests and rice paddies to weaken the enemy backfires because it turns the civilian population against the aggressor who is destroying their homes and livelihood.

In the second perspective, Dr. Richard Tucker, adjunct professor in natural resources and environment, takes the viewpoint that rules of modern warfare, such as the prohibition of chemical or nuclear weapons, have existed for hundreds of years. Commanders are required to minimize damage to citizens and property, including the natural environment. International laws for reconstruction after the war has ended have evolved throughout history, currently spearheaded by various national and international organizations. Both authors, however, agree on the difficulty or impossibility of determining blame and assigning the task of reconstruction.

Perspective #1. The Inevitable Environmental Consequences of Modern Warfare

All is fair in love and war. A clichéd expression, yes, but here the expression fits because warfare is an ugly affair, and the weapons involved are meant to destroy. Attempts to minimize environmental damage via rules and restrictions, along with efforts to place blame on belligerent forces is a difficult proposition at best due to the highly variable nature of warfare, both temporally and geographically. How and what weapons of war destroy in the course of battle depends on the nature of the conflict itself, the technology implemented, and the level of warfare the belligerents involved choose to engage. To elaborate, when two or more armed factions go to war with one another, the overall goal is to prevail over the other through overwhelming force. This force, implemented via the weapons of war, can have both intentional and unintentional impacts placed upon the surrounding environment (Westing 1990). Most environmental damage, with several notable exceptions, is unintentional and is merely the aftermath of warfare. To hold a nation-state, army, or armed faction responsible for the environmental damages associated with battle, or to place rules that limit environmental damage, is arguably an unwise waste of diplomatic resources. This essay places forward an argument that environmental damage in warfare is inevitable, and the nature of the fighting, and the belligerents involved, will ultimately determine the magnitude of environmental disturbance. Furthermore, placing blame or rules on these disturbances will only exasperate future conflict issues between previous warring factions.

Examination of warfare through the historical lens demonstrates how warfare weaponry has undergone a progressive series of technological innovations to date, with the ultimate goal of developing weapons that are ever more efficient at inflicting harm upon the opposing force, and the environment for that matter (Hammes 2004; Lind et al. 1989). This evolution of military weaponry has resulted in the historical sense as a cat and mouse game between armies, with advancements in offensive technologies results in defensive technologies advancements. Moreover, armies change their overall philosophy, or thinking, in the ways battles are fought. For example, rifled barrels and long range artillery resulted in larger battlefields; motorized transport in larger military campaigns; and aircraft in being able inflict damage well beyond the scope of the battlefield (Hupy 2008). All of these technologies change battlefield tactics and overall strategic goals. Here we will focus on the history and evolution of the strategic goals in warfare as it relates to the argument why the nature of modern warfare in itself will place its own limits on environmental damage, and how those responsible for the damages would be held accountable by default.

Warfare is, at times, summarized as an extension of politics (Van Crevald 1991). That is, when other means of resolving an issue fail, warfare often results as the lowest common denominator. Historically, this generally meant that when opposing nation states had a problem they could not resolve, each would send out armies to represent that state. When the army fell, the government of that state either negotiated peace terms, or at times was toppled by the opposing nation state army. Inflicting environmental damage upon the civilian population of the opposing nation state made no strategic sense and, with some notable exceptions, this did not occur, nor was the technology in place to render such disturbances. With the rise of the industrialized nation-state, however, came about a change in warfare, not only with what the technology of the industrialized age did to modern warfare, but also the notion that the industrialized nation contained a civilian population that supplied the military with resources and weaponry. Crippling the ability of that nation-state to produce would weaken the enemy abilities to wage war. This line of thinking first came into true prominence in the American Civil War, was practiced in earnest during World War II, and perhaps peaked in the Vietnam conflict.

Yet it was in the Vietnam conflict where this line of thinking came back to haunt the United States and their strategic goals. As stated before, warfare evolves not just technologically, but also in its ideas in response to that technology. In Vietnam, the North Vietnamese Army (NVA) and the Viet Cong (VC) insurgents knew they were up against a force that was superior to them both in a financial and technological sense. Simply put, they knew they could not defeat the U.S. military on the battlefield, so instead they set out to defeat the military by weakening support for the South Vietnamese government, along with domestic support for the U.S. war effort. The U.S. strategy, on the other hand, was in wars of the past where they were fighting an army representing a nation-state. They didn't understand that every village burned, every rice field destroyed, every forest defoliated, meant that much less support for the South Vietnamese government, and for the U.S. military presence in Vietnam. Many lessons were learned from the Vietnam conflict, with one of the most important ones being that in modern warfare, the armies you are fighting against may not represent the nation-state, and inflicting environmental damage with the sheer magnitude of modern weapons technology may not be of the best overall strategic interests, as you fail to win "the hearts and minds" of the population.

From an environmental perspective, the reader may easily imagine how the footprint of battle has changed with time; when comparing the Peloponnesian wars, to the American Civil War, to World War I, to the Vietnam conflict, the environment suffered accordingly. Yet where to establish the boundaries between disturbance from war, and economic land use is not so easy to establish. Beyond the footprint of battle, wars are very resource intensive and the swath of environmental disturbance implemented to support a war effort, in many ways, has left more of a legacy on the modern landscape than the scars of battle themselves (Hupy and Koehler 2012). Trying to point a finger at who is to blame for environmental destruction, whether it be deliberate, incidental, direct, or indirect, is a very difficult undertaking. Perhaps instead of trying to lay out the rules of conflict when politics and diplomacy fail, we should try to figure out better ways of resolving issues before the shooting starts.

Bibliography

Hammes, T. 2004. *The Sling and the Stone: On War in the 21st Century.* St. Paul: Zenith Press.

Hupy, J. P. 2008. The Environmental Footprint of War. *Environment and History* 14: 405–421.

Hupy, J. P. and T. Koehler 2012. Modern Warfare as a Significant Form of Zoogeomorphic Disturbance upon the Landscape. *Geomorphology* 157: 169–182.

Lind, W., K. Nightengale, J. Schmitt, and G. I. Wilson. 1989. The Changing Face of War: Into the Fourth Generation. *Marine Corps Gazette* 22–26.

Van Crevald, M. 1991. *The Transformation of War.* New York: The Free Press.

Westing, A. H. 1990. "Environmental Hazards of War in an Industrializing World." In *Environmental Hazards of War: Releasing Dangerous Forces in an Industrialized World*, edited by A. H. Westing, 96. London: SAGE Publications.

About the Author

Joseph Hupy is an associate professor in the Department of Geography at the University of Wisconsin—Eau Claire. His primary research interests involve examining how landscapes recover and evolve following disturbances from battle, primarily those disturbances caused by explosive munitions. In his previous research, Joe used soils as means to examine how landscapes recover and evolve, but due to the dangers of working on the ground, Joe has since turned to using unmanned aircraft to engage in high resolution remote sensing. This line of research has led to working with the military on management of training facilities.

Perspective #2. Reasons for Postwar Cleanup: Law, Ethics, and Strategy

The challenge to minimize long-term environmental damage from mass conflict has two major dimensions: first, to control the immediate impact of warfare, and second, to maximize reconstruction in the aftermath of conflict. The first task has a thousand-year history in the Just War principles. It has a strong parallel in Islamic thought (Kelsay 2007). Just War principles define when it is justified to go to war—primarily in self-defense against an aggressor—and what is justifiable conduct once the fighting is on (Plant 1992).

During fighting, the doctrine of *proportionality* holds military commanders responsible for limiting damage to what is absolutely necessary for achieving reasonable strategic goals. Specifically it emphasizes minimizing damage to civilians and property. The legal definition of "property" has within it the possibility of expanding to a broad understanding of the environmental settings of communities in conflict, but this has developed only in the late twentieth century. Since the Vietnam War, lawyers, ethicists, and ecologists have been expanding the legal definition of property to encompass environment, even ecosystems (Westing 1985; Russell 2005).

Over the centuries, the Just War debate has also included a discussion on prohibiting the use of particularly brutal weapons. This became very important by the 19th century, as warfare became more industrialized and weapons rapidly accelerated in their destructive capacity. After World War I international treaties made the first efforts to ban chemical weapons and landmines (Cameron 1998). After 1945 these efforts also included banning the use of nuclear weapons, and by the 1990s when depleted uranium (DU) weapons were first used, international lawyers added DU to the list as well.

Another dimension of the ethics of war is often overlooked: the postwar ethics of responsibility for reconstruction (May 2012). The international law of war's aftermath includes the principles that combat governments must work for a just and stable international order, and this requires reconciliation between wartime enemies. After World War I international lawyers debated whether the victorious Allies were justified in demanding heavy *reparations* from the losers, primarily Germany. The alternative principle is *reconstruction*. After World War II the Marshall Plan provided massive reconstruction resources from the United States to the ravaged lands and cities of Western and Central Europe, and the newborn United Nations undertook large-scale refugee relief and relocation.

During the Cold War era (1948–1991) local and regional wars continued to cause severe damage to both natural and human-managed environments (Bankoff 2010). Whose responsibility it was to restore these environments remained exceedingly difficult to establish, even in principle. It was challenging even to determine what the damage was. In the aftermath of the Cold War, the United Nations Environmental Program set up a Post-Conflict Environmental Assessment Project. This program has done outstanding work determining environmental damage in countries that have been convulsed in war, including Iraq and Afghanistan (UNEP 2003).

National governments, international agencies, and nongovernmental organizations (NGOs) have taken increasingly costly initiatives to heal the environmental wounds of war. NATO troops have joined aid organizations in the lengthy task of removing landmines in Afghanistan and elsewhere. The UN, governmental aid agencies and NGOs have helped restore the marshes of southern Iraq, which had been reduced by 90 percent in the 1990s. Also in Iraq agricultural lands have been restored to productivity with help from the U.S. Agency for International Development (USAID) and its counterparts in European countries. In addition, wildlife habitat in several countries has been at least partially restored by the International Union for Conservation of Nature (IUCN), the Wildlife Conservation Society in New York, and other wildlife agencies (McNeely 2000).

Finally, in the post–Cold War years the central functions of military establishments have been evolving, from long traditions of almost exclusive emphasis on fighting, to more complex roles in immediate relief efforts. Counterinsurgency campaigns, at least as far back as the Malayan "Emergency" of the 1950s and the Vietnam War, have emphasized the warrior's task of working with local communities to convince them not to support insurgents (Beckett 2001; Porch 2013). This necessitates protecting the farmlands and natural resource base of local populations. This work is associated with "greening the military," major improvements in environmental management of its bases and installations, a task that centers mostly on peacetime operations (Durant 2007; Mosher 2008).

Bibliography

Beckett, I. F. W. 2001. *Modern Insurgencies and Counter-Insurgencies*. London: Routledge.

Cameron, M., R. Lawson, and B. Tomlin, eds. 1998. *To Walk without Fear: The Global Movement to Ban Landmines*. Oxford: Oxford University Press.

Durant, R. F. 2007. *The Greening of the U.S. Military*. Washington, D.C.: Georgetown University Press.

Kelsay, J. 2007. *Arguing the Just War in Islam*. Cambridge, MA: Harvard University Press.

May, L. 2012. *After War Ends: A Philosophical Perspective*. Cambridge: Cambridge University Press.

McNeely, J. A. 2000. "War and Biodiversity: An Assessment of Impacts." In *The Environmental Consequences of War*, edited by J. E. Austin and C. E. Brook. Cambridge: Cambridge University Press.

Mosher, D. E., Beth E. Lachman, Michael D. Greenberg, Tiffany Nichols, Brian Rosen, Henry H. Willis. 2008. *Green Warriors*. Santa Monica: Rand Corporation.

Plant, G. 1992. *Environmental Protection and the Law of War*. London: Belhaven Press.

Porch, D. 2013. *Counterinsurgency*. Cambridge: Cambridge University Press.

Russell, E. 2005. "Nicking the Thin Edge of the Wedge: What History Suggests about the Environmental Law of War." *Virginia Environmental Law Journal* 24(3): 377–388.

UNEP. 2003. *Afghanistan: Post-Conflict Environmental Assessment*. Geneva: UNEP.

Westing, A. 1985. *Explosive Remnants of War: Mitigating the Environmental Effects*. London and Philadelphia: Taylor and Francis.

About the Author

Richard Tucker is adjunct professor in the School of Natural Resources and Environment, University of Michigan. His recent research and publications center on the world history of environmental consequences of wars and military operations. He is coeditor of *Natural Enemy, Natural Ally: Toward an Environmental History of War* (Oregon State University Press, 2004).

Issue/Key Question

How should Canada, the United States, and Russia deal with or prepare for increasing accessibility of the Northwest Passage? How can the marine environment best be protected?

Dilemma/Opening

The greatest threat to Arctic ecosystems is global warming and the consequent loss of sea-ice. While ice-locked, the Arctic Ocean has been little contested by adjacent nations, but without the ice the geopolitical scene will change dramatically. Already countries are jockeying for control of Arctic resources. Until 2009, sea-ice prevented the use of the Northwest Passage by ships other than ice-breakers, but now regular summer-time shipping between the Atlantic and Pacific oceans via several alternative routes through and south of the Canadian Arctic Archipelago may be a reality within 25 years.

Protection of fragile polar ecosystems and resolving conflicting claims of marine resources will become major issues. The two essays that follow look at ways of mitigating potential impacts in the Northwest Passage. Ms. Piner and Dr. Jacques focus on biological resources and the requirements of large marine ecosystem (LME) management in the Arctic Ocean. Dr. Foy draws attention to the infrastructural needs that, once implemented, will help protect the Arctic environment.

Perspective #1. Ecological Protection Is Key

The recent and rapid decline of sea ice in the Arctic has exposed long sought after maritime passageways connecting the Pacific Ocean to the Atlantic. For centuries explorers and traders have attempted navigating through this harsh Arctic environment in search of the Northwest Passage, a resource-rich shortcut connecting two world oceans. The extreme conditions of this region have contributed to the absence of heavy commercial activity and have been a prime factor in the ecological protection of the Arctic's marine ecosystems (King 2009). As climate conditions continue to change, issues involving (1) untouched oil and natural gas reserves, (2) fish stocks, and (3) territorial arrangements pressure overseeing political powers to engage in cooperative behavior to prevent militaristic and environmental conflict. Ecological protection of the Northwest Passage is essential to the global pursuits of sustainability and security and can influence diverse management policies implemented by regional and international stakeholders.

Management of LME consists of monitoring ocean space, river basins, and estuaries, to the outer margins of continental shelves and seaward (Gable 2004). The U.S. Department of Defense claims to

face multiple limitations in regards to navigating through the Arctic environment. A lack of technology for accurate ice and weather reporting and forecasting, communications, computers and intelligence, surveillance, and reconnaissance (C4ISR), as well as an insufficient fleet of ships and icebreakers, hinders the capabilities of the United States in exploring the Arctic territory in a responsible and prepared manner (US DoD 2011). Russia has invested heavily in designing and manufacturing the world's largest fleet of vessels, such as icebreakers for operations in the Arctic. Russia's technologic advancements for navigating through torrential, cold environments position it at an advantage to influence how countries build their military and industrial complexes in the Arctic and especially in the Northwest Passage (Kefferpütz 2010). However, an increase in marine vessels traveling through the Northwest Passage will have significant effects on aquatic and terrestrial life living in and migrating through this waterway.

Scientists, policymakers, and other stakeholders have given considerable attention to the effects of human induced noise on aquatic and terrestrial life in the ocean. Military sonar, energy development, and offshore construction have proven to have devastating effects on marine mammals causing auditory injuries and mass strandings (Ellison 2012). Increased anthropogenic underwater noise can alter the breeding, mating, and feeding behaviors of animals such as polar bears, narwhals, beluga whales, sea otters, and various seals and whales. Casualties of beaked whales and blue whales are documented and are most commonly associated with sonar activity (Cox 2006). The development of strategic action plans that aim to protect Arctic biodiversity and limit industrial activity will significantly reduce risks associated with increased human activity. Comprehensive guidelines for operating in the Arctic environment will ensure that Canada, the United States, and Russia approach this resource rich region with adequate and enforceable regulations.

A commercially accessible Northwest Passage could alleviate congestion in the Suez and Panama canals, as well as in the Strait of Malacca. However, environmental disasters such as oil spills and shipwrecks that occur in colder water and terrain are often more difficult to prepare for and control due to navigational hazards, severe weather, and technologic response restraints. The rate of oil decomposition in cold waters is much lower than in more temperate waters increasing the risk of wide-ranging and long-lasting effects. Species at home in the Northwest Passage that would be especially impacted by such an event include seabirds, harp seals, arctic foxes, and various types of whales. Twenty-seven Inuit tribes reside along the coast of the Northwest Passage and rely heavily on healthy marine resources for food and income (King 2009). Local communities of this region will become more vulnerable to instances of fishery collapse, oil spills, water contamination, and habitat loss as industrial interests exploit easier access to the Arctic.

The United States, Canada, and Russia can prepare for the increasing accessibility of the Northwest Passage by participating in cooperative and responsible behavior. Using scientific and local knowledge as models for policy decisions and conservation planning will promote the protection and sustainability of living marine resources of the Northwest Passage as well as the Arctic's marine environments. Arctic powers and international policymakers can incorporate the unique conditions of the Arctic as a means to improve conventional laws and regulations for shipping, resource exploration, and militaristic activities. Industrial influences impact the ecological dynamics of fragile marine ecosystems and interfere with conservation initiatives. Canada, Russia, and the United States can enhance their ecological approach in the Northwest Passage. Limits on industrial activity, enforcement of strict regulations on sonar usage, and identification of permanent key conservation zones for the migration, breeding, and feeding of Arctic species are a few of the ways international and regional stakeholders can ensure ecological protection of the Northwest Passage. It is vital that matters surrounding the Arctic are approached with seriousness and environmental preparedness as to prevent outcomes of local, regional, and global economic and environmental devastation.

Bibliography

Cox, T. M., T. J. Ragen, A.J. Read, E. Vos, R.W. Baird, K. Balcomb, . . . L. Benner. 2006. "Understanding the Impacts of Anthropogenic Sound on Beaked Whales." *Journal of Cetacean Resource Management* 7(3): 177–187.

Ellison, W. T. 2012. "A New Context-based Approach to Assess Marine Mammal Behavioral Responses to Anthropogenic Sounds." *Conservation Biology*. 26(1): 21–28.

Gable, Frank. 2004. "A Large Marine Ecosystem Approach to Fisheries Management and Sustainability: Linkages and Concepts towards Best Practices." Rhode Island: The Coastal Institute.

Kefferpütz, Roderick. 2010. "On Thin Ice? (Mis)interpreting Russian Policy in the High North." Center for European Policy Studies, CEPS Policy Brief, Thinking Ahead for Europe.

King, Hannah. 2009. "Protecting the Northwest Passage: Assessing the Threat of Year-round Shipping to the Marine Ecosystem and the Adequacy of the Current Environmental Regulatory Regimes." *Ocean and Coastal Law Journal* 14(2): 270.

U.S. Department of Defense. 2011. *Report to Congress on Arctic Operations and the Northwest Passage.*

About the Authors

Chelsea Piner is an environmental scientist, independent researcher, and aspiring archivist. She is a senior member of the University of Central Florida Political Ecology Lab and has participated in the UCF Showcase of Undergraduate Research Excellence (SURE). Ms. Piner's research has been focused primarily on habitat loss, environmental policy, keystone species, and social causes of environmental change.

Dr. Peter J. Jacques is associate professor of political science at the University of Central Florida, where he teaches global environmental politics and sustainability and directs the student research group, The Political Ecology Lab@UCF. He is managing executive editor for the flagship journal of the Association of Environmental Studies and Sciences (AESS), the *Journal of Environmental Studies and Sciences*. Dr. Jacques holds a B.A. from Montana State University and M.P.A. and Ph.D. degrees from Northern Arizona University.

Perspective #2. Investing in Maritime Infrastructure to Protect the Environment in the Northwest Passage

Changes in global climatic patterns have warmed the North America Arctic region, melting the polar ice cap, and subsequently increasing maritime traffic through the Northwest Passage. This geographic phenomenon raises global concern about international shipping and natural resources extraction in the Northwest Passage because limited infrastructure puts Northern Canada's biologically rich and productive archipelagic waters in danger. There are inadequate navigational charts and positioning equipment, poor search and rescue capabilities, and limited ports for ailing ships to seek refuge and repair, meaning a disaster is only one poor decision away (Deggim 2010; Conway 2013). Given these hazards, and that many experts believe the Northwest Passage trade routes will become more viable as polar ice melts and sea levels rise, environmental protection of that area is a major issue. Prohibiting maritime traffic and commercial activity in the passage is an unlikely environmental solution because there are economic benefits to using the passage. One potential opportunity for reducing the risk of environmental disasters is Canadian and U.S. investment in infrastructure to support shipping and maritime commerce in the Northwest Passage, similar to what Russia has done along the Northern Sea Route.

Historically, the passage was not a viable commercial trading route because of its geographic isolation, shallow waterways, and ice blockades. The lack of commercial activity in the region meant protection of the ecosystem was a nonissue. However, in 2007 the European Space Agency announced that a direct ice-free shipping route from Europe to Asia across the Arctic Ocean was discovered using satellite imagery. Then, in September 2013, the *Nordic Orion* became the first large commercial freighter to use the Northwest Passage as a trade route (Neuman 2013). Other smaller commercial ships, research vessels and cruise liners have also made the voyage, but maritime traffic has remained relatively small. However, the International Maritime Organization claims that trends and forecasts indicate polar shipping will grow in volume and diversify in nature over the coming years, making it critical to enhance infrastructure that supports safety, environmental protection, and commercial efficiency (IMO 2014).

One infrastructure deficiency is in map resources, as the Arctic is a frontier for weather forecasting, charting and navigation systems. Uncertainty and unreliability of navigation in that region makes shipping and other maritime activities risky. The National Oceanic Service (2014), states that current charting data in a significant portion of the Arctic is inadequate or nonexistent. For example, much of the Bering Sea area is only partially surveyed. Therefore, maps are unreliable, especially near shore where there are unpredictable and unknown wind and tidal patterns that could cause a ship to run aground. It is estimated that only 10 percent of the Arctic is mapped to meet modern standards (Spears and Dorey 2012). Further navigation concerns exist due to limited racon units, which are radar transponders used to mark maritime navigational hazards. Global positioning system (GPS) is also less reliable in polar regions because of limited geodetic infrastructure for accurate positioning and elevations (NOAA 2013). All of these factors lead to significant limitations when navigating in the Northwest Passage. A good geospatial foundation is needed to support sustainable shipping and commerce in the Arctic.

Another infrastructure-based risk is Canada lacking ports along the Northwest Passage for vessels to seek refuge in the event of mechanical problems or severe weather. In contrast, Russia has 16 deepwater ports along its Arctic coastline. It is widely reported that Canada needs to improve its port infrastructure to support a maritime industry along the Northwest Passage. In 2007, Prime Minister Stephen Harper announced that Canada would develop a new deepwater port at Nanisivik, on Baffin Island, but progress has been slow because of the high cost of building in the North. The only refuge options for disabled ships or a vessel trying to avoid a storm are to hide behind the many islands of the archipelago or to utilize smaller ports near mining sites. In the event of a disaster, the inadequate port infrastructure will complicate rescue, delay repairs, and impede environmental remediation, ultimately making the disaster more severe.

Search and rescue (SAR) experts understand the potential for disaster in the Northwest Passages' unforgiving environment, and the complications of a few distant ports and insufficient maps. Ultimately, it takes aircraft and rescue vessels a longer time to provide aid in the Arctic. Longer response times equate to greater causalities and damage to the environment. The Arctic is not a place where time is on your side. Despite the importance of SAR in the Arctic, it is hard to improve the situation unless the underlying maritime infrastructure issues are resolved.

One effort to improve infrastructure and many other aspects of polar shipping and commerce is the Polar Code, a mandatory international agreement designed to cover the full range of shipping-related matters relevant to navigation in waters surrounding the poles, including the protection of the environment and ecosystems of the polar regions (IMO 2014). There is also the Arctic Council (United States, Canada, Russia, Finland, Norway, Denmark, Iceland, and Sweden), a group that in 2011 signed the Nuuk Agreement, in an effort to coordinate and share the responsibilities of Arctic SAR (Conway 2013). These recent developments show promise because the nations with territory in the Northwest Passage and the Arctic are acknowledging that infrastructure demands on the Arctic are different than in other parts of the world.

It is not a matter of if, but when a disaster will threaten the environment of the Northwest Passage. The only way to protect the marine environment is to be as best prepared for that disaster as possible. This will require major changes in how shipping and maritime activities are conducted in polar regions, but first a major investment in maritime infrastructure is needed to support those industries, protect people and the environment. Canada, Russia, and the United States, as the majority territories, need to be the drivers of this effort. Even with improved infrastructure the uncertainty of global warming makes the fate of the Arctic ecosystem unknown and a pressing matter.

Bibliography

Conway, John. 2013. "Search and Rescue in the High North: An Air Force Mission?" *Air & Space Journal*: 4–24, http://www.airpower.maxwell.af.mil/digital/pdf/articles/2013-Nov-Dec/F-Conway.pdf

Deggim, Heike. 2010. *Ensuring Safe, Secure and Reliable Shipping in the Arctic Ocean*. NATO Advanced Research Workshop on Environmental Security in the Arctic Ocean, Scott Polar Research Institute, Cambridge.

European Space Agency. 2007. "Satellites Witness Lowest Arctic Ice Coverage in History." http://www.esa.int/Our_Activities/Observing_the_Earth/Envisat/Satellites_witness_lowest_Arctic_ice_coverage_in_history

International Maritime Organization. 2014. "Shipping in Polar Waters: Development of an international code of safety for ships operating in polar waters (Polar Code)." http://www.imo.org/mediacentre/hottopics/polar/Pages/default.aspx.

National Oceanic and Atmospheric Administration. 2013. *Arctic Nautical Charting Plan: A Plan to Support Sustainable Marine Transportation in Alaska and the Arctic*. Report, Office of Coast Survey Marine Chart Division.

National Oceanic Service. 2014. "Arctic Navigation." http://oceanservice.noaa.gov/economy/arctic/

Neuman, Scott. 2013. "Freighter Makes First-Of-Its-Kind Transit of Northwest Passage." National Public Radio. http://www.npr.org/blogs/thetwo-way/2013/09/27/226856198/freighter-makes-first-of-its-kind-transit-of-northwest-passage

Spears, J. and M. Dorey. 2012. "Arctic Cruise Ships: The Pressing Need for Search and Rescue." *Canadian Sailings*, October 17, 2012. http://www.canadiansailings.ca/?p=4830

About the Author

Dr. Andrew Foy is assistant professor of geospatial science at Radford University. His scientific work focuses on uncertainty in mapping and geographic information systems (GIS), as it relates to biogeography, the mapping of vegetation boundaries, and landscape change.

Appendix 3

Activities and Discussion Questions

The following investigations and activities are suited for individual student pursuit, but you might learn more and have more fun if you try them with a small group of classmates, friends, or family members. Each was designed with the goal of the National Geography Standards[1] in mind: that the geographically informed person is engaged in active inquiry that involves asking geographic questions, acquiring geographic information, and organizing that information in meaningful ways using maps and other graphics as well as the written word.

1. Analyze Volcanos as Natural Hazards

Which 10 volcanos have produced the deadliest volcanic eruptions? What aspect of the eruption actually killed people in each? Look at an atlas or Google Earth and see where these volcanos are located. Determine their geographic coordinates and plot them on an outline map of the world. What factors of physical geography explain the locations of these eruptions? Are any factors common to all or most?

A good source for this information is Volcano World (http://volcano.oregonstate.edu/deadliest-eruption).

Compare these volcanoes with the largest volcanic eruptions known in terms of types of eruptions and location. (A list can be found at http://www.volcano-live.com/large.html). Are these supervolcanos among the most deadly? Why or why not? To what degree does the spatial pattern of these supervolcanos resemble the pattern of deadly volcanoes on your map?

Look at the 16 so-called Decade Volcanos, those designated by the International Association of Volcanology and Chemistry of the Earth's Interior to currently be most hazardous to nearby communities. You can find a list at http://scienceblogs.com/eruptions/2009/04/06/the-decade-volcanoes/. Several of these are described in entries in this encyclopedia. What can be done to prevent great loss of life? Recent volcanic activity is updated on the Smithsonian Institution's Global Volcanism Program (http://www.volcano.si.edu/). Are any erupting today?

If you do not live near an active volcano, do other natural hazards occur that could threaten your community? How has your community prepared for these?

2. Consider Rivers and Their Direction of Flow

People often think it strange for a river to flow northward. Look at a map that shows the world's ten longest rivers. (These are listed in Appendix 1.) In what direction does each flow? Do any flow toward the north for part or all of its course? Check a map of your home state. What rivers, if any, flow northward? Why might people think it highly unusual for rivers to flow northward? What does determine the direction water flows?

3. Analyze Global Climate Change

Models predict long-term trends of continuing warming of global temperatures and major consequences on a global scale. Many of the features described in this encyclopedia will be affected, and global climate

---

1. Geography Education National Implementation Project (GENIP). 2012. *Geography for Life: National Geography Standards*, 2nd ed. Washington, D.C.: National Council for Geographic Education (NCGE).

change is often listed as an environmental issue. What are some of the expected, indeed ongoing, impacts of global climate change? What kind of evidence shows that changes on land and in the sea are already happening? What evidence suggests these changes are part of natural cycles rather than real change? How might predicted changes affect you and your community?

4. Investigate the Consequences of Shrinking Polar Ice and a New World Perspective in Arctic Countries

The increasing loss of sea-ice in the Arctic Ocean will open sea lanes for longer periods of time, create or enhance new chokepoints, and may lead to conflicts regarding territorial claims and resource use. The long sought Northwest Passage through the Canadian Arctic Archipelago and along the northern coast of Canada and Alaska will be a reality. Russians are increasing traffic and patrolling the Northern Sea Route from the Barents Sea north of Scandinavia along the Arctic coast of Russia to the Bering Strait. Obtain a polar projection of the Arctic Ocean, and map the current limits of sea ice. Add the Northwest Passage and the Northern Sea Route. Identify major chokepoints and potential sites of conflict. Consider territorial claims under the Law of the Convention of Sea. How might the geopolitical orientation of Canada and the United States change if they must defend open sea lanes and mineral resources on the Arctic sea floor? Two essays in Appendix 2 address issues related to the Northwest Passage. Try to expand upon these and display the results of your analysis on one or more maps.

An animated map of sea ice reduction and possible Arctic sea routes can be found at "Northern Exposure." The Economist online. http://www.economist.com/blogs/dailychart/2011/09/melting-arctic-sea-ice-and-shipping-routes.

Also, look at the map of Arctic sea routes at http://people.hofstra.edu/geotrans/eng/ch1en/conc1en/polarroutes.html. (Note that copying or distributing this map is a violation of copyright law, so just look.)

For a map of territorial claims in the Arctic, see page 36 of Van Pay, Brian. 2009. "National Maritime Claims in the Arctic, Changes in the Arctic Environment and the Law of the Seas, http://www.virginia.edu/colp/pdf/Van_Pay-Arctic-Claims.pdf.

5. Get to Know One Natural Place Very Well

Grab a notebook and choose a spot in a nearby natural area, perhaps the woods, along a river, or out in the desert where you will not be disturbed. Sit quietly for 20 minutes or so just observing nature as closely as you can. Note everything you see, hear, and smell in the area immediately surrounding you. Examine closely the ground, the surfaces of living and dead plants, and the space above you as well as the more obvious features of landscape such as landforms, rocks, plants, fungi, birds, and mammals. Identify what you can. Provide numbers and brief descriptions for each different object that you cannot identify and try to find out what they are later. Take a photo as a record of what you've discovered if you have access to a camera. How many different species did you find? Repeat the exercise several times, perhaps at different times of year. What new species can you add to your list? What changes have occurred in the landscape?

A great example of this way of learning the land can be found in *The Forest Unseen: A Year's Watch in Nature* (2012) by David George Haskell, wherein the author, a biologist, contemplates life in one square meter of ground in a Tennessee wood.

6. Make a Map of a Place Important to You

In geography, place is a central theme and is defined as locations with distinctive features that give them meaning and character to the people who interact with them. In this sense, places are creations of human beings who give them names, draw boundaries around them, and often define themselves based on their sense of this place. Is there a natural place that has much meaning for you? How do you feel when you are there? Does it help you know who you are and where you are from?

Hand draw a map of this place and its setting. You might include how you get there, other places it is close to or related to, and spots that you consider secret or private. Although your map is a sketch and will not be accurate in terms of distance and size, do indicate an approximate scale and show direction. Label important features. If you use symbols to show specific features, be sure to include a key. Write a brief account of this place and its meaning to you.

7. Write Your Own Encyclopedia Entry

Write an entry about an interesting natural feature near your home or someplace you have visited, perhaps during a winter or summer vacation, using the entries in this encyclopedia as a model. Determine the geographic coordinates. Write a description. Do some research and try to explain why this feature is located where it is.

8. Time Travel

Go back to an earlier time in the place you now live, or travel to the future. Keep a journal to record observations of your imagined time in this place, either electronically or on paper. For example, consider what your part of the world was like at the height of the last Ice Age or shortly after the Pleistocene ice sheets retreated. Another possibility is to put yourself in the place of an early European or African immigrant and describe the natural landscape that greets you and relate how it is changing now that a new people are occupying the land. Or, consider what your home area was like when your grandparents were small children. Landscape change will be a product of global climate change, so you might want to venture ahead 50 years or so and describe how the land you know now has changed. Write an introduction to your journal that describes current landscapes to provide context and something to compare to past or future scenes. Photos will also help.

9. Plan a Natural History Field Trip

Real or virtual field trips will definitely increase your appreciation of Earth's natural features. Plan a 7- to 10-day tour of significant and interesting natural sites in your state, country, or a foreign country. Some important points of interest are presented in entries in this encyclopedia. (See the list of entries by location at the front of the first volume.) You should also consult travel guides in the public library or online. Prepare an itinerary, a list of stops you will make on the trip in the order you will encounter them. For each stop, write a brief description of what you want to see there—that is, why you have chosen that particular place to visit. To make it as realistic as possible, indicate which day (1, 2, 3, etc.) of the tour you plan to be there. You may need days devoted to travel if distances between sites are great. If you can, take part or all of trip, either in person or virtually on sites such as Google Earth. Keep a journal as you go that tells what you find at each stop. Is it what you thought it would be? Different? Worthwhile? What did you learn?

10. Experience the Power of a Place through Literature

Writers often put much emphasis on place, frequently having it play a major role in shaping characters, events, and mood. In some instance authors have created such strong images of place that they color our views of distant lands we may never visit in person. Examples include classics such as William Henry Hudson's *Green Mansions* (1904), set in the tropical rainforest of Venezuela, and Mikhail Sholokhov's *And Quiet Flows the Don* (1928) about the Cossacks and the steppes of Russia. Many of James Michener's novels trace the evolution of physical as well as cultural landscapes, among them *Hawaii* (1959), *Caravans* (1963), *The Source* (1965), *Centennial* (1974), and *Chesapeake* (1978).

Select and read a novel, nonfiction account, or short story and feel the power of place that is evoked. Concentrate on the natural world and its role in the account. How would you describe the landscape presented? What is its power or spirit? How does it influence the unfolding of the plot and/or help define the characters? Could the same story have been set anywhere else?

Here are just a few of hundreds of possible choices. Most are literary classics.

Crane, Stephen. 1897. "The Open Boat." A short story with an excellent description of a seascape. The Literature Network. http://www.online-literature.com/crane/2544/

Erdrich, Louise. 1988. *Tracks*. New York: HarperCollins Publishers. The north woods of the Chippewa (Ojibway).

Hardy, Thomas. 1878. *The Return of the Native*. New York: Modern Library Classics, Random House. Egdon Heath in England becomes a character in the book.

McNickle, D'Arcy. 1978. *Wind from an Enemy Sky*. Albuquerque: University of New Mexico Press. A novel of Native America life of fictional tribe in Flathead Lake-St. Ignatius area of Montana during the time the United States was encroaching upon their land.

Mda, Zakes. 2006. *The Whale Caller*. New York: Picador, Macmillan Publishers. Story takes place on the southern coast of Western Cape, South Africa, where southern right whales come close to shore during their annual migrations.

Steinbeck, John. 1939. *Grapes of Wrath*. New York: Penguin Classics, Random House (Revised edition, 2006) and 1962. *Travels with Charley in Search of America*. New York: Penguin Books (1980)

Thoreau, Henry David. 1849. *A Week on the Concord and Merrimack Rivers*. (Reprinted as Princeton Classics Edition). Other works by Thoreau such as *Cape Cod* (1865) and "Walking," an essay published in the *Atlantic Monthly* in 1862 also describe New England landscapes in the 19th century.

Glossary

A'a: Basaltic lava that cools to form a rough-edged chunky mass.

Ablation: Loss of glacial ice through any of a variety of processes, including melting, sublimation, wind erosion, and calving.

Abyssal plain: Flat, sediment-covered ocean floor at depths greater than 13,000 ft (4,000 m). Does not include oceanic trenches.

Acadian Orogeny: Mountain-building episode that raised mountains in the New England area during the Devonian, 416–359 mya.

Accretion (of plates): Addition of one tectonic plate or microplate to another at a convergence boundary.

Acre-foot: The amount of water that would cover an acre to a depth of one foot; 325,851 gal (1,233,476 L).

Active layer: Surface layer of permafrost that thaws in summer.

Active plate margin: Edge of tectonic plate where rifting or subduction is taking place. See **Passive plate boundary**.

Adaptive radiation: Diversification of a single species into several new ones when separate populations adapt to different environments.

Air mass: Extensive body of air with uniform characteristics of temperature and humidity.

Algific: Refers to a rare habitat caused by cold air blowing out of underground passages onto talus slopes in summer.

Alkaline volcanism: Involves explosive magma with a high component of sodium, frequently occurring along subduction zones.

Allegheny Orogeny: Paleozoic (380–280 mya) mountain-building episode related to the Appalachian Mountains; equivalent to the Hercynian Orogeny in Europe.

Alluvial fan: Fan-shaped gently-sloping deposits of alluvium, usually formed where ephemeral streams exit mountains in regions with interior drainage.

Alluvium: Loose material (clay, silt, sand, gravel) transported and deposited by running water in a stream bed or on floodplains and deltas.

Alpine glacier: Body of ice moving downslope and confined within a valley. Valley glacier.

Alpine Orogeny: Mountain-building episode in Europe 65–2.5 mya that resulted in the Alps and other southern European mountains; also affected Asia.

Anadromous: Refers to fish that spend their lives in the ocean but spawn in freshwater streams.

Andesite: Coarse-grained, intrusive volcanic rock intermediate in color and composition between basalt and rhyolite; acidic.

Anoxic: Without oxygen.

Antecedent stream: A stream that was established before a slow uplift occurred, continuing to erode downward at the same pace that the rocks, by folding or faulting, uplifted beneath it.

Anticline: An upfold in layers of rock.

Antiquities Act: Act of Congress (1906), which enabled presidents to proclaim areas of scientific interest as National Monuments and prohibits excavation and destruction of objects of historical and scientific value on public lands.

Aquiclude: Impervious layer of rock or unconsolidated material that impedes passage of water.

Aquifer: Porous rock or unconsolidated sediments that hold groundwater.

Aragonite: A crystal form of calcium carbonate, common in some types of cave formations.

Archaeology: Study of human prehistory and history from cultural artifacts, including landscapes.

Archipelago: A group, chain, or other cluster of islands.

Arête: A sharp, jagged ridge that separates mountain peaks, alpine glaciers, cirques, or valleys.

Artesian: Refers to groundwater that flows to the surface due to confining pressure in the aquifer and requires no pumping.

Atlantic flyway: A major migration route along the east coast of North America and the Appalachian Mountains between boreal breeding grounds and southern wintering grounds; followed by waterfowl, shorebirds, songbirds, and raptors.

Atoll: Circular coral reef partially or fully enclosing a central lagoon.

Austral: Related to the Southern Hemisphere.

Avalonia: Microcontinent that was accreted to Eurasia during Caledonian Orogeny.

Back-arc basin: Long, narrow, underwater troughs on the side of a volcanic island arc opposite a subduction zone.

Badlands: Intricately eroded, barren terrain developed on soft sedimentary rocks and clays in drylands.

Baltica: Ancient continent that included the Eurasian Shield.

Bank: Undersea plateau, often composed of glacial till in higher latitudes, that rises close to the water's surface.

Bank-barrier reef: Flat-topped coral reef, larger than a patch reef and in deeper offshore water, often in mid-shelf regions at depths of 20–60 ft (6–18 m). Platform reef.

Barrage: Artificial dam or holding structure on a river, for irrigation, flood control, or to aid navigation.

Barrier bar or island: Exposed sand bar a short distance from shore that parallels the coast.

Barrier reef: A long, essentially linear coral reef running parallel to a coastline and usually separated from it by a lagoon.

Basalt: Fine grained, dark colored, extrusive volcanic rock; basic.

Base level: The lowest level to which a river or stream can flow. Sea level is generally the ultimate base level.

Basin, structural: Geologic structure characterized by rock layers dipping toward the center. Not necessarily a low area topographically.

Basin and Range: Refers to a landscape of fault-block mountains and intervening valleys formed by crustal extension. Specifically the Basin and Range Province in North America.

Batholith: Large, amorphous body of intrusive igneous rock, usually covering more than 40–60 mi^2 (100–155 km^2). See also **Pluton.**

Baymouth bar: Sand bar that connects opposing headlands and closes off the entry to a bay.

Biodiversity: The totality of life's variation and variability in a given region. Includes full range of variation in genes, species, communities, ecosystem functions, and landscapes.

Biodiversity hotspot: See **Hotspot, biodiversity.**

Biogeography: The study of the distribution of life, past and present, on Earth and of those processes that determine the spatial patterns of organisms. Researchers of biogeography may be botanists, ecologists, geographers, geologists, paleontologists, or zoologists by training.

Bioluminescence: Production and emission of light energy by living organisms.

Biota: All species in a given region or time period.

Bloom (algal): A population explosion among phytoplankters.

Blue hole: Water-filled sinkhole submerged beneath the sea's surface.

Bofedales: High-elevation wetlands or peatlands in the Andes Mountains.

Bog: An acidic wetland in which a dense mat of (usually) sphagnum moss and small shrubby heaths cover a spongy, peaty substrate. The vegetation mat may float on water, completely detached from the underlying peat deposit.

Bolson: Flat, interior drainage basin in drylands of Mexico.

Boreal forest: The needleleaf evergreen forest of the Northern Hemisphere that stretches across subarctic North America and Eurasia. Taiga.

Bottle tree: Sparsely branched trees with swollen trunks shaped like a bottle.

Brackish: Refers to water than is slightly salty (0.5–30 ppt), but less so than sea water.

Broadleaf deciduous forest: A vegetation type associated with humid temperate climate and dominated by trees with thin flat leaves that are shed during the nongrowing season.

Broch: Stone tower from the Iron Age, associated with dwelling sites.

Bromeliad: A plant of the Neotropical pineapple family. Many are epiphytes in the humid tropics of the Americas, but some, especially, in dry areas, are terrestrial.

Bunchgrass: A type of grass that grows in clumps rather than forming a continuous sod.

Butte: Tall, steep-sided, isolated prominence of horizontal sedimentary rock with a flat top; an erosional remnant of a mesa. See also **Mesa, Pinnacle.**

C3 grass: A cool-season perennial grass distinguished by its carbon-fixing (photosynthetic) pathway.

C4 grass: A perennial grass adapted to growing in warm climates by its particular carbon-fixing (photosynthetic) pathway.

Calcareous: Refers to rocks rich in calcium, such as limestone and dolomite.

Calcium carbonate: Major mineral component of rocks such as limestone and dolomite, $CaCO_3$.

Caldera: Large depression in the top of a volcano where an explosive eruption caused the mountain top to collapse in on itself.

Caledonian Mountains: Mountains built during the Caledonian Orogeny when ancestral North America collided with ancestral Europe. Only remnants remain, including ranges in the Appalachian Mountains, Newfoundland, Scotland (Caledonia), and Scandinavia. Also called Caledonides.

Caledonian Orogeny: Mountain building episode in the Paleozoic Era (490–390 mya) that affected the Appalachian Mountains and several mountain ranges in northern Europe.

Caliche: Hardened layer of calcium carbonate originating from a paleosol. Often called hardpan.

Calving (glacial): The breaking off of masses of ice from the edge of a glacier or ice shelf.

Cambrian: First part of the Paleozoic Era, 570–500 mya.

Carbonate: Refers to rocks, such as limestone and dolomite, with a high content of minerals containing the carbonate ion (CO_3^{2-}).

Carbonic acid: H_2CO_3; weak acid formed from water and calcium carbonate that dissolves limestone and other carbonate rocks.

Caudex: The thickened base, stem, or root of a type of succulent; frequently forms underground.

Caviomorph (rodent): Refers to a largely South American group of rodents. Includes cavies, guinea pigs, pacas, agoutis, and capybara.

Cay: See **Key.**

Cenote: In Mexico, a deep sinkhole formed by collapse of a cave roof and exposing groundwater.

Cenozoic Era: Most recent of the geologic eras, from 65 mya to present. Age of Mammals.

Chalk: A soft type of limestone.

Chaparral: Vegetation type in mediterranean climate region of the United States dominated by shrubs with sclerophyllous leaves. Called maquis in Europe and matorral in Chile.

Chemical weathering: Processes by which rocks disintegrate into smaller pieces with a change in the chemical composition. See also: **Physical Weathering.**

Chimney (volcanic): Hollow vent associated with a spatter cone.

Cinder cone: Small volcano, usually less than 1,000 ft (300 m) high, composed of cinders and ash.

Cirque: "Ice cream scoop" depression on the side of a mountain peak carved out by an alpine glacier.

Class: Taxonomic grouping ranked below phylum and above order that includes organisms with certain shared characteristics.

Climate: Typical weather (especially temperature and precipitation) patterns during a normal year that are experienced over decades or centuries. See also **Weather.**

Climate Change: Long-term global changes in weather patterns due to natural processes and human activities. Current climate change involves global warming.

Cockpit karst: Stage in development of tropical karst where the limestone landscape is pitted with closely-spaced depressions surrounded by steep-sided conical hills.

Col: A low point in a mountain ridge or arête formed where two glaciers eroded back-to-back; often creating a mountain pass.

Cold seep: An area on the seafloor where fluids rich in hydrogen sulfide and hydrocarbons such as methane leak out often forming brine pools. They are cold only in comparison to hydrothermal vents.

Cold War: Political conflict between democratic Western Bloc countries and communist Eastern Bloc governments, 1947–1991.

Columnar jointing: Refers to formation of hexagonal columns in lava as it cools.

Composite volcano: Tall, cone-shaped volcano composed of both cinders and ash from violent eruptions and quieter lava flows. Stratovolcano.

Cone karst: Limestone landscape that resembles an assemblage of steep, cone-shaped hills; developed in a tropical wet climate.

Continental climate: Climate in the interior of a continent (as opposed to coastal locations), characterized by temperature extremes.

Continental crust: Relatively thicker part of Earth's lithosphere of felsic composition and comprising the continents.

Continental divide: Boundary of major watersheds on a continent which separates drainage flowing into different oceans.

Continental glacier or icesheet: Large, moving mass of ice blanketing a significant portion of a landmass under hundreds or thousands of feet of ice.

Continental rise: A low-angle slope on the margin of a continent below the continental slope and connecting to the abyssal plain.

Continental shelf: The edge of a continent, continental crust, that is submerged in shallow seawater usually less than 650 ft (200 m) deep.

Continental slope: The steeply sloping edge of a continent between the continental shelf and the continental rise.

Convective (storms): Storms generated by the vertical rise of moist air due to heating of Earth's surface. Also called convectional.

Convergent evolution: The development of similar characteristics in unrelated species that evolve under similar environmental conditions in different geographic regions.

Cool season grass: A term for perennial grasses using the C3 photosynthetic pathway; most prevalent in temperate, high latitude, and high elevation environments. May become dormant during periods of high temperatures.

Coral (polyp): A colonial cnidarian. Individuals are essentially a tubular sac with a single opening surrounded by tentacles, much like a tiny sea anemone.

Coral reef: Limestone structures built by living organisms (stony corals and coralline red and green algae) that secrete calcium carbonate. Occur in shallow, warm, clear (low-nutrient) waters of the tropics.

Coral Triangle: The global center of coral diversity and marine biodiversity in general, this geographic region of 2,316,613 mi^2 (6,000,000 km^2) encompasses many of the islands of Southeast Asia. It extends from one apex, the Philippines, to a second, the Solomon Islands, then west along New Guinea's north shore, south again to East Timor, west to Lombok, Indonesia, and finally north along the east coast of Borneo back to the Philippines.

Cordilleran ice sheet: Alpine glaciers that merged during the Pleistocene Epoch to cover the northern part of the mountains in western North America.

Coriolis effect: Apparent force caused by Earth's rotation that affects atmospheric and oceanic circulation, deflecting movement to the right of an intended path in the northern hemisphere and to the left of an intended path in the southern hemisphere.

Corm: Swollen underground, vertical stem that stores starches.

Coulee: Deep river canyon; specifically a canyon carved into basalt on the Columbia Plateau.

Crannog: Artificial island, most often used for settlement.

Craton: Precambrian core of a continent. See also **Shield, continental**.

Crevasse filling: Sands and gravels that accumulated in a crevasse in or on glacial ice and deposited as stratified drift when the ice melted.

Cross-bedding: Refers to crisscrossing, rather than horizontal, layers in sedimentary rock, usually sandstone. Formed in desert sand dunes by winds that reverse direction or on shallow shorelines by irregular current and wave action.

Cryptic: Refers to coloration that serves to camouflage an organism.

Crystalline: Refers to rocks with crystalline structure, igneous and/or metamorphic.

Cuesta: A long, low asymmetrical ridge formed by a gently tilting layer of sedimentary rock.

Cushion plant: Low, woody plant that forms dense spreading mats in arctic and alpine environments.

Cyanobacteria: Photosynthesizing bacteria found in water and soil. Also called blue-green algae.

Cyprinids: Fish in the Cyprinidae, often called the carp family.

Dacite: Light-colored extrusive igneous rock, intermediate between dark basalt and light rhyolite.

Dalradian: Refers to sediments deposited in the Iapetus Ocean during the Paleozoic, which were subsequently metamorphosed and accreted to Europe.

Dead ice moraine: Drift deposited when the glacial ice was no longer moving and melted in place.

Deciduous: Among trees and shrubs, the habit of shedding all leaves during the nongrowing season.

Desert pavement: Surface cover of pebbles or rocks that settle in to form a tight surface after finer sediments have been blown away.

Desertscrub: Vegetation of the desert biome characterized by dominance of woody shrubs accompanied by perennial forbs, succulents, and/or ephemerals.

Diapir: Intrusion of salt that forms a surface bulge that can assume various shapes, such as domes or anticlines.

Diatreme: A type of volcanic plug or neck where the vent, which developed from an explosive eruption, is filled not with solidified magma but with an angular breccia of broken volcanic and country rock.

Dike: Vertical slab of rock from magma that injected into a crack in the rocks. It stands higher than the adjacent landscape because the rocks are more resistant to erosion.

Dipterocarp: One of many tall hardwood tropical trees in the Dipterocarpaceae.

Disjunct: In biogeography, refers to a population or distribution area geographically separated from others of the same taxon.

Distributary: One of multiple branching channels crossing a delta.

Doline, collapse: Sinkhole depression caused by surface collapse.

Doline, solution: Sinkhole depression caused by solution of surface rock such as limestone.

Dolomite: A resistant form of limestone composed of calcium magnesium carbonate, $CaMg(CO_3)_2$.

Dome, structural: Bulge in the landscape, often caused by an intrusion of igneous rock, which pushes up the overlying layers of sedimentary rock.

Drainage basin: Area that sends overland flow and groundwater to a particular stream. Watershed. Catchment basin.

Drift, glacial: All material transported and deposited by glaciers.

Dripstone: Cave formations formed as calcite is slowly deposited by dripping water.

Drip tip: The long tapering end of some leaves which serves to rid leaf surface of excess water. Characteristic of many tropical broadleaf plants.

Drumlin: Smooth, elliptical hill deposited near the terminal moraine of a continental glacier. The long axis is parallel to direction of ice flow and the end facing into ice tends to be blunt, and steeper than the opposite end which tapers downstream.

Dust Bowl: Period in American history, generally 1930s, when extreme drought on the Great Plains resulted in extensive blowing soil and dust.

Ecoregion: Geographic area with characteristic and repeating pattern of ecosystems, landforms, and soils as well as a distinct biota.

Edaphic: Refers to conditions of the soil or other substrate.

El Niño: A seasonal atmospheric and oceanic phenomenon that affects the tropical Pacific, most commonly along the west coast of South America, where in December normally cold water, high pressure, and extreme aridity are replaced by warm water, low pressure, and high humidity. Extreme, prolonged El Niños occur every 3–7 years, changing pressure and precipitation patterns across the tropical Pacific and affecting weather worldwide. Part of the El Niño Southern Oscillation (ENSO).

Endemic species: A plant or animal native to and restricted to a given geographic area.

Eocene: A geologic epoch in the Tertiary Period lasting from 56–40 mya.

Eolianite: A rock formed of cemented or solidified wind-blown sands and silts; most commonly refers to particles of marine origin.

Ephemeral: Refers to streams or lakes that only briefly and periodically hold water.

Ephemerals: Annual plants that complete their life cycles in just a few weeks.

Epiphyte: Plant, such as a fern orchid, or bromeliad, growing on another for support only and having no contact with the soil.

Erosion: The removal of fragmented surface materials.

Erratic: Rock carried by a glacier and deposited at some distance from its source region.

Escarpment: A long cliff face that separates two surfaces at different elevations.

Esker: Long, narrow sinuous ridge composed of stratified sand and gravel deposits; formed by a stream flowing within or beneath a continental glacier.

Estuary: Semienclosed inlets where freshwater streams mix with seawater.

Eustatic: Refers to a world-wide change in sea level.

Eutrophication: Abnormal growth of algae and other plant life in a freshwater body due to influx of excessive nutrients, depleting oxygen for other forms of life.

Evaporite: Minerals, such as salt or gypsum, which crystallized, or precipitated, as water evaporated.

Evapotranspiration: The transfer of water vapor to the atmosphere from a combination of evaporation and the water loss of plants via transpiration.

Evolution: Genetic change that occurs at the population level from one generation to the next.

Exclusive Economic Zone (EEZ): That offshore region extending 200 nautical miles (370 km) from the coast of a country, as defined by the UN Convention on the Law of the Seas. The political unit in question has exclusive rights to exploration and exploitation of marine and seabed resources in this zone. However, only the 12 mi (9.6 km) closest to shore, deemed territorial waters, are under the actual jurisdiction of a given country; the remainder of the EEZ is in international waters and open to navigation by all.

Exfoliation: Refers to the process whereby large slabs or sheets of rock peel off granite masses like layers of an onion.

Exfoliation dome: Large landform feature formed by exfoliation, usually with a smooth top lacking vegetation.

Family: A taxonomic group of closely related genera.

Faro: Ring-shaped coral reef that occurs in the lagoons of open atolls of the Maldives.

Fast ice: Sea-ice that is bound (fastened) to land.

Fault: Major break in the Earth's crust or rocks along which movement of Earth's crust has occurred or is occurring.

Fault-block mountain: Mountain formed by faulting, either by uplift of the mountain or downdrop of the adjacent valley.

Fauna: All the animal species in a given geographic area or time period, or a specified subset of them, such as the avifauna.

Felsenmeer: Surface of angular blocks of rock broken by frost action in alpine or subpolar climates.

Fennoscandia: The region that includes Norway, Sweden, and Finland.

Feral: Formerly domesticated plants or animals and their descendants that are no longer under the control of humans.

Finger lake: Linear lake in a glacial valley.

Firn: Granules of snow coalescing due to compression in a snow pack. Snow that did not melt during the summer and is part of the transition from snow to glacial ice.

Fissure flow: Fluid basalt lava that extruded from a fissure rather than from a volcanic cone.

Fjord: Glacially scoured U-shaped valley inundated with seawater. Also fiord.

Flood basalt: Very fluid basaltic lava, the outpouring of which covers a vast area before it cools and solidifies.

Floodplain: Low, flat area next to a stream that is built of alluvium and subject to periodic inundation.

Flora: All the plant species in a given area or time period.

Floristic kingdom: Global-scale geographic region delineated by distinct composition of its flora at the family level.

Fluvial: Referring to processes or sediments related to flowing water.

Flysch: Term used in European and Asian geology to refer to clastic marine deposits of fine grained marls, sandstones, shales, clays, and muds.

Flyways: Routes that large numbers of bird species follow on their migrations.

Foehn: A warm, dry downslope wind from a mountain area; specifically from the northern slopes of the European Alps.

Foliose lichen: Lichen with a leafy appearance.

Food web: Network of food chains from producers to consumers to decomposers.

Foreland, foredeep: A structural basin developed adjacent to and parallel to a mountain range, usually the recipient area for sediments eroded from the mountains.

Formation: A distinct, mappable geologic unit containing one or more beds with distinctive physical and chemical characteristics; the basic unit of lithostratigraphy. Formations are typically named for the geographic area where they were first described.

Frazil ice: Sharp, needle-shaped ice crystals that form in rough water. Represents the first stage in the formation of sea-ice.

Frost heaving: Refers to rocks and other material being pushed to the surface as water in ground freezes.

Fruticose lichen: Lichens that are upright and look like tiny shrubs; may be cuplike or hairlike, hanging in long strands.

Fumarole: A terrestrial hydrothermal feature that expels steam through a crack, often with hot sulfurous gasses.

Furious Fifties: The circumpolar zone between 50°S and 60°S where exceedingly strong, nearly constant westerly winds blow.

Genus (pl. genera): A taxonomic unit that groups closely related species.

Geosyncline: Large downwarp of Earth's crust that accumulates sediment; precursor to mountain building.

Geothermal field: An area within Earth's crust with abnormally high heat; often producing geothermal features, such as hot springs and geysers; frequently due to recent volcanic activity.

Geyser: A spring characterized by ejection of hot water and steam, caused by a complex configuration of underground conduits that allows water to become heated above the boiling point under intensely high pressure conditions.

Glacial lake: Lake that was present during the Pleistocene or when the continental glaciers were melting.

Glacial lobe: Finger- or tongue-like projection of a continental glacier.

Glacial outwash: Glacio-fluvial debris transported in streams derived from glacial meltwater and deposited beyond recessional and terminal moraines.

Glacial polish: Smooth, shiny surface on rocks that have been abraded by fine sediment carried in a glacier.

Glacial rebound: Slow uplift of land when the weight of glacial ice is removed. Isostatic rebound.

Glacial scour: Refers to a glacier scraping away loose soil and relatively soft rock material as it moves over a surface.

Glacial trough: U-shaped valley carved out by a glacier.

Glacier: Body of ice that slowly moves over a land surface.

Gondwana: Southern supercontinent formed by splitting of Pangaea during the mid-Miocene (200–180 mya) that encompassed present-day Africa, South America, Antarctica, Australia, India, Madagascar, and the Arabian Peninsula.

GPS: Global positioning system. A satellite-based navigation system.

Graben: Down-dropped block between two up-faulted blocks.

Grease ice: Thin soupy layer of clumped frazil ice crystals giving the appearance of an oil slick on the ocean surface. Represents the second stage in the formation of sea-ice.

Grenville Orogeny: Mountain-building episode in New England (United States) 1.3–1.1 bya.

Greywacke: Poorly sorted sandstone with a high component of silt and clay particles.

Ground moraine: Sheet of glacial till deposited as a continental glacier steadily retreats; creates swell and swale topography.

Groundwater: Water held in the pores of soil or rock, in fractures in rock, or in unconsolidated rock materials or sediments beneath the surface.

Group: A geological unit composed of two or more contiguous formations with diagnostic physical characteristics in common, sometimes deposited during same geologic time period.

Gulf Stream: See **North Atlantic Drift.**

Guyot: Flat-topped, extinct submarine volcano (seamount) that built up from the seafloor when a tectonic plate passed over a magma hotspot. The summit is at least 660 ft (200 m) bsl.

Gypsum: Soft sulfate mineral composed of calcium sulfate dihydrate, $CaSO_4 \cdot 2H_2O$. Often forms as an evaporite.

Gyre: A circular or spiraling ocean current; frequently forms beneath a subtropical high pressure area.

Halophyte: A plant adapted to living in a saline environment.

Hammock: Low mound in the Everglades sawgrass marsh that is not flooded.

Hanging trough: Tributary glaciated valley that joins a larger valley from high on a cliff or slope; U-shaped profile; caused by unequal erosion by glaciers.

Hanging valley: Tributary nonglaciated valley that joins a larger valley from high on a cliff or slope; V-shaped profile; usually caused by unequal erosion by tributary stream and main valley glacier.

Headwater stream: One of the small tributaries carrying water from a river's source area toward the main stem.

Hercynian Orogeny: Paleozoic (380–280 mya) mountain building episode in Europe; equivalent to the Allegheny Orogeny in North America.

High Plains: The flat to rolling landscape in the United States east of the Rocky Mountains, where elevations are 2,000–7,000 ft (600–2,150 m).

Hogback: Ridge formed by steeply tilted layer of resistant sedimentary rock.

Holarctic: Refers to taxa that are distributed throughout the northern hemisphere, in both North America and in Eurasia.

Holocene: Geologic epoch from end of Pleistocene approximately 12,000–10,000 years ago to present.

Hoodoo: Tall, narrow rock spire, an erosional remnant, reaching up from the base of badlands or drainage basins.

Horn: A sharp mountain peak with glacial cirques on at least three sides.

Horst: Uplifted fault block with no appreciable tilt.

Hotspot, biodiversity: A place where biodiversity and rates of endemism are high and under threat from human activity.

Hotspot, magma: Isolated plume or pool of magma not associated with subduction.

Hotspot track: Linear belts of volcanoes tracing the movement of a tectonic plate over a magma plume.

Hyphae: Long branching filaments of a fungus. Collectively known as mycelium.

Iapetus Ocean: Ocean that developed during the Paleozoic (600–400 mya). Located between the paleocontinents of Laurentia, Baltica, and Avalonia; its closure resulted in the Caledonian Orogeny. A precursor to the Atlantic Ocean.

Ice cap: Dome-shaped ice mass covering all the underlying terrain. Smaller than an ice sheet.

Ice sheet: Huge mass of glacial ice covering a large part of a continent. Currently found only in Greenland and Antarctica. A continental glacier.

Ice shelf: The end of an ice sheet that protrudes from the continent and floats on the ocean.

Ice wedge: Water that accumulates in a crack in the ground and freezes and expands; associated with permafrost and patterned ground.

Icefield: Mass of ice connecting a series of valley glaciers with intervening exposed bedrock. Smaller than an ice cap. Surface reflects underlying landforms.

Ignimbrite: Igneous rock formed by the solidification of poorly sorted mixture of volcanic ash, pumice, and other pyroclastic flow deposits.

Imbricated: Refers to rock layers that are overlapping, like tiles or fish scales.

Indicator species: Plants or animals that identify a region, ecosystem, or ecological condition.

Inselberg: An erosional remnant that stands as an isolated knob or hill on a plain, especially in savanna and desert regions. Also kopje.

Insolation: Solar radiation reaching Earth's atmosphere and surface; short wave energy from the sun.

Insubric Line: Contact zone in the Alps between the European Plate and African Plate or a subdivision of the African Plate.

Interior drainage: Refers to drainage patterns where rivers do not reach the ocean but flow inland and terminate in a basin or valley.

Interlobate moraine: Exceptionally irregular and hilly moraine deposited between two adjacent glacial lobes.

Intertropical Convergence Zone (ITCZ): Contact zone at or near the equator between Northeast and Southeast Trade Winds that shifts latitudinally with the seasons. It is the global low pressure system of the tropics that usually brings rain to the hemisphere over which it is positioned.

Invasive species: A nonnative species that spreads rapidly upon being introduced to a new area and potentially or actually causes ecological harm.

Iron Curtain: Ideological barrier between democratic Western Europe and communist Eastern Europe and the former Soviet Union.

Isostacy, isostatic: State of equilibrium between the lithosphere and the asthenosphere that maintains tectonic plates at levels in accord with their thicknesses and densities.

Isthmus: A relatively narrow strip of land between two water bodies, connecting two larger land areas.

Joint: Minor break or crack in rock; differs from a fault in that there is no movement.

Jurassic: Geologic period of the Mesozoic Era about 200–146 mya.

Karst: Landscape that develops by solution in limestone, usually including sinkholes, subsurface drainage, caves, and springs.

Katabatic wind: A downslope flow of dense air under the pull of gravity.

Kavir: Salt marsh in Iran, usually covered with a salt crust.

Kettle: Depression in glacial deposits caused by a block of buried ice that subsequently melted. Kettle lake if filled with water.

Key: Sandy island or islet formed on top of coral reef. Cay.

Knickpoint: An abrupt change of slope in the profile of a river channel resulting in waterfalls or rapids.

Krummholz: Stunted, misshapen trees at subarctic or subalpine treeline between forest and tundra.

La Niña: Part of the El Niño Southern Oscillation (ENSO) when cooler than normal water spills westward across the equatorial Pacific, often bringing drought to the western Pacific. Conditions and effects are opposite to those of El Niño. See **El Niño.**

Laccolith: A flat-bottomed mass of intrusive igneous rock formed by magma filling the bedding plane between layers of sedimentary rock, forcing the overlying layers to bulge upward. Often eroded to expose the core.

Lacustrine: Referring to processes or sediments related to lakes or their basins.

Lahar: Debris flow of pyroclastic material and other rock material of various sizes combined with water that moves rapidly down the slope of a volcano and into surrounding valleys. Usually associated with erupting stratovolcanoes that melt their cap of ice; these often deadly flows look like wet concrete.

Lake effect: Large lake's climatic modification of adjacent areas, such as moderating temperature ranges and increasing precipitation amounts.

Lake effect snow: Increased snowfall on the downwind sides of lakes, such as Lake Erie, when winter winds evaporate moisture from the relatively warm lake.

Lapies: Surface of limestone chemically weathered into furrows and ridges.

Laramide Orogeny: Mountain building episode that raised the Rocky Mountains. Began in late Cretaceous 80–70 mya and ended 55–35 mya.

Laterite: Highly leached, brick-red tropical soil characterized by high concentration of iron and aluminum oxides. Can form into a rock-hard substance (hardpan) when exposed to sun.

Latitude: Distance north or south of the Equator measured in degrees.

Laurentia: Ancestral North America; forms ancient core of today's continent.

Laurentide Ice Sheet: Continental glacier that covered much of North America multiple times during the Pleistocene Epoch.

Lava: Magma, either molten or solidified, extruded onto the Earth's surface.

Lava dome: A circular mound formed when viscous magma is extruded from a volcano vent. The material builds up around the vent rather than flowing downslope.

Lava lake: Pool of molten, fluid magma exposed to the atmosphere in a volcanic crater.

Lava tube: A type of cave developed in lava either when the channel in which lava is flowing crusts over or when a stream of lava flows beneath the surface.

Leaching: The process whereby dissolved material is washed downward through the substrate.

Leaf Succulent: Plant that stores moisture in its leaves. Large leaf succulents are large plants; small leaf succulents are small plants with small leaves.

Lee: Side of a mountain or island that is protected from the prevailing winds by the land and experiences downslope flows of air masses. Often a rain shadow. See **Windward.**

Left-lateral: A strike-slip fault at which a viewer looking along the length of the fault sees the left side as having been displaced toward him while opposite side appears to have moved away from him.

Leucogranite: Light-colored granite with almost no dark colored minerals.

Levee, natural: Sediments that build up as a ridge along the banks of a river during periodic floods, raising the banks higher than the surrounding landscape.

Littoral: In lakes and rivers refers to the shallow near-shore zone often home to wetlands. On coasts refers to a somewhat vaguely defined area which extends from high tide mark out beyond the intertidal zone to the edge of the continental shelf.

Little Ice Age: Cool period between AD 1550 and 1850; time of glacial advance after the warmer climates of the Medieval Climatic Optimum.

Loess: Fine-textured windblown sediment (silt) derived from deserts or glacial deposits.

Longitude: Distance east or west of the Prime Meridian, measured in degrees.

Longshore Current: Current running approximately parallel to a shoreline and downwind, usually carrying sediment.

Maar: Broad, shallow crater created during an explosion caused by groundwater contacting hot magma.

Macaronesia: Collectively, five mid-Atlantic archipelagos: the Azores, Madeira, Selvagems, Canaries, and Cape Verde islands.

Machair: Lime-rich meadow in Scotland formed on fine shell material.

Magma: Molten and semimolten rock material within the Earth's crust or mantle. See also **Lava**.

Magma chamber: Subsurface reservoir of molten rock.

Magmatic arc: Curvilinear pool of magma above a subduction zone giving rise to volcanoes and/or plutons.

Main stem: The major section (final large channel) of a river into which all tributaries flow.

Mangrove: Salt-tolerant plant, usually woody, that grows in the intertidal zone. Mangroves occur in 19 plant families. Also, the tropical or subtropical forest or swamp habitat of such trees and shrubs.

Mantle: The highly viscous part of Earth's interior between the crust and the outer core.

Mantle plume: Upwelling of magma from Earth's mantle at a relatively stationary location away from tectonic plate boundaries. See **Hotspot, magma.**

Maquis: See **Chaparral**.

Mass wasting: Processes by which rock or debris moves downslope under the force of gravity.

Massif: A large block of the lithosphere bounded by faults, usually older and more resistant than surrounding rock.

Meander: A sinuous bend in a river.

Medieval Climatic Optimum: A period from roughly AD 800 to 1300 when temperatures in the Northern Hemisphere were warmer than during the Little Ice Age that followed but cooler than now.

Mediterranean climate: Climate characterized by mild temperatures and summer drought; named for the Mediterranean Sea region, where this regime is typical. Elsewhere found along west coasts of continents in both hemispheres between 25° and 35° latitude.

Megafauna: The largest wild animals of a region, usually considered those weighing more than 100 lbs (45 kg). Most commonly used to refer to those large terrestrial vertebrates that became extinct at the end of the Pleistocene Epoch.

Member (geological): Named subdivision of a formation.

Mesa: Prominence composed of horizontal sedimentary rock, broader than it is tall, usually flat-topped. See also **Butte**, **Pinnacle**.

Mesozoic: The middle of the three geologic eras. Lasted approximately 251–65 mya.

Messinian Salinity Crisis: Period in the late Mesozoic Era (5.6–5.3 mya) when the Mediterranean Sea was an enclosed evaporative basin, and salt and gypsum accumulated to great depths.

Meta-plutonic: Intrusive igneous rocks that have been metamorphosed.

Meta-sedimentary: Sedimentary rocks that have been metamorphosed.

Meta-volcanic: Volcanic rocks that have been metamorphosed.

Meteor: Rock debris of extraterrestrial origin hurtling through space and the trail of visible light it produces. Shooting star.

Meteorite: Rock debris or meteor from outer space that survives its descent to Earth.

Microclimate: Highly localized climate that is distinct from the regional climate. May cover only a very small area and result from differences in aspect, topography, or elevation.

Microcontinent: A fragment of continental crust that forms a small tectonic plate.

Microphyllous: Small-leaved.

Microplate: Small piece of continental or oceanic crust. Minor tectonic plate.

Middle America: Mexico, Central America, and the Caribbean combined.

Misfit river: River or stream that does not fit the size of its valley, indicating that the volume of the river has greatly decreased or that factors other than running water produced the valley. Underfit river.

Mogote: Steep-sided residual limestone hill in karst landscape.

Mohorovicic Discontinuity (Moho): Boundary between crustal rocks and the mantle.

Molasse: Sedimentary layers associated with erosion and deposition from a rising mountain mass. Used to describe regions of the European Alps and Asian mountain regions.

Monadnock: Erosional remnant on a peneplain; usually a rounded mountain.

Monocline: A single dip or step-like drop in otherwise horizontal rock layers. A type of fold.

Monsoon: A system of seasonal wind reversal, usually associated with Asia and resulting in a long rainy season and a short dry season.

Monsoonal: A pattern of wind flow and precipitation resembling the Asian monsoon, but not as strongly developed.

Moraine: Unsorted piles of boulders, gravel, sand, and clay that were deposited directly from a melting glacier. See also **Ground moraine, Recessional moraine, Terminal moraine.**

Moulin kame: Conical hill of stratified sands and gravels, deposited as meltwater funneled through a hole in the top of a glacier.

Mudflow: Fast-flowing thick mixture of sediments and water, caused by violent storms or by volcanic activity that melts glaciers. See also **Lahar.**

Muskeg: Bogland in the boreal forest of North America, especially one in which the spongy mat of vegetation floats on water. See also **Bog.**

Mychorrhizae: Mutualistic relationship between fungi (i.e., mychorrhizal fungi) and the roots of a vascular plant.

Nappe: Sheet-like unit or slice of rock folded and thrust a large distance over other rocks; European term for thrust sheet.

Native Corporations (Alaska): Refers to ownership of Alaska lands by native Alaskans.

NATURA 2000: An ecological network in the European Union.

The Nature Conservancy: A nonprofit organization based in the United States that works to preserve landscapes and habitats.

Nearctic: The biotic region encompassing North America as far south as the Mexican Plateau. Also refers to the fauna of that region, which corresponds to the Nearctic Zoogeographic Province.

Needleleaf evergreen forest: A vegetation type largely confined to the Northern Hemisphere that is dominated by spruce, fir, and pines that maintain needles throughout the year.

Neotropical: The biotic region extending from southern Mexico and the Caribbean to southern South America. Also the plant and animal taxa restricted to or originating in that region.

Normal fault: A fault where the hanging wall slides down an inclined fault plane relative to the footwall, as movement would be expected ("normal") by gravity alone.

Nuées ardente: Extremely hot, glowing, often fatal, cloud of gas and ash that descends rapidly from an erupting volcano.

Nunatak: Area, usually a jagged mountain peak, surrounded by, but exposed above, an icefield.

Oasis: Area in an otherwise arid region where water is available. Can range in size from a few acres to sites capable of supporting large villages or cities.

Oceanic crust: Relatively thin part of Earth's lithosphere composed of basic rocks and underlying ocean basins.

Octocorals: Marine organisms (cnidarians) in the subclass Octocorallia. They are formed by colonial polyps embedded in a soft matrix, each polyp having eight tentacles, and include soft corals, sea pens, and sea fans among others.

Oligotrophic: Refers to a body of water with few dissolved nutrients, high oxygen content, and a sparse growth of algae or other plants.

Oolite: Inorganically precipitated calcareous nodule; forms oolitic limestone when many are cemented together.

Ophiolite: Sequence of oceanic crust and mantle.

Order: Taxonomic rank that is a major subdivision of a Class. Contains similar families.

Ordovician: Early part of the Paleozoic Era, 500–430 mya.

Orogeny: Mountain building event.

Orographic effect: The forced rising of air masses over a land barrier such as a mountain or edge of a plateau. Usually results in increased cloud cover and rainfall on the windward side.

Outlet glacier: A river of ice flowing from an ice cap or ice sheet to the sea.

Outwash plain: Flat landscape created by stratified sand and gravel and other sediment deposited by meltwater from a glacier. See **Glacial outwash**.

Overthrust fault: A fault in which the hanging wall appears to have been pushed up a gently inclined fault plane by compression. A low-angle thrust fault where displacement of upthrust block is measured in miles (kilometers). See also **Thrust fault**.

Pachycauly: Refers to drought-adapted plants with swollen bases, stems, or trunks as a means of storing moisture.

Pacific Ring of Fire: Zone of earthquake and volcanic activity surrounding the Pacific Ocean.

Pack ice: Large area of floating ice formed over several years and consisting of consolidated patches of sea-ice. Usually several meters thick. Also known as drift ice.

Pahoehoe: Very fluid lava that cools into rope-like shapes.

Paleontology: Study of animals in the past, through fossils and other remains.

Paleosol: Old or fossil soil; indicates erosion intervals between rock formations.

Paleozoic: Oldest of the three geologic eras following the Precambrian. Lasted from approximately 545–251 mya and ended with Permian-Triassic mass extinctions.

Pancake ice: Round patches of sea-ice 1–10 ft (30 cm–1m) in diameter and up to 4 in (10 cm) thick. The rims are raised by the collision of pancakes and consequent addition of frazil ice at the edges.

Pangaea: The supercontinent consisting of all land masses that developed in the Paleozoic and lasted until the Cretaceous, roughly between 300 and 200 mya.

Parthenogenic: Populations consisting of only females, needing no males to reproduce. Known primarily in lizards.

Passive plate margin: Plate boundary where no subduction or tectonic activity is taking place; also called stable plate margin.

Patch reef: Small, isolated reef platform in shallow water, usually in a lagoon.

Patterned ground: Polygons, stone stripes, and other geometric forms developed in surface materials by freeze-thaw activity on ground overlying permafrost.

Peneplain: Region eroded almost level.

Perched water table: Zone of saturation above the main water table, caused by a lens or layer of impermeable material.

Periglacial: Refers to areas affected by cold and ice near glaciers, or in high latitudes or high elevations.

Permafrost: Ground that is permanently frozen, where only the top layer thaws in summer.

Permian: Last period in the Paleozoic Era, 300–251 mya.

pH: The negative logarithm of the concentration of hydrogen ions in solution used as a measure of acidity (0–7) or alkalinity (7–14).

Photosynthesis: Process by which plants convert light energy into chemical energy by manufacturing carbohydrates from water and carbon dioxide in the presence of sunlight and chlorophyll.

Phreatophyte: A desert plant that avoids drought by extending long roots into the saturated zone or capillary fringe near the water table.

Phyllite: A fine-grained metamorphic rock, intermediate between slate and schist.

Phylum (pl. phyla): Basic subdivision of a kingdom, with a taxonomic rank below kingdom and above class. Groups together all classes with same body plan. The term "division" has traditionally been used for this category by botanists. Kingdom Animalia currently has 35 phyla; Plantae has 12.

Physical weathering: Processes by which rocks disintegrate into smaller pieces of the same type of rock by mechanical or non-chemical means. See also **Chemical weathering**.

Physiography, physiographic: Refers to the configuration of the landscape together with the underlying rock types and geologic structure that control that configuration.

Phytoplankton: Algae and some cyanobacteria, usually microscopic, that float in water and are the chief producers in aquatic ecosystems, the beginning of food chains.

Pillow basalt or lava: Lava that erupted under water, forming rounded clumps of igneous rock.

Pingo: An ice-cored hill in regions of permafrost.

Pinnacle: Tower or spire of sedimentary rock, taller than it is broad; erosional remnant from a mesa or butte. See also **Mesa, Butte.**

Pitted outwash plain: Flat-lying layers of sand and gravel with depressions, or pits, from buried blocks of glacial ice that subsequently melted.

Plankton: A collective term for all organisms, most microscopic, that float in water without the ability to swim against tides and currents; many are able to undergo vertical migrations.

Plate, tectonic: A large slab of Earth's crust, composed of ocean crust and/or continental crust, that moves under the pressures of convectional currents in the mantle, which causes seafloor spreading and subduction; driven by Earth's internal energy. Lithospheric plate.

Plate tectonics: The theory or explanation of how Earth's crust is rearranged by the movement of large pieces of the lithosphere driven by the planet's internal energy.

Playa: A dry lake bed formed by interior drainage and evaporation of water.

Pleistocene: The first epoch of the Quaternary Period. Included Earth's most recent period of glaciation. Lasted from about 2.6 or 1.6–1.8 mya to 12,000–10,000 years ago.

Plinian: Refers to a violent volcanic eruption involving pyroclastic flows of ash and gasses.

Plug dome: Volcano where the vent becomes plugged by solidified magma, usually ending all volcanic activity. See also **Lava dome.**

Plunge pool: Deep part of a river beneath a waterfall, where the force of falling water erodes a deep basin into the river channel.

Pluton: Mass of intrusive igneous rock, usually less than 60 mi^2 (155 km^2). See also **Batholith.**

Pluvial: Refers to wetter periods during the Pleistocene in regions not cold enough for glaciers.

Pluvial lake: Lake that formed during the Pleistocene in regions that were not glaciated but received more precipitation than they do today.

Polje: A downfaulted valley in a karst landscape.

Polynya: A persistent patch of open water in sea-ice maintained by prevailing winds. Important areas for the production of new sea-ice in winter.

Ponor: Opening in a sinkhole depression where a stream flows in or out.

Ponto-Caspian: Relating to the region around the Black and Caspian seas.

Precambrian: Earliest and longest-lasting geologic unit of time; 4,550–545 mya.

Pressure ridge: A volcanic feature in basalt where internal pressure pushes upward, breaking the surface.

Primary production: The amount of carbon and energy fixed by photosynthesizing plants in a given area.

Prominence: Local relief. The height of a mountain summit above the surrounding surface (as opposed to elevation above sea level).

Proterozoic Eon: The last stage of the Precambrian just prior to the explosion of complex life-forms on Earth; 2,500–540 mya.

Pumice: Light-colored volcanic rock that cooled very quickly. Full of holes because of trapped gases, it appears frothy but is actually fine-grained glass.

Puy: French term for a volcanic hill.

Pyroclastic flow: Very hot mix of ash and gases expelled from a volcano, usually flows close to the ground due to its density.

Pyroclastics: Solid material, ranging in size from microscopic ash to large blocks of rock, expelled from a volcano.

Quaternary: The most recent major geological time period, beginning approximately 2.6 or 1.6–1.8 mya and continuing into the present; includes the Pleistocene and the Holocene epochs.

Radial drainage: River pattern wherein streams flow away from a central point; typical of an uneroded structural dome, stratovolcano, or shield volcano.

Radiolarian: Type of marine protozoa with skeletons made of silica.

Radiolarites: Rocks which contain more than 50 percent radiolarian skeletons, originating from deep-sea accumulations.

Rain shadow: The dry area on the lee side of a mountain range caused by downslope movement of air masses.

Rainforest: Forests developing in response to exceptionally high amounts of precipitation in both tropical and temperate regions.

Ramsar Wetland of International Importance: A wetland recognized as globally significant habitat under an international treaty signed in Ramsar, Iran, in 1971 and effective as of December 21, 1975.

Rebound: Rising of land due to release of weight or pressure; usually associated with glacial melting.

Recessional moraine: A ridge of glacial debris that accumulated where a glacier temporarily paused during retreat.

Rectangular drainage: Stream system pattern that is rectangular, usually controlled by right-angle faults or joints in the rock.

Reef: A structure lying just below the water surface. May be composed of solid rock or sand, or be constructed by living organisms such as coral polyps and coralline algae. See **Coral reef.**

Refugium (pl. refugia): Locale where plant or animal species survived during long periods of unfavorable conditions, such as during Pleistocene glaciations or consequent dry periods in tropics.

Relict: A species or other taxon that has survived from an earlier geologic time or climate regime, such as the Gondwanan relicts in the modern South American, African, and Australian biotas.

Relief: The difference in elevation between the lowest and highest points on a landscape or geomorphic feature.

Retention time: The amount of time it would take for the water volume of a lake to be totally replaced.

Rhizome: Horizontal stem that grows below ground surface and produces roots and shoots at nodes along its length.

Rhyodacite: Term used to refer to either rhyolite or dacite, two extrusive igneous rocks difficult to distinguish without using petrographic techniques involving microscopy.

Rhyolite: Acidic, fine-grained, silica-rich extrusive igneous rock.

Rhyolite dome: Solidified acidic magma which protrudes from and plugs the vent of a volcano.

Ria coast: Irregular coastline of narrow inlets between steep mountainous or hilly headlands.

Ridge and Valley: Landscape that develops parallel ridges and valleys due to differential erosion of hard versus softer layers of folded sedimentary rock.

Rift: A linear break in the lithosphere caused by the pulling apart (crustal extension) of tectonic plates.

Rifting: The process by which the lithosphere is pulled apart.

Right-lateral: Refers to a strike-slip fault at which a viewer looking along the length of the fault sees the right side as having been displaced toward him while opposite side appears to have moved away from him.

Ring dike: Dike that forms a circle or partial circle.

Riparian: Refers to environments along streams.

River basin. See **Drainage basin.**

Roaring Forties: The circumpolar zone between 40°S and 50°S latitude where strong westerly winds prevail.

Rock glacier: A tongue of frozen angular rocks held together by ice that slowly moves downslope from terminal moraines or talus cones.

Rodinia: An early supercontinent that existed from 1,300–1,100 mya until about 750 mya.

Rosette: A plant with leaves arranged in a circle at its base.

Salar: Salt flat (Spanish).

Salinity: Measure of the amount of dissolved matter (salts) in water. Commonly indicated in parts per thousand (ppt) or more recently in practical salinity units (psu), for which no units are designated. The average salinity of seawater thus is 35 ppt or simply 35.

Salmonids: Any fish in the salmon family, including salmon, trout, and white fish.

Salt dome: An often mushroom-shaped vertical intrusion of evaporite minerals (salts) into surrounding layers of rock that forces overlying rock to upwarp.

Salt glacier: Body of salt that extrudes through surface rock and slowly oozes or flows downslope like a glacier.

Saltation: Movement of sediment, usually sand, by bouncing or jumping along a surface.

Saltmarsh: Brackish intertidal wetland that supports salt-tolerant grasses and other halophytic plants.

Saltpetre: Potassium nitrate (KNO_3), used in fertilizers, gun powder, and meat preservatives.

Savanna: Vegetation consisting of a continuous ground layer of grasses or low shrubs above which is an open canopy of trees or large shrubs. Various types are identified according to the type and density of the canopy plants (e.g., grass savannas, palm savannas, pine savannas).

Sclerophyllous: Refers to plants with thick, leathery leaves, most commonly associated with mediterranean dry summer climate regions.

Scoria: Dark-colored lava that is full of holes from trapped gases. Adjective: **scoriaceous.**

Sea stack: Large rock structure offshore that is an erosional remnant of the adjacent headland or offshore island. Often a vertical column of sedimentary or volcanic rock.

Seafloor spreading: The process in which upwelling of magma along diverging plate boundaries at mid-oceanic ridges creates new oceanic crust, expanding the ocean floors and driving the movement of tectonic plates.

Seagrass: Flowering plants such as eelgrass and turtlegrass that live submerged in shallow seawater. Submerged aquatic vegetation (SAV).

Sea-ice: Any form of frozen seawater.

Seamount: Submarine volcano, often with a level, eroded summit.

Semideciduous forest: A broadleaf forest in which trees shed only some of their leaves during the non-growing season or which shed all their leaves for only a brief period (i.e., brevi-deciduous).

Semi-graben: An asymmetrical downfaulted block with a major fault along only one side of the rift.

Shield, continental: Exposed Precambrian core of a continent.

Shield volcano: Volcano with a low profile built up by successive basaltic lava flows; usually covers a large area. It is frequently associated with volcanism over mantle plumes (magma hotspots).

Siliceous sinter: Hot springs deposits formed from silica.

Sill (in a fjord): An underwater rise at the mouth of fjord created by the terminal moraine of the glacier that carved the fjord.

Sinkhole: Surface depression caused by solution of limestone. May be caused by collapse of underground cavities or solution of rock from the surface.

Skerry: A small reef or rocky island.

Slot canyon: Very narrow and very deep canyon.

Solifluction: Slow downslope movement of the saturated soil active layer overlying permafrost.

Sound: Generally, a deep, large but narrow and sheltered body of seawater between two pieces of land. May have been carved by glaciers or represent a former river valley now inundated by the sea. Not a precisely defined term.

Spatter cone: A small volcano that spews out liquid chunks of lava that fall and solidify close to the vent.

Species: All members of a group of similar organisms that can interbreed and produce viable offspring. The group may consist of one or more geographically discrete populations. The basic unit of taxonomy.

Species richness: The number of species found in a particular geographic area or community.

Speleothem: Any cave formation of precipitates resulting from the dripping of water through cracks in surrounding rock.

Spit: Sand bar connected on one end to an island or the mainland.

Spreading center: The place where two tectonic plates are diverging, producing a gap that allows the upwelling of magma from the asthenosphere, as at mid-oceanic ridges.

Spring tide: A tide occurring at full moon or new moon and producing the greatest tidal range at a given site.

Stable plate margin: Plate boundary where no subduction or tectonic activity is taking place; also called passive plate margin.

Steppe: A vegetation-type dominated by grasses and forbs, especially in the temperate zone or at high elevations. As a biome, the Eurasian steppe is the equivalent of the North American prairie and South American pampa. Americans often use the term steppe to denote a short-grass prairie dominated by bunchgrasses.

Stranglers: A tropical plant, often a fig, which is an epiphyte on a canopy tree of the rainforest at germination but extends its roots down to the soil as it matures. The leaves, flowers, and fruits remain confined to the forest canopy. Mistakenly thought to "strangle" the trunk of its host tree and kill it, but may overtop the host and cut off sunlight.

Stratocone: The edifice or structure of a stratovolcano or composite volcano. See also **Stratovolcano.**

Stratovolcano: Tall volcano composed of both cinders and ash from violent eruptions and quieter lava flows. See also **Composite volcano.**

Striations: Grooves gouged into rock surfaces by a glacier.

Strike valley: Valley where direction is controlled by the geologic structure, such as a rock layer or fault.

Strike-slip: Refers to a fault with horizontal movement, with little to no vertical movement.

Strombolian: Refers to a volcano with mild explosive activity, involving fluid lava flows.

Structural valley: Valley that is not carved by a river or stream but created by the geologic structure.

Structure, geological: The three-dimensional arrangement of rock or of a specific part of Earth's crust.

Subantarctic: The region just north of the Antarctic Circle. Roughly the latitudinal belt from 46°S to 66° 30'S, including the Roaring Forties and Furious Fifties. Subpolar region of the Southern Hemisphere.

Subduction: Where a heavier, usually oceanic plate, slides beneath a lighter, usually continental plate, often causing earthquakes and volcanic activity.

Sublimation: The process by which ice is converted directly to water vapor without first transforming into liquid water.

Substrate: Surface material such as soil, regolith, sediments, or bedrock.

Succession: Process by which plant communities change as they alter the site, allowing other plants to displace them.

Supercontinent: Any of the large continents in the geologic past when all or most land masses were combined.

Suture: Contact where plates or microplates have been bonded together.

Syncline: Layers of rock that have been folded downward.

Tafoni: Weathering pits or cavities, ranging in size from tiny holes to large caves, developed primarily in sandstones and granites, usually on vertical or inclined surfaces. May result in a honeycombed appearance.

Taiga: The more open needleleaf forest in the Northern Hemisphere subarctic, poleward of the closed boreal forest just south of the tundra and usually dominated by spruce (*Picea*) and larch (*Larix*). Often used as a synonym for boreal forest.

Talus: Accumulation of broken rocks at the base of a cliff or steep slope.

Tannin: A soluble astringent compound produced by many plants and giving a reddish or tea-like color to streams into which large amounts have leached. Certain tannins were once used in the tanning of leather.

Tarn: A lake in a mountain cirque.

Taxon (pl. taxa): Any group (species, genus, family, etc.) within the taxonomic hierarchy.

Tectonic: Related to the large scale movements of pieces of Earth's crust. See **Plate Tectonics**.

Tectonic window: An opening eroded through overlying rock units into a lower rock unit, usually of different geologic ages.

Temperate rainforest: Rainforest outside the tropics, with extensive amounts of rainfall. Those along the Pacific coasts of North and South America are dominated by tall conifers.

Tephra: Rock fragments of all sizes emitted in volcanic eruptions.

Tepui (Tepuy): A high, steep-sided mesa or mountain that is a remnant of the ancient sandstone beds overlying the Guiana Shield in northeastern South America.

Terminal moraine: Ridges of unsorted glacial debris (boulders, gravel, sand, clay) that mark the farthest advance of a glacier.

Terra rosa: A reddish, clayey soil that develops where limestone has weathered.

Terrace (river): A raised, level step-like landform that is the remnant of a river's former floodplain.

Terrane: A fragment of crustal material broken off one tectonic plate or microplate that becomes attached (accreted) to another.

Tertiary: The former designation (officially retired, but still widely used) for the geologic time period from approximately 65 to 2.6–1.8 mya.

Tethys Sea: Proto-Mediterranean Sea between Gondwana and Eurasia.

Thermokarst: An irregular surface of pits and hummocks developed by freeze and thaw activities on land overlying permafrost.

Tholeiite: Igneous rocks similar to basalt but richer in silica and iron; usually formed in both oceanic and continental rift areas.

Thrust fault: A fault in which the hanging wall has ridden up the inclined fault plane relative to the footwall due to compression. Reverse fault.

Tiankeng: A very large doline or surface solution depression, usually developed in tropical karst landscapes.

Tidal pool: Rocky pool of seawater left behind by the outgoing tide.

Tidewater glacier: Glacier that flows into the ocean.

Till, glacial: Unsorted sand, gravel, clay, and boulders deposited by glacial ice.

Timberline: Elevation or latitude above which trees cannot grow. Treeline.

Tower karst: Limestone landscape of sheer-cliffs and pinnacles that develops in a tropical climate.

Trachyte: Light colored extrusive igneous rock primarily composed of alkali feldspar.

Trade Winds: The steady easterly winds of the tropics that are part of the global atmospheric circulation system.

Transform fault: Fault characterized by horizontal displacement, with little to no vertical displacement. Strike-slip fault.

Transpiration: The process by which water is transported through a plant and expelled as water vapor through the leaves into the atmosphere. See also **Evapotranspiration.**

Travertine: Deposits of calcite produced at hot springs.

Trench (oceanic): Deep, linear landform feature that develops where the oceanic crust of one tectonic plate is subducting beneath another tectonic plate.

Trench fillings: Material scraped from the ocean floor or continental shelf into a subduction trench.

Tributary: A feeder stream that flows into a larger stream and not directly into the ocean or an interior basin.

Troglobite: Organism adapted to spending its entire life in the dark environs of a cave.

Trophic level: A group of organisms sharing the same position in a food chain, such as the producers or primary consumers and so forth.

Tropical dry forest: A broadleaf forest in which trees shed their leaves during the dry season. Also known as tropical seasonal forest.

Tropical weathering: Rapid decomposition of rock by chemical processes under conditions of high temperature and high amounts of precipitation.

Trough (glacial): Large U-shaped valley carved by a large alpine or valley glacier.

Tsunami: A long, often destructive wave caused by an earthquake, underwater landslide, or other disturbance.

Tufa: Deposits of calcium carbonate.

Tuff: Deposits of pyroclastics that were consolidated into rock.

Turbidites: Sediment or sedimentary rock deposited out of very muddy water.

Turbidity: Degree of cloudiness of water due to suspended sediments.

Tussock grass: A non-sod-forming perennial grass that grows in clumps or tufts. Soil trapped in the roots may raise the grass above the general ground surface. See **Bunch grass.**

Ultra prominent peak: A peak that rises more than 4,921 ft (1,500 m) above the surrounding surface level.

Unconformity: Gap in the geological record.

Underfit river: See **Misfit river.**

Upwelling: Process in which deep, cool water rises toward the surface in a large lake or ocean.

U-shaped valley: River valley that has been enlarged, deepened, widened, and rounded by a glacier.

Uvala: Series of connected sinkholes.

Valley glacier: Glacier confined to a valley. Alpine glacier.

Vegetation: The plant cover of a region described according to structure, percent cover, and appearance rather than by the species present.

Venturi effect: An increase in the velocity of fluid as it passes through a constricted area due to a reduction in pressure.

Vesicular: Refers to the texture of volcanic rock pitted on the surface and containing many cavities inside. See also **Scoria.**

Virgin forest: Forest that has never been logged.

Volcanic arc. See **Volcanic island arc.**

Volcanic island arc: String of volcanoes rising from the sea due to subduction of a plate, usually oceanic, beneath another tectonic plate. Also volcanic arc.

Volcanic neck: Solidified magma which filled the conduit of a volcano and remains standing after the volcano has been eroded away.

Volcanic plug: Solidified magma filling the conduit of a volcano, which may either prevent further eruptions or increase the buildup of pressure and cause a violent eruption.

Volcanic spine: A rigid, pointed column of solidified lava that pushes up from the throat of a volcano.

Volcanism: All constructive processes that involve molten rock, lava, or magma.

Vulcanian: Refers to a very explosive volcanic eruption involving pyroclastics.

Wacke: A sedimentary rock formed from poorly sorted, usually volcanic, sediments.

Wadi: Term used in the Middle East for a dry streambed.

Warm season grass: A perennial grass that uses the C4 photosynthetic pathway and is thus well-adapted to grow in warm or hot climate regions. A C4 grass.

Water table: Top or surface of zone saturated by groundwater.

Watershed: All of the land that drains to a particular stream. Drainage basin

Wave-cut platform: Flat bench at base of sea cliffs created by wave erosion and exposed at low tide.

Weather: State of the atmosphere (temperature, humidity, precipitation, wind, etc.) at a given point in time. See **Climate.**

Weathering: Disintegration of rock by physical or chemical means.

Welded tuff: Pyroclastics so hot that they fused together to become a solid mass.

Wetlands: Land area permanently or periodically saturated with water such that it supports a distinct ecosystem. Includes bogs, fens, marshes, and swamps.

Wilderness Area: Officially designated and protected land area in the United States in a natural state with minimal impacts from human activity.

Windward: The side of an island or mountain range that receives the force of the wind; usually wetter or stormier than the opposite, lee side. See **Orographic effect.**

World Heritage Site: A place nominated by the country in which it occurs and inscribed by the United Nations Educational, Scientific and Cultural Organization (UNESCO) under the Convention Concerning the Protection of the World's Cultural and Natural Heritage as having "outstanding universal value."

Xenarthan: An order of placental mammals more or less restricted to the Neotropics that includes armadillos, sloths, and anteaters. Formerly classified as Edentata (edentates).

Xerophyte: A plant adapted to withstand desert conditions; they usually exhibit small, often deciduous leaves, thorns, and a shallow but broad root system.

Xylopodia: Woody, thickened underground organ on the roots of certain plants from which they can regrow after fire or the dry season.

Yardang: Large solid rock erosional remnant sculpted by wind in desert areas.

Yazoo: A stream forced to parallel an alluvial river because it cannot cross the natural levee.

Zoogeographic province: A global-scale region defined according to the animal families found there, including endemic families, widespread families, and those shared with one or two other such regions. Patterns of animal family distribution are irrespective of climate or other environmental conditions. The counterparts for plants are floristic kingdoms.

Zoonosis (pl. zoonoses): An infectious disease transmitted from other vertebrates to humans.

Zooplankton: The collective term for one-celled and tiny multicelled animals that float in the water column of seas and lakes. They are unable to move against currents and tides, but can move vertically.

Recommended Resources

Abell, Robin, David M. Olson, Eric Dinerstein, Patrick Hurley, James T. Diggs, William Eichbaum, Steven Walters, Wesley Wettengel, Tom Allnut, Colby J. Loucks, Prashant Hedao, and Caroline (Lynne) Taylor. 2000. *Freshwater Ecoregions of North America: A Conservation Assessment.* Washington, D.C.: Island Press.

Adams, William M., Andrew S. Goudie, and Antony R. Orme, editors. 1996. *The Physical Geography of Africa.* Oxford: Oxford University Press.

"African Natural Heritage." 2009. African Natural Heritage Nairobi, Kenya. http://www.africannaturalheritage.org/

"Australian Rainforests." n.d. The Royal Botanic Gardens and Domain Trust. http://www.rbgsyd.nsw.gov.au/education/Resources/rainforests/Australian_Rainforests

Bargagli, R. 2005. *Antarctic Ecosystems. Environmental Contamination, Climate Change, and Human Impact.* Ecological Studies 175. Berlin: Springer-Verlag.

Batello, Caterina, Mazrio Marzot, and Adamou Harouna Touré. 2004. *The Future Is an Ancient Lake: Traditional Knowledge, Biodiversity and Genetic Resources for Food and Agriculture in Lake Chad Basin Ecosystems.* Rome: FAO.

Benke, Arthur C. and Colbert E. Cushing, editors. 2005. *Rivers of North America.* Amsterdam: Elsevier Academic Press.

"Biosphere Reserves." n.d. UNESCO. Ecological Sciences for Sustainable Development. http://www.unesco.org/new/en/natural-sciences/environment/ecological-sciences/biosphere-reserves/

"Biosphere Reserves—Learning Sites for Sustainable Development." n.d. http://www.unesco.org/new/en/natural-sciences/environment/ecological-sciences/biosphere-reserves/

Bishof, Barbie. 2013. "Ocean Surface Currents." http://oceancurrents.rsmas.miami.edu/

Biswas, Asit K., Newton V. Cordeira, Benedito P. F. Braga, and Cecilia Tortajada, editors. 1999. *Management of Latin American River Basins: Amazon, Plata, and São Francisco.* New York: United Nations University Press.

Bridges, E. M. 1990. *World Geomorphology.* Cambridge: Cambridge University Press.

Briney, Amanda. n.d. *Aquifers and the Ogallala Aquifer.* About.Com Geography. http://geography.about.com/od/physicalgeography/a/aquifers.htm

Brooks, E. G. E., D. J. Allen, and W. R. T. Darwall. 2011. *The Status and Distribution of Freshwater Biodiversity in Central Africa.* Cambridge, UK: IUCN.

Brothers, Timothy S., Jeffrey S. Wilson, and Owen P. Dwyer. 2008. *Caribbean Landscapes: An Interpretative Atlas.* Coconut Creek, FL: Caribbean Studies Press.

Bundschuh, Jochen and Guillermo E. Alvarado, editors. 2007. *Central America: Geology, Resources and Hazards.* New York: Taylor & Francis.

Burton, Tony. 2014. *Geo-Mexico: The Geography and Dynamics of Modern Mexico.* http://geo-mexico.com/

Butzer, K. W. 1976. *Geomorphology from the Earth.* New York: Harper and Row.

Camp, Vic. n.d. "How Volcanoes Work." Department of Geological Sciences, San Diego State University. http://www.geology.sdsu.edu/how_volcanoes_work/

Cascade Volcanoes Observatory. 2008. *Volcano Hazard Program.* United States Geological Survey. http://volcanoes.usgs.gov/observatories/cvo/

Caviedes, César and Gregory Knapp. 1995. *South America.* Englewood, NJ: Prentice-Hall.

"Centres of Plant Diversity: The Americas." n.d. Department of Botany, National Museum of Natural History, Smithsonian Institution. http://botany.si.edu/projects/cpd/about_project.htm

Christopherson, Robert. 2012. *Elemental Geosystems,* 8th ed. Upper Saddle River, NJ: Prentice-Hall.

Coates, Anthony G., editor. 1997. *Central America: A Natural and Cultural History.* New Haven, CT: Yale University Press.

Cousteau, Fabien. 2006. *Oceans, The Last Wilderness Revealed.* New York: American Museum of Natural History.

Cowling, R. M., D. M. Richardson, and S. M. Pierce. 1997. *Vegetation of Southern Africa.* Cambridge, UK: Cambridge University Press.

Czaya, E. 1981. *Rivers of the World.* New York: Van Nostrand Reinhold.

Dahl, Arthur Lyon. 1998. "Island Directory." http://yabaha .net/dahl/isldb/isldir.htm. Originally published as: Arthur Lyon Dahl, IUCN/UNEP Island Directory. UNEP Regional Seas Directories and Bibliographies, No. 35, Nairobi, Kenya, 1991. http://islands.unep.ch/isldir.htm [citation as suggested by the author].

Darlington, Philip J. Jr. 1957. *Zoogeography: The Geographical Distribution of Animals*. New York: John Wiley & Sons.

Dengo, G. and J. E. Case, editors. 1990. *The Caribbean Region*. The Geology of North America, Vol. H, Boulder, CO: Geological Society of America.

Department of Geology. 2014. "GEOL 102 Historical Geology, The History of Earth and Life, Spring Semester 2014." College Park, MD: University of Maryland. http://www.geol.umd.edu/~tholtz/G102/102Syl.htm

"Directory of the World Network of Biosphere Reserves (WNBR)." n.d. Man and Biosphere Programme, UNESCO. http://www.unesco.org/new/en/natural-scien ces/environment/ecological-sciences/biosphere-re serves/world-network-wnbr/wnbr/

Doran, Peter T., W. Berry Lyons, and Diane McKnight. 2005. *Life in Antarctic Deserts and Other Cold Dry Environments: Astrobiological Analogs*, New York: Cambridge University Press.

"Earth from Space." 2011. Virtual Institute of Applied Science. http://earthfromspace.photoglobe.info/index.html

"Earth Observatory." 2014. NASA. http://earthobservatory .nasa.gov/?eocn=topnav&eoci=home

Ellwood, Brooks B. 1996. *Geology and America's National Park Areas*. Upper Saddle River, NJ: Prentice Hall. http://www.geodata.us/

"Encyclopedia of Earth, The." [various dates]. *The Encyclopedia of Earth* (EoE). http://www.eoearth.org/

"Endemic Bird Areas." n.d. BirdLife International. http:// www.birdlife.org/datazone/eba

European Environment Agency. 2002. "Europe's Biodiversity— Biogeographical Regions and Seas." http://www.eea .europa.eu/publications/report_2002_0524_154909

Few, Roger. 1994. *The Atlas of Wild Places, in Search of the Earth's Last Wildernesses*. Washington, D.C.: Smithsonian Institution.

"Freshwater Ecoregions of the World." 2013. World Wildlife Fund/The Nature Conservancy. http://www.feow.org/

Gardner, H. and R. Scoggins, editors. 1983. *Mega-Geomorphology*. Oxford: Clarendon Press.

Gillespie, Rosemary G. and David A. Clague, editors. 2009. *Encyclopedia of Islands*. Berkeley: University of California Press.

"Global Volcanism Program." 2013. Smithsonian Institution, Museum of Natural History. http://www.volcano.si.edu/

Goudie, Andrew S. 2002. *The Great Warm Deserts of the World: Landscapes and Evolution*. Oxford: Oxford University Press.

Gupta, Avijit, editor. 2005. *The Physical Geography of Southeast Asia*. Oxford: Oxford University Press.

Hall, Carolyn and Héctor Pérez Brignoli. 2003. *Historical Atlas of Central America*. Norman, OK: Oklahoma University Press.

Harris, Ann G., Esther Tuttle, and Sherwood D. Tuttle 2004. *Geology of National Parks*, 6th ed. Dubuque, IA: Kendall Hunt Publishing Company.

Henry, Jim. 2007. "Geomorphic Regions of the United States., A Supplement for Undergraduate Geoscience Courses." Online Textbook. http://capone.mtsu.edu /mabolins/geomorph.htm

Herak, M. and V. T. Stringfield, editors. 1972. *Karst, Important Karst Regions of the Northern Hemisphere*. Amsterdam: Elsevier Publishing Company.

Hess, Darrel and Dennis Tasa. 2013. *McKnight's Physical Geography*, 11th ed. Upper Saddle River, NJ: Prentice-Hall.

Holzman, Barbara A. 2009. *Tropical Forest Biomes*. Greenwood Guides to Biomes of the World. Westport, CT: Greenwood Press.

Hunt, C. B. 1974. *Natural Regions of the United States and Canada*. San Francisco: W.H. Freeman.

Incorporated Research Institutions for Seismology. n.d. *Animations*. www.iris.edu/hq/programs/education_and_ outreach/animations

Interactive Outdoors, Inc. 1998–2012. *Peakware, World Mountain Encyclopedia*. http://www.peakware.com /index.html

International Rivers. 2013. Berkeley, California. http:// www.internationalrivers.org/

"Island Directory." 1998. United Nations Environmental Programme (UNEP). http://islands.unep.ch/isldir.htm

"Island Encyclopedia, The." 2010. Oceandots.com. http:// web.archive.org/web/20101223121408/http://ocean dots.com/

Johnson, David. 2009. *The Geology of Australia*, 2nd ed. New York: Cambridge University Press.

Kammerer, J. C. 1990. *Largest Rivers in the United States*. U.S. Geological Survey. http://pubs.usgs.gov/of/1987 /ofr87–242/

King, Charles L. 1962. *Morphology of the Earth*. Edinburg: Oliver and Boyd.

Kricher, John. 2006. *Galápagos, A Natural History*. Princeton, NJ: Princeton University Press.

Kricher, John. 1997. *A Neotropical Companion: An Introduction to the Animals, Plants, and Ecosystems of the New World Tropics*, 2nd ed. Princeton, NJ: Princeton University Press.

Kummel, Bernhard. 1970. *History of the Earth, An Introduction to Historical Geology*, 2nd ed. San Francisco: W. H. Freeman and Company.

Laity, Julie J. 2008. *Deserts and Desert Environments*. Chichester, UK: Wiley-Blackwell.

"Large Marine Ecosystems of the World." 2009. National Oceanic and Atmospheric Administration (NOAA). http://www.lme.noaa.gov/index.php?option=com_content&view=article&id=47&Itemid=28

Mares, Michael A. 1999. *Encyclopedia of Deserts*. Norman, OK: University of Oklahoma Press.

"Marine Ecoregions [North America]." 2011. North American Marine Protected Areas Network, Commission for Environmental Cooperation. http://www2.cec.org/nampan/ecoregions

Martin, Paul S. 2005. *Twilight of the Mammoths: Ice Age Extinctions and the Rewilding of America*. Berkeley: University of California Press.

Mignon, Pietor, editor. 2010. *Geomorphological Landscapes of the World*. New York: Springer.

Mittermeier, Russell A., Norman Myers, and Cristina Goettsch Mittermeier. 1999. *Hotspots: Earth's Biologically Richest and Most Endangered Terrestrial Ecoregions*. Mexico City: CEMEX, S.A. and Washington, D.C.: Conservation International.

"Namibia's Geological Treasures." n.d. Geological Survey of Namibia. Ministry of Mines and Energy. http://www.mme.gov.na/gsn/gsnposters.htm

National Geographic Society. 2010. *Atlas of the World*, 9th ed. Washington, D.C.: National Geographic Society.

"National Parks of Canada." 2013. Parks Canada. http://www.pc.gc.ca/progs/np-pn/recherche-search_e.asp?p=1

Nature Conservancy. 2013. "Freshwater Ecoregions of the World." www.feow.org/ecoregions/

"NOAA's Coral Reef Information Service (CoRIS)." 2013. National Oceanic and Atmospheric Administration (NOAA). http://www.coris.noaa.gov/

"North American Marine Protected Areas Network." 2011. Commission for Environmental Cooperation. http://www2.cec.org/nampan/es

"Ocean Explorer." n.d. National Oceanic and Atmospheric Administration (NOAA). http://oceanexplorer.noaa.gov/

Oliveira, Paulo S. and Robert J. Marquis. 2002. *The Cerrados of Brazil: Ecology and Natural History of a Neotropical Savanna*. Boca Raton, FL: CRC Press.

"Online Exhibits." n.d. University of California Museum of Paleontology. http://www.ucmp.berkeley.edu/exhibits/index.php

Pāvils, Gatis. 2014. "WonderMondo." http://www.wondermondo.com

Penn, James R. 2001. *Rivers of the World*. Santa Barbara, CA: ABC-CLIO.

Perillo, Gerardo M. E., M. Cintia Piccolo, and Mario Pino-Quivara, editors. 1999. *Estuaries of South America: Their Geomorphology and Dynamics*. Berlin: Springer.

"Publications, Data, and Research." n.d. Scottish National Heritage. http://www.snh.gov.uk/publications-data-and-research/

Quinn, Joyce A. 2009. *Arctic and Alpine Biomes*. Greenwood Guides to Biomes of the World. Westport, CT: Greenwood Press.

Quinn, Joyce A. 2009. *Desert Biomes*. Greenwood Guides to Biomes of the World. Westport, CT: Greenwood Press.

Rice, R. J. 1977. *Fundamentals of Geomorphology*. New York: Longman Scientific.

Roth, Richard A. 2009. *Freshwater Aquatic Biomes*. Greenwood Guides to Biomes of the World. Westport, CT: Greenwood Press.

Seeliger, U. and B. Kjerfve, editors. 2000. *Coastal Marine Ecosystems of Latin America*. Berlin: Springer.

Short, Nicholas M. and Robert W. Blair, Jr., editors. 1996. *Geomorphology from Space*. Goddard Earth Sciences Data and Information Services Center. NASA. http://disc.sci.gsfc.nasa.gov/geomorphology

Snead, Rodman E. 1980. *World Atlas of Geomorphic Features*. Huntington, NY: Robert E. Krieger Publishing Company, Inc., and Van Nostrand Reinhold Company.

"State of Coral Reef Ecosystems of the United States and Pacific Freely Associated States: 2008, The." 2012. National Oceanic and Atmospheric Administration (NOAA). http://ccma.nos.noaa.gov/ecosystems/coralreef/coral2008/

Tockner, Klement, Urs Uehlinger, and Christopher T. Robinson, editors. 2009. *Rivers of Europe*. London: Academic Press.

Veblen, Thomas T., Robert S. Hill, and Jennifer Reed. 1996. *The Ecology and Biogeography of Nothofagus Forests*. New Haven, CT: Yale University Press.

Veblen, Thomas T., Kenneth R. Young, and Antony R. Orme, editors. 2007. *The Physical Geography of South America*. New York: Oxford University Press.

Veregin, Howard, editor. 2010. *Goode's World Atlas*. 22nd ed. Englewood, NJ: Pearson Prentice Hall.

Walter, Heinrich. 1973. *Vegetation of the Earth, in Relation to Climate and the Eco-Physiological Conditions*. New York: Springer.

West, Robert C. and John P. Augelli. 1989. *Middle America: Its Lands and Peoples*. Englewood Cliffs, NJ: Prentice-Hall.

"What Are Wetlands?" 2013. Wetlands International. http://www.wetlands.org/Whatarewetlands/tabid/202/Default.aspx

White, Mary E. 1990. *The Flowering of Gondwana. The 400 Million Year Story of Australia's Plants*. Princeton, NJ: Princeton University Press.

Williams, Richard S., Jr. and Jane G. Ferrigno, editors. 2002. "*Satellite Image Atlas of Glaciers of the World*, U.S. Geological Survey Professional Paper 1386-J-3, J384–J388. http://pubs.usgs.gov/pp/p1386j/mexico/mexico-lores.pdf

Wood, Charles A. and Jürgen Kienle. 1992. *Volcanoes of North America: United States and Canada*. Cambridge: Cambridge University Press.

Woodward, Susan L. 2003. *Biomes of Earth: Terrestrial, Aquatic, and Human-Dominated*. Westport, CT: Greenwood Press.

Woodward, Susan L. 2009. *Grassland Biomes*. Greenwood Guides to Biomes of the World. Westport, CT: Greenwood Press.

Woodward, Susan L. 2009. *Marine Biomes*. Greenwood Guides to Biomes of the World. Westport, CT: Greenwood Press.

Woodward, Susan L. and Joyce A. Quinn, 2011. *Encyclopedia of Invasive Species: From Africanized Honey Bees to Zebra Mussels*. Santa Barbara, CA: Greenwood, ABC-CLIO.

"World Heritage List." n.d. World Heritage Centre, UNESCO. http://whc.unesco.org/en/list/

"World Lake Database." 1999. International Lake Environment Committee Foundation (ILEC). http://wldb.ilec.or.jp/

"World Lakes Website." 2011. LakeNet. http://www.world-lakes.org/

"World Network of Biosphere Reserves 2010: Sites for Sustainable Development." http://unesdoc.unesco.org/images/0020/002070/207049e.pdf

"World Waterfall Database." 2014. worldwaterfall database.com. http://www.worldwaterfalldatabase.com/

World Wildlife Fund. n.d. "List of Ecoregions: Terrestrial Ecoregions." http://wwf.panda.org/about_our_earth/ecoregions/ecoregion_list/

"World's 1000 Wonders, The." 2014. TheWorldWonders.com. http://www.theworldwonders.com/

Zwiefelhofer, David B. 2014. Find Latitude and Longitude. http://www.findlatitudeandlongitude.com/

Index

Note: Page numbers in **bold** indicate main entries.

About the Authors

Joyce A. Quinn retired from California State University Fresno as professor emerita after 21 years of teaching a variety of courses in physical geography and mapping techniques. She earned an MA from the University of Colorado and a PhD from Arizona State University, specializing in the effect of climate on the distribution of plants. She has traveled extensively throughout North America, Latin America, Europe, northern and southern Africa, Uzbekistan, Nepal, China, Southeast Asia, Micronesia, and elsewhere. She is a member of the Cactus and Succulent Society of America.

Susan L. Woodward is professor emerita of geography in the Department of Geospatial Science at Radford University, Virginia. Primarily a biogeographer, she received a PhD in geography from UCLA in 1976. For many years she taught undergraduate classes on physical geography as well as on the geography of South America and of Middle America. She has traveled widely in South America and Africa, always with a trained eye focused on natural landscapes.